Operator Precedence

In the following list, operators on the same line are of equal precedence. As you move down the list, each line is of lower precedence. When the order of operations is not dictated by parentheses, the operator of higher precedence executes before an operator of lower precedence. When operators have equal precedence, binary operators execute in left-to-right order, and unary operators execute in right-to-left order.

Highest Precedence

The unary operators +, -, ++, --, !, ~

The unary operators new and (*type*)

The binary operators *, /, %

The binary operators +, -

The binary (shift) operators <<, >>, >>>

The binary operators <, >, <=, >=

The binary operators ==, !=

The binary operator &

The binary operator ^

The binary operator |

The binary operator &&

The binary operator ||

The ternary (conditional) operator ? :

Assignment operators =, *=, /=, %=, +=, -=, <<=, >>=, >>>=, &=, ^=, |=

Lowest Precedence

Data Structures and Abstractions with Java™

Frank M. Carrano
University of Rhode Island

Walter Savitch
University of California at San Diego

An Alan R. Apt Book

Pearson Education, Inc.
Upper Saddle River, NJ 07458

Library of Congress Cataloging-in-Publication Data

On file

Vice President and Editorial Director, ECS: *Marcia J. Horton*
Publisher: *Alan R. Apt*
Associate Editor: *Toni D. Holm*
Editorial Assistant: *Patrick Lindner*
Vice President and Director of Production and Manufacturing: *David W. Riccardi*
Executive Managing Editor: *Vince O'Brien*
Assistant Managing Editor: *Camille Trentacoste*
Production Editor: *Chirag Thakkar*
Director of Creative Services: *Paul Belfanti*
Creative Director: *Carole Anson*
Art Director: *Heather Scott*
Audio/Visual Editor: *Xiaohong Zhu*
Cover Image and Interior Illustrations: *Lianne Dunn*
Cover Design: *John Christiana*
Copy Editor: *Rebecca Pepper*
Interior Design: *Gail Cocker-Bogusz*
Manufacturing Manager: *Trudy Pisciotti*
Manufacturing Buyer: *Lisa McDowell*
Marketing Manager: *Pamela Shaffer*
Marketing Assistant: *Barrie Reinhold*

© 2003 by Pearson Education, Inc.
Pearson Education, Inc.,
Upper Saddle River, NJ 07458

Printed in the United States of America
10   9   8   7   6   5   4   3   2

ISBN 0-13-017489-0

Pearson Education Ltd., *London*
Pearson Education Australia Pty. Ltd., *Sydney*
Pearson Education Singapore, Pte. Ltd.
Pearson Education North Asia Ltd., *Hong Kong*
Pearson Education Canada, Inc., *Toronto*
Pearson Educación de Mexico, S.A. de C.V.
Pearson Education–Japan, *Tokyo*
Pearson Education Malaysia, Pte. Ltd.
Pearson Education, Inc., *Upper Saddle River, New Jersey*

Preface

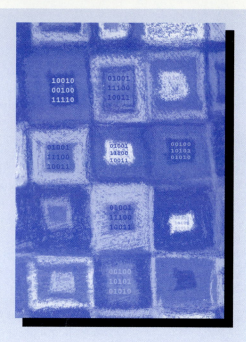

Here is the first edition of *Data Structures and Abstractions with Java*, a brand-new book for an introductory course in data structures, typically known as CS-2. Readers of *Java: An Introduction to Computer Science & Programming* by Walter Savitch can treat our new book as a sequel.

A New Approach

This book was created specifically with objects and Java in mind. It is not derived from a previous work written for another programming language. Our approach makes learning easier by focusing the reader's attention on one issue at a time, by providing flexibility in the order in which you can cover topics, and by clearly distinguishing between the specification and implementation of abstract data types, or ADTs. To accomplish these goals, we have divided the material into short, numbered segments that are organized into 30 relatively short chapters. Each segment covers a single idea. Individual chapters deal with either the specification and use of an ADT or its implementations. You can choose to cover the specification of an ADT followed by its various implementations, or you can treat the specification and use of several ADTs before you consider any implementation issues. Our organization makes it easy for you to choose the topic order that you prefer.

Features

- 30 relatively short chapters can be covered in several orders.
- Individual but consecutive chapters separate the specification and implementation of ADTs.
- Short, bite-sized segments focus attention on one issue at a time.
- Many examples illustrate new concepts.
- Highlighted notes emphasize key material and provide supplementary comments.

- Programming tips give additional programming advice.
- Numerous figures make the presentation visual and accessible.
- Questions throughout the book—and their answers—elaborate on the material presented.
- Initial chapters cover Java classes, inheritance, polymorphism, and class design.
- Java code includes `javadoc` comments.
- Appendices review Java basics, exceptions, files, and documentation.
- A Prentice Hall Companion Website at www.prenhall.com/carrano provides the Java code that appears in the book as well as any updates or corrections.
- Supplements for instructors include PowerPoint slides, laboratory materials, and answers to selected exercises and programming projects.

A Note to Students

After looking over this preface, you should read the Introduction. There you will quickly see what this book is about and what you need to know about Java before you begin. Appendices A through D review Java and serve as a primer on exceptions, files, and `javadoc` comments. Note that inside the front and back covers you will find Java's reserved words, the precedence of its operators, and a list of Unicode characters.

The topics that we cover in this book are fundamental to your future study of computer science. Even if you do not study all of these topics now, you are likely to encounter them later. We hope that you will enjoy reading the book now, and that it will serve as a useful reference for your future courses.

All of the Java code that appears in this book is available for download from the book's companion website at www.prenhall.com/carrano. There you also will find the class `SavitchIn` that you can use for keyboard input. Appendix A describes this class and provides some examples of its use.

Throughout each chapter, you will find questions that should help you to understand the material. The answers to these questions are in Appendix E at the back of the book. Unfortunately, we cannot give you answers to the exercises and programming projects that appear at the end of each chapter, even if you are not enrolled in a class. Only instructors who adopt the book can receive selected answers from the publisher. For help with these exercises and projects, you will have to contact your instructor.

An Overview

Readers of this book should have completed a programming course, preferably in Java. Appendix A covers the essentials of Java that we assume readers will know. You can use this appendix as a review or as the basis for making the transition to Java from another programming language.

The book itself begins with the Introduction, which sets the stage for the data organizations that we will study. Chapter 1 thoroughly reviews classes and methods in Java. We follow this review with a discussion of composition, inheritance, and polymorphism in Chapter 2. Chapter 3 introduces object-oriented design, presents Java interfaces, and provides an introduction to such design tools as the CRC card and the Unified Modeling Language.

Chapters 4, 5, and 6 introduce the list as an abstract data type. By dividing the material across several chapters, we were able to clearly separate the specification, use, and implementation of a list. For example, Chapter 4 specifies the list and provides several examples of its use. Chapters 5 and 6 cover implementations that use arrays, vectors, and chains of linked nodes.

In a similar fashion, we separate specification from implementation throughout the book when we discuss various other ADTs. You can cover the chapters that specify and use the ADTs and later cover the chapters that implement them. Or you can cover the chapters as they appear, implementing each ADT right after studying its specification and use. A dependency chart appears later in this preface to help you plan your path through the book.

Chapters 7 and 8 discuss iterators in the context of a list. In Chapter 7, we present the notion of an iterator, using our own interface, along with various ways to implement it. Chapter 8 continues this discussion by considering and implementing Java's iterator interfaces `Iterator` and `ListIterator`.

Chapters 9 and 10 introduce the complexity of algorithms and recursion, two topics that we integrate into future chapters. For example, Chapters 11 and 12 discuss various sorting techniques and their relative complexities. We consider both iterative and recursive versions of these algorithms.

The next two chapters, 13 and 14, return to the notion of a list. Chapter 13 discusses the sorted list, looking at two possible implementations and their efficiencies. Chapter 14 shows how to use the list as a base class for the sorted list and discusses the general design of a base class.

Chapter 15 introduces mutable objects, immutable objects, and cloning. If a client can maintain a reference to the data within an ADT, it can change that data without using the class's public methods, if the data is mutable. We consider steps that you can take to prevent the client from doing so.

Chapter 16 examines strategies for searching an array or chain in the context of a list or sorted list. This discussion is a good basis for Chapter 17, which covers the specification and use of the ADT dictionary. Chapter 18 presents implementations of the dictionary that are linked or that use arrays. Chapter 19 introduces hashing and uses it as a dictionary implementation.

Chapter 20 discusses stacks, giving examples of their use and examining the relationship between stacks and recursion. Chapter 21 implements the stack using an array, a vector, and a chain.

Chapter 22 presents queues, deques, and priority queues, and Chapter 23 considers their implementations. It is in this chapter that we discuss circularly linked and doubly linked chains.

Chapter 24 discusses trees and their possible uses. Included among the several examples of trees is an introduction to the binary search tree and the heap. Chapter 25 considers implementations of the binary tree and the general tree, and Chapter 26 focuses on the implementation of the binary search tree. Chapter 27 shows how to use an array to implement the heap. Chapter 28 introduces balanced search trees. Included in this chapter are the AVL, 2-3, 2-4, and red-black trees, as well as B-trees.

Chapters 29 and 30 discuss graphs, looking at several applications and two implementations.

Appendices A through D provide supplemental coverage of Java. As we mentioned earlier, Appendix A reviews Java up to but not including classes. Appendix B covers exception handling, and Appendix C discusses files. Appendix D considers programming style and comments. It introduces `javadoc` comments and defines the tags that we use in this book.

Appendix E contains the answers to the questions that appear throughout each chapter.

Instructor Resources

We have prepared several supplements for instructors and packaged them on a CD. Included are PowerPoint slides, laboratory materials, answers to selected exercises and programming projects, the Java code that appears in this book, and the class `SavitchIn`—described in Appendix A—for keyboard input. Note that the latter two items are also available on the Prentice Hall Companion Website at www.prenhall.com/carrano. This website also contains any updates or corrections to the book.

To obtain a copy of the Instructor's Resource CD-ROM, instructors should contact their Prentice Hall sales representative. For the name and number of your sales representative, please visit the website www.prenhall.com/replocator or call Prentice Hall Faculty Services at 1-800-526-0485. Additional information on this book and other Prentice Hall products can be found on Prentice Hall's home page at www.prenhall.com.

Contact Us

Your comments, suggestions, and corrections are always welcome. Please e-mail them to

carrano@acm.org

Acknowledgments

We thank the following reviewers for carefully reading our manuscript and making candid comments and suggestions that greatly improved our work:

David Boyd—*Valdosta State University*
Dennis Brylow—*Purdue University*
Michael Croswell—*Industry trainer/consultant*
Matthew Dickerson—*Middlebury College*
Robert Holloway—*University of Wisconsin, Madison*
John Motil—*California State University, Northridge*
Bina Ramamurthy—*SUNY, Buffalo*
David Surma—*Valpairaiso University*

Thank you to all of the people at Prentice Hall who contributed to the development and production of this book. They all worked tirelessly and cheerfully. We especially thank our publisher Alan Apt for making this project possible and for his invaluable insight and guidance during the entire process. We thank Toni Holm, associate editor, for overseeing the project and for our regular conversations that kept us grounded and on track. Jake Warde did an extraordinary job of coordinating both the reviewers of the manuscript and the creators of the supplemental materials for instructors. Thanks to our production editor, Chirag Thakkar, for producing our book on schedule. We also thank Heather Scott for her design work and Xiaohong Zhu for coordinating the art manuscript.

Special thanks go to Rebecca Pepper, our copy editor, who not only corrected our grammar but also ensured that our explanations are clear and correct. And special thanks to Lianne Dunn, who created the cover illustration and drew all of the figures in the book.

Thank you to the following people for their contributions to the supplemental materials for instructors: Steve Armstrong of Le Tourneau University, Patty Roy of Manatee Community College, and Charles Hoot of Oklahoma City University. And thanks to Nate Walker of the University of Rhode Island for preparing the Java code for distribution.

Other wonderful people have contributed in various ways. They are Doug McCreadie, Ted Emmott, Lorraine Berube, Marge White, Gérard Baudet, Joan Peckham, James Kowalski, Ed Lamagna, Bala Ravikumar, Victor Fay-Wolfe, Lisa DiPippo, Jean-Yves Hervé, James Heltshe, Brian Jepson, Ben Schomp, Patrick Lindner, James Blanding, and Tim Henry.

Thank you, everyone, for your expertise and good cheer.

FRANK M. CARRANO
WALTER SAVITCH

Chapter and Appendix Dependencies

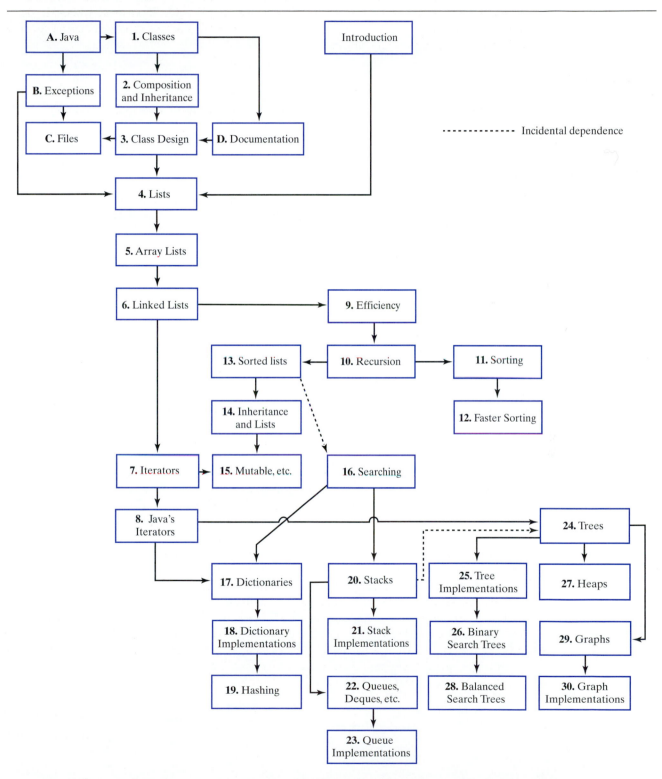

Brief Contents

Introduction 1

Chapter   1   Java Classes 5

Chapter   2   Creating Classes from Other Classes 29

Chapter   3   Designing Classes 57

Chapter   4   Lists 79

Chapter   5   List Implementations That Use Arrays 97

Chapter   6   List Implementations That Link Data 117

Chapter   7   Iterators 151

Chapter   8   Java's Iterator Interfaces 173

Chapter   9   The Efficiency of Algorithms 199

Chapter 10   Recursion 223

Chapter 11   An Introduction to Sorting 255

Chapter 12   Faster Sorting Methods 277

Chapter 13   Sorted Lists 299

Chapter 14   Inheritance and Lists 319

Chapter 15   Mutable, Immutable, and Cloneable Objects 331

Chapter 16   Searching 355

Chapter 17   Dictionaries 375

Chapter 18   Dictionary Implementations 393

Chapter 19   Hashing as a Dictionary Implementation 411

Chapter 20   Stacks 449

Chapter 21   Stack Implementations 477

Chapter 22   Queues, Deques, and Priority Queues 489

Chapter 23   Queue, Deque, and Priority Queue Implementations 511

Chapter 24   Trees 539

Chapter 25   Tree Implementations 569

Chapter 26   A Binary Search Tree Implementation 591

Chapter 27   A Heap Implementation 627

Chapter 28   Balanced Search Trees 643

Chapter 29   Graphs 673

Chapter 30   Graph Implementations 699

Appendix A   Java Essentials 715

Appendix B   Exception Handling 767

Appendix C   File Input and Output 777

Appendix D   Documentation and Programming Style 793

Appendix E   Answers to Self-Test Questions 799

Index 829

Contents

Introduction **1**

Chapter 1 **Java Classes 5**

Objects and Classes 6
Using the Methods in a Java Class 7
    References and Aliases 9
    Arguments and Parameters 10
Defining a Java Class 10
    Method Definitions 11
    Passing Arguments 14
    A Definition of the Class Name 16
    Constructors 18
    The Method toString 20
    Static Fields and Methods 20
Packages 22
    The Java Class Library 22

Chapter 2 **Creating Classes from Other Classes 29**

Composition 30
    Adapters 32
Inheritance 33
    Invoking Constructors from Within Constructors 36
    Private Fields and Methods of the Base Class 37
    Overriding and Overloading Methods 38
    Protected Access 41
    Multiple Inheritance 42
Type Compatibility and Base Classes 42
    The Class Object 44
    Abstract Classes and Methods 45
Polymorphism 46

Chapter 3 **Designing Classes 57**

Encapsulation 58
Specifying Methods 60
Java Interfaces 63
    Writing an Interface 63
    Implementing an Interface 65
    An Interface as a Data Type 66
    Type Casts Within an Interface Implementation 66
    Extending an Interface 67
    Named Constants Within an Interface 68
    Interfaces Versus Abstract Classes 69

xi

Choosing Classes 70
Identifying Classes 71
CRC Cards 72
Reusing Classes 74

Chapter 4 **Lists 79**

Specifications for the ADT List 80
Refining the Specifications 84
Using the ADT List 88
Java Class Library: The Interface List 91
Using a List Is Like Using a Vending Machine 92

Chapter 5 **List Implementations That Use Arrays 97**

Using a Fixed-Size Array to Implement the ADT List 98
An Analogy 98
The Java Implementation 100
Using Dynamic Array Expansion to Implement the ADT List 106
Expanding an Array 106
A New Implementation of a List 108
Using a Vector to Implement the ADT List 109
A Summary of Methods in the Class Vector 112
The Pros and Cons of Using an Array to Implement the ADT List 113
Java Class Library 113
The Class ArrayList 113
The Interface Serializable 114

Chapter 6 **List Implementations That Link Data 117**

Linked Data 118
Forming a Chain 119
Forming Another Chain 121
Forming Yet Another Chain 123
The Class Node 129
A Linked Implementation of the ADT List 130
Adding to the End of the List 131
Adding at a Given Position Within the List 134
The Private Method getNodeAt 136
The Method remove 137
The Method replace 140
The Method getEntry 140
The Method contains 141
The Remaining Methods 141
Using a Class Node That Has Set and Get Methods 142
Tail References 142
A Revised Implementation of the List 143
The Pros and Cons of Using a Chain to Implement the ADT List 147
Java Class Library: The Class LinkedList 147

Chapter 7 **Iterators 151**

What Is an Iterator? 152
  A Basic Iterator 153
  Iterator Methods That Modify the ADT 155
Implementing an Internal Iterator 157
Implementing an Iterator as Its Own Class 162
  An External Iterator 164
  An Inner Class Iterator 166

Chapter 8 **Java's Iterator Interfaces 173**

The Interface `Iterator` 174
Implementing the Interface `Iterator` 177
  A Linked Implementation 177
  An Array-Based Implementation 179
The Interface `ListIterator` 182
  Using the Interface `ListIterator` 185
An Array-Based Implementation of the Interface `ListIterator` 188
  The Inner Class 188
Java Class Library: `ArrayList` and `LinkedList` Revisited 194

Chapter 9 **The Efficiency of Algorithms 199**

Motivation 200
Measuring an Algorithm's Efficiency 202
  Big Oh Notation 205
Formalities 208
Picturing Efficiency 210
The Efficiency of Implementations of the ADT List 214
  The Array-Based Implementation 214
  The Linked Implementation 215
  Comparing the Implementations 216

Chapter 10 **Recursion 223**

What Is Recursion? 224
Tracing a Recursive Method 228
Recursive Methods That Return a Value 231
Recursively Processing an Array 234
Recursively Processing a Linked Chain 236
The Time Efficiency of Recursive Methods 237
  The Time Efficiency of `countDown` 238
  The Time Efficiency of Computing x^n 239
A Simple Solution to a Difficult Problem 240
A Poor Solution to a Simple Problem 245
Tail Recursion 247
Mutual Recursion 249

Chapter 11 **An Introduction to Sorting 255**

Selection Sort 256
  Iterative Selection Sort 258

Recursive Selection Sort 260
The Efficiency of Selection Sort 260
Insertion Sort 261
Iterative Insertion Sort 262
Recursive Insertion Sort 264
The Efficiency of Insertion Sort 266
Insertion Sort of a Chain of Linked Nodes 266
Shell Sort 269
The Java Code 271
The Efficiency of Shell Sort 272
Comparing the Algorithms 272

Chapter   12   **Faster Sorting Methods 277**

Merge Sort 278
Merging Arrays 278
Recursive Merge Sort 279
The Efficiency of Merge Sort 281
Iterative Merge Sort 282
Merge Sort in the Java Class Library 283
Quick Sort 283
The Efficiency of Quick Sort 284
Creating the Partition 284
Java Code for Quick Sort 287
Quick Sort in the Java Class Library 290
Radix Sort 290
Pseudocode for Radix Sort 292
The Efficiency of Radix Sort 292
Comparing the Algorithms 293

Chapter   13   **Sorted Lists 299**

Specifications for the ADT Sorted List 300
Using the ADT Sorted List 303
A Linked Implementation 304
The Method add 304
The Efficiency of the Linked Implementation 311
An Implementation That Uses the ADT List 312
Efficiency Issues 315

Chapter   14   **Inheritance and Lists 319**

Using Inheritance to Implement a Sorted List 320
Designing a Base Class 322
An Efficient Implementation of a Sorted List 326
The Method add 326

Chapter   15   **Mutable, Immutable, and Cloneable Objects 331**

Mutable and Immutable Objects 332
Companion Classes 335
Using Inheritance to Form Companion Classes 336

Cloneable Objects 339
A Sorted List of Clones 344
Cloning an Array 347
Cloning a Chain 349

Chapter 16 **Searching 355**

The Problem 356
Searching an Unsorted Array 357
    An Iterative Sequential Search of an Unsorted Array 357
    A Recursive Sequential Search of an Unsorted Array 358
    The Efficiency of a Sequential Search of an Array 360
Searching a Sorted Array 360
    A Sequential Search of a Sorted Array 360
    A Binary Search of a Sorted Array 361
    Java Class Library: The Method binarySearch 365
    The Efficiency of a Binary Search of an Array 365
Searching an Unsorted Chain 367
    An Iterative Sequential Search of an Unsorted Chain 367
    A Recursive Sequential Search of an Unsorted Chain 368
    The Efficiency of a Sequential Search of a Chain 368
Searching a Sorted Chain 369
    A Sequential Search of a Sorted Chain 369
    A Binary Search of a Sorted Chain 369
Choosing a Search Method 370

Chapter 17 **Dictionaries 375**

Specifications for the ADT Dictionary 376
    A Java Interface 379
    Iterators 380
Using the ADT Dictionary 381
    A Directory of Telephone Numbers 382
    The Frequency of Words 385
    A Concordance of Words 387
Java Class Library: The Interface Map 389

Chapter 18 **Dictionary Implementations 393**

Array-Based Implementations 394
    The Entries 394
    An Unsorted Array-Based Dictionary 395
    A Sorted Array-Based Dictionary 397
Vector-Based Implementations 400
Linked Implementations 402
    The Entries 402
    An Unsorted Linked Dictionary 403
    A Sorted Linked Dictionary 404

Chapter 19 **Hashing as a Dictionary Implementation 411**

What Is Hashing? 412

Hash Functions 415
 Computing Hash Codes 415
 Compressing a Hash Code into an Index for the Hash Table 418
Resolving Collisions 419
 Open Addressing with Linear Probing 419
 Open Addressing with Quadratic Probing 424
 Open Addressing with Double Hashing 425
 A Potential Problem with Open Addressing 426
 Separate Chaining 427
Efficiency 430
 The Load Factor 430
 The Cost of Open Addressing 431
 The Cost of Separate Chaining 432
Rehashing 434
Comparing Schemes for Collision Resolution 434
A Dictionary Implementation That Uses Hashing 435
 Entries in the Hash Table 435
 Data Fields and Constructors 436
 The Methods getValue, remove, and add 437
 Iterators 443
Java Class Library: The Class HashMap 444

Chapter 20   Stacks 449

Specifications of the ADT Stack 450
Using a Stack to Process Algebraic Expressions 453
 Checking for Balanced Parentheses, Brackets, and Braces in an Infix
  Algebraic Expression 454
 Transforming an Infix Expression to a Postfix Expression 459
 Evaluating Postfix Expressions 466
 Evaluating Infix Expressions 467
The Program Stack 470
 Recursive Methods 470
Using a Stack Instead of Recursion 471
 An Iterative Binary Search 472
Java Class Library: The Class Stack 473

Chapter 21   Stack Implementations 477

A Linked Implementation 477
An Array-Based Implementation 480
A Vector-Based Implementation 484

Chapter 22   Queues, Deques, and Priority Queues 489

Specifications of the ADT Queue 490
Using a Queue to Simulate a Waiting Line 494
 The Classes WaitLine and Customer 494
Using a Queue to Compute the Capital Gain in a Sale of Stock 500
 The Classes StockLedger and StockPurchase 500
Specifications of the ADT Deque 502

Using a Deque to Compute the Capital Gain in a Sale of Stock 504
Specifications of the ADT Priority Queue 505
Using a Priority Queue to Compute the Capital Gain in a Sale of Stock 506

Chapter   23   **Queue, Deque, and Priority Queue Implementations 511**

A Linked Implementation of a Queue 512
An Array-Based Implementation of a Queue 515
    A Circular Array 516
    A Circular Array with One Unused Location 518
A Vector-Based Implementation of a Queue 523
Circular Linked Implementations of a Queue 525
    A Two-Part Circular Linked Chain 525
A Doubly Linked Implementation of a Deque 531
Possible Implementations of a Priority Queue 534

Chapter   24   **Trees 539**

Tree Concepts 540
    Hierarchical Organizations 540
    Tree Terminology 542
Traversals of a Tree 546
    Traversals of a Binary Tree 546
    Traversals of a General Tree 549
Java Interfaces for Trees 550
    Interfaces for All Trees 550
    An Interface for Binary Trees 550
Examples of Binary Trees 552
    Expression Trees 552
    Decision Trees 554
    Binary Search Trees 557
    Heaps 560
Examples of General Trees 562
    Parse Trees 562
    Game Trees 563

Chapter   25   **Tree Implementations 569**

The Nodes in a Binary Tree 570
    An Interface for a Node 570
    An Implementation of BinaryNode 571
An Implementation of the ADT Binary Tree 572
    Creating a Basic Binary Tree 573
    The Method privateSetTree 574
    Accessor and Mutator Methods 577
    Computing the Height and Counting Nodes 577
    Traversals 578
An Implementation of an Expression Tree 583
General Trees 585
    A Node for a General Tree 585
    Using a Binary Tree to Represent a General Tree 585

Chapter 26   **A Binary Search Tree Implementation 591**

Getting Started 592
    An Interface for the Binary Search Tree 593
    Duplicate Entries 595
    Beginning the Class Definition 596
Searching and Retrieving 597
Traversing 598
Adding an Entry 598
    An Iterative Implementation 599
    A Recursive Implementation 601
Removing an Entry 606
    Removing an Entry Whose Node Is a Leaf 606
    Removing an Entry Whose Node Has One Child 607
    Removing an Entry Whose Node Has Two Children 607
    Removing an Entry in the Root 610
    An Iterative Implementation 611
    A Recursive Implementation 615
The Efficiency of Operations 618
    The Importance of Balance 619
    The Order in Which Nodes Are Added 620
An Implementation of the ADT Dictionary 621

Chapter 27   **A Heap Implementation 627**

Reprise: The ADT Heap 628
Using an Array to Represent a Heap 628
Adding an Entry 630
Removing the Root 634
Creating a Heap 637
Heapsort 639

Chapter 28   **Balanced Search Trees 643**

AVL Trees 644
    Single Rotations 645
    Double Rotations 646
    Implementation Details 650
2-3 Trees 653
    Searching a 2-3 Tree 654
    Adding Entries to a 2-3 Tree 655
    Splitting Nodes During Addition 657
2-4 Trees 658
    Adding Entries to a 2-4 Tree 659
    Comparing AVL, 2-3, and 2-4 Trees 661
Red-Black Trees 662
    Properties of a Red-Black Tree 663
    Adding Entries to a Red-Black Tree 664
    Java Class Library: The Class TreeMap 669
B-Trees 669

Chapter 29   Graphs 673

Some Examples and Terminology 674
    Road Maps 674
    Airline Routes 677
    Mazes 677
    Course Prerequisites 678
    Trees 678
Traversals 679
    Breadth-First Traversal 680
    Depth-First Traversal 680
Topological Order 683
Paths 684
    Finding a Path 686
    The Shortest Path in an Unweighted Graph 686
    The Shortest Path in a Weighted Graph 689
Java Interfaces for the ADT Graph 692

Chapter 30   Graph Implementations 699

An Overview of Two Implementations 700
    The Adjacency Matrix 700
    The Adjacency List 701
Vertices and Edges 702
    Specifying the Class Vertex 702
    The Class Edge 704
    Implementing the Class Vertex 705
An Implementation of the ADT Graph 707
    Basic Operations 707
    Graph Algorithms 710

Appendix A   Java Essentials 715

Appendix B   Exception Handling 767

Appendix C   File Input and Output 777

Appendix D   Documentation and Programming Style 793

Appendix E   Answers to Self-Test Questions 799

Index 829

Introduction

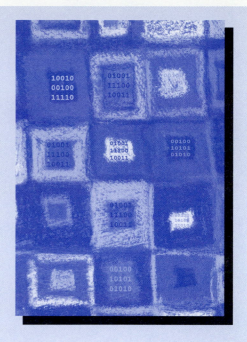

Look around and you will see ways that people organize things. When you stopped at the store this morning, you went to the back of a line to wait for the cashier. The line organized people chronologically. The first person in the line was the first to be served and to leave the line. Eventually, you reached the front of the line and left the store with a bag containing your purchases. The items in the bag were in no particular order, and some of them were the same.

At your desk, you see your to-do list. Each entry in the list has a position that might or might not be important to you. You may have written them either as you thought of them, in their order of importance, or in alphabetical order. You decide the order; the list simply provides places for your entries.

Do you see a stack of books or a pile of papers on your desk? It's easy to look at or remove the top item of the stack or to add a new item to the top of the stack. The items in a stack also are organized chronologically, with the item added most recently on top and the item added first on the bottom.

Your dictionary is an alphabetical list of words and their definitions. You search for a word and get its definition. If your dictionary is printed, the alphabetical organization helps you to locate a word quickly. If your dictionary is computerized, its alphabetical organization is hidden, but it still speeds the search.

Speaking of your computer, you have organized your files into folders, or directories. Each folder contains several other folders or files. This organization is hierarchical. If you drew a picture of it, you would get something like a family tree or a chart of a company's internal departments. These data organizations are similar and are called **trees.**

Finally, notice the road map that you are using to plan your weekend trip. The diagram of roads and towns shows you how to get from one place to another. Often, several ways are possible. One way might be shorter, another faster. The road map is an organization known as a **graph.**

1

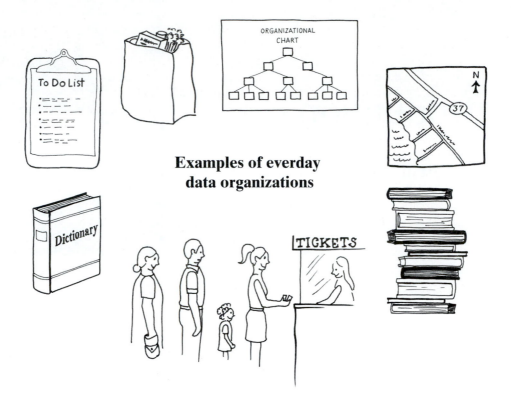

**Examples of everday
data organizations**

Computer programs also need to organize their data. They do so in ways that parallel the examples we just cited. That is, programs can use a list, a stack, a dictionary, and so on. These ways of organizing data are called abstract data types. An **abstract data type,** or **ADT,** is a specification that describes a data set and the operations on that data. Each ADT specifies what data is stored and what the operations on the data do. Since an ADT does not indicate how to store the data or how to implement the operations, we can talk about ADTs independently of any programming language. In contrast, a **data structure** is an implementation of an ADT within a programming language.

A **collection** is a general term for an ADT that contains a group of objects. Some collections allow duplicate items, some do not. Some collections arrange their contents in a certain order, while others do not. A **container** is a class that implements a collection. Some people use the terms "container" and "collection" interchangeably.

We might create an ADT **bag** consisting of an unordered collection that allows duplicates. It is like a grocery bag, a lunch bag, or a bag of potato chips. Suppose you remove one chip from a bag of chips. You don't know when the chip was placed into the bag. You don't know whether the bag contains another chip shaped exactly like the one you just removed. But you don't really care. If you did, you wouldn't store your chips in a bag!

A bag does not order its contents, but sometimes you do want to order things. ADTs can order their items in a variety of ways. The ADT **list,** for example, simply numbers its items. A list, then, has a first item, a second item, and so on. Although you can add an item to the end of a list, you can also insert an item at the beginning of the list or between existing items. Doing so renumbers the items after the new item. Additionally, you can remove an item at a particular position within a list.

Thus, the position of an item in the list does not necessarily indicate when it was added. Notice that the list does not decide where an item is placed; you make this decision.

In contrast, the ADTs **stack** and **queue** order their items chronologically. When you remove an item from a stack, you remove the one that was added most recently. When you remove an item from a queue, you remove the one that was added the earliest. Thus, a stack is like a pile of books. You can remove the top book or add another book to the top of the pile. A queue is like a line of people. People leave a line from its front and join it at its end.

Some ADTs maintain their entries in sorted order, if the items can be compared. For instance, strings can be organized in alphabetical order. When you add an item to the ADT **sorted list,** for example, the ADT determines where to place the item in the list. You do not indicate a position for the item, as you would with the ADT list.

The ADT **dictionary** contains pairs of items, much as a language dictionary contains a word and its definition. In this example, the word serves as a **key** that is used to locate the entries. Some dictionaries sort their entries and some do not.

The ADT **tree** organizes its entries according to some hierarchy. For example, in a family tree, people are associated with their children and their parents. The ADT **binary search tree** has a combined hierarchical and sorted organization that makes locating a particular entry easier.

The ADT **graph** is a generalization of the ADT tree that focuses on the relationship among its entries instead of any hierarchical organization. For example, the road map shows the existing roads and distances between towns.

This book shows you how to use and implement these data organizations. Before we begin, you need to know Java. Appendix A reviews the basic statements in Java. Chapter 1 discusses the basic construction of classes and methods. You can choose to glance at this material, read it carefully, or come back to it as necessary. Chapters 2 and 3 also focus on Java, but some or all of the material might be new to you. Chapter 2 covers techniques, including composition and inheritance, for creating new classes from existing classes. Chapter 3 discusses how to design classes, specify methods, and write Java interfaces. Using interfaces and writing comments to specify methods are essential to our presentation of ADTs.

1

Java Classes

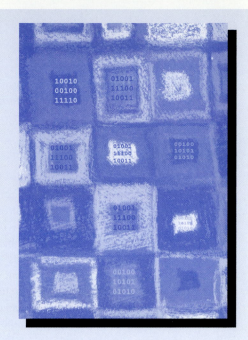

CONTENTS

Objects and Classes
Using the Methods in a Java Class
    References and Aliases
    Arguments and Parameters
Defining a Java Class
    Method Definitions
    Passing Arguments
    A Definition of the Class **Name**
    Constructors
    The Method `toString`
    Static Fields and Methods
Packages
    The Java Class Library

PREREQUISITES

Appendix   A   Java Essentials

OBJECTIVES

After studying this chapter, you should be able to

- Create an object of a class
- Call a method given its signature
- Describe the effect of a given invocation of a method
- Write a method definition
- Write a class definition
- Describe, define, and use constructors
- Describe the use of the access modifiers `public` and `private`
- Describe the use of static methods and data fields
- Create and use packages

This chapter reviews the use and creation of Java classes, methods, and packages. Even if you are familiar with this material, you should at least skim it to learn our terminology.

Objects and Classes

1.1   An **object** is a program construct that contains data and can perform certain actions. Like the objects in the world around us, the objects in a Java program interact with one another to accomplish a particular task. Thus, **object-oriented programming,** or **OOP,** views a program as a sort of world consisting of objects that interact with one another by means of actions. For example, in a program that simulates automobiles, each automobile is an object.

The actions that an object can take are called **methods**. The methods that an automobile object can perform might be moving forward, moving backward, accelerating, and so on. When you ask an object to perform an action, you **invoke,** or **call,** a method.

Objects of the same kind are said to have the same **type** and are in the same **class.** A class specifies the kind of data the objects of that class have. A class also specifies what actions the objects can take and how they accomplish those actions. When you define a class in Java, the class is like a plan or a blueprint for constructing specific objects. For example, Figure 1-1 describes a class called Automobile and shows three Automobile objects. The class is a general description of what an automobile is and what it can do.

Objects of the class Automobile are particular automobiles. Each is an **instance** of the class and is said to **instantiate** the Automobile class. Each object has a name. In Figure 1-1, the names are bobsCar, suesCar, and jakesTruck. In a Java program, bobsCar, suesCar, and jakesTruck would be variables of type Automobile. So among other things, a class is a data type.

The definition of the Automobile class says that an Automobile object has data such as its model, its year, and how much fuel is in its tank. The class definition contains no actual data—no string and no numbers. The individual objects have the data, and the class simply specifies what kind of data they have.

The Automobile class also defines methods such as goForward and goBackward. In a program that uses the class Automobile, the only actions an Automobile object can take are defined by those methods. All objects of a given class have exactly the same methods. The implementations of the methods indicate how the actions are performed and are included in the class definition. The objects themselves actually perform the method's actions, however.

The objects in a single class can have different characteristics. Even though these objects have the same types of data and the same methods, the individual objects can differ in the values of their data.

Note: An **object** is a program construct that contains data and performs actions. The objects in a Java program interact, and this interaction forms the solution to a given problem. The actions performed by objects are called **methods.**

Note: A **class** is a type or kind of object. All objects in the same class have the same kinds of data and the same methods. A class definition is a general description of what that object is and what it can do.

Figure 1-1   An outline of a class and three of its instances

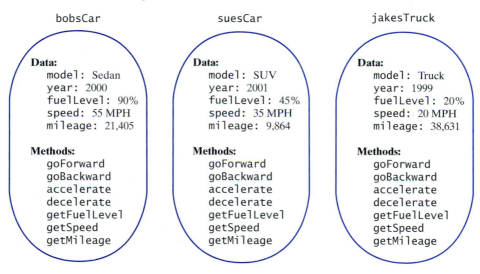

The Class Automobile

Class Name: Automobile

Data:
model_____
year_____
fuelLevel_____
speed_____
mileage_____

Methods (actions):
goForward
goBackward
accelerate
decelerate
getFuelLevel
getSpeed
getMileage

Objects (Instantiations) of the Class Automobile

bobsCar

Data:
model: Sedan
year: 2000
fuelLevel: 90%
speed: 55 MPH
mileage: 21,405

Methods:
goForward
goBackward
accelerate
decelerate
getFuelLevel
getSpeed
getMileage

suesCar

Data:
model: SUV
year: 2001
fuelLevel: 45%
speed: 35 MPH
mileage: 9,864

Methods:
goForward
goBackward
accelerate
decelerate
getFuelLevel
getSpeed
getMileage

jakesTruck

Data:
model: Truck
year: 1999
fuelLevel: 20%
speed: 20 MPH
mileage: 38,631

Methods:
goForward
goBackward
accelerate
decelerate
getFuelLevel
getSpeed
getMileage

Note: You can view a class in several different ways when programming. When you instanti-ate an object of a class, you view the class as a data type. When you implement a class, you can view it as a plan or a blueprint for constructing objects—that is, as a definition of the objects' data and actions. At other times, you can think of a class as a collection of objects that have the same type.

Using the Methods in a Java Class

1.2   Let's assume that someone has written a Java class called Name to represent a person's name. We will describe how to use this class and, in doing so, we will show you how to use a class's methods.

The program component that uses a class is called the **client** of the class. We will reserve the term "user" to mean a person who uses a program.

To declare a variable of data type `Name`, you would write, for example,

```
Name joe;
```

At this point, the variable `joe` contains nothing in particular; it is uninitialized. To create a specific object of data type `Name`—that is, to create an instance of `Name`—called `joe`, you write

```
joe = new Name();
```

The `new` operator creates an instance of `Name` by invoking a special method within the class, known as a **constructor.** The memory address of the new object is assigned to `joe`, as Figure 1-2 illustrates. We will show you how to define constructors a bit later, in Segment 1.17. Note that you can combine the previous two Java statements into one:

```
Name joe = new Name();
```

Figure 1-2   A variable that references an object

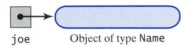

joe   Object of type `Name`

1.3   Suppose that a person's name has only two parts: a first name and a last name. The data associated with the object `joe` then consists of two strings that represent the first and last names. Since you want to be able to set a person's name, the `Name` class should have methods that give you this capability. To set `joe`'s first and last names, you use two methods from the class `Name`—`setFirst` and `setLast`—as follows:

```
joe.setFirst("Joseph");
joe.setLast("Brown");
```

A method defined within a class is usually invoked by an object such as `joe`. You write the name of the **calling object** (`joe`) first, followed by a dot, the name of the method to be invoked, and finally a set of parentheses that contain **arguments.** In this example, the arguments are strings that represent inputs to the methods. The methods set the object's data fields to the specific values given as arguments.

The methods `setFirst` and `setLast` are examples of **void methods,** in that they do not return a value. A second kind of method—the **valued method**—returns a single value. For example, the method `getFirst` returns a string that is the invoking object's first name. Similarly, the method `getLast` returns the last name.

You can invoke a valued method anywhere that you can use a value of the type returned by the method. For example, `getFirst` returns a value of type `String`, and so you can use a method invocation such as `joe.getFirst()` anywhere that it is legal to use a value of type `String`. Such places could be in an assignment statement, like

```
String hisName = joe.getFirst();
```

or within a `println` statement like

```
System.out.println("Joe's first name is " + joe.getFirst());
```

Notice that the methods `getFirst` and `getLast` have no arguments in their parentheses. Any method—valued or void—can require zero or more arguments.

Note: **Valued methods** return a single value; **void methods** do not return a value. For example, the valued method `getFirst` returns the string that represents the first name. The void method `setFirst` sets the first name to a given string but does not return a value.

Question 1 Write a Java statement that creates an object of type `Name` to represent your name.

Question 2 Write a Java statement that uses the object you created in Question 1 to display your name in the form *last name, comma, first name.*

Question 3 Which methods of the class `Automobile`, as given in Figure 1-1, are most likely valued methods, and which are most likely void methods?

References and Aliases

1.4　Java has eight primitive data types: `byte`, `short`, `int`, `long`, `float`, `double`, `char`, and `boolean`. A variable of a primitive type actually contains the primitive value. All other data types are **reference, or class, types.** The `String` variable `greeting` in

```
String greeting = "Hello";
```

is a variable of a reference type or, more simply, a **reference variable.** A reference variable contains the address in memory of an actual object. This address is called a **reference.** It is not important here to know that `greeting` contains a reference to the string `"Hello"` instead of the actual string. In such cases, it is easier to talk about the string `greeting`, when in fact this is not an accurate description of that variable. The chapters in this book make the distinction between an object and a reference to an object when it is important to do so.

Now suppose that you write

```
Name jamie = new Name("Jamie", "Jones");
Name friend = jamie;
```

The two variables `jamie` and `friend` reference the same instance of `Name`, as Figure 1-3 shows. We say that `jamie` and `friend` are **aliases,** because they are two different names for the same object. You can use `jamie` and `friend` interchangeably when referencing the object.

Figure 1-3　Aliases of an object

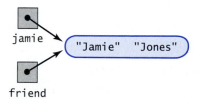

For example, if you use the variable `jamie` to change Jamie Jones's last name, you can use the variable `friend` to access it. Thus, the statements

```
jamie.setLast("Smith");
System.out.println(friend.getLast());
```

display *Smith*. Also note that the boolean expression jamie == friend is true, since both variables contain the same address.

Arguments and Parameters

1.5   Earlier you saw that an object of a class usually invokes the methods defined within the class. For example, you saw that the statements

```
Name joe = new Name();
joe.setFirst("Joseph");
joe.setLast("Brown");
```

set the first and last names for the object joe. The strings "Joseph" and "Brown" are the arguments. These arguments must correspond to the formal parameters of the method definition. In the case of setFirst, for example, the formal parameter is the string firstName. The argument is the string "Joseph". The argument is plugged in for the corresponding formal parameter. Thus, in the body of the method, firstName represents the string "Joseph" and behaves like a local variable.

A method invocation must provide exactly as many arguments as there are formal parameters in the corresponding method definition. In addition, the arguments in the invocation must correspond to the formal parameters in the method's definition with respect to both the order in which they occur and their data types. In some cases, however, Java will perform an automatic type conversion when the data types do not match.

 Programming Tip: The arguments in the invocation of a method must correspond to the formal parameters in the method's definition with respect to number, order, and data type.

Defining a Java Class

1.6   We now show you how to write the Java class Name that represents a person's name. You store a class definition in a file whose name is the name of the class followed by .java. Thus, the class Name should be in the file Name.java. (While not absolutely necessary, we will store only one class per file.)

The data in a Name object consists of the person's first and last names as strings. The methods in the class will enable you to set and look at these strings. The class has the following form:

```
public class Name
{
   private String first;   // first name
   private String last;    // last name

   < Definitions of methods are here >
   ...
} // end Name
```

The word public simply means that there are no restrictions on where the class is used. That is, the class Name is available for use in any other Java class. The two strings first and last are called the class's **data fields** or **instance variables** or **data members.** Each object of this class will have these two data fields inside of it. The word private that precedes the declaration of each data field means that only the methods within the class can refer to the data fields by their names first and last. No other class will be able to do this. The words `public` and `private` are examples of an **access modifier** or **visibility modifier,** which specifies where a class, data field, or method can be used.

1.7   Since the data fields are private, how will a class that uses the class `Name` be able to change or look at them? You can define methods in a class that look at or change its data fields. You declare such methods to be public, so that anyone can use them. A method that enables you to look at the value of a data field is called an **accessor method** or **query method.** A method that changes the value of a data field is called a **mutator method.** Java programmers typically begin the names of accessor methods with `get` and the names of mutator methods with `set`. Because of this convention, accessor methods are sometimes called **get methods** or **getters,** and mutator methods are called **set methods** or **setters.** For example, the class `Name` will have methods that include `getFirst`, `getLast`, `setFirst`, and `setLast`.

You may think that accessor methods and mutator methods defeat the purpose of making data fields private. On the contrary, they give the class control over its data fields. For example, a mutator method can check that any change to a data field is appropriate and warn you if there is a problem. The class would be unable to make this check if its data fields were public, since anyone could alter the fields.

Note: An **accessor (query) method** enables you to look at the value of a data field. A **mutator method** changes the value of a data field. Typically, you begin the names of accessor methods with `get` and the names of mutator methods with `set`.

Programming Tip: You should make each data field in a class private by beginning its declaration with the access modifier private. You cannot make any direct reference to a private data field's name outside of the class definition. The programmer who uses the class is forced to manipulate the data fields only via methods in the class. The class then can control how a programmer accesses or changes the data fields. Within any of the class's method definitions, however, you can use the name of the data field in any way you wish. In particular, you can directly change the value of the data field.

Question 1   Is the method `setFirst` an accessor method or a mutator method?

Question 2   Should a typical accessor method be valued or void?

Question 3   Should a typical mutator method be valued or void?

Question 4   What is a disadvantage of making a data field in a class public?

Method Definitions

1.8   The definition of a method has the following general form:

access-modifier   use-modifier   return-type   method-name (*parameter-list*)
{
   method-body
}

Any class can use a public method, but a private method can be used only by the class that defines it. Chapter 2 discusses the access modifier `protected`, and the section "Packages" of this chapter shows when you can omit the access modifier.

> **Note:** **Access (visibility) modifiers**
> The words `public` and `private` are examples of access modifiers that specify where a class, method, or data field can be used.

The **use modifier** is optional and in most cases is omitted. Briefly, a `final` method cannot be overridden in a derived class. An `abstract` method has no definition and must be overridden in a derived class. A `static` method is shared by all instances of the class. You will encounter these use modifiers later in this or the next chapters.

Next comes the return type, which for a valued method is the data type of the value that the method returns. For a void method, the return type is `void`. You then write the name of the method and a pair of parentheses that contain an optional list of **formal parameters** and their data types. The formal parameters, or simply **parameters,** specify values or objects that are inputs to the method.

So far, we have described the first line of the method definition, which is called the method's **signature** or **heading** or **declaration.** After the signature is the method's **body**—which is simply a sequence of Java statements—enclosed in curly braces.

1.9   As an example of a valued method, here is the definition of the method `getFirst`:

```
public String getFirst()  ◄——— Signature
{
   return first;          ⎫ Body
} // end getFirst         ⎭
```

This method returns the string in the data field `first`. The return type of this method is, therefore, `String`. A valued method must always execute a `return` statement as its last action. The data type of the value returned must match the data type declared as the return type in the method's heading. Notice that this particular method does not have formal parameters.

1.10   Now let's look at an example of a void method. The void method `setFirst` sets the data field `first` to a string that represents a first name. The method definition is as follows:

```
public void setFirst(String firstName)
{
   first = firstName;
} // end setFirst
```

This method does not return a value, so its return type is `void`. The method has one formal parameter, `firstName`, that has the data type `String`. It represents the string that the method should assign to the data field `first`. The declaration of a formal parameter always consists of a data type and a parameter name. If you have more than one formal parameter, you separate their declarations with commas.

1.11   Notice that the bodies of the previous two method definitions refer to the data field `first` by name. This is perfectly legal. Exactly whose data field is involved here? Remember that each object of this class contains a data field `first`. The data field `first` that belongs to the object invoking the method is the one involved. Java has a name for this invoking object when you want to refer to it within the body of a method definition. It is simply `this`. For example, in the method `setFirst` you could write the statement

    first = firstName;

as

    this.first = firstName;

People use `this` either for clarity or when they want to give the parameter the same name as the data field. For example, you could name `setFirst`'s parameter `first` instead of `firstName`. Clearly, the statement

    first = first;

in the method's body would not work correctly, so instead you would write

    this.first = first;

We typically will not use `this`.

Note: Members
Both the data fields and the methods are sometimes called **members** of the object, because they belong to the object.

Note: Naming classes and methods
The normal convention when naming classes and methods is to start all method names with a lowercase letter and to start all class names with an uppercase letter. Use a noun or descriptive phrase to name a class. Use a verb or action phrase to name a method.

Note: Local variables
A variable declared within a method definition is called a **local variable**. The value of a local variable is not available outside of the method definition. If two methods each have a local variable of the same name, the variables are different, even though they have the same name.

1.12   Methods should be self-contained units. You should design methods separately from the incidental details of other methods of the class and separately from any program that uses the class. One incidental detail is the name of the formal parameters. Fortunately, formal parameters behave like local variables, and so their meanings are confined to their respective method definitions. Thus, you can choose the formal parameter names without any concern that they will be the same as some other identifier used in some other method. For team programming projects, one programmer can write a method definition while another programmer writes another part of the program that uses that method. The two programmers need not agree on the names they use for formal parameters or local variables. They can choose their identifier names completely independently without any concern that some, all, or none of their identifiers might be the same.

Note: **Use of the terms "parameter" and "argument"**
The use of the terms "formal parameter" and "argument" in this book is consistent with common usage, but people also use the terms "parameter" and "argument" interchangeably. Some people use the term "parameter" for both what we call (formal) parameters and what we call arguments. Other people use the term "argument" for both what we call (formal) parameters and what we call arguments.

Passing Arguments

1.13   When a formal parameter has a primitive type such as int, the parameter is initialized to the value of the corresponding argument in the method invocation. The argument in a method invocation can be a literal constant—like 2 or 'A'—or it can be a variable or any expression that yields a value of the appropriate type. Note that the method cannot change the value of an argument that has a primitive data type. Such an argument serves as an input value only. This mechanism is known as the **call-by-value** parameter mechanism.

When a formal parameter has a class type, the corresponding argument in the method invocation must be an object of that class type. The formal parameter is initialized to the memory address of that object.[1] Thus, the formal parameter will serve as an alternative name for the object. This implies that the method can change the data in the object, if the class has mutator methods. The method, however, cannot replace an object that is an argument with another object.

1.14   **Example.** For example, if you adopt a child, you might give that child your last name. Suppose that you add the following method giveLastNameTo to the class Name that makes this change of name:

```
public void giveLastNameTo(Name child)
{
   child.setLast(last);
} // end giveLastNameTo
```

Notice that the formal parameter of this method has the type Name.

Now if Jamie Jones adopts Jane Doe, the following statements would change Jane's last name to Jones:

```
public static void main(String[] args)[2]
{
   Name jamie = new Name("Jamie", "Jones");
   Name jane = new Name("Jane", "Doe");
   jamie.giveLastNameTo(jane);
   . . .
} // end main
```

Figure 1-4 shows the argument jane and the parameter child as the method giveLastNameTo executes.

---

1. The parameter mechanism for parameters of a class type is similar to **call-by-reference** parameter passing. If you are familiar with this terminology, be aware that parameters of a class type in Java behave a bit differently from call-by-reference parameters in other languages.
2. If you are not familiar with main methods and application programs, consult the beginning of Appendix A.

Figure 1-4   The method `giveLastNameTo` modifies the object passed to it as an argument

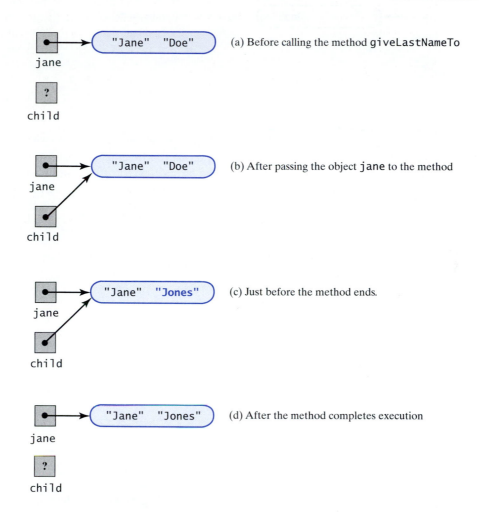

1.15   What happens if you change the method definition to allocate a new name, as follows?

```java
public void giveLastNameTo2(Name child)
{
   child = new Name(child.getFirst(), last);
} // end giveLastNameTo2
```

With this change, the invoking statement

```java
jamie.giveLastNameTo2(jane);
```

has no effect on `jane`, as Figure 1-5 illustrates. The parameter `child` behaves like a local variable, so its value is not available outside of the method definition.

Figure 1-5   A method cannot replace an object passed to it as an argument

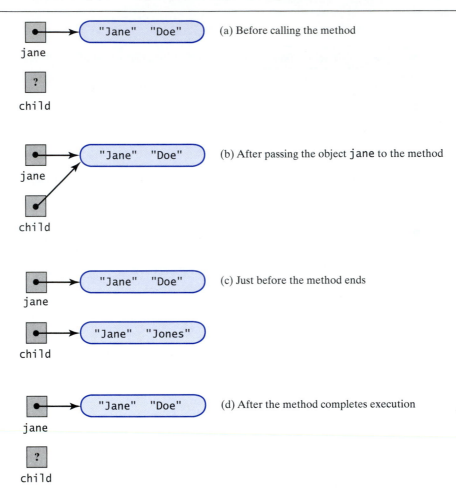

Question 8   Consider a method definition that begins with the statement

public void process(**int** number, Name aName)

If jamie is defined as in Segment 1.14 and you invoke this method with the statement

someObject.process(5, jamie);

what values are given to the parameters within the definition of the method?

Question 9   In Question 8, can the method process change the data fields in jamie?

Question 10   In Question 8, can the method process assign a new object to jamie?

A Definition of the Class Name

1.16   A complete definition for the class Name follows:

```
public class Name
{
```

```java
  private String first;  // first name
  private String last;   // last name

  public Name()
  {
  } // end default constructor

  public Name(String firstName, String lastName)
  {
    first = firstName;
    last = lastName;
  } // end constructor

  public void setName(String firstName, String lastName)
  {
    setFirst(firstName);
    setLast(lastName);
  } // end setName

  public String getName()
  {
    return toString();
  } // end getName

  public void setFirst(String firstName)
  {
    first = firstName;
  } // end setFirst

  public String getFirst()
  {
    return first;
  } // end getFirst

  public void setLast(String lastName)
  {
    last = lastName;
  } // end setLast

  public String getLast()
  {
    return last;
  } // end getLast

  public void giveLastNameTo(Name aName)
  {
    aName.setLast(last);
  } // end giveLastNameTo

  public String toString()
  {
    return first + " " + last;
  } // end toString
} // end Name
```

We typically place data field declarations at the beginning of the class, but some people place them last. Java also allows you to intermix method definitions and data field declarations. Let's examine some other details of this class definition.

Constructors

1.17   Segment 1.2 mentioned that you create an object by using the `new` operator to invoke a special method called a constructor. A **constructor** allocates memory for the object and initializes the data fields. The method definition of a constructor has certain special properties. A constructor

- Has the same name as the class
- Has no return type, not even `void`
- Has any number of formal parameters, including no parameters

A class can have several constructors that differ in the number or type of parameters.

A constructor without parameters is called the **default constructor.** A class can have only one default constructor. The definition of the default constructor for `Name` is

```java
public Name()
{
} // end default constructor
```

This particular default constructor has an empty body, but it need not be empty. It could explicitly initialize the data fields `first` and `last` to values other than the ones Java assigns by default.

Programming Tip: In the absence of any explicit initialization within a constructor, data fields are set to default values: Object types are `null`, primitive numeric types are zero, and `boolean` types are false. If a class depends on a data field's initial value, its constructor should set these values explicitly. Standard default values have been known to change.

If you do not define any constructors for a class, Java will automatically provide a default constructor—that is, a constructor with no parameters. If you define a constructor that has parameters but you do not define a default constructor—one without parameters—Java will not provide a default constructor for you. Because classes are often reused again and again, and because eventually you might want to create a new object without specifying parameters, your classes typically should include a default constructor.

Programming Tip: Once you start defining constructors, Java will not define any other constructors for you. Most of the classes you define should include a default constructor.

1.18   The class `Name` contains a second constructor, one that initializes the data fields to values given as arguments when the client invokes the constructor:

```java
public Name(String firstName, String lastName)
{
   first = firstName;
   last = lastName;
} // end constructor
```

This constructor has two parameters, `firstName` and `lastName`. You invoke it with a statement such as

```
Name jill = new Name("Jill", "Jones");
```

that passes first and last names as arguments.

1.19   After creating the object `jill`, you can change the values of its data fields by using the class's set (mutator) methods. You saw that this step was in fact necessary for the object `joe` in Segment 1.2 since `joe` was created by the default constructor and had default values—probably `null`—as its first and last names. In either case, you should not invoke a constructor again to alter the data fields of an object unless the class does not provide set methods.

Let's see what would happen in the case of `jill` if you did invoke the constructor a second time. After you created the object, the variable `jill` contained the memory address of that object, as Figure 1-6a illustrates. If you now write the statement

```
jill = new Name("Jill", "Smith");
```

a new object is created, and `jill` contains its memory address. The original object is lost, because no program variable has its address, as shown in Figure 1-6b.

What happens to a memory location when the variables in your program no longer reference it? Periodically, the Java run-time environment **deallocates** such memory locations by returning them to the operating system so that they can be used again. In effect, the memory is recycled. This process is called **automatic garbage collection.**

Note: Memory leak
If the Java runtime environment did not track and recycle memory that a program no longer references, a program could use all the memory available to it and subsequently fail. If you use another programming language—C++, for example—you would be responsible for returning unneeded memory to the operating system for reuse. A program that failed to return such memory would have what is known as a **memory leak.** Java programs do not have this problem.

Figure 1-6   An object (a) after its initial creation; (b) after its reference is lost

1.20   Notice the method `setName` in the class definition. Although `setName` could use assignment statements to initialize `first` and `last`, it instead invokes the methods `setFirst` and `setLast`. Since these methods are members of the class, `setName` can invoke them without preceding the name with an object variable and a dot. If you prefer, you can use `this`, and write the invocation as

```
this.setFirst(firstName);
```

When the logic of a method's definition is complex, you should divide the logic into smaller pieces and implement each piece as a separate method. Your method can then invoke these other methods. Such helping methods, however, might be inappropriate for a client to use. If so, declare them as private instead of public so that only your class can invoke them.

Although it generally is a good idea for methods to call other methods to avoid repeating code, you need to be careful if you call public methods from the body of a constructor. For example, it is tempting to have the constructor mentioned in Segment 1.18 call `setName`. But another class derived from your class could change the effect of `setName` and hence of your constructor. Segment 2.17 in the next chapter elaborates on this issue.

Programming Tip: If a helping method is not appropriate for public use, declare it as private.

Question 11   What is a default constructor?

Question 12   How do you invoke a constructor?

Question 13   What happens if you do not define constructors for a class?

Question 14   What happens if you do not define a default constructor but you do define a constructor that has parameters?

Question 15   What happens when an object no longer has a variable that references it?

The Method `toString`

1.21   The last method in the class is `toString`. This method returns a string that is the person's full name. You can use this method, for example, to display the name that the object `jill` represents by writing

```
System.out.println(jill.toString());
```

What is remarkable about `toString` is that Java will invoke it automatically when you write

```
System.out.println(jill);
```

For this reason, providing a class with a method `toString` is a good idea in general. If you fail to do so, Java will provide its own `toString` method, which produces a string that will have little meaning to you. The next chapter provides more detail about the `toString` method.

Static Fields and Methods

1.22   **Static fields.** Sometimes you need a data field that does not belong to any one object. For example, a class could track how many invocations of the class's methods are made by all objects of the class. Such a data field is called a **static field, static variable,** or **class variable.** You declare a static field by adding the reserved word `static`. For example, the declaration

```
private static int numberOfInvocations = 0;
```

defines one copy of `numberOfInvocations` that every object of the class can access. Objects can use a static field to communicate or to perform some joint action. In this example, each method increments `numberOfInvocations`. Such static fields normally should be private to ensure that access occurs only through appropriate accessor and mutator methods.

The definition of a named constant provides another example of a static field. The statement

public static final double PI = 3.14159;

defines a static field PI. The class has one copy of PI, rather than each object of the class having its own copy, as Figure 1-7 illustrates. Since PI is also declared as final, its value cannot change. But static fields in general can change value if you omit the modifier final.

Figure 1-7   A static field PI versus a nonstatic field radius

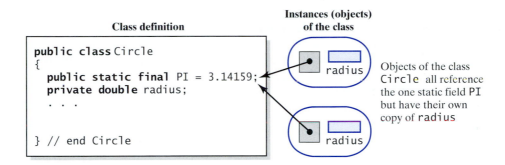

1.23   **Static methods.** Sometimes you need a method that does not belong to an object of any kind. For example, you might need a method to compute the maximum of two integers or a method to compute the square root of a number. These methods have no obvious object to which they should belong. In these cases, you can define the method as static by adding the reserved word static to the signature of the method.

A **static method** or **class method** is still a member of a class. However, you use the class name instead of an object name to invoke the method. For example, Java's predefined class Math contains several standard mathematical methods, such as max and sqrt. All of these methods are static, so you do not need—and in fact have no real use for—an object of the class Math. You call these methods by using the class name in place of a calling object. Thus, you write statements such as

```
int maximum = Math.max(2, 3);
double root = Math.sqrt(4.2);
```

The definition of a static method cannot reference any data field in its class that is not static. It can, however, reference its class's static fields. Likewise, it cannot invoke a nonstatic method of the class, unless it creates a local object of the class and uses it to invoke the nonstatic method. However, a static method can call other static methods within its class. Since every application program's main method is static, these restrictions apply to main methods.

Programming Tip: **Every class can have a main method**
You can include a test of a class as a main method in the class's definition. Anytime you suspect something is wrong, you can easily test the class definition. Since you—and others—can see what tests you performed, flaws in your testing will become apparent. If you use the class as a program, the main method is invoked. When you use the class to create objects in another class or program, the main method is ignored.

Question 16   What happens if you do not declare a constant data field as static?

Packages

1.24   Using several related classes is more convenient if you group them together within a Java **package.** To identify a class as part of a particular package, you begin the file that contains the class with a statement like

```
package myStuff;
```

You then place all of the files within one directory or folder and give it the same name as the package.

To use a package in your program, you begin the program with a statement such as

```
import myStuff.*;
```

The asterisk makes all public classes within the package available to the program. You could, however, replace the asterisk with the name of a particular class in the package that you want to use. You probably have already used packages provided by Java, such as the package `java.io`.

Why did we just say "public classes"? What other kind of class is there? You can use an access modifier to control access to a class just as you can control access to a data field or method. A public class—whether it is within a package or not—is available to any other class. If you omit the class's access modifier entirely, the class is available only to other classes within the same package. This kind of class is said to have **package access.** Similarly, if you omit the access modifier on data fields or methods, they are available by name inside the definition of any class within the same package but not outside of the package. You use package access in situations where you have a package of cooperating classes that act as a single encapsulated unit. If you control the package directory, you control who is allowed package access.

The Java Class Library

1.25   Java comes with a collection of many classes that you can use in your programs. For example, Segment 1.23 mentioned the class `Math`, which contains several standard mathematical methods such as `sqrt`. This collection is known as the **Java Class Library,** and sometimes as the **Java Application Programming Interface,** or **API.** The classes in this library are distributed among several standard packages. For example, the class `Math` is a part of the package `java.lang`.

From time to time, we will mention classes within the Java Class Library that are like or relevant to the classes that we will define.

CHAPTER SUMMARY

- An object is a program construction that contains data and can perform certain actions. When the program is run, the objects interact with one another to accomplish a particular task. The actions performed by objects are called methods. A class is a type or kind of object. All objects in the same class have the same kinds of data and the same methods.

- An access modifier, such as `public` or `private`, specifies where you can use a class, method, or data field.

- A private data field is not accessible by name outside of the class definition. Within any of the class's method definitions, you can use the data field name in any way you wish. In particular, you can directly change the value of the data field. However, outside of the class definition, you cannot make any direct reference to the data field name. The programmer who uses the class is forced to manipulate the data fields only via methods in the class. The class then can control how a programmer accesses or changes the data fields.

- A public method that returns the data in a private data field is called an accessor method. A public method that changes the data in a private data field is called a mutator method.

- Valued methods return a single value; void methods do not return any value.

- A method invocation must provide exactly the same number of arguments as there are formal parameters in the corresponding method definition. In addition, the arguments in the invocation must correspond to the method's formal parameters in its definition with respect to the order in which they occur and their data types. In some cases, however, Java will perform an automatic type conversion when the data types do not match.

- When a formal parameter has a primitive type such as `int`, the parameter is initialized to the value of the corresponding argument in the method invocation. When a formal parameter has a class type, the corresponding argument in the method invocation must be an object of that class type. The formal parameter is initialized to the memory address of that object.

- A valued method must always execute a `return` statement as its last action. The data type of the value returned must match the data type declared as the return type in the method's signature.

- A variable declared within a method definition is called a local variable. The value of a local variable is not available outside of the method definition. If two methods each have a local variable of the same name, the variables are different, even though they have the same name. Java does not give an initial value to a local variable, regardless of its data type.

- A constructor allocates memory for the object and initializes the data fields. A constructor has the same name as the class, has no return type, not even `void`, and has any number of formal parameters, including zero parameters.

- A constructor without parameters is called the default constructor. A class can have only one default constructor. If you do not define any constructors for a class, Java automatically provides a default constructor.

- When the logic of a method's definition is complex, you should divide the logic into smaller pieces and implement each piece as a separate method. Your method can then invoke these other methods. If such helping methods are inappropriate for a client to use, declare them as private instead of public so that only your class can invoke them.

- Every class can have a `main` method. If you use the class as a program, the `main` method is invoked. When you use the class to create objects in another class or program, the `main` method is ignored.

- A static field or static method is associated with the class and not the individual objects of the class.

- A package is a group of related classes that you place into a single directory or folder. Classes within a package can access by name any field or method within any other class in the package, if the field or method has no access modifier or is not private.

PROGRAMMING TIPS

- All data fields in a class should be private.

- You cannot make any direct reference to a private data field's name outside of the class definition.

- Provide public methods to look at or change the data fields in an object.

- When you invoke a method, the arguments must correspond to the method's formal parameters in its definition with respect to number, order, and data type.

- In the absence of any explicit initialization within a constructor, data fields are set to default values: Object types are **null**, primitive numeric types are zero, and **boolean** types are false.

- Once you start defining constructors, Java will not define any other constructors for you. Most of the classes you define should include a default constructor.

- If a helping method is not appropriate for public use, declare it as private.

- Include a test of a class as a **main** method in the class's definition. Anytime you suspect something is wrong, you can easily test the class definition.

EXERCISES

(Several exercises involve the class Name, as given in Segment 1.16.)

1. What is the difference between how a method handles a parameter of a primitive type and a parameter of a reference (class) type?

2. If you remove the default constructor from the class Name, what happens if you write the statement

   ```
   Name me = new Name();
   ```

3. If you remove all constructors from the class Name, what happens if you write the statement

   ```
   Name me = new Name();
   ```

4. Implement another constructor for the class Name that has as its only parameter an instance of Name. The constructor should create a new name object whose data fields have the same values as its parameter's data fields.

5. Suppose that jack and jill are two distinct objects of the class Name.

   a. Write Java statements that create a variable friend as an alias of jack.
   b. What is the value of the boolean expression friend == jack? Why?
   c. What happens to the last names of jack and jill after the following statements execute? Explain your answer.

   ```
   jill.giveLastNameTo(friend);
   jack.giveLastNameTo(jill);
   ```

6. Add the following methods to the class Name, as defined in this chapter:

   ```
   /** Task: Changes the last name to the last name of aName. */
   public void changeLastNameTo(Name aName)

   /** Task: Changes the last name to the string newLastName. */
   public void changeLastNameTo(String newLastName)
   ```

7. Write a static method `readName` suitable for a client of the class `Name` that returns a `Name` object. This object should have a first and last name that `readName` reads as strings from the keyboard.

1. Define a class called `Counter`. An object of this class is used to count things, so it records a count that is a nonnegative whole number. Include methods to set the counter to a given integer, to increase the count by 1, and to decrease the count by 1. Be sure that no method allows the value of the counter to become negative. Also include an accessor method that returns the current count value and a method that displays the count on the screen.

Write a program to test your class definition.

2. Write a class called `Person` that has two data fields, one for the person's name and one for the person's age. Include set and get methods for each of these data fields. Also include methods to test whether

- Two `Person` objects are equal—that is, have the same name and age
- One person is older than another

Finally, include a `toString` method that returns a string consisting of a person's name and age.

Write a test program that demonstrates each method.

3. Define a class `GenericCoin` that represents a coin with no value or name. The coin should have a heads side and a tails side and should be able to tell you which side is up. You should be able to "toss" the coin so that it lands randomly either heads up or tails up.

a. Write a program that tosses two coins 50 times each. Record and report how many times each coin lands heads up. Also report which coin landed heads up most often.

b. Write a program that plays a simple coin-toss game. You ask the user to guess whether the coin will be heads or tails. Then you toss the coin, tell the user the results, announce whether the user's guess was correct, and tabulate the results. The user can continue playing the game for as long as desired. When the user quits, display a summary of the game, including the number of coin tosses, the number of heads, the number of tails, the number of correct guesses, and the percentage of guesses that were correct. If desired, use graphics to illustrate the result of each coin toss.

4. Many games depend on the roll of two dice. Define a class `Die` that represents one n-sided die. The default value for n is 6. You should be able to roll the die and determine the value of its upper face. Use random numbers to simulate the roll of the die. If desired, use graphics to display this face.

5. The largest positive integer of type `int` is 2,147,483,647. Another integer type, `long`, represents integers up to 9,223,372,036,854,775,807. Imagine that you want to represent even larger integers.

Design and implement a class `Huge` of very large nonnegative integers. The largest integer should contain at least 30 digits. Provide operations for the class that

- Set the value of a nonnegative integer (provide both set methods and constructors)

- Return the value of a nonnegative integer as a string
- Read a large nonnegative integer (skip leading zeros, but remember that zero is a valid number)
- Write a large nonnegative integer (do not write leading zeros, but if the integer is zero, write a single zero)
- Add two nonnegative integers to produce the sum as a third integer
- Multiply two nonnegative integers to produce the product as a third integer

You should handle overflow when reading, adding, or multiplying integers. An integer is too large if it exceeds MAX_SIZE digits, where MAX_SIZE is a named constant that you define.

Write a test program that demonstrates each method.

6. Write a Java class CalendarDate that represents a calendar date consisting of a month, day, and year. You can use three integers to represent a date. For example, July 4, 1776, is month 7, day 4, and year 1776. Include reasonable constructors, set and get methods, and a toString method. In addition, provide methods that

- Determine whether two dates are equal
- Get the day of the week for the current date
- Determine whether the current year is a leap year
- Advance the current date by one day

A year is a leap year if it is divisible by 4 but not by 100. If the year is divisible by 100, it is a leap year only if it is also divisible by 400.

To determine the day of the week, you can use the following algorithm. First, define the following integers:

- M represents the month. M is 1 for March, 2 for April, and so on. M is 11 for January and 12 for February, but for these two months, subtract 1 from the year before proceeding.
- D represents the day of the month (1 through 31).
- C is the first two digits of the year (after any adjustment for January and February).
- Y is the last two digits of the year (after any adjustment for January and February).

Now compute
$$F = (26 M - 2)/10 + D + Y + Y/4 + C/4 - 2 C$$
All divisions are integer divisions in the sense that you discard any remainders. Now let
$$W = F \text{ (modulo 7)}$$
That is, you divide F by 7 and retain only the remainder. (The modulo operator is % in Java.) W now represents the day of the week: 0 is Sunday, 1 is Monday, and so on.

Write a test program that demonstrates each method in your class.

7. Write a Java class Time that represents the time of day in hours and minutes on a 24-hour clock. Include constructors, set and get methods, a method that advances the time by a given number of minutes, and a toString method. Provide another method, similar to toString, that returns the current time in 12-hour notation. For example, toString might return the string "13:05", while the other method returns the string "1:05pm". Optionally, you can write a method that displays the time on a digital or analog clock face.

8. A **magic square** is a square two-dimensional array of positive integers such that the sum of each row, column, and diagonal is the same constant. For example,

16	3	2	13
5	10	11	8
9	6	7	12
4	15	14	1

is a magic square because the sum of the integers in each row is 34, the sum of the integers in each column is 34, and the sum of the integers in each of the two diagonals $(16 + 10 + 7 + 1$ and $4 + 6 + 11 + 13)$ is 34. The size of this magic square array is 4 because it has 4 rows and 4 columns.

Write a Java class Square to represent an n-by-n square array of integers. Include methods that set or return the square's size n, read integers into the square, display the square, and determine whether the square is a magic square.

Write a test program that demonstrates each method.

2

Creating Classes from Other Classes

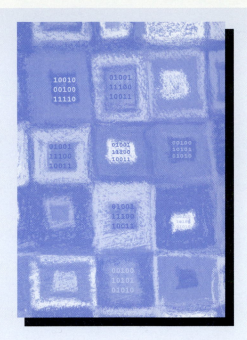

CONTENTS

Composition
    Adapters
Inheritance
    Invoking Constructors from Within Constructors
    Private Fields and Methods of the Base Class
    Overriding and Overloading Methods
    Protected Access
    Multiple Inheritance
Type Compatibility and Base Classes
    The Class `Object`
    Abstract Classes and Methods
Polymorphism

PREREQUISITES

Chapter   1   Java Classes

OBJECTIVES

After studying this chapter, you should be able to

- Use an instance of an existing class in the definition of a new class
- Use inheritance to derive a new class from an existing class
- Override and overload method definitions
- Describe the purpose and methods of the class `Object`
- Describe the purpose of an abstract class
- Determine which overridden method an object invokes

A major advantage of object-oriented programming is the ability to use existing classes when defining new classes. That is, you use classes that you or someone else has written to create new classes, rather than reinventing everything yourself. We begin this chapter with two ways to accomplish this feat.

In the first way, you simply declare an instance of an existing class as a data field of your new class. In fact, you have done this already if you have ever defined a class that had a string as a data field. Since your class is composed of objects, this technique is called composition.

The second way is to use inheritance, whereby your new class inherits properties and behaviors from an existing class, augmenting or modifying them as desired. This technique is more complicated than composition, so we will devote more time to it. As important as inheritance is in Java, you should not ignore composition as a valid and desirable technique in many situations.

Both composition and inheritance define a relationship between two classes. These relationships are often called, respectively, *has a* and *is a* relationships. You will see why when we discuss them in this chapter.

Polymorphism is another key feature of object-oriented programming. In fact object-oriented programming is usually described in terms of its main features: encapsulation, inheritance, and polymorphism. Used in conjunction with inheritance, polymorphism enables different objects to call methods having the same name and get different actions.

Composition

2.1   Chapter 1 introduced you to the class Name to represent a person's name. It defined constructors, accessor methods, and mutator methods that involved the first and last names. The data fields in Name are instances of the class String. A class uses **composition** when it has a data field that is an instance of another class. And since the class Name has an instance of the class String as a data field, the relationship between Name and String is called a ***has a*** relationship.

Let's create another class that uses composition. Consider a class of students, each of whom has a name and an identification number. Thus, the class Student contains two instances of objects as data fields: an instance of the class Name and an instance of the class String:

```
private Name    fullName;
private String id;
```

Figure 2-1 shows an object of type Student. Notice that it contains a Name object and a String object and that the Name object contains two String objects.

Figure 2-1   A Student object is composed of other objects

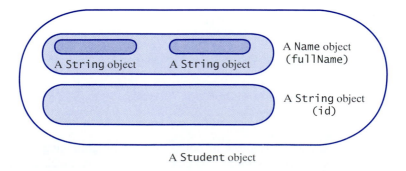

A Student object

For methods, we give the class Student constructors, accessors, mutators, and toString. Recall that the method toString is invoked when you use System.out.println to display an object, so it is a handy method to include in your class definitions.

Note: **Composition** (*has a*)

A class uses composition when it has objects as data fields. The class's implementation has no special access to such objects and must behave as a client would. That is, the class uses an object's methods to manipulate the object's data. Since the class "has a," or contains, an instance (object) of another class, the classes are said to have a *has a* relationship.

2.2   Look at the definition of the class Student, and then we will make a few more observations.

```java
public class Student
{
  private Name fullName;
  private String id;    // identification number

  public Student()
  {
    fullName = new Name();
    id = "";
  } // end default constructor

  public Student(Name studentName, String studentId)
  {
    fullName = studentName;
    id = studentId;
  } // end constructor

  public void setStudent(Name studentName, String studentId)
  {
    setName(studentName); // or fullName = studentName;
    setId(studentId);     // or id = studentId;
  } // end setStudent

  public void setName(Name studentName)
  {
    fullName = studentName;
  } // end setName

  public Name getName()
  {
    return fullName;
  } // end getName

  public void setId(String studentId)
  {
    id = studentId;
  } // end setId

  public String getId()
  {
    return id;
  } // end getId
```

```
    public String toString()
    {
        return id + " " + fullName.toString();
    } // end toString
}   // end Student
```

The method `setStudent` is useful when we create a student object by using the default constructor or if we want to change both the name and identification number that we gave to a student object earlier. Notice that the method invokes the other set methods from this class to initialize the data fields. For example, to set the field `fullName` to the parameter `studentName`, `setStudent` uses the statement

```
    setName(studentName);
```

We could also write this statement as

```
    this.setName(studentName);
```

where `this` refers to the instance of `Student` that invokes the method `setStudent`. Or we could write the assignment statement

```
    fullName = studentName;
```

Implementing methods in terms of other methods is usually desirable. It might not be desirable when implementing constructors, however, as you will see later in this chapter.

Suppose that we want `toString` to return a string composed of the student's identification number and name. It must use methods in the class `Name` to access the name as a string. For example, `toString` could return the desired string by using either

```
    return id + " " + fullName.getFirst() + " " + fullName.getLast();
```

or, more simply,

```
    return id + " " + fullName.toString();
```

The data field `fullName` references a `Name` object whose private fields are not accessible by name in the implementation of this class. We can access them indirectly via the accessor methods `getFirst` and `getLast` or by invoking `Name`'s `toString` method.

Question 1   What data fields would you use in the definition of a class `Address` to represent a student's address?

Question 2   Add a data field to the class `Student` to represent a student's address. What new methods should you define?

Question 3   What existing methods need to be changed in the class `Student` as a result of the added field that Question 2 described?

Adapters

2.3   Suppose that you have a class, but the names of its methods do not suit your application. Or maybe you want to simplify some methods or eliminate others. You can use composition to write a new class that has an instance of your existing class as a data field and defines the methods that you want. Such a new class is called an **adapter class.**

For example, suppose that instead of using objects of the class `Name` to name people, we want to use simple nicknames. We could use strings for nicknames, but since we cannot alter them, a class of nicknames would be more flexible. The following class has an instance of the class `Name` as a data field, a default constructor, and set and get methods. We use the first-name field of the class `Name` to store the nickname.

```
public class NickName
{
  private Name nick;

  public NickName()
  {
    nick = new Name();
  } // end default constructor

  public void setNickName(String nickName)
  {
    nick.setFirst(nickName);
  } // end setNickName

  public String getNickName()
  {
    return nick.getFirst();
  } // end getNickName
} // end NickName
```

Notice how this class uses the methods of the class `Name` to implement its methods. A `NickName` object now has only `NickName`'s methods, and not the methods of `Name`.

Inheritance

2.4 **Inheritance** is a major component of object-oriented programming that enables you to organize classes. The name comes from the notion of inherited traits like eye color, hair color, and so forth, but it is perhaps clearer to think of inheritance as a classification system. Inheritance allows you to define a general class and then later to define more specialized classes simply by adding to or revising the details of the older, more general class definition. This saves work, because the specialized class inherits all the properties of the general class and you need only program the new or revised features.

For example, you might define a generic class for vehicles and then define more specific classes for particular types of vehicles, such as automobiles, wagons, and boats. Similarly, the class of automobiles includes the classes of cars and trucks. Figure 2-2 illustrates this hierarchy of classes. The `Vehicle` class is the **base class** for the other **derived classes.** The `Automobile` class is the base class for the derived classes `Car` and `Truck`. Another term for base class is **superclass,** and another term for derived class is **subclass.**

Figure 2-2   A hierarchy of classes

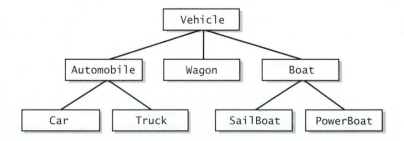

As you move up in the diagram, the classes are more inclusive. A car is an automobile and, therefore, is also a vehicle. However, a vehicle is not necessarily a car. A sailboat is a boat and is also a vehicle, but a vehicle is not necessarily a sailboat.

2.5   Java and other programming languages use inheritance to organize classes in this hierarchical way. A programmer can then use an existing class to write a new one that has more features. For example, the class of vehicles has certain properties—like miles traveled—that its data fields record. The class also has certain behaviors—like going forward—that its methods define. The classes `Automobile`, `Wagon`, and `Boat` inherit these properties and behaviors. Everything that is true of all `Vehicle` objects, such as miles traveled, is described only once and inherited by the classes `Automobile`, `Wagon`, and `Boat`. Without inheritance, descriptions like miles traveled would have to be repeated for each of the derived classes `Automobile`, `Wagon`, `Boat`, `Car`, `Truck`, and so on. The derived classes then add to or revise the properties and behaviors that they inherit.

Note: Inheritance

Inheritance is a way of organizing classes so that common properties and behaviors can be defined only once for all the classes involved. Thus, you can define a general class and then later define more specialized classes simply by adding to or revising the details of the older, more general class definition.

Since the `Automobile` class is derived from the `Vehicle` class, it inherits all the data fields and methods of that class. The `Automobile` class would have additional fields for such things as the amount of fuel in the fuel tank, and it would also have some added methods. Such fields and methods are not in the `Vehicle` class, because they do not apply to all vehicles. For example, wagons have no fuel tank.

Inheritance gives an instance of a derived class all the behaviors of the base class. For example, an automobile will be able to do everything that a vehicle can do; after all, an automobile *is a* vehicle. In fact, inheritance is known as an ***is a*** relationship between classes. Since the derived class and the base class share properties, you should use inheritance only when it makes sense to think of an instance of the derived class as also being an instance of the base class.

Note: An *is a* relationship

Inheritance makes an instance of a derived class behave like an instance of its base class. Thus, you should use inheritance only when this *is a* relationship between classes is meaningful.

Question 4   Revise the hierarchy in Figure 2-2 to categorize vehicles according to whether they have wheels.

2.6   **Example.** Let's construct an example of inheritance within Java. Suppose we are designing a program that maintains records about students, including those in grade school, high school, and college. We can organize the records for the various kinds of students by using a natural hierarchy that begins with students. College students are then one subclass of students. College students divide into two smaller subclasses: undergraduate students and graduate students. These subclasses might further subdivide into still smaller subclasses. Figure 2-3 diagrams this hierarchical arrangement.

A common way to describe derived classes is in terms of family relationships. For example, the class of students is said to be an **ancestor** of the class of undergraduate students. Conversely, the class of undergraduate students is a **descendant** of the class of students.

Figure 2-3   A hierarchy of student classes

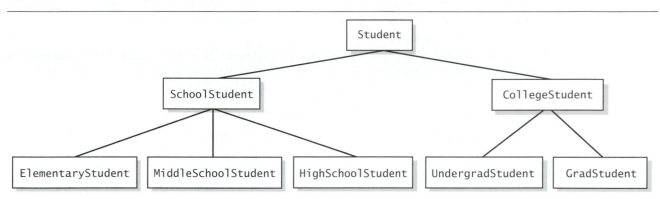

Although our program may not need any class corresponding to students in general, thinking in terms of such classes can be useful. For example, all students have names, and the methods of initializing, changing, and displaying a name will be the same for all student records. In Java, we can define a class called Student that includes data fields for the properties that belong to all subclasses of students, such as college students and high school students. The class definition can also contain all the methods that manipulate the data fields for the class Student. In fact, we have already defined such a Student class in Segment 2.2.

2.7   Now consider a class for college students. A college student is a student, so we use inheritance to derive the class CollegeStudent from the class Student. You define a derived class by adding data fields and methods to an existing class, the base class. In our example, Student is the base class and CollegeStudent is the derived class. The derived class has—that is, inherits—all the data fields and methods of the base class. In addition, the derived class defines whatever data fields and methods you wish to add.

To indicate that CollegeStudent is a derived class of Student, we write the phrase extends Student on the first line of the class definition. Thus, the class definition of CollegeStudent begins

```
public class CollegeStudent extends Student
```

When you define a derived class, you write only the added data fields and the added methods. For example, the class CollegeStudent has all the data fields and methods of the class Student, but we do not mention them in the definition of CollegeStudent. In particular, every object of the class CollegeStudent has a data field called fullName, but we do not declare the data field fullName in the definition of the class CollegeStudent.

Suppose that we create a new object of the class CollegeStudent as follows:

```
CollegeStudent cs = new CollegeStudent();
```

The object cs has a data field fullName. Because fullName is a private data field, it is not legal to write cs.fullName outside of the definition of the class Student. However, the data field is there. We can access and change this data field by using Student's methods, since the class CollegeStudent inherits all public methods from the base class Student. For example, we can write

```
cs.setName(new Name("Warren", "Peace"));
```

even though setName is a method of the base class Student. Since we have used inheritance to construct CollegeStudent from the class Student, every college student *is a* student. That is, a CollegeStudent object "knows" how to perform Student behaviors.

2.8   A derived class, like `CollegeStudent`, can also add some data fields and/or methods to those it inherits from its base class. For example, `CollegeStudent` adds the data field `year` and the methods `setYear` and `getYear`. We can set the graduation year of the object `cs` by writing

```
cs.setYear(2007);
```

Suppose that we also add a data field that represents the degree sought and the methods to access and change it. We could also add fields for an address and grades, but to keep it simple, we will not. Let's look at the class and focus on the constructors first.

```java
public class CollegeStudent extends Student
{
  private int    year;   // year of graduation
  private String degree; // degree sought

  public CollegeStudent()
  {
    super();      // must be first
    year = 0;
    degree = "";
  } // end default constructor

  public CollegeStudent(Name studentName, String studentId,
                        int graduationYear, String degreeSought)
  {
    super(studentName, studentId); // must be first
    year = graduationYear;
    degree = degreeSought;
  } // end constructor

  public void setStudent(Name studentName, String studentId,
                         int graduationYear, String degreeSought)
  {
    setName(studentName); // NOT fullName = studentName;
    setId(studentId);     // NOT id = studentId;
    // or setStudent(studentName, studentId); (see Segment 2.15)

    year = graduationYear;
    degree = degreeSought;
  } // end setStudent

  < The methods setYear, getYear, setDegree, getDegree go here. >
  . . .

  public String toString()
  {
    return super.toString() + ", " + degree + ", " + year;
  } // end toString
} // end CollegeStudent
```

Invoking Constructors from Within Constructors

2.9   **Calling the base class's constructor.** Constructors typically initialize a class's data fields. In a derived class, how can the constructor initialize data fields inherited from the base class? One way is to call the base class's constructor. The derived class's constructor can use the reserved word `super` as a name for the constructor of the base class, also known as the superclass.

Notice that the default constructor in the class `CollegeStudent` begins with the statement

```
super();
```

This statement invokes the default constructor of the base class. The new default constructor must invoke the base class's default constructor to properly initialize the data fields that are inherited from the base class. Actually, if you do not invoke `super`, Java will do it for you. In this book, we will always invoke `super` explicitly, to make the action a bit clearer. Note that the call to `super` must occur first in the constructor. You can use `super` to invoke a constructor only from within another constructor.

In like fashion, the initializing constructor invokes a corresponding constructor in the base class with the statement

```
super(studentName, studentId);
```

Programming Tip: **Calling the constructor of the base class**

The constructor of a derived class automatically calls the constructor of the base class. However, you can use `super` within the definition of the constructor of a derived class to call the constructor of the base class explicitly. When you do, `super` must always be the first action taken in the constructor definition. You cannot use the name of the constructor instead of `super`.

2.10   **(Optional) Using `this` to invoke a constructor.** You can use the reserved word `this` much as you use `super`, except that it calls a constructor of the same class instead of a constructor of the base class. For example, consider the following definition of a constructor that we might add to the class `CollegeStudent` in Segment 2.8:

```java
public CollegeStudent(Name studentName, String studentId)
{
    this(studentName, studentId, 0, "");
} // end constructor
```

The one statement in the body of this constructor definition is a call to the constructor whose definition begins

```java
public CollegeStudent(Name studentName, String studentId,
                      int graduationYear, String degreeSought)
```

As with `super`, any use of `this` must be the first action in a constructor definition. Thus, a constructor definition cannot contain both a call using `super` and a call using `this`. What if you want both a call with `super` and a call with `this`? In that case, you would use a call with `this` and have the constructor that is called with `this` have `super` as its first action.

Private Fields and Methods of the Base Class

2.11   **Accessing inherited data fields.** The class `CollegeStudent` also has a `setStudent` method with four parameters, `studentName`, `studentId`, `graduationYear`, and `degreeSought`. To initialize the inherited data fields `fullName` and `id`, the method invokes the inherited methods `setName` and `setId`:

```java
setName(studentName); // NOT fullName = studentName
setId(studentId);     // NOT id = studentId
```

Recall that `fullName` and `id` are private data fields in the definition of the base class `Student`. Only the definition of a method in the class `Student` can access `fullName` and `id` directly. Although the class `CollegeStudent` inherits these data fields, none of its methods can access them directly by name. Thus, `setStudent` cannot use an assignment statement such as

```
id = studentId; // ILLEGAL in setStudent
```

to initialize the data field `id`. Instead it must use some public mutator method such as `setId`.

Programming Tip: A data field that is private in a base class is not accessible by name within the definition of a method for any other class, including a derived class. Even so, a derived class inherits the data fields of its base class.

The fact that a private data field of a base class cannot be accessed in the definition of a method of a derived class often seems wrong to people. To do otherwise, however, would make the access modifier `private` pointless: Anytime you wanted to access a private data field, you could simply create a derived class and access it in a method of that class. Thus, all private data fields would be accessible to anybody who wanted to put in a little extra effort.

2.12   **Private methods of the base class.** Although a derived class cannot access the private data fields of its base class by name, it can access them indirectly by using set and get methods. In contrast, a derived class cannot invoke a base class's private methods at all. While a derived class inherits the data fields of its base class, its does not inherit the base class's private methods.

This should not be a problem, since you should use private methods only as helpers within the class in which they are defined. If you want to use a base class's method in a derived class, you should make the method either protected or public. We discuss protected methods later in this chapter.

Programming Tip: A derived class does not inherit and cannot invoke a private method of the base class.

Overriding and Overloading Methods

2.13   The set and get methods of the class `CollegeStudent` are straightforward, so we will not bother to look at them. However, we have provided the class with a method `toString`. Why did we do this, when our new class inherits a `toString` method from its base class `Student`? Clearly the string that the base class's `toString` method returns can include the student's name and identification number, but it cannot include the year and degree that are associated with the derived class. Thus, we need to write a new method `toString`.

But why not have the new method invoke the inherited method? We can do this, but we'll need to distinguish between the method that we are defining for `CollegeStudent` and the method inherited from `Student`. As you can see from the class definition in Segment 2.8, the new method `toString` contains the statement

```
return super.toString() + ", " + degree + ", " + year;
```

Since `Student` is the superclass, we write

```
super.toString()
```

to indicate that we are invoking the superclass's `toString`. If we omitted `super`, `toString` would invoke itself recursively. Here we are using `super` as if it were an object. In contrast, we used `super` with parentheses as if it were a method within the constructor definitions.

If you glance back at Segment 2.2, you will see that Student's toString method appears as follows:

```java
public String toString()
{
   return id + " " + fullName.toString();
} // end toString
```

This method calls the toString method defined in the class Name, since the object fullName is an instance of the class Name.

2.14 **Overriding a method.** In the previous segment, you saw that the class CollegeStudent defines a method toString and also inherits a method toString from its base class Student. Both of these methods have no parameters. The class, then, has two methods with the same name and the same parameters.

When a derived class defines a method with the same signature—that is, the same name, the same return type, and the same number and types of parameters—as a method in the base class, the definition in the derived class is said to **override** the definition in the base class. Objects of the derived class that invoke the method will use the definition in the derived class. For example, if cs is an instance of the class CollegeStudent,

```java
cs.toString()
```

uses the definition of the method toString in the class CollegeStudent, not the definition of toString in the class Student, as Figure 2-4 illustrates. As you've already seen, however, the definition of toString in the derived class can invoke the definition of toString in the base class by using super.

Figure 2-4 The method toString in CollegeStudent overrides the method toString in Student

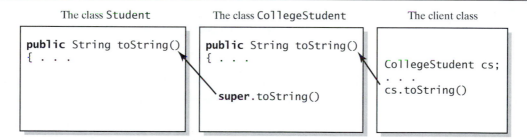

Note: **Overriding a method definition**
A method in a derived class overrides a method in the base class when both methods have the same signature—that is, the same name, the same return type, and the same number and types of parameters.

Programming Tip: You can use super in a derived class to call an overridden method of the base class.

2.15 **Overloading a method.** Suppose that a derived class has a method with the same name as a method in its base class, but the methods do not have identical parameters. The derived class would have both methods—the one it defines and the one it inherits from the base class. Java is able to distinguish between these methods since their parameters differ in number or data type. We say that the method in the derived class **overloads** the method in the base class.

For example, the base class `Student` and the derived class `CollegeStudent` each have a method named `setStudent`. The methods are not exactly the same, however, as they have a different number of parameters. In `Student`, the method's signature is

```
public void setStudent(Name studentName, String studentId)
```

whereas in `CollegeStudent` it is

```
public void setStudent(Name studentName, String studentId,
                       int graduationYear, String degreeSought)
```

An instance of the class `Student` can invoke only `Student`'s version of the method, but an instance of `CollegeStudent` can invoke either method. Again, Java can distinguish between the two methods because they have different parameters.

Within the class `CollegeStudent`, the implementation of `setStudent` can invoke `Student`'s `setStudent` to initialize the fields `fullName` and `id` by including the statement

```
setStudent(studentName, studentId);
```

instead of making calls to the methods `setName` and `setId`, as we did in Segment 2.11. Since the two versions of `setStudent` have different parameter lists, we do not need to preface the call with `super` to distinguish the two methods. However, we are free to do so by writing

```
super.setStudent(studentName, studentId);
```

Overloading methods is not restricted to cases of inheritance. One class can have several methods with the same name as long as they differ in their parameters.

Note: **Overloading a method definition**
A method in a class overloads a method in either the same class or its base class when both methods have the same name but differ in the number or types of parameters. Overloaded methods must have the same return type.

Overloading and overriding are easy to confuse, but they are both legal. It is more important to learn the concepts than to distinguish between the terms.

2.16   **Multiple use of super.** As we have already noted, within the definition of a method of a derived class, you can call an overridden method of the base class by prefacing the method name with `super` and a dot. However, if the base class is itself derived from some other superclass, you cannot repeat the use of `super` to invoke a method from that superclass.

For example, suppose that the class `UndergradStudent` is derived from the class `CollegeStudent`, which is derived from the class `Student`. You might think that you can invoke a method of the class `Student` within the definition of the class `Undergraduate`, by using `super.super`, as in

```
super.super.toString(); // ILLEGAL!
```

As the comment indicates, this repeated use of `super` is not allowed in Java.

Programming Tip: `super`
Although a method in a derived class can invoke an overridden method defined in the base class by using `super`, the method cannot invoke an overridden method that is defined in the base class's base class. That is, the construct `super.super` is illegal.

Question 5   Are the two definitions of the constructors for the class Student (Segment 2.2) an example of overloading or overriding?

Question 6   If you add the method

```
public void setStudent(Name studentName, String studentId)
```

to the class CollegeStudent, and let it give some default values to the fields year and degree, are you overloading or overriding setStudent? Why?

2.17   **The final modifier.** Suppose that a constructor calls a method other than another constructor. For simplicity, imagine that this method—call it m—is in the same class C as the constructor. Now imagine that we derive a new class from C and we override the method m. If we invoke the constructor of our new class, it will call the base class's constructor, which will call our overridden version of the method m. This method might use data fields that the constructor has not yet initialized, causing an error. Even if no error occurs, we will, in effect, have altered the behavior of the base class's constructor.

To specify that a method definition cannot be overridden with a new definition in a derived class, you make it a **final method** by adding the final modifier to the method signature. For example, you can write

```
public final void m()
{
   . . .
}
```

Note that private methods are automatically final methods, since you cannot override them in a derived class.

Programming Tip: If a constructor invokes a method in its class, declare that method to be final so that no subclass can override the method and hence change the behavior of the constructor.

You can declare an entire class as a **final class,** in which case you cannot use it as base class to derive any other class from it. Java's String class is an example of a final class.

Programming Tip: String cannot be the base class for any other class because it is a final class.

Protected Access

2.18   You know that you control access to a class's data fields and methods by using an access modifier like public or private. As you saw in Chapter 1, you can omit the access modifier entirely when the class is within a package and you want the class to be available only to other classes in the package. You also have one other choice for controlling access: You can use the access modifier protected for methods and data fields.

A method or data field that is modified by protected can be accessed by name only within

- Its own class definition C
- Any class derived from C
- Any class within the same package as C

For example, if a method is marked protected in class C, you can invoke it from within any method definition in a class derived from class C. However, with classes that are not derived from C or that are not in the same package as C, a protected method behaves as if it were private.

You should continue to declare all data fields as private. If you want a derived class to have access to a data field in the base class, define protected accessor or mutator methods within the base class.

Note that package access is more restricted than protected access and gives more control to the programmer defining the classes. If you control the package directory, you control who is allowed package access.

Figure 2-5 illustrates the various kinds of access modifiers.

Figure 2-5   Public, private, protected, and package access

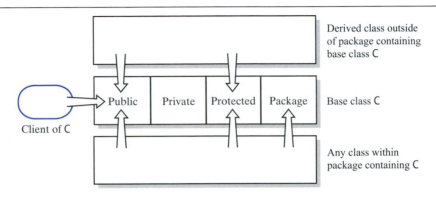

 Programming Tip: When you design a class, consider the classes derived from it, either now or in the future. They might need access to your class's data fields. If your class does not have public accessor or mutator methods, provide protected versions of such methods.

Multiple Inheritance

2.19   Some programming languages allow one class to be derived from two different base classes. That is, you can derive class C from classes A and B. This feature, known as **multiple inheritance,** is not allowed in Java. In Java a derived class can have only one base class. You can, however, derive class B from class A and then derive class C from class B, since this is not multiple inheritance.

A derived class can implement any number of interfaces—which we describe in Chapter 3—in addition to extending any one base class. This capability gives Java an approximation to multiple inheritance without the complications that arise with multiple base classes.

Type Compatibility and Base Classes

2.20   **Object types of a derived class.** Previously, you saw the class CollegeStudent, which was derived from the class Student. In the real world, every college student is also a student. This relationship holds in Java as well. Every object of the class CollegeStudent is also an object of the class Student. Thus, if we have a method that has a formal parameter of type Student, the argument in an invocation of this method can be an object of type CollegeStudent.

Specifically, suppose that the method in question is in some class and begins as follows:

public void someMethod(Student scholar)

Within the body of someMethod, the object scholar can invoke public methods that are defined in the class Student. For example, the definition of someMethod could contain the expression scholar.getId(). That is, scholar has Student behaviors.

Now consider an object joe of CollegeStudent. Since the class CollegeStudent inherits all the public methods of the class Student, joe can invoke those inherited methods. That is, joe can behave like an object of Student. (It happens that joe can do more, since it is an object of CollegeStudent, but that is not relevant right now.) Therefore, joe can be the argument of someMethod. That is, for some object o, we can write

    o.someMethod(joe);

No automatic type casting has occurred here. An object of the class CollegeStudent also is an object of the class Student. Thus, joe also is of type Student. The object joe need not be, and is not, type-cast to an object of the class Student.

We can take this idea further. Suppose that we derive the class UndergradStudent from the class CollegeStudent. In the real world, every undergraduate is a college student, and every college student is also a student. Once again, this relationship holds in Java. Every object of the class UndergradStudent is also an object of the class CollegeStudent and so is also an object of the class Student. Thus, if we have a method that has a formal parameter of type Student, the argument in an invocation of this method can be an object of type UndergradStudent. Thus, an object can actually have several types as a result of inheritance.

Note: An object of a derived class has more than one type. Everything that works for objects of an ancestor class also works for objects of any descendant class.

2.21   Because an object of a derived class also has the types of all of its ancestor classes, you can assign an object of a class to a variable of any ancestor type, but not the other way around. For example, since the class UndergradStudent is derived from the class CollegeStudent, which is derived from the class Student, the following are legal:

    Student amy = **new** CollegeStudent();
    Student brad = **new** UndergradStudent();

However, the following statements are all illegal:

    CollegeStudent cs = **new** Student();   // ILLEGAL!
    UndergradStudent ug = **new** Student();   // ILLEGAL!
    UndergradStudent ug2 = **new** CollegeStudent(); // ILLEGAL!

This makes perfectly good sense. For example, a college student is a student, but a student is not necessarily a college student. Some programmers find the phrase "is a" to be useful in deciding what types an object can have and what assignments to variables are legal.

Question 7   If HighSchoolStudent is a derived class of Student, can you assign an object of HighSchoolStudent to a variable of type Student? Why or why not?

Question 8   Can you assign an object of Student to a variable of type HighSchoolStudent? Why or why not?

The Class `Object`

2.22   As you have already seen, if you have a class A and you derive class B from it, and then you derive class C from B, an object of class C is of type C, type B, and type A. This works for any chain of derived classes no matter how long the chain is.

Java has a class—named `Object`—that is at the beginning of every chain of derived classes. This class is an ancestor of every other class, even those that you define yourself. Every object of every class is of type `Object`, as well as being of the type of its class and also of the types of all the other ancestor classes. If you do not derive your class from some other class, Java acts as if you had derived it from the class `Object`.

 Note: Every class is a descendant class of the class `Object`.

The class `Object` contains certain methods, among which are `toString`, `equals`, and `clone`. Every class inherits these methods, either from `Object` directly or from some other ancestor class that ultimately inherited the methods from the class `Object`.

The inherited methods `toString`, `equals`, and `clone`, however, will almost never work correctly in the classes you define. Typically, you need to override the inherited method definitions with new, more appropriate definitions. Thus, whenever you define the method `toString` in a class, for example, you are actually overriding `Object`'s method `toString`.

2.23   **The `toString` method.** The method `toString` takes no arguments and is supposed to return all the data in an object as a `String`. However, you will not automatically get a nice string representation of the data. The inherited version of `toString` returns a value based upon the invoking object's memory address. You need to override the definition of `toString` to cause it to produce an appropriate string for the data in the class being defined. You might want to look again at the `toString` methods in Segments 2.2 and 2.8.

2.24   **The `equals` method.** The method `equals` has the following definition in the class `Object`:

```java
public boolean equals(Object obj)
{
  return (this == obj);
} // end equals
```

The expression `x.equals(y)` is `true` if x and y reference the same object. You might, however, want an `equals` method in your class that returns true if the two distinct objects that x and y reference are equal in some sense. If so, you need to override `equals` in your class.

For example, consider an `equals` method for the class `Name` that we defined in Chapter 1. As you recall, `Name` has two data fields, `first` and `last`, that are instances of `String`. We could decide that two `Name` objects are equal if they have equal first names and equal last names. The following method determines whether two `Name` objects are equal by comparing their data fields:

```java
public boolean equals(Object otherObject)
{
  boolean result = false;

  if (otherObject instanceof Name) // NOT instanceOf
  {
    Name otherName = (Name) otherObject;
    String otherFirst = otherName.first;
    String otherLast = otherName.last;
```

```
      result = first.equals(otherFirst) && last.equals(otherLast);
   } // end if

   return result;
} // end equals
```

Notice the use of the operator instanceof, which returns true if the object on its left is an instance of the class on its right. If we pass an object to this equals method that is not an instance of the class Name, the method returns false. Otherwise, the method compares the data fields. Notice that we first must cast[1] the type of the parameter otherObject from Object to Name so that we can access Name's data fields.

Question 9 The previous method equals invokes an equals method. To what class does that method belong?

Question 10 If sue and susan are two instances of the class Name, what if statement can determine whether they represent the same name?

2.25 **The clone method.** Another method inherited from the class Object is the method clone. This method takes no arguments and returns a copy of the calling object. The returned object is supposed to have data identical to that of the calling object, but it is a different object (an identical twin or a "clone"). As with other methods inherited from the class Object, we need to override the method clone before it can behave properly in our class. However, in the case of the method clone, there are other things we must do as well. A discussion of the method clone appears in Chapter 15.

Abstract Classes and Methods

2.26 The class Student defined in Segment 2.2 is a base class for other classes such as CollegeStudent. We really do not need to create objects of type Student, although it is certainly legal to do so. We might, however, want to prevent a client from creating objects of type Student. To do so, we can declare the class to be an **abstract class** by including the reserved word abstract in the signature of the class definition, as follows:

```
public abstract class Student
{
   . . .
```

Often when programmers define an abstract class, they declare one or more methods that have no body. The intention in doing so is to require that every derived class implement such methods in an appropriate way for that class. For example, we might want every derived class of Student to implement a display method. We certainly cannot write a display method for a future class that is not yet defined, but we can require one. To do so, we declare display to be an **abstract method** by including the reserved word abstract in the signature of the method, as follows:

```
public abstract void display();
```

Note that the method signature is followed by a semicolon; the method has no body.

---

1. Segment A.17 of Appendix A reviews type casts.

Note: An abstract class will be the base class of another class. Thus, an abstract class is sometimes called an **abstract base class.**

2.27   If a class has at least one abstract method, Java requires that you declare the class itself as abstract.
This makes sense, for otherwise you could create an object of an incomplete class. In our example,
the object would have a method `display` without an implementation.

   What if the derived class of an abstract class does not implement all of the abstract methods?
Java will treat the derived class as abstract and prevent you from creating an object of its type. For
example, if the class `CollegeStudent`, which is derived from `Student`, did not implement `display`,
`CollegeStudent` would have to be abstract.

Programming Tip: A class with at least one abstract method must be declared as an abstract
class.

   Even after we've made the class `Student` abstract by adding the abstract method `display`, not
all of its methods are abstract. All the method definitions, except for the method `display`, are
exactly the same as in our original definition. They are full definitions that do not use the reserved
word `abstract`. When it makes sense to implement a method in an abstract class, you should do so.
In this way, you include as much detail as possible in the abstract class, detail that need not be
repeated in derived classes.

2.28   **Example.** Let's add another method to the class `Student`, one that invokes the abstract method
`display`. Before you complain about invoking a method that has no body, remember that `Student`

is an abstract class. When we finally derive a class from `Student` that is not abstract, `display` will
be implemented.

   The method we have in mind serves mainly as an example, rather than doing anything useful. It
skips the specified number of lines before displaying an object:

```
/** Task: Displays the object after skipping
 *        numberOfLines lines. */
public void displayAt(int numberOfLines)
{
  for (int count = 0; count < numberOfLines; count++)
    System.out.println();
  display();
} // end displayAt
```

The method `displayAt` invokes the abstract method `display`. Here the abstract method serves as a
placeholder for a method that will be defined in a future derived class. If `display` were not
abstract, we would have to give it a body that really would be useless, since every derived class
would override it.

Question 11   Suppose that you change the name of the previous method `displayAt` to `dis-
play`. Does the resulting method overload or override the method `display()`? Why?

Polymorphism

2.29   "Polymorphism" comes from a Greek word meaning "many forms." Polymorphism is common in
English, and its use in a programming language makes the programming language more like a

human language. For example, the English instruction "Play your favorite sport" means different things to different people. To one person it means to play baseball. To another person it means to play soccer. In Java, **polymorphism** allows the same program instruction to mean different things in different contexts. In particular, one method name, used as an instruction, can cause different actions depending on the kind of object performing the action.

Originally, overloading a method name was considered polymorphism. However, the modern usage of the term refers to an object determining at execution time which action of a method it will use for a method name that is overridden either directly or indirectly.

Note: **Polymorphism**

One method name in an instruction can cause different actions according to the kinds of objects that invoke the method.

2.30

Example. For example, a method named `display` can display the data in an object. But the data it displays and how much it displays depend on the kind of object invoking the method. Let's add the method `display` to the class `Student` of Segment 2.2 and assume that neither the method nor the class is abstract. Thus, `display` has an implementation within the class `Student`. Now add to the class the method `displayAt` as it appears in Segment 2.28.

If the only class around were `Student`, these changes would not be exciting. But we derived the class `UndergradStudent` from the class `CollegeStudent`, which we derived from the class `Student`. The class `UndergradStudent` inherits the method `displayAt` from the class `Student`. In addition, `UndergradStudent` overrides the method `display` defined in `Student` by providing its own implementation. So what? you might be wondering.

Well, look at the poor compiler's job when it encounters the following Java statements:[2]

```
UndergradStudent ug = new UndergradStudent(. . .);
ug.displayAt(2);
```

The method `displayAt` was defined in the class `Student`, but it calls the method `display` that is defined in the class `UndergradStudent`. The code for `displayAt` could have been compiled with the class `Student` *before* the class `UndergradStudent` was even written. In other words, this compiled code could use a definition of the method `display` that was not even written at the time that `displayAt` was compiled. How can that be?

When the code for `displayAt` is compiled, the call to `display` produces an annotation that says, "use the appropriate definition of `display`." Then, when we invoke `ug.displayAt(2)`, the compiled code for `displayAt` reaches this annotation and replaces it with an invocation of the version of `display` that goes with `ug`. Because in this case `ug` is of type `UndergradStudent`, the version of `display` that is used will be the definition in the class `UndergradStudent`.

2.31 The decision as to which method definition to use depends on the invoking object's place in the inheritance chain. *It is not determined by the type of the variable naming the object.* For example, consider the following code:

```
UndergradStudent ug = new UndergradStudent(. . .);
Student s = ug;
s.displayAt(2);
```

---

2. The arguments of the constructor are not relevant to the examples in this section, so we have replaced them with ellipses to save space.

As we noted in Segment 2.21, assigning an object of the class UndergradStudent to a variable of type Student is perfectly legal. Here, the variable s is just another name for the object that ug references, as Figure 2-6 illustrates. That is, s and ug are aliases. But the object still remembers that it was created as an UndergradStudent. In this case, s.displayAt(2) ultimately will use the definition of display given in UndergradStudent, not the definition of display given in Student.

A variable's **static type** is the type that appears in its declaration. For example, the static type of the variable s is Student. The static type is fixed and determined when the code is compiled. The type of object that a variable references at a point in time during execution is called its **dynamic type.** A variable's dynamic type can change as execution progresses. When the assignment s = ug executes in the previous code, the dynamic type of s is UndergradStudent. A variable of a reference type is called a **polymorphic variable,** since its dynamic type can differ from its static type and change during execution.

To determine which definition of display to use in our example, Java examines the code to see which class's constructor created the object. That is, Java uses the dynamic type of the variable s to make this determination.

Figure 2-6   The variable s is another name for an undergraduate object

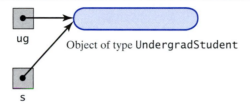

 Note: An object, not its reference, determines which method is invoked.

This way of handling a call to a method that might be overridden later is called **dynamic binding** or **late binding,** because the *meaning* of the method invocation is not bound to the *location* of the method invocation until you run the program. If Java did not use dynamic binding when you ran the preceding code, you would not see the data for an undergraduate student. Instead you would see only what the method display of the class Student provided.

 Note: Dynamic binding
Dynamic binding is the process that enables different objects to use different method actions for the same method name.

2.32   Java is so good at figuring out which definition of a method to use that even a type cast will not fool it. Recall that you use a type cast to change the type of a value to some other type. The meaning of s.displayAt(2) will always be appropriate for an UndergradStudent, even if we use a type cast to change the type of ug to the type Student, as in the following statements:

```
UndergradStudent ug = new UndergradStudent(. . .);
Student s = (Student) ug;
s.displayAt(2);
```

Despite the type cast, `s.displayAt(2)` will use the definition of `display` given in `UndergradStudent`, not the definition of `display` given in `Student`. The object, not its name, determines which method to use.

To see that dynamic binding really is a big deal, consider the following code:

```
UndergradStudent ug = new UndergradStudent(. . .);
Student s = ug;
s.displayAt(2);
GradStudent g = new GradStudent(. . .);
s = g;
s.displayAt(2);
```

The two lines shown in color are identical, yet each one invokes a different version of `display`. The first line displays an `UndergradStudent` and the second displays a `GradStudent`, as Figure 2-7 illustrates. An object remembers what method definitions it had when the new operator created it. You can place the object in a variable of a different (but ancestor) class type, but that has no effect on which method definition the object uses for an overridden method.

Let's pursue this process a bit more to see that it is even more dramatic than it may appear at first glance. Note that objects of the classes `UndergradStudent` and `GradStudent` inherit the method `displayAt` from the class `Student` and do not override it. Thus, the text of the method definition is even the same for objects of the classes `UndergradStudent` and `GradStudent`. It is the method `display`, invoked in the definition of `displayAt`, that is overridden.

Note: Objects know how they are supposed to act

When an overridden method (or a method that uses an overridden method) is invoked, the action of that method is the one defined in the class whose constructor created the object. This action is not determined by the static type of the variable naming the object. A variable of any ancestor class can reference an object of a descendant class, but the object always remembers which method actions to use for every method name, because Java uses dynamic binding.

Figure 2-7   An object, not its name, determines its behavior

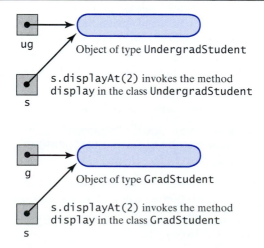

2.33   **Type checking and dynamic binding.** You need to be aware of how dynamic binding interacts with Java's type checking. For example, if `UndergradStudent` is a derived class of the class `Student`, we can assign an object of type `UndergradStudent` to a variable of type `Student`, as in

```
Student s = new UndergradStudent();
```

But that is not the end of the story.

Although we can assign an object of type `UndergradStudent` to a variable of type `Student`, we can invoke a method that is in the class `Student` only when the calling object is the variable s (of type `Student`). However, if the method is overridden in the definition of the class `UndergradStudent` and the object named by the variable s is of type `UndergradStudent`, it is the version of the method defined in `UndergradStudent` that will be used. In other words, the variable determines what method names can be used, but the object determines which definition of the method name will be used. If we want to use a method name that was first introduced in the class `UndergradStudent` with the object named by the variable s of type `Student`, we must use a type cast.

2.34   **Example.** For example, recall that `UndergradStudent` is a derived class of `Student`. The following statements are legal:

```
Student s = new UndergradStudent(. . .);
s.setName(new Name("Jamie", "Jones"));
s.display();
```

The definition of `display` given in the class `UndergradStudent` is used. *Remember, the object, not the variable, determines which definition of a method will be used.*

On the other hand, the following is illegal:

```
s.setDegree(2); // ILLEGAL
```

because `setDegree` is not the name of a method in the class `Student`. *Remember, the variable determines which method names can be used.*

The variable s is of type `Student`, but it references an object of type `UndergradStudent`. That object can still invoke the method `setDegree`, but the compiler does not know this. To make the invocation legal, we need a type cast, such as the following:

```
UndergradStudent ug = (UndergradStudent) s;
ug.setDegree(2); // LEGAL
```

You may think this is all just a silly exercise, because you would never assign an object of type `UndergradStudent` to a variable of type `Student`. Not so. You may not often make such an assignment directly, but you frequently will do so unwittingly. Recall that we can have an argument of type `UndergradStudent` for a method parameter of type `Student` and that a formal parameter behaves like a local variable that is assigned the value of its corresponding argument. In this case an object of type `UndergradStudent` (the argument in the method invocation) is assigned to a variable of type `Student` (the formal parameter in the method definition).

2.35   **Example.** If we add an appropriate `toString` method to the class `Student`, we can display a student object by using the `toString` method, as follows:

```
Name joe = new Name("Joe", "Student");
Student s = new Student(joe, 123456789);
System.out.println(s.toString());
```

But thanks to dynamic binding, we do not even need to write `toString` in our invocation of `System.out.println`. The following will work just as well and will produce exactly the same output:

```
Student s = new Student(joe, 123456789);
System.out.println(s);
```

The method invocation `System.out.println(s)` invokes the method `println` with the calling object `System.out`. One definition of the method `println` has a single parameter of type `Object`. The definition is equivalent to the following:

```
public void println(Object theObject)
{
   System.out.println(theObject.toString());
} // end println
```

(By the way, the invocation of the method `println` inside the braces is a different, overloaded definition of the method `println` that has a parameter of type `String`, not `Object`.)

This definition of `println` existed before the class `Student` was defined. Yet the invocation

```
System.out.println(s);
```

with an object `s` of type `Student`—and hence also of type `Object`—uses `Student`'s `toString`, not `Object`'s `toString`. Dynamic binding is what makes this work.

Question 12 Is a method `display` with no parameters that is defined explicitly in each of the classes `Student`, `CollegeStudent`, and `UndergradStudent` an example of overloading or overriding? Why?

Question 13 Is overloading a method name an example of polymorphism?

Question 14 In the following code, will the two invocations of `displayAt` produce the same output?

```
Student s = new UndergradStudent(. . .);
s.displayAt(2);
s = new GradStudent(. . .);
s.displayAt(2)
```

CHAPTER SUMMARY

- When you use composition to define a class, you use objects of one or more existing classes as data fields. The new class treats these objects as it would any other client of the existing classes.

- Composition defines a *has a* relationship between two classes.

- Inheritance groups classes that have properties and behaviors in common. The common properties and behaviors are defined only once for all the classes. Thus, you can define a general class—the base class—and later define more specialized classes—the derived classes—by simply adding to or revising the details of the older, more general class definition.

- Use inheritance when you have an *is a* relationship between two classes.

- A method in a derived class overrides a method in the base class when both methods have the same name, the same return type, and the same number and types of parameters.

- A method in a class overloads a method in either the same class or its base class when both methods have the same name but differ in the number or types of parameters.

- Everything that works for objects of an ancestor class also works for objects of any descendant class.

- A protected method can be accessed by name within its own class, a derived class, or a class within its class's package. Other classes cannot invoke it; the protected method behaves as if it were private.

- Every class is a descendant of the class `Object`.

- An abstract class has no instances and serves only as a base class. Any class that omits the definition of one or more of its methods must be declared abstract.

- Polymorphism is the concept whereby an object determines at execution time which action of a method it will use for an overridden method name. Dynamic binding is the process that implements polymorphism.

- When an overridden method (or a method that uses an overridden method) is invoked, the action of that method is the one defined in the class whose constructor created the object. This action is not determined by the type of the variable naming the object. A variable of any ancestor class can hold an object of a descendant class, but the object always remembers which method actions to use for every method name, because Java uses dynamic binding.

- The variable that names an object determines which method names an object can invoke. The object, not its name, determines which definition of a method it will use.

PROGRAMMING TIPS

- The constructor of a derived class automatically calls the constructor of the base class. However, you can use `super` within the definition of the constructor of a derived class to call the constructor of the base class explicitly. When you do, `super` must always be the first action taken in the constructor definition. You cannot use the name of the constructor instead of `super`.

- A data field or method that is private in a base class is not accessible by name in the definition of a method for any other class, including a derived class.

- A derived class cannot invoke a private method of the base class by name.

- You can use `super` in a derived class to call an overridden method of the base class.

- A method in a derived class cannot invoke an overridden method that is defined in the base class's base class. That is, the construct `super.super` is illegal.

- If a constructor invokes a method in its class, declare that method to be final so that no subclass can override the method and hence change the behavior of the constructor.

- `String` cannot be the base class for any other class because it is a final class.

- When you design a class, consider the classes derived from it, either now or in the future. They might need access to your class's data fields. If your class does not have public accessor or mutator methods, provide protected versions of such methods.

- A class with at least one abstract method must be declared an abstract class.

EXERCISES

1. Given the class `Student` defined in Segment 2.2, write Java statements that create a `Student` object for Jill Jones. Do this in two ways, using a different constructor each time. Jill's ID number is 8001.

2. If joe is an object of the class Student, as defined in Segment 2.2, is it legal to write joe.getFirst() to get joe's first name? Why or why not?

3. Consider the class Student defined in Segment 2.2.

    a. Add a constructor that has three String parameters representing the student's first name, last name, and identification number.

    b. Add a method getFirst that returns a student's first name.

4. Consider the class NickName as defined in Segment 2.3. Why is composition a more appropriate way to reuse the class Name than inheritance?

5. Revise the hierarchy in Figure 2-2 to include categories of land, sea, air, and space vehicles.

6. Consider the class CollegeStudent as defined in Segment 2.8. The method toString contains the invocation super.toString(). What string does this invocation return?

7. The class CollegeStudent has the method setStudent. Does this method overload or override the setStudent method in the class Student? Explain.

8. The class CollegeStudent has no definitions for methods that set or get the student's name. Why?

9. Can you omit the call to super in the default constructor of the class CollegeStudent? Can you omit it in the second constructor? Give reasons for your answers.

10. Suppose that joe is an object of the class CollegeStudent. Write Java statements that display joe's name. Repeat this in two other distinct ways.

11. You could revise the constructor in the class Student as follows:

```
public Student(Name studentName, String studentId)
{
    setStudent(studentName, studentId);
} // end constructor
```

The derived class CollegeStudent could override setStudent, thereby affecting this constructor. How can you prevent any derived class of Student from overriding setStudent?

12. Given the class Student and its derived class CollegeStudent, which of the following statements are legal and which are not?

    a. Student bob = new Student();
    b. Student bob = new CollegeStudent();
    c. CollegeStudent bob = new Student();
    d. CollegeStudent bob = new CollegeStudent();

13. Assuming that you have added an equals method to the class Name, as described in Segment 2.24, write an equals method for the class Student and one for the class CollegeStudent.

14. An abstract class can have methods that are implemented as well as other methods that are not. A method without an implementation—that is, without a body—is abstract.

    a. What is the purpose of an abstract method?
    b. What is the purpose of an abstract class?

15. Consider the following Java statements:

```
jillJones = new Name("Jill", "Jones");
joeCool = new Name("Joseph", "Cool");
Student jill = new Student(jillJones, "2222");
CollegeStudent joe = new CollegeStudent(joeCool, "33", 2004,
                                        "B.S.");
```

a. Can joe be the argument of a method whose parameter's type is Student? Why or why not?

b. Can jill be the argument of a method whose parameter's type is CollegeStudent? Why or why not?

c. Is jill.getYear() legal? Why or why not?

d. Is joe.getId() legal? Why or why not?

16. Suppose that the class Student has the methods display and displayAt, as described in Segment 2.28. Suppose also that the class CollegeStudent has a method display. Assume that jill and joe are defined as in Exercise 15. Which version of the method display will displayAt invoke when each of the following statements executes?

a. jill.displayAt(2);

b. joe.displayAt(2);

c. Student s = joe;
   s.displayAt(2);

d. Student s = (Student)joe;
   s.displayAt(2);

17. Imagine two classes, A and B.
Class A has a private data field theData and the following methods:

```
public void w();
public void x();
protected void y();
private void z();
```

Class B extends class A and has the following methods:

```
public void x();
protected void r();
private void s();
```

Suppose that the client declares instances of these classes, as follows:

```
A inA = new A();
B inB = new B();
```

a. Which of the objects inA and inB can access the field theData?

b. Which of these objects can invoke the method w?

c. Which of these objects can invoke the method y?

d. Which of these objects can invoke the method r?

e. Which of these objects can invoke the method z?

f. Which version of the method x does inB.x() invoke?

g. Which methods are available to the implementation of the class B?

h. Which methods are available to clients of B?

PROJECTS

1. Implement the class Die, as described in Project 4 of Chapter 1. Then implement a class TwoDice that represents two six-sided dice. You should be able to roll the dice and determine the sum of their face values. You should also be able to determine various special cases, such as a pair of ones (snake eyes) or a pair of sixes (box cars).

2. Design and implement a class to play a game that uses dice. Use the class TwoDice that Project 1 describes.

   You can use the following simple game or choose one of your own. Players take turns in rolling the dice. For each player, maintain a cumulative sum of the face values of the rolled dice. Double the value of any matching pair of dice. The first player to reach a certain number, such as 50 or 100, wins.

3. Define the class Address to represent a person's mailing address. Include data fields for at least the street address, city, and state. Provide reasonable constructors and set and get methods. Next add an Address field to the class Student, as defined in Segment 2.2. Add methods to Student that access or modify the address. Revise any existing methods of Student to accommodate this new field.

4. Define the class Transcript to record a student's grades for a semester. Begin by creating other classes such as Course and Grade. A Course object could contain the title, number of credits, and grade for a course. A Grade object could contain a letter grade and the quality points that the grade represents. The class Transcript then contains an instance of Course for each course taken by a student in one semester.

   Now add an instance of Transcript as a data field of the class Student. Add appropriate methods to Student that deal with the transcript.

5. Textile designers often use computers to create new patterns. Design and implement a class SquarePattern that represents a pattern for a fabric square of a given dimension. Methods in the class should enable you to create objects that have different patterns. Use this class in another class Fabric that represents a piece of fabric whose pattern is composed of various squares. Your classes should be able to display the patterns on the screen.

6. The class Name given in Segment 1.16 of Chapter 1 represents a person's first and last names. Derive the class ProperName from Name, adding data fields for a middle initial and a title such as Ms., Mr., Dr., or Sir. Provide reasonable constructors and set and get methods for the new fields. Override the toString method so that it behaves correctly for the new class.

   Explain why inheritance is appropriate in the definition of ProperName but is not a reasonable choice for the definition of the class NickName that Segment 2.3 describes.

7. Project 1 in Chapter 1 describes the class Counter that records a nonnegative integer count. Given this class, define a class GraphicCounter by using either composition or inheritance. You should be able to display a GraphicCounter object on the screen, as Figure 2-8 illustrates. Provide the class with reasonable methods.

   Use the class to create an application or applet that behaves like a timer. You set the timer to an initial value in seconds and, at a signal, it counts down to zero. You should see the timer's value change as it counts.

Figure 2-8   A graphic counter for Project 7

42

8. Project 3 of Chapter 1 asked you to define a class GenericCoin. Each GenericCoin object can be tossed so that it randomly lands either heads up or tails up. Derive a class Coin from GenericCoin that adds a monetary value and a name as data fields. Provide your class with appropriate methods.

Write a program that tests your class and shows that your new coins inherit the behaviors of a GenericCoin object. In particular, your new coins can be tossed.

Now write a program that creates ten of each kind of coin (for example, ten pennies, ten nickels, and so on). Toss each coin once and form two groups, one for heads and one for tails. Compute the monetary value of the coins in each group.

9. Design and implement the classes Student, CollegeStudent, UndergradStudent, and GradStudent according to the hierarchy shown in Figure 2-3. Although you can use aspects of these classes that you saw in this chapter, make the classes Student and CollegeStudent abstract classes.

The classes UndergradStudent and GradStudent should each ensure that the degree field of CollegeStudent is set to a legal value. For example, you could restrict an undergraduate student to B.A. and B.S. degree programs and a graduate student to M.S. and Ph.D. programs.

Designing Classes

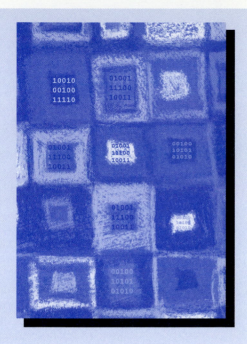

CONTENTS

Encapsulation
Specifying Methods
Java Interfaces
    Writing an Interface
    Implementing an Interface
    An Interface as a Data Type
    Type Casts Within an Interface Implementation
    Extending an Interface
    Named Constants Within an Interface
    Interfaces Versus Abstract Classes
Choosing Classes
    Identifying Classes
    CRC Cards
Reusing Classes

PREREQUISITES

Chapter   1   Java Classes
Chapter   2   Creating Classes from Other Classes
Appendix D   Documentation and Programming Style

OBJECTIVES

After studying this chapter, you should be able to

- Describe encapsulation, information hiding, and data abstraction
- Write specifications for methods that include preconditions and postconditions
- Write a Java interface for a class
- Choose appropriate classes and methods during the design of a program, including classes that might be written already

Object-oriented programming embodies three design concepts: encapsulation, inheritance, and polymorphism. We have already discussed inheritance and polymorphism. Now, building on our earlier discussion of classes, this chapter introduces encapsulation as a way to hide the details of an implementation during the design of a class. We go on to emphasize the importance of specifying how a method should behave before you implement it and of expressing your specifications as comments in your program.

We introduce Java interfaces as a way to separate the declarations of a class's behavior from its implementation. Finally, we present, at an elementary level, some techniques for identifying the classes necessary for a particular solution.

Encapsulation

3.1   What is the most useful description of an automobile, if you want to learn to drive one? It clearly is not a description of how its engine goes through a cycle of taking in air and gasoline, igniting the gasoline/air mixture, and expelling exhaust. Such details are unnecessary when you want to learn to drive. In fact, such details can get in your way. If you want to learn to drive an automobile, the most useful description of an automobile has such features as the following:

- If you press your foot on the accelerator pedal, the automobile will move faster.
- If you press your foot on the brake pedal, the automobile will slow down and eventually stop.
- If you turn the steering wheel to the right, the automobile will turn to the right.
- If you turn the steering wheel to the left, the automobile will turn to the left.

Just as you need not tell somebody who wants to drive a car how the engine works, you need not tell somebody who uses a piece of software all the fine details of its Java implementation. Likewise, suppose that you create a software component for another programmer to use in a program. You should describe the component in a way that tells the other programmer how to use it but that spares the programmer all the details of how you wrote the software.

3.2   **Encapsulation** is one of the design principles of object-oriented programming. "Encapsulation" sounds as though it means putting things into a capsule, and that image is indeed correct. Encapsulation hides the fine detail of what is inside the "capsule." For this reason, encapsulation is often called **information hiding.** But part of what is in the capsule is visible. In an automobile, certain things are visible—like the pedals and steering wheel—and others are hidden under the hood. The automobile is encapsulated so that the details are hidden, and only the controls needed to drive the automobile are visible, as Figure 3-1 shows. Similarly, you should encapsulate your Java code so that details are hidden and only the necessary controls are visible.

Encapsulation encloses data and methods into a class and hides the implementation details that are not necessary for using the class. If a class is well designed, its use does not require an understanding of its implementation. A programmer can use the class's methods without knowing the details of how they are coded. The programmer needs to know only how to provide a method with appropriate arguments and can leave it up to the method to perform the right action. In this way, the programmer is spared having to worry about the internal details of the class definition. The programmer who uses encapsulated software to write more software has a simpler task. As a result, software is produced more quickly and with fewer errors.

 Note: **Encapsulation** is a design principle of object-oriented programming that encloses data and methods into a class, thereby hiding the details of a class's implementation. A programmer receives only enough information to be able to use the class. A well-designed class can be used as though the body of every method was hidden from view.

Figure 3-1   An automobile's controls are visible to the driver, but its inner workings are hidden

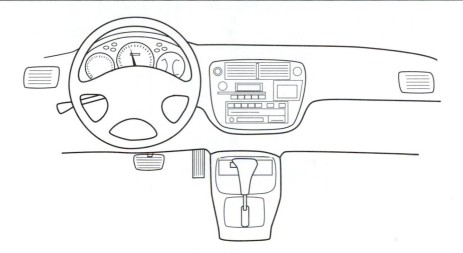

3.3   **Abstraction** is a process that asks you to focus on *what* instead of *how*. When you design a class, you practice **data abstraction.** You focus on what you want to do with or to the data without worrying about how you will accomplish these tasks and how you will represent the data. Abstraction asks you to focus on what data and operations are important. When you abstract something, you identify the central ideas. For example, an abstract of a book is a brief description of the book, as opposed to the entire book.

When designing a class, you should not think about any method's implementation. That is, you should not worry about *how* the class's methods will accomplish their goals. This separation of specification from implementation allows you to concentrate on fewer details, thereby making your task easier and less error-prone. Detailed, well-planned specifications facilitate an implementation that is more likely to be successful.

Note: The process of **abstraction** asks you to focus on *what* instead of *how*.

3.4   When done correctly, encapsulation divides a class definition into two parts, which we will call the **client interface** and the **implementation.** The client interface describes everything a programmer needs to know to use the class. It consists of the signatures for the public methods of the class, the comments that tell a programmer how to use these public methods, and any publicly defined constants of the class. The client interface part of the class definition should be all you need to know to use the class in your program.

The implementation consists of all data fields and the definitions of all methods, including those that are public, private, and protected. Although you need the implementation to run a client (a program that uses the class), you should not need to know anything about the implementation to write the client. Figure 3-2 illustrates an encapsulated implementation of a class and the client interface. Although the implementation is hidden from the client, the interface is visible and provides the client well-regulated communication with the implementation.

Figure 3-2   An interface provides well-regulated communication between a hidden implementation and a client

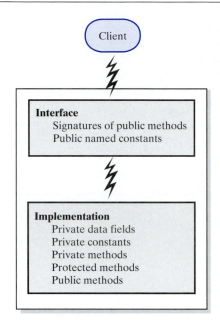

The client interface and implementation are not separated in the definition of a Java class. They are mixed together. You can, however, create a separate **Java interface** as a companion to your class. A Java interface contains the signatures for a class's public methods and can define public named constants. A later section of this chapter describes how to write and use a Java interface. We will write a number of Java interfaces in the rest of the book.

Question 1   How does a client interface differ from a class implementation?

Question 2   Think of an example, other than an automobile, that illustrates encapsulation. What part of your example corresponds to a client interface and what part to an implementation?

Specifying Methods

3.5   Separating the purpose of a class and its methods from their implementations is vital to a successful software project. You should specify what each class and method does without concern for its implementation. Writing descriptions enables you to capture your ideas initially and to develop them so that they are clear enough to implement. Your written descriptions should reach the point where they are useful as comments in your program. You need to go beyond a view that sees comments as something you add after you write the program to satisfy an instructor or boss.

Let's focus on comments that you write for a class's methods. Although organizations tend to have their own style for comments, the developers of Java have specified a commenting style that you should follow. If you include comments written in this style in your program, you can run a utility program called `javadoc` to produce documents that describe your classes. This documentation tells people what they need to know to use your class but omits all the implementation details, including the bodies of all method definitions.

The program javadoc extracts the heading for your class, the signatures for all public methods, and comments that are written in a certain form. Each such comment must appear immediately before a public class definition or the signature of a public method and must begin with /** and end with */. Certain **tags** that begin with the symbol @ appear within the comments to identify various aspects of the method. For example, you use @param to identify a parameter, @return to identify a return value, and @throws to indicate an exception that the method throws. You will see some examples of these tags within the comments in this chapter. Appendix D provides the details for writing comments acceptable to javadoc.

Rather than talk further about the rules for javadoc here, we want to discuss some important aspects of specifying a method. First, you need to write a concise statement of the method's purpose or task. Beginning this statement with a verb will help you to avoid many extra words that you really do not need.

In thinking about a method's purpose, you need to consider its input parameters, if any, and describe them. You also need to describe the method's results. Does it return a value, does it cause some action, or does it affect the state of an argument? In writing such descriptions, you should keep in mind the following ideas.

3.6 A **precondition** is a statement of the conditions that must be true before a method begins execution. The method should not be used, and cannot be expected to perform correctly, unless the precondition is satisfied. A precondition can be related to the description of a method's parameters. For example, a method that computes the square root of x can have $x \geq 0$ as a precondition.

A **postcondition** is a statement of what is true after a method completes its execution. For a valued method, the postcondition will describe the value returned by the method. For a void method, the postcondition will describe actions taken and any changes to the calling object. In general, the postcondition describes all the effects produced by a method invocation.

Thinking in terms of a postcondition can help you to clarify a method's purpose. Notice that going from precondition to postcondition leaves out the *how*—that is, we separate the method's specification from its implementation.

Programming Tip: When a method cannot satisfy its postcondition, even though its precondition is met, it can throw an exception. (See Appendix B for a discussion of exceptions.)

3.7 **Responsibility.** A precondition defines responsibility. If the client is responsible for ensuring that certain conditions are met before calling the method, the method need not check the conditions. On the other hand, if the method is responsible for enforcing the conditions, the client does not check them. A clear statement of who must check a given set of conditions increases the probability that someone will do so and avoids duplication of effort.

For example, you could specify the square root method that we mentioned in Segment 3.6 by writing the following comments before its signature:

```
/** Task: Computes the square root of a number.
 *  @param x  a real number >= 0
 *  @return the square root of x
 */
```

In this case, the method assumes that the client will provide a nonnegative number as an argument.

On the other hand, the method could assume responsibility for checking the argument. In that case, its comments could read as follows:

```
/** Task: Computes the square root of a number.
 *  @param x  a real number
```

```
*   @return the square root of x if x >= 0
*   @throws ArithmeticException if x < 0
*/
```

Although we've integrated the precondition and postcondition into the previous comments, we could identify them separately, as we did for the task.

Programming Tip: Specify each public method fully in comments placed before the method's signature. State whether a method or its client is responsible for ensuring that the necessary conditions are met for the successful execution of the method. In this way, checking is done but not duplicated. During debugging, however, a method should always check that its precondition has been met.

3.8   **Assertions.** Preconditions and postconditions are examples of assertions. An **assertion** is a statement of truth about some aspect of your program's logic. You can think of it as a boolean expression that is true, or that at least should be true, at a certain point. If an assertion is false, something is wrong with your program. You can state assertions that are not obvious as comments within your code. For example, if at some point in a method's definition, you know that the variable sum should be positive, you could write the following comment:

```
// Assertion: sum > 0
```

Such comments point out aspects of the logic that might not be clear. Additionally, they provide places for you to check the accuracy of your code during debugging.

Programming Tip: Assertions written as comments within a method's body identify aspects of your logic that you can check during debugging.

3.9   When you use inheritance and polymorphism to override a method in a base class, the method in the derived class could be inconsistent with the method in the base class. Preconditions and postconditions will help you to avoid this problem. A postcondition must apply to all versions of a method throughout the subclasses. An overridden method can add to a postcondition—that is, it can do more—but it should not do less. However, an overridden method cannot augment its precondition. In other words, it cannot require more than a version of the method in a base class requires.

Question 3   Assume that you have a class Circle that has a data field radius and the following method to compute the circle's area:

public double area();

What precondition and postcondition can you write for this method?

Question 4   Suppose that you have an array of positive integers. The following statements find the largest integer in the array. What assertion can you write as a comment after the if statement in the following loop?

```
int max = 0;
for (int index = 0; index < array.length; index++)
{
  if (array[index] > max)
    max = array[index];
  // Assertion:
}
```

Java Interfaces

3.10   Earlier in this chapter we spoke in general terms about the client interface, which tells you all you need to know to use a particular class in your program. An interface consists of the class's public constants and the signatures for its public methods. Although a Java class intermixes its interface with its implementation, you can write a separate interface.

A **Java interface** is a program component that contains public constants, signatures for public methods, and, ideally, comments that describe them. You would write a Java interface in addition to writing the class, meaning that the method signatures appear in two separate files. When you write a class that conforms to an interface, we say that the class **implements** the interface. A class that implements an interface must define a body for every method that the interface specifies.

Java provides some interfaces for you. Others you will write yourself. For example, Java provides an interface called `Comparable`. Any class that implements this `Comparable` interface must implement the following method:

```
public int compareTo(Object otherObject)
```

Briefly, this method compares two objects and returns an integer that signals the result of the comparison. For example, Java's class `String` implements the `Comparable` interface and so has a method `compareTo` that compares two strings.

Note: The method `compareTo` compares two objects and returns a signed integer that indicates the result of the comparison. For example, if x and y are two instances of the same class that implements the interface `Comparable`, `x.compareTo(y)` returns

- A negative integer if x is less than y
- Zero if x equals y
- A positive integer if x is greater than y

If x and y have different types, `x.compareTo(y)` throws the exception `ClassCastException`.

Writing an Interface

3.11   A Java interface begins like a class definition, except that you use the word `interface` instead of `class`. That is, an interface begins with the statement

```
public interface interface-name
```

rather than

```
public class class-name
```

The interface can contain any number of public method signatures, each followed by a semicolon. For example, Java's `Comparable` interface is simply

```
public interface Comparable
{
  public int compareTo(Object otherObject);
} // end Comparable
```

Our example has only one method signature. Note that an interface does not declare the constructors for a class. Also note that methods within an interface are public by default, so you can omit `public` from their signatures.

You store an interface definition in a file whose name is the name of the interface followed by .java. For example, the interface Comparable is in the file Comparable.java.

Note: An interface can declare data fields, but they must be public. By convention, a class's data fields are private, so any data fields in an interface should represent named constants. Thus, they should be public and final.

Note: A Java interface is a good place to provide comments that specify each method's purpose, parameters, precondition, and postcondition. In this way, you can specify a class in one file and implement it in another.

3.12   **Example.** Recall the class Name that we presented in Segment 1.16 of Chapter 1. The following statements define a Java interface for this class. We have included comments for only the first two methods to save space:

```java
public interface NameInterface
{
   /** Task: Sets the first and last names.
    *  @param firstName  a string that is the desired first name
    *  @param lastName   a string that is the desired last name */
   public void setName(String firstName, String lastName);

   /** Task: Gets the full name.
    *  @return a string containing the first and last names */
   public String getName();

   public void setFirst(String firstName);
   public String getFirst();

   public void setLast(String lastName);
   public String getLast();

   public void giveLastNameTo(NameInterface child);

   public String toString();
} // end NameInterface
```

This interface provides a client with a handy summary of the methods' specifications. The client should be able to use the class that implements NameInterface without looking at the class.

Notice that the parameter of the method giveLastNameTo has NameInterface as its data type instead of Name, as it did in Chapter 1. You should write an interface independently of any class that will implement it. We will talk about interfaces as data types beginning with Segment 3.15.

Programming Tip: **Naming an interface**
Interface names, particularly those that are standard in Java, often end in "able," such as Comparable or Cloneable. That ending does not always provide a good name, so endings such as "er" or "Interface" are also used. Just as Java's exception names end in "Exception," we will usually end our interface names with "Interface."

Implementing an Interface

3.13 Any class that implements an interface must state so at the beginning of its definition by using an implements clause. For example, if a class C implements the Comparable interface, it would begin as follows:

> **public class** C **implements** Comparable

The class then must provide a definition for each method declared in the interface. In this example, the class C must implement the method compareTo.

   The implementation of the class Name given in Chapter 1 could implement NameInterface as given in the previous segment. You would simply add an implements clause to the first line of the class definition, so that it reads as follows:

> **public class** Name **implements** NameInterface

The class Name must now implement every method declared in NameInterface. Using an interface is a way to guarantee that a class has defined certain methods.

   Figure 3-3 illustrates the three files that contain NameInterface, Name, and their client.

Figure 3-3   The files for an interface, a class that implements the interface, and the client

The interface	The class	The client
```public interface NameInterface { . . . }```	```public class Name implements NameInterface { . . . }```	```public class Client { . . . NameInterface joe; . . . joe = new Name(); }```
NameInterface.java	Name.java	Client.java

3.14 Several classes can implement the same interface, perhaps in different ways. For example, many classes implement the Comparable interface and provide their own version of the compareTo method.

   Additionally, a class can implement more than one interface. If it does, you simply list all the interface names, separated by commas. If the class is derived from another class, the implements clause always follows the extends clause. Thus, you could write

> **public class** C **extends** B **implements** Comparable, AnotherInterface

As Segment 2.19 mentioned, you cannot derive a class from more than one base class. A Java interface serves a function similar to a base class, even though it is not a class. By allowing a class to implement any number of interfaces, Java approximates multiple base classes without the complications they cause.

Question 5   Write a Java interface for the class Student given in Segment 2.2 of Chapter 2.

Question 6   What revision(s) should you make to the class Student so that it implements the interface you wrote for the previous question?

An Interface as a Data Type

3.15   You can use a Java interface as you would a data type when you declare a variable, a data field, or a method's parameter. For example, a method could have a parameter whose type is `Comparable`:

```
public void myMethod(Comparable entry)
```

Any argument that you pass to this method must be an object of a class that implements the `Comparable` interface. Thus, by using `Comparable` as the parameter's type, you ensure that the method's argument will be able to invoke the method `compareTo`. In general, a method can be sure that its parameter can invoke particular methods, namely those declared in an interface, if its data type is the interface.

What if a class `D` does not begin with the phrase `implements Comparable`, yet still implements the method `compareTo`? You could not pass an instance of `D` to `myMethod`.

Note: By using an interface as an object's type, you ensure that the object will have a certain set of methods.

3.16   A variable declaration such as

```
NameInterface myName;
```

makes `myName` a reference variable. Now `myName` can reference any object of any class that implements `NameInterface`. So if you have

```
myName = new Name("Coco", "Puffs");
```

then `myName.getFirst()` returns a reference to the string `"Coco"`. If the class `AnotherName` also implements `NameInterface`, and you later write

```
myName = new AnotherName("April", "MacIntosh");
```

then `myName.getFirst()` returns a reference to the string `"April"`.

Chapter 2 introduced polymorphic variables when discussing inheritance. In that discussion, you saw that you could write

```
A item = new B();
```

if the class `B` is derived from the class `A`. The variable `item` is polymorphic, since its dynamic type can differ from its static type. Here you see that the variable `myName` also is polymorphic. Thus, polymorphic variables can occur as a result of using either inheritance or interfaces.

Type Casts Within an Interface Implementation

3.17   Implementing an interface can involve a complication. For example, notice that in the `Comparable` interface, the type of `compareTo`'s parameter is `Object`. We want the parameter to have the same type as the calling object, but the type of the calling object is unknown until we define a class that implements the interface. Since we want the interface to be general, we have to settle for making the parameter of type `Object`. Thus, in any class that implements the interface, a type cast probably will be needed within the body of the definition of the method.

3.18   **Example.** The following class represents data about a pet and implements the interface `Comparable`. Look for the type cast in the definition of `compareTo`.

```
public class Pet implements Comparable
{
```

```
    private String name;
    private int     age;      // in years
    private double weight;    // in pounds

    /** Task: Compares the weight of two pets. */
    public int compareTo(Object other)
    {
        Pet otherPet = (Pet)other;
        return weight - otherPet.weight;
    } // end compareTo

    < Other methods are here. >
} // end Pet
```

Since other's data type is `Object`, we need to cast it to `Pet` to be able to access the data field `weight`.

We might use the class `Pet` in a program by writing the following statements. Note that type casting is not necessary here:

```
Pet dog = new Pet("Fido", 5, 55.6);
Pet cat = new Pet("Fluffy", 6, 10.3);

if (dog.compareTo(cat) < 0)
    System.out.println("Dog weighs less than cat.");
```

 Question 7   Revise the class `Name` given in Segment 1.16 of Chapter 1 so that it implements the interface `Comparable`.

Extending an Interface

3.19   Once you have an interface, you can derive another interface from it by using inheritance. In fact, you can derive an interface from several interfaces, even though you cannot derive a class from several classes.

When an interface extends another interface, it has all the methods of the inherited interface. Thus, you can create an interface that consists of the methods in an existing interface plus some new methods. For example, working with our pet theme, suppose that we have the following interface:

```
public interface Nameable
{
    public void setName(String petName);
    public String getName();
} // end Nameable
```

We can extend `Nameable` to create the interface `Callable`:

```
public interface Callable extends Nameable
{
    public void come(String petName);
} // end Callable
```

A class that implements `Callable` must implement the methods `come`, `setName`, and `getName`.

3.20   You also can combine several interfaces into a new interface and add even more methods if you like. For example, suppose that in addition to the previous two interfaces, we define the following interfaces:

```
public interface Capable
{
  public void hear();
  public void respond();
} // end Capable

public interface Trainable extends Callable, Capable
{
  public void sit();
  public void speak();
  public void lieDown();
} // end Trainable
```

A class that implements `Trainable` must implement the methods `setName`, `getName`, `come`, `hear`, and `respond`, as well as the methods `sit`, `speak`, and `lieDown`.

Note: A Java interface can be derived from several interfaces, even though you cannot derive a class from several classes.

Question 8   Suppose that the class `Pet` in Segment 3.18 contains the method `setName`, yet does not implement the interface `Nameable` of Segment 3.19. Could you pass an instance of `Pet` as the argument of the method with the following signature?

```
public void enterShow(Nameable pet)
```

Named Constants Within an Interface

3.21   An interface can contain named constants, that is, public data fields that you initialize and declare as final. If you want to implement several classes that share a common set of named constants, you can define the constants in an interface that the classes implement. In this way, the classes do not have their own set of constants. You save a bit of memory, but more importantly, you have only one set of constants to keep current.

3.22   **Example.** For example, imagine classes for various geometric forms like circles, spheres, and cylinders. Each of these forms has a radius, and each involves the constant π. We could define the following interface that our classes would implement:

```
public interface Circular
{
  public static final double PI = 3.14159;

  public void setRadius(double newRadius);
  public double getRadius();
} // end Circular
```

Although an interface could contain constants exclusively, this interface recognizes that a radius will exist, and so declares both set and get methods for it.

Now a class `Circle` that implements this interface could appear as follows:

```java
public class Circle implements Circular
{
  private double radius;

  public void setRadius(double newRadius)
  {
    radius = newRadius;
  } // end setRadius

  public double getRadius()
  {
    return radius;
  } // end getRadius

  public double getArea()
  {
    return PI*radius*radius;
  } // end getArea
} // end Circle
```

The class implements the methods `setRadius` and `getRadius` and uses the constant `PI` in the method `getArea`. The class does not define its own copy of `PI` but does declare `radius` as a data field. An interface cannot contain an ordinary data field like `radius`, since it is private.

Interfaces Versus Abstract Classes

3.23 The purpose of an interface is similar to that of an abstract base class. However, an interface is not a base class. In fact, it is not a class of any kind. When should you use an interface and when should you use an abstract class? Use an abstract base class if you want to provide a method definition or declare a private data field that your classes will have in common. Otherwise, use an interface. Remember that a class can implement several interfaces but can extend only one abstract class.

3.24 **Example.** Consider the example from the previous section that involved π and a radius. Instead of defining an interface, let's define an abstract class:

```java
public abstract class CircleBase
{
  public static final double PI = 3.14159;
  private double radius;

  public void setRadius(double newRadius)
  {
    radius = newRadius;
  } // end setRadius

  public double getRadius()
  {
    return radius;
  } // end getRadius

  public abstract double getArea();
} // end CircleBase
```

This class defines the constant PI just as the interface did in the previous section. But here we also declare the data field radius that descendant classes will inherit. Since the data field is private, the class CircleBase must implement set and get methods so that its descendant classes can access radius. If CircleBase simply declared setRadius and getRadius as abstract—omitting their implementations—a descendant class would be unable to implement them.

If the definition of CircleBase stopped here, it would not be abstract, but it still would be a useful base class. However, this class also declares the abstract method getArea, which its descendant classes must implement in their own way.

The following class is derived from the base class CircleBase. It implements the abstract method getArea. In doing so, it invokes the inherited method getRadius to access the inherited data field radius. Circle cannot reference the data field radius by name.

```
public class Circle extends CircleBase
{
  public double getArea()
  {
    double radius = getRadius();
    return PI*radius*radius;
  } // end getArea
} // end Circle
```

In this method, radius is simply a local variable.

Choosing Classes

We have talked about specifying classes and implementing classes, but up to now, we have chosen the class to specify or implement. If you must design an application from scratch, how will you determine the classes you need? In this section, we introduce you to some techniques that software designers use in choosing and designing classes. Although we will mention these techniques in subsequent chapters from time to time, our intent is simply to expose you to these ideas. Future courses will develop ways to select and design classes.

3.25   Imagine that we are designing a registration system for your school. Where should we begin? A useful way to start would be to look at the system from a functional point of view, as follows:

- **Who or what will use the system?** A human user or a software component that interacts with the system is called an **actor.** So a first step is to list the possible actors. For a registration system, two of the actors could be a student and the registrar.
- **What can each actor do with the system?** A **scenario** is a description of the interaction between an actor and the system. For example, a student can add a course. This basic scenario has variations that give rise to other scenarios. For instance, what happens when the student attempts to add a course that is closed? Our second step, therefore, is to identify scenarios. One way to do this is to complete the question that begins "What happens when...".
- **Which scenarios involve common goals?** For example, the two scenarios we just described are related to the common goal of adding a course. A collection of such related scenarios is called a **use case.** Our third step, then, is to identify the use cases.

You can get an overall picture of the use cases involved in a system you are designing by drawing a **use case diagram.** Figure 3-4 is a use case diagram for our simple registration system. Each actor—the student and the registrar—appears as a stick figure. The box represents the registration system, and the ovals within the box are the use cases. A line joins an actor and a use case if an interaction exists between the two.

Figure 3-4   A use case diagram for a registration system

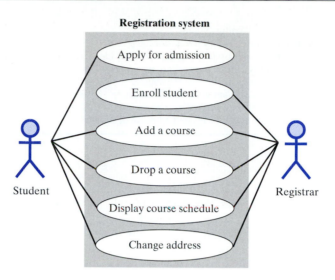

Some use cases in this example involve one actor, and some involve both. For example, only the student applies for admission, and only the registrar enrolls a student. However, both the student and the registrar can add a course to a student's schedule.

 Note: Use cases depict a system from the actors' points of view. They do not necessarily suggest classes within the system.

Identifying Classes

3.26   Although drawing a use case diagram is a step in the right direction, it does not identify the classes that are needed for your system. Several techniques are possible, and you will probably need to use more than one.

One simple technique is to describe the system and then identify the nouns and verbs in the description. The nouns can suggest classes, and the verbs can suggest appropriate methods within the classes. Given the imprecision of natural language, this technique is not foolproof, but it can be useful.

For example, we could write a sequence of steps to describe each use case in Figure 3-4. Figure 3-5 gives a description of the use case for adding a course from the point of view of a student. Notice the alternative actions taken in Steps 2a and 4a when the system does not recognize the student or when a requested course is closed.

What classes does this description suggest? Looking at the nouns, we could decide to have classes to represent a student, a course, a list of all courses offered, and a student's schedule of courses. The verbs suggest actions that include determining whether a student is eligible to register, determining whether a course is closed, and adding a course to a student's schedule. One way to assign these actions to classes is to use CRC cards, which we describe next.

Figure 3-5   A description of a use case for adding a course

```
System:   Registration
Use case: Add a course
Actor:     Student
Steps:
       1. Student enters identifying data.
       2. System confirms eligibility to register.
          a. If ineligible to register, ask student to enter identification data again.
       3. Student chooses a particular section of a course from a list of course offerings.
       4. System confirms availability of the course.
          a. If course is closed, allow student to return to Step 3 or quit.
       5. System adds course to student's schedule.
       6. System displays student's revised schedule of courses.
```

CRC Cards

3.27   A simple technique to explore the purpose of a class uses index cards. Each card represents one class. You begin by choosing a descriptive name for a class and writing it at the top of a card. You then list the names of the public methods that represent the class's **responsibilities.** You do this for each class in the system. Finally, you indicate the interactions, or **collaborations,** among the classes. That is, you write on each class's card the names of other classes that have some sort of interaction with the class. Because of their content, these cards are called **class-responsibility-collaboration,** or **CRC, cards.**

For example, Figure 3-6 shows a CRC card for the class CourseSchedule that represents the courses in which a student has enrolled. Notice that the small size of each card forces you to write brief notes. The number of responsibilities must be small, which suggests that you think at a high level and consider small classes. The size of the cards also lets you arrange them on a table and move them around easily while you search for collaborations.

Figure 3-6   A class-responsibility-collaboration (CRC) card

```
                     CourseSchedule

    Responsibilities
        Add a course
        Remove a course
        Check for time conflict
        List course schedule


    Collaborations
        Course
        Student
```

    Question 9   Write a CRC card for the class Student given in Segment 2.2 of Chapter 2.

3.28   **The Unified Modeling Language.** The use case diagram in Figure 3-4 is part of a larger notation known as the **Unified Modeling Language,** or **UML.** Designers use the UML to illustrate a software system's necessary classes and their relationships. The UML gives people an overall view of a complex system more effectively than either a natural language or a programming language can. English, for example, can be ambiguous, and Java code provides too much detail. Providing a clear picture of the interactions among classes is one of the strengths of the UML.

Besides the use case diagram, the UML provides a **class diagram** that places each class description in a box analogous to a CRC card. The box contains a class's name, its **attributes** (data fields), and **operations** (methods). For example, Figure 3-7 shows a box for the class `CourseSchedule`. Typically, you omit from the box such common operations as constructors, get methods, and set methods.

Figure 3-7   A class representation that can be a part of a class diagram

```
┌─────────────────────────┐
│      CourseSchedule      │
├─────────────────────────┤
│  courseCount            │
│  courseList             │
├─────────────────────────┤
│  addCourse(course)      │
│  removeCourse(course)   │
│  isTimeConflict()       │
│  listSchedule()         │
└─────────────────────────┘
```

 Question 10   How would the class `Name`, given in Segment 1.16 of Chapter 1, appear in a class diagram of the UML?

3.29   In a class diagram, lines join the boxes to show the relationships among the classes, including any inheritance hierarchy. For example, the class diagram in Figure 3-8 shows that the classes `UndergradStudent` and `GradStudent` are each derived from the class `Student`. An arrow with a hollow head points to the base class. Within the UML, the base class `Student` is said to be a **generalization** of `UndergradStudent` and `GradStudent`.

Figure 3-8   UML notation for a base class `Student` and two derived classes

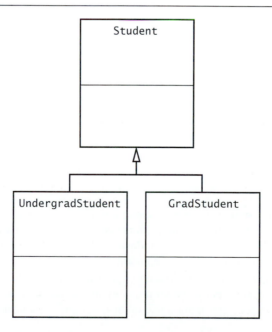

An **association** is a line that represents a relationship between instances of two classes. Basically, an association represents what a CRC card calls a collaboration. For example, relationships exist among the classes Student, CourseSchedule, and Course. Figure 3-9 shows how the UML pictures these relationships. The association (line) between the classes CourseSchedule and Course, for example, indicates a relationship between objects of the class CourseSchedule and objects of the class Course. This association has an arrow pointing toward Course. The arrow indicates responsibilities. Thus, a CourseSchedule object should be able to tell us the courses it contains, but a Course object need not be able to tell us to which schedules it belongs. The UML calls this aspect of the notation the **navigability.**

This particular arrow is said to be **unidirectional,** since it points in one direction. An association with arrowheads on both ends is called **bidirectional.** For example, a Student object can determine its course schedule, and a CourseSchedule object can determine to which student it belongs. You can assume that the navigability of an association without arrowheads is unspecified at the present stage of the design.

At the ends of the association are numbers. At the end of the line beginning at CourseSchedule and extending to Course, you see the notation 0..10. This notation indicates that each CourseSchedule object is associated with between zero and ten courses. If you follow the line in the other direction, you encounter an asterisk. It has the same meaning as the notation 0..infinity. Each Course object can be associated with many, many course schedules—or with none at all. The figure also indicates a relationship between one Student object and one CourseSchedule object. This notation on the ends of an association is called the association's **cardinality** or **multiplicity.**

Figure 3-9   Part of a UML class diagram with associations

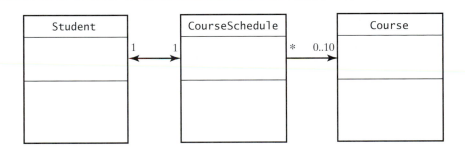

Question 11   Combine Figures 3-8 and 3-9 into one class diagram. Then add a class AllCourses that represents all courses offered this semester. What new association(s) do you need to add?

Reusing Classes

3.30   When you first start to write programs, you can easily get the impression that each program is designed and written from scratch. On the contrary, most software is created by combining already existing components with new components. This approach saves time and money. In addition, the existing components have been used many times and so are better tested and more reliable.

For example, a highway simulation program might include a new highway object to model a new highway design, but it would probably model automobiles by using an automobile class that had already been designed for some other program. As you identify the classes that you need for your project, you should see whether any of the classes exist already. Can you use them as is, or would they serve as a good base class for a new class?

3.31   As you design new classes, you should take steps to ensure that they are easily reusable in the future. You must specify exactly how objects of that class interact with other objects. This is the principle of encapsulation that we discussed in the first section of this chapter. But encapsulation is not the only principle you must follow. You must also design your class so that the objects are general and not tailored too much for one particular program. For example, if your program requires that all simulated automobiles move only forward, you should still include a reverse in your automobile class. Some other simulation may require automobiles to back up.

Admittedly, you cannot foresee all the future uses of your class. But you can and should avoid dependencies that will restrict its use later by another programmer. Chapter 14 describes the design of a class with its future use in mind.

Using the principles that this chapter discusses to design a reusable class with an interface that has comments suitable for `javadoc` takes work. Hacking together a solution to your specific problem would take less time. But the payback for your effort will come later on, when you or another programmer needs to reuse an interface or a class. If you planned for the future when you wrote those components, every use of them will be faster and easier. Actual software developers use these principles to save time over the long term, because saving time saves them money. You should use them, too.

CHAPTER SUMMARY

- Encapsulation is a design principle of object-oriented programming that encloses data and methods into a class, thereby hiding the details of a class's implementation. Only enough information to allow a programmer to use the class is given. The programmer should be able to use a well-designed class as if the body of every method is hidden from view.

- Abstraction is a process that asks you to focus on *what* instead of *how*.

- The method `compareTo` compares two objects and returns a negative integer, zero, or a positive integer according to whether the comparison is less than, equal to, or greater than.

- An interface declares the public methods that a class must implement and can contain public named constants.

- A class that implements an interface has an `implements` clause at the start of the class definition. The class must implement all the methods declared in the interface.

- A Java class can implement any number of interfaces. This feature gives Java an approximation to multiple inheritance, a concept that Java does not support.

- Use cases depict a system from the point of view of one or more actors. Use cases do not necessarily suggest classes within the system.

- A class-responsibility-collaboration (CRC) card lists a class's name, actions, and other classes that collaborate with it.

- A class diagram depicts the relationships among classes and, for each class, lists its name, data fields, and methods. The notation used is a part of the Unified Modeling Language (UML).

PROGRAMMING TIPS

- Specify each public method fully in comments placed before the method's signature. State whether a method or its client is responsible for ensuring that the necessary conditions are met for the successful execution of the method. In this way, checking is done but not duplicated. However, during debugging, a method should always check that its precondition has been met.

● A method that cannot satisfy its postcondition, even though its precondition is met, can throw an exception.

● Assertions written as comments within a method's body identify aspects of your logic that you can check during debugging.

● Interface names, particularly those that are standard in Java, often end in "able," such as `Comparable` or `Cloneable`. That ending does not always provide a good name, so endings such as "er" or "Inter-face" are also used. Just as Java's exception names end in "Exception," we will usually end our interface names with "Interface."

EXERCISES

1. Consider the class `Circle`, as given in Segment 3.22.

   a. Is the client or the method `setRadius` responsible for ensuring that the circle's radius is positive?
   b. Write a precondition and a postcondition for the method `setRadius`.
   c. Write comments for the method `setRadius` in a style suitable for `javadoc`.
   d. Revise the method `setRadius` and its precondition and postcondition to change the responsibility mentioned in your answer to Part *a*.

2. Revise the class `Circle` as given in Segment 3.22, so that it also implements the interface `Comparable`. Implement the method `compareTo` so that circles are compared according to their radii.

3. Repeat Exercise 2, but instead use the class `Circle` as given in Segment 3.24.

4. Consider the interface `NameInterface` defined in Segment 3.12. We provided comments for only two of the methods. Write comments in `javadoc` style for each of the other methods.

5. Write a Java interface for the class `CollegeStudent` given in Segment 2.8 of Chapter 2.

6. What revision(s) should you make to the class `CollegeStudent` so that it implements the interface that you wrote for the previous exercise?

7. Revise the classes `Student` and `CollegeStudent` so that each class implements the interface `Comparable` and, therefore, implements the method `compareTo`.

PROJECTS

1. Design a class `Fraction` of fractions. Each fraction is signed and has a numerator and a denominator that are integers. Your class should be able to add, subtract, multiply, and divide two fractions. These methods should have a fraction as a parameter and should return the result of the operation as a fraction.

   The class should also be able to find the reciprocal of a fraction, compare two fractions, determine whether two fractions are equal, and convert a fraction to a string. Your class should handle zero denominators.

Fractions should always occur in lowest terms, and the class should be responsible for this requirement. For example, if the user tries to create a fraction such as 4/8, the class should set the fraction to 1/2. Likewise, the results of all arithmetic operations should be in lowest terms. Note that a fraction can be improper—that is, have a numerator that is larger than its denominator. Such a fraction, however, should be in lowest terms.

Begin by writing a CRC card for this class. Then write a Java interface that declares each public method. Include `javadoc`-style comments to specify each method.

2. Write a Java class `Fraction` that implements both the interface you designed in Project 1 and the `Comparable` interface. Begin with reasonable constructors. Design and implement useful private methods, and include comments that specify them.

   To reduce a fraction such as 4/8 to lowest terms, you need to divide both the numerator and the denominator by their greatest common denominator. The greatest common denominator of 4 and 8 is 4, so when you divide the numerator and denominator of 4/8 by 4, you get the fraction 1/2. The following recursive algorithm determines the greatest common denominator of two positive integers:

   ```
   Algorithm gcd(integerOne, integerTwo)
   if (integerOne % integerTwo == 0)
     result = integerTwo
   else
     result = gcd(integerTwo, integerOne % integerTwo)
   return result
   ```

   It will be easier to determine the correct sign of a fraction if you force the fraction's denominator to be positive. However, your implementation must handle negative denominators that the client might provide.

   Write a program that adequately demonstrates your class.

3. A mixed number contains both an integer portion and a fractional portion. Design a class `MixedNumber` of mixed numbers that uses the class `Fraction` that you designed in Project 1. Provide operations for `MixedNumber` that are analogous to those of `Fraction`. That is, provide operations to set, retrieve, add, subtract, multiply, and divide mixed numbers. The fractional portion of any mixed number should be in lowest terms and have a numerator that is strictly less than its denominator.

   Write a Java interface, including `javadoc` comments, for this class.

4. Implement the class `MixedNumber` that you designed in Project 3. Use the operations in `Fraction` whenever possible. For example, to add two mixed numbers, convert them to fractions, add the fractions by using `Fraction`'s add operation, and then convert the resulting fraction to mixed form. Use analogous techniques for the other arithmetic operations.

   Handling the sign of a mixed number can be a messy problem if you are not careful. Mathematically, it makes sense for the sign of the integer part to match the sign of the fraction. But if you have a negative fraction, for example, the `toString` method for the mixed number could give you the string `"-5 -1/2"`, instead of `"-5 1/2"`, which is what you would normally expect. Here is a possible solution that will greatly simplify computations.

   Represent the sign of a mixed number with a character data field. Once this sign is set, make the integer and fractional parts positive. When a mixed number is created, if the given integer part is not zero, take the sign of the integer part as the sign of the mixed number and ignore the signs of the fraction's numerator and denominator. However, if the given integer part is zero, take the sign of the given fraction as the sign of the mixed number.

5. Consider two identical pails. One pail hangs from a hook on the ceiling and contains a blue liquid. The other pail is empty and rests on the floor directly below the first pail. Suddenly a small hole develops in the bottom of the full pail. Blue liquid streams from the full pail and falls into the empty pail on the floor, as Figure 3-10 illustrates. Liquid continues to fall until the upper pail is empty. Notice that the outline of the pails is black; only the liquid is blue.

   Design classes for a program that illustrates this action. When the program begins execution, it should display both pails in their original condition before the leak occurs. Decide whether the leak will occur spontaneously or at a user signal, such as pressing the Return key or clicking the mouse. If the latter, you could have the user position the cursor on the pail bottom to indicate where the leak will occur.

   Write CRC cards and Java interfaces that include comments in javadoc style.

6. Implement your design for the leaking pail, as described in Project 5.

Figure 3-10   A leaking pail (Project 5)

4

Lists

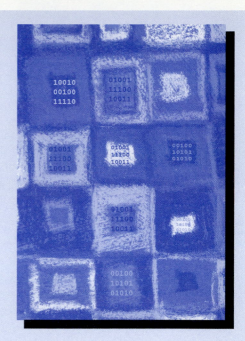

CONTENTS

Specifications for the ADT List
    Refining the Specifications
Using the ADT List
Java Class Library: The Interface **List**
Using a List Is Like Using a Vending Machine

PREREQUISITES

Introduction
Chapter   1   Java Classes
Chapter   3   Designing Classes
Appendix   B   Exception Handling

OBJECTIVES

After studying this chapter, you should be able to

- Describe the concept of an abstract data type (ADT)
- Describe the ADT list
- Use the ADT list in a Java program

This chapter builds on the concepts of encapsulation and data abstraction that were presented in the previous chapter, and it develops the notion of an abstract data type, or ADT. As an example of an abstract data type, we specify and use the ADT list. In doing so we will provide a Java interface for our list. Knowing just this interface, you will be able to use a list in a Java program. You do not need to know how the entries in the list are represented or how the list operations are implemented. Indeed, your program will not depend on these specifics. As you will see, this important program feature is what data abstraction is all about.

Specifications for the ADT List

4.1   A list provides a way to organize data. We can have to-do lists, gift lists, address lists, grocery lists, even lists of lists. These lists provide a useful way for us to organize our lives, as illustrated in Figure 4-1. Each list has a first item, a last item, and usually items in between. That is, the items in a list have a position: first, second, and so on. An item's position might be important to you, or it might not. When adding an item to your list, you might always add it at the end, or you might insert it between two other items already in the list.

Figure 4-1   A to-do list

Everyday lists such as to-do lists, gift lists, address lists, and grocery lists have entries that are strings. What can you do to such lists?

- Typically, you **add** a new entry **at the end** of the list.
- Actually, you can **add** a new entry **anywhere:** at the beginning, the end, or in between items.
- You can cross out an entry—that is, **remove** it.
- You can **remove all** entries.
- You can **replace** an entry.
- You can **look at** any entry.
- You can determine whether the list **contains** a particular entry.
- You can **count** the number of entries in the list.
- You can determine whether the list is **empty** or **full.**
- You can **display** all of the entries in the list.

4.2   When you work with a list, you determine where an entry is or should be. You probably are not conscious of its exact position: Is it tenth? Fourteenth? However, when your program uses a list, a convenient way to identify a particular entry is by the entry's position within the list. It could be first, that is, at position 1, or second (position 2), and so on. This convention allows you to describe, or specify, the operations on a list more precisely.

At this point, you should *not* be thinking about how to represent a list in your program or how to implement its operations. For the moment, forget about arrays, for example. You first need to clearly know what the list operations do: Focus on *what* the operations do, not on *how* they do them. That is, you need a detailed set of specifications before you can use a list in a program. In fact, you should specify the list operations before you even decide on a programming language.

At this point, the list is an abstract data type. An **abstract data type,** or **ADT,** consists of data having the same type and the operations on that data. An ADT describes its data and specifies its operations. It does not indicate how to store the data or how to implement the operations. Thus, we can discuss ADTs independently of a programming language. In contrast, a **data structure** is an implementation of an ADT within a programming language.

4.3   To specify the ADT list, we describe its data and specify the operations on that data. Unlike common lists whose entries are strings, the ADT list is more general and has entries that are objects of the same type. The following is a specification of the ADT list:

ABSTRACT DATA TYPE LIST

DATA

- A collection of objects in a specific order and having the same data type
- The number of objects in the collection

OPERATIONS

add(newEntry)

Task: Adds newEntry to the end of the list.
Input: newEntry is an object.
Output: None.

add(newPosition, newEntry)

Task: Adds newEntry at position newPosition within the list.
Input: newPosition is an integer, newEntry is an object.
Output: None.

remove(givenPosition)

Task: Removes from the list the entry at position givenPosition.
Input: givenPosition is an integer.
Output: None.

clear()

Task: Removes all entries from the list.
Input: None.
Output: None.

replace(givenPosition, newEntry)

Task: Replaces the entry at position givenPosition with newEntry.
Input: givenPosition is an integer, newEntry is an object.
Output: None.

getEntry(givenPosition)

Task: Retrieves the entry at position givenPosition in the list.
Input: givenPosition is an integer.
Output: Returns a reference to the entry at position givenPosition.

contains(anEntry)

Task: Determines whether the list contains anEntry.
Input: anEntry is an object.
Output: Returns true if anEntry is in the list, or false if not.

getLength()

Task: Gets the number of entries currently in the list.
Input: None.
Output: Returns the number of entries currently in the list as an int.

isEmpty()

Task: Determines whether the list is empty.
Input: None.
Output: Returns true if the list is empty, or false if not.

isFull()

Task: Determines whether the list is full.
Input: None.
Output: Returns true if the list is full, or false if not.

display()

Task: Displays all entries that are in the list in the order in which they occur, one per line.
Input: None.
Output: None.

We have only begun to specify the behaviors of these list operations, as the specifications just given leave some details to the imagination. Some examples will help us to better understand these operations so that we can improve the specifications. We'll need precise specifications before we implement the operations.

 Programming Tip: After designing a draft of an ADT, confirm your understanding of the operations and their design by writing some pseudocode that uses the ADT.

4.4

E

Example. When you first declare a new list, it is empty and its length is zero. If you add three objects—a, b, and c—one at a time and in the order given, to the end of the list, the list will appear as

a
b
c

The object a is first, and c is last. To save space here, we will sometimes write a list's contents on one line. For example, we might write

a b c

to represent this list.

The following pseudocode represents the previous three additions to the specific list myList:

myList.add(a)
myList.add(b)
myList.add(c)

At this point, myList is not empty, so myList.isEmpty() is false. Since the list contains three entries, myList.getLength() is 3. Notice that adding entries to the end of a list does not change the positions of entries already in the list. Figure 4-2 illustrates these add operations as well as the operations that we describe next.

Figure 4-2   The effect of ADT list operations on an initially empty list

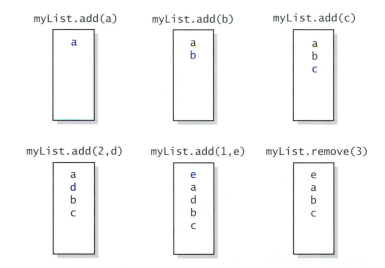

4.5   Now suppose that we add entries at various positions within the list. For example,

myList.add(2, d)

places d at position 2 within the list. Doing so, however, moves b to position 3 and c to position 4, so that the list now contains

a d b c

If we add e to the beginning of the list by writing

    myList.add(1, e)

the current entries in the list move to the next higher position. The list then contains

    e a d b c

Look at Figure 4-2 again to see the effect of these operations.

4.6 We can retrieve the second entry in this list by writing

    ref2 = myList.getEntry(2)

This expression returns a reference to the second entry. Remember that we are writing pseudocode here. Later examples in Java will show you that a type cast is likely to be necessary.

What happens when we remove an entry? For example,

    myList.remove(3)

removes the third entry—d in the previous example—from the list. The list then contains

    e a b c

Notice that entries after the one that was removed move to the next lower position within the list. Figure 4-2 illustrates this change to the list.

What if an application requires us to remove an entry from a list but retain the entry for another purpose? Our interpretation of remove would force us to first use getEntry to obtain a reference to the entry and then use remove to remove the entry from the list. We could refine the specification of remove to return a reference to the object removed from the list. To use this version of remove, we would write a pseudocode statement such as

    ref3 = myList.remove(3)

This change makes remove more versatile, as the client could either save or ignore the returned reference.

We can replace the third entry b of our list with f by writing

    myList.replace(3, f)

No other entries move or change. We could refine the specification of replace to return a reference to the object that was replaced. So if we wrote

    ref = myList.replace(3, f)

ref would reference the former entry b.

 Note: The objects in an ADT list have an order determined by the client of the list. To add, remove, or retrieve an entry, you must specify the entry's position within the list.

Refining the Specifications

4.7 The previous specifications ignore at least three difficulties that might arise during the use of the ADT list:

- The operations add, remove, replace, and getEntry are well behaved when the given position is valid for the current list. What happens when one of these operations receives an invalid position number?
- The methods remove, replace, and getEntry are not meaningful for empty lists. What happens when an empty list invokes one of these operations?

- A list could become full, depending on the list's implementation. What happens when the client tries to add an entry to a full list?

You as class designer need to make decisions about how to handle unusual conditions and include these decisions in your specifications. The documentation for the ADT list should reflect both these decisions and the detail that the previous examples demonstrate.

4.8   In general, you can address unusual situations in several ways. Your method could

- Assume that the invalid situations will not occur. This assumption is not as naive as it might sound. A method could state as an assumption—that is, a precondition—restrictions to which a client must adhere. It is then up to the client to enforce the precondition by checking that the precondition is satisfied before invoking the method. Notice that the client has methods such as `isEmpty` and `getLength` to help with this task. As long as the client obeys the restriction, the invalid situation will not occur.
- Ignore the invalid situations. A method could simply do nothing when given invalid data. Doing absolutely nothing, however, leaves the client wondering what happened.
- Make reasonable assumptions and act in a predictable way. For example, if a client tries to remove the sixth entry from a three-entry list, the `remove` method could either remove the last entry instead or return `null`.
- Return a boolean value that indicates the success or failure of an operation.
- Throw an exception.

As Appendix B shows, throwing an exception is often a desirable way for a Java method to react to unusual events that occur during its execution. The method can simply report a problem without deciding what to do about it. The exception enables each client to do what is needed in its own particular situation. To handle errors in this way, you must write `try-catch` blocks to use the method. For simplicity, we adopt the philosophy that methods should throw exceptions only in truly exceptional circumstances, when no other reasonable solution exists. Future chapters will include some examples of handling exceptions.

4.9   After you have identified all unusual circumstances, you should specify how your methods will behave under each of these circumstances. For example, it would be reasonable for the add method to throw an exception if it tries to add an entry at an invalid position. However, it might be just as reasonable for the method to return false in these situations.

Your documentation for your ADT should describe these specifications. As your specifications become more detailed, they increasingly should reflect your choice of programming language. Ultimately, you can write a Java interface (see Chapter 3) for the class that will implement the ADT.

Note: A first draft of an ADT's specifications often overlooks or ignores situations that you really need to consider. You might intentionally make these omissions to simplify this first draft. Once you have written the major portions of the specifications, you can concentrate on the details that make the specifications complete.

4.10   The following Java interface contains the methods for an ADT list and detailed comments that describe their behaviors. Recall that a class interface does not include data fields, constructors, private methods, or protected methods. We assume that items in the list will be objects—that is, instances of a class. For example, we could have a list of strings. To accommodate entries of any class type, the list methods use `Object` as the type of entry. As we discussed previously, all classes ultimately are derived from `Object`.

For lists of primitive types, we could replace each occurrence of `Object` with the desired type. Another possibility, however, would be to place instances of an appropriate wrapper class in our list. For example, instead of instances of the primitive type `int`, we could use instances of the wrapper class `Integer`. (Appendix A discusses wrapper classes.)

```java
/** An interface for the ADT list.
 *  Entries in the list have positions that begin with 1.
 */
public interface ListInterface
{
  /** Task: Adds a new entry to the end of the list.
   *  @param newEntry  the object to be added as a new entry
   *  @return true if the addition is successful, or false if not */
  public boolean add(Object newEntry);

  /** Task: Adds a new entry at a specified position within
   *        the list. Entries originally at and above the specified
   *        position are at the next higher position within the list.
   *        The list's size is increased by 1.
   *  @param newPosition  an integer that specifies the desired
   *                      position of the new entry; newPosition >= 1
   *                      and newPosition <= getLength()+1
   *  @param newEntry     the object to be added as a new entry
   *  @return true if the addition is successful, or false if not */
  public boolean add(int newPosition, Object newEntry);

  /** Task: Removes the entry at a given position from the list.
   *        Entries originally at positions higher than the given
   *        position are at the next lower position within the list,
   *        and the list's size is decreased by 1.
   *  @param givenPosition  an integer that indicates the position of
   *                        the entry to be removed; givenPosition >= 1
   *                        and givenPosition <= getLength()
   *  @return either the entry at position givenPosition, if the removal
   *          was successful, or null */
  public Object remove(int givenPosition);

  /** Task: Removes all entries from the list. */
  public void clear();

  /** Task: Replaces the entry at a given position in the list.
   *  @param givenPosition  an integer that indicates the position of the
   *                        entry to be replaced; givenPosition >= 1
   *                        and givenPosition <= getLength()
   *  @param newEntry  the object that will replace the entry at the
   *                   position givenPosition
   *  @return true if the replacement occurs, or false if either the
   *          list was empty or givenPosition is invalid */
  public boolean replace(int givenPosition, Object newEntry);

  /** Task: Retrieves the entry at a given position in the list.
   *  @param givenPosition  an integer that indicates the position of
   *                        the desired entry; givenPosition >= 1
   *                        and givenPosition <= getLength()
   *  @return a reference to the indicated list entry, if found,
```

```
 *              otherwise returns null */
public Object getEntry(int givenPosition);

/** Task: Determines whether the list contains a given entry.
 *  @param anEntry  the object that is the desired entry
 *  @return true if the list contains anEntry, or false if not */
public boolean contains(Object anEntry);

/** Task: Gets the length of the list.
 *  @return the integer number of entries currently in the list */
public int getLength();

/** Task: Determines whether the list is empty.
 *  @return true if the list is empty, or false if not */
public boolean isEmpty();

/** Task: Determines whether the list is full.
 *  @return true if the list is full, or false if not */
public boolean isFull();

/** Task: Displays all entries that are in the list, one per
 *         line, in the order in which they occur in the list. */
public void display();
} // end ListInterface
```

Question 1 Write pseudocode statements that add some objects to a list, as follows. First add c, then a, then b, and then d such that the order of the objects in the list will be a, b, c, d.

Question 2 Write pseudocode statements that exchange the third and seventh entries in a list of ten objects.

Note: The entries in a list of *n* entries are numbered from 1 to *n*. Although you cannot add a new entry at position 0, you can add one at position $n + 1$.

4.11   After specifying an ADT and writing a Java interface for its operations, you should write some Java statements that use the ADT. In this way, you check both the suitability and your understanding of the specifications. It is better to revise the design or documentation of the ADT now instead of after you have written its implementation. An added benefit of doing this task carefully is that you can use these same Java statements later to test your implementation.

The following section looks at several examples that use a list. These examples can be part of a program that tests your implementation.

Programming Tip: **Write a test program before you implement a class**

Writing Java statements that test a class's methods will help you to fully understand the specifications for the methods. Obviously, you must understand a method before you can implement it correctly. If you are also the class designer, your use of the class might help you see desirable changes to your design or its documentation. You will save time if you make these revisions before you have implemented the class. Since you must write a program that tests your implementation sometime, why not get additional benefits from the task by writing it now instead of later?

Using the ADT List

Imagine that we hire a programmer to implement the ADT list in Java, given the interface and specifications that we have developed so far. If we assume that these specifications are clear enough for the programmer to complete the implementation, we can use the ADT's operations in a program without knowing the details of the implementation. That is, we do not need to know *how* the programmer implemented the list to be able to use it. We only need to know *what* the ADT list does.

This section assumes that we have an implementation for the list and demonstrates how we can use a list in our program.

4.12   **Example.** Imagine that we are organizing a local road race. Our job is to note the order in which the runners finish the race. Since each runner wears a distinct identifying number, we can add each runner's number to the end of a list as the runners cross the finish line. Figure 4-3 illustrates such a list.

Figure 4-3   A list of numbers that identify runners in the order in which they finished a race

The following Java program shows how we can perform this task by using the ADT list. It assumes that the class `AList` implements the Java interface `ListInterface` that you saw in the previous section. Since `ListInterface` assumes that the items in the list are objects, we will treat each runner's identifying number as a string.

```java
public class ListClient
{
   public static void main(String[] args)
   {
      testList();
   } // end main

   public static void testList()
   {
      ListInterface runnerList = new AList(); // has only methods
                                              // in ListInterface
      runnerList.add("16"); // winner
      runnerList.add(" 4"); // second place
```

```
            runnerList.add("33"); // third place
            runnerList.add("27"); // fourth place
            runnerList.display();
        } // end testList
    } // end ListClient
```

The output from this program is

```
16
 4
33
27
```

Notice that the data type of runnerList is ListInterface instead of AList. While either type is correct, using ListInterface obliges runnerList to call only methods in the interface.

4.13   **Example.** The previous example uses the list method display to display the items in the list. We might want our output in a different form, however. The following method is an example of how a client could display the items in a list without using the method display. Notice the use of the list methods getLength and getEntry. Also notice that the data type of the input parameter aList is ListInterface. Thus, we can use as the argument of the method an instance of any class that implements ListInterface. That is, the method works for any implementation of the ADT list.

```
public static void displayList(ListInterface aList)
{
    int numberOfEntries = aList.getLength();
    System.out.println("The list contains " + numberOfEntries +
                    " entries, as follows:");

    for (int position = 1; position <= numberOfEntries; position++)
        System.out.println(aList.getEntry(position) +
                        " is entry " + position);

    System.out.println();
} // end displayList
```

Assuming the list runnerList from the example in Segment 4.12, the expression display-List(runnerList) produces the following output:

```
The list contains 4 entries, as follows:
16 is entry 1
 4 is entry 2
33 is entry 3
27 is entry 4
```

4.14   **Example.** A professor wants an alphabetical list of the names of the students who arrive for class today. As each student enters the room, the professor adds the student's name to a list. It is up to the professor to place each name into its correct position in the list so that the names will be in alphabetical order. The ADT list does *not* choose the order of its entries.

The following Java statements place the names Amy, Ellen, Bob, Drew, Aaron, and Carol in an alphabetical list. The comment at the end of each statement shows the list after the statement executes.

```
// make an alphabetical list of the names
// Amy, Ellen, Bob, Drew, Aaron, Carol
ListInterface alphaList = new AList();
```

```
alphaList.add(1, "Amy");     // Amy
alphaList.add(2, "Ellen");   // Amy Ellen
alphaList.add(2, "Bob");     // Amy Bob Ellen
alphaList.add(3, "Drew");    // Amy Bob Drew Ellen
alphaList.add(1, "Aaron");   // Aaron Amy Bob Drew Ellen
alphaList.add(4, "Carol");   // Aaron Amy Bob Carol Drew Ellen
```

After initially adding Amy to the beginning of the list and Ellen to the end of the list (at position 2), the professor inserts

- Bob between Amy and Ellen at position 2
- Drew between Bob and Ellen at position 3
- Aaron before Amy at position 1
- Carol between Bob and Drew at position 4

This technique of inserting each name into a collection of alphabetized names is called an **insertion sort.** We will discuss this and other ways of ordering items in a later chapter.

If we now remove the entry at position 4—Carol—by writing

```
alphaList.remove(4);
```

Drew and Ellen will then be at positions 4 and 5, respectively. Thus, `alphaList.getEntry(4)` would return a reference to Drew.

Finally, suppose that we want to replace a name in this list. We cannot replace a name with just any name and expect that the list will remain in alphabetical order. Replacing Bob with Ben by writing

```
alphaList.replace(3, "Ben");
```

would maintain alphabetical order, but replacing Bob with Nancy would not. The list's alphabetical order resulted from our original decisions about where to add names to the list. The order did not come about automatically as a result of list operations. That is, the client, not the list, maintained the order. We could, however, design an ADT that maintains its data in alphabetical order. You will see an example of such an ADT in Chapter 13.

Question 3   Suppose that `alphaList` contains a list of the four strings Amy, Ellen, Bob, and Drew. Write Java statements that swap Ellen and Bob and that then swap Ellen and Drew so that the list will be in alphabetical order.

4.15

Example. Let's look at a list of objects that are not strings. Suppose that we have the class `Name` from Chapter 1 that represents a person's first and last names. The following statements indicate how we could make a list of the names Amy Smith, Tina Drexel, and Robert Jones:

```
// make a list of names as you think of them
ListInterface nameList = new AList();
Name amy = new Name("Amy", "Smith");
nameList.add(amy);
nameList.add(new Name("Tina", "Drexel"));
nameList.add(new Name("Robert", "Jones"));
```

Now let's retrieve the name that is second in the list:

```
Name secondName = (Name)nameList.getEntry(2);
```

Notice that we must type-cast the object that `getEntry` returns. To accommodate entries of any class type, the list methods use `Object` as the type of entry. In particular, the return type of `getEntry` is `Object`. Thus, we must type-cast the returned entry to the data type of the entries in the list. That type is `Name` in this example.

Earlier we said that an ADT has data of the same type. As you will see in the next chapters, the implementations of the ADT list will not enforce this requirement. As this example just showed, you must know the data type of an entry in a list when you retrieve or remove it so that you can perform any necessary type cast. Although Java will let you place objects of various types in the same list, you would need to keep track of their data types. In general, requiring an ADT's entries to have the same type makes life easier.

Programming Tip: **Type-cast returned objects**
ADT entries that a method returns are of type `Object` and must be type-cast to their actual type.

Question 4   The example in Segment 4.13 used `getEntry` to retrieve an entry from a list.

a.   Why was a type cast to `String` not necessary?
b.   Would a type cast to `String` be wrong?

4.16   **Example.** Let's talk a bit more about the previous example. The variable `secondName` is a reference

to the second object of type `Name` in the list. Using this reference, we can modify the object. For example, we could change its last name by writing

```
secondName.setLast("Doe");
```

If the class `Name` did not have set methods like `setLast`, we would be unable to modify the objects in this list. For instance, if we had a list of strings, we would not be able to alter one of the strings in this way. Once we create an object of the class `String`, we cannot alter it. We could, however, replace an entire object in the list—regardless of its type—by using the ADT list operation `replace`.

A class, such as `Name`, that has set methods is a class of **mutable objects.** A class, such as `String`, without set methods is a class of **immutable objects.** Chapter 15 talks about such classes in more detail.

Java Class Library: The Interface List

4.17   The standard package `java.util` contains an interface for the ADT list that is similar to our interface. Its name is `List`. The major difference between a list in the Java Class Library and our ADT list is the numbering of a list's entries. A list in the Java Class Library uses the same numbering scheme as a Java array: The first entry is at position, or index, 0. In contrast, we begin our list at position 1.

The interface `List` also declares more methods than our interface does. The following method signatures are for a selection of methods that are similar to the ones you have seen in this chapter. We have used blue to indicate where they differ from our methods.

```
public boolean add(Object newEntry)
public void add(int index, Object newEntry)
public Object remove(int index)
public void clear()
public Object set(int index, Object anEntry)  // like replace
public Object get(int index)                  // like getEntry
public boolean contains(Object anEntry)
public int size()                             // like getLength
public boolean isEmpty()
```

The second add method is a void method. It throws an exception if `index` is out of range, instead of returning a boolean value, as our add method does. The method `set` is like our `replace` method, but it returns a reference to the entry that was replaced in the list instead of returning a boolean value. The other differences are simply in the method names used. For example, the interface `List` uses `get` for our `getEntry` and `size` for our `getLength`.

You can learn more about the interface `List` at

`http://java.sun.com/products/jdk/1.4/docs/api/index.html`

Using a List Is Like Using a Vending Machine

4.18   Imagine that you are in front of a vending machine, as Figure 4-4 depicts; better yet, take a break and go buy something from one!

Figure 4-4   A vending machine

When you look at the front of a vending machine, you see its interface. By inserting coins and pressing buttons, you are able to make a purchase. Here are some observations that we can make about the vending machine:

● You can perform only the specific tasks that the machine's interface presents to you.
● You must understand these tasks—that is, you must know what to do to buy a soda.
● You cannot see or access the inside of the machine, because a steel shell encapsulates it.
● You can use the machine even though you do not know what happens inside.
● If someone replaced the machine's inner mechanism with an improved version, leaving the interface unchanged, you could still use the machine in the same way.

You, as the user of a vending machine, are like the client of the ADT list that you saw earlier in this chapter. The observations that we just made about the user of a vending machine are similar to the following observations about a list's client:

● The client can perform only the operations specific to the ADT list. These operations often are declared within a Java interface.

- The client must adhere to the specifications of the operations that the ADT list provides. That is, the author of the client must understand how to use these operations.
- The client cannot access the data within the list without using an ADT operation. The principle of encapsulation hides the data within the ADT.
- The client can use the list, even though it cannot access the list's entries directly—that is, even though the programmer does not know how the data is stored.
- If someone changed the implementation of the list's operations, the client could still use the list in the same way, as long as the interface did not change.

4.19   In the examples of the previous section, each list is an instance of a class that implements the ADT list. That is, each list is an object whose behaviors are the operations of the ADT list. You can think of each such object as the vending machine that we just described. Each object encapsulates the list's data and operations just as the vending machine encapsulates its product (soda cans) and delivery system.

Some ADT operations have inputs analogous to the coins you insert into a vending machine. Some ADT operations have outputs analogous to the change, soda cans, messages, and warning lights that a vending machine provides.

Now imagine that you are the designer of the front, or interface, of the vending machine. What can the machine do, and what should a person do to use the machine? Will it help you or hinder you to think about how the soda cans will be stored and transported within the machine? We maintain that you should ignore these aspects and focus solely on how to use the machine—that is, on your design of the interface. Ignoring extraneous details makes your task easier and increases the quality of your design.

Recall that abstraction as a design principle asks you to focus on *what* instead of *how*. When you design an ADT, and ultimately a class, you use data abstraction to focus on what you want to do with or to the data without worrying about how you will accomplish these tasks. We practiced data abstraction at the beginning of this chapter when we designed the ADT list. We referred to each entry in our list by its position within the list. As we chose the methods that a list would have, we did not consider how we would represent the list. Instead, we focused on what each method should do.

Ultimately, we wrote a Java interface that specified the methods in detail. We were then able to write a client that used the list, again without knowledge of its implementation. If someone wrote the implementation for us, our program would presumably run correctly. If someone else gave us a better implementation, we could use it without changing our already-written client. This feature of the client is a major advantage of abstraction.

CHAPTER SUMMARY

- An abstract data type, or ADT, consists of both data and a set of operations on the data. An ADT provides a way to design a new data type independently of the choice of programming language.

- A list is an ADT whose data consists of ordered entries. Each entry is identified by its position within the list.

- A Java program manipulates or accesses a list's entries by using only the operations defined for the ADT list. The manifestation of the ADT in a programming language encapsulates the data and operations. That is, the particular data representations and method implementations are hidden from the client.

- When you use data abstraction to design an ADT, you focus on what you want to do with or to the data without worrying about how you will accomplish these tasks. That is, you ignore the details of how you represent data and how you manipulate it.

PROGRAMMING TIPS

- After designing a draft of an ADT, confirm your understanding of the operations and their design by writing some pseudocode that uses the ADT.

- After specifying an ADT and writing a Java interface for its operations, write some Java statements that use the ADT. In this way, you check both the suitability and your understanding of the specifications. An added benefit of doing this task carefully is that later you can use these same Java statements to test your implementation.

- ADT entries that a method returns are of type `Object` and must be type-cast to their actual type.

EXERCISES

1. If `myList` is an empty list, what does it contain after the following statements execute?

    ```
    myList.add("alpha");
    myList.add(1, "beta");
    myList.add("gamma");
    myList.add(2, "delta");
    myList.add(4, "alpha");
    myList.remove(2);
    myList.remove(2);
    myList.replace(3, "delta");
    ```

2. Suppose that you want an operation for the ADT list that removes the first occurrence of a given object from the list. The signature of the method could be as follows:

    public boolean remove(Object anObject)

    Write comments that specify this method.

3. Write Java statements at the client level that return the position of a given object in the list `myList`. Assume that the object is in the list.

4. Suppose that you want an operation for the ADT list that returns the position of a given object in the list. The signature of the method could be as follows:

    public int getPosition(Object anObject)

    Write comments that specify this method.

5. Suppose that the ADT list did not have a method `replace`. Write Java statements at the client level that replace an object in the list `nameList`. The object's position in the list is `givenPosition` and the replacement object is `newObject`.

6. Suppose that the ADT list did not have a method `contains`. Suppose further that `nameList` is a list of `Name` objects, where `Name` is as defined in Chapter 1. Write Java statements at the client level that determine whether the `Name` object `myName` is in the list `nameList`.

7. Suppose that you have a list that is created by the following statement:

    ListInterface studentList = **new** AList();

    Imagine that someone has added to the list several instances of the class `Student` that Chapter 2 defined.

    a. Write Java statements that display the last names of the students in the list in the same order in which the students appear in the list. Do not alter the list.
    b. Write Java statements that interchange the first and last students in the list.

8. Consider a class `Coin` that represents a coin. The class has methods such as `getValue`, `toss`, and `isHeads`. The method `getValue` returns the value, or denomination, of a coin. The method `toss` simulates a coin toss in which the coin lands either heads up or tails up. The method `isHeads` returns true if a coin is heads up.

Suppose that `coinList` is an ADT list of coins that have randomly selected denominations. Toss each of these coins. If the result of a coin toss is heads, move the coin to a second list called `headsList`; if it is tails, leave the coin in the original list. When you are finished tossing coins, compute the total value of the coins that came up heads. Assume that the list `headsList` has been created for you and is empty initially.

PROJECTS

1. The introduction to this book spoke of a bag as a way to organize data. A grocery bag, for example, contains items in no particular order. Some of them might be duplicate items. The ADT bag, like the grocery bag, is perhaps the simplest of data organizations. It holds objects but does not arrange or organize them further.

Design an ADT bag. Many operations are analogous to those of the ADT list, but the entries do not have positions. In addition to these basic operations, include the following:

- A union operation that combines the contents of two bags into a third bag
- An intersection operation that creates a bag of those items that occur in both of two bags
- A difference operation that creates a bag of the items that would be left in one bag after removing those that also occur in another bag

Specify each ADT operation by stating its purpose, by describing its parameters, and by writing preconditions, postconditions, and a pseudocode version of its signature. Then write a Java interface for the ADT bag that includes `javadoc`-style comments.

2. You might have a piggy bank or some other receptacle to hold your spare coins. The piggy bank holds the coins but gives them no other organization. And certainly the bank can contain duplicate coins. The piggy bank is like the ADT bag that you designed in Project 1, but it is simpler. It has only three operations: You can add a coin to the bank, remove one (you shake the bank, so you have no control over what coin falls out), or determine whether the bank is empty.

Design the ADT piggy bank, assuming that you have the ADT bag from Project 1 and the class `Coin` from Exercise 8. Write a Java interface for the ADT piggy bank that includes `javadoc`-style comments.

3. Santa Claus allegedly keeps lists of those who are naughty and those who are nice. On the naughty list are the names of those who will get coal in their stockings. On the nice list are those who will receive gifts. Each object in this list contains a name (an instance of `Name`, as defined in Chapter 1) and a list of that person's gifts (an instance of an ADT list).

Design an ADT for the objects in the nice list. What operations should this ADT have? After you design the ADT, implement it by writing a Java class. Assume that you have an implementation of the ADT list—that is, assume that the class `AList` implements `ListInterface`, as given in this chapter. Finally, create some instances of your class and place them on Santa's nice list.

4. A recipe contains a title, a list of ingredients, and a list of directions. An entry in the list of ingredients contains an amount, a unit, and a description. For example, *2 cups of flour* could be an entry in this list.

Implement a class of recipes, assuming that the class `AList` implements `ListInterface`, as given in this chapter. The amount of an ingredient can be a `double` value or an instance of the class `MixedNumber`, which was described in Project 3 of Chapter 3.

5

List Implementations That Use Arrays

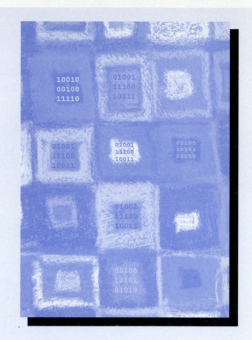

CONTENTS

Using a Fixed-Size Array to Implement the ADT List
    An Analogy
    The Java Implementation
Using Dynamic Array Expansion to Implement the ADT List
    Expanding an Array
    A New Implementation of a List
Using a Vector to Implement the ADT List
    A Summary of Methods in the Class **Vector**
The Pros and Cons of Using an Array to Implement the ADT List
Java Class Library
    The Class **ArrayList**
    The Interface **Serializable**

PREREQUISITES

Chapter   3   Designing Classes
Chapter   4   Lists

OBJECTIVES

After studying this chapter, you should be able to

- Implement the ADT list by using a fixed-size array, an array that you expand dynamically, or an instance of **Vector**
- Discuss the advantages and disadvantages of the three implementations presented

You have seen several examples of how to use the ADT list in a program. This chapter presents three different ways that you can implement a list in Java. Each of these ways involves an array. You will see a completely different implementation in the next chapter.

We begin by using an ordinary Java array to represent the entries in a list. With this implementation, your list could become full, just as a handwritten list can fill a page. We then offer two other implementations that do not suffer from this problem. When you use all of the space in an array, Java enables you to move the data to a larger array. The effect is to have an array that apparently expands to meet your needs. Alternately, you can use an instance of the Java class Vector to represent the list entries. The result is like using an array that can expand, since the underlying implementation of Vector uses such an array. But this list implementation is simpler to write than one that uses an array, because Vector does the work for you.

Using a Fixed–Size Array to Implement the ADT List

We begin by using an analogy to describe how a fixed-size array could represent a list. In doing so, we show how the add and remove methods would work. Subsequently, we present a corresponding Java implementation for the list.

An Analogy

5.1   Imagine a classroom—call it room A—containing 40 desks in a fixed position. If a course is restricted to 30 students, 10 desks are idle and wasted. If we lift the enrollment restriction, we can accommodate only 10 more students, even if 20 more want to take the course.

An array is like this classroom, and each desk is like one array location. Suppose that we number the 40 desks in the room sequentially, beginning with zero, as Figure 5-1 illustrates. Although desks are arranged in rows in typical classrooms, we will ignore this detail and treat the desks as a one-dimensional array.

Figure 5-1   A classroom that contains desks in a fixed position

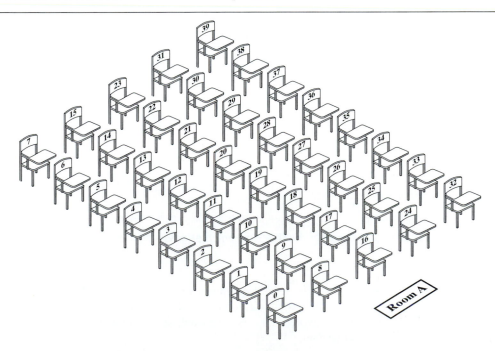

Suppose that the first student who arrives at the classroom sits at desk 0; the second student sits at desk 1, and so on. Eventually, 30 students occupy the desks numbered 0 through 29. They are organized by arrival time. The instructor knows immediately who arrived first (that person is at desk 0) and who arrived last (that person is at desk 29). Additionally, the instructor could ask for the name of the student seated at any particular desk, just as a programmer can access any array element directly. Thus, the instructor could ask for each student's name in order of arrival—by polling desks 0 through 29—or in reverse order—by polling desks 29 through 0. This action is called a **traversal,** or **iteration,** of the data. When you use an array to organize data in this manner, the implementation is said to be **array based.**

Instead of arranging the students in room A by arrival time, suppose that we arrange them alphabetically by name. Doing so requires a **sorting algorithm,** such as the ones that Chapters 11 and 12 will discuss. That is, the ADT list does not choose the order of its entries; the client must do so.

5.2   **Adding a new student.** Imagine that we have already arranged the students in room A alphabetically by name. Suppose that a new student wants to join the students already in the room. Recall that the 30 occupied desks are numbered sequentially from 0 to 29. Since 40 desks are in the room, the desk numbered 30 is available. When the students were arranged by arrival time, we would simply have assigned the new student to desk 30. Since the students are now arranged alphabetically by name, we must do more work.

Suppose that the new student belongs between the two students that occupy desks 10 and 11. That is, the new student's name is alphabetically between the names of the two students that occupy desks 10 and 11. Since the desks are in fixed positions, the new student must occupy desk 11. Before the new student can be seated, the student currently at desk 11 needs to move to desk 12, as Figure 5-2 illustrates. This requirement, however, causes a chain reaction: The student currently at desk 12 needs to move to desk 13, and so on. That is, each student seated in desks 11 through 29 must move to the next higher-numbered desk. If only one student moves at a time, the student in desk 29 must move to desk 30 before the student in desk 28 can move to desk 29, and so on. As you can see, adding a new student requires moving several other students. However, we do not disturb the students seated in the desks that are before the new student's desk—desks 0 through 10 in our example.

Figure 5-2   Seating a new student between two existing students: at least one other student must move

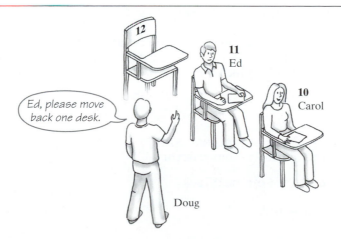

    Question 1   In the previous example, under what circumstance could you add a new student alphabetically by name without moving any other student?

5.3   **Removing a student.** Now imagine that the student in desk 5 of room A drops the course. The desk stays in its fixed location within the room. If we still want students to sit in consecutively numbered desks, several students will need to move. In fact, each student in desks 6 through 30 must move to the next lower-numbered desk, beginning with the student in desk 6. That is, if only one student moves at a time, the student in desk 6 must move to desk 5 before the student in desk 7 moves to desk 6, and so on.

Question 2   What is an advantage of moving students as just described so that the vacated desk does not remain vacant?

Question 3   What is an advantage of leaving the vacated desk vacant?

The Java Implementation

5.4   The Java array-based implementation for the ADT list incorporates some of the ideas that our class-room example illustrates. The implementation is a class AList[1] that implements the interface List-Interface that you saw in Chapter 4. The private data fields are

- An array of objects
- An integer that counts the number of entries in the list
- An integer constant that defines the size of the array

The Java definitions for these items appear as follows:

```
private Object[] entry; // array of list entries
private int length;     // current number of entries in list
private static final int MAX_SIZE = 50; // max length of list
```

Each ADT operation corresponds to a public method within the class.

5.5   The class AList has the following form. Notice the overall organization of the class, the private data, the default constructor, and the simple implementations of the methods clear, getLength, isEmpty, isFull, and display. We will provide implementations for the other methods shortly.

```
public class AList implements ListInterface
{
  private Object[] entry; // array of list entries
  private int length;     // current number of entries in list
  private static final int MAX_SIZE = 50; // max length of list

  public AList()
  {
    length = 0;
    entry = new Object[MAX_SIZE];
  } // end default constructor

  public AList(int maxSize)
  {
    length = 0;
```

---

1. Ordinarily we would name this class ArrayList. But as you will see at the end of this chapter, Java already provides a class with that name. Although we certainly could have named our class ArrayList as well, we chose a different name to avoid confusion.

```java
      entry = new Object[maxSize];
   } // end constructor

   public boolean add(Object newEntry)
   { < Implementation deferred >
   } // end add

   public boolean add(int newPosition, Object newEntry)
   { < Implementation deferred >
   } // end add

   public Object remove(int givenPosition)
   { < Implementation deferred >
   } // end remove

   public void clear()
   {
      length = 0;
      < But see Question 4. >
   } // end clear

   public boolean replace(int givenPosition, Object newEntry)
   { < Implementation deferred >
   } // end replace

   public Object getEntry(int givenPosition)
   { < Implementation deferred >
   } // end getEntry

   public boolean contains(Object anEntry)
   { < Implementation deferred >
   } // end contains

   public int getLength()
   {
      return length;
   } // end getLength

   public boolean isEmpty()
   {
      return length == 0;
   } // end isEmpty

   public boolean isFull()
   {
      return length == entry.length;
   } // end isFull

   public void display()
   {
      for (int index = 0; index < length; index++)
         System.out.println(entry[index]);
   } // end display

   < This class will define two private methods that will be discussed later. >
} // end AList
```

Question 4   The method `clear` sets `length` to zero. Although the list methods will correctly behave as though the list is empty, the objects that were in the list will remain allocated. Suggest at least two ways to deallocate these objects.

5.6   **The first add method.** Now consider the implementations that we deferred. Adding a new entry to the end of the list is easy; we simply add the entry to the array immediately after its last occupied location. Of course, since we are using a fixed-size array, adding a new entry is possible only if the array has available space. If the array is full, our implementation returns false. Thus, the first add method has the following implementation:

```
public boolean add(Object newEntry)
{
  boolean isSuccessful = true;

  if (!isFull())
  {
    // position of new entry will be after last entry in list,
    // that is, at position length+1; corresponding array index is
    // 1 less than position, so index is length
    entry[length] = newEntry;
    length++;
  }
  else
    isSuccessful = false;

  return isSuccessful;
} // end add
```

5.7   **The second add method.** Adding a new entry at an arbitrary position within the list is like adding a student to room A in our example in Segment 5.2. Although that example positions students alphabetically by their names, remember that the list's client—not the list itself—determines the desired position of each entry. Thus, if that position is before the end of the list, we need to shift existing entries to vacate the desired location so that it can accommodate the new entry. If the addition is to the end of the list, no such shift is necessary. In either case, space must be available in the array to accommodate a new entry.

The following implementation of add uses a private method `makeRoom` to handle the details of moving data within the array. Remember that we can add to the list at positions that range from 1 to the length of the list plus 1.

```
public boolean add(int newPosition, Object newEntry)
{
  boolean isSuccessful = true;

  if (!isFull() && (newPosition >= 1)
                && (newPosition <= length+1))
  {
    makeRoom(newPosition);
    entry[newPosition-1] = newEntry;
    length++;
  }
  else
    isSuccessful = false;

  return isSuccessful;
} // end add
```

Now we must implement the private method makeRoom. Typically, the method shifts list entries toward the end of the array, beginning with the last entry, as Figure 5-3 illustrates. (For simplicity, our figures and discussion portray the objects as if they were actually in the array. In reality, the array contains references to the objects.) However, if newPosition is length + 1, the addition is at the end of the array, so no shift is necessary. In this case, makeRoom does nothing, since its for statement exits immediately.

```
/** Task: Makes room for a new entry at newPosition.
 *   Precondition: 1 <= newPosition <= length+1;
 *                 length is list's length before addition. */
private void makeRoom(int newPosition)
{
    // move each entry to next higher position, starting at end of
    // list and continuing until the entry at newPosition is moved
    for (int index = length; index >= newPosition; index--)
      entry[index] = entry[index-1];
}   // end makeRoom
```

Notice that the add method enforces the preconditions of makeRoom.

Figure 5-3   Making room to insert Carla as the third entry in an array

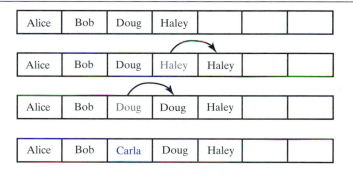

Question 5   You could implement the first add method, which adds an entry to the end of the list, by invoking the second add method, as follows:

```
public boolean add(Object newEntry)
{
    return add(length+1, newEntry);
} // end add
```

Discuss the pros and cons of this revised approach.

Question 6   Suppose that myList is a list that contains the five entries a b c d e.

a.   What does myList contain after executing myList.add(5, w)?
b.   Starting with the original five entries, what does myList contain after executing myList.add(6, w)?
c.   Which of the operations in Parts *a* and *b* of this question require elements in the array to shift?

Question 7   If `myList` is a list of five entries, each of the following statements adds a new entry to the end of the list:

```
myList.add(newEntry);
myList.add(6, newEntry);
```

Which way requires fewer operations?

5.8   **The remove method.** Removing a list entry at an arbitrary position is like a student leaving room A in our example in Segment 5.3. We need to shift existing entries to avoid a gap in the array, except when removing the list's last entry. The following implementation uses a private method `removeGap` to handle the details of moving data within the array:

```java
public Object remove(int givenPosition)
{
  Object result = null;   // return value

  if ((givenPosition >= 1) && (givenPosition <= length))
  {
    result = entry[givenPosition-1]; // get entry to be removed

    // move subsequent entries toward entry to be removed,
    // unless it is last in list
    if (givenPosition < length)
      removeGap(givenPosition);

    length--;
  } // end if

  return result;   // return reference to removed entry,
                   // or null if givenPosition is invalid
} // end remove
```

Question 8   When a list is empty, the data field `length` contains zero. What does the remove method return in this case? Why?

The following private method `removeGap` shifts list entries toward the entry that is removed, as Figure 5-4 illustrates. Beginning with the entry after the one to be removed and continuing until the end of array, `removeGap` moves each entry to its next lower position.

```java
/** Task: Shifts entries that are beyond the entry to be removed
 *        to next lower position.
 *  Precondition: 1 <= givenPosition <= length;
 *                length is list's length before removal. */
private void removeGap(int givenPosition)
{
  for (int index = givenPosition; index < length; index++)
    entry[index-1] = entry[index];
} // end removeGap
```

Note that no shift is necessary if the deletion is at the end of the array. In that case, the last entry in the list is at position `length`, since the first entry is at position 1. Thus, `givenPosition` would equal `length`, and so the `for` statement in `removeGap` would exit immediately. Also notice that the remove method enforces the preconditions of `removeGap`. In particular, `removeGap` is not invoked when the list is empty.

Figure 5-4   Removing Bob by shifting array entries

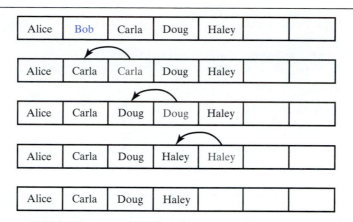

5.9   **The methods `replace` and `getEntry`.** Replacing a list entry and retrieving a list entry are two straightforward operations when an array is used to represent the entries. You simply replace or retrieve the object that is in the indicated array location.

The following methods implement these two operations:

```
public boolean replace(int givenPosition, Object newEntry)
{
  boolean isSuccessful = true;

  if ((givenPosition >= 1) && (givenPosition <= length))
    entry[givenPosition-1] = newEntry;
  else
    isSuccessful = false;

  return isSuccessful;
} // end replace

public Object getEntry(int givenPosition)
{
  Object result = null;  // result to return

  if ((givenPosition >= 1) && (givenPosition <= length))
    result = entry[givenPosition-1];

  return result;
} // end getEntry
```

 Question 9   What is an advantage of using an array to organize data? What is a disadvantage?

5.10   **The method `contains`.** The method `getEntry` locates the entry at a given position by going directly to the appropriate array element. In contrast, the method `contains` must search the array for a given entry. Beginning at index zero, the method examines each array element until it either locates the desired entry or reaches the end of the array without success. In the following implementation, we use a local boolean variable to terminate the loop when we find the desired entry:

```java
public boolean contains(Object anEntry)
{
  boolean found = false;
  for (int index = 0; !found && (index < length); index++)
  {
    if (anEntry.equals(entry[index]))
      found = true;
  } // end for

  return found;
} // end contains
```

This way of looking for a particular entry in an array is called a **sequential search.** Chapter 16 discusses this technique further and presents another algorithm that is generally faster.

Note: Using a fixed-size array to implement the ADT list limits the size of the list. Some lists naturally have a finite size, so this implementation is both appropriate and useful. For other lists, one of the other implementations given in this chapter and the next one would be more fitting.

Using Dynamic Array Expansion to Implement the ADT List

5.11   An array, of course, has a fixed size. You decide on a maximum size for your array when you write your program. Segment 5.4 of the previous section used an array of MAX_SIZE memory locations to represent the entries in the list. When the array, and hence the list, becomes full, the method isFull returns true and the add methods return false.

The fixed-size array in the previous implementation of the ADT list is like our classroom. If the room contains 40 desks but only 30 students, we waste 10 desks. If 40 students register for the course, the room is full and cannot accommodate anyone else. Likewise, if we do not use all locations in an array, we waste memory. If we need more, we are out of luck. For example, the implementation in the previous section denies a request to add to a list that already contains MAX_SIZE entries.

Some applications can use a list that has a limited length. For example, a list of airline passengers and a list of ticket holders to a movie should not exceed a known maximum. For other applications, however, the length of a list can grow without bound. We will now show you how a list can be as long as you want but still use an array to represent its entries.

Expanding an Array

5.12   One way to accommodate additional students is to use a larger room. Suppose that you are seated at your desk waiting for class to start. The professor arrives and announces that the class must move to a larger room. Suppose that the students leave one room and move to another without changing desk numbers. That is, a student at desk *n* in the old room will occupy desk *n* in the new room.

In a similar manner, when an array becomes full, you can move its contents to a larger array. This process is called the **dynamic expansion** of an array. Figure 5-5 shows two arrays: an original array of five consecutive memory locations and another array—twice the size of the original array—that is in another part of the computer's memory. If you copy the data from the original smaller array to the first five locations in the new larger array, the result will be like expanding the original array. The only glitch in this scheme is the name of the new array: You want it to be the same as the name of the old array. This is possible, as you will see momentarily.

Figure 5-5   The dynamic expansion of an array copies the array's contents to a larger second array

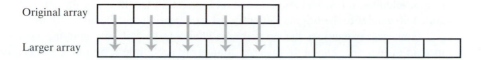

5.13   Let's work with a simple array of integers:

```
int[] myArray = new int[INITIAL_SIZE];
```

where `INITIAL_SIZE` is an integer constant like `MAX_SIZE`. At this point, `myArray` references the array in Figure 5-6a. Next, we'll save the reference to this array by writing

```
int[] oldArray = myArray; // save reference to myArray
```

Both `oldArray` and `myArray` contain the same value, namely the address of the array. That is, `old-Array` and `myArray` each reference the array, as Figure 5-6b illustrates. For example, `oldArray[0]` and `myArray[0]` reference the same location: the first location of the array.

Now we'll allocate a new, larger array, but we'll let only `myArray` reference it:

```
myArray = new int[2*oldArray.length];   // double size of array
```

Figure 5-6c illustrates the two arrays.

Figure 5-6   (a) An array; (b) the same array with two references; (c) the two arrays, with the reference to the original array now referencing a new, larger array

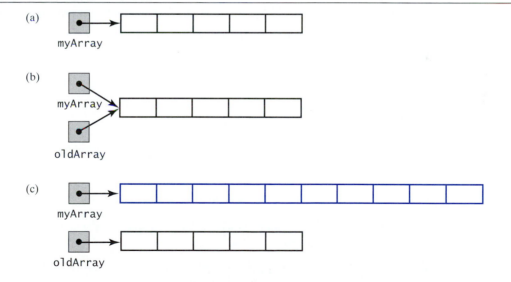

Finally, we'll copy the data from the original array (`oldArray`) to the new array (`myArray`):

```
for (int index = 0; index < oldArray.length; index++)
    myArray[index] = oldArray[index];
```

5.14   Expanding the size of an array is not as attractive as it might first seem. Each time you expand an array, you must copy its contents. If you were to expand an array by one element each time you needed additional space in the array, the process would be expensive. For example, if a 50-element array represented a list of 50 entries, adding an entry to the list would require that you copy the array to a 51-element array. Adding another entry would require that you copy the 51-element array to a 52-element array, and so on. Each add operation would cause the array to be copied. If you added 50 entries to the original 50-entry list, you would copy the array 50 times.

However, expanding the array by *m* elements spreads the copying cost over *m* additions instead of just one. Doubling the size of an array each time it becomes full is a typical approach. For example, when you add an entry to a full list of 50 entries, you copy the 50-element array to a 100-element array before completing the addition. The next 49 additions then can be made quickly without copying the array. Thus, you will have added 50 entries to the original list but will have copied the array only once.

Note: During dynamic array expansion, the elements of an array are copied to a larger array. You should expand the array sufficiently to reduce the impact of the cost of copying.

A New Implementation of a List

5.15   You can use these ideas to revise the implementation of the ADT list that the previous section presented. Only `isFull` and the two add methods are affected in the revised implementation. To begin, change the method `isFull` to always return false. Since we will expand the array when it becomes full, the list is never full.

Instead of ignoring an addition when the array is full, each of the revised add methods doubles the array by calling a new private method `doubleArray`. To detect when the array is full, we define another private method `isArrayFull`, whose implementation is the same as the method `isFull` in the class `AList`. (See Segment 5.5.) For example, the first add method would appear as follows:

```
public boolean add(Object newEntry)
{
  if (isArrayFull())
    doubleArray();

  // add new entry after last current entry
  entry[length] = newEntry;
  length++;

  return true;
} // end add
```

You would make similar changes to the second add method.

Question 10   Revise the second add method that adds an entry at a given position within the list by using dynamic array expansion.

5.16   The private method `doubleArray` incorporates our recent discussion of expanding an array, and appears as follows:

```
/** Task: Doubles the size of the array of list entries. */
private void doubleArray()
{
  Object[] oldList = entry;       // save reference to array of
                                  // list entries
  int oldSize = oldList.length;   // save old max size of array

  entry = new Object[2*oldSize];  // double size of array
```

```
    // copy entries from old array to new, bigger array
    for (int index = 0; index < oldSize; index++)
       entry[index] = oldList[index];
} // end doubleArray
```

This completes the revised implementation. We will call the new class `DynamicArrayList`.

5.17   If the method `isFull` always returns false, why bother implementing it? The short answer is that `isFull` is in `ListInterface`, so any class that implements `ListInterface` must define it. If `DynamicArrayList` did not implement `isFull`, we would have to declare the class as abstract. Thus, we would not be able to create an instance of `DynamicArrayList`. Should we omit `isFull` from `ListInterface`? If we do, our array-based implementation `AList` can still define `isFull`. That is, a class that implements an interface can contain methods that are not specified in the interface. However, let's see what happens if we do omit `isFull` from `ListInterface`.

Suppose that `AList` implements `isFull`, but `DynamicArrayList` does not. If the client uses `isFull`, changing from one implementation of the ADT list (`AList`) to another (`DynamicArrayList`) would not be as simple as it should be. We would need to modify the client so that it did not use `isFull`. In addition, any instance of `ListInterface`, such as `myList` in the statement

```
ListInterface myList = new AList();
```

would be unable to invoke `isFull`, even though `AList` implements it.

Programming Tip: A class implementing a single interface that declares the operations of an ADT should define the methods declared in the interface as its only public methods. The class can also define private methods and protected methods.

Using a Vector to Implement the ADT List

5.18   One way to let a list grow as needed is to use dynamic array expansion, as the previous section describes. Another way uses an instance of Java's `Vector` class to represent the list's entries. The class `Vector` provides the capabilities of an array that expands dynamically, but it hides the details of the process.

`Vector`, which is in the package `java.util`, has methods that manipulate its entries in ways that are useful to an implementation of the ADT list. If we store our list entries in an instance of `Vector`, we can use `Vector`'s methods to manipulate our list entries. Figure 5-7 shows a client interacting with a list by using the methods in `ListInterface`. The implementations of these methods in turn interact with `Vector`'s methods to produce the desired effects on the list.

Figure 5-7   A client uses the methods given in `ListInterface`, but the implementation of the list uses `Vector` methods to perform its operations

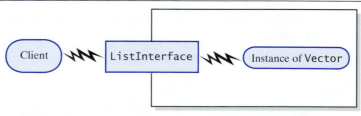

Implementation of a list

5.19 We begin the class that implements `ListInterface` as follows:

```
import java.util.Vector;
public class VectorList implements ListInterface
{
   private Vector entry; // entries in list
   . . .
```

We must provide the `import` statement to indicate that the code that follows uses the class `Vector` from the package `java.util`. Often programmers will replace `Vector` in this statement with an asterisk to make all classes in the package `java.util` available to their programs.

The data field `entry` is now an instance of `Vector` instead of an array, as it was earlier in this chapter. Since a vector keeps track of the number of entries it contains, a data field `length` is not required. Any time that we want the number of entries in the vector, and hence the list, we can write `entry.size()`.

The constructors for our class create an instance of `Vector` by invoking `Vector`'s constructors. Our default constructor simply invokes `Vector`'s default constructor:

```
public VectorList()
{
   entry = new Vector();
} // end default constructor
```

Here, `Vector`'s default constructor creates a vector that can hold 10 entries. This vector will double in size after it becomes full.

Our second constructor enables the client to specify the initial capacity of the list. It invokes a corresponding constructor of `Vector`:

```
public VectorList(int initialSize)
{
   entry = new Vector(initialSize);
} // end constructor
```

Here `Vector`'s constructor creates a vector that can hold `initialSize` entries. This vector also will double in size after it becomes full.

5.20 To add to the end of a list, you use `Vector`'s `addElement` method. This method adds a given object to the end of a vector. If necessary, the vector increases its capacity to accommodate the new entry. Thus, our add method does not test whether the vector is full:

```
public boolean add(Object newEntry)
{
   entry.addElement(newEntry);
   return true;
} // end add
```

To add an entry at a given position in the list, we use `Vector`'s `insertElementAt` method. This method acts much the same as the add method for the ADT list. However, `Vector` numbers its entries from 0 instead of from 1:

```
public boolean add(int newPosition, Object newEntry)
{
   boolean isSuccessful = true;

   if ((newPosition >= 1) && (newPosition <= entry.size()+1))
      entry.insertElementAt(newEntry, newPosition-1);
```

```
   else
      isSuccessful = false;

   return isSuccessful;
} // end add
```

5.21   Similarly, remove uses Vector's method removeElementAt. Since removeElementAt is a void method and remove is not, remove must retrieve the entry to be deleted before it is actually removed from the list. We use the method elementAt to retrieve an entry from a vector at a given index. Thus, the following statements are the heart of remove's implementation:

```
result = entry.elementAt(givenPosition-1);
entry.removeElementAt(givenPosition-1);
```

The remove method then has the following implementation:

```
public Object remove(int givenPosition)
{
   Object result = null;   // return value

   if ((givenPosition >= 1) && (givenPosition <= entry.size()))
   {
      result = entry.elementAt(givenPosition-1);
      entry.removeElementAt(givenPosition-1);
   } // end if

   return result;
} // end remove
```

5.22   The method clear uses the statement
```
entry.removeAllElements();
```
to remove all entries from the vector and hence from the list.
    The method replace uses the statement
```
entry.setElementAt(newEntry, givenPosition-1);
```
to replace a designated entry in the list.
    The method getEntry uses the statement
```
result = entry.elementAt(givenPosition-1);
```
to retrieve a particular entry from the list.
    The implementations of the methods contains, getLength, isEmpty, and display are simple and left as exercises. As in the previous section, the method isFull always returns false.

5.23   Java's class Vector and our class VectorList are similar in their functionality. VectorList simply invokes methods of the class Vector in its implementation of ListInterface. VectorList is an example of an adapter class, which we described in Segment 2.3 of Chapter 2.
    Writing VectorList is certainly easier than writing either of the other two array-based implementations that this chapter describes. However, since VectorList uses an instance of Vector instead of an array, its methods typically are less efficient than those of the other implementations.

 Note: Implementations of the ADT list that use either dynamic array expansion or an instance of Vector let the list grow as needed.

A Summary of Methods in the Class `Vector`

5.24   We conclude this section with a description of the methods—including constructors—that we used from the class `Vector`. Descriptions of other methods in this class are available at

> http://java.sun.com/products/jdk/1.4/docs/api/index.html

public `Vector()`

Creates an empty vector with an initial capacity of 10. When the vector needs to increase its capacity, the capacity doubles.

public `Vector(int initialCapacity)`

Creates an empty vector with the specified initial capacity. When the vector needs to increase its capacity, the capacity doubles.

public void `addElement(Object newElement)`

Adds `newElement` to the end of the vector and increases its size by 1. The capacity of the vector is increased if that is required.

public void `insertElementAt(Object newElement, int index)`

Inserts `newElement` into the vector at the specified index. Each element in the vector with an index greater than or equal to `index` is shifted upward to have an index that is 1 greater than the value it had previously. The value of `index` must be greater than or equal to zero and less than or equal to the current size of the vector. The method throws `ArrayIndexOutOfBoundsException` if `index` is not in this range. The capacity of the vector is increased if that is required. Note that you can use this method to add an element after the last current element.

public void `removeElementAt(int index)`

Deletes the element at the specified index. Each element in the vector with an index greater than or equal to `index` is shifted downward to have an index that is 1 less than the value it had previously. The value of `index` must be greater than or equal to `zero` and less than the current size of the vector. The method throws `ArrayIndexOutOfBoundsException` if `index` is not in this range.

public void `removeAllElements()`

Removes all elements from the vector and sets its size to zero.

public void `setElementAt(Object newElement, int index)`

Replaces the element at the specified index to `newElement`. The element previously at that position is discarded. The value of `index` must be greater than or equal to `zero` and less than the current size of the vector. The method throws `ArrayIndexOutOfBoundsException` if `index` is not in this range.

public `Object elementAt(int index)`

Returns the element at the specified index. The value of `index` must be greater than or equal to `zero` and less than the current size of the vector. Throws `ArrayIndexOutOfBoundsException` if `index` is not in this range.

public boolean `contains(Object anEntry)`

Returns true if `anEntry` is an element of the vector; otherwise, returns false.

public boolean `isEmpty()`

Returns true if the vector is empty (that is, has a size of `zero`); otherwise, returns false.

public int `size()`

Returns the number of elements in the vector.

The Pros and Cons of Using an Array to Implement the ADT List

5.25   This chapter discussed three implementations of the ADT list. Since Java's class `Vector` uses an array in its implementation, all of this chapter's implementations are based on an array.

An array is simple to use and enables you to access any element immediately, if you know its index. Thus, the list's retrieval operation `getEntry` is easy to write and quick to execute. Adding to the end of a list, and hence to the array, is equally easy and fast.

On the other hand, using a fixed-size array limits the size of a list, which is usually a disadvantage. Using either dynamic array expansion or a vector enables you to increase the array's size but requires copying data.

Regardless of whether the array has a size that is fixed or dynamic, adding or removing entries that are between other entries requires shifting elements in the array. This data movement degrades the time efficiency of these operations, particularly when the list is long and the position of the addition or removal is near the beginning of the list. The implementation in the next chapter avoids this particular disadvantage but has disadvantages of its own.

You should realize that the elements that we shift in the array are references, and so do not occupy much space nor take much time to move. Some languages other than Java store the data itself within the array. In that case, moving large, complex objects can be quite time-consuming.

 Note: When you use an array or vector to implement the ADT list,

- Retrieving an entry is fast
- Adding an entry at the end of a list is fast
- Adding or removing an entry that is between other entries requires shifting elements in the array
- Increasing the size of the array or vector requires copying elements

---

Java Class Library

The Java Class Library has a class that is similar the class `AList` that we defined in this chapter. It also has a special interface that enables you to write objects to a file with little effort. We introduce both of these components in this section.

The Class `ArrayList`

5.26   Chapter 4 described the interface `List` that is in the standard Java package `java.util`. Recall that the methods in this interface are similar to the methods in our `ListInterface`. Other than some name changes, the major difference is in the numbering of the entries in a list. The first entry in our lists is at position 1, whereas the first entry in a list that adheres to the interface `java.util.List` is at index 0.

The same package `java.util` that contains the interface `List` also contains a class `ArrayList` that implements `List`. This class uses dynamic array expansion, as we described earlier in this chapter. `ArrayList` is actually quite similar to the class `Vector`. Both classes are in the same package, and both implement the interface `List`. However, `Vector` contains all the methods of `ArrayList` as well as some others. You can learn more about these classes at

```
http://java.sun.com/products/jdk/1.4/docs/api/index.html
```

The Interface Serializable

5.27   You can represent an object as a sequence of bytes that you write to a file by using a process called **object serialization.** This process is possible for any instances of a class that implements the interface Serializable. This interface, which is in the package java.io, is empty, so you have no additional methods to implement. Adding only the words implements Serializable to the class's definition is enough.

For example, we could begin the class AList as follows:

```
public class AList implements ListInterface, Serializable
{
    . . .
```

The Serializable interface tells the compiler that instances of AList can be **serialized,** that is, can be written to a file using object serialization.

If the list myList is an instance of AList, any objects that are in myList must also belong to a class that implements Serializable. Such objects are serialized when myList is serialized. To serialize an object such as myList, you use the method writeObject from the class ObjectOutputStream. To reconstruct an object, you use the method readObject from the class ObjectInputStream. Appendix C provides an example of serialization and more information about writing and reading files.

Programming Tip: A class that represents a collection of objects should implement the interface Serializable. By simply adding the word "Serializable" to the list of interfaces that a class implements, you can provide clients of that class with an easy way to place instances of the class in a file.

CHAPTER SUMMARY

- The three implementations of the ADT list in this chapter use an array to store the items in a list.

- Using an array results in relatively simple implementations of the list.

- An array provides direct access to any of its elements, so a method such as **getEntry** has a simple, efficient implementation.

- Using a fixed-size array can result in a full list. Using either dynamic array expansion or an instance of **Vector** avoids this drawback.

- Adding an entry to or removing an entry from an array-based list typically requires that other entries shift by one position within the array.

- Expanding the size of an array requires copying the contents of the array to a larger array.

- Using an instance of **Vector** has the same advantages and disadvantages as using dynamic array expansion but results in an implementation that is much easier to write.

- Object serialization enables you to write objects to a file. Such objects must belong to a class that implements the interface Serializable.

PROGRAMMING TIPS

- A class implementing a single interface that declares the operations of an ADT should define the methods declared in the interface as its only public methods. The class can also define private methods and protected methods.

● A class that represents a collection of objects should implement the interface **Serializable**. By simply adding the word "**Serializable**" to the list of interfaces that a class implements, you can provide clients of that class with an easy way to place instances of the class in a file.

EXERCISES

1. Add a constructor to each of the classes `AList`, `DynamicArrayList`, and `VectorList` that creates a list from a given array of objects.

2. Suppose that you want an operation for the ADT list that removes the first occurrence of a given object from the list. The signature of the method could be as follows:

    public boolean remove(Object anObject)

    The method returns true if the list contained anObject and that object was removed. Write an implementation of this method for each of the three classes described in this chapter.

3. Suppose that you want an operation for the ADT list that returns the position of a given object in the list. The signature of the method could be as follows:

    public int getPosition(Object anObject)

    Write an implemention of this method for each of the three classes described in this chapter.

4. Exercise 5 in the previous chapter asked you to write statements at the client level that replace an object in a given list. Write a method at the client level that performs such a replacement. How does your method compare with the method `replace` of the ADT list?

5. Implement a method `replace` for the ADT list that returns the replaced object. Do this for each of the three classes described in this chapter.

6. Suppose that a list contains `Comparable` objects. Implement the following methods for each of the three classes described in this chapter.

    a. The method `getMin` that returns the smallest object in the list.
    b. The method `removeMin` that removes and returns the smallest object in the list.

7. Implement an `equals` method for the ADT list that returns true when the entries in one list equal the entries in a second list. In particular, add this method to the classes `AList` and `VectorList`.

8. Implement the methods `contains`, `getLength`, and `isEmpty` in the class `VectorList`.

9. Implement the method `display` in the class `VectorList` in two ways. One way uses the vector method `elementAt`. Another way uses the list method `getEntry`.

PROJECTS

1. Complete the implementation of the class `DynamicArrayList`.

2. Complete the implementation of the class `VectorList`.

3. Write a class that implements the interface `ListInterface` by using an instance of the class `ArrayList`. Compare your new class with the class `VectorList`.

4. Implement the interface `ListInterface` by using an array in which you ignore the first array location. Thus, you store the list's i^{th} entry in the array location at index `i`.

5. Implement as the class `Bag` the ADT bag that Project 1 of Chapter 4 described. Represent the bag as an array that you expand dynamically as necessary. Using `Bag`, implement a class `PiggyBank` as described in Project 2 of Chapter 4.

6. Repeat Project 5, but instead use an instance of `Vector` to represent the bag.

7. A set is a special bag that does not allow duplicates. Project 1 of Chapter 4 describes the ADT bag. Specify the operations for the ADT set. Implement the set by using

    a. An array that you expand dynamically as necessary
    b. An instance of `Vector`
    c. An instance of `Bag`

6

List Implementations
That Link Data

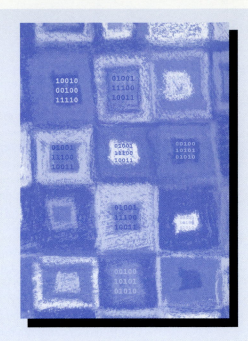

CONTENTS

Linked Data
    Forming a Chain
    Forming Another Chain
    Forming Yet Another Chain
The Class **Node**
A Linked Implementation of the ADT List
    Adding to the End of the List
    Adding at a Given Position Within the List
    The Private Method **getNodeAt**
    The Method **remove**
    The Method **replace**
    The Method **getEntry**
    The Method **contains**
    The Remaining Methods
    Using a Class **Node** That Has Set and Get Methods
Tail References
    A Revised Implementation of the List
The Pros and Cons of Using a Chain to Implement the ADT List
Java Class Library: The Class **LinkedList**

PREREQUISITES

Chapter   4   Lists
Chapter   5   List Implementations That Use Arrays

OBJECTIVES

After studying this chapter, you should be able to

- Implement the ADT list by using a linked organization of data
- Discuss the advantages and disadvantages of a linked implementation of the list

Using an array to implement the ADT list has both advantages and disadvantages, as you saw in Chapter 5. An array can either have a fixed size or be moved to a larger array. A fixed-size array can lead to a full list. Although dynamic array expansion can provide as much space as the list needs, you must move data each time you expand the array. In addition, any array requires you to move data either to make room for a new entry or to close up a gap after a deletion.

This chapter uses a data organization that avoids moving data. As a result, adding or removing list entries require less effort than these operations would with an array. As you will see, however, this new implementation has its own drawbacks.

Linked Data

6.1   In Chapter 5, we used the analogy of a classroom to describe how data is stored in an array. Here we use a classroom to show you another way to organize data.

Imagine an empty classroom—room L—that is assigned to a course. All available desks are in the hallway. Any student that registers for the course receives a desk, takes it into the room, and sits at it. Assume that the room can accommodate all of the desks in the hall.

Each desk in the hallway has a number stamped on its back. This number—called an **address**—never changes and is not considered when desks are given to students. Thus, the room will eventually contain desks whose addresses are not sequential in general.

Now imagine that Jill is among 30 students who are seated in room L at exactly 30 desks. Taped to each desktop is a blank piece of paper. As Jill entered the room, the instructor wrote on her paper the desk number (address) of another desk in the room. For example, the paper on Jill's desk might contain the number 20. If her desk is desk 15, we say that desk 15 **references** desk 20 and that desks 15 and 20 are **linked.** Since the desks are linked to one another, we say that they form a **chain** of desks.

Figure 6-1 shows a chain of five desks. No desk references the first desk in the chain, but the instructor remembers its desk number, 22. Notice that the last desk in the chain does not reference another desk; the piece of paper on this desk is blank.

Figure 6-1   A chain of five desks

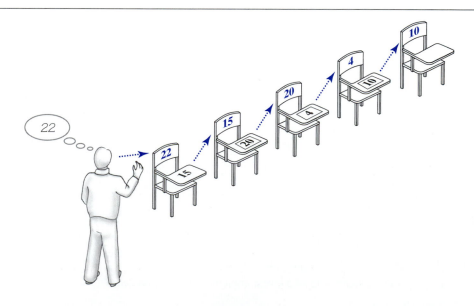

6.2   The chain of desks provides an order for the desks. Suppose that first in the chain is the student who arrived most recently. Written on this student's desk is the desk number of the student who arrived just before. With one exception, everyone's desk references the desk of the student who arrived just before. The exception is the person who arrived first. That person sits at the last desk, which does not reference another desk.

    The instructor knows the address of the first desk in the chain and so can ask questions of the student at that first desk. Then by looking at the address, or desk number, that is written on the paper on first desk, the instructor can locate the second desk in the chain and can question its occupant. Continuing in this way, the instructor can visit every desk in the order in which they appear in the chain. Ultimately, the instructor reaches the desk that references no other desk. The only way the instructor can locate the student in this last desk is to begin at the first desk. The instructor can traverse this chain in only one order. In Chapter 5, however, the instructor in room A was able to ask questions of any student in any order.

Forming a Chain

6.3   How did the instructor form the chain of desks in the first place? Let's return to the time when room L was empty and all available desks were in the hallway.

    Suppose that you arrive first. You get a desk from the hallway and enter the room. The instructor notes your desk's number (address) and leaves the paper on your desk blank to indicate that no other student has arrived. The room appears as in Figure 6-2.

Figure 6-2   One desk in the room

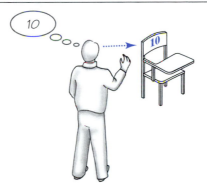

6.4   When the second student arrives, the instructor writes your desk's number on the new desk's paper and then remembers the number of the new (second) desk. Let's assume that the instructor can remember only one desk number at a time. The room appears as in Figure 6-3.

6.5   When the third student arrives, the instructor writes the memorized desk number, which is that of the second desk, on the new desk's paper and then remembers the number of the new (third) desk. The room appears as in Figure 6-4.

6.6   After all the students have arrived, the instructor knows only the desk number of the student who arrived most recently. On that student's desk is the desk number of the student who arrived just previously. In general, written on each student's desk is the number of the desk that belongs to the previous student that arrived. Since you were the first student to arrive, the paper on your desk is still blank. In Figures 6-1 through 6-4, you are the person at desk 10.

Figure 6-3   Two linked desks, with the newest desk first

Figure 6-4   Three linked desks, with the newest desk first

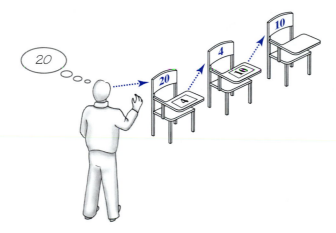

Question 1   The instructor knows the address of only one desk.

    a.   Where in the chain is that desk: first, last, or somewhere else?
    b.   Who is sitting at that desk: the student who arrived first, the student who arrived last, or someone else?

Question 2   Where in the chain of desks is a new desk added: at the beginning, at the end, or somewhere else?

6.7   The following pseudocode details the steps that the instructor took to form a chain of students in the order of their arrival:

    newDesk *represents the new student's desk*
    New student sits at newDesk
    Instructor memorizes address of newDesk

```
while (students arrive)
{
    newDesk represents the new student's desk
    New student sits at newDesk
    Instructor writes memorized address on newDesk
    Instructor memorizes address of newDesk
}
```

Notice that the chain of desks organizes the students in reverse order of their arrival times. The instructor places each new desk at the beginning of the chain. When done, the instructor knows the address of the first desk in the chain; seated at this desk is the last student to arrive.

Forming Another Chain

6.8   Suppose that the instructor wants to organize the chain in a different way, so that the first student to arrive will be first in the chain and the last student to arrive will be last. Once again, suppose that you are the first student to arrive. You are accommodated as you were in the previous example. That is, the instructor notes your desk's number (address) and leaves the paper on your desk blank. So far, the situation is the same as the one shown in Figure 6-2.

When the second student arrives, the instructor writes the number of the second desk on the paper that is on your desk and leaves the new desk's paper blank. (Recall that in the previous chain your paper remained blank the entire time.) Note that the instructor remembers only the address of your desk, since you were the first student to arrive. Figure 6-5 shows the chain at this point.

Figure 6-5   Two linked desks, with the newest desk last

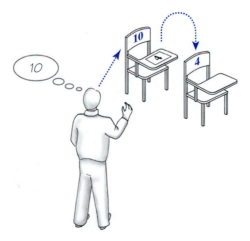

When the third student arrives, the instructor needs to write the number of the third desk on the paper that is on the second desk. The instructor no longer knows the address of the second desk but can determine it by looking at the paper on your desk. Again, the instructor leaves the new desk's paper blank, as you can see in Figure 6-6.

Figure 6-6   Three linked desks, with the newest desk last

6.9   For each new student, the instructor must write the number of the new desk on the paper that is on the last desk in the chain. To locate the last desk, the instructor begins with the first desk, determines the address of the second desk, then determines the address of the third desk, and so on until the address of the last desk is known. That is, the instructor has to traverse the chain of desks each time to be able to link a new desk to the end of the chain of desks. After all of the students have arrived, the instructor still remembers your desk number, since you were the first student to arrive. Figure 6-7 shows the room after five students have arrived.

Figure 6-7   Five linked desks, with the newest desk last

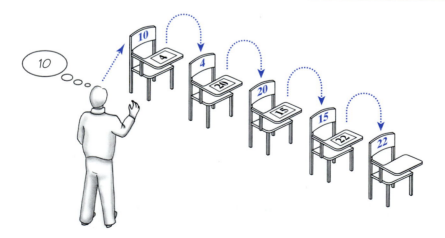

Written on the paper that is on your desk is the desk number for the second student to arrive. That is, your desk—which is first in the chain—references the desk of the second student to arrive. The second desk references the desk of the third student to arrive. Except for the last desk, each desk references the desk that belongs to the student who arrived next. The paper on the last student's desk is blank.

Question 3 The instructor remembers the address of only one desk.

a. Where in the chain is that desk: first, last, or somewhere else?
b. Who is sitting at that desk: the student who arrived first, the student who arrived last, or someone else?

Question 4 Where in the chain of desks is a new desk added: at the beginning, at the end, or somewhere else?

6.10   The following pseudocode details the steps that the instructor took to add a desk to the end of the chain:

> newDesk *represents the new student's desk*
> *New student sits at* newDesk
> *Instructor memorizes address of* newDesk
> **while** (*students arrive*)
> {
>   newDesk *represents the new student's desk*
>   *New student sits at* newDesk
>   *Instructor traverses the chain to locate its last desk*
>   *Instructor writes address of* newDesk *on this last desk*
> }

You can see that the instructor performed more work this time: Each new desk is added to the end of the chain, which requires the instructor to traverse the entire chain to locate the last desk. It is much easier to add a desk to the beginning of the chain than to its end. Notice that the chain of desks organizes the students in order of their arrival times. When done, the instructor knows the address of the first desk on the chain; seated at this desk is the first student to arrive.

Question 5 What is an advantage of using a linked organization of data? What is a disadvantage?

Forming Yet Another Chain

6.11   Organizing students chronologically by their arrival times required the instructor to add each new student to the beginning or end of the chain of desks. No student or desk currently in the room had to move.

Suppose that the instructor instead wants to organize the students alphabetically by their names. We can examine the details of the necessary algorithm by considering room L after a few students enter the room and the instructor has organized them alphabetically. Assume that the students' desks are linked, that the instructor knows the address of the first desk in the chain, and that this desk is occupied by the student whose name is alphabetically earliest.

6.12   **Adding to a particular place in a chain.** Imagine that a new student wants to join the students in room L. The student gets any available desk from the hallway. The instructor needs to link this new desk to the desks currently in the room so that the new student is in the correct position within the current arrangement of students. This link can be made without moving any current student in the room. To simplify our discussion, when we mention an address *on* a desk, we mean the address that is written on the paper that is on the desk. In contrast, a desk's address is the fixed address that is stamped on the back of each desk.

The details of how to insert a new desk into the chain depend on where in the chain the desk belongs. Consider the following cases:

- Case 1: The new desk belongs before all current desks.
- Case 2: The new desk belongs between two current desks.
- Case 3: The new desk belongs after all current desks.

As you will see, the last case is really not a special case.

6.13   **Case 1.** Figure 6-8 depicts Case 1 before we add the new desk to the beginning of the chain. In this figure,

- `newDesk` represents the new student's desk
- `firstDesk` represents the first desk in the chain

Figure 6-8   A chain of desks just prior to adding a new desk to the beginning of the chain

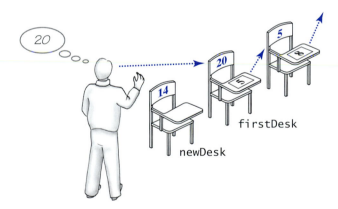

Recall that the instructor, or **head** of the chain, knows the address of the first desk. Two steps are necessary in this case:

1. Place the address of `firstDesk` on `newDesk`. (`newDesk` now references `firstDesk`.)
2. Give the address of `newDesk` to the instructor (head).

Figure 6-9 illustrates the result of these steps. Notice that this case is like the situation described in Segment 6.4.

Figure 6-9   The addition of a new desk to the beginning of a chain of desks

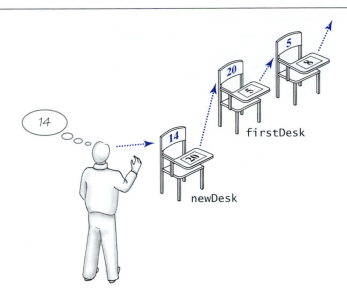

6.14   **Case 2.** Figure 6-10 shows Case 2 before we add the new desk between two desks currently in the chain, where

- newDesk represents the new student's desk
- deskBefore represents the desk that will be before newDesk in the final arrangement
- deskAfter represents the desk currently after deskBefore; its address is on deskBefore

Figure 6-10   Two consecutive desks within a chain of desks just prior to adding a new desk between them

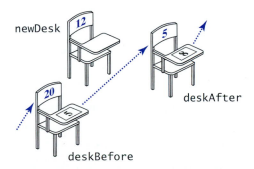

The following steps are necessary to place the new desk between the two consecutive desks desk-Before and deskAfter:

1. Copy the address on deskBefore (that is, deskAfter's address) and place it on newDesk.
2. Place the address of newDesk on deskBefore.

Figure 6-11 illustrates the result of these steps.

Figure 6-11   The addition of a new desk between two other desks

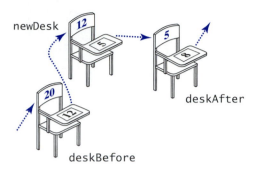

6.15   **Case 3.** When the new desk belongs after all current desks, the situation is like Case 2, except that `deskAfter` does not exist. Remember that the paper on the desk of the last student is blank. That desk is `deskBefore` and does not reference any other.

In this situation, Step 1 of Case 2 copies blank from `deskBefore` to `newDesk`. This step, together with the other step of Case 2, is exactly what needs to happen so that `newDesk` is last in the arrangement of desks. Thus, we can handle Case 3 in the same way that we handle Case 2.

Question 6   If a chain of desks organizes students alphabetically by name, how can you find the student whose name is alphabetically first? Alphabetically last?

6.16   **Removing an item from a chain.** Students who leave room L return their desks to the hall. Such desks can be reassigned to other students who enter either room L or other rooms that share this hallway. Suppose that you leave room L because you want to drop the course. If you simply move your desk to the hallway, you will not actually remove yourself from the chain of desks in the room: Either another desk or the instructor will still reference your desk. You need to disconnect your desk from the chain, but the details of how you do this depend on where it is in the chain. Here are the possible cases:

- Case 1: The desk to be removed is first in the chain of desks.
- Case 2: The desk to be removed is between two current desks.
- Case 3: The desk to be removed is last in the chain of desks.

Once again, you will see that the last case is not really a special case.

6.17   **Case 1.** Figure 6-12 illustrates Case 1 before we remove the first desk from the chain. The following steps are necessary to remove the first desk:

1. By asking the instructor, locate the first desk.
2. Give the address that is written on the first desk to the instructor. This is the address of the second desk in the chain.
3. Return the first desk to the hallway.

Figure 6-13 shows the chain after the first two steps take place. Notice that the first desk is no longer a part of the chain. Technically, it still references the second desk. But if this desk is ever used again, a new address will be written on its paper.

Figure 6-12   A chain of desks just prior to removing its first desk

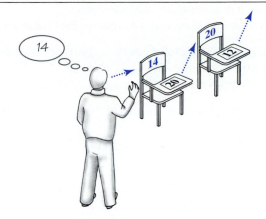

Figure 6-13   A chain of desks just after removing its first desk

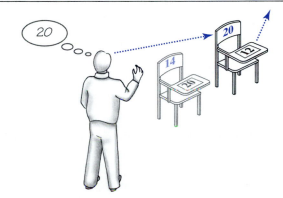

6.18   **Case 2.** Figure 6-14 shows Case 2 before we remove a desk that is between two current desks, where

- `deskToRemove` is the desk to be removed
- `deskBefore` is the desk before the one to be removed
- `deskAfter` is the desk after the one to be removed

Figure 6-14   A chain of desks just prior to removing a desk between two other desks

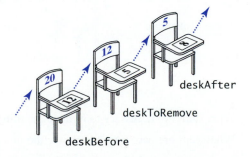

Note that the address on deskBefore is the address of deskToRemove and the address on deskToRemove is that of the next desk, deskAfter. We'll assume that we can determine the address of deskBefore, and from it determine the other addresses.

The following steps are necessary to remove deskToRemove:

1. Copy the address on deskToRemove to deskBefore. (deskBefore now references deskAfter, which is the desk currently after deskToRemove.)
2. Return deskToRemove to the hallway.

Figure 6-15 shows the chain after the first of these steps takes place.

Figure 6-15   A chain of desks just after removing a desk between two other desks

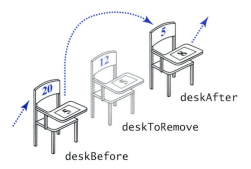

6.19   **Case 3.** Finally, when the desk to be removed is last in the chain of desks, we can proceed as for Case 2. Remember that the paper on the last desk in the chain is blank because that desk does not reference any other desk. Therefore, Step 1 of Case 2 would copy a blank from the last desk to deskBefore, as 6-16 illustrates. This action is exactly what needs to happen so that deskBefore is last in the chain of desks.

Figure 6-16   Before and after removing the last desk from a chain

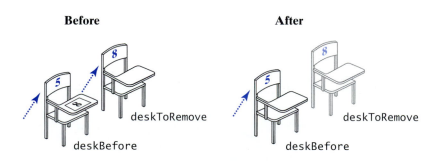

Question 7   What steps are necessary to remove the third desk in a chain of five desks?

Question 8   What steps are necessary to remove the first desk in a chain of five desks?

The Class Node

6.20   The previous section described how you can organize data without physically moving it. This section expresses these ideas in Java by implementing the ADT list. Recall that a list is a collection of objects that are organized by their positions in the collection.

We begin by defining the Java equivalent of a desk, the **node.** Nodes are objects that you typically link together to form a data structure. Our particular nodes have two data fields each: one to reference an entry in the list and one to reference another node. An entry in the list is analogous to a person who sits at a desk. The reference to another node is analogous to the desk address written on the paper that is on each desk.

6.21   The class that represents these nodes can have the following form:

```
class Node
{
   private Object data; // entry in list
   private Node   next; // link to next node

   < Constructors >
   . . .
   < Accessor and mutator methods: getData, setData, getNextNode, setNextNode >
   . . .
} // end Node
```

Let's focus on the data fields. The field `data` is of type `Object`, so the entries in the list are objects. In this case, `data` contains a reference to the desired object. However, if the entries in the list had a primitive data type such as `int`, `data` would be of type `int` and would actually contain the list entry. Sometimes we will call this field the **data portion** of the node.

The field `next` contains a reference to another node. Notice that its data type is `Node`, which is the class that we are currently defining! Such a circular definition might surprise you, but it is perfectly legal in Java. It also enables one node to reference another node, just as one desk referenced another desk in the first section of this chapter. Notice that a desk did not reference a student. Likewise, a node does not reference a list entry but rather references an entire node that contains a list entry. Sometimes we will call this field the **link portion** of the node. Figure 6-17 illustrates two nodes that are linked and contain either integers or references to objects.

Figure 6-17   Two linked nodes with (a) primitive data; (b) object data

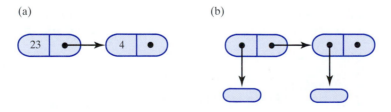

6.22   The rest of the class definition is uneventful. Constructors to initialize the node are useful, and since the data fields are private, methods to access and alter their contents are necessary. But are they really? If we intend `Node` to be for public use, like our other classes, such methods are necessary; however, `Node` is an implementation detail of the ADT list that should be hidden from the list's client.

One way to hide Node from the world is to define it within a package that also contains the class that implements the list. Another way—the way we will use here—is to define Node within the class that implements the list. Such a class is declared to be private and is called an **inner class**. The data fields of an inner class are accessible directly by the **outer class** without the need for accessor and mutator methods. Thus, we can simplify the definition of Node greatly:

```java
private class Node
{
  private Object data; // data portion
  private Node   next; // link to next node

  private Node(Object dataPortion)
  {
    data = dataPortion;
    next = null;
  } // end constructor

  private Node(Object dataPortion, Node nextNode)
  {
    data = dataPortion;
    next = nextNode;
  } // end constructor
} // end Node
```

We did not include a default constructor because we will not need one. In a moment, you will see how to use this class as an inner class. Later, in Segment 6.42, we will talk about a definition of Node that does have set and get methods.

A Linked Implementation of the ADT List

6.23   In the example in the first section of this chapter, the instructor remembered the address of the first desk in a chain of desks. Similarly, the linked implementation for the ADT list uses a chain of nodes and must "remember" the address of the first node in this chain. The implementation does so by recording a reference to the first node in a data field called the **head reference.** Here is an outline of a class definition that implements the ADT list and contains the class Node as an inner class. Recall that Chapter 4 introduced the interface ListInterface.

```java
public class LList[1] implements ListInterface
{
  private Node firstNode; // reference to first node
  private int  length;    // number of entries in list

  public LList()
  {
    clear();
  } // end default constructor

  public final void clear()
  {
```

---

[1]. We named this class LList instead of LinkedList to avoid confusion with Java's class LinkedList in the package java.util. You will see Java's LinkedList later in this chapter.

```
        firstNode = null;
        length = 0;
    } // end clear
```

    < Implementations of the public methods `add, remove, replace, getEntry, contains,`
       `getLength, isEmpty, isFull,` *and* `display` *go here.* >
    . . .

```
    // --------------private!----------------------------
    /** Task: Returns a reference to the node at a given position.
     *  Precondition: List is not empty; 1 <= givenPosition <= length. */
    private Node getNodeAt(int givenPosition)
    {
        < Implementation deferred >
    } // end getNodeAt

    private class Node // private inner class
    {
        < See Segment 6.22. >
    } // end Node
} // end LList
```

The data field `firstNode` is the head reference of the chain of nodes. Just like the instructor who knew the address of the first desk in the chain of desks, `firstNode` references the first node in the chain of nodes. Another data field, `length`, records the number of entries in the current list. This number is also the number of nodes in the chain. The default constructor simply initializes these data fields by calling `clear`. So initially, a list is empty, `firstNode` is `null`, and `length` is 0.

As we mentioned in Chapter 2, when a constructor calls another public method such as `clear`, that method should be `final` so that no subclass can override it, thereby changing the effect of the constructor.

Adding to the End of the List

6.24   We will now implement the public methods of the class `LList`, beginning with the first add method. This method adds a new entry to the end of the list. Recall from Segment 6.10 the steps that we took when the instructor added a new desk to the end of the chain. Initially when the first student arrived, we had the following steps:

    `newDesk` *represents the new student's desk*
    New student sits at `newDesk`
    Instructor memorizes address of `newDesk`

Here are the analogous steps that add must take to add the first entry to an initially empty list. Note that a new desk is analogous to a new node and the instructor is analogous to `firstNode`.

    `newNode` *references a new instance of* `Node`
    Place data in `newNode`
    `firstNode` = *address of* `newNode`

In Java, these steps appear as follows, where `newEntry` references the entry to be added to the list:

```
Node newNode = new Node(newEntry);
firstNode = newNode;
```

Figure 6-18 illustrates these steps. Notice that in Part *b* of this figure, both `firstNode` and `newNode` reference the same node. After the insertion of the new node is complete, only `firstNode` should reference it. We could set `newNode` to `null`, but as you will see shortly, `newNode` is a local variable of the method `add`. As such, `newNode` will not exist after `add` ends its execution. The same is true of the local variable `newEntry`.

Figure 6-18   (a) An empty list and a new node; (b) after adding a new node to a list that was empty

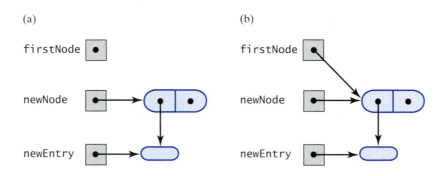

6.25   Now, to add a desk to the end of the chain, the instructor took the following steps:

> `newDesk` *represents the new student's desk*
> *New student sits at* `newDesk`
> *Instructor locates the last desk in the chain*
> *Instructor writes address of* `newDesk` *on this last desk*

The analogous steps that `add` must take to add a new entry to the end of a list are

> `newNode` *references a new instance of* `Node`
> *Place data in* `newNode`
> *Locate last node in chain*
> *Place address of* `newNode` *in this last node*

That is, we make the last node in the chain reference the new node.
In Java, these steps appear as follows:

```
Node newNode = new Node(newEntry);
Node lastNode = getNodeAt(length); // get reference to last node
lastNode.next = newNode; // make last node reference new node
```

The method `getNodeAt` is a private method of the class `LList` that locates and returns a reference to the node at a given position within the list. Its specifications are given near the end of Segment 6.23. Notice that `lastNode` is an instance of `Node`, so `lastNode.next` is that node's data field `next`.

Figure 6-19 illustrates this addition to the end of a chain of nodes. To simplify the figure, we have omitted the actual entries in the list. These entries are objects that the nodes reference.

As in Figure 6-18, we are left with external references into the chain of nodes that we do not want. Again, since these reference variables `newNode` and `lastNode` will be local to the method, they will not exist for long. If they did persist, we would set these variables to `null` after the addition was complete.

Figure 6-19   A chain of nodes (a) just prior to adding a node at the end; (b) just after adding a node at the end

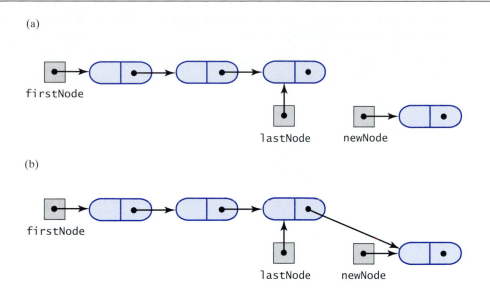

(a)

firstNode

lastNode   newNode

(b)

firstNode

lastNode   newNode

6.26   **The Java method.** Assuming that we have the private method getNodeAt, we can complete the method add based on the previous thoughts:

```java
public boolean add(Object newEntry)
{
    Node newNode = new Node(newEntry);

    if (isEmpty())
        firstNode = newNode;
    else                            // add to end of nonempty list
    {
        Node lastNode = getNodeAt(length);
        lastNode.next = newNode; // make last node reference new node
    } // end if

    length++;
    return true;
}   // end add
```

This method first creates a new node for the new entry. If the list is empty, it adds the new node by making firstNode reference it. If the list is not empty, however, we must locate the end of the list. Since we have a reference only to the first node, we must traverse the list until we locate the last node and obtain a reference to it. We will define a private method getNodeAt to accomplish this task. Since the data field length contains the size of the list, and since we identify list entries by their positions within the list beginning with 1, the last node is at position length. We need to pass this value to getNodeAt. Once getNodeAt gives us a reference to the last node, we can set the last node's link to reference the new node.

The method getNodeAt does the messy work; we will examine its implementation later, in Segment 6.33. In the meantime, we can implement the public methods knowing only what getNodeAt does, and not how it does it.

Adding at a Given Position Within the List

6.27   The second add method adds a new entry at a specified position within the list. After creating a new node that newNode references, we determine whether the existing list is empty. If it is, we add the new node to the list by writing firstNode = newNode, as we did in the first add method. If the list is not empty, we must consider two cases:

- Case 1: Adding the entry to the beginning of the list
- Case 2: Adding the entry at a position other than the beginning of the list

6.28   **Case 1.** In the context of desks in a room, the necessary steps for the first case are

> newDesk *represents the new student's desk*
> *New student sits at* newDesk
> *Place the address of the first desk on* newDesk *(the instructor knows the address of the first desk)*
> *Give the address of* newDesk *to the instructor*

As a result of these steps, the new desk references the current first desk in the chain and becomes the new first desk.

Here are the analogous steps that add must take to add to the beginning of a list:

> newNode *references a new instance of* Node
> *Place data in* newNode
> *Set* newNode*'s link to* firstNode
> *Set* firstNode *to* newNode

That is, we make the new node reference the first node in the chain, making it the new first node. Figure 6-20 illustrates these steps, and the following Java statements implement them:

```
Node newNode = new Node(newEntry);
newNode.next = firstNode;
firstNode = newNode;
```

Figure 6-20   A chain of nodes (a) just prior to adding a node at the beginning; (b) just after adding a node at the beginning

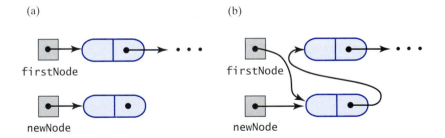

Adding a node to an empty chain, as Figure 6-18 depicts, is actually the same as adding a node to the beginning of a chain.

Question 9   The code that we developed in Segment 6.24 to add a node to an empty chain is

```
Node newNode = new Node(newEntry);
firstNode = newNode;
```

The code that we just developed to add to the beginning of a chain is

```
Node newNode = new Node(newEntry);
newNode.next = firstNode;
firstNode = newNode;
```

Why do these statements work correctly when the chain is empty?

6.29   **Case 2.** In the second case, we add an entry to the list at a position other than the beginning. The necessary steps for the second case in the context of desks in a room are

> newDesk *references the new student's desk*
> deskBefore *represents the desk that will be before the new desk*
> deskAfter *represents the desk after* deskBefore; *its address is on* deskBefore
> *Place the address of* deskAfter *on* newDesk
> *Place the address of* newDesk *on* deskBefore

Here, the analogous steps that add must take are

> newNode *references the new node*
> nodeBefore *references the node that will be before the new node*
> *Set* nodeAfter *to* nodeBefore*'s link*
> *Set* newNode*'s link to* nodeAfter
> *Set* nodeBefore*'s link to* newNode

The following Java statements implement these steps:

```
Node newNode = new Node(newEntry);
Node nodeBefore = getNodeAt(newPosition-1);
Node nodeAfter = nodeBefore.next;
newNode.next = nodeAfter;
nodeBefore.next = newNode;
```

Figure 6-21a shows the chain after the first three statements execute, and Figure 6-21b shows it after the node has been added.

Figure 6-21   A chain of nodes (a) just prior to adding a node between two adjacent nodes; (b) just after adding a node between two adjacent nodes

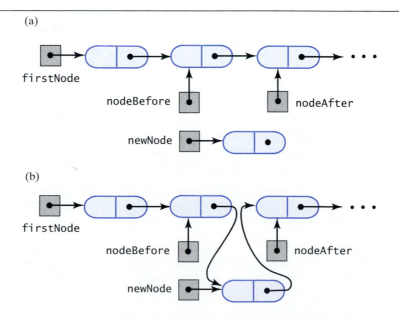

6.30   **The Java method.** The following implementation of the add method summarizes these ideas:

```java
public boolean add(int newPosition, Object newEntry)
{
  boolean isSuccessful = true;

  if ((newPosition >= 1) && (newPosition <= length+1))
  {
    Node newNode = new Node(newEntry);

    if (isEmpty() || (newPosition == 1)) // case 1
    {
      newNode.next = firstNode;
      firstNode = newNode;
    }
    else              // case 2: newPosition > 1, list is not empty
    {
      Node nodeBefore = getNodeAt(newPosition-1);
      Node nodeAfter = nodeBefore.next;
      newNode.next = nodeAfter;
      nodeBefore.next = newNode;
    } // end if

    length++;
  }
  else
    isSuccessful = false;
  return isSuccessful;
} // end add
```

6.31   **An out-of-memory error.** One of the list implementations given in Chapter 5 used a fixed-size array to represent the list entries. You saw that the array—and therefore the list—could become full. With a linked implementation, the list cannot become full. Anytime you add a new entry, you create a new node for that entry. It is possible, however, for your program to use all of your computer's memory. If this occurs, your request for a new node will cause the error OutOfMemoryError. You could interpret this condition as a full list; however, an OutOfMemoryError is fatal, and the client will not have the opportunity to react to it.

The Private Method getNodeAt

6.32   To complete our implementation of the add methods, we need to implement the method getNodeAt, which returns a reference to the node at a given position within the list. Since the method returns a reference to a node, the method is an implementation detail that we would not want a client to use. Thus, getNodeAt should be a private method. Recall the specifications for this method:

```java
/** Task: Returns a reference to the node at a given position.
 *  Precondition: List is not empty; 1 <= givenPosition <= length. */
private Node getNodeAt(int givenPosition)
```

Segments 6.2 and 6.9 discussed how an instructor locates a particular desk within a chain of desks by beginning at the head of the chain and traversing it from one desk to another. The technique is the same here. The data field firstNode contains a reference to the first node in the list. That node contains a reference to the second node in the list, and so on.

We can use a temporary variable `currentNode` to reference the nodes, one at a time, as we traverse the chain from the first node to the desired node. Initially, we set `currentNode` to `first-Node` so that it references the first node in the chain. If we are seeking the first node, we are done. Otherwise, we move to the next node by executing

```
currentNode = currentNode.next;
```

If we are seeking the second node, we are done. Otherwise, we move to the next node by executing

```
currentNode = currentNode.next;
```

once again. We continue in this manner until we locate the node at the desired position within the list.

6.33   The implementation for `getNodeAt` follows:

```
/** Task: Returns a reference to the node at a given position.
 *  Precondition: List is not empty; 1 <= givenPosition <= length. */
private Node getNodeAt(int givenPosition)
{
   Node currentNode = firstNode;

   // traverse the list to locate the desired node
   for (int counter = 1; counter < givenPosition; counter++)
      currentNode = currentNode.next;

   return currentNode;
} // end getNodeAt
```

Within the for loop, `currentNode` should never become `null`, if the method's precondition is met. Thus, `currentNode.next` never executes if `currentNode` is `null`. Notice that the previous add methods enforce this method's precondition.

Programming Tip: If `ref` is a reference to a node in a chain, before you use it to access `ref.data` or `ref.next`, be sure that `ref` is not `null`.

The Method remove

6.34   The `remove` method removes the entry at a specified position within a nonempty list. We must consider two cases:

● Case 1: Removing the entry at the beginning of the list
● Case 2: Removing an entry at a position other than the beginning of the list

6.35   **Case 1.** Segment 6.17 discussed the first case in the context of desks in a room. The necessary steps then were

By asking the instructor, locate the first desk.
Give the address that is written on the first desk to the instructor. This is the address of the second desk in the chain.
Return the first desk to the hallway.

Here the analogous steps are

Set `firstNode` *to the link in the first node.*
Since references to the first node no longer exist, the system automatically recycles its memory.

Figure 6-22 illustrates these steps, and the following Java statement implements them:

```
firstNode = firstNode.next;
```

Figure 6-22   A chain of nodes (a) just prior to removing the first node; (b) just after removing the first node

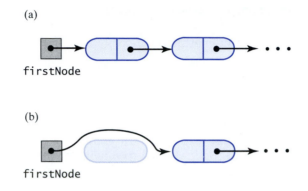

(a)

firstNode

(b)

firstNode

6.36   **Case 2.** In the second case, we remove an entry at a position other than the beginning of the list. Segment 6.18 discussed this case in the context of desks in a room. The necessary steps then were

> *Locate the desk before* deskToRemove; *call it* deskBefore. *The address on* deskBefore *is the address of* deskToRemove.
> *The address on* deskToRemove *is that of the next desk,* deskAfter, *in the chain.*
> *Copy the address on* deskToRemove *to* deskBefore. *(*deskBefore *now references* deskAfter, *which is the desk currently after* deskToRemove.*)*
> *Return* deskToRemove *to the hallway.*

Here the analogous steps are

> *Let* nodeBefore *reference the node before the one to be removed.*
> *Set* nodeToRemove *to* nodeBefore*'s link;* nodeToRemove *now references the node to be removed.*
> *Set* nodeAfter *to* nodeToRemove*'s link;* nodeAfter *now references the node after the one to be removed.*
> *Set* nodeBefore*'s link to* nodeAfter. *(*nodeToRemove *is now disconnected from the chain.)*
> *Set* nodeToRemove *to* null.
> *Since references to the disconnected node no longer exist, the system automatically recycles its memory.*

The following Java statements implement these steps:

```
Node nodeBefore = getNodeAt(givenPosition-1);
Node nodeToRemove = nodeBefore.next;
Node nodeAfter = nodeToRemove.next;
nodeBefore.next = nodeAfter;
nodeToRemove = null;
```

Figure 6-23a illustrates the chain after the first three statements execute, and Figure 6-23b shows it after the node is removed.

Figure 6-23 A chain of nodes (a) just prior to removing an interior node; (b) just after removing an interior node

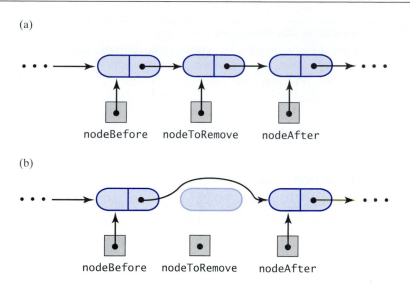

(a)

nodeBefore   nodeToRemove   nodeAfter

(b)

nodeBefore   nodeToRemove   nodeAfter

6.37   **The Java method.** The remove method has the following implementation. Recall that the method returns the entry that it deletes from the list. Notice that we use the private method getNodeAt, which we wrote originally for the add methods. Also notice that we do not set nodeToRemove to null after disconnecting the node. As we have mentioned before, nodeToRemove is local to the remove method and does not exist after the method completes executing. So although we could set nodeToRemove to null, doing so is not necessary.

```java
public Object remove(int givenPosition)
{
  Object result = null;                  // return value

  if (!isEmpty() && (givenPosition >= 1) && (givenPosition <= length))
  {
    if (givenPosition == 1)           // case 1: remove first entry
    {
      result = firstNode.data;        // save entry to be removed
      firstNode = firstNode.next;
    }
    else                              // case 2: givenPosition > 1
    {
      Node nodeBefore = getNodeAt(givenPosition-1);
      Node nodeToRemove = nodeBefore.next;
      Node nodeAfter = nodeToRemove.next;
      nodeBefore.next = nodeAfter; // disconnect the node to be removed
      result = nodeToRemove.data;  // save entry to be removed
    }  // end if

    length--;
  } // end if
```

```
        return result;                   // return removed entry, or null
                                         // if operation fails
    }  // end remove
```

> **Note:**   **Allocating and deallocating memory**
> When you use the new operator, you create, or **instantiate,** an object. At that time, the Java run-time environment **allocates,** or assigns, memory to the object. When you create a node for a linked chain, we sometimes say that you have allocated the node. After the method remove removes a node from a chain, you have no way to reference it, so you cannot use it. As Segment 1.19 noted, the Java run-time environment automatically deallocates and recycles the memory associated with such nodes without explicit instruction from the programmer.

The Method `replace`

6.38   Replacing, or revising, a list entry requires us to simply replace the data portion of a node with other data. The implementation appears as follows:

```java
public boolean replace(int givenPosition, Object newEntry)
{
    boolean isSuccessful = true;

    if (!isEmpty() && (givenPosition >= 1) && (givenPosition <= length))
    {
        Node desiredNode = getNodeAt(givenPosition);
        desiredNode.data = newEntry;
    }
    else
        isSuccessful = false;

    return isSuccessful;
} // end replace
```

Question 10   Compare the effort involved in replacing an entry in a list using the previous method replace and the method replace given in Segment 5.9.

The Method `getEntry`

6.39   Retrieving a list entry is also straightforward:

```java
public Object getEntry(int givenPosition)
{
    Object result = null;  // result to return

    if (!isEmpty() && (givenPosition >= 1) && (givenPosition <= length))
        result = getNodeAt(givenPosition).data;

    return result;
} // end getEntry
```

The method getNodeAt returns a reference to the desired node, so
```
    getNodeAt(givenPosition).data
```
is the data portion of that node.

Although our implementations of getEntry and replace are easy to write, each does more work than if we had used an array to represent the list. Here, getNodeAt starts at the first node in the chain and moves from node to node until it reaches the desired one. In Segment 5.9, you saw that replace and getEntry can reference the desired array element directly without involving any other array element.

The Method contains

6.40   To determine whether a list contains a given entry, you must look at the entries in the list, one at a time. In Chapter 5, where we used an array to represent the list's entries, we examined each array element—starting at index zero—until we either found the desired entry or discovered that it was not in the array.

We use the same general approach here to search a chain for a particular piece of data. We begin at the first node, and if that does not contain the entry we are seeking, we look at the second node, and so on. When searching an array, we use an index. To search a chain, we use a reference to a node. For example, currentNode could reference the node that we want to examine. Initially, we want currentNode to reference the first node in the chain, so we set it to firstNode. To make currentNode reference the next node, we would execute the statement

```
currentNode = currentNode.next;
```

Thus, the method contains has the following implementation:

```java
public boolean contains(Object anEntry)
{
   boolean found = false;
   Node currentNode = firstNode;
   while (!found && (currentNode != null))
   {
      if (anEntry.equals(currentNode.data))
         found = true;
      else
         currentNode = currentNode.next;
   } // end while

   return found;
} // end contains
```

The method has the same general form as the corresponding method in Segment 5.10.

The Remaining Methods

6.41   The method isFull should always return false. The only time a list whose implementation is linked could appear full is when the system cannot provide memory to the add method for a new node. In that case, an OutOfMemoryError occurs, which is fatal. A client would not have the opportunity to call isFull.

The implementations of the methods getLength and isEmpty are the same as for the array-based implementation that you saw in Chapter 5. We leave the implementation of display as an exercise.

Question 11   Write an implementation for the method `display` that displays the entries in the list, one per line. Assume that the objects in the list belong to a class that implements the method `toString`. You should look at the previous implementation of the method `contains` for an idea of how to construct the necessary loop. Here, however, the loop does not end until the entire chain is traversed.

Question 12   The implementation of `isEmpty` compares the data field `length` with zero. What is another equally brief implementation of this method?

Using a Class Node That Has Set and Get Methods

6.42   Since `Node` is an inner class, the class `LList` can access `Node`'s private data fields directly by name. Doing so makes the implementation somewhat easier to write, read, and understand, particularly for novice Java programmers. However, some computer scientists feel that you should access a class's data fields only by calling accessor and mutator (set and get) methods.

Suppose that we had included the methods `getData`, `setData`, `getNextNode`, and `setNextNode` in the class `Node`, as described earlier in Segment 6.21. We could then revise the implementation of `LList` by making changes such as the following:

- Change `currentNode.data` to `currentNode.getData()`
- Change `currentNode.next` to `currentNode.getNextNode()`
- Change
  `desiredNode.data = newEntry;`
  to
  `desiredNode.setData(newEntry);`
- Change
  `nodeBefore.next = nodeAfter;`
  to
  `nodeBefore.setNextNode(nodeAfter);`

If we had written `Node` and `LList` in this way, `Node` could be either a private inner class or a public class. Here `Node` is an implementation detail that we want to hide, so making it an inner class is appropriate. But if we ever changed our mind and wanted to use `Node` as a public class, we could do so without revising it and `LList`.

Question 13   What changes to the class `LList` are necessary to enable a client to serialize instances of the class?

Tail References

6.43   **The problem.** Imagine that we have a collection of data from which we will create a list. That is, our data will be the list's entries. If the data is in the order in which the entries will appear in the list, we create the list by repeatedly adding the next entry to the end of the list.

We could do this by using the implementation of the add method that we presented in Segment 6.26. However, if you examine that method, you will discover that it invokes the private method `getNodeAt` to locate the last node in the chain and hence the last entry in the list. To accomplish this task, `getNodeAt` must begin at the first entry and traverse the chain until it locates the last node.

Given a reference to the last node, add can insert the new entry at the end of the list. This reference, however, is not retained when the method completes its task. Thus, if we add another entry to the end of the list, add will invoke `getNodeAt` again to traverse the list from its beginning. Since we plan to add entries repeatedly to the end of the list, many repetitious traversals will occur.

6.44   **A solution.** In such cases, maintaining a reference to the end of the chain—as well as a reference to the beginning of the chain—is advantageous. We call such a reference to the end of a chain a **tail reference.** Figure 6-24 illustrates a linked chain with both head and tail references.

Figure 6-24   A linked chain with a head reference and a tail reference

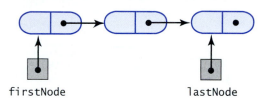

The tail reference, like the head reference, is a private data field of the class. The private data fields in our revised implementation then would be

```
private Node firstNode; // head reference to first node
private Node lastNode;  // tail reference to last node
private int  length;    // number of entries in list
```

Question 14   Examine the implementation of the class `LList` given in the previous section. Which methods would require a new implementation if you used both a head reference and a tail reference?

A Revised Implementation of the List

By examining the class `LList`, you should find that the constructor, both `add` methods, and the `remove` method are the ones that might alter the head and tail references, and thus those methods will need to be revised. The rest of the original implementation remains the same. Let's examine these revisions.

6.45   **The constructor.** The default constructor initializes both the head and tail references:

```
public LList()
{
   firstNode = null;
   lastNode = null;
   length = 0;
} // end default constructor
```

Here, and in the rest of the revision, changes from the original implementation appear in color.

6.46   **Adding to the end of the list.** Adding to the end of an empty list requires both the head and tail references to reference the new solitary node. Thus, after creating a new node that `newNode` references, the add method would execute

```
firstNode = newNode;
lastNode = newNode;
```

Adding to the end of a nonempty list no longer requires a traversal to locate the last entry: The tail reference `lastNode` provides this information. After making the addition, the tail reference must change to refer to the new last entry. The following statements perform these steps, as Figure 6-25 illustrates:

```
lastNode.next = newNode;
lastNode = newNode;
```

Figure 6-25   Adding a node to the end of a nonempty chain that has a tail reference

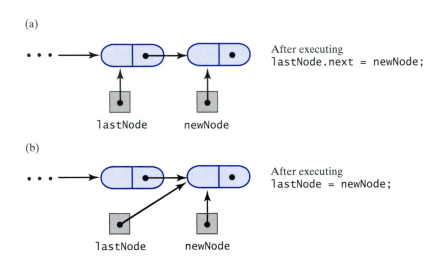

(a)

After executing
`lastNode.next = newNode;`

lastNode   newNode

(b)

After executing
`lastNode = newNode;`

lastNode   newNode

The first add method reflects the previous comments:

```
public boolean add(Object newEntry)
{
  Node newNode = new Node(newEntry);

  if (isEmpty())
    firstNode = newNode;
  else
    lastNode.next = newNode;

  lastNode = newNode;
  length++;
  return true;
}  // end add
```

6.47   **Adding to the list at a given position.** Adding to a list by position affects the tail reference only when we are adding to an empty list or adding to the end of a nonempty list. Other cases do not affect the tail reference, so we treat them as we did in Segment 6.30 when we did not have a tail reference.

Thus, the implementation of the method that adds by position is

```java
public boolean add(int newPosition, Object newEntry)
{
  boolean isSuccessful = true;

  if ((newPosition >= 1) && (newPosition <= length+1))
  {
    Node newNode = new Node(newEntry);

    if (isEmpty())
    {
      firstNode = newNode;
      lastNode = newNode;
    }
    else if (newPosition == 1)
    {
      newNode.next = firstNode;
      firstNode = newNode;
    }
    else if (newPosition == length + 1)
    {
      lastNode.next = newNode;
      lastNode = newNode;
    } // end if
    else
    {
      Node nodeBefore = getNodeAt(newPosition-1);
      Node nodeAfter = nodeBefore.next;
      newNode.next = nodeAfter;
      nodeBefore.next = newNode;
    } // end if

    length++;
  }
  else
    isSuccessful = false;

  return isSuccessful;
} // end add
```

6.48   **Removing an entry from a list.** Removing an entry can affect the tail reference in two cases:

- Case 1: If the list contains one entry and we remove it, an empty list results and we must set both the head and tail references to null.
- Case 2: If the list contains several entries and we remove the last one, we must change the tail reference so that it references the new last entry.

Figure 6-26 illustrates these two cases, and the following method implements them:

Figure 6-26   Removing the last node from a chain that has both head and tail references when the chain
contains (a) one node; (b) more than one node

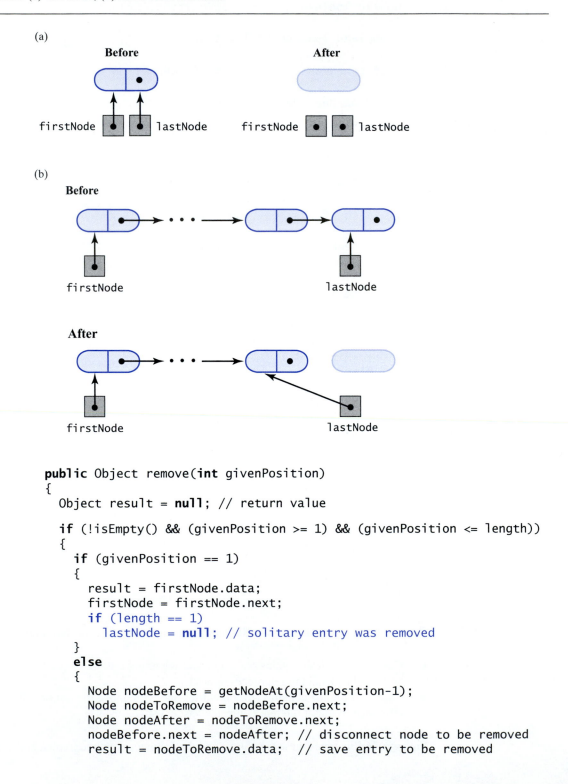

```
public Object remove(int givenPosition)
{
  Object result = null; // return value

  if (!isEmpty() && (givenPosition >= 1) && (givenPosition <= length))
  {
    if (givenPosition == 1)
    {
      result = firstNode.data;
      firstNode = firstNode.next;
      if (length == 1)
        lastNode = null; // solitary entry was removed
    }
    else
    {
      Node nodeBefore = getNodeAt(givenPosition-1);
      Node nodeToRemove = nodeBefore.next;
      Node nodeAfter = nodeToRemove.next;
      nodeBefore.next = nodeAfter; // disconnect node to be removed
      result = nodeToRemove.data;  // save entry to be removed
```

```
            if (givenPosition == length)
               lastNode = nodeBefore; // last node was removed
         } // end if

            length--;
         } // end if
      return result;
   } // end remove
```

The Pros and Cons of Using a Chain to Implement the ADT List

6.49   This chapter has showed you how to use a chain in the implementation of the ADT list. One of the greatest advantages of this approach is that the chain, and therefore the list, can grow as large as necessary. As long as memory is available, you can add as many nodes to a chain as you wish. Although you can also use dynamic array expansion—as Chapter 5 describes—to allow the list to grow, each time a larger array is necessary, you must copy the entries from the full array to the new array. No such copying is required when you use a chain.

   In addition, a chain allows you to add and remove nodes without moving any existing entries that are already in the list. With an array, adding and removing entries usually requires that other entries be moved within the array. However, you must traverse a chain from its beginning to determine where to make the addition or deletion.

   Retrieving an existing entry from a chain requires a similar traversal to locate the desired entry. When you use an array instead of a chain, you can access any element directly by position, without searching the array. Lastly, a chain requires more memory than an array. Although both data structures contain references to data objects, each node in a chain also contains a reference to another node.

Java Class Library: The Class LinkedList

6.50   Recall from Chapter 4 that the standard Java package java.util contains the interface List. This interface is like our ListInterface, but some methods have different names and the list entries begin at position 0 instead of 1. This same package contains the class LinkedList. This class implements the interface List and contains additional methods that add, remove, and retrieve entries at the beginning or end of a list. These additional methods are as follows:

public void addFirst(Object newEntry)
Adds newEntry to the beginning of the list.

public void addLast(Object newEntry)
Adds newEntry to the end of the list.

public Object removeFirst()
Removes and returns the first entry in the list.

public Object removeLast()
Removes and returns the last entry in the list.

public Object getFirst()
Returns the first entry in the list.

public Object getLast()
Returns the last entry in the list.

Descriptions of other methods in this class are available at

http://java.sun.com/products/jdk/1.4/docs/api/index.html

CHAPTER SUMMARY

- You can form a chain of linked data by using objects called nodes. Each node has two parts. One part contains either data of a primitive type or a reference to a data object. A second part references the next node in the chain. The last node, however, references no other node and contains **null**. A head reference external to the chain references the first node.

- You can add or remove any node that is linked to other nodes in a chain by changing at most two references.

- Adding or removing a node that is linked to other nodes in a chain must consider a special case: when the node will be or is first in the chain.

- Locating a particular node in a chain of linked nodes requires a traversal of the chain. Beginning at the first node, you move from node to node sequentially until you reach the desired node.

- Adding or removing a node that is last in a chain of linked nodes requires a traversal of the entire chain. Maintaining a tail reference to the last node eliminates the need for a traversal when adding a node at the end of the chain. A tail reference, however, makes removing the last node a bit more difficult.

PROGRAMMING TIP

- If **ref** is a reference to a node in a chain, be sure that **ref** is not **null** before you use it to access **ref.data** or **ref.next**.

EXERCISES

1. Add a constructor to the class LList that creates a list from a given array of objects. Consider at least two different ways to implement such a constructor. Which way does the least amount of work?

2. Suppose that you want an operation for the ADT list that removes the first occurrence of a given object from the list. The signature of the method could be as follows:

    public boolean remove(Object anObject)

    The method returns true if the list contained anObject and the object was removed. Write an implementation of this method for the class LList.

3. Suppose that you want an operation for the ADT list that returns the position of a given object in the list. The signature of the method could be as follows:

    public int getPosition(Object anObject)

    Write an implementation of this method for the class LList.

4. Implement a replace method for the class LList that returns the replaced object.

5. Implement an equals method for the class LList that returns true when the entries in one list equal the entries in a second list.

6. Suppose that a list contains `Comparable` objects. Implement the following methods for the class `LList`.

a. The method `getMin` that returns the smallest object in the list.
b. The method `removeMin` that removes and returns the smallest object in the list.

---

1. Revise the inner class `Node` so that it has the set and get methods mentioned in Segment 6.42. Then revise the class `LList` so that it invokes these set and get methods instead of accessing the private data fields `data` and `next` directly by name.

2. Create a Java interface that contains the six methods described in Segment 6.50 and the three methods described in Exercises 2, 3, and 4. Then extend this interface and `ListInterface` to form `DoubleEndedListInterface`. Write a class that implements `DoubleEndedListInterface`. Represent the list's entries by using a chain of nodes that has both a head reference and a tail reference. Write a program that thoroughly tests your class.

3. Repeat Project 2, but do not use a tail reference.

4. Implement the ADT bag that Project 1 of Chapter 4 describes. Represent the bag as a chain of linked nodes.

5. A set is a special bag that does not allow duplicates. Project 1 of Chapter 4 describes the ADT bag. Specify the operations for the ADT set. Implement the set by using a chain of linked nodes.

6. Adding nodes to or removing nodes from a linked chain requires a special case when the operation is at the beginning of the chain. To eliminate the special case, you can add a **dummy head node** at the beginning of the chain. The dummy head node is always present but does not contain a list entry. The chain, then, is never empty, and so the head reference is never `null`, even when the list is empty. Modify the class `LList`, as presented in this chapter, by adding a dummy head node to the chain.

7

Iterators

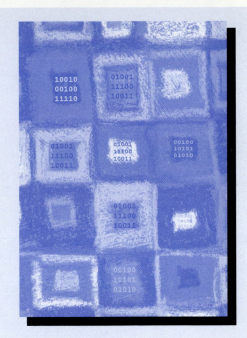

CONTENTS

What Is an Iterator?
  A Basic Iterator
  Iterator Methods That Modify the ADT
Implementing an Internal Iterator
Implementing an Iterator as Its Own Class
  An External Iterator
  An Inner Class Iterator

PREREQUISITES

Chapter   4   Lists
Chapter   6   List Implementations That Link Data
Appendix   B   Exception Handling

OBJECTIVES

After studying this chapter, you should be able to

- Describe the concept of iterator

- Use an iterator to traverse or manipulate a list

- Implement in Java an internal iterator, an external iterator, and an inner class iterator for a list

- Describe the pros and cons of the three kinds of iterators just mentioned

An iterator is an object that traverses a collection of data. During the traversal, you can look at the data entries, modify them, add entries, and remove entries. This chapter talks about iterators and applies them to the ADT list. You can add iterator methods to the operations of the ADT list, or you can define an iterator as a separate class that interacts with the ADT list. This separate class can be external to the ADT list or hidden within its implementation. We will look at all of these approaches.

This chapter creates an iterator that is easy to understand and is useful as well. The Java Class Library also contains two iterator interfaces, `Iterator` and `ListIterator`, that we will explore in the next chapter.

What Is an Iterator?

7.1   How would you count the number of lines on this page? You could use your finger to point to each line as you counted it. Your finger would keep your place on the page. If you paused at a particular line, your finger would be on the current line and there would be a previous line and a next line. If you think of this page as a list of lines, you would be traversing the list as you counted the lines.

An **iterator** is a program component that enables you to step through, or **traverse,** a collection of data such as a list, beginning with the first entry. During one complete traversal, or **iteration,** each data item is considered once. You control the progress of the iteration by repeatedly asking the iterator to advance to the next entry in the list. At any time during the iteration, you can ask the iterator to give you a reference to the current entry. You also can modify the list as you traverse it.

You are familiar with iteration because you have written loops. For example, if `nameList` is a list of strings, we can write the following `for` loop to display the entire list:

```java
int listSize = nameList.getLength();
for (int position = 1; position <= listSize; position++)
    System.out.println(nameList.getEntry(position));
```

Here, `position` is a simple iterator. Using it, the loop **iterates** through the entries in the list. Instead of simply displaying each entry, we could do other things to or with it.

7.2   Notice that the previous loop is at the client level, since it uses the ADT operation `getEntry` to access the list. For an array-based implementation of the list, `getEntry` can retrieve the desired array element directly and quickly. But if a linked chain of nodes represents the list's entries, `getEntry` must move from node to node until it locates the desired one. For example, to retrieve the nth entry in the list, `getEntry` would begin at the first node in the chain and then move to the second node, the third node, and so on until it reached the nth node. At the next repetition of the loop, `getEntry` would retrieve the $n + 1^{st}$ entry in the list by beginning again at the first node in the chain and stepping from node to node until it reached the $n + 1^{st}$ node. This wastes time.

Iteration is such a common operation that we could include it as part of the ADT list. Doing so would enable a more efficient implementation than we are able to achieve at the client level. Notice that the operation `display` of the ADT list performs an iteration. But `display` only displays the list. What if we want to do something else with the list's entries as we traverse them? We do not want to add another operation each time we think of another way to use an iteration. Yet we should encapsulate a list traversal.

We need an iterator that steps through a collection of data at our command and retrieves or modifies the entries. The iterator should keep track of its progress; that is, it should know where it is in the collection and whether it has accessed each entry.

Note: **Iterators**

An **iterator** is a program component that steps through, or **traverses,** a collection of data. The iterator keeps track of its progress during the traversal, or **iteration.** It can tell you whether a next entry exists and if so, return a reference to it. During one cycle of the iteration, each data item is considered once.

A Basic Iterator

7.3   Let's specify some methods that are appropriate for an iterator by writing the following Java interface. Our methods can throw an exception, so we begin by importing the exception from the package `java.util`.

```java
import java.util.NoSuchElementException;
public interface BasicIteratorInterface
{
   /** Task: Determines whether the iteration has completed its traversal
    *         and gone beyond the last entry in the collection of data.
    *  @return true if the iteration has another entry to return */
   public boolean hasCurrent();

   /** Task: Advances the current position of the iteration by 1.
    *  @return true if the iteration has another entry to return  */
   public boolean advance();

   /** Task: Retrieves the current entry in the iteration.
    *  @return a reference to the current entry in the iteration,
    *          if one exists
    *  @throws NoSuchElementException, if no current entry exists */
   public Object getCurrent() throws NoSuchElementException;

   /** Task: Sets the iteration to begin with the first entry in
    *         the collection. */
   public void reset();
} // end BasicIteratorInterface
```

This interface is of our own design. Java provides other iterator interfaces that we will examine in the next chapter. Using our interface should help you to understand iterators in general and Java's iterators in particular.

You will notice that our interface specifies that an exception be thrown when the iterator does not find an expected entry. We do this to be consistent with Java's iterator interfaces. Because `NoSuchElementException` is a run-time exception, the `throws` clause in a method's signature is optional. Additionally, you do not have to write `try` and `catch` blocks when you invoke the method. (See Appendix B if you need more information about exceptions.)

7.4   **Example.** Let's demonstrate these methods with the ADT list. The simplest, but not the best, way to implement an iterator interface is to define the iterator methods within the class that implements the ADT in question. Such an iterator is called an **internal iterator.** In this case, we will define a class that implements the two interfaces `ListInterface`, introduced in Chapter 4, and `BasicIteratorInterface`. Let's call the resulting class `ListWithInternalIterator`.

Suppose that we want to use this class to create a list of names. We will use strings for the names, but we could also use instances of the class `Name` that Chapter 1 presented. The following Java statements create such a list:

```java
String jamie = "Jamie";
String joey = "Joey";
String rachel = "Rachel";

ListWithInternalIterator nameList = new ListWithInternalIterator();
nameList.add(jamie);
nameList.add(joey);
nameList.add(rachel);
```

At this point, nameList contains the names

> Jamie
> Joey
> Rachel

We now invoke nameList.reset() to initialize the iterator. The following sequence of events demonstrates the iterator methods; this sequence is illustrated in Figure 7-1:

- nameList.hasCurrent() returns true because a current entry—the first one in the list—exists.
- nameList.getCurrent() returns the string *Jamie*.
- nameList.advance() advances the iteration to the next name in the list and returns true.
- nameList.getCurrent() returns the string *Joey*.
- nameList.advance() advances the iteration to the next name in the list and returns true.
- nameList.getCurrent() returns the string *Rachel*.
- nameList.advance() advances the iteration beyond the end of the list and returns false.
- nameList.hasCurrent() returns false.

Figure 7-1   The effect of iterator methods on a list

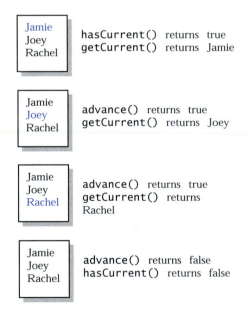

7.5   **Example.** We can use the iterator to display the entries in the list. The following Java statements display the list nameList that Segment 7.4 defined:

```java
nameList.reset();
while (nameList.hasCurrent())
{
  System.out.println(nameList.getCurrent());
  nameList.advance();
} // end while
```

Compare this code with the `for` loop given in Segment 7.1. Both loops are independent of the implementation of the list. But this loop potentially can take less time to execute than the `for` loop. Since this iterator keeps track of its position within the list, `getCurrent` can access and return the current entry in the iteration faster, in general, than `getEntry` can in the `for` loop. As we noted in Segment 7.2, when a linked chain of nodes implements a list, `getEntry` must move from node to node until it reaches the desired one.

Question 1   Assume that `nameList` is an instance of `ListWithInternalIterator` and contains at least three entries. Write Java statements that

a. Display the third entry.
b. Display the even-numbered entries in the list. That is, display the second entry, the fourth entry, and so on.

Iterator Methods That Modify the ADT

7.6   Some iterators let you add, remove, or replace entries during a traversal. We can define a more extensive interface that includes such methods. Our new interface extends the previous `BasicIteratorInterface` as follows. Although it is not necessary to repeat the declarations of the methods in `BasicIteratorInterface`, we do so for reference.

```java
import java.util.NoSuchElementException;
public interface IteratorInterface extends BasicIteratorInterface
{
  public boolean hasCurrent();
  public boolean advance();
  public Object getCurrent() throws NoSuchElementException;
  public void reset();

  /** Task: Adds a new entry immediately after the current entry,
   *          if one exists.
   *   @param newEntry  the object that is the new entry
   *   @throws NoSuchElementException, if no current entry exists */
  public void addAfterCurrent(Object newEntry)
                            throws NoSuchElementException;

  /** Task: Removes the current entry, if one exists, and
   *          advances the iteration to the next entry.
   *   @throws NoSuchElementException, if no current entry exists */
  public void removeCurrent() throws NoSuchElementException;

  /** Task: Replaces the current entry with a new entry.
   *   @param newEntry  the object that replaces the current entry
   *   @throws NoSuchElementException, if no current entry exists */
  public void replaceCurrent(Object newEntry)
                            throws NoSuchElementException;
} // end IteratorInterface
```

Note: An iterator can add, remove, or replace entries during a traversal.

7.7 **Example.** Once again, assume that the list `nameList` contains the names

> Jamie
> Joey
> Rachel

and that we invoke `nameList.reset()`. Figure 7-2 illustrates the following sequence of events:

- `nameList.hasCurrent()` returns true because a current entry—the first one in the list—exists.
- `nameList.getCurrent()` returns the string *Jamie*.
- `nameList.advance()` advances the iteration to the next name in the list and returns true.
- `nameList.getCurrent()` returns the string *Joey*.
- `nameList.removeCurrent()` removes *Joey* from the list.
- `nameList.getCurrent()` returns the string *Rachel*.

Figure 7-2   The effect of iterator methods on a list

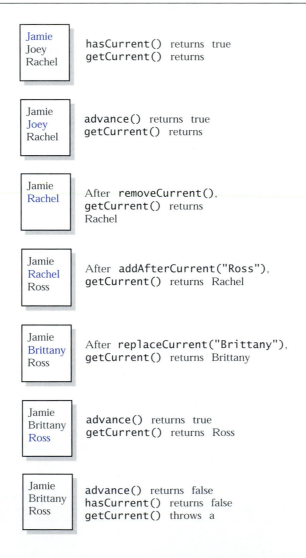

- nameList.addAfterCurrent("Ross") adds the string *Ross* after *Rachel*.
- nameList.getCurrent() returns the string *Rachel*.
- nameList.replaceCurrent("Brittany") replaces *Rachel* with *Brittany*.
- nameList.getCurrent() returns the string *Brittany*.
- nameList.advance() advances the iteration to the next name in the list and returns true.
- nameList.getCurrent() returns the string *Ross*.
- nameList.advance() advances the iteration beyond the end of the list and returns false.
- nameList.hasCurrent() returns false.
- nameList.getCurrent() throws a NoSuchElementException.

7.8   The iterator methods addAfterCurrent and removeCurrent enable us to alter the list, with a predictable effect on the iteration. What happens if we alter the list by using the list operations add or remove? Subsequent calls to the iterator's methods could be unpredictable. For example, if we know the position of the current entry and use remove instead of removeCurrent to delete it, further iteration might not be reliable. You should be careful when using add and remove during an iteration.

Question 2   Beginning with the list nameList that contains the names *Jamie, Joey,* and *Rachel,* describe the effect of the following Java statements:

```
nameList.reset();
String name = (String) nameList.getCurrent();
nameList.removeCurrent();
nameList.advance();
nameList.addAfterCurrent(name);
System.out.println(nameList.getCurrent());
nameList.display();
```

Implementing an Internal Iterator

7.9   In this section we modify the linked implementation of the list given in Chapter 6 by including the methods that IteratorInterface specifies. In doing so, we provide our list with an internal iterator. The resulting class has the following form. The differences between this class and the class outlined in Segment 6.23 appear in color.

```java
import java.util.NoSuchElementException;
public class LinkedListWithInternalIterator
                     implements ListInterface, IteratorInterface
{
  private Node firstNode;
  private int  length;
  private Node currentNode; // current node in iteration
  private Node priorNode;   // node before the current node

  public LinkedListWithInternalIterator()
  {
    clear();
  } // end default constructor

  public final void clear()
  {
    firstNode = null;
    length = 0;
```

```
                currentNode = null;
                priorNode = null;
            } // end clear
```

> *< Implementations of the remaining methods of the ADT list go here;*
> *you can see them in Chapter 6, beginning at Segment 6.24. >*
>   . . .
> *< Implementations of the methods in IteratorInterface go here;*
> *you will see them soon. >*
>   . . .
> *< Implementation of the private class Node (Segment 6.22) goes here. >*
>   . . .

```
            } // end LinkedListWithInternalIterator
```

Just as you can use your finger to keep track of your place on this page, our iterator implementation uses a reference to keep track of the iterator's position within the list entries. This reference, which we call currentNode, is an added data field of the class. As you will see, the removeCurrent method will need a reference to the node before the current one. This reference is the data field priorNode. The default constructor initializes the references to the first, current, and previous nodes to null by calling the method clear.

7.10   **The method hasCurrent.** The methods in IteratorInterface work with the current entry in the list as the iteration progresses. Each method begins by determining whether the current entry in the iteration exists, so we begin by implementing the method hasCurrent:

```
public boolean hasCurrent()
{
  return currentNode != null;
} // end hasCurrent
```

7.11   **The method getCurrent.** The method getCurrent retrieves the current entry. If the list is empty or the iterator has already reached the end of the list, no current entry will exist. In that case, the method throws an exception. We have chosen to throw an exception because the iterators that Java specifies throw exceptions. For simplicity, we use an exception provided by Java, namely NoSuchElementException.

```
public Object getCurrent() throws NoSuchElementException
{
  if (hasCurrent())
    return currentNode.data; // or return currentNode.getData()
  else
    throw new NoSuchElementException("getCurrent(): " +
                                    "no current entry");
} // end getCurrent
```

The definition of the private class Node given in Segment 6.22 of Chapter 6 did not include set and get methods for the private data fields data and next, since we can access them directly by name. As we mentioned in Segment 6.42, however, it can be a good idea to include set and get methods when defining a private inner class. If we had done so, we could write currentNode.get-Data() instead of currentNode.data, for example. Although we will continue to use the class Node in both this chapter and the next without set and get methods, as it was defined in Segment 6.22, we will add set and get methods to the private classes we create from now on.

7.12 **The method `replaceCurrent`.** To replace the current entry, the method `replaceCurrent` uses a similar implementation:

```java
public void replaceCurrent(Object newEntry) throws NoSuchElementException
{
  if (hasCurrent())
    currentNode.data = newEntry;
  else
    throw new NoSuchElementException("replaceCurrent(): " +
                                     "no current entry");
} // end replaceCurrent
```

Question 3   Consider a list of strings whose first two entries are *Jim* and *Judy,* and an iterator that is at the beginning of the list. If the iterator calls the method `replaceCurrent` with the string *Ben* as its argument, what does a subsequent call to `getCurrent` return?

7.13 **The method `advance`.** Before we advance `currentNode` so that it references the next entry in the list, we must copy its value to `priorNode`. In this way, the method `remove` will have references to both the current entry and to the entry that precedes it. Recall that you need both references to remove a node from a linked chain. Advancing the current entry's reference to the next entry is also straightforward. The only subtlety involves the return value: If `currentNode` references the last entry, advancing it makes `currentNode` `null` and the return value false.

```java
public boolean advance()
{
  boolean result = false;

  if (hasCurrent())
  {
    priorNode = currentNode;
    currentNode = currentNode.next;
    result = hasCurrent();
  }
  return result;
} // end advance
```

Question 4   If `currentNode` references the last entry in a list, a call to `hasCurrent` would return true. What would a call to `advance` return? Why?

7.14 **The method `removeCurrent`.** Removing the current entry takes a bit more care. Recall from Segment 6.34 of Chapter 6 that removing a node from a chain of linked nodes considers two cases. If the node to be removed—that is, the current node—is not first in the chain, you need a reference to the node before the current node. We have maintained such a reference in `priorNode`. Notice that we can determine whether the current node is first because `priorNode` is `null` in that case. The following implementation uses these observations:

```java
public void removeCurrent() throws NoSuchElementException
{
  if (hasCurrent())
  {
    length--;

    if (priorNode == null) // current node is first in list
    {
      firstNode = currentNode.next;
      currentNode = firstNode;
    }
```

```
        else                    // current node is not first in list
        {
          priorNode.next = currentNode.next;
          currentNode = currentNode.next;
        } // end if
      }
      else                      // no current node
        throw new NoSuchElementException("removeCurrent(): " +
                                         "no current entry");
    } // end removeCurrent
```

Figures 7-3 and 7-4 illustrate the steps in this method. After the method removes the current node, `currentNode` references the node that was after the one just removed, if such a node exists. Thus, if there is an entry after the one removed, it becomes the current entry. Otherwise, when the removed node was last in the list, `currentNode` becomes `null`.

Figure 7-3   Before and after removing the current entry when its node is first in the chain

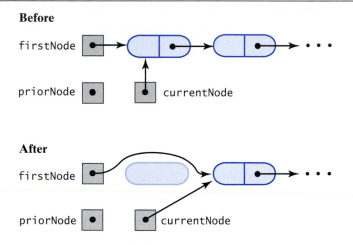

Figure 7-4   Before and after removing the current entry when its node is not first in the chain

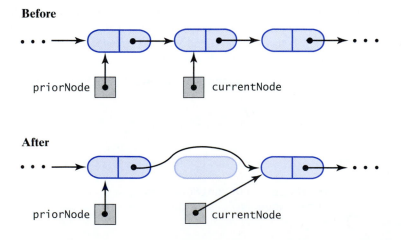

Question 5   Describe how Figure 7-3 would appear if the list contained only one entry.

Question 6   Describe how Figure 7-4 would appear if the current entry was last in the list.

Question 7   If `currentNode` references the last entry in a list, which list entry does a call to `removeCurrent` remove?

Question 8   Following the call to `removeCurrent` in Question 7, what will a subsequent call to `hasCurrent` return? Why?

7.15   **The method `addAfterCurrent`.** Finally, when a current entry exists, adding an entry after it requires one case, as Figure 7-5 illustrates. Note that this addition does not change the reference to the current node. What was the current entry before the addition is still the current entry afterward.

Figure 7-5   Before and after adding an entry after the current entry

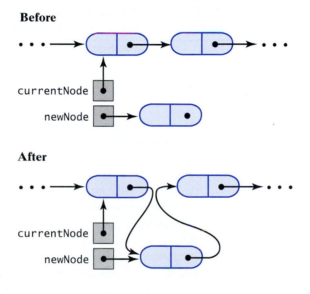

```java
public void addAfterCurrent(Object newEntry)
                          throws NoSuchElementException
{
  if (hasCurrent())
  {
    Node newNode = new Node(newEntry);
    newNode.next = currentNode.next;
    currentNode.next = newNode;
    length++;
  }
  else
    throw new NoSuchElementException("addAfterCurrent(): " +
                                    "no current entry");
} // end addAfterCurrent.
```

Question 9   Describe how Figure 7-5 would appear if the current entry was last in the list.

7.16   **The method reset.** The last iterator method is `reset`:

```java
public void reset()
{
   currentNode = firstNode;
   priorNode = null;
} // end reset
```

We can use this method to set the iteration to the beginning of the list.

Note: **Internal iterators**

An internal iterator results when you implement the iterator methods within the class that implements the ADT. Thus, an internal iterator can access an ADT's data fields directly without using the public methods of the ADT. However, you can have only one instance of such an iterator at a time. As you will see in the next section, this restriction is a disadvantage.

Implementing an Iterator as Its Own Class

7.17   An internal iterator might be easy to understand and use, but only one iteration of a list can occur at any time. Why would you want more than one iteration to be in progress simultaneously? Imagine a printed list of names that are not distinct and are in no particular order. Using an internal iterator is like running one finger down that list to count the names. Now suppose that you want to count the number of times each name occurs in the list. You can use two fingers, as follows. With your left hand, use one finger to point to the first name in the list. With your right hand, use one finger to point to each of the names in the list, starting with the first one. As you traverse the list with your right hand, compare each name to the name that your left hand marks. In this way, you can count the number of times the first name occurs in the list. Now move your left-hand finger to the next name in the list and use your right hand to point to the beginning of the list. Repeat the previous process to count the number of times that the second name appears in the list. Try it with the names in Figure 7-6. (Since your left hand will encounter Jane three times, you will repeat the computation needlessly unless you are careful. We consider this detail a bit later.)

Each of your two fingers can traverse the list independently of the other. They are like two independent iterators that traverse the same list. An internal iterator would not give you this capability. Instead you must implement the iterator methods as a class separate from the class that implements the ADT—such as a list—to which you will apply the iterator. The two classes must, of course, interact in some way. The iterator, then, is an object separate from the list, and you can have several such iterator objects in existence at the same time.

The iterator class can be public and separate from the class that implements the ADT. An instance of such an iterator class is called an **external iterator.** The iterator class can also be a private inner class of the class that implements the ADT. An instance of this inner class is called an **inner class iterator.** You use both of these iterators in the same way. But as you will see, an inner class iterator usually can execute faster than an external iterator.

Figure 7-6   Counting the number of times that Jane appears in a list of names

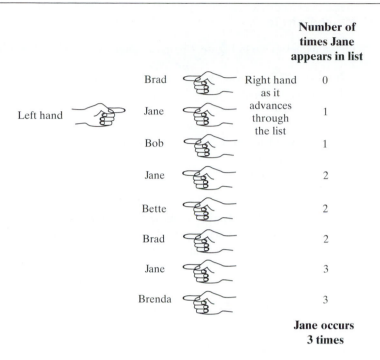

Let's write some code that counts the occurrences of each name in the list in Figure 7-6. Let

7.18   Suppose that nameIterator is either an external iterator or an inner class iterator that is associated with the list of names shown in Figure 7-6. We could invoke the methods in IteratorInterface just as the internal iterator did in Segment 7.4, replacing nameList with nameIterator. Thus, for example,

- nameIterator.hasCurrent() returns true because a current entry exists.
- nameIterator.getCurrent() returns the string *Brad*.

Let's write some code that counts the occurrences of each name in the list in Figure 7-6. Let nameIterator correspond to your left hand in the figure. Now we'll define a second iterator, countingIterator, that corresponds to your right hand. For each name that your left hand marks, your right hand traverses the entire list to count the occurrences of that name. Thus, we have the following nested loops:

```
while (nameIterator.hasCurrent())
{
   String currentName = (String)nameIterator.getCurrent();

   int nameCount = 0;
   countingIterator.reset();
   while (countingIterator.hasCurrent())
   {
      String nextName = (String)countingIterator.getCurrent();
      if (currentName.equals(nextName))
         nameCount++;

      countingIterator.advance();
   } // end while
```

```
        System.out.println(currentName + " occurs " +
                            nameCount + " times.");
        nameIterator.advance();
    } // end while
```

With the names given in Figure 7-6, these statements produce the following output:

> Brad occurs 2 times.
> Jane occurs 3 times.
> Bob occurs 1 times.
> Jane occurs 3 times.
> Bette occurs 1 times.
> Brad occurs 2 times.
> Jane occurs 3 times.
> Brenda occurs 1 times.

As you can see, since `nameIterator` (your left hand) encounters *Brad* twice and *Jane* three times, the computation in the inner loop is repeated needlessly. For example, we compute that *Brad* occurs twice each time `nameIterator` encounters *Brad*.

If we are allowed to destroy the list, we can remove the duplicate entries—and thereby prevent the repeated computations—by modifying the `if` statement as follows:

```
if (currentName.equals(nextName))
{
  nameCount++;
  if (nameCount > 1)
    countingIterator.removeCurrent();
} // end if
```

When `nameCount` exceeds 1, the current entry of `countingIterator` must be a name that the iterator has already encountered in the list. Thus, we remove that entry. The iteration continues with the next entry, which is the new current entry. Exercise 9 at the end of this chapter considers the case when we cannot destroy the list.

An External Iterator

7.19   Suppose that the iterator class `ExternalIterator` implements the interface `IteratorInterface`. After creating a list `nameList`, we would create an instance of the iterator, as follows:

```
ExternalIterator nameIterator = new ExternalIterator(nameList);
```

This invocation of `ExternalIterator`'s constructor connects the iterator `nameIterator` to the list `nameList` by making one of the class's data fields reference `nameList`. The class has an integer as another data field that indicates the current position of the iteration within the list.

Thus, the class `ExternalIterator` could begin as follows:

```
public class ExternalIterator implements IteratorInterface
{
  private ListInterface list;  // reference to list
  private int currentPosition; // iterator position

  public ExternalIterator(ListInterface aList)
  {
```

```
            list = aList;
            currentPosition = 1;
        } // end constructor


            . . .

    } // end ExternalIterator
```

In addition to connecting the iterator to the list in question, the constructor begins the iteration at the first entry in the list.

7.20   The class `ExternalIterator` has no special access to the private data fields of the class that implements the list. It is a client of the list and so can process the list only by using the list's ADT operations. Figure 7-7 shows an external iterator with a reference to an ADT but with no knowledge of the ADT's implementation. The implementations of the iterator methods will use methods specified in `ListInterface`. The resulting implementations are rather straightforward but take longer to execute, in general, than the corresponding implementations for an internal iterator.

Figure 7-7   An external iterator with a reference to an ADT, an indicator of its position within the iteration, and no knowledge of the ADT's implementation

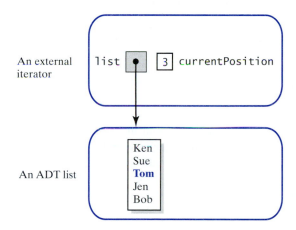

For example, to retrieve the current entry in the iteration, `getCurrent` uses the list's `getEntry` method:

```
public Object getCurrent() throws NoSuchElementException
{
    if (hasCurrent())
        return list.getEntry(currentPosition);
    else
        throw new NoSuchElementException("getCurrent(): " +
                                         "no current entry");
} // end getCurrent
```

The list method `getEntry` must traverse the linked chain of nodes to locate the node that contains the current entry. In contrast, the implementation of `getCurrent` in Segment 7.11 simply returned `currentNode.data`.

We leave as exercises the implementations of the other methods in `IteratorInterface`. These implementations are independent of the implementation of the list and are actually simpler than those in the previous internal iterator. In general, however, they take longer to execute.

Note: **External iterators**

An external iterator must access an ADT's data by using the public methods of the ADT. Thus, the typical external iterator takes longer to perform its operations than do other kinds of iterators. On the other hand, the implementation of an external iterator is usually straightforward. Additionally, you can have several independent external iterators in existence at the same time for a given ADT.

To provide an iterator for an existing implementation of an ADT that cannot be altered, you must use an external iterator.

An Inner Class Iterator

7.21   The internal iterator is efficient because it has direct access to the list's private data fields. But you can have only one such iteration in progress at a time. The external iterator as a public class allows multiple and distinct iterations to exist simultaneously. However, since the iterator can access the list's data fields only indirectly via ADT operations, the iteration takes more time than one performed by an internal iterator. The solution is to define the separate iterator class as an inner class of the ADT. Because the iterator is a separate class, you can have multiple iterations in progress at the same time. Moreover, since the iterator is an inner class, it has direct access to the ADT's data fields. For these reasons, an inner class iterator is usually preferable to an internal or external iterator.

To achieve our goal, we start by rearranging the pieces of the class that contained an internal iterator. We began that implementation in Segment 7.9. We will take the implementations of the methods specified in `IteratorInterface` and place them into a new inner class, `IteratorForLinkedList`. The outer class `LinkedListWithIterator` will be much like the class `LList` of Chapter 6 (Segment 6.23). It needs another method, however, that the client can use to create an iterator. This method, `getListIterator`, has the following simple implementation:

```
public IteratorInterface getListIterator()
{
   return new IteratorForLinkedList();
} // end getListIterator
```

We will show you how to use this method shortly.

To accommodate this new method, we create the following new interface that extends `ListInterface` instead of changing it:

```
public interface ListWithIteratorInterface extends ListInterface
{
   public IteratorInterface getListIterator();
} // end ListWithIteratorInterface
```

This interface has all the list methods of `ListInterface` and the new method `getListIterator`.

Because a class can implement more than one interface, we can define the class LinkedListWithIterator without using our new interface. Having the interface, however, enables us to declare an object of type ListWithIteratorInterface and know that the object will have the list methods and the method getListIterator.

7.22   Now we can outline our new classes:

```java
import java.util.NoSuchElementException;
public class LinkedListWithIterator implements
                                    ListWithIteratorInterface
{
  private Node firstNode;
  private int  length;

  < Implementations of the constructor and methods of the ADT list go here;
      you can see them in Chapter 6, beginning at Segment 6.23. >
  . . .
  public IteratorInterface getListIterator()
  {
    return new IteratorForLinkedList();
  } // end getListIterator

  private class IteratorForLinkedList implements IteratorInterface
  {
    private Node currentNode; // current node in iteration
    private Node priorNode;   // node before the current node

    public IteratorForLinkedList()
    {
      currentNode = firstNode;
      priorNode = null;
    } // end default constructor

    < Implementations of the methods in IteratorInterface go here. >
    . . .
  } // end IteratorForLinkedList

  < Implementation of the private class Node (Segment 6.22) goes here. >
  . . .
} // end LinkedListWithIterator
```

The implementations of the methods declared in IteratorInterface appear within the inner class IteratorForLinkedList. They are the same as the implementations in the class LinkedListWith-InternalIterator, given in Segments 7.10 through 7.16.

7.23   **Example: Using an iterator to display a list.** Since we've defined an interface ListWithIterra-torInterface that includes the method getListIterator and the methods of ListInterface, we can use it to create a new list:

```java
ListWithIteratorInterface myList = new LinkedListWithIterator();
```

Now if we add entries to this list, we can display them by using our iterator.

We first create an iterator object by invoking the new list method getListIterator:

```java
IteratorInterface myIterator = myList.getListIterator();
```

We then write a loop that is similar to the one you saw in Segment 7.5. Here the iterator object instead of the list object invokes the iterator methods:

```java
while (myIterator.hasCurrent())
{
    System.out.println(myIterator.getCurrent());
    myIterator.advance();
} // end while
```

Figure 7-8 illustrates an inner class iterator such as `myIterator`. The iterator has direct access to the ADT's underlying data structure—a linked chain, in this example. Thus, the iterator can quickly retrieve the current entry in the iteration.

Figure 7-8   An inner class iterator with direct access to the linked chain that implements the ADT

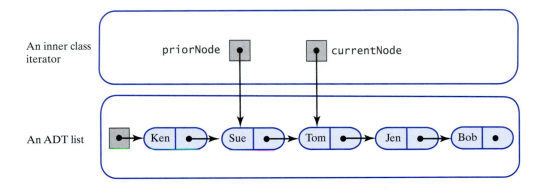

 Note: Inner class iterators
An inner class iterator has direct access to an ADT's data, so it is as efficient as an internal iterator with about the same implementation effort. The advantage is that you can have several iterator objects in existence at the same time. These iterators can traverse a list independently of one another.

CHAPTER SUMMARY

- An iterator is a program component that enables you to traverse a collection of data. During the traversal, you can look at the data entries, modify them, add entries, and remove entries.

- An internal iterator results when you add the iterator's operations to the class that implements the ADT. As such, it can efficiently access an ADT's data.

- An internal iterator allows only one iteration of a list at any time.

- An external iterator is an object of a public class that implements the iterator methods. This class is separate from but interacts with the class that implements the ADT. An external iterator must access an ADT's data by using the public methods of the ADT. Thus, the typical external iterator takes longer to perform its operations than other kinds of iterators. On the other hand, implementing an external iterator is usually straightforward.

- An external iterator enables you to have several iterators that traverse an ADT's data independently.

- An inner class iterator is an instance of an inner class defined within the class that implements the ADT to be traversed. The inner class implements the iterator methods and has direct access to the ADT's private data. Thus, its methods can execute as quickly as those of an internal iterator with about the same implementation effort. In addition, you can have several independent iterator objects in existence at the same time.

- Typically, an inner class iterator is preferable to other types of iterators.

EXERCISES

1. Describe the main advantage of an internal iterator over an external iterator, the main advantage of an external iterator over an internal iterator, and how an inner class iterator has both advantages.

2. Suppose that `nameList` is a list that contains the following strings: *Kyle, Cathy, Sam, Austin, Sara.* What output is produced by the following sequence of statements?

```java
IteratorInterface nameIterator = nameList.getListIterator();
System.out.println(nameIterator.getCurrent());
nameIterator.advance();
nameIterator.advance();
System.out.println(nameIterator.getCurrent());
nameIterator.replaceCurrent("Brittany");
nameIterator.advance();
nameIterator.removeCurrent();
System.out.println(nameIterator.getCurrent());
nameList.display();
```

3. Repeat Exercise 2, but instead use the following statements:

```java
IteratorInterface nameIterator = nameList.getListIterator();
nameIterator.removeCurrent();
nameIterator.removeCurrent();
nameIterator.advance();
System.out.println(nameIterator.getCurrent());
nameIterator.advance();
nameIterator.replaceCurrent("Brittany");
nameList.display();
System.out.println(nameIterator.getCurrent());
nameIterator.advance();
System.out.println(nameIterator.getCurrent());
```

4. Suppose that `nameList` is a list of at least one string and that `nameIterator` is defined as follows:

```java
IteratorInterface nameIterator = nameList.getListIterator();
```

Write Java statements that use `nameIterator` to display only the last string in the list. Do this in two ways, as follows:

a. Use the method `hasCurrent`.

b. Do not use the method `hasCurrent`.

5. Consider adding a method `getNext` to `BasicInteratorInterface` with the following specifications:

```
/** Task: Retrieves the current entry in the iteration and then
 *   advances the current position of the iteration by 1.
 *   @return the current entry in the iteration, if one exists
 *   @throws NoSuchElementException, if no current entry
 *            exists */
public Object getNext() throws NoSuchElementException;
```

Implement this method by using methods in `BasicInteratorInterface`.

6. Given a list of strings and an iterator `nameIterator` whose data type is `IteratorInterface`, write statements that remove all occurrences of the string *CANCEL* from the list.

7. Given a list of strings and an iterator `nameIterator` whose data type is `IteratorInterface`, write statements that add the string *Bob* after the first occurrence of the string *Sam*.

8. Given a list of strings and an iterator object `nameIterator` whose data type is `IteratorInterface`, write statements that remove any duplicates in the list.

9. Given a list of strings and an iterator object `nameIterator` whose data type is `IteratorInterface`, count the number of times each string occurs in a list of strings without altering the list. Assume that you have an implementation of the ADT set. A set is an ADT that rejects duplicate entries. It includes the following methods add and `contains`:

```
/** Task: Adds an entry to the set if it is not already present.
 *   @param newEntry  an object to be added as a new entry
 *   @return true if the entry was added */
public boolean add(Object newEntry);

/** Task: Determines whether the set contains a given entry.
 *   @param anEntry  the object that is the desired entry */
 *   @return true if the set contains anEntry */
public boolean contains(Object anEntry);
```

10. Given a list of strings and an iterator `nameIterator`, write Java code that shows how calls to the method add can cause conflict or inconsistency for an iterator. Assume the implementation given in Segment 7.9 and illustrate your code with pictures similar to those of Figures 7-3 and 7-4.

11. When an iterator is at the last item in a list, a call to advance returns false. A subsequent call to `hasCurrent` would then also return false, and a call to `getCurrent` would throw an exception. Consider the following alternate approach. When the iterator is at the last item in a list, a call to advance moves the iterator to the first item in the list. Describe the major drawback to such an approach.

12. Consider adding a method `addBeforeCurrent(Object newEntry)` to the `IteratorInterface` of Segment 7.6. The method would be similar to `addAfterCurrent` except that the new entry is inserted immediately before the current entry if one exists. Show how this might be implemented in the internal iterator of Segment 7.9.

PROJECTS

1. Revise the class AList, which uses an array to implement the ADT list, as follows. Have the class implement the interface IteratorInterface as an inner class. The class AList is given in Segments 5.5 through 5.10 of Chapter 5.

2. Complete the implementation of the class ExternalIterator that was begun in Segment 7.19.

3. Write Java code that uses iterators to rearrange a list of strings so that they are alphabetical. For example, if you rearrange the list given in Segment 7.17, the resulting list should be *Bette, Bob, Brad, Brad, Brenda, Jane, Jane, Jane*.

4. Implement the internal iterator of Segment 7.9 along with the method addBeforeCurrent described in Exercise 12. Use this iterator to write code that reverses a list of strings, as follows: Repeatedly remove the first string from the list and add it before the current first string of a new list.

Java's Iterator Interfaces

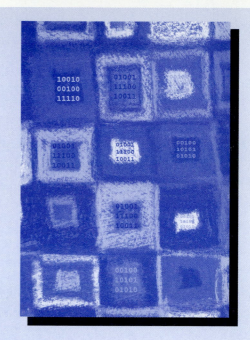

CONTENTS

The Interface `Iterator`
Implementing the Interface `Iterator`
    A Linked Implementation
    An Array-Based Implementation
The Interface `ListIterator`
    Using the Interface `ListIterator`
An Array-Based Implementation of the Interface `ListIterator`
    The Inner Class
Java Class Library: `ArrayList` and `LinkedList` Revisited

PREREQUISITES

Chapter   5   List Implementations That Use Arrays
Chapter   6   List Implementations That Link Data
Chapter   7   Iterators
Appendix B   Exception Handling

OBJECTIVES

After studying this chapter, you should be able to

- Use an iterator that implements the Java interface `Iterator`
- Implement the interface `Iterator` as an inner class
- Use an iterator that implements the Java interface `ListIterator`
- Implement the interface `ListIterator` as an inner class

The previous chapter showed you how to define and use an iterator to traverse a collection of data. During the traversal, you can look at the data entries, modify them, add entries, and remove entries. You saw several ways to implement an iterator, and you learned that using an inner class for the iterator is desirable. This approach allows the iterator direct and efficient access to the ADT's underlying data structure. It also enables you to have several independent iterators in existence simultaneously.

In the previous chapter we implemented our own iterator interface. This chapter discusses and implements two iterator interfaces that Java provides, `Iterator` and `ListIterator`.

The Interface `Iterator`

8.1   Although the iterator we implemented in the previous chapter is useful and easy to understand, you still should be familiar with the iterator interfaces that Java provides. The Java Class Library provides two interfaces for iterators—`Iterator` and `ListIterator`—in the package `java.util`.

The interface `Iterator` specifies only three iterator methods—`hasNext`, `next`, and `remove`. These methods traverse a collection of data from its beginning. We still have a current entry in a list, and initially it is the first entry. The iterator marks the current entry much as your finger can point to an entry in a list or to a line on this page.

The method `hasNext` determines whether a current entry exists and returns true or false accordingly. It behaves just as our method `hasCurrent` does in the previous chapter. (See Segment 7.10.)

If a current entry exists, the method `next` returns a reference to the current entry and then advances the iterator's marker to the next entry in the list, as Figure 8-1 illustrates. Thus, `next` combines the behaviors of our methods `getCurrent` and `advance` from `BasicIteratorInterface`. (See Segment 7.3.) Repeated calls to `next` traverse through the list.

The method `remove` removes the entry that `next` just returned. When you implement the `Iterator` interface, you do not have to provide a `remove` operation—it is optional—but you do need to define a method `remove`, because it appears in the interface. Such a method would simply throw the exception `UnsupportedOperationException` if the client invokes it.

Note that `Iterator` does not include a method that resets the iteration to the list's beginning.

Figure 8-1   The effect of a call to `next` on a list

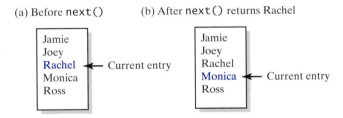

8.2   As you read through the specifications of the methods in the interface `Iterator`, compare the methods with those in our `BasicIteratorInterface`.

```
package java.util;
public interface Iterator
{
    /** Task: Determines whether the iteration has completed its traversal
     *           and gone beyond the last entry in the collection of data.
```

```
     *    @return true if the iteration has another entry to return */
     boolean hasNext();

     /** Task: Retrieves the current (next) entry in the collection
     *            and advances the iteration by one position.
     *    @return a reference to the current entry in the iteration,
     *            if one exists
     *    @throws NoSuchElementException if the iteration had reached the
     *            end already, that is, if hasNext() is false */
     Object next();

     /** Task: Removes from the collection of data the last entry
     *            that next() returned. A subsequent call to next() will
     *            behave as it would have before the removal.
     *    Precondition: next() has been called, and remove() has not
     *            been called since then. The collection has not been
     *            altered during the iteration except by calls to this
     *            method.
     *    @throws IllegalStateException if next() has not been called,
     *            or if remove() was called already after the last
     *            call to next().
     *    @throws UnsupportedOperationException if this iterator does
     *            not permit a remove operation. */
     void remove();   // Optional
} // end Iterator
```

All of the exceptions mentioned in this interface are run-time exceptions, and so they do not have to appear within a `throws` clause of the methods' signatures. Also, you do not have to write `try` and `catch` blocks when you invoke these methods.

8.3

E

Example. Let's look at an example of how these methods work with the ADT list. Assume that we have implemented the interface `Iterator` as an inner class of the class that implements the ADT list. Further, assume that the list class has the method `getListIterator`. If `nameList` is a list containing the following names:

Jamie
Joey
Rachel

and `nameIterator` is defined as

```
     Iterator nameIterator = nameList.getListIterator();
```

the following sequence of events demonstrates the iterator methods:

- `nameIterator.hasNext()` returns true because a next entry exists.
- `nameIterator.next()` returns the string *Jamie* and advances the iteration.
- `nameIterator.next()` returns the string *Joey* and advances the iteration.
- `nameIterator.remove()` removes *Joey* from the list.
- `nameIterator.next()` returns the string *Rachel* and advances the iteration.
- `nameIterator.hasNext()` returns false because the iteration is beyond the end of the list.
- `nameIterator.next()` causes a `NoSuchElementException`.

Figure 8-2 illustrates these events.

Figure 8-2   The effect of iterator methods on a list

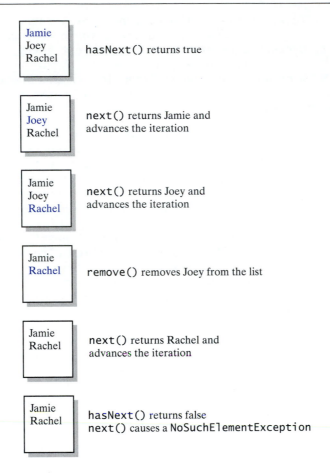

Question 1   Assume that `nameList` is a list that contains at least three entries and that `nameIterator` is defined as in Segment 8.3. If `nameIterator` is at the beginning of the list, write Java statements that display the list's third entry.

Question 2   Given `nameList` and `nameIterator` as described in Question 1, write statements that display the even-numbered entries in the list. That is, display the second entry, the fourth entry, and so on.

Question 3   Given `nameList` and `nameIterator` as described in Question 1, write statements that remove all entries from the list.

8.4
Example. Let's consider two situations that cause the exception `IllegalStateException`. If the iteration is at the beginning of the list and we write

```
nameIterator.hasNext();
nameIterator.remove();
```

an IllegalStateException occurs because next was not called before we called remove. Similarly, if we write

```
nameIterator.next();
nameIterator.remove();
nameIterator.remove();
```

the second remove causes an IllegalStateException because remove had been called already since the most recent call to next.

Note: Java's Iterator interface specifies three methods: hasNext, next, and remove.

Implementing the Interface Iterator

8.5   In this section, we will implement the interface Iterator by adding an inner class to each of two implementations of the ADT list. First, we will use a linked implementation of the list but will provide only the iterator operations hasNext and next. Then we will use an array-based list and implement all three methods of Iterator.

As we did in Segment 7.21 of Chapter 7, we will define another interface that the list class can implement. It includes the operations of the ADT list and the method getListIterator. In this case, the method returns an instance of Iterator instead of returning an instance of IteratorInterface, as the method in Chapter 7 did.

```
import java.util.*;
public interface ListWithIteratorInterface extends ListInterface
{
   public Iterator getListIterator();
} // end ListWithIteratorInterface
```

A Linked Implementation

8.6   In this implementation, we do not want our iterator to support the remove method. We begin as we did in Segment 7.22 with the class LinkedListWithIterator, but we revise ListWithIteratorInterface as in Segment 8.5. Additionally, the inner class IteratorForLinkedList implements Iterator instead of IteratorInterface and has a different implementation.

```
import java.util.NoSuchElementException;
import java.util.iterator;
public class LinkedListWithIterator implements
                                        ListWithIteratorInterface
{
   private Node firstNode;
   private int  length;

   < Implementations of the constructor and methods of the ADT list go here;
       you can see them in Chapter 6, beginning at Segment 6.23. >
   . . .
   public Iterator getListIterator()
   {
```

```
      return new IteratorForLinkedList();
   } // end getListIterator

   private class IteratorForLinkedList implements Iterator
   {
      private Node currentNode; // current node in iteration

      public IteratorForLinkedList()
      {
         currentNode = firstNode;
      } // end default constructor
```

< Implementations of methods in the interface *Iterator go here. >*
      . . .
```
   } // end IteratorForLinkedList
```

< Implementation of the private class Node (Segment 6.22) goes here. >
      . . .
```
} // end LinkedListWithIterator
```

8.7 **The method hasNext.** Now consider the implementations of the methods in the inner class IteratorForLinkedList. The method hasNext has the same implementation as hasCurrent did in Segment 7.10 for our interface IteratorInterface:

```
public boolean hasNext()
{
   return currentNode != null;
} // end hasNext
```

8.8 **The method next.** The implementation of next is a bit more involved. If hasNext returns true, next should return the entry at currentNode and then advance currentNode. But if hasNext returns false, the method next should throw an exception.

```
public Object next() throws NoSuchElementException
{
   if (hasNext())
   {
      Node returnNode = currentNode;   // get current node
      currentNode = currentNode.next; // advance iteration

      return returnNode.data;          // return data in current node
   }
   else
      throw new NoSuchElementException("Iteration has ended; " +
                                       "illegal call to next.");
} // end next
```

8.9 **The method remove.** Even though we decided not to support a remove operation for this iterator, we must implement the method because it is declared in the interface Iterator. If the client invokes remove, the method simply throws the exception UnsupportedOperationException.

```
public void remove() throws UnsupportedOperationException
{
   throw new UnsupportedOperationException("remove() is not " +
                                           "supported by this iterator");
} // end remove
```

This exception is in the package java.lang and so is included automatically in every Java program. Thus, the second import statement at the beginning of the class LinkedListWithIterator in Segment 8.6 is unnecessary.

Note: The remove method
An iterator that does not allow the removal of items during a traversal is not unusual. In such cases, the remove method is implemented, but it throws an exception if invoked.

An Array-Based Implementation

8.10   For the array-based implementation, our iterator will support the remove method. Let's begin with an array-based implementation of the ADT list. The class has the same data fields and methods as the classes AList and DynamicArrayList given in Chapter 5. But since our new class implements the interface ListWithIteratorInterface, it also includes the method getListIterator. This method returns an instance of Iterator instead of returning an instance of our interface IteratorInterface, as it did in Segment 7.21. Our class also contains the inner class IteratorForArrayList, which implements the interface Iterator. The class has the following form:

```java
import java.util.*;
public class ArrayListWithIterator implements ListWithIteratorInterface
{
  private Object[] entry; // array of list entries
  private int length;
  private static final int INITIAL_SIZE = 25;

  < Implementations of the constructor and methods of the ADT list go here;
      you can see them in Chapter 5, beginning at Segment 5.5. >
  . . .
  public Iterator getListIterator()
  {
    return new IteratorForArrayList();
  } // end getListIterator

  private class IteratorForArrayList implements Iterator
  {
    < Implementations of methods in the interface Iterator go here. >
    . . .
  } // end IteratorForArrayList
} // end ArrayListWithIterator
```

We now examine the inner class in detail.

8.11   **Beginning the inner class.** Just as you can use your finger to keep track of your place on this page, our iterator implementation uses an index to keep track of the iterator's position within the array of list entries. This index, which we call currentIndex, is a data field of the inner class IteratorForArrayList. The constructor initializes currentIndex to zero.

What makes the implementation of Iterator a bit tricky is the requirement that the client call next before each call to remove. In contrast, our iterator in Chapter 7 allowed us to call removeCurrent repeatedly to remove several entries from the list. Therefore, the implementation here needs an additional data field—a boolean flag—that enables the remove method to know whether next was called. We name this data field wasNextCalled. Thus, the inner class begins as follows:

```java
private class IteratorForArrayList implements Iterator
{
  private int currentIndex;
  private boolean wasNextCalled; // needed by remove

  public IteratorForLinkedList()
  {
    currentIndex = 0;
    wasNextCalled = false;
  } // end default constructor
  . . .
```

8.12   **The method hasNext.** The implementation of hasNext is straightforward. The iterator can retrieve the next entry if currentIndex < length. Notice that this expression is false when the list is empty.

```java
public boolean hasNext()
{
  return currentIndex < length;
} // end hasNext
```

8.13   **The method next.** The implementation of the method next follows the same logic as the version given in Segment 8.8. If hasNext returns true, next returns entry[currentIndex], increments currentIndex, and sets the flag wasNextCalled to true. On the other had, if hasNext returns false, next throws an exception.

```java
public Object next() throws NoSuchElementException
{
  if (hasNext())
  {
    wasNextCalled = true;
    Object currentEntry = entry[currentIndex];
    currentIndex++;
    return currentEntry;
  }
  else
    throw new NoSuchElementException("next() called after " +
                                     "iteration has reached end.");
} // end next
```

8.14   **The method remove.** The iterator's method remove removes from the list the entry that the most recent call to next returned. Contrast this with the ADT operation remove, which removes the entry at a specified position within the list. Remember that a call to the iterator's method remove is valid only if next has been called since the last call to remove. The class's data field wasNext-Called helps us to implement this aspect of the method. Notice that we must also prevent a subsequent call to remove that is not preceded by a call to next. We do that by throwing an IllegalStateException. In addition, a subsequent call to next must behave as it would have before the removal took place.

Although the inner class has direct access to the array entry, removing an entry from the list involves shifting elements within the array. Since we have already developed that code for the list's remove method, we will call it from the implementation of the iterator's remove method. To do that, we need the position number of the list entry to be removed, rather than its array index. Recall from Segments 4.10 and 5.6 that the position number of an entry in a list begins at 1, so it is 1 larger than the corresponding array index.

Figure 8-3 illustrates how to use currentIndex in this implementation. The figure shows the array of list entries and the index currentIndex just before the call to next, just after the call to next but before the call to remove, and just after the call to remove. Notice that next returns a reference to the current entry—*Chris* in the figure—in the iteration and then increments currentIndex (Figure 8-3b). The method remove must remove this entry from the list. Since currentIndex is now 1 larger than the index of *Chris*, it is the position number of the list entry that must be removed. After the entry is removed, the next entry—*Deb* in the figure—moves to the next lower-numbered position in the array. Thus, remove decrements currentIndex so that it remains the index of the next entry in the iteration (Figure 8-3c).

Figure 8-3   The array of list entries and currentIndex (a) just before the call to next();
(b) just after the call to next() but before the call to remove(); (c) after the call to remove()

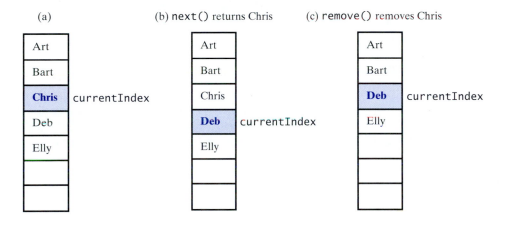

The method remove has the following implementation within the inner class IteratorForArrayList:

```
public void remove() throws IllegalStateException
{
   if (wasNextCalled)
   {
      // currentIndex was incremented by the call to next, so it
      // is the position number of the entry to be removed
      ArrayListWithIterator.this.remove(currentIndex);
      currentIndex--;   // index of next entry to be removed
      wasNextCalled = false;
   }
   else
      throw new IllegalStateException("next not called for " +
                                   "this invocation of remove");
} // end remove
```

This method calls the list's method remove. We precede the call with ArrayListWithIterator.this to distinguish between the two versions of remove.

An inner class can refer to its outer class's data fields and methods by name alone, if it does not also use the same names for its own definitions. For example, the method next in Segment 8.13 referred to the array entry directly by name since no other entry exists. But we could have written ArrayListWithIterator.this.entry instead.

Question 4   Consider the list and the calls to next and remove in Figure 8-3.

a.   What would a call to next return if it occurred after the call to remove in Figure 8-3c?
b.   What would a call to next return if it occurred after the call to next in Figure 8-3b?

The Interface `ListIterator`

8.15   The Java Class Library provides a second interface for iterators—ListIterator—in the package java.util. This type of iterator enables you to traverse a list in either direction and to modify the list during the iteration. In addition to the three methods hasNext, next, and remove that the interface Iterator specifies, ListIterator contains methods that work with the entry before the current one as well as methods that change, add, or replace list entries during the traversal. This added capability makes the interface harder to understand and to implement.

We begin by looking at the interface:

```
package java.util;
public interface ListIterator extends Iterator
{
  /** Task: Determines whether the iteration has completed its traversal
   *        and gone beyond the last entry in the collection of data.
   *  @return true if the iteration has another entry to visit when
   *        traversing the list forward; otherwise returns false */
  boolean hasNext();

  /** Task: Retrieves the current (next) entry in the collection
   *        and advances the iteration by one position.
   *  @return a reference to the current entry in the iteration, if
   *        one exists
   *  @throws NoSuchElementException if the iteration had reached the
   *        end already, that is, if hasNext() is false */
  Object next();

  /** Task: Removes from the list the last entry that either next()
   *        or previous() has returned.
   *  Precondition: next() or previous() has been called, but the
   *        iterator's remove() or add() method has not been called
   *        since then. That is, you can call remove only once per
   *        call to next() or previous(). The list has not been altered
   *        during the iteration except by calls to the iterator's
   *        remove() or add() method.
   *  @throws IllegalStateException if next() or previous() has not
   *        been called, or if remove() or add() has been called
   *        already after the last call to next() or previous()
   *  @throws UnsupportedOperationException if this iterator does not
   *        permit a remove operation */
  void remove(); // Optional
```

```
// The previous three methods are in the interface Iterator; they are
// duplicated here for reference and to show new behavior for remove.

  /** Task: Determines whether the iteration has completed its traversal
   *        and gone before the first entry in the collection of data.
   *  @return true if the iteration has another entry to visit when
   *        traversing the list backward; otherwise returns false */
  boolean hasPrevious();

  /** Task: Retrieves the previous entry in the list and moves the
   *        iteration back to this previous entry.
   *  @return a reference to the entry before the iterator's
   *        current entry, if one exists
   *  @throws NoSuchElementException if the iterator has no previous
   *        entry */
  Object previous();

  /** Task: Gets the index of the current (next) entry.
   *  @return the index of the list entry that a subsequent call to
   *        next() would return. If next() would not return an entry
   *        because the iterator is at the end of the list, returns
   *        the size of the list. Note that the iterator numbers
   *        the list entries from 0 instead of 1. */
  int nextIndex();

  /** Task: Gets the index of the entry before the current one.
   *  @return the index of the list entry that a subsequent call to
   *        previous() would return. If previous() would not return
   *        an entry because the iterator is at the beginning of the
   *        list, returns -1. Note that the iterator numbers the
   *        list entries from 0 instead of 1. */
  int previousIndex();

  /** Task: Adds an entry to the list just before the entry, if any,
   *        that next() would have returned before the addition. This
   *        addition is just after the entry, if any, that previous()
   *        would have returned. After the addition, a call to
   *        previous() will return the new entry, but a call to next()
   *        will behave as it would have before the addition.
   *        Further, the addition increases by 1 the values that
   *        nextIndex() and previousIndex() will return.
   *  @param newEntry  an object to be added to the list
   *  @throws ClassCastException if the class of newEntry prevents the
   *        addition to this list
   *  @throws IllegalArgumentException if some other aspect of newEntry
   *        prevents the addition to this list
   *  @throws UnsupportedOperationException if this iterator does not
   *        permit an add operation */
  void add(Object newEntry); // Optional

  /** Task: Replaces the last entry in the list that either next()
   *        or previous() has returned.
   *  Precondition: next() or previous() has been called, but remove()
   *        or add() has not been called since then.
   *  @param newEntry  an object that is the replacement entry
```

```
 *   @throws ClassCastException if the class of newEntry prevents the
 *           addition to this list
 *   @throws IllegalArgumentException if some other aspect of newEntry
 *           prevents the addition to this list
 *   @throws IllegalStateException if next() or previous() has not
 *           been called, or if remove() or add() has been called
 *           already after the last call to next() or previous()
 *   @throws UnsupportedOperationException if this iterator does not
 *           permit a set operation */
  void set(Object newEntry); // Optional
} // end ListIterator
```

Notice that `ListIterator` extends `Iterator`. Thus, `ListIterator` would include the methods `hasNext`, `next`, and `remove` from the interface `Iterator`, even if we did not write them explicitly. We have done so for your reference and to indicate `remove`'s additional behavior.

All of the exceptions mentioned in this interface are run-time exceptions, so they do not have to appear within a `throws` clause of the methods' signatures. In addition, you do not have to write `try` and `catch` blocks when you invoke these methods.

8.16   **The current entry.** Both `ListIterator` and `Iterator` use the idea of a current entry in a list. Initially, the current entry is the first entry in the list. The iterators mark the current entry, much as your finger can point to an entry in a list or to a line on this page. Recall that the method `hasNext` determines whether a current entry exists. If one exists, `next` returns a reference to the current entry and advances the iterator's marker to the next entry in the list, as Figure 8-1 illustrated. Repeated calls to `next` step through the list. So far, nothing is different from what you learned about the interface `Iterator` earlier in this chapter.

8.17   **The previous entry.** `ListIterator` also provides access to the entry just before the current one—that is, to the previous entry. The method `hasPrevious` determines whether a previous entry exists. If so, the method `previous` returns a reference to the previous entry and moves the iterator's marker back by one entry so that it "points" to the entry it just returned. Figure 8-4 shows the effect of `previous` on a list. Intermixing calls to `previous` and `next` enables you to move back and forth within the list. If you call `next` and then call `previous`, each method returns the same entry. Like `next`, `previous` throws an exception when called after it has completed its traversal of the list.

Figure 8-4   The effect of a call to `previous()` on a list

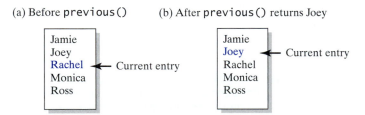

(a) Before `previous()`   (b) After `previous()` returns Joey

8.18   **The indices of the current and previous entries.** As Figure 8-5 shows, the methods `nextIndex` and `previousIndex` each return the index of the entry that a subsequent call to `next` or `previous`, respectively, would return. Note that the iterator numbers the list's entries beginning with 0, instead of 1 as the ADT list operations do. If a call to `next` would throw an exception because the iterator is at the end of the list, `nextIndex` returns the size of the list. Similarly, if a call to `previous` would throw an exception because the iterator is at the beginning of the list, `previousIndex` returns −1.

Figure 8-5   The indices returned by the methods `nextIndex` and `previousIndex`

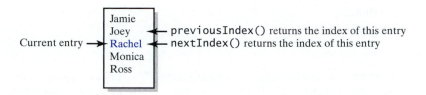

 Note: The interface `ListIterator` specifies nine methods, including the three methods that `Iterator` specifies. They are `hasNext`, `next`, `remove`, `hasPrevious`, `previous`, `nextIndex`, `previousIndex`, `add`, and `set`.

Using the Interface `ListIterator`

8.19   **Example: Traversals.** Let's look at an example of the methods that work with the current and previous entries and then use it to describe the remaining methods in the interface. We make the following assumptions:

- The interface `ListIterator` is implemented as an inner class of the class that implements the ADT list.
- The method `getListIterator` is added to the ADT list.
- The list `nameList` contains the following names:

  Jamie
  Doug
  Jill

- The iterator `traverse` is defined as follows:
  ```
  ListIterator traverse = nameList.getListIterator();
  ```

Since `traverse` is at the beginning of the list, the Java statements

```
System.out.println("nextIndex     " + traverse.nextIndex());
System.out.println("hasNext       " + traverse.hasNext());
System.out.println("previousIndex " + traverse.previousIndex());
System.out.println("hasPrevious   " + traverse.hasPrevious());
```

produce the output

```
nextIndex     0
hasNext       true
previousIndex -1
hasPrevious   false
```

If we then execute the statements

```
System.out.println("next      " + traverse.next());
System.out.println("nextIndex " + traverse.nextIndex());
System.out.println("hasNext   " + traverse.hasNext());
```

the output is

```
next      Jamie
nextIndex 1
hasNext   true
```

Finally, the statements

```
System.out.println("previousIndex " + traverse.previousIndex());
System.out.println("hasPrevious   " + traverse.hasPrevious());
System.out.println("previous      " + traverse.previous());
System.out.println("nextIndex     " + traverse.nextIndex());
System.out.println("hasNext       " + traverse.hasNext());
System.out.println("next          " + traverse.next());
```

produce the output

```
previousIndex 0
hasPrevious   true
previous      Jamie
nextIndex     0
hasNext       true
next          Jamie
```

Question 5   Suppose that `traverse` is an iterator as defined in Segment 8.19, but the contents of `nameList` are unknown. Write Java statements that display the names in `nameList` in reverse order, beginning at the end of the list.

8.20   **Example: The method set.** The method `set` replaces the entry that either `next` or `previous` just returned. At the end of the previous segment, `next` had just returned *Jamie*, so the current entry is *Doug*. Thus,

```
traverse.set("Bob");
```

replaces *Jamie* with *Bob*. Since *Jamie* was the first entry in the list, the list now appears as

```
Bob
Doug
Jill
```

Note that this replacement operation does not affect the position of the iterator within the list. Thus, calls to `nextIndex` and `previousIndex`, for example, are not affected. In this case, since the current entry is *Doug*, `nextIndex` returns 1 and `previousIndex` returns 0. Also note that we can call `set` again; doing so here will replace *Bob*.

Question 6   If the iteration's current entry is *Doug*, write Java statements that replace *Jill* with *Jennifer.*

8.21   **Example: The method add.** The method `add` inserts an entry into the list just before the current entry. Thus, the insertion is made immediately before the entry, if any, that `next` would have returned before `add` was called and just after the entry, if any, that `previous` would have returned. Note that if the list is empty, `add` inserts a new entry as the only entry in the list.

If the current entry is *Doug*, the statement

```
traverse.add("Kerry");
```

adds *Kerry* to the list just before *Doug*—that is, at index 1 or, equivalently, at list position 2. After this addition, the list is as follows:

Bob
Kerry
Doug
Jill

A call to `next` at this point returns *Doug,* since `next` would have returned *Doug* had we not called `add`. If, however, we call `previous` instead of `next`, the new entry *Kerry* will be returned. Furthermore, the addition increases by 1 the values that `nextIndex` and `previousIndex` will return. Thus, immediately after the addition, `nextIndex` will return 2 and `previousIndex` will return 1.

Question 7   If the iteration's current entry is *Doug,* write Java statements that add *Miguel* right after *Doug.*

8.22   **Example: The method `remove`.** The method `remove` is similar to `remove` in the interface `Iterator`, which you saw earlier in this chapter. But in the interface `ListIterator`, `remove` is affected by the method `previous` as well as by `next`. Thus, `remove` removes the list entry that the last call to either `next` or `previous` returned.
If the list contains

Bob
Kerry
Doug
Jill

and the iterator `traverse` is at *Doug,* the statements

```
traverse.previous();
traverse.remove();
```

remove *Kerry* from the list, since `previous` returns *Kerry*. The iterator's current entry is still *Doug.*
Notice that both `set` and `remove` will throw the exception `IllegalStateException` if neither `next` nor `previous` has been called, or if either `remove` or `add` has been called already since the last call to `next` or `previous`. As you will see in the next section, this behavior complicates the implementation somewhat.

8.23   **The optional methods `set`, `add`, and `remove`.** Finally, the methods `set`, `add`, and `remove` are optional in the sense that you can choose not to provide one or more of these operations. In that case, however, each such operation must have an implementation that throws the exception `UnsupportedOperationException` if the client invokes the operation.
An iterator of type `ListIterator` that does not support `set`, `add`, and `remove` is still useful, since it enables you to traverse a list in both directions. The implementation of such an iterator, which we leave as an exercise, is much simpler than the complete implementation that we present in the next section.

Note: An iterator of type `ListIterator` that does not support `set`, `add`, and `remove` is simpler to implement and enables you to traverse a list in both directions.

An Array-Based Implementation of the Interface `ListIterator`

8.24   As we did for the interface `Iterator` earlier in this chapter, we will implement the interface `ListIterator` as an inner class of a class that uses an array to represent the ADT list. First, we define an interface for the list class that includes the operations of the ADT list and the method `getListIterator`. In this case, the method returns an instance of `ListIterator` instead of `Iterator`.

```java
import java.util.*;
public interface ListWithListIteratorInterface extends ListInterface
{
  public ListIterator getListIterator();
} // end ListWithListIteratorInterface
```

8.25   **The class that implements the ADT list.** Chapter 5 presented several classes that implemented the ADT list by using an array. `AList` used a fixed-size array, and `DynamicArrayList` used dynamic expansion. Our new class can have the data fields and public methods of either `AList` or `DynamicArrayList` and includes the method `getListIterator`. It also contains the inner class `IteratorForArrayList` that implements the interface `ListIterator`. The class has the following form:

```java
import java.util.*;
public class ArrayListWithListIterator implements
                                     ListWithListIteratorInterface
{
  private Object[] entry; // array of list entries
  private int length;     // current number of entries in list
  private static final int INITIAL_SIZE = 25;

  < Implementations of the constructor and methods of the ADT list go here;
     you can see them in Chapter 5, beginning at Segment 5.5. >
  . . .
  public ListIterator getListIterator()
  {
    return new IteratorForArrayList();
  } // end getListIterator

  private class IteratorForArrayList implements ListIterator
  {
    < Implementations of the methods in ListIterator go here. >
    . . .
  } // end IteratorForArrayList
} // end ArrayListWithListIterator
```

The Inner Class

8.26   **The data fields.** We begin implementing the inner class `IteratorForArrayList` by thinking about how the methods `set` and `remove` will throw the exception `IllegalStateException`. This aspect of the implementation can be a bit confusing. These methods throw an `IllegalStateException` if either

- `next` or `previous` was not called or
- `remove` or `add` has been called already since the last call to `next` or `previous`

We will need several boolean flags as data fields to record whether these methods have been called. As you will see later, only the following three flags are necessary:

```
private boolean wasNextCalled;
private boolean wasPreviousCalled;
private boolean wasAddCalled;
```

We will be able to deduce whether `remove` has been called by examining only these flags.

In addition to these three data fields, we need a marker for the current position of the iterator. Thus, the inner class begins as follows:

```
private class IteratorForArrayList implements ListIterator
{
  private int currentIndex;
  private boolean wasNextCalled;
  private boolean wasPreviousCalled;
  private boolean wasAddCalled;

  public IteratorForArrayList()
  {
    currentIndex = 0;
    wasNextCalled = false;
    wasPreviousCalled = false;
    wasAddCalled = false;
  } // end default constructor
  . . .
```

8.27 **The method `hasNext`.** The method `hasNext` has the same implementation that it had earlier in Segment 8.12. Recall that it returns true if the iterator has not reached the end of the list.

```
public boolean hasNext()
{
  return currentIndex < length;
} // end hasNext
```

8.28 **The method `next`.** The implementation of `next` is similar to the one given in Segment 8.13. Here, however, it has other boolean flags to set. When `next` is called, a prior call to `previous` will be irrelevant to `remove` and `set`. Thus, we set `wasPreviousCalled` to false. Also, the `set` method cares when add is called after `next`. For `set` to detect a subsequent call to add, we must make `was-AddCalled` false.

```
public Object next() throws NoSuchElementException
{
  if (hasNext())
  {
    wasNextCalled = true;
    wasPreviousCalled = false;
    wasAddCalled = false;

    Object currentEntry = entry[currentIndex];
    currentIndex++;
    return currentEntry;
  }
  else
```

```
                throw new NoSuchElementException("next() called after iteration " +
                                                "has reached end.");
      } // end next
```

8.29   **The methods hasPrevious and previous.** The methods hasPrevious and previous have implementations that are analogous to those of hasNext and next, respectively.

```
        public boolean hasPrevious()
        {
          return (currentIndex > 0) && (currentIndex <= length);
        } // end hasPrevious

        public Object previous()
        {
          if (hasPrevious())
          {
            wasPreviousCalled = true;
            wasNextCalled = false;
            wasAddCalled = false;

            currentIndex--;
            return entry[currentIndex];
          }
          else
            throw new NoSuchElementException("previous() called after " +
                                             "iteration has reached beginning.");
        } // end previous
```

8.30   **The methods nextIndex and previousIndex.** The method nextIndex returns either the index of
the current entry or the size of the list if the iteration has passed the end of the list.

```
        public int nextIndex()
        {
          int result;

          if (hasNext())
            result = currentIndex;
          else
            result = length;

          return result;
        } // end nextIndex
```

The method previousIndex returns either the index of the entry just before the current entry or –1
if the iteration is at the beginning of the list.

```
        public int previousIndex()
        {
          int result;
```

```
if (hasPrevious())
  result = currentIndex - 1;
else
  result = -1;

return result;
} // end previousIndex
```

8.31   **The method add.** The method add adds an entry to the list just before the iterator's current entry, as Figure 8-6 illustrates. If `currentIndex` is the index of the current entry within the array, we use the list's add method to add an entry at position `currentIndex+1` within the list. Recall that entries after the new entry will be shifted and renumbered. Therefore, we need to increment `currentIndex` so that it will continue to indicate the iterator's current entry. Thus, add has the following implementation:

```
public void add(Object newEntry)
{
  wasAddCalled = true;
  currentIndex++;
  ArrayListWithListIterator.this.add(currentIndex, newEntry);
} // end add
```

Figure 8-6   The array of list entries and `currentIndex` (a) just before the call to add; (b) just after the call to add

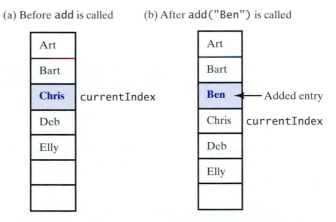

8.32   **The method remove.** The logic for the remove method when a call to next precedes the call to remove is like the logic for the remove method in the interface `Iterator`, which you saw in Segment 8.14. Recall that Figure 8-3 illustrated the array of list entries and the index `currentIndex` before and after the calls to next and remove. Figure 8-7 provides a similar illustration when a call to `previous` precedes the call to `remove`. Notice that `previous` returns a reference to the previous entry—*Bart*—in the iteration and decrements `currentIndex` (Figure 8-7b). The method `remove` must remove this entry from the list. Notice that `currentIndex` is now 1 smaller than the position number of the list entry that must be removed. After the entry *Bart* has been removed, the next entry—*Chris*—moves to the next lower-numbered position in the array. Thus, `currentIndex` remains the index of the next entry in the iteration and so is unchanged (Figure 8-7c).

Figure 8-7   The array of list entries and `currentIndex` (a) just before the call to `previous()`; (b) just after the call to `previous()` but before the call to `remove()`; (c) after the call to `remove()`

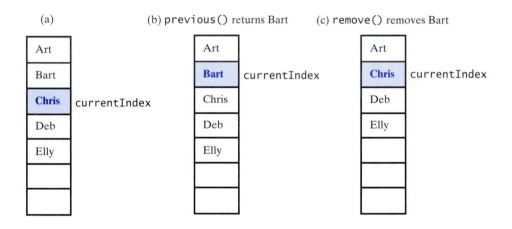

Remember, `remove` must throw an exception if neither `next` nor `previous` has been called or if either `remove` or `add` has been called already since the last call to `next` or `previous`. We can test the fields `wasNextCalled` and `wasPreviousCalled` to determine whether either `next` or `previous`, respectively, has been called. And we can look at the flag `wasAddCalled` to determine whether `add` was called after `next` or `previous`. But what about `remove`? If, as its last action, `remove` sets both the field `wasNextCalled` and the field `wasPreviousCalled` to false, it can detect whether it is being called a second time by testing these fields. Here is a summary of the logic necessary to detect when `remove` should throw an exception:

- If the flags `wasNextCalled` and `wasPreviousCalled` are both false, `next` and `previous` have not been called, or `remove` has been called already since the call to `next` or `previous`.

- If the flag `wasAddCalled` is `true`, `add` has been called since the call to `next` or `previous`.

Figure 8-8 shows calls to `remove` in various contexts and the state of the boolean flags. In Part *a*, `remove` causes an exception because it is not preceded by a call to either `next` or `previous`. In Parts *b* and *c*, the first call to `remove` is legal, but the second call causes an exception. Each of the remaining calls to `remove` causes an exception.

Figure 8-8   Possible contexts in which the method `remove()` is called

(a)
```
                           ◄── wasNextCalled is false, wasPreviousCalled is false
    traverse.remove();  ◄── Causes an exception
```

(b)
```
    traverse.next();
                           ◄── wasNextCalled is true, wasAddCalled is false
    traverse.remove();  ◄── wasNextCalled is false, wasPreviousCalled is false
    traverse.remove();  ◄── Causes an exception
```

(c)
```
    traverse.previous();
                           ◄── wasPreviousCalled is true, wasAddCalled is false
    traverse.remove();  ◄── wasPreviousCalled is false, wasNextCalled is false
    traverse.remove();  ◄── Causes an exception
```

(d)
```
    traverse.next();
                           ◄── wasNextCalled is true, wasAddCalled is false
    traverse.add(...);  ◄── wasAddCalled is true
    traverse.remove();  ◄── Causes an exception
```

(e)
```
    traverse.previous();
                           ◄── wasPreviousCalled is true, wasAddCalled is false
    traverse.add(...);  ◄── wasAddCalled is true
    traverse.remove();  ◄── Causes an exception
```

The following implementation of `remove` reflects this discussion:

```java
public void remove() throws IllegalStateException
{
  if (wasNextCalled && !wasAddCalled)
  {
    // next() called, but add() not called;
    // currentIndex is 1 more than the index of the entry
    // returned by next(), so it is the position number of
    // the entry to be removed
    ArrayListWithListIterator.this.remove(currentIndex);
    currentIndex--;
    wasNextCalled = false;
```

```
            wasPreviousCalled = false;
          }
          else if (wasPreviousCalled && !wasAddCalled)
          {
            // previous() called, but add() not called;
            // currentIndex is the index of the entry returned by
            // previous(), so is 1 less than the position number of
            // the entry to be removed
            ArrayListWithListIterator.this.remove(currentIndex+1);
            wasNextCalled = false;
            wasPreviousCalled = false;
          }
          else
            throw new IllegalStateException("next or previous not " +
                                 "called for this invocation of remove");
        } // end remove
```

8.33   **The method set.** The method set replaces the current entry of the iteration. It uses currentIndex, as updated by either of the methods next or previous. Since the method next returns entry[currentIndex] and then increments currentIndex, the method set would replace the object in entry[currentIndex-1] after a call to next. Likewise, since previous returns entry[currentIndex-1] and then decrements currentIndex, the method set would replace entry[currentIndex] after a call to previous.

The following implementation of set reflects these observations and uses the same logic that we used in remove to determine whether to throw IllegalStateException:

```
          public void set(Object newEntry)
          {
            if (wasNextCalled && !wasAddCalled)
              entry[currentIndex-1] = newEntry;
            else if (wasPreviousCalled && !wasAddCalled)
              entry[currentIndex] = newEntry;
            else
              throw new IllegalStateException("next() or previous() not " +
                        "called for this invocation of set(), " +
                        "OR remove() or add() was called after next() " +
                        "or previous(), but before set().");
          } // end set
```

 Note: Implementing the entire interface ListIterator is more complex than implementing the interface Iterator. However, the implementation is easier when the associated ADT has an array-based implementation rather than a linked implementation.

Java Class Library: ArrayList and LinkedList Revisited

8.34   In a sense, this entire chapter has been about the Java Class Library, since the interfaces Iterator and ListIterator are components of it. In this last section, we want to focus on another feature of the classes ArrayList and LinkedList that we mentioned in Chapters 5 and 6, respectively. Each of these classes contains methods that are analogous to our method `getListIterator`. In particular, both classes contain the following methods:

```
public Iterator iterator();
public ListIterator listIterator(int index);
```

The method `iterator` returns an iterator that adheres to the `Iterator` interface. The method `listIterator` returns an iterator that begins at the list element indicated by `index`, where zero indicates the first entry in the list. This iterator has the methods specified in the `ListIterator` interface.

In addition, `ArrayList` has the method

```
public ListIterator listIterator();
```

which has the same effect as `listIterator(0)`.

CHAPTER SUMMARY

- The interface **Iterator** specifies three methods: **hasNext**, **next**, and **remove**. An iterator that implements this interface need not provide a **remove** operation. Instead, the method **remove** would throw the exception **UnsupportedOperationException**.

- The interface **ListIterator** specifies nine methods, including the three methods that **Iterator** specifies. They are **hasNext**, **next**, **remove**, **hasPrevious**, **previous**, **nextIndex**, **previous-Index**, **add**, and **set**. The methods **remove**, **add**, and **set** are optional in the sense that they can throw the exception **UnsupportedOperationException** instead of affecting the list.

- You can implement each of the interfaces **Iterator** and **ListIterator** as an inner class of the class that defines the collection to be iterated. This approach enables you to have several independent iterators that traverse an ADT. It also allows the iterator direct access to the underlying data structure, so its implementation can be efficient.

EXERCISES

1. Suppose that `nameList` is a list that contains the following strings: *Kyle, Cathy, Sam, Austin, Sara.* What output is produced by the following sequence of statements?

```
Iterator nameIterator = nameList.getListIterator();
System.out.println(nameIterator.next());
nameIterator.next();
System.out.println(nameIterator.next());
nameIterator.remove();
System.out.println(nameIterator.next());
nameList.display();
```

2. Repeat Exercise 1, but instead use the following statements:

```
Iterator nameIterator = nameList.getListIterator();
nameIterator.next();
nameIterator.remove();
nameIterator.next();
nameIterator.next();
nameIterator.remove();
System.out.println(nameIterator.next());
nameList.display();
System.out.println(nameIterator.next());
System.out.println(nameIterator.next());
```

3. Suppose that nameList is a list of at least one string and that nameIterator is defined as follows:

```
Iterator nameIterator = nameList.getListIterator();
```

Write Java statements that use nameIterator to display only the last string in the list.

4. Given nameList and nameIterator as described in Exercise 3, write statements that use nameIterator to remove all the entries from the list.

5. Given a list of strings and an iterator nameIterator whose data type is Iterator, remove all occurrences of the string *CANCEL* from the list.

6. Given a list of strings and an iterator nameIterator whose data type is Iterator, write statements that remove any duplicates in the list.

7. Given a list of strings and an iterator nameIterator whose data type is Iterator, count the number of times each string occurs in the list, without altering the list. Assume that you have an implementation of the ADT set with the methods add and contains. The ADT set will reject duplicate entries.

8. Suppose that nameList is a list that contains the following strings: *Kyle, Cathy, Sam, Austin, Sara*. What output is produced by the following sequence of statements?

```
ListIterator nameIterator = nameList.getListIterator();
System.out.println(nameIterator.next());
nameIterator.next();
nameIterator.next();
System.out.println(nameIterator.next());
nameIterator.set("Brittany");
nameIterator.previous();
nameIterator.remove();
System.out.println(nameIterator.next());
nameList.display();
```

9. Repeat Exercise 8, but instead use the following statements:

```
ListIterator nameIterator = nameList.getListIterator();
nameIterator.next();
nameIterator.remove();
nameIterator.next();
nameIterator.next();
nameIterator.previous();
nameIterator.remove();
System.out.println(nameIterator.next());
nameIterator.next();
nameIterator.set("Brittany");
System.out.println("Revised list:");
nameList.display();
System.out.println(nameIterator.previous());
System.out.println(nameIterator.next());
```

10. Given a list of strings and an iterator nameIterator whose data type is ListIterator, write statements that add the string *Bob* after the first occurrence of the string *Sam*.

11. Implement the interface `Iterator` as an external iterator.

12. If you wanted to implement the interface `ListIterator` as an inner class iterator by using a linked implementation, what difficulties would you face?

PROJECTS

1. Revise the class `LinkedListWithIterator` given in Segment 8.6 so that the inner class `IteratorForLinkedList` provides a `remove` operation.

2. Implement all of the methods in the interface `ListIterator` as an external iterator.

3. Implement the interface `ListIterator` as an inner class, but do not support the operations `remove`, `add`, and `set`.

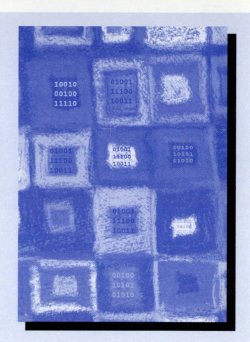

CHAPTER

9

The Efficiency of Algorithms

CONTENTS

Motivation
Measuring an Algorithm's Efficiency
    Big Oh Notation
Formalities
Picturing Efficiency
The Efficiency of Implementations of the ADT List
    The Array-Based Implementation
    The Linked Implementation
    Comparing the Implementations

PREREQUISITES

Chapter   1   Java Classes
Chapter   5   List Implementations That Use Arrays
Chapter   6   List Implementations That Link Data

OBJECTIVES

After studying this chapter, you should be able to

- Determine the efficiency of a given algorithm
- Compare the expected execution times of two methods, given the efficiencies of their algorithms

With amazing frequency, manufacturers introduce new computers that are faster and have larger memories than their recent predecessors. Yet we—and likely your computer science professors—ask you to write code that is efficient in its use of time and space (memory). We have to admit that such efficiency is not as pressing an issue as it was fifty years ago, when computers were much slower and their memory size was much smaller than they are now. (Computers had small memories, but they were physically huge, occupying entire rooms.) Even so, efficiency remains an issue—in some circumstances, a critical issue.

This chapter will introduce you to the terminology and methods that computer scientists use to measure the efficiency of an algorithm. With this background, you not only will have an intuitive feel for efficiency, but also will be able to talk about efficiency in a quantitative way.

Motivation

9.1   Perhaps you think that you are not likely to write a program in the near future whose execution time is noticeably long. You might be right, but we are about to show you some simple Java code that does take a long time to perform its computations.

Imagine that we are defining a Java class to represent extremely large integers. Of course, we will need to represent the many digits possible in one of these integers, but that is not the subject of this example. We want a method for our class that adds two large integers—that is, two instances of our class—and a method that multiplies two large integers. Suppose that we have implemented the add method successfully and are about to design a multiply method.

As you know, multiplication is equivalent to repeated addition. So if we want to compute the product 7562 times 423, for example, we could add 7562 to an initially zero variable 423 times. Remember that our add method works, so we can readily use it in our implementation of multiply.

9.2   Let's write some simple Java code to test our idea. Realize that this code is simply an experiment to verify our approach of repeated addition and does not use anything that we might already have written for our class.

If we use long integers in our experiment, we could write the following statements:

```java
long firstOperand  = 7562;
long secondOperand =  423;
long product = 0;

for (; secondOperand > 0; secondOperand--)
  product = product + firstOperand;

System.out.println(product);
```

If you execute this code, you will get the right answer of 3,198,726. Now change the second operand from 423 to 100,000,000 (that is, a 1 followed by eight zeros), and execute the code again. Again, you will get the correct answer, which this time is 756,200,000,000 (7562 followed by eight zeros). However, you should notice a delay in seeing this result. Now try 1,000,000,000, which is a 1 followed by nine zeros. Again you will get the correct answer—7562 followed by nine zeros—but you will have to wait even longer for the result. The wait might be long enough for you to suspect that something is broken. If not, try 1 followed by ten zeros!

What's our point? Our class is supposed to deal with really large integers. The integers in our little experiment, while large, are not *really* large. Even so, the previous simple code takes a noticeably long time to execute. Should you use a faster computer? Should you wait for an even faster computer to be invented? We have a better solution.

9.3   The delay in our example is caused by the excessive number of additions that the code must perform. Instead of adding 7562 to an initially zero variable one billion times, we could save time by adding one billion to an initially zero variable 7562 times. This approach won't always be faster, because one operand might not be much smaller than the other. Besides, we can do much better.

Consider again the product 7562 * 421. The second operand, 423, has three digits: A hundreds digit 4, a tens digit 2, and a ones digit 3. That is, 423 is the sum 400 + 20 + 3. Thus,

$$7562 * 423 = 7562 * (400 + 20 + 3)$$
$$= 7562 * 400 + 7562 * 20 + 7562 * 3$$
$$= 756200 * 4 + 75620 * 2 + 7562 * 3$$

Now we can replace the three previous multiplications with additions, so that the desired product is the sum

$$(756200 + 756200 + 756200 + 756200) + (75620 + 75620) + (7562 + 7562 + 7562)$$

There are three parenthesized terms, one for each digit in the second operand. Each of these terms is the sum of d integers, where d is a digit in the second operand. We can conveniently compute this sum from the right—involving first 7562, then 75620, and finally 756200—because 75620 is 10 * 7562, and 756200 is 10 * 75620.

9.4   We can use these observations to write pseudocode that will compute this type of sum. Let the operands of the multiplication be `firstOperand` and `secondOperand`. The following pseudocode computes the product of these operands by using addition.

```
secondOperandLength = number of digits in secondOperand
product = 0

for (; secondOperandLength > 0; secondOperandLength--)
{
   digit = rightmost digit of secondOperand

   for (; digit > 0; digit--)
      product = product + firstOperand

   Drop rightmost digit of secondOperand
   Tack 0 onto end of firstOperand
}
// Assertion: product is the result
```

If we use this pseudocode to compute 7562 * 423, `firstOperand` is 7562 and `secondOperand` is 423. The pseudocode computes the sum

$$(7562 + 7562 + 7562) + (75620 + 75620) + (756200 + 756200 + 756200 + 756200)$$

from left to right. The outer loop specifies the number of parenthesized groups as well as their contents, and the inner loop processes the additions within the parentheses.

9.5   Here is some Java code for you to try based on the previous pseudocode. Again, this is an experiment to verify an approach and is not the implementation of a method in our class of large integers. As such, we will implement the last two steps of the pseudocode by dividing by 10 and multiplying by 10.

```
long firstOperand =  7562;
long secondOperand = 100000000;

int secondOperandLength = 9;
long product = 0;
```

```
for (; secondOperandLength > 0; secondOperandLength--)
{
  long digit = secondOperand - (secondOperand/10) * 10;

  for (; digit > 0; digit--)
    product = product + firstOperand;

  secondOperand = secondOperand/10; // discard last digit
  firstOperand = 10 * firstOperand; // tack zero on right
} // end for

System.out.println(product);
```

You should find that this code executes faster than the code in Segment 9.2 after you change secondOperand to 100000000.

Note: As this example shows, even a simple program can be noticeably inefficient.

Measuring an Algorithm's Efficiency

9.6   The previous section should have convinced you that a program's efficiency matters. How can we measure efficiency so that we can compare various approaches to solving a problem? In the previous section, we asked you to run two programs and observe that one was noticeably slower than the other. In general, having to implement several ideas before you can choose one requires too much work to be practical. Besides, a program's execution time depends in part on the particular computer and the programming language used. It would be much better to measure an *algorithm's* efficiency before you implement it.

For example, suppose that you want to go to a store downtown. Your options are to walk, drive your car, ask a friend to take you, or take a bus. What is the best way? First, what is your concept of best? Is it the way that saves money, your time, your friend's time, or the environment? Let's say that the best option for you is the fastest one. After defining your criterion, how do you evaluate your options? You certainly do not want to try all four options so you can discover which is fastest. That would be like writing four different programs that perform the same task so you can measure which one is fastest. Instead you would investigate the "cost" of each option, considering the distance and the speed at which you can travel, the amount of other traffic, the number of stops at traffic lights, the weather, and so on.

9.7   The same considerations apply when deciding what algorithm is best. Again, we need to define what we mean by best. An algorithm has both time and space requirements, called its **complexity,** that we can measure. Typically we analyze these requirements separately and talk about an algorithm's **time complexity**—the time it takes to execute—or its **space complexity**—the memory it needs to execute. So a "best" algorithm might be the fastest one or the one that uses the least memory.

The process of measuring the complexity of algorithms is called the **analysis of algorithms.** When we measure an algorithm's complexity, we are not measuring how involved or difficult it is. We will concentrate on the time complexity of algorithms, because it is usually more important than space complexity. You should realize that an inverse relationship often exists between an algorithm's time and space complexities. If you revise an algorithm to save execution time, you usually will need more space. If you reduce an algorithm's space requirement, it likely will require more time to execute. Sometimes, however, you will be able to save both time and space.

Your measure of the complexity of an algorithm should be easy to compute, certainly easier than implementing the algorithm. You should express this measure in terms of the size of the problem. For example, if you are searching a collection of data, the problem size is the number of items in the collection. Such a measure enables you to compare the relative cost of algorithms as a function of the size of the problem. Typically, we are interested in large problems; a small problem is likely to take little time, even if the algorithm is inefficient.

9.8   Realize that you cannot compute the actual time requirement of an algorithm. After all, you have not implemented the algorithm in Java and you have not chosen the computer. Instead, you find a function of the problem size that behaves like the algorithm's actual time requirement. That is, as the time requirement increases, the value of the function increases, and vice versa. The value of the function is said to be **directly proportional** to the time requirement. Such a function is called a **growth-rate function** because it measures how an algorithm's time requirement grows as the problem size grows. By comparing the growth-rate functions of two algorithms, you can determine whether one algorithm is faster than the other.

You could estimate the maximum time that an algorithm could take—that is, its **worst-case time.** If you can tolerate this worst-case time, your algorithm is acceptable. You also could estimate the minimum or **best-case time.** If the best-case time is still too slow, you need another algorithm. For many algorithms, the worst and best cases rarely occur. A more useful measure is the **average-case time** requirement of an algorithm. This measure, however, is usually harder to find than the best and worst cases. Typically, we will find the worst-case time.

9.9   **Example.** Consider the problem of computing the sum $1 + 2 + \ldots + n$ for any positive integer n. Figure 9-1 contains pseudocode showing three ways to solve this problem. Algorithm A computes the sum $0 + 1 + 2 + \ldots + n$ from left to right. Algorithm B computes $0 + (1) + (1 + 1) + (1 + 1 + 1) + \ldots + (1 + 1 + \ldots 1)$. Finally, Algorithm C uses an algebraic identity to compute the sum.

Figure 9-1   Three algorithms for computing the sum $1 + 2 + \ldots + n$ for an integer $n > 0$

Algorithm A	Algorithm B	Algorithm C

sum = 0
for i = 1 *to* n
   sum = sum + i
	sum = 0
	for i = 1 *to* n
	  { **for** j = 1 *to* i
	     sum = sum + 1
	  }
		sum = n * (n + 1) / 2

Which algorithm—A, B, or C—is fastest? We can begin to answer this question by considering both the size of the problem and the effort involved. The integer n is a measure of the problem size: As n increases, the sum involves more terms. To measure the effort, or time requirement, of an algorithm, we must find an appropriate growth-rate function. To do so, we begin by counting the number of operations required by the algorithm. Figure 9-2 tabulates the number of assignments, additions, multiplications, and divisions that Algorithms A, B, and C require. These counts do not include the operations that control the loops. We have ignored these operations here to make counting easier, but as you will see later in Segment 9.14, doing so will not affect our final conclusion about algorithm speed.

Figure 9-2   The number of operations required by the algorithms in Figure 9-1

	Algorithm A	Algorithm B	Algorithm C
Assignments	$n + 1$	$1 + n(n + 1)/2$	1
Additions	n	$n(n + 1)/2$	1
Multiplications			1
Divisions			1
Total operations	$2n + 1$	$n^2 + n + 1$	4

Question 1   For any positive integer n, the identity

$$1 + 2 + \ldots + n = n(n + 1)/2$$

is one that you will encounter while analyzing algorithms. Can you derive it? If you can, you will not need to memorize it. *Hint*: Write $1 + 2 + \ldots + n$. Under it write $n + (n - 1) + \ldots + 1$. Then add terms from left to right.

Question 2   Can you derive the values in Figure 9-2? *Hint*: For Algorithm B, use the identity given in Question 1.

Note: Useful identities

$1 + 2 + \ldots + n = n(n + 1)/2$
$1 + 2 + \ldots + (n - 1) = n(n - 1)/2$

9.10   The various operations listed in Figure 9-2 probably take different amounts of time to execute. However, if we assume that they each require the same amount of time, we will still be able to determine which algorithm is fastest. For example, Algorithm A requires $n + 1$ assignments and n additions. If each assignment takes no more than $t_=$ time units and each addition takes no more than t_+ time units, Algorithm A requires no more than $(n + 1)\, t_= + n\, t_+$ time units. If we replace $t_=$ and t_+ with the larger of the two values and call it t, Algorithm A requires no more than $(2n + 1)\, t$ time units. Whether we look at a time estimate such as $(2n + 1)\, t$ or the total number of operations $2n + 1$, we can draw the same conclusion: Algorithm A requires time directly proportional to $2n + 1$ in the worst case. Thus, Algorithm A's growth-rate function is $2n + 1$.

Using similar reasoning, we can conclude that Algorithm B requires time directly proportional to $n^2 + n + 1$, and Algorithm C requires time that is constant and independent of the value of n. Figure 9-3 plots these time requirements as a function of n. You can see from this figure that as n grows, Algorithm B requires the most time.

9.11   Typical growth-rate functions are algebraically simpler than the ones you have just seen. Why? Recall that since you are not likely to notice the effect of an inefficient algorithm when the problem is small, you should focus on large problems. Thus, if we care only about large values of n when comparing the algorithms, we can consider only the dominant term in each growth-rate function.

For example, $n^2 + n + 1$ behaves like n^2 when n is large because n^2 is much larger than $n + 1$ in that case. In other words, the difference between the value of $n^2 + n + 1$ and that of n^2 is relatively small and can be ignored when n is large. So instead of using $n^2 + n + 1$ as Algorithm B's growth-rate function, we can use n^2—the term with the largest exponent—and say that Algorithm B requires time proportional to n^2. Likewise, Algorithm A requires time proportional to n. On the other hand, Algorithm C requires time that is independent of n.

Figure 9-3   The number of operations required by the algorithms in Figure 9-1 as a function of n

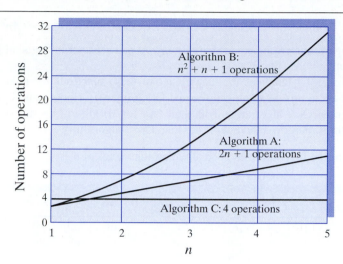

Big Oh Notation

9.12   Computer scientists use a notation to represent an algorithm's complexity. Instead of saying that Algorithm A has a worst-case time requirement proportional to n, we say that A is **O(n).** We call this notation **Big Oh** since it uses the capital letter O. We read O(n) as either "Big Oh of n" or "order of at most n." Similarly, since Algorithm B has a worst-case time requirement proportional to n^2, we say that B is O(n^2). Algorithm C always requires four operations. Regardless of the problem size n, this algorithm requires the same time, be it worst case, best case, or average case. We say that Algorithm C is O(1). We will discuss Big Oh notation more carefully and introduce other notations in the next section.

9.13   **Example.** Imagine that you are at a wedding reception, seated at a table of n people. In preparation for the toast, the waiter pours champagne into each of n glasses. That task is O(n). Someone makes a toast. It is O(1), even if the toast seems to last forever, because it is independent of the number of guests. If you clink your glass with everyone at your table, you have performed an O(n) operation. If everyone at your table does likewise, they collectively have performed an O(n^2) operation.

9.14   **Example.** In Segment 9.9, we ignored the operations that control the loops in the algorithms. Obviously this simplification affects the total number of operations, but even if we counted them, we would get the same growth-rate functions that you saw in the previous segment. For example, Algorithm A contains the for statement

```
for i = 1 to n
```

This statement represents an assignment to i, additions to i, and comparisons with n. In total, the loop-control logic requires 1 assignment, n additions, and $n + 1$ comparisons, for a total of $2n + 2$ additional operations. So Algorithm A actually requires $4n + 3$ operations instead of only $2n + 1$. What is important, however, is not the exact count of operations, but the general behavior of the algorithm. The functions $4n + 3$ and $2n + 1$ are each directly proportional to n. For large values of n, the difference between these two functions is negligible. We do not have to count every operation to see that Algorithm A requires time that increases linearly with n. Thus, Algorithm A is O(n).

9.15   The growth-rate functions that you are likely to encounter grow in magnitude as follows when $n > 10$:

$$O(1) < O(\log \log n) < O(\log n) < O(\log^2 n) < O(n) < O(n \log n) < O(n^2) < O(n^3) < O(2^n) < O(n!)$$

The logarithms given here are base 2. As you will see later in Segment 9.20, the choice of base does not matter.

Figure 9-4 tabulates the magnitudes of these functions for increasing values of the problem size n. From this data you can see that $O(\log \log n)$, $O(\log n)$, and $O(\log^2 n)$ algorithms are much faster than $O(n)$ algorithms. Although $O(n \log n)$ algorithms are significantly slower than $O(n)$ algorithms, they are markedly faster than $O(n^2)$ algorithms.

Figure 9-4   Typical growth-rate functions evaluated at increasing values of n

n	$\log (\log n)$	$\log n$	$(\log n)^2$	n	$n \log n$	n^2	n^3	2^n	$n!$
10	2	3	11	10	33	10^2	10^3	10^3	10^5
10^2	3	7	44	100	664	10^4	10^6	10^{30}	10^{94}
10^3	3	10	99	1000	9966	10^6	10^9	10^{301}	10^{1435}
10^4	4	13	177	10,000	132,877	10^8	10^{12}	10^{3010}	$10^{19,335}$
10^5	4	17	276	100,000	1,660,964	10^{10}	10^{15}	$10^{30,103}$	$10^{243,338}$
10^6	4	20	397	1,000,000	19,931,569	10^{12}	10^{18}	$10^{301,030}$	$10^{2,933,369}$

Note: When analyzing the time efficiency of an algorithm, consider large problems. For small problems, the difference between the execution times of two solutions to the same problem is usually insignificant.

9.16   **Example.** Segments 9.2 and 9.5 showed you two ways to perform a computation. One way was noticeably slow. You should now be able to predict this behavior without actually running the code.

The first way—call it Method 1—used this loop:

```
long product = 0;
for (; secondOperand > 0; secondOperand--)
   product = product + firstOperand;
```

How many times is `firstOperand` added to `product`? If `secondOperand` contains an integer n, then n such additions occur. When n is large, so is the number of additions required to compute the solution. From our discussion in the previous section, we can say that Method 1 is $O(n)$.

The second way—call it Method 2—used the following code, where `secondOperandLength` is the number of digits in `secondOperand`:

```
long product = 0;
for (; secondOperandLength > 0; secondOperandLength--)
{
   long digit = secondOperand - (secondOperand/10) * 10;

   for (; digit > 0; digit--)
     product = product + firstOperand;

   secondOperand = secondOperand/10;
   firstOperand = 10 * firstOperand;
} // end for
```

How many times is firstOperand added to product this time? Each digit of the second operand can be at most 9, so the inner for loop adds firstOperand to product at most nine times. The loop, in fact, executes once for each digit in secondOperand. Since secondOperand contains secondOperandLength digits, the loop adds firstOperand to product at most 9 * secondOperandLength times.

If secondOperand contains an integer n, as it does in Method 1, how does n affect secondOperandLength here? The data in Figure 9-5 can help us answer this question. The figure tabulates $\log_{10} n$ truncated to an integer—which we denote as $\lfloor \log_{10} n \rfloor$—for two-digit, three-digit, and four-digit values of the integer n. (Note that $\lfloor 4.9 \rfloor$, for example, is 4.) You can see that the number of digits in n is $1 + \lfloor \log_{10} n \rfloor$. Therefore, the number of additions that Method 2 requires—at most 9 * secondOperandLength—is at most $9 * (1 + \lfloor \log_{10} n \rfloor)$.

Figure 9-5   The number of digits in an integer n compared with the integer portion of $\log_{10} n$

n	Number of Digits	$\lfloor \log_{10} n \rfloor$
10 – 99	2	1
100 – 999	3	2
1000 – 9999	4	3

Now we need to compare our analyses of Methods 1 and 2. Method 1 requires n additions. Method 2 requires at most $9 * (1 + \lfloor \log_{10} n \rfloor)$ additions. Which approach requires the fewest additions? Let's see if we can answer this question by looking at the data in Figure 9-6. For values of n greater than 18,

$$n > 9 * (1 + \lfloor \log_{10} n \rfloor)$$

Figure 9-6   The values of two logarithmic growth-rate functions for various ranges of n

n	$\lfloor \log_{10} n \rfloor$	$9 * (1 + \lfloor \log_{10} n \rfloor)$
10 – 99	1	18
100 – 999	2	27
1000 – 9999	3	36
10,000 – 99,999	4	45
100,000 – 999,999	5	54

As n increases, n is much larger than $9 * (1 + \lfloor \log_{10} n \rfloor)$. Since Method 1 is O($n$), it requires many more additions than Method 2 when n is large, and so it is much slower. In fact, Method 2 is O(log n) in its worst case. Figure 9-4 shows that an O(n) algorithm is slower than an O(log n) algorithm.

Note: **Floors and ceilings**
The **floor** of a number x, denoted as $\lfloor x \rfloor$, is the largest integer less than or equal to x. For example, $\lfloor 4.9 \rfloor$ is 4. When you **truncate** a real number to an integer, you actually are computing the number's floor by discarding any fractional portion. The **ceiling** of a number x, denoted as $\lceil x \rceil$, is the smallest integer greater than or equal to x. For example, $\lceil 4.1 \rceil$ is 5.

Formalities

9.17 Big Oh notation has a formal mathematical meaning that can justify some of the sleight-of-hand we used in the previous sections. You saw that an algorithm's actual time requirement is directly proportional to a function f of the problem size n. For example, $f(n)$ might be $n^2 + n + 1$. In this case, we would conclude that the algorithm is of order at most n^2—that is, $O(n^2)$. We essentially have replaced $f(n)$ with a simpler function—let's call it $g(n)$. In this example, $g(n)$ is n^2.

What does it really mean to say that a function $f(n)$ is of order at most $g(n)$—that is, that $f(n) = O(g(n))$? In simple terms, it means that Big Oh provides an upper bound on a function's growth rate. More formally, we have the following mathematical definition.

Note: Formal definition of Big Oh

An algorithm's time requirement $f(n)$ is of order at most $g(n)$—that is, $f(n) = O(g(n))$—in case a positive real number c and positive integer N exist such that $f(n) \leq c\, g(n)$ for all $n \geq N$.

Figure 9-7 illustrates this definition. You can see that when n is large enough—that is, when $n \geq N$—$f(n)$ does not exceed $c\, g(n)$. The opposite is true for smaller values of n.

Figure 9-7 An illustration of the definition of Big Oh

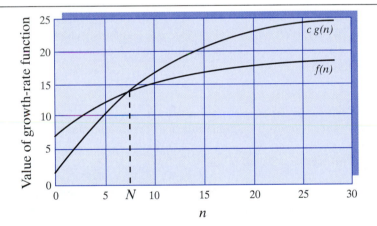

9.18 **Example.** In Segment 9.14, we said that an algorithm that uses $4n + 3$ operations is $O(n)$. We now can show that $4n + 3 = O(n)$ by using the formal definition of Big Oh.

When $n \geq 3$, $4n + 3 \leq 4n + n = 5n$. Thus, if we let $f(n) = 4n + 3$, $g(n) = n$, $c = 5$, and $N = 3$, we have shown that $4n + 3 = O(n)$. That is, if an algorithm requires time directly proportional to $4n + 3$, it is $O(n)$.

Other values for the constants c and N will also work. For example, $4n + 3 \leq 4n + 3n = 7n$ when $n \geq 1$. Thus by choosing $c = 7$ and $N = 1$, we have shown that $4n + 3 = O(n)$.

You need to be careful when choosing $g(n)$. For example, we just found that $4n + 3 \leq 7n$ when $n \geq 1$. But $7n < n^2$ when $n \geq 7$. So why wouldn't we let $g(n) = n^2$ and conclude that our algorithm is $O(n^2)$? Although we could draw this conclusion, it is not as good—or **tight**—as it can be. You want the upper bound on $f(n)$ to be as small as possible, and you want it to involve simple functions like the ones given in Figure 9-4.

9.19

Example. Show that $4n^2 + 50n - 10 = O(n^2)$. It is easy to see that

$$4n^2 + 50n - 10 \leq 4n^2 + 50n \text{ for any } n$$

Since $50n \leq 50n^2$ for $n \geq 50$,

$$4n^2 + 50n - 10 \leq 4n^2 + 50n^2 = 54n^2 \text{ for } n \geq 50$$

Thus, with $c = 54$ and $N = 50$, we have shown that $4n^2 + 50n - 10 = O(n^2)$.

Note: To show that $f(n) = O(g(n))$, replace the smaller terms in $f(n)$ with larger terms until only one term is left.

Question 3   Show that $3n^2 + 2^n = O(2^n)$. What values of c and N did you use?

9.20

Example. Show that $\log_b n = O(\log_2 n)$. Let $L = \log_b n$ and $B = \log_2 b$. From the meaning of a logarithm, we can conclude that $n = b^L$ and $b = 2^B$. Combining these two conclusions, we have

$$n = b^L = (2^B)^L = 2^{BL}$$

Thus, $\log_2 n = BL = B \log_b n$ or, equivalently, $\log_b n = (1/B) \log_2 n$ for any $n \geq 1$. Taking $c = 1/B$ and $N = 1$ in the definition of Big O, we reach the desired conclusion.

It follows from this example that the general behavior of a logarithmic function is the same regardless of its base. Often the logarithms used in growth-rate functions are base 2. But since the base really does not matter, we typically omit it.

Note: The base of a log in a growth-rate function is usually omitted, since $O(\log_a n) = O(\log_b n)$.

9.21   **Identities.** The following identities hold for Big Oh notation:

$$O(k f(n)) = O(f(n)) \text{ for a constant } k$$
$$O(f(n)) + O(g(n)) = O(f(n) + g(n))$$
$$O(f(n)) O(g(n)) = O(f(n) g(n))$$

By using these identities and ignoring smaller terms in a growth-rate function, you can usually determine the order of an algorithm's time requirement with little effort. For example, if the growth-rate function is $4n^2 + 50n - 10$,

$$O(4n^2 + 50n - 10) = O(4n^2) \text{ by ignoring the smaller terms}$$
$$= O(n^2) \text{ by ignoring the multiplier}$$

9.22   **The complexities of program constructs.** The time complexity of a sequence of statements in an algorithm or program is the sum of the statements' individual complexities. However, it is sufficient to take instead the largest of these complexities. Thus, if $S_1, S_2, \ldots, S_k$ is a sequence of statements, and if f_i is the growth-rate function for statement S_i, the complexity is $O(\max(f_1, f_2,..., f_k))$.

The time complexity of the if statement

```
if (condition)
    S₁
else
    S₂
```

is the sum of the complexity of the condition and the complexity of S_1 or S_2, whichever is largest.

The time complexity of a loop is the complexity of its body times the number of times the body executes. Thus, the complexity of a loop such as

> **for** i = 1 *to* n
>   S

is $O(n f(n))$, where f is the growth-rate function for S.

9.23   **Other notations.** Although we will use Big Oh notation most often in this book, other notations are sometimes useful when describing an algorithm's time requirement $f(n)$. We mention them here primarily to expose you to them. Beginning with the definition of Big Oh that you saw earlier, we define **Big Omega** and **Big Theta**.

- **Big Oh.** $f(n)$ is of order at most $g(n)$—that is, $f(n) = O(g(n))$—in case positive constants c and N exist such that $f(n) \leq c\ g(n)$ for all $n \geq N$. The time requirement $f(n)$ is not larger than $c\ g(n)$. Thus, an analysis that uses Big Oh produces a maximum time requirement for an algorithm.
- **Big Omega.** $f(n)$ is of order at least $g(n)$—that is, $f(n) = \Omega(g(n))$—in case $g(n) = O(f(n))$. In other words, in case positive constants c and N exist such that $f(n) \geq c\ g(n)$ for all $n \geq N$. The time requirement $f(n)$ is not smaller than $c\ g(n)$. Thus, a Big Omega analysis produces a minimum time requirement for an algorithm.
- **Big Theta.** $f(n)$ is of order $g(n)$—that is, $f(n) = \Theta(g(n))$—in case $f(n) = O(g(n))$ and $g(n) = O(f(n))$. Another way to say the same thing is $f(n) = O(g(n))$ and $f(n) = \Omega(g(n))$. The time requirement $f(n)$ is the same as $g(n)$. A Big Theta analysis assures that the time estimate is as good as possible. Even so, Big Oh is the more common notation.

Picturing Efficiency

9.24   Much of an algorithm's work occurs during its repetitive phases, that is, during the execution of loops or as a result of recursive calls. In this section, we will illustrate the time efficiency of several examples.

We begin with the loop in Algorithm A of Figure 9-1, which appears in pseudocode as follows:

> **for** i = 1 *to* n
>   sum = sum + i

The body of this loop requires a constant amount of execution time, and so it is $O(1)$. Figure 9-8 represents that time with one icon for each repetition of the loop, and so a row of n icons represents the loop's total execution time. This algorithm is $O(n)$: Its time requirement grows as n grows.

Figure 9-8   An $O(n)$ algorithm

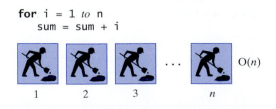

9.25 Algorithm B in Figure 9-1 contains nested loops, as follows:

```
for i = 1 to n
{
  for j = 1 to i
    sum = sum + 1
}
```

When loops are nested, you examine the innermost loop first. Here, the body of the inner loop requires a constant amount of execution time, and so it is O(1). If we again represent that time with an icon, a row of i icons represents the time requirement for the inner loop. Since the inner loop is the body of the outer loop, it executes n times. Figure 9-9 illustrates the time requirement for these nested loops, which is proportional to $1 + 2 + \ldots + n$. Question 1 asked you to show that

$$1 + 2 + \ldots + n = n(n + 1) / 2$$

Thus, the computation is $O(n^2)$.

Figure 9-9 An $O(n^2)$ algorithm

```
for i = 1 to n
{  for j = 1 to i
      sum = sum + 1
}
```

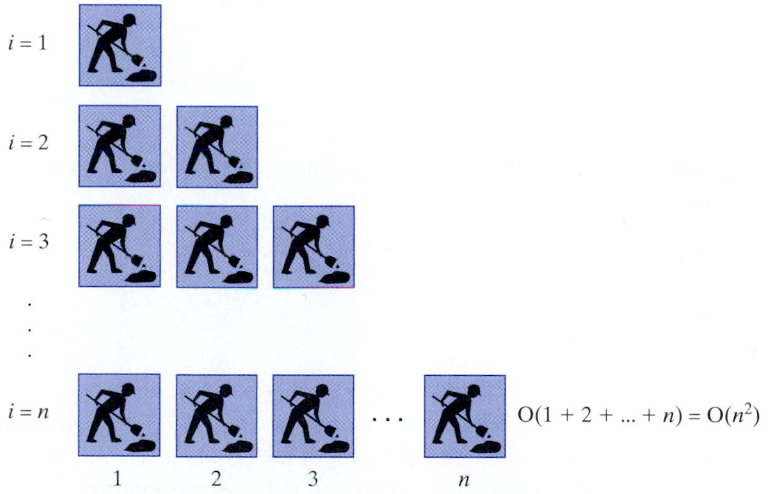

9.26 The body of the inner loop in the previous segment executes a variable number of times that depends on the outer loop. Suppose we change the inner loop so that it executes the same number of times for each repetition of the outer loop, as follows:

```
for i = 1 to n
{
  for j = 1 to n
    sum = sum + 1
}
```

Figure 9-10 illustrates these nested loops and shows that the computation is $O(n^2)$.

Figure 9-10   Another $O(n^2)$ algorithm

```
for i = 1 to n
{   for j = 1 to n
        sum = sum + 1
}
```

$i = 1$ ...

$i = 2$ ...

$i = 3$ ...

$\vdots$

$i = n$ ... $O(n * n) = O(n^2)$

    1   2   3 n

Question 4   Using Big Oh notation, what is the order of the following computation's time requirement?

```
for i = 1 to n
{
   for j = 1 to 5
      sum = sum + 1
}
```

9.27   Let's get a feel for the growth-rate functions in Figure 9-4. As we mentioned, the time requirement for an $O(1)$ algorithm is independent of the problem size n. We can apply such an algorithm to larger and larger problems without affecting the execution time. This situation is ideal, but not typical.

For other orders, what happens if we double the problem size? The time requirement for an $O(\log n)$ algorithm will change, but not by much. An $O(n)$ algorithm will need twice the time, an $O(n^2)$ algorithm will need four times the time, and an $O(n^3)$ algorithm will need eight times the time. Doubling the problem size for an $O(2^n)$ algorithm squares the time requirement. Figure 9-11 tabulates these observations.

Question 5   Suppose that you can solve a problem of a certain size on a given computer in time T by using an $O(n)$ algorithm. If you double the size of the problem, how fast must your computer be to solve the problem in the same time?

Question 6   Repeat Question 5, but instead use an $O(n^2)$ algorithm.

Figure 9-11   The effect of doubling the problem size on an algorithm's time requirement

Growth-Rate Function for Size n Problems	Growth-Rate Function for Size $2n$ Problems	Effect on Time Requirement
1	1	No effect
$\log n$	$1 + \log n$	Negligible
n	$2n$	Doubles
$n \log n$	$2n \log n + 2n$	Doubles and then adds $2n$
n^2	$(2n)^2$	Quadruples
n^3	$(2n)^3$	Multiplies by 8
2^n	2^{2n}	Squares

9.28   Now suppose that your computer can perform one million operations per second. How long will it take an algorithm to solve a problem whose size is one million? We cannot answer this question exactly without knowing the algorithm, but the computations in Figure 9-12 will give you a sense of how the algorithm's Big Oh would affect our answer. An $O(\log n)$ algorithm would take a fraction of a second, whereas an $O(2^n)$ algorithm would take billions of years!

Figure 9-12   The time to process one million items by algorithms of various orders at the rate of one million operations per second

Growth-Rate Function f	$f(10^6)/10^6$
$\log n$	0.0000199 seconds
n	1 second
$n \log n$	19.9 seconds
n^2	11.6 days
n^3	31,709.8 years
2^n	$10^{301,016}$ years

Note: You can use $O(n^2)$, $O(n^3)$, or even $O(2^n)$ algorithms as long as your problem size is small. For example, at the rate of one million operations per second, an $O(n^2)$ algorithm would take one second to solve a problem whose size is 1000. An $O(n^3)$ algorithm would take one second to solve a problem whose size is 100. And an $O(2^n)$ algorithm would take about one second to solve a problem whose size is 20.

Question 7   The following algorithm determines whether an array contains duplicates within its first n items:

Algorithm hasDuplicates(array, n)
```
for (index = 0 to n-2)
  for (rest = index+1 to n-1)
    if (array[index] equals array[rest])
      return true
return false
```

What is the Big Oh of this algorithm in the worst case?

The Efficiency of Implementations of the ADT List

We now consider the time efficiency of two implementations of the ADT list that we discussed in previous chapters.

The Array-Based Implementation

One of the implementations of the ADT list given in Chapter 5 used a fixed-size array to represent the list's entries. We can now determine the efficiency of the list operations when implemented in this way.

9.29   **Adding to the end of the list.** Let's begin with the operation that adds a new entry to the end of the list. Segment 5.6 provided the following implementation for this operation:

```
public boolean add(Object newEntry)
{
  boolean isSuccessful = true;

  if (!isFull())
  {
    entry[length] = newEntry;
    length++;
  }
  else
    isSuccessful = false;

  return isSuccessful;
} // end add
```

Each step in this method—determining whether the list is full, assigning a new entry to an array element, and incrementing the length—is an $O(1)$ operation. By applying your knowledge of the material presented in Segments 9.21 and 9.22, you can show that this method is $O(1)$. Intuitively, since you know that the new entry belongs at the end of the list, you know what array element should contain the new entry. Thus, you can make this assignment independently of any other entries in the list.

9.30   **Adding to the list at a given position.** The ADT list has another method that adds a new entry to a list, but this one adds the entry at a position that the client specifies:

```
public boolean add(int newPosition, Object newEntry)
{
  boolean isSuccessful = true;

  if (!isFull() && (newPosition >= 1)
                && (newPosition <= length+1))
  {
    makeRoom(newPosition);
    entry[newPosition-1] = newEntry;
    length++;
  }
  else
    isSuccessful = false;

  return isSuccessful;
} // end add
```

The method's general form is similar to the previous add method in that it determines whether the list is full, assigns the new entry to an array element, and increments the length. Once again, these are all O(1) operations, as are the initial comparisons that check the value of newPosition. What is different here is making room in the array for the new entry. This task is accomplished by the private method makeRoom:

```
private void makeRoom(int newPosition)
{
   for (int index = length; index >= newPosition; index--)
      entry[index] = entry[index-1];
} // end makeRoom
```

The worst case occurs when newPosition is 1 because the method must shift all of the list elements. If the list contains n entries, the body of the loop is repeated n times in the worst case. Therefore, the method makeRoom is O(n). This observation implies that the method add is also O(n).

Question 8   What is the Big Oh of the method remove in the worst case? (See Segment 5.8.) Assume an array-based implementation, and use an argument similar to the one we just made for add.

Question 9   What is the Big Oh of the method replace in the worst case? (See Segment 5.9.)

Question 10   What is the Big Oh of the method getEntry in the worst case? (See Segment 5.9.)

Question 11   What is the Big Oh of the method contains in the worst case? (See Segment 5.10.)

Question 12   What is the Big Oh of the method display in the worst case? (See Segment 5.5.)

The Linked Implementation

9.31   **Adding to the end of the list.** Now consider the linked implementation of the ADT list as given in Chapter 6. Let's begin with the method in Segment 6.26 that adds to the end of the list:

```
public boolean add(Object newEntry)
{
   Node newNode = new Node(newEntry);

   if (isEmpty())
      firstNode = newNode;
   else
   {
      Node lastNode = getNodeAt(length);
      lastNode.next = newNode;
   } // end if

   length++;
   return true;
} // end add
```

Except for the call to getNodeAt, the statements in this method are all O(1) operations.

We need to examine `getNodeAt`:

```java
private Node getNodeAt(int givenPosition)
{
   Node currentNode = firstNode;
   for (int counter = 1; counter < givenPosition; counter++)
     currentNode = currentNode.next;
   return currentNode;
} // end getNodeAt
```

Except for the loop, the method contains all O(1) operations. In the worst case, `givenPosition` is *n*, so the loop, and therefore the method, is O(*n*). We can conclude that the method add is also O(*n*). This result makes intuitive sense since, to add at the end of the list, the method must traverse the chain of linked nodes to locate the last one.

9.32   **Adding to the list at a given position.** The analysis of the second add method is essentially the same as that of the one in the previous segment. To add a new entry at a given position, the method must traverse the chain of linked nodes to determine the point of insertion. In the worst case, the traversal goes to the end of the chain. If you look at the method's implementation in Segment 6.30 of Chapter 6, you will see that it calls the method `getNodeAt`, which you just saw is O(*n*). Reaching the conclusion that the second add method is O(*n*) is straightforward.

Question 13   What is the Big Oh of the linked implementation of the method `remove` in the worst case? (See Segment 6.37.) Use an argument similar to the one we just made for add.

9.33   **Retrieving an entry.** Consider the method `getEntry` that retrieves the item at a given position within a list:

```java
public Object getEntry(int givenPosition)
{
   Object result = null; // result to return

   if (!isEmpty() && (givenPosition >= 1) && (givenPosition <= length))
     result = getNodeAt(givenPosition).data;

   return result;
} // end getEntry
```

This method uses the method `getNodeAt` to locate the desired entry in the chain of linked nodes. We saw that `getNodeAt` is O(*n*), so `getEntry` is also O(*n*).

Question 14   What is the Big Oh of the method `replace` in the worst case? (See Segment 6.38.)

Question 15   What is the Big Oh of the method `contains` in the worst case? (See Segment 6.40.)

Question 16   What is the Big Oh of the method `display` in the worst case? (See Appendix E for the answer to Question 11 of Chapter 6.)

Comparing the Implementations

9.34   Figure 9-13 summarizes the orders of the ADT list's operations for the implementations that use an array and a chain of linked nodes. These orders represent the worst-case behaviors of these operations.

For an array-based implementation of the ADT list, the operations add by position, and remove, contains, and display are each O(n). The other operations are each O(1). For a linked implementation, all operations are O(n) except for clear, getLength, isEmpty, and isFull. These four operations are each O(1).

As you can see, many of the operations have the same Big Oh for both implementations. However, operations that add to the end of a list, replace an entry, or retrieve an entry are much faster when you use an array to represent a list than when you use linked nodes. If your application uses these particular operations frequently, an array-based implementation could be attractive.

Adding a tail reference to the linked implementation, as was done in Segments 6.43 through 6.48 of Chapter 6, makes adding to the end of the list an O(1) operation. Exercise 5 at the end of this chapter asks you to analyze this implementation.

Figure 9-13   The time efficiencies of the ADT list operations for two implementations, expressed in Big Oh notation

Operation	Array	Linked
add(newEntry)	O(1)	O(n)
add(newPosition, newEntry)	O(n)	O(n)
remove(givenPosition)	O(n)	O(n)
replace(givenPosition, newEntry)	O(1)	O(n)
getEntry(givenPosition)	O(1)	O(n)
contains(anEntry)	O(n)	O(n)
display()	O(n)	O(n)
clear(), getLength(), isEmpty(), isFull()	O(1)	O(1)

Programming Tip: When choosing an implementation for an ADT, you should consider the operations that your application requires. If you use a particular operation frequently, you want its implementation to be efficient. Conversely, if you rarely use an operation, you can afford to use a class that has an inefficient implementation of that operation.

CHAPTER SUMMARY

- An algorithm's complexity is described in terms of the time and space required to execute it.

- An algorithm's time requirement $f(n)$ is of order at most $g(n)$—that is, $f(n) = O(g(n))$—in case positive constants c and N exist such that $f(n) \leq c\, g(n)$ for all $n \geq N$.

- The relationships among typical growth-rate functions are as follows:

- $O(1) < O(\log \log n) < O(\log n) < O(\log^2 n) < O(n) < O(n \log n) < O(n^2) < O(n^3) < O(2^n) < O(n!)$

- For an array-based implementation of the ADT list, the operations add by position, and **remove**, **contains**, and **display** are each O(n). The other operations are each O(1). For a linked implementation, all operations are O(n) except for **clear**, **getLength**, **isEmpty**, and **isFull**. These four operations are each O(1).

EXERCISES

1. Using Big Oh notation, indicate the time requirement of each of the following tasks in the worst case. Describe any assumptions that you make.

   a. After arriving at a party, you shake hands with each person there.
   b. Each person in a room shakes hands with everyone else in the room.
   c. You climb a flight of stairs.
   d. You slide down the banister.
   e. After entering an elevator, you press a button to choose a floor.
   f. You ride the elevator from the ground floor up to the nth floor.
   g. You read a book twice.

2. Describe a way to climb from the bottom of a flight of stairs to the top in $O(n^2)$ time.

3. Using Big Oh notation, indicate the time requirement of each of the following tasks in the worst case.

   a. Display all the integers in an array of integers.
   b. Display all the integers in a chain of linked nodes.
   c. Display the nth integer in an array of integers.
   d. Compute the sum of the first n even integers in an array of integers.

4. Chapter 5 describes an implementation of the ADT list that uses an array that can expand dynamically. Using Big Oh notation, what is the time efficiency of the method doubleArray, as given in Segment 5.16?

5. Suppose that you alter the linked implementation of the ADT list to include a tail reference, as described in Segments 6.43 through 6.48. The time efficiencies of what methods, if any, are affected by this change? Use Big Oh notation to describe the efficiencies of any affected methods.

6. By using the definition of Big Oh, show that

   a. $6n^2 + 3$ is $O(n^2)$
   b. $n^2 + 17n + 1$ is $O(n^2)$
   c. $5n^3 + 100 n^2 - n - 10$ is $O(n^3)$
   d. $3n^2 + 2^n$ is $O(2^n)$

7. In the worst case, Algorithm X requires $n^2 + 9n + 5$ operations and Algorithm Y requires $5n^2$ operations. What is the Big Oh of each algorithm?

8. Plot the number of operations required by Algorithms X and Y of Exercise 7 as a function of n. What can you conclude?

9. Show that $O(\log_a n) = O(\log_b n)$ for $a, b > 1$. *Hint*: $\log_a n = \log_b n / \log_b a$.

10. Suppose that your implementation of a particular algorithm appears in Java as follows:

```
for (int pass = 1; pass <= n; pass++)
{
    for (int index = 0; index < n; index++)
    {
        for (int count = 1; count < 10; count++)
        {
            . . .
        } // end for
    } // end for
} // end for
```

The algorithm involves an array of *n* items. The previous code shows the only repetition in the algorithm, but it does not show the computations that occur within the loops. These computations, however, are independent of *n*. What is the order of the algorithm?

11. Repeat Exercise 10, but replace 10 with n in the inner loop.

12. Using Big Oh notation, indicate the time requirement of the methods in `IteratorInterface` when implemented as an internal iterator of the ADT list. The implementation begins at Segment 7.9.

13. Using Big Oh notation, indicate the time requirement of the methods in `IteratorInterface` when implemented as an external iterator of the ADT list. The implementation begins at Segment 7.19. Consider both linked and array-based implementations of the list.

14. Using Big Oh notation, indicate the time requirement of the methods in Java's interface `Iterator`, as implemented in Chapter 8. The linked implementation begins at Segment 8.6, and the array-based implementation begins at Segment 8.10.

15. Using Big Oh notation, indicate the time requirement of the methods in Java's interface `ListIterator`, as implemented in Chapter 8. The array-based implementation begins at Segment 8.24.

16. If $f(n)$ is $O(g(n))$ and $g(n)$ is $O(h(n))$, use the definition of Big Oh to show that $f(n)$ is $O(h(n))$.

17. Segment 9.15 and the chapter summary showed the relationships among typical growth-rate functions. Indicate where the following growth-rate functions belong in this ordering:

a. $n^2 \log n$
b. $\sqrt{n}$
c. $n^2/\log n$

18. Show that $7n^2 + 5n$ is not $O(n)$.

19. Suppose that you have a dictionary whose words are not sorted in alphabetical order. As a function of the number, *n*, of words, what is the efficiency of searching for a particular word in this dictionary?

20. Repeat Exercise 19 for a dictionary whose words are sorted alphabetically. Compare your results with those for Exercise 19.

21. Consider a football player who runs windsprints on a football field. He begins at the 0-yard line and runs to the 1-yard line and then back to the 0-yard line. Then he runs to the 2-yard line and back to the 0-yard line, runs to the 3-yard line and back to the 0-yard line, and so on until he has reached the 10-yard line and returned to the 0-yard line.

    a. How many total yards does he run?

    b. How many total yards does he run if he reaches the n-yard line instead of the 10-yard line?

    c. How does his total distance run compare to that of a sprinter who simply starts at the 0-yard line and races to the n-yard line?

22. Exercise 3 in Chapter 4 asked you to write Java statements at the client level that return the position of a given object in a list. Using Big Oh notation, compare the time requirement of these statements with that of the method `getPosition` in Exercise 3 of Chapter 5 and Exercise 3 of Chapter 6.

PROJECTS

For the following projects, you should know how to time a section of code in Java. One approach is to use the class `java.util.Date`. A Date object contains the time at which it was constructed. This time is stored as a `long` integer equal to the number of milliseconds that have passed since 00:00:00.000 GMT on January 1, 1970. By subtracting the starting time in milliseconds from the ending time in milliseconds, you get the run time—in milliseconds—of a section of code.

For example, suppose that `thisMethod` is the name of a method you wish to time. The following statements will compute the number of milliseconds that `thisMethod` requires to execute:

```
Date current = new Date();              // get current time
long startTime = current.getTime();
thisMethod();                           // code to be timed
current = new Date();                   // get current time
long stopTime = current.getTime();
long elapsedTime = stopTime - startTime; // milliseconds
```

1. Write a Java program that implements the three algorithms in Figure 9-1 and times them for various values of n. The program should display a table of the run times of each algorithm for various values of n.

2. Consider the following two loops:

```
// Loop A
for (i = 1; i <= n; i++)
   for (j = 1; j <= 10000; j++)
      sum = sum + j;

// Loop B
for (i = 1; i <= n; i++)
   for (j = 1; j <= n; j++)
      sum = sum + j;
```

Although loop A is $O(n)$ and loop B is $O(n^2)$, loop B can be faster than loop A for small values of n. Design and implement an experiment to find the value of n for which loop B is faster.

3. Repeat Project 2, but use the following for loop B:

```
// Loop B
for (i = 1; i <= n; i++)
  for (j = 1; j <= n; j++)
    for (k = 1; k <= n; k++)
      sum = sum + k;
```

10
Recursion

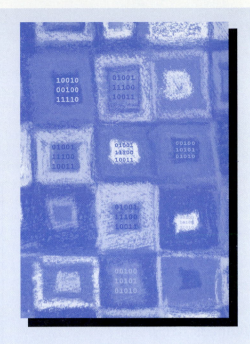

CONTENTS

What Is Recursion?
Tracing a Recursive Method
Recursive Methods That Return a Value
Recursively Processing an Array
Recursively Processing a Linked Chain
The Time Efficiency of Recursive Methods
    The Time Efficiency of countDown
    The Time Efficiency of Computing x^n
A Simple Solution to a Difficult Problem
A Poor Solution to a Simple Problem
Tail Recursion
Mutual Recursion

PREREQUISITES

Chapter   1   Java Classes
Chapter   5   List Implementations That Use Arrays
Chapter   6   List Implementations That Link Data
Chapter   9   The Efficiency of Algorithms

OBJECTIVES

After studying this chapter, you should be able to

- Determine whether a given recursive method will end successfully in a finite amount of time
- Write a recursive method
- Estimate the time efficiency of a recursive method
- Identify tail recursion and replace it with iteration

Repetition is a major feature of many algorithms. In fact, repeating things rapidly is a key ability of computers. Two problem-solving processes involve repetition; they are called iteration and recursion. In fact, most programming languages provide two kinds of repetitive constructs, iterative and recursive.

You know about iteration because you know how to write a loop. Regardless of the loop construct you use—for, while, or do—your loop contains the statements that you want to repeat and a mechanism for controlling the number of repetitions. You might have a counted loop that counts repetitions as 1, 2, 3, 4, 5, or 5, 4, 3, 2, 1. Or the loop might execute repeatedly while a boolean variable or expression is true. Iteration often provides a straightforward and efficient way to implement a repetitive process.

At times, iterative solutions are elusive or hopelessly complex. Discovering or verifying such solutions is not a simple task. In these cases, recursion can provide an elegant alternative. Some recursive solutions can be the best solutions, some provide insight for finding a better iterative solution, and some should not be used at all because they are grossly inefficient. Recursion, however, remains an important problem-solving strategy.

This chapter will show you how to think recursively.

What Is Recursion?

10.1   You can build a house by hiring a contractor. The contractor in turn hires several subcontractors to complete portions of the house. Each subcontractor might hire other subcontractors to help. You use the same approach when you solve a problem by breaking it into smaller problems. In one special variation of this problem-solving process, the smaller problems are identical except for their size. This special process is called **recursion.**

Suppose that you can solve a problem by solving an identical but smaller problem. How will you solve the smaller problem? If you use recursion again, you will need to solve an even smaller problem that is just like the original problem in every other respect. How will replacing a problem with another one ever lead to a solution? One key to the success of recursion is that eventually you will reach a smaller problem whose solution you know because either it is obvious or it is given. The solution to this smallest problem is probably not the solution to your original problem, but it can help you reach it. Either just before or just after you solve a smaller problem, you usually contribute a portion of the solution. This portion, together with the solutions to the other, smaller problems, provides the solution to the larger problem.

Let's look at an example.

10.2   **Example: The countdown.** It's New Year's Eve and the giant ball is falling in Times Square. The crowd counts down the last ten seconds: "10, 9, 8, . . ." Suppose that I ask you to count down to 1 beginning at some positive integer like 10. You could shout "10" and then ask a friend to count down from 9. Counting down from 9 is a problem that is exactly like counting down from 10, except that there is less to do. It is a smaller problem.

To count down from 9, your friend shouts "9" and asks a friend to count down from 8. This sequence of events continues until eventually someone's friend is asked to count down from 1. That friend simply shouts "1." No other friend is needed. You can see these events in Figure 10-1.

In this example, I've asked you to complete a task. You saw that you could contribute a part of the task and then ask a friend to do the rest. You know that your friend's task is just like the original task, but it is smaller. You also know that when your friend completes this smaller task, your job will be done. What is missing from the process just described is the signal that each friend gives to the previous person at the completion of a task.

When you count down from 10, I need you to tell me when you are done. I don't care how—or who—does the job, as long as you tell me when it is done. I can take a nap until I hear from you. Likewise, when you ask a friend to count down from 9, you do not care how your friend finishes the job. You just want to know when it is done so you can tell me that you are done. You can take a nap while you are waiting.

 Note: Recursion is a problem-solving process that breaks a problem into identical but smaller problems.

Figure 10-1   Counting down from 10

Ultimately, we have a group of napping people waiting for someone to say "I'm done." The first person to make that claim is the person who shouts "1," as Figure 10-1 illustrates, since that person needs no help in counting down from 1. At this time in this particular example, the problem is solved, but I don't know that because I'm still asleep. The person who shouted "1" says "I'm done" to the person who shouted "2." The person who shouted "2" says "I'm done" to the person who shouted "3," and so on, until you say "I'm done" to me. The job is done; thanks for your help; I have no idea how you did it, and I don't need to know!

10.3   What does any of this have to do with Java? In the previous example, you play the role of a Java method. I, the client, have asked you, the recursive method, to count down from 10. When you ask a friend for help, you are invoking a method to count down from 9. But you do not invoke another method; you invoke yourself!

Note: A method that calls itself is a **recursive method.** The invocation is a **recursive call** or **recursive invocation.**

The following Java method counts down from a given positive integer, displaying one integer per line.

```java
/** Task: Counts down from a given positive integer.
 *  @param integer  an integer > 0 */
public static void countDown(int integer)
{
  System.out.println(integer);
  if (integer > 1)
    countDown(integer - 1);
} // end countDown
```

Since the given integer is positive, the method can display it immediately. This step is analogous to you shouting "10" in the previous example. Next the method asks whether it is finished. If the given integer is 1, there is nothing left to do. But if the given integer is larger than 1, we need to count down from integer – 1. We've already noted that this task is smaller but otherwise identical to the original problem. How do we solve this new problem? We invoke a method, but countDown is such a method. It does not matter that we have not finished writing it at this point!

10.4   Will the method countDown actually work? Shortly we will trace the execution of countDown both to convince you that it works and to show you how it works. But traces of recursive methods are messy, and you usually do not have to trace them. If you follow certain guidelines when writing a recursive method, you can be assured that it will work.

In designing a recursive solution, you need to answer certain questions:

Note: **Questions to answer when designing a recursive solution**

- What part of the solution can you contribute directly?
- What smaller but identical problem has a solution that, when taken with your contribution, provides the solution to the original problem?
- When does the process end? That is, what smaller but identical problem has a known solution, and have you reached this problem, or **base case?**

For the method countDown, we have the following answers to these questions:

- The method countDown displays the given integer as the part of the solution that it contributes directly. This happens to occur first here, but it need not always occur first.
- The smaller problem is counting down from integer – 1. The method solves the smaller problem when it calls itself recursively.

- The `if` statement asks if the process has reached the base case. Here the base case occurs when `integer` is 1. Because the method displays `integer` before checking it, nothing is left to do once the base case is identified.

Note: **Design guidelines for successful recursion**

To write a recursive method that behaves correctly, you generally should adhere to the following design guidelines:

- The method definition must contain logic that involves a parameter to the method and leads to different cases. Typically, such logic includes an `if` statement or a `switch` statement.
- One or more of these cases should provide a solution that does not require recursion. These are the **base cases,** or **stopping cases.**
- One or more cases must include a recursive invocation of the method. These recursive invocations should in some sense take a step toward a base case by using "smaller" arguments or solving "smaller" versions of the task performed by the method.

Programming Tip: **Infinite recursion**

A recursive method that does not check for a base case, or that misses the base case, will execute "forever." This situation is known as infinite recursion.

10.5   Before we trace the method `countDown`, we should note that we could have written it in other ways. For example, a first draft of this method might have looked like this:

```java
public static void countDown(int integer)
{
  if (integer == 1)
    System.out.println(integer);
  else
  {
    System.out.println(integer);
    countDown(integer - 1);
  } // end if
} // end countDown
```

Here, the programmer considered the base case first. The solution is clear and perfectly acceptable, but you might want to avoid the redundant `println` statement that occurs in both cases.

10.6   Removing the redundancy just mentioned could result in either the version given earlier in Segment 10.3 or the following one:

```java
public static void countDown(int integer)
{
  if (integer >= 1)
  {
    System.out.println(integer);
    countDown(integer - 1);
  } // end if
} // end countDown
```

When `integer` is 1, this method will produce the recursive call `countDown(0)`. This turns out to be the base case for this method, and nothing is displayed.

All three versions of `countDown` produce correct results; there are probably others as well. Choose the one that is clearest to you.

10.7   The version of `countDown` just given in Segment 10.6 provides us an opportunity to compare it with the following iterative version:

```java
// Iterative version.
public static void countDown(int integer)
{
  while (integer >= 1)
  {
    System.out.println(integer);
    integer--;
  } // end while
} // end countDown
```

The two methods have a similar appearance. Both compare `integer` with 1, but the recursive version uses an `if`, and the iterative version uses a `while`. Both methods display `integer`. Both compute `integer - 1`.

Programming Tip: An iterative method contains a loop. A recursive method calls itself. Although some recursive methods contain a loop *and* call themselves, if you have written a `while` statement within a recursive method, be sure that you did not mean to write an `if` statement.

Question 1   Write a recursive void method that skips *n* lines of output, where *n* is a positive integer. Use `System.out.println()` to skip one line.

Question 2   Describe a recursive algorithm that draws a given number of concentric circles. The innermost circle should have a given diameter. The diameter of each of the other circles should be 4/3 the diameter of the circle just inside it.

Tracing a Recursive Method

10.8   Now let's trace the method `countDown` given in Segment 10.3:

```java
public static void countDown(int integer)
{
  System.out.println(integer);
  if (integer > 1)
    countDown(integer - 1);
} // end countDown
```

Suppose that the client invokes this method with the statement

```java
countDown(3);
```

This call is like any other call to a nonrecursive method. The argument 3 is copied into the parameter `integer` and the following statements are executed:

```java
System.out.println(3);
if (3 > 1)
  countDown(3 - 1); // first recursive call
```

A line containing 3 is displayed, and the recursive call `countDown(2)` occurs, as Figure 10-2a shows.

Execution of the method is suspended until the results of `countDown(2)` are known. In this particular method definition, no statements appear after the recursive call. So although it appears that nothing will happen when execution resumes, it is here that the method returns to the client.

Figure 10-2   The effect of the method call `countDown(3)`

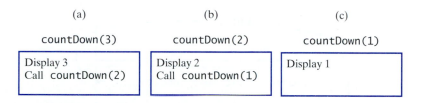

(a)	(b)	(c)
countDown(3)	countDown(2)	countDown(1)
Display 3 Call countDown(2)	Display 2 Call countDown(1)	Display 1

10.9   Continuing our trace, `countDown(2)` causes the following statements to execute:

```
System.out.println(2);
if (2 > 1)
    countDown(2 - 1); // second recursive call
```

A line containing 2 is displayed, and the recursive call `countDown(1)` occurs, as shown in Figure 10-2b. Execution of the method is suspended until the results of `countDown(1)` are known.

The call `countDown(1)` causes the following statements to execute:

```
System.out.println(1);
if (1 > 1)
```

A line containing 1 is displayed, as Figure 10-2c shows, and no other recursive call occurs.

Figure 10-3 illustrates the sequence of events from the time that `countDown` is first called. The numbered arrows indicate the order of the recursive calls and the returns from the method. After 1 is displayed, the method completes execution and returns to the point (arrow 4) after the call `countDown(1)`. Execution continues from there and the method returns to the point (arrow 5) after the call `countDown(2)`. Ultimately, a return to the point after the initial recursive call in the client occurs.

Although tracking these method returns seems like a formality that has gained us nothing, it is an important part of any trace because some recursive methods will do more than simply return to their calling method. You will see an example of such a method shortly.

10.10   Figure 10-3 appears to show multiple copies of the method `countDown`. In reality, however, multiple copies do not exist. Instead, for each call to a method—be it recursive or not—Java records the state of the method, including the values of its parameters and local variables. Each record, called an **activation record,** is analogous to a piece of paper. The records are placed into an ADT called a **stack,** much as you would stack papers one on top of the other. The record of the currently executing method is on top of the stack. In this way, Java can suspend the execution of a recursive method and invoke it again with new argument values. The boxes in Figure 10-3 correspond roughly to activation records, although the figure does not show them in the order in which they would appear in a stack. Figure 10-4 illustrates the activation records that enter and leave the stack as a result of the call countDown(3).

Figure 10-3   Tracing the recursive call countDown(3)

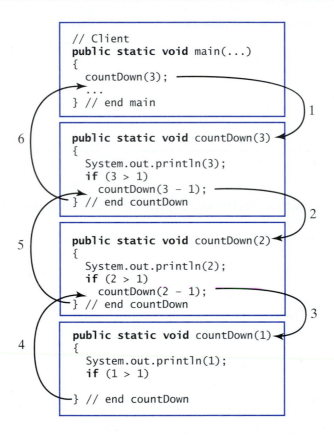

 Note: The stack of activation records
A recursive method uses more memory than an iterative method, in general, because a stack of activation records is used to implement the recursion.

 Programming Tip: Stack overflow
Too many recursive calls can cause the error message "stack overflow." This means that the stack of activation records has become full. In essence, the method has used too much memory. Infinite recursion or large-size problems are the likely causes of this error.

 Question 3   Write a recursive void method countUp(n) that counts up from 1 to *n*, where *n* is a positive integer. *Hint*: A recursive call will occur before you display anything.

Figure 10-4   The stack of activation records during the execution of a call to countDown(3)

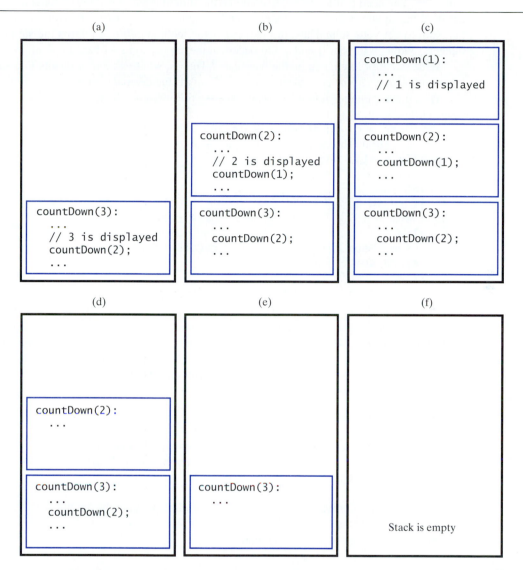

Recursive Methods That Return a Value

10.11   The recursive method countDown in the previous sections is a void method. Valued methods can also be recursive. The guidelines for successful recursion given in Segment 10.4 apply to valued methods as well, with an additional note. Recall that a recursive method must contain a statement such as an if that chooses among several cases. Some of these cases lead to a recursive call, but at least one case has no recursive call. For a valued method, each of these cases must provide a value for the method to return.

10.12   **Example: Compute the sum 1 + 2 + . . . + _n_ for any integer _n_ > 0.** The given value for this problem is the integer _n_. Beginning with this fact will help us to find the smaller problem because its input will also be a single integer. The sum always starts at 1, so that can be assumed.

Suppose that I have given you a positive integer *n* and asked you to compute the sum of the first *n* integers. You need to ask a friend to compute the sum of the first *m* integers for some positive integer *m*. What should *m* be? Well, if your friend computes $1 + \ldots + (n - 1)$, you can simply add *n* to that sum to get your sum. Thus, if sumOf(n) is the method call that returns the sum of the first *n* integers, adding *n* to your friend's sum occurs in the expression sumOf(n-1) + n.

What small problem can be the base case? That is, what value of *n* results in a sum that you know immediately? One possible answer is 1. If *n* is 1, the desired sum is 1.

With these thoughts in mind, we can write the following method:

```
/** @param n   an integer > 0
 *   @return the sum 1 + 2 + ... + n */
public static int sumOf(int n)
{
  int sum;
  if (n == 1)
    sum = 1;                    // base case
  else
    sum = sumOf(n - 1) + n; // recursive call
  return sum;
} // end sumOf
```

10.13   The definition of the method sumOf satisfies the design guidelines for successful recursion. You should be confident that the method will work correctly without tracing its execution. However, a trace will be instructive here because it will not only show you how a valued recursive method works, but also demonstrate actions that occur after a recursive call is complete.

Suppose that the client invokes this method with the statement

```
System.out.println(sumOf(3));
```

The computation occurs as follows:

1. sumOf(3) is sumOf(2) + 3; sumOf(3) suspends execution, and sumOf(2) begins.
2. sumOf(2) is sumOf(1) + 2; sumOf(2) suspends execution, and sumOf(1) begins.
3. sumOf(1) returns 1.

Once the base case is reached, the suspended executions resume, beginning with the most recent. Thus, sumOf(2) returns 1 + 2, or 3; then sumOf(3) returns 3 + 3, or 6. Figure 10-5 illustrates this computation as a stack of activation records.

Question 4   Write a recursive valued method that computes the product of the integers from 1 to *n*, where *n* > 0.

Note: Should you trace a recursive method?
We have shown you how to trace the execution of a recursive method primarily to show you how recursion works and to give you some insight into how a typical compiler implements recursion. Should you ever trace a recursive method? Usually no. You certainly should not trace a recursive method while you are writing it. If the method is incomplete, your trace will be, too, and you are likely to become confused. If a recursive method does not work, follow the suggestions given in the next programming tip. You should trace a recursive method only as a last resort.

Figure 10-5   The stack of activation records during the execution of a call to `sumOf(3)`

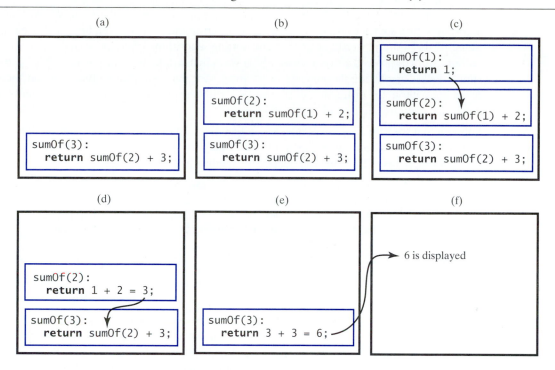

 Programming Tip: **Debugging a recursive method**

If a recursive method does not work, answer the following questions. Any "no" answers should guide you to the error.

- Does the method have at least one parameter?
- Does the method contain a statement that tests a parameter and leads to different cases?
- Did you consider all possible cases?
- Does at least one of these cases cause at least one recursive call?
- Do these recursive calls involve smaller arguments, smaller tasks, or tasks that get closer to the solution?
- If these recursive calls produce or return correct results, will the method produce or return a correct result?
- Is at least one of the cases a base case that has no recursive call?
- Are there enough base cases?
- Does each base case produce a result that is correct for that case?
- If the method returns a value, does each of the cases return a value?

10.14   Our previous examples were simple so that you could study the construction of recursive methods. Since you could have solved these problems iteratively with ease, should you actually use their recursive solutions? Nothing is inherently wrong with these recursive methods. However, given the way that typical present-day systems execute recursive methods, a stack overflow is likely for large values of *n*. Iterative solutions to these simple examples would not have this difficulty and are easy to write. Realize, however, that future operating systems might be able to execute these recursive methods without difficulty.

Recursively Processing an Array

Later in this book we will talk about searching an array for a particular item. We will also look at algorithms that **sort,** or arrange, the items in an array into either ascending or descending order. Some of the more powerful searching and sorting algorithms often are stated recursively. In this section, we will process arrays recursively in ways that will be useful to us later. We have chosen a simple task—displaying the integers in an array—for our examples so that you can focus on the recursion without the distraction of the task. We will consider more complex tasks later in this book and in the exercises at the end of this chapter.

10.15   Suppose that we have an array of integers and we want a method that displays it. So that we can display all or part of the array, the method will display the array elements whose indices range from first through last. Thus, we can declare the method as follows:

```
/** Task: Displays the integers in an array.
 *  @param array  an array of integers
 *  @param first  the index of the first element displayed
 *  @param last   the index of the last element displayed,
 *                first <= last */
public static void displayArray(int[] array, int first, int last)
```

This task is simple and could readily be implemented using iteration. You might not imagine, however, that we could also implement it recursively in a variety of ways. But we can and will.

10.16   **Starting with `array[first]`.** An iterative solution would certainly start at the first element, `array[first]`, so it is natural to have our first recursive method begin there also. If I ask you to display the array, you could display `array[first]` and then ask a friend to display the rest of the array. Displaying the rest of the array is a smaller problem than displaying the entire array. You wouldn't have to ask a friend for help if you had to display only one element—that is, if first and last were equal. This is the base case. Thus, we could write the method displayArray as follows:

```
public static void displayArray(int array[], int first, int last)
{
  System.out.print(array[first] + " ");
  if (first < last)
    displayArray(array, first+1, last);
} // end displayArray
```

For simplicity, we assume that the integers will fit on one line. Notice that the client would follow a call to displayArray with System.out.println() to get to the next line.

10.17   **Starting with `array[last]`.** Strange as it might seem, we can begin with the last element in the array and still display the array from its beginning. Rather than displaying the last element right away, you would ask a friend to display the rest of the array. After the elements `array[first]` through `array[last-1]` had been displayed, you would display `array[last]`. The resulting output would be the same as in the previous segment.

The method that implements this plan follows:

```
public static void displayArray(int array[], int first, int last)
{
  if (first <= last)
  {
    displayArray(array, first, last-1);
    System.out.print (array[last] + " ");
  }
} // end displayArray
```

10.18   **Dividing the array in half.** A common way to process an array recursively divides the array into two pieces. You then process each of the pieces separately. Since each of these pieces is an array that is smaller than the original array, each defines the smaller problem necessary for recursion. Our first two examples also divided the array into two pieces, but one of the pieces contained only one element. Here we divide the array into two approximately equal pieces. To divide the array, we find the element at or near the middle of the array. The index of this element is

```
int mid = (first + last)/2;
```

Figure 10-6 shows two arrays and their middle elements. Suppose that we include `array[mid]` in the left "half" of the array, as the figure shows. In Part *b*, the two pieces of the array are equal in length; in Part *a* they are not. This slight difference in length doesn't matter.

Figure 10-6   Two arrays with their middle elements within their left halves

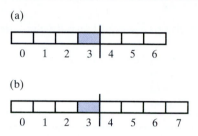

Once again, the base case is an array of one element. You can display it without help. But if the array contains more than one element, you divide it into halves. You then ask a friend to display one half and another friend to display the other half. These two friends, of course, represent two recursive calls in the following method:

```
public static void displayArray(int array[], int first, int last)
{
  if (first == last)
    System.out.print(array[first] + " ");
  else
  {
    int mid = (first + last)/2;
    displayArray(array, first, mid);
    displayArray(array, mid+1, last);
  }
} // end displayArray
```

Question 5   In Segment 10.18, suppose that the array's middle element is not in either half of the array. Instead you can recursively display the left half, display the middle element, and then recursively display the right half. What is the implementation of `displayArray` if you make these changes?

Note: When you process an array recursively, you can divide it into two pieces. For example, the first or last element could be one piece, and the rest of the array could be the other piece. Or you could divide the array into halves.

10.19   **Displaying a list.** In Chapter 5, we used an array to implement the ADT list. We implemented the list's `display` method iteratively, but here we'll use recursion instead. Since `display` has no parameters and our recursive `displayArray` methods do, we write `displayArray` as a private method that `display` calls. Since the array, `entry`, of list entries is a data field of the class that implements the list, it need not be a parameter of `displayArray`. The arguments in the call to `displayArray` would be zero for the first index and `length-1` for the last index, where `length` is a data field of the list's class. Finally, `display` is not a static method, so `displayArray` cannot be static.

We can use any version of `displayArray` given previously. Using the version in Segment 10.16, the revised methods appear as follows:

```
public void display()
{
  displayArray(0, length-1);
  System.out.println();
} // end display

private void displayArray(int first, int last)
{
  System.out.print(entry[first] + " ");
  if (first < last)
    displayArray(first+1, last);
} // end displayArray
```

Note: A recursive method that is part of an implementation of an ADT often is private, because its necessary parameters make it unsuitable as an ADT operation.

Recursively Processing a Linked Chain

10.20   Again, for simplicity, let's recursively display the data in a chain of linked nodes. Once again, we'll implement the method `display` for the ADT list, but this time let's use the linked implementation from Chapter 6. As it did in Segment 10.19, `display` will call a private recursive method. We will name that method `displayChain`. Since `displayChain` will be recursive, it needs a parameter. That parameter should represent the chain, so it will be a reference to the first node in the chain.

Dividing a linked chain into pieces is not as easy as dividing an array, since we cannot access any particular node without traversing the chain from its beginning. Hence, the most practical approach displays the data in the first node and then recursively displays the data in the rest of the chain.

Suppose that we name `displayChain`'s parameter `nodeOne`. Then `nodeOne.data` is the data in the first node, and `nodeOne.next` is a reference to the rest of the chain. What about the base case? Although a one-element array was a fine base case for `displayArray`, using an empty chain as the base case is easier here because we can simply compare `nodeOne` to `null`. Thus, we have the following implementations for the methods `display` and `displayChain`:

```
public void display()
{
  displayChain(firstNode);
  System.out.println();
} // end display

private void displayChain(Node nodeOne)
{
```

```
    if (nodeOne != null)
    {
      System.out.print(nodeOne.data + " ");
      displayChain(nodeOne.next);
    }
  } // end displayChain
```

Note: When you write a method that processes a chain of linked nodes recursively, you use a reference to the chain's first node as the method's parameter. You then process the first node followed by the rest of the chain.

10.21 **Displaying a chain backwards.** Suppose that you want to traverse a chain of linked nodes in reverse order. In particular, suppose that you want to display the object in the last node, then the one in the next-to-last node, and so on working your way toward the beginning of the chain. Since each node references the next node but not the previous one, using iteration for this task would be difficult. You could traverse to the last node, display its contents, go back to the beginning and traverse to the next-to-last node, and so on. Clearly, however, this is a tedious and time-consuming approach. Alternatively, you could traverse the chain once and save a reference to each node. You could then use these references to display the objects in the chain's nodes in reverse order. A recursive solution would do this for you.

If a friend could display the nodes in reverse order, beginning with the second node, you could display the first node and complete the task. The following recursive solution implements this idea:

```
public void displayBackward()
{
  displayChainBackward(firstNode);
  System.out.println();
} // end displayBackward

private void displayChainBackward(Node nodeOne)
{
  if (nodeOne != null)
  {
    displayChainBackward(nodeOne.next);
    System.out.print(nodeOne.data + " ");
  }
} // end displayChainBackward
```

Question 6   Trace the previous method displayBackward for a chain of three nodes.

The Time Efficiency of Recursive Methods

Chapter 9 showed you how to measure an algorithm's time requirement by using Big Oh notation. We used a count of the algorithm's major operations as a first step in determining an appropriate growth-rate function. For the iterative examples we examined, that process was straightforward. We will use a more formal technique here to measure the time requirement of a recursive algorithm and thereby choose the right growth-rate function.

The Time Efficiency of `countDown`

10.22   As a first example, consider the `countDown` method given in Segment 10.3. The size of the problem of counting down to 1 from a given integer is directly related to the size of that integer. Since Chapter 9 used n to represent the size of the problem, we will rename the parameter `integer` in count-Down to n to simplify our discussion. Here is the revised method:

```java
public static void countDown(int n)
{
   System.out.println(n);
   if (n > 1)
      countDown(n - 1);
} // end countDown
```

When n is 1, `countDown` displays 1. This is the base case and requires a constant amount of time. When $n > 1$, the method requires a constant amount of time for both the `println` statement and the comparison. In addition, it needs time to solve the smaller problem represented by the recursive call. If we let $t(n)$ represent the time requirement of `countDown(n)`, we can express these observations by writing

$t(n) = 1 + t(n - 1)$ for $n > 1$
$t(1) = 1$

The equation for $t(n)$ is called a **recurrence relation,** since the definition of the function t contains an occurrence of itself—that is, a recurrence. What we need is an expression for $t(n)$ that is not given in terms of itself. One way to find such an expression is to pick a value for n and to write out the equations for $t(n)$, $t(n - 1)$, and so on, until we reach $t(1)$. From these equations, we should be able to guess at an appropriate expression to represent $t(n)$. We then need only to prove that we are right. This might sound harder than it is.

10.23   **Solving a recurrence relation.** To solve the previous recurrence relation for $t(n)$, let's begin with $n = 4$. We get the following sequence of equations:

$t(4) = 1 + t(3)$
$t(3) = 1 + t(2)$
$t(2) = 1 + t(1) = 1 + 1 = 2$

Substituting 2 for $t(2)$ in the equation for $t(3)$ results in

$t(3) = 1 + 2 = 3$

Substituting 3 for $t(3)$ in the equation for $t(4)$ results in

$t(4) = 1 + 3 = 4$

It appears that

$t(n) = n$ for $n \geq 1$

We can start with a larger value of n, get the same result, and convince ourselves that it is true. But we need to *prove* that this result is true for every $n \geq 1$. This is not hard to do.

To prove that $t(n) = n$ for $n \geq 1$, we begin with the recurrence relation for $t(n)$, since we know it is true:

$t(n) = 1 + t(n - 1)$ for $n > 1$

We need to replace $t(n - 1)$ on the right side of the equation. Now if $t(n - 1) = n - 1$ when $n > 1$, the following would be true for $n > 1$:

$t(n) = 1 + n - 1 = n$

Thus, if we can find an integer k that satisfies the equation $t(k) = k$, the next higher integer will also satisfy it. So will the next one and the next one. Since we are given that $t(1) = 1$, all integers larger than 1 will satisfy the equation. This proof is an example of a **proof by induction.**

To conclude, we now know that countDown's time requirement is given by the function $t(n) = n$. Thus, the method is O(n).

Question 7   What is the Big Oh of the method sumOf given in Segment 10.12?

Question 8   Computing x^n for some real number x and an integral power $n \geq 0$ has a simple recursive solution:

$x^n = x\, x^{n-1}$
$x^0 = 1$

a.   What recurrence relation describes this algorithm's time requirement?
b.   By solving this recurrence relation, determine the Big Oh of this algorithm.

The Time Efficiency of Computing x^n

10.24   We can compute x^n for some real number x and an integral power $n \geq 0$ more efficiently than the approach that Question 8 suggests. To reduce the number of recursive calls and therefore the number of multiplications, we can express x^n as follows:

$x^n = (x^{n/2})^2$ when n is even and positive
$x^n = x\, (x^{(n-1)/2})^2$ when n is odd and positive
$x^0 = 1$

This computation could be implemented by a method power(x, n) that contains the recursive call power(x, n/2). Since integer division in Java truncates its result, this call is appropriate regardless of whether n is even or odd. Thus, power(x, n) would invoke power(x, n/2) once, square the result, and, if n is odd, also multiply the result by x. These multiplications are O(1) operations.

The recurrence relation that represents the method's time requirement to compute x^n is then

$t(n) = 1 + t(n/2)$ when $n \geq 2$
$t(1) = 1$
$t(0) = 1$

10.25   Since the recurrence relation involves $n/2$, our discussion will be simpler if n is a power of 2. So let's begin at $n = 16$ and write the following sequence of equations:

$t(16) = 1 + t(8)$
$t(8) = 1 + t(4)$
$t(4) = 1 + t(2)$
$t(2) = 1 + t(1)$

By substituting repeatedly, we get the following:
$t(16) = 1 + t(8) = 1 + (1 + t(4)) = 2 + (1 + t(2)) = 3 + (1 + t(1)) = 4 + t(1)$

Since $16 = 2^4$, $4 = \log_2 16$. This fact, together with the base case $t(1) = 1$, leads us to guess that

$t(n) = 1 + \log_2 n$

Now we need to prove that this guess is, in fact, true for $n \geq 1$. It is true for $n = 1$, because

$$t(1) = 1 + \log_2 1 = 1$$

For $n > 1$, we know that the recurrence relation for $t(n)$ is true:

$$t(n) = 1 + t(n/2)$$

We need to replace $t(n/2)$. If our guess $t(n) = 1 + \log_2 n$ were true for all values of $n < k$, we would have $t(k/2) = 1 + \log_2 (k/2)$, since $k/2 < k$. Thus,

$$
\begin{aligned}
t(k) &= 1 + t(k/2) \\
&= 1 + (1 + \log_2 (k/2)) \\
&= 2 + \log_2 (k/2) \\
&= \log_2 4 + \log_2 (k/2) \\
&= \log_2 (4k/2) \\
&= \log_2 (2k) \\
&= \log_2 2 + \log_2 k \\
&= 1 + \log_2 k
\end{aligned}
$$

To summarize, we assumed that $t(n) = 1 + \log_2 n$ for all values of $n < k$ and showed that $t(k) = 1 + \log_2 k$. Thus, $t(n) = 1 + \log_2 n$ for all $n \geq 1$. Since power's time requirement is given by $t(n)$, the method is O(log n).

A Simple Solution to a Difficult Problem

10.26   The Towers of Hanoi is a classic problem in computer science whose solution is not obvious. Imagine three poles and a number of disks of varying diameters. Each disk has a hole in its center so that it can fit over each of the poles. Suppose that the disks have been placed on the first pole in order from largest to smallest, with the smallest disk on top. Figure 10-7 illustrates this initial configuration for three disks.

Figure 10-7   The initial configuration of the Towers of Hanoi for three disks.

The problem is to move the disks from the first pole to the third pole so that they remain piled in their original order. But you must adhere to the following rules:

1. Move one disk at a time. Each disk you move must be a topmost disk.
2. No disk may rest on top of a disk smaller than itself.
3. You can store disks on the second pole temporarily, as long as you observe the previous two rules.

10.27   The solution is a sequence of moves. For example, if three disks are on pole 1, the following sequence of seven moves will move the disks to pole 3, using pole 2 temporarily:

Move a disk from pole 1 to pole 3
Move a disk from pole 1 to pole 2
Move a disk from pole 3 to pole 2

Move a disk from pole 1 to pole 3
Move a disk from pole 2 to pole 1
Move a disk from pole 2 to pole 3
Move a disk from pole 1 to pole 3

Figure 10-8 illustrates these moves.

Figure 10-8   The sequence of moves for solving the Towers of Hanoi problem with three disks

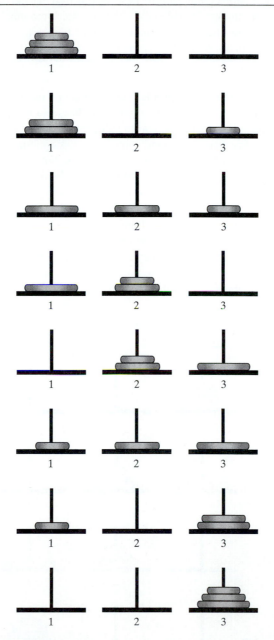

 Question 9   We discovered the previous solution for three disks by trial and error. Using the same approach, what sequence of moves solves the problem for four disks?

With four disks, the problem's solution requires 15 moves, so it is somewhat difficult to find by trial and error. With more than four disks, the solution is much more difficult to discover. What we need is an algorithm that produces a solution for any number of disks. Even though discovering a solution by trial and error is hard, finding a recursive algorithm to produce the solution is fairly easy.

> **Note:** Invented in the late 1800s, the Towers of Hanoi problem was accompanied by this legend. A group of monks was said to have begun moving 64 disks from one tower to another. When they finish, the world will end. When you finish reading this section, you will realize that the monks—or their successors—could not have finished yet. By the time they do, it is quite plausible that the disks, if not the world, will have worn out!

10.28   A recursive algorithm solves a problem by solving one or more smaller problems of the same type. The problem size here is simply the number of disks. So imagine that the first pole has four disks, as in Figure 10-9a, and that I ask you to solve the problem. Eventually, you will need to move the bottom disk, but first you need to move the three disks on top of it. Ask a friend to move these three disks—a smaller problem—according to our rules, but make the destination pole 2. Allow your friend to use pole 3 as a spare. Figure 10-9b shows the final result of your friend's work.

When your friend tells you that the task is complete, you move the one disk left on pole 1 to pole 3. Moving one disk is a simple task. You don't need help—or recursion—to do it. This disk is the largest one, so it cannot rest on top of any other disk. Thus, pole 3 must be empty before this move. After the move, the largest disk will be first on pole 3. Figure 10-9c shows the result of your work.

Now ask a friend to move the three disks on pole 2 to pole 3, adhering to the rules. Allow your friend to use pole 1 as a spare. When your friend tells you that the task is complete, you can tell me that your task is complete as well. Figure 10-9d shows the final results.

Figure 10-9   The smaller problems in a recursive solution for four disks

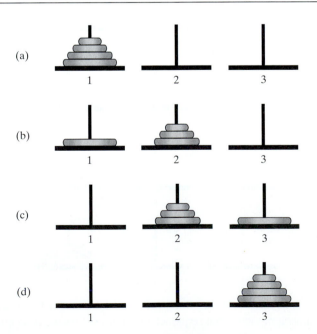

10.29   Before we write some pseudocode to describe the algorithm, we need to identify a base case. If only one disk is on pole 1, we can move it directly to pole 3 without using recursion. With this as the base case, the algorithm is as follows:

> *Algorithm to move* `numberOfDisks` *disks from* `startPole` *to* `endPole` *using* `tempPole`
>   *as a spare according to the rules of the Towers of Hanoi problem*
> ```
> if (numberOfDisks == 1)
> ```
>   *Move disk from* `startPole` *to* `endPole`
> ```
> else
> {
> ```
>   *Move all but the bottom disk from* `startPole` *to* `tempPole`
>   *Move disk from* `startPole` *to* `endPole`
>   *Move all disks from* `tempPole` *to* `endPole`
> ```
> }
> ```

At this point, we can develop the algorithm further by writing

> *Algorithm* `solveTowers(numberOfDisks, startPole, tempPole, endPole)`
> ```
> if (numberOfDisks == 1)
> ```
>   *Move disk from* `startPole` *to* `endPole`
> ```
> else
> {
>    solveTowers(numberOfDisks-1, startPole, endPole, tempPole)
> ```
>   *Move disk from* `startPole` *to* `endPole`
> ```
>    solveTowers(numberOfDisks-1, tempPole, startPole, endPole)
> }
> ```

If we choose zero disks as the base case instead of one disk, we can simplify the algorithm a bit, as follows:

> *Algorithm* `solveTowers(numberOfDisks, startPole, tempPole, endPole)`
> ```
> if (numberOfDisks > 0)
> {
>    solveTowers(numberOfDisks-1, startPole, endPole, tempPole)
> ```
>   *Move disk from* `startPole` *to* `endPole`
> ```
>    solveTowers(numberOfDisks-1, tempPole, startPole, endPole)
> }
> ```

Although somewhat easier to write, the second version of the algorithm executes many more recursive calls.

Question 10   For two disks, how many recursive calls are made by each of the two algorithms just given?

Your knowledge of recursion should convince you that both forms of the algorithm are correct. Recursion has enabled us to solve a problem that appeared to be difficult. But is this algorithm efficient? Could we do better if we used iteration?

10.30   **Efficiency.** Let's look at the efficiency of our algorithm. How many moves occur when we begin with *n* disks? Let $m(n)$ denote the number of moves that `solveTowers` needs to solve the problem for *n* disks. Clearly,

$$m(1) = 1$$

For $n > 1$, the algorithm uses two recursive calls to solve problems that have $n - 1$ disks each. The required number of moves in each case is $m(n - 1)$. Thus, you can see from the algorithm that

$$m(n) = m(n - 1) + 1 + m(n - 1) = 2\,m(n - 1) + 1$$

From this equation, you can see that $m(n) > 2\,m(n - 1)$. That is, solving the problem with n disks requires more than twice as many moves as solving the problem with $n - 1$ disks.

It appears that $m(n)$ is related to a power of 2. Let's evaluate the recurrence for $m(n)$ for a few values of n:

$$m(1) = 1, m(2) = 3, m(3) = 7, m(4) = 15, m(5) = 31, m(6) = 63$$

It seems that

$$m(n) = 2^n - 1$$

We can prove this conjecture by using mathematical induction, as follows.

10.31   **Proof by induction that $m(n) = 2^n - 1$.** We know that $m(1) = 1$ and $2^1 - 1 = 1$, so the conjecture is true for $n = 1$. Now assume that it is true for $n = 1, 2, \ldots, k$, and consider $m(k + 1)$.

$$
\begin{aligned}
m(k + 1) &= 2\,m(k) + 1 && \text{(use the recurrence relation)}\\
&= 2\,(2^k - 1) + 1 && \text{(we assumed that } m(k) = 2^k - 1)\\
&= 2^{k+1} - 1
\end{aligned}
$$

Since the conjecture is true for $n = k + 1$, it is true for all $n \geq 1$.

10.32   **Exponential growth.** The number of moves required to solve the Towers of Hanoi problem grows exponentially with the number of disks n. That is, $m(n) = O(2^n)$. This rate of growth is alarming, as you can see from the following values of 2^n:

$$
\begin{aligned}
2^5 &= 32\\
2^{10} &= 1024\\
2^{20} &= 1{,}048{,}576\\
2^{30} &= 1{,}073{,}741{,}824\\
2^{40} &= 1{,}099{,}511{,}627{,}776\\
2^{50} &= 1{,}125{,}899{,}906{,}842{,}624\\
2^{60} &= 1{,}152{,}921{,}504{,}606{,}846{,}976
\end{aligned}
$$

Remember the monks mentioned at the end of Segment 10.27? They are making $2^{64} - 1$ moves. It should be clear that you can use this exponential algorithm only for small values of n, if you want to live to see the results.

Before you condemn recursion and discard our algorithm, you need to know that you cannot do any better. Not you, not the monks, not anyone. We demonstrate this observation next by using mathematical induction.

10.33   **Proof that Towers of Hanoi cannot be solved in fewer than $2^n - 1$ moves.** We have shown that our algorithm for the Towers of Hanoi problem requires $m(n) = 2^n - 1$ moves. Since we know that at least one algorithm exists—we found one—there must be a fastest one. Let $M(n)$ represent the number of moves that this optimal algorithm requires for n disks. We need to show that $M(n) = m(n)$ for $n \geq 1$.

Our algorithm solves the problem with one disk in one move. We cannot do better, so we have that $M(1) = m(1) = 1$. If we assume that $M(n - 1) = m(n - 1)$, consider n disks. Looking back at Figure 10-9b, you can see that at one point in our algorithm the largest disk is isolated on one pole and $n - 1$ disks are on another. This configuration would have to be true of an optimal algorithm as well, for there is no other way to move the largest disk. Thus, the optimal algorithm must have moved these $n - 1$ disks from pole 1 to pole 2 in $M(n - 1) = m(n - 1)$ moves.

After moving the largest disk (Figure 10-9c), the optimal algorithm moves $n - 1$ disks from pole 2 to pole 3 in another $M(n - 1) = m(n - 1)$ moves. Altogether, the optimal algorithm makes at least $2 M(n - 1) + 1$ moves. Thus,

$$M(n) \geq 2 M(n - 1) + 1$$

Now apply the assumption that $M(n - 1) = m(n - 1)$ and then the recurrence for $m(n)$ given in Segment 10.30 to get

$$M(n) \geq 2 m(n - 1) + 1 = m(n)$$

We have just shown that $M(n) \geq m(n)$. But since the optimal algorithm cannot require more moves than our algorithm, the expression $M(n) > m(n)$ cannot be true. Thus, we must have $M(n) = m(n)$ for all $n \geq 1$.

10.34 Finding an iterative algorithm to solve the Towers of Hanoi problem is not as easy as finding a recursive algorithm. We now know that any iterative algorithm will require at least as many moves as the recursive algorithm. An iterative algorithm will save the overhead—space and time—of tracking the recursive calls, but it will not really be more efficient than solveTowers. An algorithm that uses both iteration and recursion to solve the Towers of Hanoi problem is discussed in the section "Tail Recursion," and an entirely iterative algorithm is the subject of Project 2 at the end of this chapter.

A Poor Solution to a Simple Problem

Some recursive solutions are so inefficient that you should avoid them. The problem that we will look at now is simple, occurs frequently in mathematical computations, and has a recursive solution that is so natural that you are likely to be tempted to use it. Don't!

10.35 **Example: Fibonacci numbers.** Early in the 13th century, the mathematician Leonardo Fibonacci proposed a sequence of integers to model the number of descendants of a pair of rabbits. Later named the **Fibonacci sequence,** these numbers occur in surprisingly many applications.

The first two terms in the Fibonacci sequence are 1 and 1. Each subsequent term is the sum of the preceding two terms. Thus, the sequence begins as 1, 1, 2, 3, 5, 8, 13, . . . Typically, the sequence is defined by the equations

$$F_0 = 1$$
$$F_1 = 1$$
$$F_n = F_{n - 1} + F_{n - 2} \text{ when } n \geq 2$$

You can see why the following recursive algorithm would be a tempting way to generate the sequence:

```
Algorithm Fibonacci(n)
if (n <= 1)
   return 1
else
   return Fibonacci(n-1) + Fibonacci(n-2)
```

10.36 This algorithm makes two recursive calls. That fact in itself is not the difficulty. Earlier, you saw perfectly good algorithms—displayArray in Segment 10.18 and solveTowers in Segment 10.29—that make several recursive calls. The trouble here is that the same recursive calls are made repeatedly. A call to Fibonacci(n) invokes Fibonacci(n-1) and then Fibonacci(n-2). But the call to `Fibonacci(n-1)` has to compute `Fibonacci(n-2)`, so the same Fibonacci number is computed twice.

Things get worse. The call to `Fibonacci(n-1)` calls `Fibonacci(n-3)` as well. The two previous calls to `Fibonacci(n-2)` each invoke `Fibonacci(n-3)`, so `Fibonacci(n-3)` is computed three times. Figure 10-10a illustrates the dependency of F_6 on previous Fibonacci numbers and so indicates the number of times a particular number is computed repeatedly by the method `Fibonacci`. In contrast, Figure 10-10b shows that an iterative computation of F_6 computes each prior term once. The recursive solution is clearly less efficient. The next segments will show you just how inefficient it is.

Figure 10-10 The computation of the Fibonacci number F_6 (a) recursively; (b) iteratively

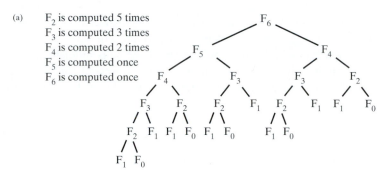

(a) F_2 is computed 5 times
F_3 is computed 3 times
F_4 is computed 2 times
F_5 is computed once
F_6 is computed once

(b) $F_0 = 1$
$F_1 = 1$
$F_2 = F_1 + F_0 = 2$
$F_3 = F_2 + F_1 = 3$
$F_4 = F_3 + F_2 = 5$
$F_5 = F_4 + F_3 = 8$
$F_6 = F_5 + F_4 = 13$

10.37 **The time efficiency of the algorithm `Fibonacci`.** We can investigate the efficiency of the `Fibonacci` algorithm by using a recurrence relation, as we did in Segments 10.22 through 10.25. First, notice that F_n requires one add operation plus the operations that F_{n-1} and F_{n-2} require. So if $t(n)$ represents the time requirement of the algorithm in computing F_n, we have

$$t(n) = 1 + t(n - 1) + t(n - 2) \text{ for } n \geq 2$$
$$t(1) = 1$$
$$t(0) = 1$$

This recurrence relation looks like the recurrence for the Fibonacci numbers themselves. It should not surprise you then that $t(n)$ is related to the Fibonacci numbers. In fact, if you look at Figure 10-10a and count the occurrences of the Fibonacci numbers F_2 through F_6, you will discover a Fibonacci sequence.

To find a relationship between $t(n)$ and F_n, let's expand $t(n)$ for a few values of n:

$$t(2) = 1 + t(1) + t(0) = 1 + F_1 + F_0 = 1 + F_2 > F_2$$
$$t(3) = 1 + t(2) + t(1) > 1 + F_2 + F_1 = 1 + F_3 > F_3$$
$$t(4) = 1 + t(3) + t(2) > 1 + F_3 + F_2 = 1 + F_4 > F_4$$

We guess that $t(n) > F_n$ for $n \geq 2$. Notice that $t(0) = 1 = F_0$ and $t(1) = 1 = F_1$. These do not satisfy the strict inequality of our guess.

We now prove that our guess is indeed fact. (You can skip the proof on your first reading.)

10.38   **Proof by induction that $t(n) > F_n$ for $n \geq 2$.** Since the recurrence relation for $t(n)$ involves two recursive terms, we need two base cases. In the previous segment, we already showed that $t(2) > F_2$ and $t(3) > F_3$. Now if $t(n) > F_n$ for $n = 2, 3, \ldots, k$, we need to show that $t(k + 1) > F_{k+1}$. We can do this as follows:

$$t(k + 1) = 1 + t(k) + t(k - 1) > 1 + F_k + F_{k-1} = 1 + F_{k+1} > F_{k+1}$$

We can conclude that $t(n) > F_n$ for all $n \geq 2$.

Since we know that $t(n) > F_n$ for all $n \geq 2$, we can say that $t(n) = \Omega(F_n)$. Recall that the Big Omega notation means that $t(n)$ is at least as large as the Fibonacci number F_n. It turns out that we can compute F_n directly without using the recurrence relation given in Segment 10.35. It can be shown that

$$F_n = (a^n - b^n)/\sqrt{5}$$

where $a = (1 + \sqrt{5})/2$ and $b = (1 - \sqrt{5})/2$. Since $|1 - \sqrt{5}| < 2$, we have $|b| < 1$ and $|b^n| < 1$. Therefore, we have

$$F_n > (a^n - 1)/\sqrt{5}$$

Thus, $F_n = \Omega(a^n)$, and since we know that $t(n) = \Omega(F_n)$, we have $t(n) = \Omega(a^n)$. Some arithmetic shows that the previous expression for a equals approximately 1.6. We conclude that $t(n)$ grows exponentially with n.

10.39   At the beginning of this section, we observed that each Fibonacci number is the sum of the preceding two Fibonacci numbers in the sequence. This observation should lead us to an iterative solution that is $O(n)$. Although the clarity and simplicity of the recursive solution makes it a tempting choice, it is much too inefficient to use.

Programming Tip: Do not use a recursive solution that repeatedly solves the same problem in its recursive calls.

Question 11   To compute the Fibonnaci number F_8 in the least time, should you do so recursively, iteratively, or directly by evaluating the expression

$$F_n = (a^n - b^n)/\sqrt{5}$$

as given in Segment 10.38?

Tail Recursion

10.40   **Tail recursion** occurs when the last action performed by a recursive method is a recursive call. For example, the following method countDown from Segment 10.6 is tail recursive:

```java
public static void countDown(int integer)
{
   if (integer >= 1)
   {
      System.out.println(integer);
```

```
      countDown(integer - 1);
   } // end if
} // end countDown
```

A method that implements the algorithm Fibonacci given in Segment 10.35 will not be tail recursive, even though a recursive call *appears* last in the method. A closer look reveals that the last *action* is an addition.

The tail recursion in a method simply repeats the method's logic with changes to parameters and variables. Thus, you can perform the same repetition by using iteration. Converting a tail-recursive method to an iterative one is usually a straightforward process. For example, consider the recursive method countDown just given. First replace the if statement with a while statement. Then, instead of the recursive call, assign the call's argument integer – 1 to the method's formal parameter integer. Doing so gives us the following iterative version of the method:

```
public static void countDown(int integer)
{
   while (integer >= 1)
   {
      System.out.println(integer);
      integer = integer - 1;
   } // end while
} // end countDown
```

This method is essentially the same as the iterative method given in Segment 10.7.

Because converting tail recursion to iteration is often uncomplicated, some compilers convert tail-recursive methods to iterative methods to save the overhead involved with recursion. Most of this overhead involves memory, not time. If you need to save space, you should consider replacing tail recursion with iteration.

10.41 **Example.** Let's replace the tail recursion in the algorithm solveTowers given in Segment 10.29:

```
Algorithm solveTowers(numberOfDisks, startPole, tempPole, endPole)
if (numberOfDisks > 0)
{
   solveTowers(numberOfDisks-1, startPole, endPole, tempPole)
   Move disk from startPole to endPole
   solveTowers(numberOfDisks-1, tempPole, startPole, endPole)
}
```

This algorithm contains two recursive calls. The second one is tail recursive, since it is the algorithm's last action. Thus, we could try replacing the second recursive call with appropriate assignment statements and use a loop to repeat the method's logic, including the first recursive call, as follows:

```
Algorithm solveTowers(numberOfDisks, startPole, tempPole, endPole)
while (numberOfDisks > 0)
{
   solveTowers(numberOfDisks-1, startPole, endPole, tempPole)
   Move disk from startPole to endPole
   numberOfDisks = numberOfDisks - 1
   startPole = tempPole
   tempPole = startPole
   endPole = endPole
}
```

This isn't quite right, however. Obviously, assigning `endPole` to itself is superfluous. Assigning `tempPole` to `startPole` and then assigning `startPole` to `tempPole` destroys `startPole` but leaves `tempPole` unchanged. What we need to do is exchange `tempPole` and `startPole`. Let's look at what is really happening here.

The only instruction that actually moves disks is *Move disk from* `startPole` *to* `endPole`. This instruction moves the largest disk that is not already on `endPole`. The disk to be moved is at the bottom of a pole, so any disks that are on top of it need to be moved first. Those disks are moved by the first recursive call. If we want to omit the second recursive call, what would we need to do instead before repeating the first recursive call? We must make sure that `startPole` contains the disks that have not been moved to `endPole`. Those disks are on `tempPole` as a result of the first recursive call. Thus, we need to exchange the contents of `tempPole` and `startPole`.

Making these changes results in the following revised algorithm:

```
Algorithm solveTowers(numberOfDisks, startPole, tempPole, endPole)
while (numberOfDisks > 0)
{
   solveTowers(numberOfDisks-1, startPole, endPole, tempPole)
   Move disk from startPole to endPole
   numberOfDisks--
   Exchange the contents of tempPole and startPole
}
```

This revised algorithm is unusual in that its loop contains a recursive call. The base case for this recursion occurs when `numberOfDisks` is zero. Even though the method does not contain an `if` statement, it does detect the base case, ending the recursive calls.

 Note: In a tail-recursive method, the last action is a recursive call. This call performs a repetition that can be done more efficiently by using iteration. Converting a tail-recursive method to an iterative one is usually a straightforward process.

Mutual Recursion

10.42   Some recursive algorithms make their recursive calls indirectly. For example, we might have the following chain of events: Method A calls Method B, Method B calls Method C, and Method C calls Method A. Such recursion—called **mutual recursion** or **indirect recursion**—is more difficult to understand and trace, but it does arise naturally in certain applications.

For example, the following rules describe strings that are valid algebraic expressions:

- An algebraic expression is either a term or two terms separated by a + or – operator.
- A term is either a factor or two factors separated by a * or / operator.
- A factor is either a variable or an algebraic expression enclosed in parentheses.
- A variable is a single letter.

Suppose that the methods `isExpression`, `isTerm`, `isFactor`, and `isVariable` determine whether a string is, respectively, an expression, a term, a factor, or a variable. The method `isExpression` calls `isTerm`, which in turn calls `isFactor`, which then calls `isVariable` and `isExpression`. Figure 10-11 illustrates these calls.

Project 5 describes another example of mutual recursion. For a more detailed discussion of algebraic expressions, see Chapter 20.

Figure 10-11   An example of mutual recursion

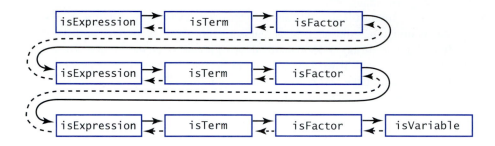

CHAPTER SUMMARY

- Recursion is a problem-solving process that breaks a problem into identical but smaller problems.

- The definition of a recursive method must contain logic that involves a parameter to the method and leads to different cases. One or more of these cases are base cases, or stopping cases, because they provide a solution that does not require recursion. One or more cases include a recursive invocation of the method that takes a step toward a base case by solving a "smaller" version of the task performed by the method.

- For each call to a method, Java records the values of the method's parameters and local variables in an activation record. The records are placed into an ADT called a stack that organizes them chronologically. The record most recently added to the stack is of the currently executing method. In this way, Java can suspend the execution of a recursive method and invoke it again with new argument values.

- A recursive method that processes an array often divides the array into portions. Recursive calls to the method work on each of these array portions.

- A recursive method that processes a chain of linked nodes needs a reference to the chain's first node as its parameter.

- A recursive method that is part of an implementation of an ADT often is private, because its necessary parameters make it unsuitable as an ADT operation.

- A recurrence relation expresses a function in terms of itself. You can use a recurrence relation to express the work done by a recursive method.

- Any solution to the Towers of Hanoi problem with n disks requires at least $2^n - 1$ moves. A recursive solution to this problem is clear and efficient.

- Each number in the Fibonacci sequence—after the first two—is the sum of the previous two numbers. Computing a Fibonacci number recursively is quite inefficient, as the required previous numbers are computed several times each.

- Tail recursion occurs when the last action made by a recursive method is a recursive call. This recursive call performs a repetition that can be done more efficiently by using iteration. Converting a tail-recursive method to an iterative one is usually a straightforward process.

- Indirect recursion results when a method calls a method that calls a method, and so on until the first method is called again.

PROGRAMMING TIPS

- An iterative method contains a loop. A recursive method calls itself. Although some recursive methods contain a loop *and* call themselves, if you have written a `while` statement within a recursive method, be sure that you did not mean to write an `if` statement.

- A recursive method that does not check for a base case, or that misses the base case, will not terminate normally. This situation is known as infinite recursion.

- Too many recursive calls can cause the error message "stack overflow." This means that the stack of activation records has become full. In essence, the method uses too much memory. Infinite recursion or large-size problems are the likely causes of this error.

- Do not use a recursive solution that repeatedly solves the same problem in its recursive calls.

- If a recursive method does not work, answer the following questions. Any "no" answers should guide you to the error.
  - Does the method have at least one parameter?
  - Does the method contain a statement that tests a parameter and leads to different cases?
  - Did you consider all possible cases?
  - Does at least one of these cases cause at least one recursive call?
  - Do these recursive calls involve smaller arguments, smaller tasks, or tasks that get closer to the solution?
  - If these recursive calls produce or return correct results, will the method produce or return a correct result?
  - Is at least one of the cases a base case that has no recursive call?
  - Are there enough base cases?
  - Does each base case produce a result that is correct for that case?
  - If the method returns a value, does each of the cases return a value?

EXERCISES

1. Consider the method `displayRowOfCharacters` that displays any given character the specified number of times on one line. For example, the call
   ```
   displayRowOfCharacters('*', 5);
   ```
   produces the line
   ```
   *****
   ```
   Implement this method in Java by using recursion.

2. Describe a recursive algorithm that draws concentric circles, given the diameter of the outermost circle. The diameter of each inner circle should be three-fourths the diameter of the circle that encloses it. The diameter of the innermost circle should exceed 1 inch.

3. Write a method that asks the user for integer input that is between 1 and 10, inclusive. If the input is out of range, the method should recursively ask the user to enter a new input value.

4. The factorial of a positive integer n—which we denote as $n!$—is the product of n and the factorial of $n - 1$. The factorial of 0 is 1. Write two different recursive methods that each return the factorial of n.

5. Write a recursive method that writes a given array backward. Consider the last element of the array first.

6. Repeat Exercise 5, but instead consider the first element of the array first.

7. A palindrome is a string that reads the same forward and backward. For example *deed* and *level* are palindromes. Write an algorithm in pseudocode that determines whether a string is a palindrome.

8. For three disks, how many recursive calls are made by each of the two solveTowers algorithms given in Segment 10.29?

9. Write a recursive method that counts the number of nodes in a chain of linked nodes.

10. If n is a positive integer in Java, n%10 is its rightmost digit and n/10 is the integer obtained by dropping the rightmost digit from n. Using these facts, write a recursive method that displays an integer n in decimal. Now observe that you can display n in any base between 2 and 9 by replacing 10 with the new base. Revise your method to accommodate a given base.

11. Consider the method contains of the class AList, as given in Segment 5.10. Write a private recursive method that contains can call, and revise the definition of contains accordingly.

12. Repeat Exercise 11, but instead use the class LList and Segment 6.40.

13. Write four different recursive methods that each compute the sum of integers in an array of integers. Model your methods after the displayArray methods given in Segments 10.15 through 10.18 and described in Question 5.

14. Write a recursive method that returns the smallest integer in an array of integers. If you divide the array into two pieces—halves, for example—and find the smallest integer in each of the two pieces, the smallest integer in the entire array will be the smaller of the these two integers. Since you will be searching a portion of the array—for example, the elements array[first] through array[last]—it will be convenient for your method to have three parameters: the array and two indices, first and last. You can refer to the method displayArray in Segment 10.18 for inspiration.

PROJECTS

1. Implement the two solveTowers algorithms given in Segment 10.29. Represent the towers by either single characters or strings. Each method should display directions that indicate the moves that must be made. Insert counters into each method to count the number of times it is called. These counters can be data fields of the class that contains these methods. Compare the number of recursive calls made by each method for various numbers of disks.

2. You can get a solution to the Towers of Hanoi problem by using the following iterative algorithm. Beginning with pole 1 and moving from pole to pole in the order pole 1, pole 3, pole 2, pole 1, and so on, make at most one move per pole according to the following rules:

   ● Move the topmost disk from a pole to the next possible pole in the specified order. Remember that you cannot place a disk on top of a smaller one.
   ● If the disk that you are about to move is the smallest of all the disks and you just moved it to the present pole, do not move it. Instead, consider the next pole.

This algorithm should make the same moves as the recursive algorithms given in Segment 10.29 and pictured in Figure 10-8. Thus, this iterative algorithm is O(2^n) as well.

    Implement this algorithm.

3. Write an application or applet that animates the solution to the Towers of Hanoi problem. The problem asks you to move n disks from one pole to another, one at a time. You move only the top disk on a pole, and you place a disk only on top of larger disks on a pole. Since each disk has certain characteristics, such as its size, it is natural to define a class of disks.

    Design and implement an ADT tower that includes the following operations:
- Add a disk to the top of the disks on the pole
- Remove the topmost disk

Also, design and implement a class that includes a recursive method to solve the problem.

4. Java's class Graphics has the following method to draw a line between two given points:

```
/** Task: Draws a line between the points (x1, y1) and
 *        (x2, y2). */
public void drawLine(int x1, int y1, int x2, int y2)
```

Graphics uses a coordinate system that measures points from the top left corner.

    Write a recursive method that draws a picture of a 12-inch ruler. Mark inches, half inches, quarter inches, and eighth inches. Mark the half inches with marks that are smaller than those that mark the inches. Mark the quarter inches with marks that are smaller than those that mark the half inches, and so on. Your picture need not be full size. *Hint*: Draw a mark in the middle of the ruler and then draw rulers to the left and right of this mark.

5. Imagine a row of n lights that can be turned on or off only under certain conditions, as follows. The first light can be turned on or off anytime. Each of the other lights can be turned on or off only when the preceding light is on and all other lights are off. If all the lights are on initially, how can you turn them off? For three lights numbered 1 to 3, you can take the following steps, where 1 is a light that is on and 0 is a light that is off:

```
1 1 1   All on initially
0 1 1   Turn off light 1
0 1 0   Turn off light 3
1 1 0   Turn on light 1
1 0 0   Turn off light 2
0 0 0   Turn off light 1
```

    You can solve this problem in general by using mutual recursion, as follows:

Algorithm turnOff(n)
// *Turn off* n *lights that are initially on.*
if (n == 1)
  Turn off light 1
else
{
  if (n > 2)
    turnOff(n - 2)

> *Turn off light* n
> ```
> if (n > 2)
>    turnOn(n - 2)
> turnOff(n - 1)
> }
> ```
>
> *Algorithm* `turnOn(n)`
> `// Turn on` n *lights that are initially off.*
> ```
> if (n == 1)
> ```
>   *Turn on light 1*
> `else`
> ```
> {
>    turnOn(n - 1)
>    if (n > 2)
>       turnOff(n - 2)
> ```
>   *Turn on light* n
> ```
>    if (n > 2)
>       turnOn(n - 2)
> }
> ```
>
> **a.** Implement these algorithms in Java so that it produces a list of directions to turn off *n* lights that initially are on.
> **b.** What recurrence relation expresses the number of times that lights are switched on or off during the course of solving this problem for *n* lights?

An Introduction to Sorting

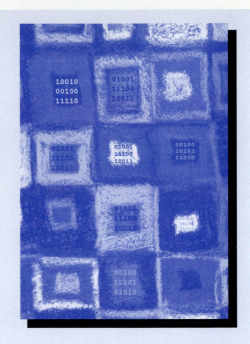

CONTENTS

Selection Sort
    Iterative Selection Sort
    Recursive Selection Sort
    The Efficiency of Selection Sort
Insertion Sort
    Iterative Insertion Sort
    Recursive Insertion Sort
    The Efficiency of Insertion Sort
    Insertion Sort of a Chain of Linked Nodes
Shell Sort
    The Java Code
    The Efficiency of Shell Sort
Comparing the Algorithms

PREREQUISITES

Chapter   4   Lists
Chapter   5   List Implementations That Use Arrays
Chapter   6   List Implementations That Link Data
Chapter   9   The Efficiency of Algorithms
Chapter 10 Recursion

OBJECTIVES

After studying this chapter, you should be able to

- Sort an array into ascending order by using the following methods: selection sort, insertion sort, and Shell sort
- Sort a chain of linked nodes into ascending order by using an insertion sort
- Determine the efficiency of a sort and discuss the relative efficiencies of the various methods

We are all familiar with arranging objects in order from smallest to largest or from largest to smallest. We not only order numbers this way, but we also can arrange people by age, height, or name, books by title, author, or height, and so on. Arranging things into either ascending or descending order is called **sorting.** You can sort any collection of items that can be compared with one another. Likewise, in Java you can sort any objects that are Comparable—that is, objects of any class that implements the interface Comparable and, therefore, defines the method compareTo. Exactly how you compare two objects depends on the nature of the objects. For example, you can arrange a row of books on your bookshelf in several ways: by title, by author, by height, by color, and so on. The designer of a class of book objects would choose one of these ways when implementing the method compareTo.

Suppose you have a collection of elements that need to be sorted in some way. For example, you might want to arrange a list of numbers from lowest to highest or from highest to lowest, or you might want to create a list of strings in alphabetical order. This chapter discusses and implements a few simple algorithms that sort items into ascending order. That is, our algorithms rearrange the first n entries in a collection so that

entry $1 \leq$ entry $2 \leq \ldots \leq$ entry n

With only small changes to our algorithms, you will be able to sort entries into descending order.

Sorting an array is usually easier than sorting a chain of linked nodes. For this reason, typical sorting algorithms sort an array. In particular, our algorithms will rearrange the first n values in an array a so that

a[0] $\leq$ a[1] $\leq$ a[2] $\leq \ldots \leq$ a[n – 1]

However, we also will use one of our algorithms to sort a chain of linked nodes. Thus, we could add a sort method to the ADT list and use one of our algorithms to implement the method.

Sorting is such a common and important task that many sorting algorithms exist. This chapter examines some basic algorithms for sorting data. Although most of our examples will sort integers, the Java implementations given will sort any Comparable objects.

The efficiency of a sorting algorithm is significant, particularly when large amounts of data are involved. We will examine the performance of the algorithms in this chapter and find that they are relatively slow. The next chapter will present algorithms that usually are much faster.

Selection Sort

11.1   Imagine that you want to rearrange the books on your bookshelf by height, with the shortest book on the left. You might begin by tossing all of the books onto the floor. You then could return them to the shelf one by one, in their proper order. If you first return the shortest book to the shelf, and then the next shortest, and so on, you would perform a kind of **selection sort.** But using the floor—or another shelf—to store your books temporarily uses extra space needlessly.

Instead, approach your intact bookshelf and *select* the shortest book. Since you want it to be first on the shelf, you remove the first book on the shelf and put the shortest book in its place. You still have a book in your hand, so you put it into the space formerly occupied by the shortest book. That is, the shortest book has traded places with the first book, as Figure 11-1 illustrates. You now ignore the shortest book and repeat the process for the rest of the bookshelf.

Figure 11-1   Before and after exchanging the shortest book and the first book

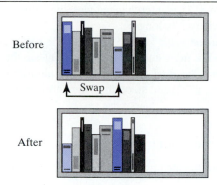

Before

Swap

After

In terms of an array a, the selection sort finds the smallest element in the array and exchanges it with a[0]. Then, ignoring a[0], the sort finds the next smallest element and swaps it with a[1], and so on. Notice that we use only one array and sort by making elements trade places with other elements.

We could have copied the array into a second array and then moved the elements back to the original array in their proper order. But that would be like using the floor to store books temporarily. Fortunately, all of that extra space is unnecessary.

Figure 11-2   A selection sort of an array of integers into ascending order

a[0]	a[1]	a[2]	a[3]	a[4]
15	8	10	2	5

15	8	10	2	5

2	8	10	15	5

2	8	10	15	5

2	5	10	15	8

2	5	10	15	8

2	5	8	15	10

2	5	8	15	10

2	5	8	10	15

11.2   Figure 11-2 shows how a selection sort rearranges an array of integers by interchanging values. Beginning with the original array, the sort locates the smallest value in the array, that is, the 2 in a[3]. The value in a[3] is interchanged with the value in a[0]. After that interchange, the smallest value is in a[0] where it belongs.

The next smallest value is the 5 in a[4]. The sort then interchanges the value in a[4] with the value in a[1]. So far, the values in a[0] and a[1] are the smallest in the array and are in their correct position within the final sorted array. The algorithm then interchanges the next smallest element—the 8—with a[2], and so on until the entire array is sorted.

Iterative Selection Sort

11.3   The following pseudocode describes an iterative algorithm for the selection sort:

Algorithm selectionSort(a, n)
// Sorts the first n elements of an array a.

```
for (index = 0; index < n - 1; index++)
{
   indexOfNextSmallest = the index of the smallest value among
          a[index], a[index+1],..., a[n - 1]
   Interchange the values of a[index] and a[indexOfNextSmallest]
   // Assertion: a[0] ≤ a[1] ≤...≤ a[index], and these are the smallest
   // of the original array elements. The remaining array elements begin at a[index+1].
}
```

Notice that during the last iteration of the for loop, the value of index is n – 2, even though the last array element is a[n – 1]. Once the elements a[0] through a[n – 2] are in their correct places, only the one element a[n – 1] remains to be positioned. But since the other elements are correctly positioned, it must already be in the correct place as well.

Note: Notation
In mathematics, one-letter variable names are common. Recognizing this, and seeking to save some space, we use a here to represent an array within the text and pseudocode. Within Java code elsewhere, we have tried to avoid one-letter identifiers, using them only sparingly. However, the code that you will see in this chapter and the next uses a to represent an array simply to maintain consistency with the text.

11.4   One way to organize methods that sort an array is to create a class of static methods that perform the various sorts. For the moment, the following class contains the public method selectionSort and two private methods that assist in sorting. It is easy to see that the definition of selectionSort is a direct translation of the previous pseudocode into Java code.

```
/***********************************************************************
 * Class for sorting an array of Comparable objects from smallest to
 * largest.
 ***********************************************************************/
public class SortArray
{
   /** Task: Sorts the first n objects in an array into ascending order.
    *   @param a   an array of Comparable objects
```

```
 *    @param n   an integer > 0 */
public static void selectionSort(Comparable[] a, int n)
{
  for (int index = 0; index < n - 1; index++)
  {
    int indexOfNextSmallest = indexOfSmallest(a, index, n-1);
    swap(a, index, indexOfNextSmallest);
    // Assertion: a[0] <= a[1] <= . . . <= a[index] <= all other a[i]
  } // end for
} // end selectionSort

/** Task: Determines the index of the smallest value in an array.
 *    @param a        an array of Comparable objects
 *    @param first    an integer > 0 that is the index of the first
 *                    array element to consider
 *    @param last     an integer > 0 that is the index of the last
 *                    array element to consider
 *    @return the index of the smallest value among
 *            a[first], a[first+1], . . . , a[last] */
private static int indexOfSmallest(Comparable[] a, int first, int last)
{
  Comparable min = a[first];
  int indexOfMin = first;
  for (int index = first+1; index <= last; index++)
  {
    if (a[index].compareTo(min) < 0)
    {
      min = a[index];
      indexOfMin = index;
      // Assertion: min is the smallest of a[first] through a[index].
    } // end if
  } // end for

  return indexOfMin;
} // end indexOfSmallest

/** Task: Swaps the array elements a[i] and a[j].
 *    @param a  an array of Comparable objects
 *    @param i  an integer >= 0 and < a.length
 *    @param j  an integer >= 0 and < a.length */
private static void swap(Comparable[] a, int i, int j)
{
  Comparable temp = a[i];
  a[i] = a[j];
  a[j] = temp;
} // end swap
} // end SortArray
```

The method indexOfSmallest searches the array elements a[first] through a[last] and returns the index of the smallest among them. The method uses two local variables, min and index-OfMin. At any point in the search, min references the smallest value found so far. That value occurs at a[indexOfMin]. At the end of the search, the method returns indexOfMin.

Notice that for our purposes here, we could have assumed that last is always n - 1 and omitted it as a parameter. However, this general version will be useful in other settings.

Question 1   Trace the steps that a selection sort takes when sorting the following array into ascending order: 9 6 2 4 8.

Recursive Selection Sort

11.5   Selection sort also has a natural recursive form. Often recursive algorithms that involve arrays operate on a portion of the array. Such algorithms use two parameters, `first` and `last`, to designate the portion of the array composed of the elements `a[first]` through `a[last]`. The recursive selection sort algorithm uses this notation as well:

> ***Algorithm*** `selectionSort(a, first, last)`
> *// Sorts the array elements* `a[first]` *through* `a[last]` *recursively.*
>
> `if (first < last)`
> `{`
>   `indexOfNextSmallest = ` *the index of the smallest value among*
>   `a[first], a[first+1], ..., a[last]`
>   *Interchange the values of* `a[first]` *and* `a[indexOfNextSmallest]`
>   `// Assertion:` a[0] ≤ a[1] ≤ ... ≤ a[first] *and these are the smallest*
>   `// ` *of the original array elements. The remaining array elements begin at* `a[first+1]`.
>   `selectionSort(a, first+1, last)`
> `}`

Notice that we consider only arrays of two or more elements. After we place the smallest element into the first position of the array, we ignore it and sort the rest of the array by using a selection sort.

11.6   When we implement the previous recursive algorithm in Java, its signature will differ from the signature of the iterative method `selectionSort` given in Segment 11.4. We could, however, provide the following method to simply invoke the recursive method:

```
public static void selectionSort(Comparable[] a, int n)
{
   selectionSort(a, 0, n-1); // invoke recursive method
} // end selectionSort
```

Whether you make the recursive method `selectionSort` private or public is up to you, but making it public provides the client with a choice of two ways in which to invoke the sort. In a similar fashion, you could revise the iterative selection sort given in Segment 11.4 to use the parameters `first` and `last` and then provide the method just given to invoke it.

With these observations in mind, we will make the subsequent sorting algorithms more general by giving them three parameters—a, `first`, and `last`—so that they sort the elements `a[first]` through `a[last]`.

The Efficiency of Selection Sort

11.7   In the iterative method `selectionSort`, the for loop executes $n - 1$ times, so it invokes the methods `indexOfSmallest` and `swap` $n - 1$ times each. In the $n - 1$ calls to `indexOfSmallest`, `last` is $n - 1$ and `first` ranges from 0 to $n - 2$. Each time `indexOfSmallest` is invoked, its loop executes `last - first` times. Thus, this loop executes a total of

$$(n - 1) + (n - 2) + \ldots + 1$$

times. This sum is $n(n - 1)/2$, so the selection sort is $O(n^2)$. Notice that our discussion does not depend on the nature of the data in the array. It could be wildly out of order, nearly sorted, or completely sorted; in any case, selection sort would be $O(n^2)$.

The recursive selection sort performs the same operations as the iterative selection sort, and so it is also $O(n^2)$.

Note: The time efficiency of selection sort

Selection sort is $O(n^2)$ regardless of the initial order of the elements in an array.

Insertion Sort

11.8 Another intuitive sorting algorithm is the **insertion sort.** Suppose again that you want to rearrange the books on your bookshelf by height, with the shortest book on the left. If the leftmost book on the shelf were the only book, your shelf would be sorted. But you also have all the other books to sort. Consider the second book. If it is taller than the first book, you now have two sorted books. If not, you remove the second book, slide the first book to the right, and *insert* the book you just removed into the first position on the shelf. The first two books are now sorted.

Now consider the third book. If it is taller than the second book, you now have three sorted books. If not, remove the third book and slide the second book to the right, as Parts *a* through *c* of Figure 11-3 illustrate. Now see whether the book in your hand is taller than the first book. If so, insert the book into the second position on the shelf, as shown in Figure 11-3d. If not, slide the first book to the right, and insert the book in your hand into the first position on the shelf. If you repeat this process for each of the remaining books, your bookshelf will be arranged by the heights of the books.

Figure 11-3   The placement of the third book during an insertion sort

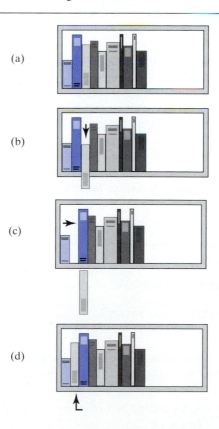

Figure 11-4 shows the bookshelf after several steps of the insertion sort. The books on the left side of the shelf are sorted. You remove the next unsorted book from the shelf and slide sorted books to the right, one at a time, until you find the right place for the book in your hand. You then insert this book into its new sorted location.

Figure 11-4   An insertion sort of books

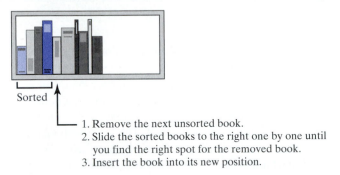

Sorted

1. Remove the next unsorted book.
2. Slide the sorted books to the right one by one until you find the right spot for the removed book.
3. Insert the book into its new position.

Iterative Insertion Sort

11.9   An insertion sort of an array **partitions**—that is, divides—the array into two parts. One part is sorted and initially contains just the first element in the array. The second part contains the remaining elements. The algorithm removes the first element from the unsorted part and inserts it into its proper sorted position within the sorted part. Just as you did with the bookshelf, you choose the proper position by comparing the unsorted element with the sorted elements, beginning at the end of the sorted part and continuing toward its beginning. As you compare, you shift array elements in the sorted part to make room for the insertion.

Figure 11-5 illustrates these steps for a sort that has already positioned the first three elements of the array. The 3 is the next element that must be placed into its proper position within the sorted region. Since 3 is less than 8 and 5 but greater than 2, the 8 and 5 are shifted to make room for the 3.

Figure 11-6 illustrates an entire insertion sort of an array of integers. At each pass of the algorithm, the sorted part expands by one element as the unsorted part shrinks by one element. Eventually, the unsorted part is empty and the array is sorted.

The following iterative algorithm describes an insertion sort of the elements at indices `first` through `last` of the array a. The loop in the algorithm processes the unsorted part and invokes another method—`insertInOrder`—to perform the insertions.

Algorithm `insertionSort(a, first, last)`
// Sorts the array elements a[first] *through* a[last] *iteratively.*

```
for (unsorted = first+1 through last)
{
   firstUnsorted = a[unsorted]
   insertInOrder(firstUnsorted, a, first, unsorted-1)
}
```

Algorithm `insertInOrder(element, a, begin, end)`
// Inserts element *into the sorted array elements* a[begin] *through* a[end].

```
index = end
while ( (index >= begin) and (element < a[index]) )
```

```
{
    a[index+1] = a[index] // make room
    index--
}
// Assertion: a[index+1] is available.

a[index+1] = element     // insert
```

Figure 11-5   An insertion sort inserts the next unsorted element into its proper location within the sorted portion of an array

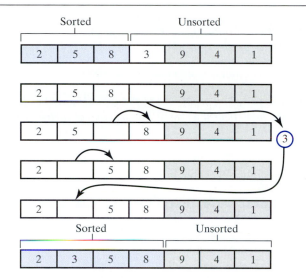

Figure 11-6   An insertion sort of an array of integers into ascending order

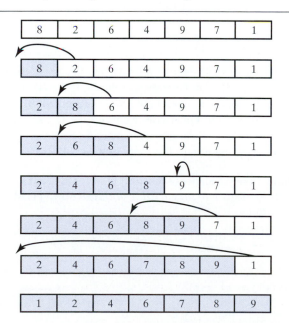

Question 2   Trace the steps that an insertion sort takes when sorting the following array into ascending order: 9 6 2 4 8.

Recursive Insertion Sort

11.10   You can describe an insertion sort recursively as follows. If you sort all but the last item in the array—a smaller problem than sorting the entire array—you then can insert the last item into its proper position within the rest of the array. The following pseudocode describes a recursive insertion sort:

> *Algorithm* `insertionSort(a, first, last)`
> *// Sorts the array elements* `a[first]` *through* `a[last]` *recursively.*
>
> **if** *(the array contains more than one element)*
> {
>   *Sort the array elements* `a[first]` *through* `a[last-1]`
>   *Insert the last element* `a[last]` *into its correct sorted position within the rest of*
>   *the array*
> }

We can implement this algorithm in Java as follows:

```java
public static void insertionSort(Comparable[] a, int first, int last)
{
   if (first < last)
   {
      // sort all but the last element
      insertionSort(a, first, last-1);

      // insert the last element in sorted order
      insertInOrder(a[last], a, first, last-1);
   } // end if
} // end insertionSort
```

11.11   **The algorithm `insertInOrder`: first draft.** The recursive method `insertInOrder` inserts an element into a sorted portion of the array, as follows. If the element to insert is greater than or equal to the last item in the sorted portion of the array, the element belongs immediately after this last item, as Figure 11-7a illustrates. Otherwise, we move the last sorted item to the next higher position in the array and insert the element into the remaining portion, as shown in Figure 11-7b.

We can describe these steps more carefully as follows:

> *Algorithm* `insertInOrder(element, a, first, last)`
> *// Inserts* `element` *into the sorted array elements* `a[first]` *through* `a[last]`.
> *// First draft.*
>
> **if** `(element >= a[last])`
>   `a[last+1] = element`
> **else**
> {
>   `a[last+1] = a[last]`
>   `insertInOrder(element, a, first, last-1)`
> }

Figure 11-7   Inserting the first unsorted element into the sorted portion of the array. (a) The element is greater than or equal to the last sorted element; (b) the element is smaller than the last sorted element

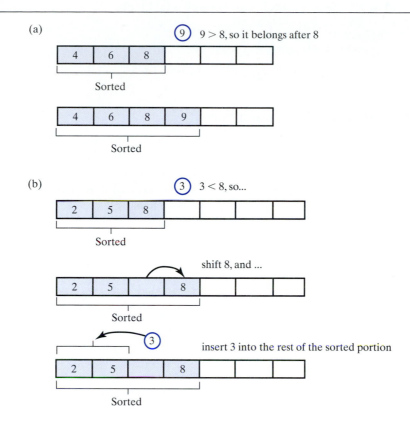

11.12   **The algorithm `insertInOrder`: final draft.** This algorithm is not quite right. The `else` clause will work only if we have more than one element in the remaining portion of the array—that is, if `first` < `last`. If `first` and `last` were equal, for example, the recursive call would be equivalent to

```
insertInOrder(element, a, first, first-1);
```

which is incorrect.

Will `last` ever equal `first`, if they were not equal to begin with? Yes. When `element` is less than all elements a[first], . . . , a[last], each recursive call decreases `last` by 1 until eventually `last` equals `first`. What should we do when this happens? Since the sorted portion consists of one element a[last], we will move a[last] to the next higher position and place `element` in a[last].

The following revised algorithm reflects these changes:

Algorithm `insertInOrder(element, a, first, last)`
// Inserts element *into the sorted array elements* a[first] *through* a[last].

```
if (element >= a[last])
   a[last+1] = element
else if (first < last)
```

```
      {
        a[last+1] = a[last]
        insertInOrder(element, a, first, last-1)
      }
      else // first == last and element < a[last]
      {
        a[last+1] = a[last]
        a[last] = element
      }
```

The Efficiency of Insertion Sort

11.13   Look back at the iterative algorithm `insertionSort` given in Segment 11.9. For an array of *n* elements, `first` is 0 and `last` is *n* − 1. The `for` loop then executes *n* − 1 times, and so the method `insertInOrder` is invoked *n* − 1 times. Thus, within `insertInOrder`, `begin` is 0 and `end` ranges from 0 to *n* − 2. The loop within `insertInOrder` executes at most `end` − `begin` + 1 times each time the method is invoked. Thus, this loop executes a total of

$$1 + 2 + \ldots + (n - 1)$$

times. This sum is $n\,(n - 1)/2$, so the insertion sort is $O(n^2)$. The recursive insertion sort performs the same operations as the iterative insertion sort, so it is also $O(n^2)$.

This analysis provides a worst-case scenario. In the best case, the loop in `insertInOrder` would exit immediately. Such is the case if the array is sorted already. In the best case, then, insertion sort is $O(n)$. In general, the more sorted an array is, the less work `insertInOrder` needs to do. This fact and its relatively simple implementation make the insertion sort popular for applications in which the array does not change much. For example, some customer databases add only a small percentage of new customers each day.

The next chapter will use the insertion sort when the array size is small.

Note: **The time efficiency of insertion sort**

Insertion sort is at best $O(n)$ and at worst $O(n^2)$. The closer an array is to sorted order, the less work an insertion sort does.

Insertion Sort of a Chain of Linked Nodes

11.14   Usually you will sort arrays, but sometimes you might need to sort a chain of linked nodes. When you do, the insertion sort is one that is easy to understand.

Figure 11-8 shows a chain whose nodes contain integers that are sorted into ascending order. To begin to see how we can construct an insertion sort for this chain, imagine that we want to insert a node into this chain so that the integers in the nodes remain in sorted order.

Figure 11-8   A chain of integers sorted into ascending order

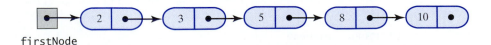

firstNode

Suppose that the node to be inserted into the chain contains the integer 6. We need to locate where in the chain the new node belongs. If we adapt the algorithm `insertInOrder` given in Segment 11.9, we would begin at the end of the chain and compare 6 with the integer 10. Since 6 belongs before 10, we would then compare 6 with 8. Since 6 belongs before 8, we compare 6 with 5 and discover that 6 belongs between 5 and 8. Can we use the same approach here? We *could*, but we would need to traverse the entire chain to reach the last node. Having a tail reference would not help, because once we've looked at the last node, we then need to look at the next-to-last node. But we cannot locate that node knowing just the last node. We would need to traverse the chain again and stop just before the last node.

A better way is to start at the beginning of the chain and make comparisons as we move toward the end of the chain until we find the correct insertion point. Thus, we would compare 6 with 2, then with 3, with 5, and finally with 8 to determine that 6 belongs between 5 and 8. Recall from Chapter 6 that during a traversal you can save a reference to the node before the current one, as Figure 11-9 illustrates. Doing so will allow us to make the insertion. Also remember that inserting at the beginning of the chain differs somewhat from inserting anywhere else in the chain.

Figure 11-9   During the traversal of a chain to locate the insertion point, save a reference to the node before the current one

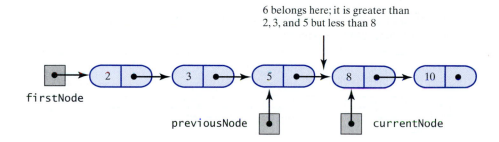

11.15   Imagine that we plan to add a sort method to a class `LinkedChainList` that implements the ADT list. Assume that this class has an inner class `Node` that has set and get methods for its private data fields. We would add the following method to `LinkedChainList` to insert the node that `nodeToInsert` references into the sorted chain that `firstNode` references.

```java
private void insertInOrder(Node nodeToInsert)
{
   Comparable item = (Comparable) nodeToInsert.getData();
   Node currentNode = firstNode;
   Node previousNode = null;

   // locate insertion point
   while ( (currentNode != null) &&
           (item.compareTo(currentNode.getData()) > 0) )
   {
      previousNode = currentNode;
      currentNode = currentNode.getNextNode();
   } // end while

   // make the insertion
   if (previousNode != null)
   { // insert between previousNode and currentNode
```

```
            previousNode.setNextNode(nodeToInsert);
            nodeToInsert.setNextNode(currentNode);
        }
        else // insert at beginning
        {
            nodeToInsert.setNextNode(firstNode);
            firstNode = nodeToInsert;
        } // end if
    } // end insertInOrder
```

11.16   Now that the hard part is done, we can use this method to implement an insertion sort. We can use
the same strategy that we used to sort an array: Divide the chain into two parts. The first part is
sorted, and it initially contains only the first node. The second part is unsorted and initially is the
rest of the chain. Of course, we cannot divide a chain of only one node into two pieces, but such a
chain is already sorted!

Figure 11-10 illustrates how to make this division. We first make the variable unsortedPart
reference the second node and then set the link portion of the first node to null. To sort the nodes,
we use the method insertInOrder to take each node from the unsorted part and insert it into the
sorted part. Notice that our plan relinks existing nodes instead of creating new ones.

Figure 11-10 Breaking a chain of nodes into two pieces as the first step in an insertion sort:
(a) the original chain; (b) the two pieces

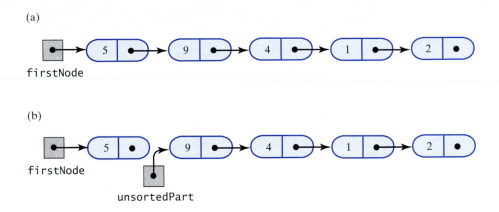

The method to perform the insertion sort appears as follows. We assume that length is a data
field that contains the number of nodes currently in the list. Notice that unsortedPart always references the rest of the chain.

```
public void insertionSort()
{
    // if one item is in list, there is nothing to do
    if (length > 1)
    { // Assertion: firstNode != null.

        // break list into 2 pieces: sorted and unsorted
        Node unsortedPart = firstNode.getNextNode();
        firstNode.setNextNode(null);
```

```
    while (unsortedPart != null)
    {
        Node nodeToInsert = unsortedPart;
        unsortedPart = unsortedPart.getNextNode();
        insertInOrder(nodeToInsert);
    } // end while
} // end if
} // end insertionSort
```

Question 3   In the previous method `insertionSort`, if you move the line

`unsortedPart = unsortedPart.getNextNode();`

after the call to `insertInOrder`, will the method still work? Explain.

11.17   **The efficiency of an insertion sort of a chain.** For a chain of n nodes, the number of comparisons that the method `insertInOrder` makes is at most the number of nodes in the sorted portion of the chain. The method `insertionSort` calls `insertInOrder` $n - 1$ times. The first time it does so, the sorted portion contains one item, so one comparison is made. The second time, the sorted portion contains two items, so at most two comparisons are made. Continuing in this fashion, you can see that the maximum number of comparisons is

$$1 + 2 + \ldots + (n - 1)$$

This sum is $n\,(n - 1)/2$, so this insertion sort is $O(n^2)$.

Note: Sorting a chain of linked nodes can be difficult. The insertion sort, however, provides a reasonable way to perform this task.

Shell Sort

11.18   The sorting algorithms that we have discussed so far are simple and often useful, but they are too inefficient to use on large arrays. The Shell sort is a variation of the insertion sort that is faster than $O(n^2)$.

During an insertion sort, an array element moves to an adjacent location. When an element is far from its correct sorted position, it must make many such moves. So when an array is completely scrambled, an insertion sort takes a good deal of time. But when an array is almost sorted, an insertion sort is more efficient. In fact, Segment 11.13 showed that the more sorted an array is, the less work the method `insertInOrder` needs to do.

By capitalizing on these observations, Donald Shell devised an improved insertion sort, now called the **Shell sort.** Shell wanted elements to move beyond their adjacent locations. To do so, he sorted subarrays of elements at equally spaced indices. Instead of moving to an adjacent location, an element moves several locations away. The result is an array that is almost sorted—one that can be sorted efficiently by using an ordinary insertion sort.

11.19   For example, Figure 11-11 shows an array and the subarrays obtained by considering every sixth element. The first subarray contains the integers 10, 9, and 7; the second subarray contains 16 and 6; and so on. There happen to be six of these subarrays.

Now we sort each of the six subarrays separately by using an insertion sort. Figure 11-12 shows the sorted subarrays and the state of the original array as a result. Notice that the array is "more sorted" than it was originally.

Figure 11-11   An array and the subarrays formed by grouping elements whose indices are 6 apart

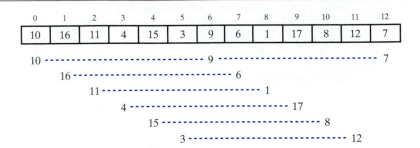

Figure 11-12   The subarrays of Figure 11-11 after they are sorted, and the array that contains them

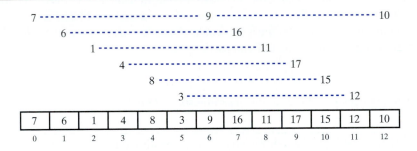

11.20   Now we form new subarrays, but this time we reduce the separation between indices. Shell suggested that the initial separation between indices be $n/2$ and that you halve this value at each pass until it is 1. The array in our example has 13 elements, so we began with a separation of 6. We now reduce the separation to 3. Figure 11-13 shows the resulting subarrays, and Figure 11-14 shows the subarrays after they are sorted.

Figure 11-13   The subarrays of the array in Figure 11-12 formed by grouping elements whose indices are 3 apart

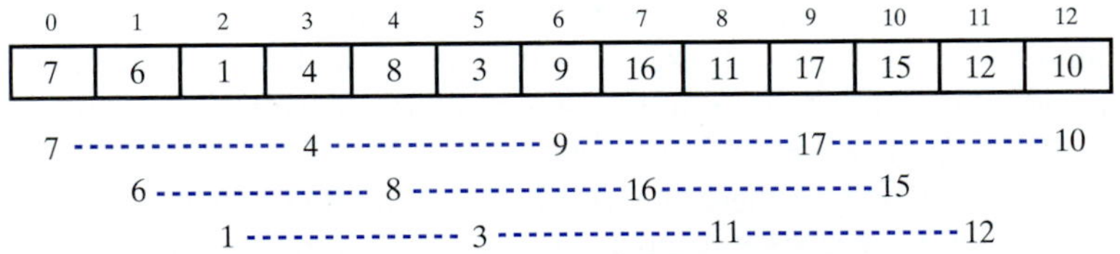

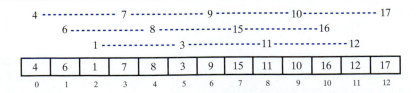

Figure 11-14   The subarrays of Figure 11-13 after they are sorted, and the array that contains them

Dividing the current separation 3 by 2 results in 1. Therefore, the final step is simply an ordinary insertion sort of the entire array. Thus, the array will be sorted regardless of what we have done to it beforehand. That is, Shell sort will work if you use any sequence of index separations, as long as the last one is 1. But not just any sequence will make Shell sort efficient, as you will see in Segment 11.22.

Question 4   Apply the Shell sort to the array 9 8 2 7 5 4 6 3 1, with index separations of 4, 2, and 1. What are the intermediate steps?

The Java Code

11.21   The heart of the Shell sort is the adaptation of the insertion sort to work on a subarray of equally spaced elements. By combining and modifying the two algorithms that describe the insertion sort, as given in Segment 11.9, we obtain the following method that sorts array elements whose indices are separated by an increment of space.

```java
/** Task: Sorts equally spaced elements of an array into
 *        ascending order.
 *  @param a      an array of Comparable objects
 *  @param first  an integer >= 0 that is the index of the first
 *                array element to consider
 *  @param last   an integer >= first and < a.length that is the
 *                index of the last array element to consider
 *  @param space  the difference between the indices of the
 *                elements to sort */
private static void incrementalInsertionSort(Comparable[] a, int first,
                                             int last, int space)
{
  int unsorted, index;

  for (unsorted = first + space; unsorted <= last;
       unsorted = unsorted + space)
  {
    Comparable firstUnsorted = a[unsorted];

    for (index = unsorted - space; (index >= first) &&
                  (firstUnsorted.compareTo(a[index]) < 0);
                  index = index - space)
    {
      a[index + space] = a[index];
    } // end for

    a[index + space] = firstUnsorted;
  } // end for
} // end incrementalInsertionSort
```

A method to perform a Shell sort will invoke `incrementalInsertionSort` and supply any sequence of spacing factors. For example, we might write the following method, using the spacing that Segment 11.20 described:

```
public static void shellSort(Comparable[] a, int first, int last)
{
   int n = last - first + 1; // number of array elements

   for (int space = n/2; space > 0; space = space/2)
   {
      for (int begin = first; begin < first + space; begin++)
         incrementalInsertionSort(a, begin, last, space);
   } // end for
} // end shellSort
```

Question 5   Trace the steps that a Shell sort takes when sorting the following array into ascending order: 9 6 2 4 8 7 5 3.

The Efficiency of Shell Sort

11.22   Since Shell sort uses an insertion sort repeatedly, it certainly seems like much more work than using only one insertion sort. Actually, however, it is not. Although we used an insertion sort several times instead of just once, the initial sorts are of arrays that are much smaller than the original one, the later sorts are on arrays that are partially sorted, and the final sort is on an array that is almost entirely sorted. Intuitively, this seems good. But even though Shell sort is not very complicated, its analysis is.

Since `incrementalInsertionSort` involves a loop and is called from within nested loops, Shell sort uses three nested loops. Often such algorithms are $O(n^3)$, but it turns out that the worst-case behavior of the Shell sort is still $O(n^2)$. If n is a power of 2, the average-case behavior is $O(n^{1.5})$. And if you tweak the spacing a bit, you can make the Shell sort even more efficient.

One improvement is to avoid even values of `space`. Figure 11-11 provided an example of the subarrays when `space` was 6. The first subarray contained 10, 9, and 7, for instance. Later, after we halved `space`, the first subarrray contained 7, 4, 9, 17, and 10, as Figure 11-13 shows. Notice that these two subarrays have elements in common, namely the 10, 9, and 7. Thus, the comparisons that you make when `space` is even will be repeated on the next pass when the increment is `space/2`.

To avoid this inefficiency, simply add 1 to `space` whenever it is even. This simple change results in consecutive increments that have no factor in common. The worst-case behavior of the Shell sort is then $O(n^{1.5})$. Other sequences for `space` result in even greater efficiencies, although the proof that this is the case remains elusive. An improved Shell sort can be a reasonable choice for moderately large arrays.

Note: **The time efficiency of Shell sort**

The Shell sort, as implemented in this chapter, is $O(n^2)$ in the worst case. By adding 1 to `space` anytime that it is even, you can improve the worst-case behavior to $O(n^{1.5})$.

Comparing the Algorithms

11.23   Figure 11-15 summarizes the time efficiencies of the three sorting algorithms presented in this chapter. Generally, the selection sort is the slowest algorithm. The Shell sort, by capitalizing on the best case behavior of the insertion sort, is the fastest.

Figure 11-15 The time efficiencies of three sorting algorithms, expressed in Big Oh notation

	Best Case	Average Case	Worst Case
Selection sort	$O(n^2)$	$O(n^2)$	$O(n^2)$
Insertion sort	$O(n)$	$O(n^2)$	$O(n^2)$
Shell sort	$O(n)$	$O(n^{1.5})$	$O(n^{1.5})$

CHAPTER SUMMARY

- A selection sort of an array selects the smallest element and swaps it with the first one. Ignoring the new first element, the sort then finds the smallest element in the rest of the array and swaps it with the second element, and so on.

- Typically, you perform a selection sort iteratively, although a simple recursive form is possible.

- A selection sort is $O(n^2)$ in all cases.

- An insertion sort divides an array into two portions, sorted and unsorted. Initially, the array's first element is in the sorted portion. The sort takes the next unsorted element and compares it with elements in the sorted portion. As the comparisons continue, each sorted element is shifted by one position toward the end of the array until the unsorted element's correct position is located. The sort then inserts the element into its correct position, which has been vacated by the shifts.

- You can perform an insertion sort either iteratively or recursively.

- An insertion sort is $O(n^2)$ in the worst case but is $O(n)$ in the best case. The more sorted an array is, the less work an insertion sort does.

- You can use an insertion sort to sort a chain of linked nodes, a task that typically is difficult.

- The Shell sort is a modification of the insertion sort that sorts subarrays of elements that are equally spaced within the array. The strategy efficiently arranges the array so that it is almost sorted, enabling an ordinary insertion sort to quickly finish the job.

- The worst-case behavior of Shell sort, as implemented in this chapter, is $O(n^2)$. With a simple change, its worst-case behavior can be improved to at least $O(n^{1.5})$.

EXERCISES

1. Sort the array of integers 5 7 4 9 8 5 6 3 into ascending order by using a selection sort. Write the contents of the array each time that the sort changes it.

2. Repeat Exercise 1, but use an insertion sort instead.

3. Repeat Exercise 1, but use a Shell sort instead.

4. Revise the selection sort so that it selects the largest, instead of the smallest, element in the array and sorts the array into ascending order.

5. Repeat Exercise 4, but this time sort the array into descending order.

6. A **bubble sort** can sort an array of n elements into ascending order by making $n-1$ passes through the array. On each pass, it compares two adjacent elements and swaps them if they are out of order. For example, on the first pass, it compares the first and second elements, then the second and third elements, and so on. At the end of the first

pass, the largest element is in its proper position at the end of the array. We say that it has bubbled to its correct spot. Each subsequent pass ignores the elements at the end of the array, since they are sorted and are larger than any of the remaining elements. Thus, each pass makes one fewer comparison than the previous pass. Figure 11-16 gives an example of a bubble sort.

Implement the bubble sort

a. Iteratively
b. Recursively

Figure 11-16 A bubble sort of an array (see Exercise 6)

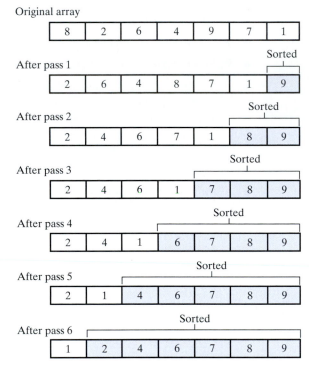

7. How does the efficiency of the bubble sort compare to the other sorting algorithms in this chapter?

8. The bubble sort in Exercise 6 always makes *n* passes. However, it is possible for the array to become sorted before all *n* passes are complete. For example, a bubble sort of the array

    9 2 1 6 4 7 8

is sorted after only two passes:

    2 1 6 4 7 8 9 (end of pass 1)
    1 2 4 6 7 8 9 (end of pass 2)

But since a swap occurred during the second pass, the sort needs to make one more pass to check that the array is in order. Additional passes, such as the ones that the algorithm in Exercise 6 would make, are unnecessary.

You can skip these unnecessary passes and even make the last pass do less work, as follows. During the first pass, the last swap is of the 9 and 8. The second pass checks up to the 8. But during the second pass, the last swap is of the 6 and 4. You now know that 6, 7, 8, and 9 are sorted. The third pass needs only to check up to the 4, instead of the 7, as an ordinary bubble sort would do. No swaps occur during the third pass, so the index of the last swap during this pass is taken as zero, indicating that no further passes are necessary. Implement this revised bubble sort.

9. Devise an algorithm that determines whether a given array of integers is sorted into ascending order.

10. Which recursive algorithms in this chapter are tail recursive?

11. Revise the implementation of the Shell sort given in Segment 11.21 so that space is not even.

12. As Segment 11.22 suggests, you can improve the efficiency of the Shell sort by adding 1 to space any time that it is even.

    a. By looking at several examples, convince yourself that consecutive increments do not have a common factor.
    b. Subtracting 1 from space any time that it is even does not produce consecutive increments without common factors. Find an example of n that demonstrates this phenomenon.

13. Suppose you want to find the largest element in an unsorted array of n elements. Algorithm A searches the entire array sequentially and records the largest element seen so far. Algorithm B sorts the array into descending order, and then reports the first element as the largest. Compare the time efficiency of the two approaches.

PROJECTS

1. Graphical demonstrations of various sorting algorithms are instructive, as they provide insight into how an algorithm behaves. Consider a collection of vertical lines of varying lengths, such as the ones in Figure 11-17a. Create a sorting demonstration that sorts the lines by length, as shown in Figure 11-17b. You should draw the configuration of lines after every swap or move that a given sorting algorithm makes. If you delay execution very briefly after each redraw, the result will be an animation of the sort.

    You could begin by drawing 256 lines, each one pixel wide but of different lengths—and perhaps different colors—arranged from shortest to longest so that they appear as a triangle. The user then should exercise an option to scramble the lines. At a user signal, your sorting algorithm should sort the lines.

    You can provide individual demonstrations, perhaps as applets, for each sort algorithm. Or you can include all the algorithms in one program that asks the user to choose an algorithm. Each sort should start with the same scrambled lines so the user can compare methods. You might also choose a sort algorithm at random and see whether the user can guess which one it is.

2. Revise the implementations of the insertion sort and the Shell sort so that they count the number of comparisons made during a sort. Use your implementations to compare the two sorts on various arrays of random Integer objects. Also, compare the Shell sort as implemented in Segment 11.21 with a revised Shell sort that adds 1 to space any time that it is even.

Figure 11-17 An animated sorting demonstration that sorts vertical lines
(a) before its execution; (b) after its execution

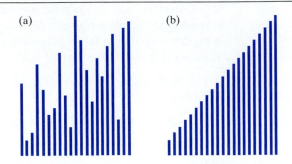

(a)   (b)

3. Implement any three sorting algorithms given in this chapter. Use your implementations to compare the run times of the three sorts on various arrays of random Integer objects. See the projects at the end of Chapter 9 for a description of how to time a block of Java code.

12

Faster Sorting Methods

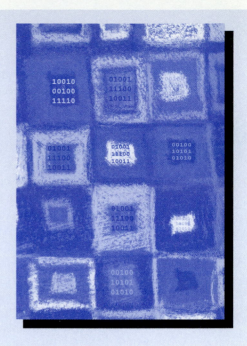

CONTENTS

Merge Sort
    Merging Arrays
    Recursive Merge Sort
    The Efficiency of Merge Sort
    Iterative Merge Sort
    Merge Sort in the Java Class Library
Quick Sort
    The Efficiency of Quick Sort
    Creating the Partition
    Java Code for Quick Sort
    Quick Sort in the Java Class Library
Radix Sort
    Pseudocode for Radix Sort
    The Efficiency of Radix Sort
Comparing the Algorithms

PREREQUISITES

Chapter   4   Lists
Chapter   5   List Implementations That Use Arrays
Chapter   9   The Efficiency of Algorithms
Chapter 10   Recursion
Chapter 11   An Introduction to Sorting

OBJECTIVES

After studying this chapter, you should be able to

- Sort an array into ascending order by using the following methods: merge sort, quick sort, and radix sort
- Determine the efficiency of a sort and discuss the relative efficiencies of the various methods

The sorting methods that you saw in the previous chapter often are sufficient when you want to sort small arrays. They even can be a reasonable choice if you need to sort a larger array once. Additionally, the insertion sort is a good way to sort a chain of linked nodes. However, when you need to sort very large arrays frequently, those methods take too much time. This chapter presents sorting algorithms that are much faster in general than the methods in Chapter 11.

Merge Sort

12.1   The **merge sort** divides an array into halves, sorts the two halves, and then merges them into one sorted array. The algorithm for merge sort is usually stated recursively. You know that a recursive algorithm expresses the solution to a problem in terms of a smaller version of the same problem. When you divide a problem into two or more smaller but *distinct* problems, solve *each* new problem, and then combine their solutions to solve the original problem, the strategy is said to be a **divide and conquer** algorithm. That is, you divide the problem into pieces and conquer each piece to reach a solution. Although divide and conquer algorithms often are expressed recursively, this is not a requirement.

When expressed recursively, a divide and conquer algorithm has two or more recursive calls. Most of the recursive solutions that you have seen so far do not use the divide and conquer strategy. For example, Segment 11.5 gave a recursive version of the selection sort. Even though that algorithm considers smaller and smaller arrays, it contains only one recursive call.

The real effort of a merge sort occurs during the merge step, so we will begin there.

Merging Arrays

12.2   Imagine that you have two distinct arrays that are sorted. Merging two sorted arrays is not difficult, but it does require an additional array. Processing both arrays from beginning to end, you compare an element in one array with an element in the other and copy the smaller element to a new third array, as Figure 12-1 shows. After reaching the end of one array, you simply copy the remaining elements from the other array to the new third array.

Figure 12-1   Merging two sorted arrays into one sorted array

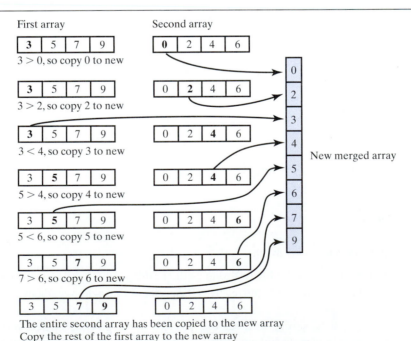

Recursive Merge Sort

12.3   **The algorithm.** In a merge sort, you merge two sorted arrays that are actually halves of the original array. That is, you divide the array into halves, sort each half, and merge the sorted halves into a second temporary array, as Figure 12-2 shows. You then copy the temporary array back to the original array.

Figure 12-2   The major steps in a merge sort

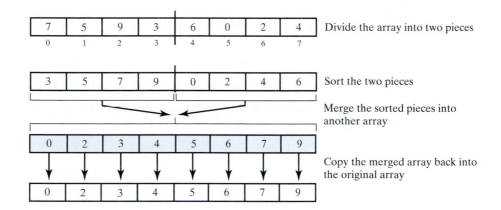

This sounds like a simple plan, but how did we sort the two halves of the array? By using a merge sort, of course! If mid is the index of the approximate midpoint of an array of n elements, we need to sort the elements indexed by 0 through mid, and then the elements indexed by mid + 1 through n – 1. Since we perform these sorts by recursive calls to the merge sort algorithm, the algorithm needs two parameters—first and last—to specify the first and last indices of the subrange of the array to be sorted. We will use the notation a[first..last] to mean the array elements a[first], a[first+1],..., a[last].

Merge sort has the following recursive formulation:

Algorithm mergeSort(a, first, last)
// Sorts the array elements a[first] *through* a[last] *recursively.*

```
if (first < last)
{
   mid = (first + last)/2
   mergeSort(a, first, mid)
   mergeSort(a, mid+1, last)
   Merge the sorted halves a[first..mid] and a[mid+1..last]
}
```

Notice that the algorithm considers only arrays of two or more elements.
The following pseudocode describes the merge step:

Algorithm merge(a, first, mid, last)
// Merges the adjacent subarrays a[first..mid] *and* a[mid+1..last].

```
beginHalf1 = first
endHalf1 = mid
beginHalf2 = mid + 1
endHalf2 = last
Allocate tempArray
```

```
// While both subarrays are not empty, compare an element in one subarray with
// an element in the other; then copy the smaller item into the temporary array
index = 0  // next available location in tempArray
while ( (beginHalf1 <= endHalf1) and (beginHalf2 <= endHalf2) )
{
    if (a[beginHalf1] < a[beginHalf2])
    {
        tempArray[index] = a[beginHalf1]
        beginHalf1++
    }
    else
    {
        tempArray[index] = a[beginHalf2]
        beginHalf2++
    }
    index++
}
// Assertion: One subarray has been completely copied to tempArray.

Copy remaining elements from other subarray to tempArray
Copy elements from tempArray to array a
```

Implementing a recursive merge sort is straightforward, and we leave it as a programming project.

12.4   **Tracing the steps in the algorithm.** Let's examine what happens when we invoke mergeSort on the array halves. Figure 12-3 shows that mergeSort divides an array into two pieces and then recursively divides each of those pieces into two pieces until each piece contains only one element. At this point in the algorithm, the merge steps begin. Two pieces of one element each are merged to form a two-element subarray. Two pieces of two elements each are merged to form a four-element subarray, and so on.

Figure 12-3   The effect of the recursive calls and the merges during a merge sort

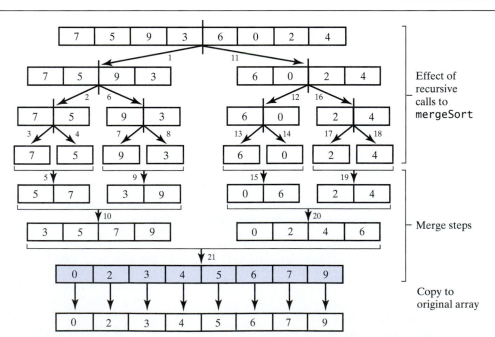

Numbers on the arrows indicate the order in which the recursive calls and the merges occur. Notice that the first merge occurs after four recursive calls to mergeSort and before other recursive calls to mergeSort. Thus, the recursive calls to mergeSort are interwoven with calls to merge. You can see that the actual sorting takes place during the merge steps and not during the recursive calls.

As you will see, we can use these observations in two ways. First, we can determine the algorithm's efficiency. Second, we can formulate the mergeSort algorithm iteratively.

Note: Merge sort rearranges the elements in an array during its merge steps.

Question 1   Trace the steps that a merge sort takes when sorting the following array into ascending order: 9 6 2 4 8 7 5 3.

The Efficiency of Merge Sort

12.5   Assume for now that n is a power of 2, so that we can divide n by 2 evenly. The array in Figure 12-3 has $n = 8$ elements. The initial call to mergeSort makes two recursive calls to mergeSort, dividing the array into two subarrays of $n/2$, or 4, elements each. Each of the two recursive calls to merge-Sort makes two recursive calls to mergeSort, dividing the two subarrays into four subarrays of $n/2$, or 2, elements each. Finally, recursive calls to mergeSort divide the four subarrays into eight subarrays of $n/2$, or 1, element each. It takes three levels of recursive calls to obtain subarrays of one element each. Notice that the original array contained 2^3 elements. The exponent 3 is the number of levels of recursive calls.

Now consider the merge steps, because that is where the real work occurs. From Figure 12-1, you can see that the merge step makes at most n comparisons among the n elements in the two subarrays. Now look at the merge steps in Figure 12-3. Four merges of one-element subarrays occur, each requiring 2—that is, $n/4$—comparisons, for a total of $4(n/4)$, or n, comparisons. At the next level, two merges of two-element subarrays occur, each requiring 4—that is, $n/2$—comparisons, for a total of $2(n/2)$, or n, comparisons. At the last level, one merge of four-element subarrays occur, requiring 8—that is, n—comparisons.

In general, if n is 2^k, k levels of recursive calls occur, so there are k levels of merges. The merges at each level require n comparisons, so in total, $n * k$ comparisons are necessary. Since k is $\log_2 n$, mergeSort is $O(n \log n)$.

When n is not a power of 2, we can find an integer k so that $2^{k-1} < n < 2^k$. For example, when n is 15, k is 4. Thus,

$$k - 1 < \log_2 n < k$$

so if we round $\log_2 n$ up, we will get k. Therefore, the merge sort is $O(n \log n)$. Notice that the merge steps perform the same amount of work regardless of the initial order of the array. Merge sort is $O(n \log n)$ in the worst, best, and average cases.

A disadvantage of merge sort is the need for the temporary array during the merge step. At the beginning of Chapter 11, we spoke of sorting the books on your bookshelf by height. We were able to do so without the extra space that another shelf or the floor would provide. You can see now that the merge sort would require this extra space. Later in this chapter, you will see another algorithm that sorts in $O(n \log n)$ time without a second array.

> **Note:**   **The time efficiency of merge sort**
> Merge sort is O(n log n) in all cases. Its need for a temporary array is a disadvantage.

12.6   **Determining efficiency another way.** In Chapter 10, we used a recurrence relation to determine the efficiency of recursive algorithms. We can use the same technique here. If $t(n)$ represents the time requirement of mergeSort, the two recursive calls each require time $t(n/2)$. The merge step makes n comparisons and $2n$ assignments, and so it is O(n). Thus, we have the following:

$$t(n) = t(n/2) + t(n/2) + n$$
$$\quad\quad = 2\ t(n/2) + n \text{ when } n > 1$$
$$t(1) = 0$$

As a first step in solving this recurrence relation, we evaluate it for a specific value of n. Since $t(n)$ involves $n/2$, choosing n to be a power of 2—8, for example—is convenient. We then have

$$t(8) = 2\ t(4) + 8$$
$$t(4) = 2\ t(2) + 4$$
$$t(2) = 2\ t(1) + 2 = 2$$

By substituting repeatedly, we get the following for $t(8)$:

$$t(8) = 2\ t(4) + 8$$
$$\quad\quad = 2\ [2\ t(2) + 4] + 8$$
$$\quad\quad = 4\ t(2) + 8 + 8$$
$$\quad\quad = 4\ [2\ t(1) + 2] + 8 + 8$$
$$\quad\quad = 8 + 8 + 8$$
$$\quad\quad = 8 * 3$$

Since $8 = 2^3$, $3 = \log_2 8$, so we guess that

$$t(n) = n \log_2 n$$

Just as we did in Chapter 10, we now need to prove that our guess is in fact true. We leave this proof as an exercise.

Iterative Merge Sort

12.7   Once we have the merge algorithm, developing the recursive merge sort is easy. Developing an iterative merge sort is not as simple. We begin by making some observations about the recursive solution.

The recursive calls simply divide the array into n one-element subarrays, as you can see in Figure 12-3. Although we do not need recursion to isolate the elements in an array, the recursion controls the merging process. To replace the recursion with iteration, we will need to control the merges. Such an algorithm will be more efficient of both time and space, since it will eliminate the recursive calls and, therefore, the stack of activation records. But an iterative merge sort will be trickier to code without error.

Basically, an iterative merge sort starts at the beginning of the array and merges pairs of individual elements to form two-element subarrays. Then it returns to the beginning of the array and merges pairs of the two-element subarrays to form four-element subarrays, and so on. However, after merging all pairs of subarrays of a particular length, we might have elements left over. Merging these requires some care. Project 2 at the end of this chapter asks you to develop an iterative merge sort. You will see there that you can save much of the time necessary to copy the temporary array back to the original array during the merges.

Merge Sort in the Java Class Library

12.8   The class `Arrays` in the package `java.util` defines several versions of a static method `sort` to sort an array into ascending order. For an array of objects, `sort` uses a merge sort. The method

```
public static void sort(Object[] a);
```

sorts an entire array a of objects, while the method

```
public static void sort(Object[] a, int first, int last);
```

sorts the subarray that the indices `first` and `last` define. For both methods, objects in the array must define the `Comparable` interface.

The merge sort used here skips the merge step if none of the elements in the left half of the array are greater than the elements in the right half. Since both halves are sorted already, the merge step is unnecessary in this case.

Question 2   Modify the merge algorithm given in Segment 12.3 so that it skips any unnecessary merges, as just described.

Quick Sort

12.9   We now look at another divide and conquer strategy for sorting an array. The **quick sort** divides an array into two pieces, but unlike merge sort, these pieces are not necessarily halves of the array. Instead, quick sort chooses one element in the array—called the **pivot**—and rearranges the array elements so that

- The pivot is in the position that it will occupy in the final sorted array
- Elements in positions before the pivot are ≤ the pivot
- Elements in positions after the pivot are ≥ the pivot

This arrangement is called a **partition** of the array.

Creating the partition divides the array into two pieces, which we will call *Smaller* and *Larger*, separated by the pivot, as Figure 12-4 illustrates. Since the elements in *Smaller* are less than or equal to the pivot, and the elements in *Larger* are greater than or equal to the pivot, the pivot is in its correct and final position within the sorted array. If we now sort the two subarrays *Smaller* and *Larger*—by using quick sort, of course—the original array will be sorted. The following algorithm describes our sorting strategy:

> *Algorithm* `quickSort(a, first, last)`
> // *Sorts the array elements* `a[first]` *through* `a[last]` *recursively.*
>
> ```
> if (first < last)
> {
> ```
>   *Choose a pivot*
>   *Partition the array about the pivot*
>   `pivotIndex = ` *index of pivot*
>   `quickSort(a, first, pivotIndex-1)` *// sort Smaller*
>   `quickSort(a, pivotIndex+1, last)`   *// sort Larger*
> ```
> }
> ```

Figure 12-4   A partition of an array during a quick sort

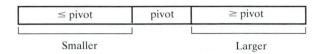

The Efficiency of Quick Sort

12.10   Notice that creating the partition—which accounts for most of quickSort's work—occurs before the recursive calls to quickSort. Contrast this with merge sort, where most of the work occurs during the merge phase *after* the recursive calls to mergeSort. Like merging, partitioning will require *n* comparisons, so it will be an O(*n*) task. Thus, we can assess the efficiency of quick sort, even though we have not yet developed a partitioning strategy.

The ideal situation occurs when the pivot moves to the center of the array, so the two subarrays that the partition forms are the same size. If every recursive call to quickSort forms a partition with equal-sized subarrays, the quick sort will be like merge sort in that the recursive calls halve the array. Thus, quick sort would be O(*n* log *n*), and this would be its best case.

This ideal situation might not always occur, however. In the worst case, each partition has one empty subarray. Although one recursive call will have nothing to do, the other call must sort *n* – 1 elements instead of *n*/2. The result is *n* levels of recursive calls instead of *n* log *n*. Thus, in the worst case, quick sort is O(n^2).

The choice of pivots, then, affects quick sort's efficiency. Some pivot-selection schemes can lead to worst-case behavior if the array is already sorted or nearly sorted. In practice, nearly sorted arrays can occur more frequently than you might imagine. As you will see later, our pivot-selection scheme will avoid the worst case.

Although we will not prove it, quick sort is O(*n* log *n*) in the average case. While merge sort is always O(*n* log *n*), quick sort is generally faster in practice and does not require the additional memory that merge sort needs for merging.

Note: **The time efficiency of quick sort**

Quick sort is O(*n* log *n*) in the average case but O(n^2) in the worst case. You can avoid the worst case by a careful choice of pivot.

Creating the Partition

12.11   Various strategies are possible for choosing a pivot and for creating the partition. For now, we will assume that you have chosen a pivot, and so we will describe how to create a partition independently of your pivot-selection strategy. Later, our actual pivot-selection scheme will suggest minor changes to this partitioning process.

After choosing a pivot, swap it with the last element in the array so that the pivot is not in your way while you create the partition. Figure 12-5a shows an array after this step. Starting at the beginning of the array and moving toward the end (left to right in the figure), look for the first element that is greater than or equal to the pivot. In Figure 12-5b, that element is 5 and occurs at the index indexFromLeft. In a similar fashion, starting at the next-to-last element and moving toward the beginning of the array (right to left in the figure), look for the first element that is less than or equal to the pivot. In Figure 12-5b, that element is 2 and occurs at the index `indexFromRight`. Now, if `indexFromLeft` is less than `indexFromRight`, swap the two elements at those indices. Figure 12-5c shows the result of this step.

Continue the searches from the left and from the right. Figure 12-5d shows that the search from the left stops at 4 and the search from the right stops at 1. Since `indexFromLeft` is less than `index-FromRight`, swap 4 and 1. The array now appears as in Figure 12-5e.

Continue the searches again. Figure 12-5f shows that the search from the left stops at 6 while the search from the right goes beyond the 6 to stop at 1. Since `indexFromLeft` is not less than `indexFromRight`, no swap is necessary and the searches end. The only remaining step is to place the pivot between the subarrays *Smaller* and *Larger* by swapping a[`indexFromLeft`] and a[`last`], as Figure 12-5g shows. The completed partition appears in Figure 12-5h.

Figure 12-5   A partitioning strategy for quick sort

12.12   **Elements equal to the pivot.** Notice that both of the subarrays *Smaller* and *Larger* can contain elements equal to the pivot. This might seem a bit strange to you. Why not always place any elements that equal the pivot into the same subarray? Such a strategy would tend to make one subarray larger than the other. However, to enhance quick sort's performance, we want the subarrays to be as nearly equal in size as possible.

Notice that both the search from the left and the search from the right stop when they encounter an element that equals the pivot. This means that rather than leaving such elements in place, they are swapped. It also means that such an element has an equal chance of landing in each of the subarrays.

12.13   **Pivot selection.** Ideally, the pivot should be the median value in the array, so that the subarrays *Smaller* and *Larger* each have the same—or nearly the same—number of elements. To find the median value, we must sort the array and get the value in the middle. But sorting the array is the original problem, so this circular logic is doomed. Besides, we want to choose a pivot quickly.

Instead, we will take as our pivot the median of three elements in the array: the first element, the middle element, and the last element. One way to accomplish this task is to sort only those three elements and use the middle element of the three as the pivot. Figure 12-6 shows an array both before and after its first, middle, and last elements are sorted. The pivot is the 5. This pivot selection strategy is called **median-of-three pivot selection.**

Figure 12-6   Median-of-three pivot selection: (a) The original array; (b) the array with its first, middle, and last elements sorted

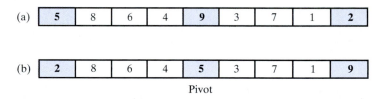

12.14   **Adjusting the partition algorithm.** Median-of-three pivot selection suggests some minor adjustments to our partitioning scheme. Previously, we swapped the pivot with the last element in the array. But here, the first, middle, and last elements in the array are sorted, so we know that the last element is at least as large as the pivot. Thus, the last element belongs in the subarray *Larger*. We can simply leave the last element in place. To get the pivot out of the way, we can swap it with the next-to-last element, a[last-1], as Figure 12-7 shows. Thus, the partition algorithm can begin its search from the right at index last − 2.

Figure 12-7   (a) The array with its first, middle, and last elements sorted; (b) the array after positioning the pivot and just before partitioning

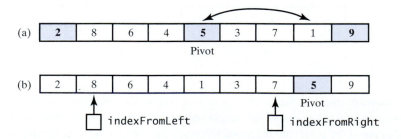

Also notice that the first element is at least as small as the pivot, and so it belongs in the subarray *Smaller*. Thus, we can leave the first element in place and have the partition algorithm begin its search from the left at index first + 1. Figure 12-7b shows the status of the array at this point, just prior to partitioning.

This scheme provides a side benefit that simplifies the loops for the two searches. The search from the left looks for an element that is greater than or equal to the pivot. That search will terminate because, at worst, it will stop at the pivot. The search from the right looks for an element that is less than or equal to the pivot. That search will terminate because, at worst, it will stop at the first element. Thus, the loops need not do anything special to prevent the searches from going beyond the ends of the array.

After the search loops end, we need to position the pivot between the subarrays *Smaller* and *Larger*. We do this by swapping the elements a[indexFromLeft] and a[last-1].

Note: Quick sort rearranges the elements in an array during the partitioning process. After each step in this process, one element—the pivot—is placed in its correct sorted position. The elements in each of the two subarrays that are before and after the pivot will remain in their respective subarrays.

Java Code for Quick Sort

12.15   **Pivot selection.** Median-of-three pivot selection requires us to sort three elements. We do this with simple comparisons and swaps, as follows:

```
/** Task: Sorts the first, middle, and last elements of an
 *         array into ascending order.
 *  @param a       an array of Comparable objects
 *  @param first   the integer index of the first array element;
 *                 first >= 0
 *  @param mid     the integer index of the middle array element
 *  @param last    the integer index of the last array element;
 *                 last - first >= 2, last < a.length */
private static void sortFirstMiddleLast(Comparable[] a, int first,
                                        int mid, int last)
{
  order(a, first, mid); // make a[first] <= a[mid]
  order(a, mid, last);  // make a[mid]   <= a[last]
  order(a, first, mid); // make a[first] <= a[mid]
} // end sortFirstMiddleLast

/** Task: Orders two given array elements into ascending order
 *         so that a[i] <= a[j].
 *  @param a  an array of Comparable objects
 *  @param i  an integer >= 0 and < array.length
 *  @param j  an integer >= 0 and < array.length */
private static void order(Comparable[] a, int i, int j)
{
  if (a[i].compareTo(a[j]) > 0)
    swap(a, i, j);
} // end order
```

```
/** Task: Swaps the array elements array[i] and array[j]. */
private static void swap(Comparable[] array, int i, int j)
{
   Comparable temp = array[i];
   array[i] = array[j];
   array[j] = temp;
} // end swap
```

12.16 **Partitioning.** Median-of-three pivot selection assumes that the array has at least three elements. If you have only three elements, the pivot selection sorts them, so there is no need for the partition method or for quick sort. Thus, the following partition method assumes that the array contains at least four elements:

```
/** Task: Partitions an array as part of quick sort into two subarrays
 *         called Smaller and Larger that are separated by a single
 *         element called the pivot.
 *         Elements in Smaller are left of the pivot and <= pivot.
 *         Elements in Larger are right of the pivot and >= pivot.
 * @param a      an array of Comparable objects
 * @param first  the integer index of the first array element;
 *               first >= 0
 * @param last   the integer index of the last array element;
 *               last - first >= 3; last < a.length
 * @return the index of the pivot */
private static int partition(Comparable[] a, int first, int last)
{
   int mid = (first + last)/2;
   sortFirstMiddleLast(a, first, mid, last);

   // Assertion: The pivot is a[mid]; a[first] <= pivot and
   // a[last] >= pivot, so do not compare these two array elements
   // with pivot.

   // move pivot to next-to-last position in array
   swap(a, mid, last-1);
   int pivotIndex = last-1;
   Comparable pivot = a[pivotIndex];

   // determine subarrays Smaller = a[first..endSmaller]
   //                 and Larger  = a[endSmaller+1..last-1]
   // such that elements in Smaller are <= pivot and
   // elements in Larger are >= pivot; initially, these subarrays are empty

   int indexFromLeft = first+1;
   int indexFromRight = last - 2;

   boolean done = false;
   while (!done)
   {
      // starting at beginning of array, leave elements that are < pivot;
      // locate first element that is >= pivot; you will find one,
      // since last element is >= pivot
      while (a[indexFromLeft].compareTo(pivot) < 0)
         indexFromLeft++;
```

```
// starting at end of array, leave elements that are > pivot;
// locate first element that is <= pivot; you will find one,
// since first element is <= pivot

while (a[indexFromRight].compareTo(pivot) > 0)
  indexFromRight--;

// Assertion: a[indexFromLeft] >= pivot and
//            a[indexFromRight] <= pivot.

if (indexFromLeft < indexFromRight)
{
  swap(a, indexFromLeft, indexFromRight);
  indexFromLeft++;
  indexFromRight--;
}
else
  done = true;
} // end while

// place pivot between Smaller and Larger subarrays
swap(a, pivotIndex, indexFromLeft);
pivotIndex = indexFromLeft;

// Assertion:
// Smaller = a[first..pivotIndex-1]
// Pivot = a[pivotIndex]
// Larger = a[pivotIndex + 1..last]

return pivotIndex;
}  // end partition
```

12.17 **The quick sort method.** Before completing the Java code for quick sort, we need to think about small arrays. You have seen that the array should contain at least four elements before you call the partition method. But simply agreeing to use quick sort only on large arrays is not enough. The pseudocode given for quick sort in Segment 12.9 shows that partitioning even a very large array will eventually lead to a recursive call that involves an array as small as two elements. The code for quick sort needs to screen out these small arrays and use another way to sort them. An insertion sort is a good choice for small arrays. In fact, using it instead of quick sort on arrays of as many as ten elements is reasonable. The following method implements quick sort with these observations in mind. The method assumes a constant MIN_SIZE that specifies the size of the smallest array on which we will use a quick sort.

```
/** Task: Sorts an array into ascending order. Uses quick sort with
 *        median-of-three pivot selection for arrays of at least
 *        MIN_SIZE elements, and uses insertion sort for other arrays. */
public static void quickSort(Comparable[] a, int first, int last)
{
  if (last - first + 1 < MIN_SIZE)
    insertionSort(a, first, last);
  else
  {
    // create the partition: Smaller | Pivot | Larger
    int pivotIndex = partition(a, first, last);
```

```
          // sort subarrays Smaller and Larger
          quickSort(a, first, pivotIndex-1);
          quickSort(a, pivotIndex+1, last);
      } // end if
   }  // end quickSort
```

Question 3 Trace the steps that the method `quickSort` takes when sorting the following array into ascending order: 9 6 2 4 8 7 5 3. Assume that `MIN_SIZE` is 4.

Quick Sort in the Java Class Library

12.18 The class `Arrays` in the package `java.util` uses a quick sort to sort arrays of primitive types into ascending order. The method

public static void sort(*type*[] a);

sorts an entire array a, while the method

public static void sort(*type*[] a, **int** first, **int** last);

sorts the subarray that the indices `first` and `last` define. Note that *type* is either byte, char, double, float, int, long, or short.

Radix Sort

12.19 The sorting algorithms that you have seen so far sort objects that can be compared. The **radix sort** does not compare objects, but to work, it must restrict the data that it sorts. For this restricted data, the radix sort is O(n), and so it is faster than any other sort in this chapter. However, it is not suitable as a general-purpose sorting algorithm, because it treats array elements as if they were strings that have the same length.

Let's look at an example of a radix sort of the following three-digit positive integers:

123 398 210 019 528 003 513 129 220 294

Notice that 19 and 3 are padded with zeros to make them three-digit integers. The radix sort begins by grouping the integers according to their rightmost digits. Since a digit can have one of 10 values, we need 10 groups, or **buckets.** If bucket *d* corresponds to the digit *d*, we place 123 into bucket 3, 398 into bucket 8, and so on. Figure 12-8a shows the result of this process. Notice that each bucket must retain the order in which it receives the integers.

Looking at the buckets sequentially, we see that the integers are now in the following order:

210 220 123 003 513 294 398 528 019 129

Beginning with empty buckets, we now group these integers by their middle digits. Thus, 210 goes into bucket 1, 220 goes into bucket 2, 123 goes into bucket 2, and so on. Figure 12-8b shows the result of this pass.

The integers in the buckets are now in this order:

003 210 513 019 220 123 528 129 294 398

Starting again with empty buckets, we group these integers by their leftmost digits. Thus, 003 goes into bucket 0, 210 goes into bucket 2, 513 goes into bucket 5, and so on. Figure 12-8c shows the result of this pass.

The integers in the buckets are now in their final sorted order:

003 019 123 129 210 220 294 398 513 528

Figure 12-8   Radix sort: (a) Original array and buckets after first distribution; (b) reordered array and buckets after second distribution; (c) reordered array and buckets after third distribution; (d) sorted array

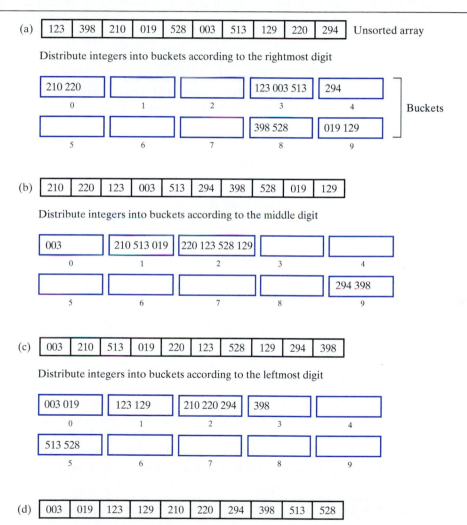

Note: **Origin of the radix sort**

During the early days of computing, data was stored on punched cards. Each card had 80 columns in which to store 80 characters. Each column had 12 rows that were the possible positions for holes. A machine called a card sorter distributed the cards among 12 bins according to any column chosen by the machine's operator. These bins are analogous to the buckets in a radix sort. After running a stack of cards through the card sorter, the operator would gather the cards a bin at a time to create a new stack. The stack would be run through the sorter again to sort the next column of holes. By repeating this process, the operator could sort the cards.

Pseudocode for Radix Sort

12.20   Our previous description of radix sort assumed that the integers to be sorted each contain the same number of digits. Actually, this requirement is unnecessary as long as you get 0 when you ask for a digit that does not exist. For example, if you ask for the hundreds digit of a two-digit integer, you should get 0. The following algorithm describes a radix sort of an array of positive decimal integers:

Algorithm `radixSort(a, first, last, maxDigits)`
// Sorts the array of positive decimal integers `a[first..last]` *into ascending order;*
// `maxDigits` *is the number of digits in the longest integer.*

for (i = 1 *to* maxDigits)
{
   Clear bucket[0], bucket[1], . . . , bucket[9]
   for (index = first *to* last)
   {
      digit = i^{th} *digit from the right of* a[index]
      Place a[index] *at end of* bucket[digit]
   }
   Place contents of bucket[0], bucket[1], . . . , bucket[9] *into the array* a
}

Question 4   Trace the steps that the algorithm `radixSort` takes when sorting the following array into ascending order:

6340   1234   291   3   6325   68   5227   1638

The Efficiency of Radix Sort

12.21   If an array contains *n* integers, the inner loop in the previous algorithm iterates *n* times. If each integer contains *d* digits, the outer loop iterates *d* times. Thus, the radix sort is O(*d* * *n*). The *d* in this expression tells us that the actual running time for a radix sort depends on the size of the integers. But on a computer, the typical integer is restricted in size to about 10 decimal digits or 32 bits. As long as *d* is fixed and is much smaller than *n*, radix sort is simply an O(*n*) algorithm.

Note: Although radix sort is an O(*n*) algorithm for certain data, it is not appropriate for all data.

Question 5   One of the difficulties with the radix sort is that the number of buckets depends on the kind of strings you are sorting. You saw that sorting integers requires 10 buckets; sorting words requires at least 26 buckets. If you use radix sort to alphabetize an array of words, what changes would be necessary to the given algorithm?

Comparing the Algorithms

12.22   Figure 12-9 summarizes the efficiencies of the sorting algorithms presented in this chapter and the previous chapter. Although a radix sort is fastest, it is not always applicable. The merge sort and quick sort are generally faster than any of the other algorithms.

Figure 12-9   The time efficiency of various sorting algorithms, expressed in Big Oh notation

	Average Case	Best Case	Worst Case
Radix sort	$O(n)$	$O(n)$	$O(n)$
Merge sort	$O(n \log n)$	$O(n \log n)$	$O(n \log n)$
Quick sort	$O(n \log n)$	$O(n \log n)$	$O(n^2)$
Shell sort	$O(n^{1.5})$	$O(n)$	$O(n^{1.5})$
Insertion sort	$O(n^2)$	$O(n)$	$O(n^2)$
Selection sort	$O(n^2)$	$O(n^2)$	$O(n^2)$

To give you an idea of how the problem size affects time efficiency, Figure 12-10 tabulates the four growth-rate functions that appear in Figure 12-9 for several values of n. You certainly could use an $O(n^2)$ sort algorithm when n is 10. When n is 100, a Shell sort is almost as fast as a quick sort in the average case. But when n is one million, an average-case quick sort is much faster than a Shell sort and much, much faster than an insertion sort.

If your array has relatively few elements or if it is nearly sorted, the insertion sort is a good choice. Otherwise, the quick sort is generally preferable.

Figure 12-10 A comparison of growth-rate functions as n increases

n	10	10^2	10^3	10^4	10^5	10^6
$n \log_2 n$	33	664	9966	132,877	1,660,964	19,931,569
$n^{1.5}$	32	10^3	31,623	10^6	31,622,777	10^9
n^2	10^2	10^4	10^6	10^8	10^{10}	10^{12}

CHAPTER SUMMARY

- Merge sort is a divide and conquer algorithm that halves an array, recursively sorts the two halves, and then merges them into one sorted array.

- Merge sort is $O(n \log n)$. However, it does use additional memory to perform the merge step.

- Quick sort is another divide and conquer algorithm that partitions an array into two subarrays that are separated by one element, the pivot. The pivot is in its correct sorted position. The elements in one sub-array are less than or equal to the pivot, while the elements in the second subarray are greater than or equal to the pivot. Quick sort recursively sorts the two subarrays.

- Quick sort is $O(n \log n)$ most of the time. Although it is $O(n^2)$ in its worst case, you usually can avoid this case by choosing appropriate pivots.

- Even though merge sort and quick sort are O(n log n) algorithms, quick sort is usually faster in practice and does not require additional memory.

- Radix sort initially distributes strings into buckets according to the character at one end of the strings. The sort then collects the strings and distributes them again among the buckets according to the character in the next position. The sort continues this process until all character positions are considered.

- Radix sort does not compare array elements. Although it is O(n), it cannot sort all types of data. Thus, it is not appropriate as a general-purpose sorting algorithm.

EXERCISES

1. Suppose that 80 90 70 85 60 40 50 95 represents an array of Integer objects. Show the steps that a merge sort takes when sorting this array.

2. Consider the method quickSort, as given in Segment 12.17, that sorts an array of objects into ascending order by using a quick sort. Suppose that 80 90 70 85 60 40 50 95 represents an array of Integer objects.

   a. What does the array look like after quickSort partitions it for the first time? (Show all intermediate results.)
   b. How many comparisons did this partition process require?
   c. The pivot is now between two subarrays called *Smaller* and *Larger*. Will the position of this particular element change during subsequent steps of the sort? Why or why not?
   d. What recursive call to quickSort occurs next?

3. Show the steps that a radix sort takes when sorting the following array of Integer objects:
   783 99 472 182 264 543 356 295 692 491 94

4. Show the steps that a radix sort takes when sorting the following array of strings into alphabetical order:
   joke book back dig desk word fish ward dish wit deed fast dog bend

5. Describe how a card player can use a radix sort to sort a hand of cards.

6. A **bucket sort** is a simple way to sort an array of n positive integers that lie between 0 and m, inclusive. You need $m + 1$ counters. Then, making only one pass through the array, you count the number of times each integer occurs in the array. For example, Figure 12-11 shows an array of integers that lie between 0 and 4 and the five counters after a bucket sort has made its pass through the array. From the counters, you can see that the array contains one 0, three 1s, two 2s, one 3, and three 4s. These counts enable you to determine that the sorted array should contain 0 1 1 1 2 2 3 4 4 4.

   a. Write a method that performs a bucket sort.
   b. How does the efficiency of a bucket sort compare to that of an insertion sort or a quick sort?

7. Consider a linked implementation of the ADT list.

   a. Implement a method that merges two sorted chains into one new sorted chain.
   b. The method described in Part *a* could be part of a merge sort of a sorted chain. Describe how you could implement such a sort.

Figure 12-11 A bucket sort of an array (see Exercise 6)

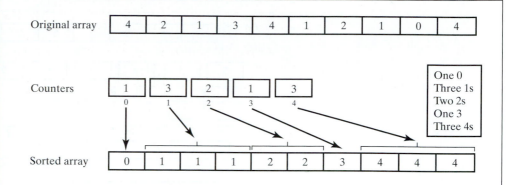

8. A sorting algorithm is **stable** if it does not change the relative order of objects that are equal. For example, if object a appears before object b in a collection of data, and a.compareTo(b) is zero, a stable sorting algorithm will leave object a before object b after sorting the data. Stability is important to certain applications. For example, suppose that you sort a group of people first by name and then by age. A stable sorting algorithm will ensure that people of the same age will remain in alphabetical order.

   What sorting algorithms in Chapters 11 and 12 are stable?

9. Segment 12.6 showed that you can determine the efficiency of merge sort by solving the recurrence relation

   $$t(n) = 2\, t(n/2) + n \text{ when } n > 1$$
   $$t(1) = 0$$

   Prove by induction that $t(n) = n \log_2 n$.

PROJECTS

1. Implement the recursive algorithm for merge sort.

2. Segment 12.7 introduced you to an iterative merge sort. This project continues that discussion by providing more details about the merge steps.

   a. If n is a power of 2, as it is in Figure 12-3, you would merge pairs of individual elements, starting at the beginning of the array. Then you would return to the beginning of the array and merge pairs of two-element subarrays. Finally, you would merge one pair of four-element subarrays. Notice that the subarrays in each pair of subarrays contain the same number of elements.

   In general, n might not be a power of 2. After merging a certain number of pairs of subarrays, you might have too few elements left to make up a complete pair of subarrays. In Figure 12-12a, after merging pairs of single elements, one element is left over. You then merge one pair of two-element subarrays, and merge the leftover two-element subarray with the leftover single element. Parts b and c of Figure 12-12 show two other possibilities.

Figure 12-12 Special cases in an iterative merge sort after merging one-element subarrays

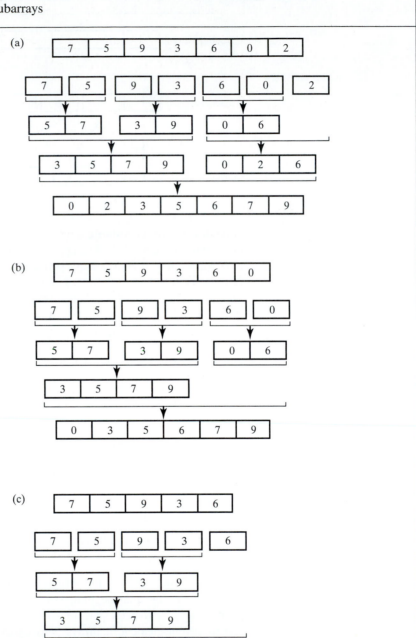

Implement an iterative merge sort. Use the algorithm merge that was given in Segment 12.3. A private method that uses merge to merge the pairs of subarrays is useful. After the method completes its task, you can handle the leftovers that we just described.

b. Merging two subarrays requires an additional temporary array. While you need to use this extra space, you can save much of the time that our earlier merge algorithm spends in copying elements from the temporary array back to the original array. If *a* is the original array and *t* is the temporary array, you first merge subarrays of *a* into the array *t*. Instead of copying *t* back to *a* and continuing the merge, you determine subarrays of *t* and merge them into *a*. If you can do this an even number of times, no additional copying is necessary. Make these changes to the iterative merge sort that you wrote in Part *a*.

3. Revise the implementation of quick sort as follows. If the array has 7 elements, choose the middle element as the pivot. For arrays of between 8 and 40 elements, use the median-of-three pivot-selection scheme described in Segment 12.15. For larger arrays, the pivot is the median of 9 elements that are about equally spaced, including the first, last, and middle elements. For arrays of fewer than 7 elements, use insertion sort instead of quick sort.

4. Extend Project 1 of Chapter 11 to provide graphical demonstrations of the merge sort and quick sort algorithms introduced in this chapter.

5. The **median** of a collection of data is the middle value. One way to find the median is to sort the data and take the value that is at—or nearly at—the center of the collection. But sorting does more than necessary to find the median. You need to find only the kth smallest element in the collection for an appropriate value of k. To find the median of n items, you would take k as $n/2$ rounded up—that is, $\lceil n/2 \rceil$.

You can use the partitioning strategy of quick sort to find the kth smallest element in an array. After choosing a pivot and forming the subarrays *Smaller* and *Larger*, as described in Segments 12.15 and 12.16, you can draw the following conclusion:

1. If *Smaller* contains k or more elements, it must contain the kth smallest element.
2. If *Smaller* contains $k - 1$ elements, the kth smallest element is the pivot.
3. If *Smaller* contains fewer than $k - 1$ elements, the kth smallest element is in *Larger*.

You now can develop a recursive solution to finding the kth smallest element. Cases 1 and 3 correspond to the recursive calls. Case 2 is the base case.

Implement a recursive method that finds the kth smallest element in an unsorted array. Use your method to find the median in the array.

6. Implement a merge sort of the objects in a chain of linked nodes.

7. Implement a radix sort of the strings in a chain of linked nodes.

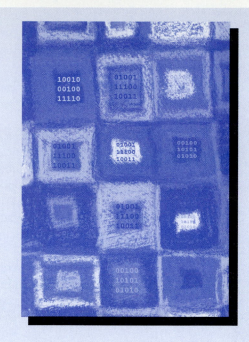

CONTENTS

Specifications for the ADT Sorted List
    Using the ADT Sorted List
A Linked Implementation
    The Method **add**
    The Efficiency of the Linked Implementation
An Implementation That Uses the ADT List
    Efficiency Issues

PREREQUISITES

Chapter   4   Lists
Chapter   6   List Implementations That Link Data
Chapter   9   The Efficiency of Algorithms
Chapter   10   Recursion

OBJECTIVES

After studying this chapter, you should be able to

- Use a sorted list in a program
- Describe the differences between the ADT list and the ADT sorted list
- Implement the ADT sorted list by using a chain of linked nodes
- Implement the ADT sorted list by using the operations of the ADT list

Chapter 4 introduced you to the ADT list. The entries in a list are ordered simply by their positions within the list. Thus, a list has a first entry, a second entry, and so on.

This ADT enables you to order entries according to any criterion you want—alphabetical or chronological, for instance. In fact, Chapter 4 showed you an example that used a list to organize names in alphabetical order. To do so, the client had to determine where in the list a particular entry belonged.

If your application creates a list and then at some point needs to sort the list's entries into numerical or alphabetical order, for example, you can add a sort operation to the ADT list. You can use one of the algorithms given in Chapters 11 and 12 to implement this operation. But when your application requires only sorted data, having an ADT that orders the data for you would be more convenient than the ADT list. The sorted list is such an ADT.

When you either add an entry to or remove an entry from a sorted list, you provide only the entry. You do not specify where in the list the entry belongs or exists. The ADT determines this for you.

This chapter describes the operations of the ADT sorted list, provides examples of using a sorted list, and presents two possible Java implementations. One of these implementations uses the ADT list, but it is not especially efficient. Chapter 14 addresses the reuse of a class and provides a more efficient implementation of the sorted list as it discusses the use of inheritance.

Specifications for the ADT Sorted List

13.1   The ADT list leaves it up to the client to arrange the objects in a given collection. The client can maintain the objects in any order that meets its needs. Suppose that you want a list of names or other strings that are in alphabetical order. You could certainly use the ADT list for this task, but you would have to determine the position that each string should have within the list. Wouldn't it be more convenient if the list itself alphabetized the entries as you added them? What you need is a different ADT, namely the **sorted list.**

Recall that to use the add operation of the ADT list, you must specify both the new entry and its desired position within the list. Such an operation is not desirable for the ADT sorted list, since the sorted list is responsible for organizing its entries. If you were allowed to specify a new entry's position, you might destroy the order of the sorted list's entries. Instead, the add operation of the ADT sorted list requires only the new entry. The operation compares the new entry to other entries in the sorted list to determine the new entry's position. Thus, the entries in a sorted list must be objects that can be compared with one another.

What, then, can you place in a sorted list? One possibility is strings, since the class String provides a compareTo method for comparing two strings. In general, you can have a sorted list of any objects that are instances of a class that has a compareTo method. As you saw in Segment 3.13 and again at the beginning of Chapter 11, such classes implement the interface Comparable. Since Java's wrapper classes, such as Integer and Double, implement the Comparable interface, you can place instances of them into a sorted list.

13.2   Let's examine the possible operations for this ADT. For simplicity, we will allow the sorted list to contain duplicate items. Insisting that the sorted list contain only unique items is somewhat more complicated, and we will leave this variation as an exercise.

We've already mentioned that you can add an entry to the sorted list. Since the sorted list determines the position of a new entry, you could ask the ADT for this position. That is, you could ask for the position of an existing entry or for the position in which a proposed entry would occur if you added it to the list. You could also ask the ADT whether it contained a particular entry. And clearly you should be able to remove an entry.

Let's specify these operations more carefully.

ABSTRACT DATA TYPE SORTED LIST

DATA

- A collection of objects in sorted order and having the same data type
- The number of objects in the collection

OPERATIONS

`add(newEntry)`

> Task: Adds `newEntry` to the sorted list so that the list remains sorted.
> Input: `newEntry` is the object to be added.
> Output: None.

`remove(anEntry)`

> Task: Removes the first or only occurrence of `anEntry` from the sorted list.
> Input: `anEntry` is the object to be removed.
> Output: Returns true if `anEntry` was located and removed, or false if not. In the latter case, the list remains unchanged.

`getPosition(anEntry)`

> Task: Gets the position of the first or only occurrence of `anEntry`.
> Input: `anEntry` is the object to be found.
> Output: Returns the position of `anEntry` if it occurs in the list. Otherwise, returns the position where `anEntry` would occur in the list, but as a negative integer.

The following operations behave as they do for the ADT list and are described in Chapter 4:

```
getEntry(givenPosition)
contains(anEntry)
remove(givenPosition)
clear()
getLength()
isEmpty()
isFull()
display()
```

13.3 The first two methods are straightforward, but `getPosition` deserves some comment. Given an entry in the sorted list, the method `getPosition` returns the entry's position number within the list, as you would expect. We number the entries beginning with 1, just as we do for the ADT list. But what if the given entry is not in the sorted list? In this case, `getPosition` returns the position number where the entry belongs in the list. The returned number is negative, however, to signal that the entry is not in the list. For example, if `missingObject` is not in the sorted list `sList` but belongs at position 3, `sList.getPosition(missingObject)` would return –3.

The sorted list also has some, but not all, of the operations of an ADT list. We have already mentioned that adding an entry at a given position is not possible, because otherwise the client could destroy the order of the sorted list. For the same reason, the list's `replace` method is not available to a sorted list. The other operations of the ADT list, however, are useful for a sorted list as well, including the ones that retrieve or remove the entry at a given position. The methods `getEntry` and `remove` each have a position number as a parameter, but they will not alter the relative order of the entries in the sorted list.

Although the list's `remove` method returns the object removed from the list, it is not necessary for the sorted list's `remove` method to do so. The client already has at least a copy of this entry to be able to invoke sorted list's `remove`.

13.4   The following Java interface specifies these operations in more detail:

```java
public interface SortedListInterface
{
    /** Task: Adds a new entry to the sorted list in its proper order.
     *  @param newEntry  the object to be added as a new entry
     *  @return true if the addition is successful */
    public boolean add(Comparable newEntry);

    /** Task: Removes a specified entry from the sorted list.
     *  @param anEntry  the object to be removed
     *  @return true if anEntry was located and removed */
    public boolean remove(Comparable anEntry);

    /** Task: Gets the position of an entry in the sorted list.
     *  @param anEntry  the object to be found
     *  @return the position of the first or only occurrence of
     *          anEntry if it occurs in the list; otherwise returns
     *          the position where anEntry would occur in the list,
     *          but as a negative integer */
    public int getPosition(Comparable anEntry);

    // The following methods are described in Segment 4.10 of
    // Chapter 4 as part of the ADT list:

    public Object getEntry(int givenPosition);
    public boolean contains(Object anEntry);
    public Object remove(int givenPosition);
    public void clear();
    public int getLength();
    public boolean isEmpty();
    public boolean isFull();
    public void display();
} // end SortedListInterface
```

Note: The ADT sorted list can add, remove, or locate an entry, given the entry as an argument. The sorted list has several operations that are the same as ADT list operations, namely `getEntry`, contains, remove (by position), clear, getLength, isEmpty, isFull, and display. However, a sorted list will not let you add or replace an entry by position.

Using the ADT Sorted List

13.5 **Example.** To demonstrate the operations of the ADT sorted list that the previous section specifies, we first create a sorted list of strings. We begin by declaring and allocating the list nameList, where we assume that SortedList is an implementation of the ADT operations specified by the interface SortedListInterface:

```
SortedListInterface nameList = new SortedList();
```

Next, we add names in an arbitrary order, realizing that the ADT will sort them alphabetically:

```
nameList.add("Jamie");
nameList.add("Brenda");
nameList.add("Sarah");
nameList.add("Tom");
nameList.add("Carlos");
```

Displaying the sorted list by writing

```
nameList.display();
```

results in the following output:

Brenda
Carlos
Jamie
Sarah
Tom

13.6 Assuming the list just given, here are some examples of the ADT operations on the sorted list:

nameList.getPosition("Jamie") returns 3, the position of *Jamie* in the list
nameList.contains("Jill") returns false, because *Jill* is not in the list
nameList.getPosition("Jill") returns –4, because *Jill* belongs at position 4 in the list
nameList.getEntry(2) returns *Carlos*, because he is at position 2 in the list

Now remove *Tom* and the first name in the list by writing

```
nameList.remove("Tom");
nameList.remove(1);
```

The list now contains

Carlos
Jamie
Sarah

Removing the last entry, *Tom*, did not change the positions of the other entries in the list, but removing the first entry did. *Carlos* is now at position 1, instead of 2.

Question 1   Suppose that wordList is an unsorted list of words. Using the operations of the ADT list and the ADT sorted list, create a sorted list of these words.

Question 2   Imagine that you have a sorted list that is not empty. Write Java statements that

a. Display the last entry in the sorted list.
b. Add the sorted list's first entry to the sorted list again.

A Linked Implementation

As with all ADTs, you have a choice of several ways in which to implement the sorted list. You could store a sorted list's entries in, for example, an array, a chain of linked nodes, an instance of a vector, or an instance of an ADT list. In this chapter, we will consider a chain of linked nodes and an instance of an ADT list. In the next chapter, we will use inheritance to develop a completely different implementation.

13.7   **An outline of the class.** An implementation that uses a chain of linked nodes to store the entries in a sorted list has several details in common with the linked implementation of the ADT list that you studied in Chapter 6. In particular, it has the same data fields, similar constructors, and the same implementations for several of its methods. Although our implementation also could use the same definition of the inner class Node, we will use a definition that includes get and set methods. Thus, we have the following outline of a class definition that implements the ADT sorted list:

```java
public class SortedLinkedList implements SortedListInterface
{
  private Node firstNode; // reference to first node of chain
  private int  length;    // number of entries in sorted list

  public SortedLinkedList()
  {
    firstNode = null;
    length = 0;
  } // end default constructor

  < Implementations of the sorted list operations go here. >
  . . .

  private class Node
  {
    private Object data;
    private Node    next;

    < Constructors >
    . . .

    < Accessor and mutator methods: getData, setData, getNextNode, setNextNode >
    . . .
  } // end Node
} // end SortedLinkedList
```

The Method add

13.8   **Locating the insertion point.** Adding an entry to a sorted list requires that you determine where in the list the new entry belongs. Since the entries are sorted, you compare the new entry with the entries in the sorted list until you reach an entry that is no smaller than the new entry. Figure 13-1 depicts a chain of linked nodes that contain names sorted alphabetically. The figure shows where the additional names *Ally, Cathy, Luke, Sue,* and *Tom* would be inserted into the chain and the comparisons that would have to occur to determine those locations.

Figure 13-1 Insertion points of names into a sorted chain of linked nodes

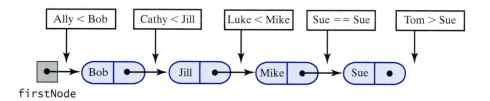

You can see from the figure that, as strings, *Ally* is less than *Bob,* and so it would be inserted at the beginning of the chain. To determine where to insert *Luke,* you would find that *Luke* is greater than both *Bob* and *Jill* but less than *Mike.* Thus, *Luke* belongs before *Mike* in the chain. *Sue,* on the other hand, is already in one of the nodes. You would discover that *Sue* is greater than *Bob, Jill,* and *Mike* but not greater than *Sue.* So you would insert the new entry *Sue* just before the existing entry *Sue.* Finally, *Tom* is greater than all the current names in the list, so you would add it to the end of the chain.

Note: Given a sorted list with entries in ascending order, you insert a new entry just before the first entry that is not smaller than the new entry.

13.9 **The algorithm.** Recall from Segment 6.27 that you handle the addition of a new node to the beginning of a chain differently from the addition at other points in the chain. Adding to the beginning is easy, since `firstNode` references the first node in the chain. To add anywhere else, you need a reference to the node that will ultimately occur before the new node. Thus, while you traverse the chain of linked nodes to discover where the new entry belongs, you must retain a reference to the node prior to the one under consideration.

A high-level algorithm that describes our strategy follows:

Algorithm **add(newEntry)**
// Adds a new entry to the sorted list.

Allocate a new node containing `newEntry`
Search chain until either you find a node containing `newEntry` *or you pass the point*
    where it should be
Let `nodeBefore` *reference the node before the insertion point*
if *(the chain is empty or the new node belongs at the beginning of the chain)*
    Add new node to beginning of chain

else
    Insert new node after the node referenced by `nodeBefore`

Increment length of sorted list

13.10 **An iterative implementation of add.** A Java implementation of the previous algorithm follows. We use a private method getNodeBefore to search the chain for the node before the insertion point.

```java
public boolean add(Comparable newEntry)
{
  Node newNode = new Node(newEntry);
  Node nodeBefore = getNodeBefore(newEntry);

  if (isEmpty() || (nodeBefore == null)) // add before first node
  {
    newNode.setNextNode(firstNode);
    firstNode = newNode;
  }
  else                     // add between nodeBefore and currentNode
  {
    Node nodeAfter = nodeBefore.getNextNode();
    newNode.setNextNode(nodeAfter);
    nodeBefore.setNextNode(newNode);
  } // end if

  length++;
  return true;
} // end add
```

13.11 **The private method getNodeBefore.** We still need to implement the private method getNodeBefore. We will need two references as we traverse the list. Clearly we need a reference to the current node so we can compare its entry to the desired entry. But we also must retain a reference to the previous node, because it is this reference that the method returns. In the following implementation, these references are currentNode and nodeBefore:

```java
/** Task: Determines the node that is before the node
 *        that should or does contain a given entry.
 *  @param anEntry  the object to be located
 *  @return either a reference to the node that is before the node
 *          that contains or should contain anEntry, or null,
 *          if no prior node exists (that is, if anEntry is or
 *          belongs at the beginning of the list) */
private Node getNodeBefore(Comparable anEntry)
{
  Node currentNode = firstNode;
  Node nodeBefore = null;

  while ( (currentNode != null) &&
          ( anEntry.compareTo(currentNode.getData()) > 0) )
  {
    nodeBefore = currentNode;
    currentNode = currentNode.getNextNode();
  } // end while

  return nodeBefore;
} // end getNodeBefore
```

Recall that the method `compareTo` returns an integer that indicates the result of the comparison. The integer is negative if the invoking object is less than `compareTo`'s argument, zero if they are equal, or positive if the invoking object is greater than `compareTo`'s argument.

Question 3   Suppose that you use the previous method add to add an entry to a sorted list. If the entry is already in the list, where in the list will add insert it? Before the first occurrence of the entry, after the first occurrence of the entry, after the last occurrence of the entry, or somewhere else?

13.12   **Thinking recursively.** Using recursion to process a chain of linked nodes can be an attractive alternative to an iterative approach. The basic concept is easy, but the implementation is a bit difficult due to the way Java passes arguments to methods, as you will see.

Recall from Segment 10.20 that you can process the chain's first node and then process the rest of the chain recursively. Thus, to add a new node to a sorted chain of linked nodes, you use the following logic:

if (*the chain is empty or the new node belongs at the beginning of the chain*)
   Add the new node to the beginning of the chain

else
   Ignore the first node and add the new node to the rest of the chain

Figure 13-2   Recursively adding *Luke* to a sorted chain of names

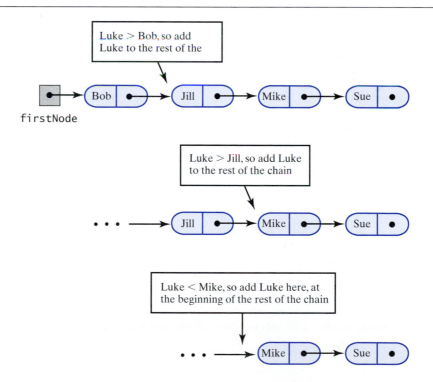

Figure 13-2 illustrates the logic needed to recursively add the name *Luke* to a sorted chain of names. Since *Luke* is greater than *Bob*, you recursively consider the subchain that begins at *Jill*. *Luke* is also greater than *Jill*, so you now consider the subchain beginning at *Mike*. Finally, *Luke* is less than *Mike*, so you make the actual addition at the beginning of this subchain—that is, before *Mike*. Adding to the beginning of a chain—or subchain—is the base case of this recursion. Happily, the beginning of a chain is the easiest place to make an addition.

If `currentNode` initially references the chain and later references the rest of the chain, we can add some detail to the previous logic, as follows:

```
if ( (currentNode == null) or
        newEntry.compareTo(currentNode.getData()) <= 0)
{
    currentNode = new Node(newEntry, currentNode)
}
else
    Recursively add newEntry to the chain beginning at currentNode.getNextNode()
```

13.13   **A recursive implementation of add.** The example in Segment 10.20 displayed the contents of a chain. Since that operation does not alter the chain, its recursive formulation was straightforward. Obviously, in our present situation, the method add does alter the chain. Getting the recursive method to make these changes is the challenge in Java.

Let's look at the recursive implementation of the method add before we describe why it works. You learned in Segment 10.19 that you write a private method to perform the recursion and you write a public method—typically the one that implements the ADT operation—to invoke this private method. Thus, we have the following method definitions:

```
public boolean add(Comparable newEntry)
{
    firstNode = add(newEntry, firstNode);
    length++;
    return true;
} // end add

private Node add(Comparable newEntry, Node currentNode)
{
    if ( (currentNode == null) ||
            newEntry.compareTo(currentNode.getData()) <= 0)
    {
        currentNode = new Node(newEntry, currentNode);
    }
    else
    {
        Node nodeAfter = add(newEntry, currentNode.getNextNode());
        currentNode.setNextNode(nodeAfter);
    } // end if

    return currentNode;
} // end add
```

The private method add adds `newEntry` to the subchain that begins at `currentNode`.

Question 4   Repeat Question 3, but instead use the previous method add.

13.14   **Tracing an addition to the list's beginning.** Suppose that `nameList` is the sorted list that the chain in Figure 13-3a represents. Let's invoke `nameList.add("Ally")` to add *Ally* to this list. This addition will occur at the beginning of the chain. The public method add will call the private method add with the invocation add("Ally", firstNode). The reference in the argument firstNode is copied to the parameter currentNode, and so it also references the first node in the chain, as Figure 13-3b illustrates.

Since *Ally* will be added to the beginning of the chain, the statement

```
currentNode = new Node("Ally", currentNode);
```

executes and creates a new node for *Ally*. This node is linked to the original chain, as Figure 13-3c shows. Notice that firstNode is unchanged even though it is the argument that corresponds to the parameter currentNode.

The private method now returns the value of currentNode, and the public method add assigns that value to firstNode. Thus, the chain with the completed addition appears as in Figure 13-3d.

Figure 13-3   Recursively adding a node at the beginning of a chain

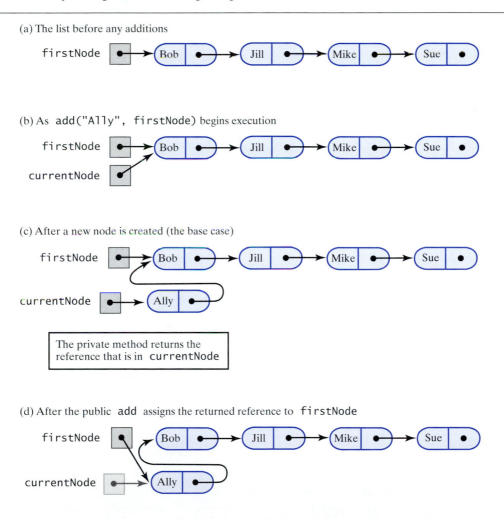

13.15   **Tracing an addition to the list's interior: the recursive calls.** What happens when the addition is not at the beginning of the original chain? Let's trace what happens when we add *Luke* to the chain in Figure 13-4a. The public method add calls the private method add with the invocation add("Luke", firstNode). As in the previous segment, the reference in firstNode is copied to the parameter currentNode, and so it also references the first node in the chain, as Figure 13-4a illustrates.

Figure 13-4   Recursively adding a node between existing nodes in a chain

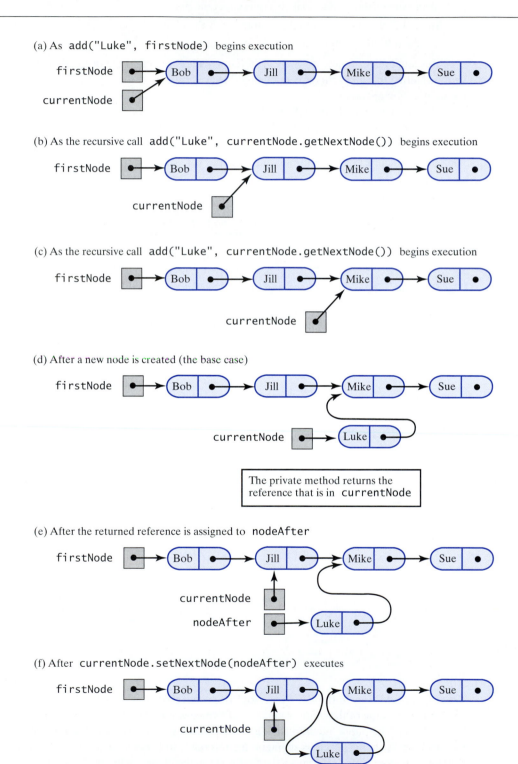

Since *Luke* comes after *Bob*, another recursive call occurs:

```
add("Luke", currentNode.getNextNode())
```

The second argument is a reference to the chain's second node, the one containing *Jill*. This reference is copied to the parameter `currentNode`, as Figure 13-4b depicts.

Luke comes after *Jill*, so the recursive process is repeated again, and `currentNode` references the chain's third node—*Mike*'s node—as shown in Figure 13-4c. *Luke* is less than *Mike,* so no recursive call occurs. We are at the base case. A new node is created that contains *Luke* and references *Mike*'s node, as Figure 13-4d illustrates.

13.16   **Tracing the returns from the recursive method.** Having just created a new node, the private method add returns a reference to it, as Figure 13-4d indicates. The statement that invoked add now resumes execution:

```
nodeAfter = add("Luke", currentNode.getNextNode());
```

Thus, `nodeAfter` is assigned a reference to the new node containing *Luke*, as Figure 13-4e illustrates.

At this point, `currentNode` references *Jill*'s node, as it did in Part *b* of the figure. The next statement to execute is

```
currentNode.setNextNode(nodeAfter);
```

Thus, the data field `next` in *Jill*'s node is changed to reference *Luke*'s node, as shown in Figure 13-4f.

The private method add now returns a reference to *Jill*'s node. If we continue the trace, we will make *Bob*'s node reference *Jill*'s node and `firstNode` reference *Bob*'s node, even though these references are already in place.

13.17   Projects 1 and 2 at the end of this chapter ask you to complete the iterative and recursive implementations. Notice that many of the sorted list operations are the same as operations of the ADT list and so would have implementations like those you saw in Chapter 6.

Note: Since the ADTs sorted list and list share many of the same operations, portions of their implementations are identical.

Question 5   What changes to the class `SortedLinkedList` are necessary to enable a client to serialize instances of the class?

The Efficiency of the Linked Implementation

13.18   If you consider the analysis of the linked implementation of the ADT list given in Chapter 9, you will see that the efficiency of adding to a list depends on the efficiency of the method `getNodeAt`. This method locates the insertion point by traversing the chain of nodes. It is an $O(n)$ operation. The add method for the sorted list does its own traversal of the list to locate where to make the addition. This traversal is also $O(n)$, making the addition to a sorted list an $O(n)$ operation.

In fact, the operations of the sorted list have the same efficiencies as the corresponding operations for a list. Figure 13-5 summarizes these efficiencies for a sorted list. Deriving these results is left as an exercise.

Figure 13-5   The worst-case efficiencies of the operations on the ADT sorted list for two implementations

ADT Sorted List Operation	Array	Linked
`add(newEntry)`	O(n)	O(n)
`remove(anEntry)`	O(n)	O(n)
`getPosition(anEntry)`	O(n)	O(n)
`getEntry(givenPosition)`	O(1)	O(n)
`contains(anEntry)`	O(n)	O(n)
`remove(givenPosition)`	O(n)	O(n)
`display()`	O(n)	O(n)
`clear(), getLength(), isEmpty(), isFull()`	O(1)	O(1)

An Implementation That Uses the ADT List

As we noted in Segment 13.17, the linked implementation of the ADT sorted list repeats much of the corresponding implementation of the ADT list. Can we avoid this duplication of effort and reuse portions of the list's implementation? The answer to this question is yes, as you will soon see.

You can certainly use the ADT list to create and maintain an alphabetical list of strings. It is natural, then, to consider using the ADT list when implementing the ADT sorted list. Basically, you can take one of two approaches to this use of the ADT list. Here we will use a list as a data field within the class that implements the sorted list. Figure 13-6 shows an instance of such a sorted list. Recall from Segment 2.1 that this approach is called composition and illustrates the *has-a* relationship between two classes. The next chapter considers the second approach, using inheritance to derive the sorted list from the list.

Figure 13-6   An instance of a sorted list that contains a list of its entries

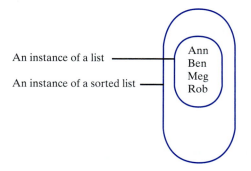

An instance of a list

An instance of a sorted list

Ann
Ben
Meg
Rob

13.19   Our class `SortedList` will implement the interface `SortedListInterface`. We begin this class by declaring a list as a data field and defining a default constructor. We assume that the class `LList`, as discussed in Chapter 6, is an implementation of the interface `ListInterface` for the ADT list. Thus, our class begins as follows:

```
public class SortedList implements SortedListInterface
{
    private ListInterface list;
```

```
public SortedList()
{
   list = new LList();
} // end default constructor
   . . .
} // end SortedList
```

13.20   **The method add.** The implementations of the operations of the ADT sorted list are brief, as the list does most of the work. To add a new entry to the sorted list, we first use the method getPosition, which is an operation of the sorted list. We assume, of course, that it is already implemented, even though we have not written it yet. Recall that getPosition determines the position of an existing entry within a sorted list, or the position at which we should insert a new entry that does not occur in the sorted list. The method uses the sign of the integer it returns to indicate whether the entry exists in the list already. When adding an entry to a sorted list that can contain duplicate entries, it does not matter whether the entry exists in the sorted list already. Thus, we can ignore the sign of the integer that getPosition returns. Notice that the following implementation uses the method abs of the class Math to discard this sign. It also uses the add operation of the ADT list. (In this section, calls to ADT list operations will appear in color.)

```
public boolean add(Comparable newEntry)
{
   int newPosition = Math.abs(getPosition(newEntry));
   return list.add(newPosition, newEntry);
} // end add
```

Question 6   Repeat Question 3, but instead use the previous method add.

13.21   **The method remove.** We also use getPosition to remove an object from a sorted list. This time, however, we do need to know whether the given entry exists in the sorted list. If it does not exist, we cannot remove it. In such cases, remove returns false. Also, notice that the method uses the operation remove of the ADT list to make the deletion. Thus, the method has the following implementation:

```
public boolean remove(Comparable anEntry)
{
   boolean result = false;
   int position = getPosition(anEntry);
   if (position > 0)
   {
      list.remove(position);
      result = true;
   } // end if

   return result;
} // end remove
```

Question 7   If a sorted list contains five duplicate objects and you use the previous method remove to remove one of them, what will be removed from the list: the first occurrence of the object, the last occurrence of the object, or all occurrences of the object?

13.22   **The logic for getPosition.** Implementing getPosition is somewhat harder than implementing the previous two methods. To determine where in the list anEntry is or belongs, we need to compare anEntry to the entries already in the list, beginning with the first one. If anEntry is in the list, we obviously compare entries until we find a match. However, if anEntry is not in the list, we want to stop the search at the point where it belongs in the sorted list. We take advantage of the sorted order of the objects by using logic similar to the logic described in Segment 13.8.

For example, suppose that the sorted list contains the four names *Brenda*, *Carlos*, *Sarah*, and *Tom*. If we want to determine where *Jamie* belongs in the sorted list, we discover that, as strings,

Jamie > Brenda
Jamie > Carlos
Jamie < Sarah

Thus, *Jamie* belongs after *Carlos* but before *Sarah*—that is, at position 3 in the sorted list, as Figure 13-7 illustrates.

Figure 13-7   A sorted list in which *Jamie* belongs after *Carlos* but before *Sarah*

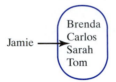

To compare anEntry to an entry in the sorted list, we first use the list operation getEntry to return the entry at a given position within the sorted list. Then the expression

anEntry.compareTo(list.getEntry(position))

makes the comparison.

13.23   **The implementation of getPosition.** In the following implementation of getPosition, the while loop determines anEntry's position in the sorted list, and the if statement determines whether anEntry is in the list.

```java
public int getPosition(Comparable anEntry)
{
   int position = 1;
   int length = list.getLength();

   // determine position of anEntry
   while ( (position <= length) &&
           (anEntry.compareTo(list.getEntry(position)) > 0) )
   {
      position++;
   } // end while

   // determine whether anEntry is in list
   if ( (position > length) ||
        (anEntry.compareTo(list.getEntry(position)) != 0) )
   {
      position = -position; // anEntry is not in list
   } // end if

   return position;
} // end getPosition
```

Question 8   Assume that the sorted list `nameList` contains the four names *Brenda*, *Carlos*, *Sarah*, and *Tom* as strings. By tracing the code for `getPosition`, determine what `getPosition` returns when `anEntry` represents

a. *Carlos*;   **b.** *Alan*;   **c.** *Wendy*;   **d.** *Tom*;   **e.** *Jamie*.

Question 9   Since you can determine whether a given entry is in a particular sorted list by testing the sign of the integer that `getPosition` returns, you can use `getPosition` to implement the method `contains`. Write such an implementation.

13.24   Each of the remaining methods—`contains`, `remove`, `getEntry`, `clear`, `getLength`, `isEmpty`, `isFull`, and `display`—has the same specifications as in the ADT list. Each simply can invoke the corresponding list method. For example, the method `getLength` has the following implementation in `SortedList`:

```
public int getLength()
{
   return list.getLength();
} // end getLength
```

Question 10   You can implement the method `contains` by invoking either `getPosition`, as Question 9 suggests, or the ADT list's `contains` method. Which of these implementations is more efficient when the entry sought is not present in the sorted list? Why?

Efficiency Issues

Except perhaps for some subtle logic in `getPosition`, you can write the previous implementation quickly and with few, if any, errors. Saving human time is an attractive feature of using an existing class to build another. But does the implementation use computer time efficiently? In this particular implementation, several methods invoke `getPosition`, so their efficiency depends on `getPosition`'s efficiency.

13.25   **The efficiency of `getPosition`.** As we examine `getPosition`, as given in Segment 13.23, we note that the list method `getLength` is an O(1) operation. Therefore, we need not be concerned with it. On the other hand, a loop examines the entries in the list one at a time by invoking `getEntry` until the desired entry is located. Thus, the efficiency of `getPosition` depends in part on the efficiency of `getEntry`. However, the efficiency of `getEntry` depends upon which implementation of the ADT list you use. We will examine two list implementations that lead to rather different efficiencies for `getPosition`.

Chapter 9 discussed the efficiencies of the ADT list operations. Figure 13-8 recalls the efficiencies of the list operations that we need to complete our analysis of the sorted list. If you use an array to represent the entries in a list, `getEntry` is an O(1) operation. The loop in `getPosition` is therefore O(n) in the worst case and leads us to conclude that the array-based implementation of `getPosition` is O(n).

If you use a chain of linked nodes to contain the entries in a list, the method `getEntry` is O(n). Since `getPosition`'s loop invokes `getEntry`, we see that `getPosition` is O(n^2). Each time that `getEntry` retrieves the next entry in the list, it starts its search at the beginning of the chain. This fact is the cause of `getPosition`'s inefficiency.

Figure 13-8   The worst-case efficiencies of selected ADT list operations for array-based and linked implementations

ADT List Operation	Array	Linked
getEntry(givenPosition)	O(1)	O(n)
add(newPosition, newEntry)	O(n)	O(n)
remove(givenPosition)	O(n)	O(n)
contains(anEntry)	O(n)	O(n)
display()	O(n)	O(n)
clear(), getLength(), isEmpty(), isFull()	O(1)	O(1)

13.26   **The efficiency of add.** The implementation of the sorted list method add given in Segment 13.20 contains the following statements:

```
int newPosition = Math.abs(getPosition(newEntry));
return list.add(newPosition, newEntry);
```

For an array-based implementation of the ADT list, both getPosition and the list operation add are O(n) operations. Thus, the sorted list operation add is O(n). For a linked implementation of the list, getPosition is O(n^2) and dominates the list operation add, which is only O(n). Thus, the sorted list operation add is O(n^2).

13.27   Figure 13-9 summarizes the efficiencies of the sorted list operations for array-based and linked implementations of the ADT list. Confirmation of these results is left as an exercise. As you can see, the implementation of the sorted list given in this section is easy to write but is not very efficient if the underlying list uses a chain of linked nodes. The next chapter will show you how you can reuse the ADT list in the implementation of the sorted list without sacrificing efficiency.

 Question 11   Give an advantage and a disadvantage of using composition in the implementation of the class SortedList.

Figure 13-9   The worst-case efficiencies of the ADT sorted list operations when implemented using an instance of the ADT list

ADT Sorted List Operation	List Implementation Array	Linked
add(newEntry)	O(n)	O(n^2)
remove(anEntry)	O(n)	O(n^2)
getPosition(anEntry)	O(n)	O(n^2)
getEntry(givenPosition)	O(1)	O(n)
contains(anEntry)	O(n)	O(n)
remove(givenPosition)	O(n)	O(n)
display()	O(n)	O(n)
clear(), getLength(), isEmpty(), isFull()	O(1)	O(1)

Note: Using containment to implement the ADT sorted list
When you use an instance of an ADT list to represent the entries in the ADT sorted list, you must use the list's operations to access the sorted list's entries, instead of accessing them directly. This approach leads to an inefficient implementation of the sorted list when the underlying list uses a chain of linked nodes to store its entries.

CHAPTER SUMMARY

- The ADT sorted list maintains its entries in sorted order. It, not the client, determines where to place an entry.

- The ADT sorted list can add, remove, or locate an entry, given the entry as an argument.

- The sorted list has several operations that are the same as the corresponding operations of the ADT list. However, a sorted list will not let you add or replace an entry by position.

- A chain of linked nodes provides a reasonably efficient implementation of the sorted list.

- An implementation of the sorted list that uses an ADT list as a data field is easy to write. However, depending upon how the ADT list is implemented, its efficiency can suffer.

EXERCISES

1. Suppose that nameList is a sorted list of names. Using the operations of the ADT list and the ADT sorted list, create a list of these names without changing their order.

2. As specified in this chapter, the sorted list can contain duplicate entries. Specify a sorted list of unique items. For example, add could return true if it added an entry to the list but return false if the entry is in the list already.

3. Consider an array-based implementation of the sorted list. To implement the method add, you must add an entry to a sorted array so that the array remains sorted.

   a. Describe the steps in this implementation.
   b. On which sort have you based your logic?
   c. Analyze the worst-case efficiency of this implementation of add.

4. Derive the worst-case efficiencies of the sorted list operations for both array-based and linked implementations, as given in Figure 13-5.

5. Derive the worst-case efficiencies of the sorted list operations when implemented using an instance of the ADT list, as given in Figure 13-9.

6. Consider an array-based implementation of the sorted list. Let the array entry be the data field that represents the list's entries. If a constructor is given an array of unsorted list entries, the constructor must place them into entry in sorted order. To do so, it could repeatedly use the sorted list's add method to add the entries to the sorted list (and hence to the array entry) in their proper order. Or it could copy the entries to entry and sort them by using a sort algorithm from Chapters 11 and 12.

   a. If you use the first approach, what sort are you actually using?
   b. Would you ever want to use the second approach? Explain.

7. Consider the implementation of the sorted list that uses an instance of the ADT list. In particular, consider the method `contains`. One implementation of `contains` could invoke `getPosition` (see Question 9). Another implementation could simply invoke `list.contains`. Compare the efficiencies of these two implementations.

8. Write a linked implementation of the sorted list method `contains`. Your search of the chain should end when it either locates the desired entry or passes the point at which it should have occurred.

9. Compare the efficiency of the method `contains` that Exercise 8 describes and the list's version of `contains`. Consider the worst case, average case, and best case.

10. Segment 12.2 described how to merge two sorted arrays into one sorted array. Add an operation to the ADT sorted list that merges two sorted lists. Implement the merge in three ways, as follows:

    a. Use only sorted list operations.
    b. Assume an array-based implementation.
    c. Assume a linked implementation.

PROJECTS

1. Complete the linked implementation of the ADT sorted list that was begun in this chapter. Use iteration instead of recursion.

2. Repeat Project 1, but use recursion wherever possible.

3. Implement the ADT sorted list by using an array to represent the ADT's entries. Use dynamic array expansion so that the sorted list can grow as large as necessary.

4. Implement the ADT sorted list by using an instance of `Vector` to represent the ADT's entries. Recall that Chapter 5 presented a similar implementation for the ADT list.

5. Exercise 2 asks you to specify an ADT sorted list of unique items. Implement such an ADT using one of the implementations described in this chapter or in the previous projects.

6. Add an iterator to the ADT sorted list by defining an inner class within the class that implements the ADT.

7. A **polynomial** in x is an algebraic expression that involves integer powers of x, as follows:

$$P(x) = a_n x^n + a_{n-1} x^{n-1} + \ldots + a_1 x + a_0$$

The a's are called **coefficients.** The **degree** of the polynomial is n, the highest exponent of x that appears in $P(x)$. Although a_n cannot be zero in a degree n polynomial, any other coefficient can be zero.

Specify an ADT polynomial that includes operations such as `getDegree`, `getCoefficient`, `setCoefficient`, `add`, and `subtract`. Implement this ADT by using a sorted list. The sorted list should not contain any coefficients that are zero.

Inheritance and Lists

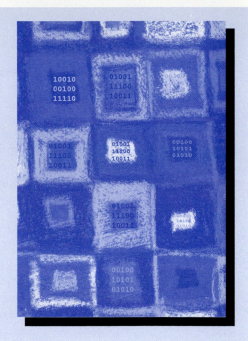

CONTENTS

Using Inheritance to Implement a Sorted List
Designing a Base Class
An Efficient Implementation of a Sorted List
    The Method **add**

PREREQUISITES

Chapter   2   Creating Classes from Other Classes
Chapter   4   Lists
Chapter   6   List Implementations That Link Data
Chapter   13   Sorted Lists

OBJECTIVES

After studying this chapter, you should be able to

- Describe how a class implementation that uses inheritance differs from one that uses composition
- Design a class that contains protected methods to make it suitable for use as a base class
- Write an efficient implementation of a sorted list by using inheritance

Chapter 13 introduced you to the ADT sorted list, which maintains its entries in a sorted order. As with many other ADTs, you can implement the sorted list by using either an array or a chain of linked nodes. The advantage of such implementations is their time efficiency. However, they require you to repeat a portion of the implementation of the ADT list, since the ADTs sorted list and list have several operations in common.

In an attempt to avoid this duplication of effort, Chapter 13 used an instance of the ADT list to contain the entries of the sorted list. This list was a data field of the class implementing the sorted list. The result was an implementation that you could write quickly, because the implementation of the list had done most of the work. But since the sorted list operations used the list in the same way that a client would, the sorted list operations were inefficient of time. This inefficiency was more pronounced when the ADT list had a linked implementation.

Instead of using composition, as we did in Chapter 13, what if we use inheritance? This chapter looks at the implications of deriving a sorted list from a list. In doing so we find that a subclass (derived class) can be more efficient if it can access the underlying data structures of its superclass (base class). This is possible if the superclass includes methods that enable future subclasses to access or modify its data fields. A class designer should plan for the future use of a class as well as a present need.

Using Inheritance to Implement a Sorted List

14.1   Recall the implementation of the class `SortedList` that we developed in Chapter 13. `SortedList` has an instance of another class, `LList` in this case, as a data field. `SortedList` and `LList` have a *has-a* relationship. Several of `SortedList`'s methods—namely `remove` (by position), `getEntry`, `contains`, `clear`, `getLength`, `isEmpty`, `isFull`, and `display`—behave like `LList`'s methods. If `SortedList` inherited these methods from `LList`, we would not have to implement them again. Thus, we could revise `SortedList` as follows:

```
public class SortedList extends LList
                        implements SortedListInterface
{
  public boolean add(Comparable newEntry)
  {
    int newPosition = Math.abs(getPosition(newEntry));
    return super.add(newPosition, newEntry);
  } // end add

  < Implementations of remove(anEntry) and getPosition(anEntry) go here. >
  . . .
} // end SortedList
```

First, you can see that `SortedList` is derived from `LList`. Also notice that we have omitted the data field `list` and the default constructor that appeared in Segment 13.19. To revise the `add` method given in Segment 13.20, we simply replaced `list` with `super`. That is, we wrote

```
super.add(newPosition, newEntry);
```

to invoke the add operation of the ADT list instead of

```
list.add(newPosition, newEntry);
```

as we did in Chapter 13. Coincidentally, `SortedList`'s add method overrides and hides the other add method in `LList` that adds to the end of a list.

We would make similar changes to the methods `remove` and `getPosition`. The remaining methods of the sorted list are inherited from `LList`, and so they do not appear explicitly in `SortedList`.

14.2   **A pitfall.** This implementation contains a pitfall that is the direct result of using inheritance. Although `SortedList` conveniently inherits methods such as `isEmpty` from `LList`, it also inherits two methods that can destroy the order of a sorted list. These two methods appear in `ListInterface` as follows:

```
/** Task: Adds newEntry to the list at position newPosition. */
public boolean add(int newPosition, Object newEntry);

/** Task: Replaces the entry at givenPosition with newEntry. */
public boolean replace(int givenPosition, Object newEntry);
```

If a client writes

```
SortedList sList = new SortedList();
```

sList can invoke any method declared in either SortedListInterface or ListInterface, includ-ing the previous methods add and replace. Thus, a client could destroy the order of the entries in a sorted list either by adding an entry out of order or by replacing an entry.

14.3   **Possible ways to avoid the pitfall.** What can we do to avoid this pitfall? Here are three possibilities:

- Declare the sorted list as an instance of SortedListInterface. For example, if the client writes

```
SortedListInterface sList = new SortedList();
```

sList can invoke only methods declared within SortedListInterface. Notice that the list operations add and replace do not appear in SortedListInterface. Although this can be a good programming practice, that is all it is. A client need only ignore this practice and define the data type of sList as SortedList to have all operations of the ADT list available to it. You have already seen how a client can sabotage the sorted list in this case.

- Implement the list's add and replace methods within the class SortedList, but have them return false. For example, add could appear as follows:

```
public boolean add(int newPosition, Object newEntry)
{
   return false;
} // end add
```

This version of add overrides and hides the version that LList implements. If the client invokes this method, the sorted list will remain unchanged. The client can detect that the method was unsuccessful, but not why.

If the list's method were a void method, we could give the overriding version an empty body, but then the client would be unaware that the method did not do anything.

- Implement the list's add and replace methods within the class SortedList and have them throw an exception when invoked. For example, add could appear as follows:

```
public boolean add(int newPosition, Object newEntry)
{
   throw new UnsupportedOperationException("Illegal attempt to " +
            "add at a specified position within a sorted list.");
} // end add
```

This version of add also overrides and hides the version that LList implements. If the client invokes this method, an exception occurs. This approach is a common practice, and it is the one we prefer.

Question 1   As a variation of the second possibility just given, you could implement the ADT list's two add methods so that each one calls the add method specified in SortedListInterface. In this way, the new entry is added in its correct position within the sorted list. Is this a good idea?

Programming Tip: If your class inherits methods that are inappropriate, you can override them with methods that throw an exception when invoked. In such a case, examine your design and consider whether inheritance was the right choice. Do the benefits of inheritance outweigh the inconvenience of overriding the inappropriate methods, or would composition provide a cleaner design?

14.4   **Efficiency.** The implementation of SortedList given here has the same efficiency—or inefficiency in this case—as the version that uses composition given in the previous chapter. If LList had been designed with inheritance in mind, SortedList could access LList's underlying data structure and provide faster operations. To this end, we revise the class LList in the next section.

Note: The implementation of the sorted list that extends the class LList is as inefficient as the implementation that used composition given in the previous chapter.

Question 2   Give an advantage and a disadvantage of using inheritance in the way shown in this section to implement the class SortedList.

Designing a Base Class

14.5   Let's examine the class LList that we developed in Chapter 6 as a linked implementation of the ADT list. Recall that the class places each of the list's entries into its own node. These nodes are linked so that the first entry's node references the node of the second entry, and so on. A data field firstNode of the class references the first node, and another data field length counts the number of entries in the list.

Like most classes, LList has data fields that are private. The client cannot access these fields directly by name. The class designer must decide whether to provide public methods that give the client indirect access to the data fields. In the case of LList, the public method getLength enables the client to get the length of the list. The client, however, cannot directly change the list's length. Only other member methods, such as add and remove, can alter the length. In addition, LList denies the client access to the field firstNode by not providing public accessor or mutator methods for this field. This design is appropriate, as firstNode is an implementation detail that should be hidden from the client.

14.6   The following excerpt of the class LList shows aspects of the class that are relevant to this discussion:

```
public class LList implements ListInterface
{
  private Node firstNode; // reference to first node
  private int  length;    // number of entries in list
```

```
                 public LList()
                 {
                   firstNode = null;
                   length = 0;
                 } // end default constructor

                 public int getLength()
                 {
                   return length;
                 } // end getLength
```

< *Implementations of the public methods* add, remove, clear, replace, getEntry,
contains, isEmpty, isFull, *and* display *go here.* >
. . .

```
                 /** Task: Returns a reference to the node at a given position. */
                 private Node getNodeAt(int givenPosition)
                 {
                   . . .
                 } // end getNodeAt

                 private class Node
                 {
                   private Object data;
                   private Node next;
                   . . .
                 } // end Node
               } // end LList
```

Each node is represented by the private class Node, which is defined within LList and hidden from the client. The method getNodeAt facilitates the implementation of other member methods by returning a reference to the node at a given position. We do not want the client to have access to this node, since it is part of the underlying representation of the list, so we make the method private.

14.7 So far, nothing should be new to you. Now imagine that we want LList to serve as a base class for another class that you are developing. You saw in the previous section of this chapter that a subclass of LList has the same access rights as a client of LList. That is, a subclass cannot access the data field firstNode, the method getNodeAt, or the class Node, as Figure 14-1 illustrates. If we want to extend the capability of LList and do so efficiently, the subclass will need access to these aspects of the class—that is, to the underlying data structure.

We can revise LList to make it more suitable as a base class by providing its subclasses access to items that are hidden from a client. We begin by reviewing protected access, which we discussed in Segment 2.18.

Note: **Protected access**
You can access a protected method or data field by name only within its own class definition C, within a class derived from C, or within any class in the same package as C.

Figure 14-1 A derived class of the class LList cannot access or change anything that is private within LList

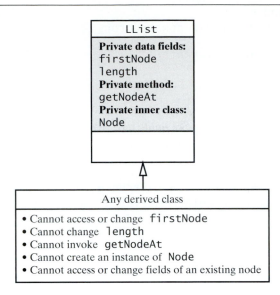

We make the following changes to LList:

1. To enable a subclass to access the data fields by name without giving this access to the client, we could declare firstNode and length to be protected. It is more typical, however, to keep them private and to provide protected methods for only the access we desire. The subclass will need to access or change the head reference firstNode, so we provide protected methods get-FirstNode and setFirstNode:

```java
protected Node getFirstNode()
{
   return firstNode;
} // end getFirstNode

protected void setFirstNode(Node newFirstNode)
{
   firstNode = newFirstNode;
} // end setFirstNode
```

2. Since getLength is public, the subclass can get the value of length, but it might also need to change it. Typically, such changes will simply increment or decrement the number of items in the list. For convenience, we provide the following three protected methods:

```java
protected void setLength(int newLength)
{
   length = newLength;
} // end setLength
```

```
protected void incrementLength()
{
   length++;
} // end incrementLength

protected void decrementLength()
{
   length--;
} // end decrementLength
```

3. Next, we make getNodeAt protected instead of private. The client still cannot use this method, but the implementations of the class and any subclass can.

4. We make the class Node protected instead of private, and we do the same for its constructors. We could also make Node's data fields data and next protected instead of private, but just as we did for LList, we instead make them private and provide protected accessor and mutator methods. If Node already has private set and get methods for data and next, we can simply make them protected. Otherwise, we add the following four protected methods:

```
protected void setData(Object dataPortion)
{
   data = dataPortion;
} // end setData

protected Object getData()
{
   return data;
} // end getData

protected void setNextNode(Node nextNode)
{
   next = nextNode;
} // end setNextNode

protected Node getNextNode()
{
   return next;
} // end getNextNode
```

Node will remain hidden from the client but will be available to any subclass of LList. Making these changes to the class LList results in a new class, which we will name LinkedListBase. Figure 14-2 illustrates this class and the access that a derived class has to it. The next section shows how to use LinkedListBase as the base class for a sorted list.

Programming Tip: **Planning for the future**

When designing a class, you should plan for its future use as well as a present need. Decide whether you want any future subclass to manipulate your class's data fields. If you do, provide protected mutator methods. If public accessor methods are not already in your design, provide protected accessor methods as well.

Figure 14-2   Access available to a class derived from the class `LinkedListBase`

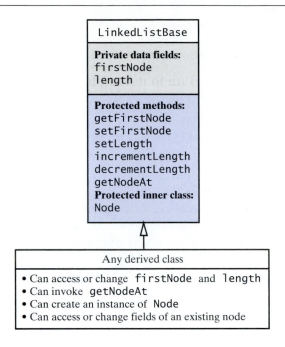

LinkedListBase

Private data fields:
firstNode
length

Protected methods:
getFirstNode
setFirstNode
setLength
incrementLength
decrementLength
getNodeAt
Protected inner class:
Node

↑

Any derived class
• Can access or change `firstNode` and `length`
• Can invoke `getNodeAt`
• Can create an instance of `Node`
• Can access or change fields of an existing node

Question 3   Imagine a subclass of the class `LinkedListBase`. Implement a method within the subclass that adds an entry to the beginning of the list.

An Efficient Implementation of a Sorted List

14.8   Instead of calling ADT list operations to perform operations on an ADT sorted list, our implementation will execute faster if it can be similar to the linked implementation that we wrote in the previous chapter, beginning at Segment 13.7. The class `LinkedListBase` will enable us to manipulate the list's underlying data structure faster than if we had to rely solely on the operations of the ADT list to do so. Thus, we want our class to extend `LinkedListBase`. We begin it by writing

> **public class** SortedList **extends** LinkedListBase
> **implements** SortedListInterface

As before, we will design a sorted list of `Comparable` objects.

The Method add

14.9   The add operation in our new class is quite similar to the one given in Segment 13.10. Instead of referencing the first node in the chain by its name `firstNode`, we must invoke LList's protected methods `getFirstNode` and `setFirstNode`. And instead of incrementing the length of the list by writing `length++`, we must invoke `LList`'s protected method `incrementLength`. Thus, our revised method appears as follows (changes to the add method of Segment 13.10 appear in color):

```java
public boolean add(Comparable newEntry)
{
   Node newNode = new Node(newEntry);
   Node nodeBefore = getNodeBefore(newEntry);

   if (isEmpty() || nodeBefore == null)
   {
      newNode.setNextNode(getFirstNode());
      setFirstNode(newNode);
   }

   else
   {
      Node nodeAfter = nodeBefore.getNextNode();
      newNode.setNextNode(nodeAfter);
      nodeBefore.setNextNode(newNode);
   } // end if

   incrementLength();
   return true;
} // end add
```

Whereas the methods `getNextNode` and `setNextNode` were private in the previous chapter, here they are protected, yet they can be invoked in the same way.

14.10   **The private method `getNodeBefore`.** We still need to implement the private method `getNodeBefore`. The implementation is like the one given in Segment 13.11, but it uses `getFirstNode()` instead of `firstNode`:

```java
private Node getNodeBefore(Comparable anEntry)
{
   Node currentNode = getFirstNode();
   Node nodeBefore = null;

   while ( (currentNode != null) &&
           (anEntry.compareTo(currentNode.getData()) > 0) )
   {
      nodeBefore = currentNode;
      currentNode = currentNode.getNextNode();
   } // end while

   return nodeBefore;
} // end getNodeBefore
```

14.11   **Efficiency.** This version of the method add executes faster than the versions given in Segments 14.1 and 13.20. Those earlier versions can use only the operations of the ADT list—that is, the public methods of the class `LList`. Recall that those add methods first invoke `getPosition` to determine where in the list the new entry belongs, and then they invoke the list's add method. The implementation of `getPosition` given in Segment 13.23 traverses the sorted list to determine the position for the new entry. Within the $O(n)$ loop that performs this traversal is an invocation of the method `getEntry`. When `getEntry` has a linked implementation, it also traverses the sorted list, and so it is O(n). Thus, getPosition is O(n^2). It follows that the add methods in Segment 14.1 and Segment 13.20 are each O(n^2).

Our improved add method in the previous segment adds a new node in its proper location by traversing the chain of nodes at most once. Even though the method must use the protected methods to manipulate the chain of linked nodes, it can add the new node as soon as it determines its proper location, without traversing the chain repeatedly. Thus, it is an O(n) operation.

14.12   **The rest of the class.** To implement remove and getPosition, we would make similar changes to their linked implementations in the class SortedLinkedList. Recall that Chapter 13 left these implementations as an exercise. Finally, we need to override the add and replace methods of the ADT list, as we did in Segment 14.3, so that they throw an exception if invoked.

Note: You can use inheritance *and* maintain efficiency if your base class provides protected access to its underlying data structure

---

CHAPTER SUMMARY

- By using the ADT list to implement the sorted list, this chapter demonstrated the difference between implementations that use composition and those that use inheritance. The basic ideas are the same as those described in Chapter 2. With composition, a class has an object as a data field. The class's methods must act as clients of the object, so they use only the object's public methods. With inheritance, a class inherits all the public methods of its base class. Its implementation, as well as its client, can use these public methods.

- A base class can provide protected methods that enable its subclasses to manipulate its data fields in ways that its client cannot. In this way, a subclass's methods can be more efficient than if they had to use only public methods, as the client must.

- By adding protected methods to the class that implements the ADT list, you can derive the sorted list from it and still have an efficient implementation.

PROGRAMMING TIPS

- If your class inherits methods that are inappropriate, you can override them with methods that throw an exception when invoked. In such a case, examine your design and consider whether inheritance was the right choice. Do the benefits of inheritance outweigh the inconvenience of overriding the inappropriate methods, or would composition provide a cleaner design?

- When designing a class, decide whether you want any future subclasses to manipulate your class's data fields. If you do, provide protected mutator methods, and if public accessor methods are not already in your design, provide protected accessor methods as well.

EXERCISES

1. Derive a class from LinkedListBase that overrides the method equals inherited from the class Object. Assuming that objects in the list have an appropriate implementation of equals, your new method should return true if each entry in one list equals the corresponding entry in a second list.

2. Repeat Exercise 1, but use the class SortedList, as described in Segment 14.8, instead of LinkedListBase.

3. The class SortedList, as described in Segment 14.8, inherits the method contains from LinkedListBase. Since this method searches an unsorted list, it is not as efficient as it could be when the desired entry is not in the list. Override this method to take advantage of the list's sorted nature.

4. Write a constructor for the class SortedList that has an instance of LList as a parameter. The new sorted list should contain all the elements of the list, but in sorted order.

5. If the class LinkedListBase had the method getListIterator, as described in Segment 7.21, what would you need to do to define an iterator for the class SortedList?

6. Compare the time efficiency of the sorted list method

    public boolean add(Comparable newEntry);

as given in Segment 14.9, with that of the list method

    public boolean add(**int** newPosition, Object newEntry);

PROJECTS

1. Complete the implementation of the class SortedList that Segment 14.8 began.

2. Revise the class DynamicArrayList, as described in Chapter 5, to make it more suitable as a base class. Then derive a class of sorted lists from it.

15

Mutable, Immutable, and Cloneable Objects

CONTENTS

Mutable and Immutable Objects
    Companion Classes
    Using Inheritance to Form Companion Classes
Cloneable Objects
A Sorted List of Clones
Cloning an Array
Cloning a Chain

PREREQUISITES

Chapter   2   Creating Classes from Other Classes
Chapter   5   List Implementations That Use Arrays
Chapter   7   Iterators
Chapter   13   Sorted Lists
Chapter   14   Inheritance and Lists
Appendix   B   Exception Handling

OBJECTIVES

After studying this chapter, you should be able to

- Distinguish among mutable and immutable objects
- Beginning with a class of immutable objects, use inheritance to define a companion class of mutable objects
- Define a method `clone` for a given class
- Implement an ADT such as a sorted list that clones the objects added to it
- Clone an array or chain of objects.

When a class has public mutator, or set, methods, a client can use these methods to alter objects of that class. Although this ability seems reasonable, it is unreasonable if the class organizes the objects in a particular way. For example, a sorted list of names maintains the names in alphabetical order. If a client can alter a name, it can destroy the order of the list.

This chapter looks at two strategies that prevent this problem. The first one simply requires a client to place only objects that have no mutator methods into the ADT. The second strategy requires the ADT to make a copy, or **clone,** of any object that a client adds to it. With this technique, the client has no reference to the copy and so cannot change it. In describing this approach, we discuss how to write methods that make clones of objects.

Mutable and Immutable Objects

15.1   Many of the classes you have studied have private data fields and public methods that either look at or change these fields. As you know, such methods are called accessor methods and mutator methods—or, alternatively, get and set methods. An object that belongs to a class that has public mutator methods is said to be **mutable** because the client can use the set methods to change the values of the object's data fields. For example, you saw the class Name of two-part names in Segment 1.16. It has the following two data fields:

```
private String first;   // first name
private String last;    // last name
```

To change these fields, the class has the mutator methods setFirst and setLast. To look at the fields, it has the accessor methods getFirst and getLast.

Note: A mutable object belongs to a class that has mutator (set) methods for its data fields.

15.2   Let's use this class to create an object for *Chris Coffee* by writing the following Java statement:

```
Name chris = new Name("Chris", "Coffee");
```

Figure 15-1 illustrates this object and the reference variable chris.

Figure 15-1   An object and its reference variable chris

chris

Now suppose we create a list and then add chris to the list by writing

```
ListInterface nameList = new LList();
nameList.add(1, chris);
```

Since chris is a mutable object, we can change its data fields by writing, for example,

```
chris.setLast("Smith");
```

After this change, the object chris represents the name *Chris Smith*. Nothing is surprising here. What might be surprising, however, is that the list has changed! That's right: If we retrieve the first item in the list by writing, for instance,

```
System.out.println(nameList.getEntry(1));
```

we will get *Chris Smith* instead of *Chris Coffee*.

15.3   How can it be that the list, which we created before changing the name, contains the changed name? Remember that in Java, the list contains references to the actual objects that the client places in it. So the list has a reference to its first item, but so does the client, since it has the variable chris, as Figure 15-2a shows.

Figure 15-2   An object in the list nameList (a) initially; (b) after the reference variable chris is used to change it

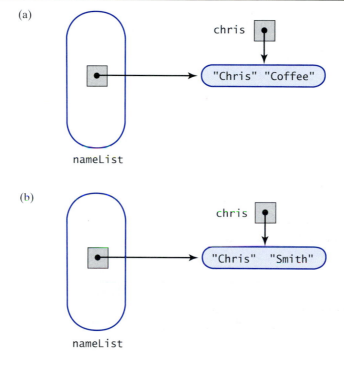

When we altered the object by executing

```
chris.setLast("Smith");
```

we changed the one and only copy of the object, as Figure 15-2b shows. Since the list still references that object, nameList.getEntry(1) returns a reference to the object. This aspect of Java can be a convenient way for the client to alter the objects it has placed in a list.

Note: When a client creates a mutable object and adds it to an ADT list, only one copy of the object ordinarily exists. Thus, if the client alters the object, the list changes. Ideally, the client will use the replace operation to revise an entry in the list, but we cannot force the client to do so.

15.4   The ability to alter mutable objects in an ADT can permit a client to destroy the ADT's integrity. For example, suppose that we create a sorted list of names instead of a list of names. If we write

```
Name jesse = new Name("Jesse", "Java");
Name rob = new Name("Rob", "Bean");
SortedListInterface alphaList = new SortedList();
alphaList.add(jesse);
alphaList.add(rob);
alphaList.display();
```

we would get the sorted list

Rob Bean
Jesse Java

assuming that the list sorts by last name. Now if we write

```
rob.setLast("Smith");
alphaList.display();
```

the list changes to

Rob Smith
Jesse Java

This sorted list is no longer alphabetical. One solution to this problem is to require the client to use immutable objects, as the next segment describes.

15.5   An **immutable** object is one whose data fields cannot be altered by a client. The class to which an immutable object belongs has no public mutator (set) methods, so once you create the object, you cannot change its data fields. If you need to change them, you will have to discard the object and create a new one with the revised fields. Such a class is said to be **read only.** A client that places immutable objects into a sorted list cannot alter those objects and thus cannot destroy the sorted order of the list.

Note: An immutable object belongs to a read-only class. Such a class has no public mutator (set) methods for its data fields.

Programming Tip: When the objects in a sorted list are mutable, a client can destroy the sorted order of the list. Placing only immutable objects in a sorted list is one way to prevent this problem.

15.6   To convert the previous class Name into a read-only class, we can change the access modifiers of the methods setFirst, setLast, and setName from public to either private or protected to prevent a client from invoking them. We could, of course, omit these methods altogether, modifying the other methods that invoke them. But having protected set methods is useful for any subclass of Name. For simplicity, we will omit Name's method giveLastNameTo.

    Let's call the resulting class ImmutableName. If we place instances of ImmutableName in a list or a sorted list, we will not be able to change these objects by using any references that we might have retained to them. Of course, we can use the replace operation of the ADT list to replace a particular item in a list, but no such operation exists for a sorted list. To change an entry in a sorted list, we would remove the entry and add a new one. In this way, the sorted list maintains its sorted order.

15.7   **Mutable or immutable?** Most classes have set methods, so their instances are mutable. The ability to change an object's data is convenient and efficient, particularly when an object's state must change often during the course of a program's execution. For example, a bank must regularly update the object that represents your checking account. If that object were immutable, it would be discarded and a new object representing the updated data would be created. But changing an object takes less time than replacing it.

On the other hand, sharing a mutable object can be dangerous. Suppose that you have two references, a and b, to the same object. If you use a to modify the object, you might get confused when you use b to reference it. But sharing immutable objects is safe, since no matter how you reference them, they remain unchanged.

Programming Tip: Use an immutable object if it will be shared. Use a mutable object if its data will change frequently.

Companion Classes

15.8   If you do need to alter an immutable object, it can be convenient to have a **companion class** of corresponding mutable objects. The classes ImmutableName and Name are examples of two such companion classes. The objects in both classes represent names, but one type of object cannot be altered, while the other can be.

To make the classes even more convenient, you could include methods that convert an object from one type to the other. For example, we might add the following method getMutable to the class ImmutableName:

```
// add getMutable to the class ImmutableName
public Name getMutable()
{
   return new Name(first, last);
} // end getMutable
```

Now, if we have an instance of ImmutableName, such as fixedName in the statement

```
ImmutableName fixedName = new ImmutableName("Maria", "Mocha");
```

and we find that we need to alter it, we can invoke getMutable as follows:

```
Name flexibleName = fixedName.getMutable();
```

The new object flexibleName has the same data fields as fixedName, but it also has set methods to change them.

Similarly, we can add the method getImmutable to the class Name, as follows:

```
// add getImmutable to the class Name
public ImmutableName getImmutable()
{
   return new ImmutableName(first, last);
} // end getImmutable
```

Figure 15-3 illustrates the two classes Name and ImmutableName.

Figure 15-3   The classes `Name` and `ImmutableName`

Name
first last
getFirst() getLast() setFirst(firstName) setLast(lastName) setName(firstName, lastName) compareTo() toString() getImmutable()

ImmutableName
first last
getFirst() getLast() compareTo() toString() getMutable()

Question 1   Write Java statements that take the following steps:
- Create an object of the class `Name`.
- Convert the object to an immutable object without changing its data fields.
- Add the object to the sorted list `nameList`.

Question 2   Write Java statements that take the following steps:

- Create an object of the class `ImmutableName`.
- Convert the object to a mutable object without changing its data fields.
- Change the last name of the new object.
- Convert the revised mutable object to an immutable object.

Note: Java's class `String` is a read-only class. That is, instances of `String` are immutable. Once you create a string, you cannot change it. Frequently, however, string applications require that you either remove a portion of a string or join two strings together. For such applications, Java provides the class `StringBuffer` of mutable strings. `StringBuffer` provides several methods that modify a string by adding, removing, or replacing substrings. Appendix A describes some of the methods that belong to these two classes.

   `String` and `StringBuffer` are a pair of companion classes. `StringBuffer` has a constructor that takes an instance of `String` as an argument and produces a mutable string with the same value. `StringBuffer` also has the method `toString` that converts a mutable instance of `String-Buffer` to an immutable instance of `String`.

Using Inheritance to Form Companion Classes

15.9   **The class `ImmutableName`.** Consider the implementation of the class `ImmutableName`. Like the class `Name`, it has data fields `first` and `last`, constructors, accessor methods `getFirst` and `getLast`, and the method `getMutable`. Additionally, it has protected methods `setFirst`, `setLast`, and `setName` that enable a subclass, but not a client, to change the data fields. Thus, the class `ImmutableName` could have the following form:

```
public class ImmutableName implements Comparable
{
   private String first;
   private String last;
```

```
    < Constructors >
    . . .

    < Accessor methods getFirst and getLast >
    . . .

    < Methods compareTo and toString >
    . . .

    public Name getMutable()
    {
      return new Name(first, last);
    } // end getMutable

// -------- protected methods -----------------------------
    protected void setFirst(String firstName)
    {
      first = firstName;
    } // end setFirst

    protected void setLast(String lastName)
    {
      last = lastName;
    } // end setLast

    protected void setName(String firstName, String lastName)
    {
      setFirst(firstName);
      setLast(lastName);
    } // end setName
} // end ImmutableName
```

15.10   **The class `Name`.** The classes `ImmutableName` and `Name` have the methods `getFirst`, `getLast`, `comp-areTo`, and `toString`. To avoid duplication of effort when creating a pair of companion classes, you should start with the class of immutable objects and use inheritance to define the class of mutable objects. Thus, we have the following definition of the class `Name`:

```
public class Name extends ImmutableName
{
  public Name()
  {
  } // end default constructor

  public Name(String firstName, String lastName)
  {
    super.setName(firstName, lastName);
  } // end constructor

  public void setName(String firstName, String lastName)
  {
    super.setName(firstName, lastName);
  } // end setName

  public void setFirst(String firstName)
  {
    super.setFirst(firstName);
  } // end setFirst
```

```java
   public void setLast(String lastName)
   {
      super.setLast(lastName);
   } // end setLast

   public void giveLastNameTo(Name aName)
   {
      aName.setLast(this.getLast()); // 'this' is optional
   } // end giveLastNameTo

   public ImmutableName getImmutable()
   {
      return new ImmutableName(getFirst(), getLast());
   } // end getImmutable
} // end Name
```

The class Name can invoke the protected methods of its base class ImmutableName. For example, the second constructor calls the protected method setName. This class provides public versions of the set methods setName, setFirst, and setLast, which override ImmutableName's protected set methods. Each of these invokes the corresponding protected method in ImmutableName. For example, the new public setName calls the base class's protected setName. Using super here to invoke this method is necessary to avoid a recursive call.

The methods giveLastNameTo and getImmutable must use get methods to access ImmutableName's data fields first and last, since they are private. Notice that the use of this to invoke the get methods is optional.

Figure 15-4 illustrates the relationship between these two classes.

Figure 15-4   The class Name is derived from the class ImmutableName

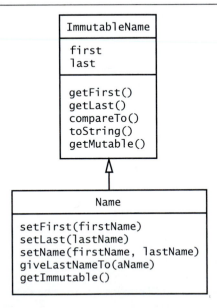

 Note: Companion classes
When creating a pair of companion classes, define the class of immutable objects and use inheritance to derive the class of mutable objects.

Question 3 When you derive the class Name from the class ImmutableName, Name inherits the method getMutable.

a. What happens when an instance of Name invokes getMutable?
b. Is this a problem?

Cloneable Objects

15.11 In Segment 15.4, we created a sorted list of mutable objects. Unfortunately, the client of this list can modify the objects so that they are no longer sorted. We said then that one solution is to always place immutable objects in a sorted list.

A more involved solution is to make a copy of the client's objects and place the copies in the ADT. The ADT then can control what the client can and cannot do to the objects. This section examines how to make a copy of an object.

15.12 In Java, a **clone** is a copy of an object. The class Object contains a protected method clone that returns a copy of an object. The method has the following signature:

```
protected Object clone() throws CloneNotSupportedException
```

Since clone is protected, and since Object is the superclass of all other classes, the implementation of any method can invoke clone. But clients cannot invoke clone unless a class overrides it and declares it public. Making copies of objects can be expensive, so it might be something that you do not want a class to do. By making clone a protected method, the designers of Java force you to think twice about cloning.

If you want your class to contain a public method clone, the class needs to state this fact by implementing the Java interface Cloneable. Such a class would begin as follows:

```
public class MyClass implements Cloneable
{ . . .
```

The interface Cloneable is simply

```
public interface Cloneable
{
}
```

The interface is empty. It declares no methods and serves only as a way for a class to indicate that it implements clone. If you forget to write implements Cloneable in your class definition, instances of your class that invoke clone will cause the exception CloneNotSupportedException. This result can be confusing at first, particularly if you did implement clone.

Programming Tip: If your program produces the exception CloneNotSupportedException even though you implemented a method clone in your class, you probably forgot to write implements Cloneable in your class definition.

Note: **The Cloneable interface**
The empty Cloneable interface is not a typical interface. A class implements it to indicate that it will provide a public clone method. Since the designers of Java wanted to provide a default

implementation of the method `clone`, they included it in the class `Object` and not in the interface `Cloneable`. But because the designers did not want every class to automatically have a public `clone` method, they made `clone` a protected method.

Note: **Cloning**

Cloning is not an operation that every class should be able to do. If you want your class to have this ability, you must

- Declare that your class implements the `Cloneable` interface
- Override the protected method `clone` that your class inherits from the class `Object`

15.13   **Example: Cloning a `Name` object.** Let's add a method `clone` to the class `Name` of Segment 15.10. Before we write one line of the method, we should add `implements Cloneable` to the first line of the class definition. Since `Name` extends `ImmutableName`, we would write

public class Name **extends** ImmutableName **implements** Cloneable

The public method `clone` within `Name` must invoke the method `clone` of its superclass by executing `super.clone()`. Because `Name`'s base class `ImmutableName` does not override `clone`, `super.clone()` invokes `Object`'s protected method `clone`. `Object`'s version of `clone` can throw an exception, so we must enclose each call to it in a `try` block and write a `catch` block to handle the exception. The method's final action should be to return the cloned object.

Thus, `Name`'s method `clone` could appear as follows:

```
public Object clone()
{
   Name theCopy = null
   try
   {
      theCopy = (Name)super.clone();
   }
   catch (CloneNotSupportedException e)
   {
      System.err.println("Name cannot clone: " + e.toString());
   }
   return theCopy;
} // end clone
```

Since `super.clone()` returns an instance of `Object`, we must cast this instance to `Name`. The `return` statement will implicitly cast `theCopy` to `Object`, as required.

The exception that `Object`'s method `clone` can throw is `CloneNotSupportedException`. Since we are writing a `clone` method for our class `Name`, this exception will never occur. Even so, we still must use `try` and `catch` blocks when invoking `Object`'s `clone` method. Instead of the `println` statement in the `catch` block, we could write the simpler statement

throw new Error(e.toString());

Programming Tip: When a public `clone` method invokes `Object`'s protected `clone` method, it must use `try` and `catch` blocks, even though a `CloneNotSupportedException` will never occur.

15.14   **Two ways to copy.** What does this method `clone` actually do? You want it to make copies of the data fields associated with the invoking object. When a data field is an object, you can copy it in one of two ways:

- You can copy the reference to the object and share the object with the clone, as illustrated in Figure 15-5a. This copy is called a **shallow copy;** the clone is a **shallow clone.**
- You can copy the object itself, as illustrated in Figure 15-5b. This copy is called a **deep copy;** the clone is a **deep clone.**

   Note: `Object`'s `clone` method returns a shallow clone.

Figure 15-5   (a) A shallow clone; (b) a deep clone

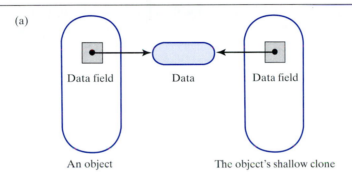

(a)

Data field   Data   Data field

An object   The object's shallow clone

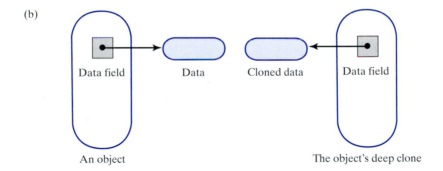

(b)

Data field   Data   Cloned data   Data field

An object   The object's deep clone

15.15   **Name's clone is shallow.** The class `Name` has the data fields `first` and `last`, which are instances of `String`. Each field contains a reference to a string. It is these references that are copied when `clone` invokes `super.clone()`. For example, Figure 15-6 illustrates the objects that the following statements create:

```
Name april = new Name("April", "Jones");
Name twin = (Name)april.clone();
```

The clone `twin` is a shallow clone because the strings that are the first and last names are not copied.

Figure 15-6 An instance of Name and its shallow clone

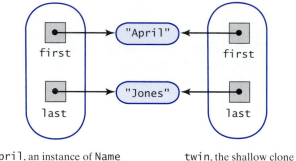

april, an instance of Name   twin, the shallow clone

A shallow clone is good enough for the class Name. Recall that instances of String are immutable. Having an instance of Name and its clone share the same strings is not a problem because no one can change the strings. This is good news since, like many classes that Java provides, String has no method clone. Thus, if we change the clone's last name by writing

```
twin.setLast("Smith");
```

twin's last name will be *Smith*, but april's will still be *Jones*, as Figure 15-7 shows. That is, set-Last changes twin's data field last so that it references *Smith*. It does not change april's last, so it still references *Jones*.

Figure 15-7 A clone after one of its data fields is changed

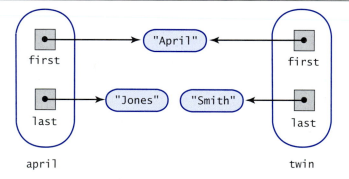

april   twin

15.16   **Example: Creating a deep clone of a single field.** Sometimes a shallow clone is unsuitable. If a class has mutable objects as data fields, you must clone the objects and not simply copy their references. For example, let's add a method clone to the class Student that we encountered in Segment 2.2. Recall that the class has the following form:

```
public class Student
{
   private Name fullName;
   private String id;
```

< *Constructors and the methods* setStudent, setName, setId, getName, getId, *and*
toString >
. . .
} // end Student

Since the class Name has set methods, the data field fullName is a mutable object. We should be sure to clone fullName within the definition of Student's clone method. We can do that because we added a clone method to Name in Segment 15.13. Thus, we can define a clone method for the class Student, as follows:

```
public Object clone()
{
  try
  {
    Student theCopy = (Student)super.clone();
    theCopy.fullName = (Name)fullName.clone();
    return theCopy;
  }
  catch (CloneNotSupportedException e)
  {
    throw new Error(e.toString());
  }
} // end clone
```

After invoking super.clone(), we clone the mutable data field fullName.

Figure 15-8 illustrates an instance of Student and the clone that this method returns. You can see that the Name object that represents the student's full name is copied, but the strings that represent the first and last names, as well as the ID number, are not.

Figure 15-8   An instance of Student and its clone, including a deep copy of fullName

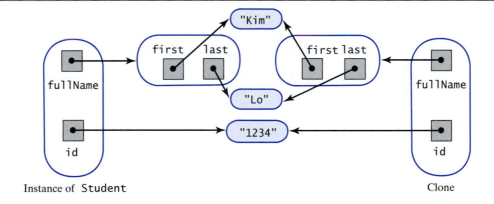

Instance of Student   Clone

Had we failed to clone the data field fullName—that is, had we omitted the statement

theCopy.fullName = (Name)fullName.clone();

the student's full name would be shared by the original instance and its clone. Figure 15-9 illustrates this situation.

Figure 15-9   A shallow copy of `fullName`

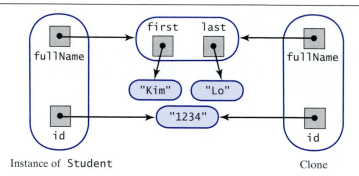

Instance of `Student`   Clone

Question 4   Suppose that x is an instance of `Student` and y is its clone; that is,

```
Student y = (Student) x.clone();
```

a.   If you change x's last name by executing

```
Name xName = x.getName();
xName.setLast("Smith");
```

does y's last name change? Explain.

b.   If you fail to clone `fullName` within `Student`'s `clone` method, will changing x's last name change y's last name as well? Explain.

Note: Within each public `clone` method, you typically perform the following tasks:

- Invoke the `clone` method of the superclass by writing `super.clone()`.
- Enclose the call to `clone` in a `try` block, and write a `catch` block to handle the possible exception `CloneNotSupportedException`. You can skip this step if `super.clone()` invokes a public `clone` method.
- Clone the mutable data fields of the object that `super.clone()` returned, when possible.
- Return the clone.

A Sorted List of Clones

Segment 15.4 talked about the danger of placing mutable objects in an ADT such as a sorted list. If the client retains a reference to any of the objects, it could alter those objects and destroy the integrity of the ADT. In the case of a sorted list, the client could destroy the sorted order of the objects.

Segment 15.5 offered one solution to this problem, namely, to place only immutable objects in the ADT. This section offers another solution that enables you to place mutable objects in the ADT.

15.17   Suppose that a client adds an object to an ADT. Imagine that the ADT clones the object before adding it to its data. The client then would be able to access or change the ADT's data only by using ADT operations. It would not have a reference to the clone that it could use to alter the clone. Of course, this scenario requires that the added object be Cloneable. Let's examine the details of such an implementation of the ADT sorted list.

Segment 13.1 noted that objects in a sorted list must be Comparable—that is, they must have a compareTo method. In this case, we also want the objects to be Cloneable. For example, the class Name in Segment 15.13 implements the interface Cloneable and, by virtue of inheritance, also implements Comparable.

15.18   Consider the method add for a sorted list. Segment 13.4 provided the following signature for this method:

public boolean add(Comparable newEntry)

Because we now want newEntry to be cloneable as well, we create our own interface, as follows, that we can use for the data type of newEntry:

```
public interface Sortable extends Comparable, Cloneable
{
   public Object clone(); // overrides Object's protected clone
   public int compareTo(Object other); // can omit this line
} // end Sortable
```

We then could write add's signature as

public boolean add(Sortable newEntry)

Note that Sortable extends two interfaces. An interface can extend more than one interface, even though a class can extend only one other class. The declaration of the public method clone is necessary, as it overrides Object's protected method clone. We could, however, omit the declaration of compareTo, since it appears in the interface Comparable, but it does not hurt to include it in Sortable as a reminder.

15.19   With these logistics out of the way, we propose the following changes to the implementation of the ADT sorted list. You can apply these changes to the implementations discussed in Chapters 13 and 14:

● In add, place a clone of the desired entry into the sorted list instead of the entry itself. That is, place newEntry.clone() into the list instead of newEntry.
● In getEntry, return a clone of the desired entry instead of the entry itself. For example, you could replace

return result;

with

return result.clone();

Let's examine these changes more closely. Suppose that a client has a reference, newEntry, to an object, and it adds the object to an ADT. The ADT clones the object and adds the clone instead of the original object, as Figure 15-10 illustrates. The client has no reference to the ADT's data. If the client modifies the object that newEntry references, the ADT is not changed.

What if getEntry did not return a clone of the desired entry but instead returned a reference to the desired entry in the ADT? As Figure 15-11 illustrates, the client would be able to change the entry within the ADT. So even though the ADT contains a clone of the client's original object, getEntry would give the client access to the clone. Thus, it is necessary for getEntry to return a clone of the desired entry. This is a clone of the clone of the client's original object, as Figure 15-12 shows.

Figure 15-10 An ADT and its client after the clone of an object is added to the ADT

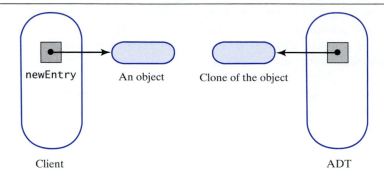

Figure 15-11 The effect of getEntry if it did not return a clone

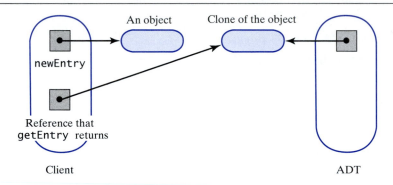

Figure 15-12 The effect of getEntry when it returns a clone

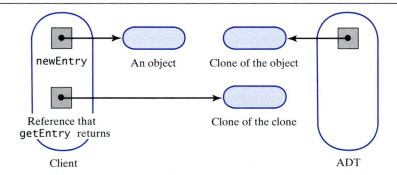

 Note: An ADT can clone the objects that a client adds to it, but you will have duplicates of each entry in the ADT. For complex objects, the time and memory needed to make each copy can be substantial.

Cloning an Array

15.20   The class `AList` that you saw in Chapter 5 used a fixed-size array to implement the ADT list. Suppose that we wanted to add a `clone` method to `AList`. While making a copy of the list, `clone` needs to copy the array and all the objects in it. As a first step, we would indicate that `AList` contains a `clone` method by beginning the class with

public class `AList` **implements** `ListInterface, Cloneable`

Now we implement `clone`. In Segment 15.16, a few statements performed all of `clone`'s tasks, so we wrote them entirely within a `try` block. Here we have more to do, so we will invoke `super.clone()` within a `try` block but perform the rest of the tasks after the `catch` block. Thus, we have the following outline for `AList`'s method `clone`:

```java
public Object clone()
{
  AList theCopy = null;

  try
  {
    theCopy = (AList)super.clone(); // not enough by itself
  }
  catch (CloneNotSupportedException e)
  {
    throw new Error(e.toString());
  } // end try/catch

  < For a deep copy, we need to do more here, as you will see. >
  . . .
  return theCopy;
} // end clone
```

The method first invokes `super.clone` and casts the returned object to `AList`. To perform a deep copy, we need to clone the data fields that are or could be mutable objects. Recall from Segment 5.4 that the fields of `AList` are

```java
private Object[] entry; // array of list entries
private int length;     // current number of entries in list
private static final int MAX_SIZE = 50; // max length of list
```

Thus, we need to clone the array `entry`.

Arrays in Java have a `clone` method; in other words, they implement `Cloneable`. So, we can add the following statement to the list's `clone` method:

```java
theCopy.entry = (Object[])entry.clone();
```

No `try` and `catch` blocks are necessary here. Only `Object`'s `clone` method contains a `throws` clause.

An array's `clone` method creates a shallow copy of each object in the array. For our deep copy, we need to clone each array element. We could attempt to write a loop whose body contains the following statement:

```java
theCopy.entry[index] = entry[index].clone(); // WRONG!
```

But this statement is wrong! The object `entry[index]` is attempting to invoke `Object`'s `clone` method, but `clone` is protected. We were able to invoke `Object`'s `clone` earlier in Segment 15.13

when we wrote `super.clone()`, but there the class invoked an inherited method. To be invoked here, `clone` would have to be a public method.

15.21   To solve our dilemma, we need to override `clone` and make it public. To this end, we define the following interface:

```
public interface Listable extends Cloneable
{
  public Object clone(); // deep copy expected
} // end Listable
```

We then insist that the objects in the list be `Listable`, that is, that their classes implement the interface `Listable`. To accomplish this, we make the following changes to `AList`. We first declare `entry` as

```
private Listable[] entry; // array of list entries
```

Next, we replace occurrences of Object within AList with Listable. We make the same change to ListInterface.

To clone the array, we use the statement

```
theCopy.entry = (Listable[])entry.clone();
```

We then clone each object in the array by writing a loop whose body is the statement

```
theCopy.entry[index] = (Listable)entry[index].clone();
```

Thus, we have the following definition of `clone` for the class `AList`:

```
public Object clone()
{
  AList theCopy = null;

  try
  {
    theCopy = (AList)super.clone(); // not enough by itself
  }
  catch (CloneNotSupportedException e)
  {
    throw new Error(e.toString());
  } // end try/catch

  theCopy.entry = (Listable[])entry.clone();
  for (int index = 0; index < length; index++)
    theCopy.entry[index] = (Listable)entry[index].clone();

  return theCopy;
} // end clone
```

Note: To make a deep clone of an array a of cloneable objects, you invoke `a.clone()` and then clone each object in the array. For example, if `myArray` is an array of `Thing` objects, and `Thing` implements `Cloneable`, you would write

```
Thing[] clonedArray = (Thing[])myArray.clone();
for (int index = 0; index < myArray.length; index++)
    clonedArray[index] = (Thing)myArray[index].clone();
```

Cloning a Chain

15.22   Now suppose that we want to add a `clone` method to a linked implementation of the ADT list, such as the class `LList` of Chapter 6 or the class `LinkedListBase` of Chapter 14. (The `clone` methods for these classes are virtually identical.) As in the previous section, the class must implement the interface `Cloneable`. Thus, `LList` would begin as follows:

```
public class LList implements ListInterface, Cloneable
{
    private Node firstNode; // reference to first node
    private int  length;    // number of entries in list
    . . .
```

We must also define the interface `Listable`, as we did in Segment 15.21, and replace occurrences of `Object` within the class `LList` and the interface `ListInterface` with `Listable`.

The first part of the `clone` method would be like the code that you saw in Segment 15.20, except that we would replace `AList` with `LList`. If we invoked only `super.clone()`, our method would produce a shallow copy of the list, as Figure 15-13 illustrates. In other words, both the original list and its clone would reference the same chain of nodes, and these nodes would reference one set of data.

Figure 15-13 A list that stores its data in a chain and its shallow clone

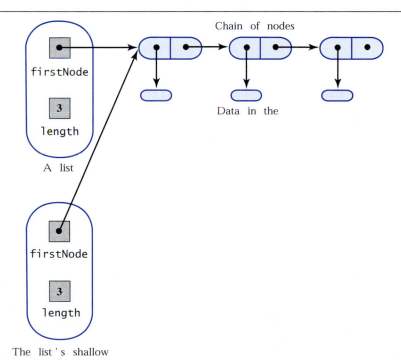

As before, `clone` needs to do more to perform a deep copy. It needs to clone the chain of nodes as well as the data that the nodes reference. Figure 15-14 shows a list with its deep clone.

Figure 15-14 A list that stores its data in a chain and its deep clone

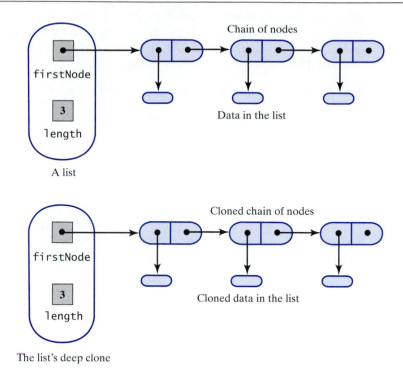

15.23   **Cloning a node.** To clone the nodes in the chain, we need to add a method `clone` to the private class `Node`. We have already replaced occurrences of `Object` with `Listable`, so next we add `implements Cloneable` to the declaration of the class `Node`. Finally, `Node`'s `clone` method begins like other `clone` methods, but then it goes on to clone the data portion of the node. We do not bother cloning the link since `LList`'s `clone` method will set it. With these changes, the revised class `Node` appears as follows (changes are indicated in color):

```
private class Node implements Cloneable
{
  private Listable data;
  private Node     next;

  private Node(Listable dataPortion)
  {
    data = dataPortion;
    next = null;
  } // end constructor

  private Node(Listable dataPortion, Node nextNode)
  {
    data = dataPortion;
    next = nextNode;
  } // end constructor
```

```
    . . .
      < Accessor and mutator methods getData, setData, getNextNode, and setNextNode
        go here. >
    . . .
    public Object clone()
    {
      Node theCopy = null;
      try
      {
        theCopy = (Node)super.clone();
      }
      catch (CloneNotSupportedException e)
      {
        throw new Error(e.toString());
      } // end try/catch

      theCopy.data = (Listable)data.clone();
      theCopy.next = null; // don't clone link; it's set later

      return theCopy;
    } // end clone
} // end Node
```

Remember that data invokes a public method clone that does not throw an exception, so data.clone() can appear outside of a try block.

15.24   **Cloning the chain.** LList's clone method invokes super.clone() in a statement such as

```
LList theCopy = (LList)super.clone();
```

The method then must clone the chain of nodes that stores the list's data. To do so, the method needs to traverse the chain, clone each node, and link the cloned nodes appropriately. We begin by cloning the first node so that we can set the data field firstNode correctly:

```
// make a copy of the first node
theCopy.firstNode = (Node)firstNode.clone();
```

Next, we traverse the rest of the chain. A reference newRef references the last node that we have added to the new chain, while the reference oldRef keeps track of where we are in the traversal of the original chain. The statement

```
newRef.setNextNode((Node)oldRef.clone()); // attach cloned node
```

clones the current node in the original chain, along with its data, and then links the clone to the end of the new chain. Recall that Node's clone method also clones the data that a node references.

The following statements incorporate the previous ideas and clone the rest of the chain:

```
Node newRef = theCopy.firstNode;       // last node in new chain
Node oldRef = firstNode.getNextNode(); // next node in old chain

for (int count = 2; count <= length; count++)
{
  newRef.setNextNode((Node)oldRef.clone()); // attach cloned node
```

```
          newRef = newRef.getNextNode();              // update references
          oldRef = oldRef.getNextNode();
      } // end for
```

15.25   The code in the previous segment assumes a nonempty chain of nodes. The complete `clone` method that follows accounts for an empty chain.

```java
public Object clone()
{
  LList theCopy = null;

  try
  {
    theCopy = (LList) super.clone();
  }
  catch (CloneNotSupportedException e)
  {
    throw new Error(e.toString());
  } // end try/catch

  // copy underlying chain of nodes

  if (firstNode == null) // if chain is empty
    theCopy.firstNode = null;
  else
  {
    // make a copy of the first node
    theCopy.firstNode = (Node)firstNode.clone();

    // make a copy of the rest of chain
    Node newRef = theCopy.firstNode;
    Node oldRef = firstNode.getNextNode();

    for (int count = 2; count <= length; count++)
    {
      // clone node and its data; link clone to new chain
      newRef.setNextNode((Node)oldRef.clone());
      newRef = newRef.getNextNode();
      oldRef = oldRef.getNextNode();
    } // end for
  } // end if

  return theCopy;
} // end clone
```

Note: To make a deep clone of a chain of linked nodes that reference cloneable objects, you must clone the nodes as well as the objects.

Question 5   The `for` statement in Segment 15.25 is controlled by the number of nodes in the chain. Revise this statement and its associated loop so it is controlled by `oldRef`.

CHAPTER SUMMARY

- An object that belongs to a class having public mutator (set) methods is mutable because the client can use the methods to change the values of the object's data fields. If a class has no mutator methods, its objects are immutable.

- Beginning with a class of immutable objects, you can use inheritance to define a companion class of mutable objects by adding mutator methods.

- The class `Object` includes a protected method `clone` that makes an identical copy of an object. A class can override `clone` and declare it public, thus making it available to a client of the class. Such a class must implement the Java interface `Cloneable`. If a class does not override `clone`, it has no `clone` method, since `clone` is protected in `Object`.

- A `clone` method should invoke `super.clone()` to ensure that all aspects of an object are copied.

- Every array has a `clone` method that copies the array and all the objects in it.

- To create a deep clone of a chain of linked nodes, you must create new nodes and clone the data objects in the original nodes.

PROGRAMMING TIPS

- When an ADT—such as a sorted list—organizes objects in a certain way, a client should not be able to destroy this organization by altering the objects directly. Yet if the client retains references to the objects, that is exactly what a client could do. To prevent this, allow the client to add only immutable objects to the ADT. Alternatively, the ADT could clone the objects added to it. In this case, the client would not have references to the clones and could not alter them.

- Use an immutable object if it will be shared. Use a mutable object if its data will change frequently.

- If you forget to write `implements Cloneable` in your class definition, instances of your class that invoke `clone` will cause the exception `CloneNotSupportedException`.

- When a public `clone` method invokes `Object`'s protected `clone` method, it must use `try` and `catch` blocks, even thought a `CloneNotSupportedException` will never occur.

EXERCISES

1. Is the class `Student` that is mentioned in Segment 15.16 mutable or immutable? Describe what you would do to create a companion class for `Student` without using inheritance.

2. **a.** Using the method `getEntry` of the ADT list, describe a client-level method that modifies the entry at a given position within a list.
   b. What must you know about the entries in the list for your method to work?
   c. Does the method `replace` of the ADT list have any advantage over your method?

3. Implement the method `compareTo` for the class `ImmutableName`.

4. The class `NickName` given in Segment 2.3 has a data field that is an instance of the class `Name` and two methods, `setNickName` and `getNickName`. Implement a method `clone` for `NickName`, assuming that `Name` implements the interface `Cloneable`.

PROJECTS

1. Using inheritance, define a pair of companion classes modeled after the class Student, as given in Segment 2.2.

2. Chapter 5 describes an implementation of the ADT list that uses an instance of the class Vector to represent the entries in the list. Write a clone method for this implementation and demonstrate that it works. Note that Vector implements the interface Cloneable.

3. Revise the linked implementation of the ADT sorted list, as given in Chapter 13, according to the suggestions about cloning given in Segment 15.19. That is, the method add should place a clone of the desired entry, instead of the entry itself, into the sorted list. Additionally, the method getEntry should return a clone of the desired entry, instead of returning the entry itself.

16

Searching

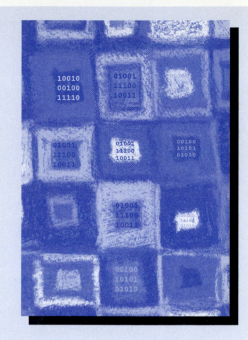

CONTENTS

The Problem
Searching an Unsorted Array
    An Iterative Sequential Search of an Unsorted Array
    A Recursive Sequential Search of an Unsorted Array
    The Efficiency of a Sequential Search of an Array
Searching a Sorted Array
    A Sequential Search of a Sorted Array
    A Binary Search of a Sorted Array
    Java Class Library: The Method `binarySearch`
    The Efficiency of a Binary Search of an Array
Searching an Unsorted Chain
    An Iterative Sequential Search of an Unsorted Chain
    A Recursive Sequential Search of an Unsorted Chain
    The Efficiency of a Sequential Search of a Chain
Searching a Sorted Chain
    A Sequential Search of a Sorted Chain
    A Binary Search of a Sorted Chain
Choosing a Search Method

PREREQUISITES

Chapter   4   Lists
Chapter   5   List Implementations That Use Arrays
Chapter   6   List Implementations That Link Data
Chapter   9   The Efficiency of Algorithms
Chapter   10   Recursion
Chapter   13   Sorted Lists

OBJECTIVES

After studying this chapter, you should be able to

- Search an array by using a sequential search
- Search an array by using a binary search
- Search a chain of linked nodes sequentially
- Determine the efficiency of a search

People are always looking for something, be it a date, a mate, or a lost sock. In fact, searching is one of the most common tasks done for us by computers. Just think of how many times you search the World Wide Web. This chapter looks at two simple search strategies, the sequential search and the binary search. You can use these strategies when implementing the method contains for either the ADT list or the ADT sorted list. A binary search is usually much faster than a sequential search when the data is in an array rather than a chain of linked nodes and when the data is sorted. Sorting data, however, usually takes much more time than searching it. This fact should influence your choice of search method in a given situation.

The Problem

16.1   Like the people in Figure 16-1, you can search your desk for a pen, your closet for your favorite sweater, or a list of names to see whether you are on it. Searching for a particular item—sometimes called the **target**—among a collection of many items is a common task.

Figure 16-1   Searching is an everyday occurrence

Let's find your name on that list. If nameList is an instance of an ADT list whose entries are names, we can search it by using the list operation contains. Recall that this method is boolean-valued and returns true if a given item is in the list.

The implementation of contains depends upon how we store the list entries. Among the implementations of the ADT list given in Chapters 5 and 6 is one that stores the list's entries in an array and another that uses a chain of linked nodes. Let's look at the array first.

Searching an Unsorted Array

16.2   As Segment 5.10 mentioned, a **sequential search** of a list compares the desired item—the target—with the first entry in the list, the second entry in the list, and so on until it either locates the desired entry or looks at all the entries without success. In an array-based implementation of the list, we search the array that contains the list's entries. We can implement this search either iteratively or recursively. This section looks at both approaches and examines their efficiencies.

Recall that our list implementation in Chapter 5 has two data fields: The array `entry`, which contains the list's entries, and the integer `length`, which is the number of entries.

An Iterative Sequential Search of an Unsorted Array

16.3   The following implementation of `contains` was given in Segment 5.10. It uses a loop to search the array `entry` containing `length` objects:

```java
public boolean contains(Object anEntry)
{
  boolean found = false;
  for (int index = 0; !found && (index < length); index++)
  {
    if (anEntry.equals(entry[index]))
      found = true;
  } // end for

  return found;
} // end contains
```

The loop exits as soon as it locates the first entry in the array that matches the desired item. In this case, `found` is true. On the other hand, if the loop examines all the entries in the array without finding one that matches `anEntry`, `found` remains false. Figure 16-2 provides an example of these two outcomes. For simplicity, our illustrations use integers.

Figure 16-2   An iterative sequential search of an array that (a) finds its target; (b) does not find its target

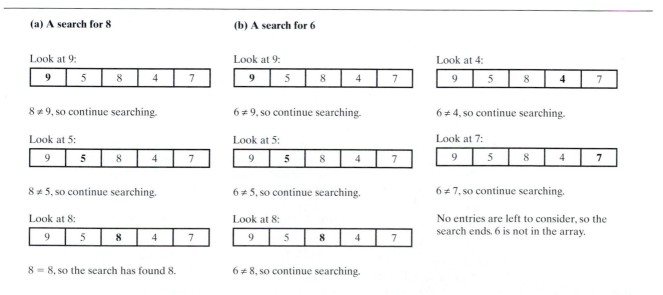

(a) A search for 8

Look at 9:

| 9 | 5 | 8 | 4 | 7 |

$8 \neq 9$, so continue searching.

Look at 5:

| 9 | 5 | 8 | 4 | 7 |

$8 \neq 5$, so continue searching.

Look at 8:

| 9 | 5 | 8 | 4 | 7 |

$8 = 8$, so the search has found 8.

(b) A search for 6

Look at 9:

| 9 | 5 | 8 | 4 | 7 |

$6 \neq 9$, so continue searching.

Look at 5:

| 9 | 5 | 8 | 4 | 7 |

$6 \neq 5$, so continue searching.

Look at 8:

| 9 | 5 | 8 | 4 | 7 |

$6 \neq 8$, so continue searching.

Look at 4:

| 9 | 5 | 8 | 4 | 7 |

$6 \neq 4$, so continue searching.

Look at 7:

| 9 | 5 | 8 | 4 | 7 |

$6 \neq 7$, so continue searching.

No entries are left to consider, so the search ends. 6 is not in the array.

Question 1   Write a method `contains` that returns the index of the first array element that equals `anEntry`. If the array does not contain such an element, return -1.

Question 2   Write a method that performs an iterative sequential search of a list by using only operations of the ADT list. The method should return true if a given item is in a given list.

A Recursive Sequential Search of an Unsorted Array

16.4   We begin a sequential search of an array by looking at the first entry in the array. If that entry is the desired one, we end the search. Otherwise we search the rest of the array. Since this new search is also sequential and since the rest of the array is smaller than the original array, we have a recursive description of a solution to our problem. Well, almost. We need a base case. An empty array could be the base case because it never contains the desired item.

For the array a, we search the n elements `a[0]` through `a[n-1]` by beginning with the first element, `a[0]`. If it is not the one we seek, we need to search the rest of the array that is, we search array elements `a[1]` through `a[n-1]`. In general, we search the array elements `a[first]` through `a[n-1]`. To be even more general, we can search array elements `a[first]` through `a[last]`, where `first ≤ last`.

16.5   The following pseudocode describes the logic of our recursive algorithm:

> **_Algorithm to search_ `a[first]` _through_ `a[last]` _for_ `desiredItem`**
> **if** (_there are no elements to search_)
>   **return false**
> **else if** (`desiredItem` _equals_ `a[first]`)
>   **return true**
> **else**
>   **return** _the result of searching_ `a[first+1]` _through_ `a[last]`

Figure 16-3 illustrates a recursive search of an array.

16.6   The method that implements this algorithm will need parameters `first` and `last`. To spare the client the detail of providing values for these parameters, and to allow the method `contains` to have the same signature as it did in Segment 16.3, we implement the algorithm as a private method `search` that `contains` invokes. Since we again assume the array-based list implementation from Chapter 5, the array `entry` takes the place of the array `a` in the previous algorithm, and `length` is the number of elements to search. Because `entry` and `length` are data fields of the class that implements the list, they are not parameters of the methods that follow.

```java
public boolean contains(Object anEntry)
{
  return search(0, length-1, anEntry);
} // end contains

/** Task: Searches entry[first] through entry[last] for anEntry.
 *   @param first        an integer index >= 0 and < length
 *   @param last         an integer index >= 0 and < length
 *   @param desiredItem  the object to be found
 *   @return true if desiredItem is found */
private boolean search(int first, int last, Object desiredItem)
{
  boolean found;
  if (first > last)
    found = false;
```

```
    else if (desiredItem.equals(entry[first]))
      found = true;
    else
      found = search(first+1, last, desiredItem);

    return found;
  } // end search
```

Figure 16-3   A recursive sequential search of an array that (a) finds its target; (b) does not find its target

---

(a) A search for 8

Look at the first entry, 9:

9	5	8	4	7

8 ≠ 9, so search the next subarray.

Look at the first entry, 5:

5	8	4	7

8 ≠ 5, so search the next subarray.

Look at the first entry, 8:

8	4	7

8 = 8, so the search has found 8.

(b) A search for 6

Look at the first entry, 9:

9	5	8	4	7

6 ≠ 9, so search the next subarray.

Look at the first entry, 5:

5	8	4	7

6 ≠ 5, so search the next subarray.

Look at the first entry, 8:

8	4	7

6 ≠ 8, so search the next subarray.

Look at the first entry, 4:

4	7

6 ≠ 4, so search the next subarray.

Look at the first entry, 7:

7

6 ≠ 7, so search an empty array.

No entries are left to consider, so the
search ends. 6 is not in the array.

Question 3   List the comparisons that the previous method search makes while searching the array of objects

o1 o2 o3 o4 o5

for o6.

Question 4   Implement at the client level a recursive method search by using only operations of the ADT list. The method should return true if a given item is in a given list.

The Efficiency of a Sequential Search of an Array

16.7   Whether you implement a sequential search iteratively or recursively, the number of comparisons will be the same. In the best case, you will locate the desired item first in the array. You will have made only one comparison, and so the search will be $O(1)$. In the worst case, you will search the entire array. Either you will find the desired item at the end of the array or you will not find it at all. In either event, you will have made n comparisons for an array of n elements. The sequential search in the worst case is therefore $O(n)$. Typically, you will look at about one-half of the elements in the array. Thus, the average case is $O(n/2)$, which is just $O(n)$.

Note: **The time efficiency of a sequential search of an array**
Best case: $O(1)$
Worst case: $O(n)$
Average case: $O(n)$

Searching a Sorted Array

A sequential search of an unsorted array is rather easy to understand and to implement. When the array contains relatively few elements, the search is efficient enough to be practical. However, when the array contains many elements, a sequential search can be time-consuming. For example, imagine that you are looking through a jar of coins for one minted during the year of your birth. A sequential search of 10 coins is not a problem. With 1000 coins, the search could be lengthy; with 1 million coins, it is overwhelming. A faster search method would be welcome. Fortunately, faster searches are possible.

A Sequential Search of a Sorted Array

16.8   Suppose that before you begin searching your coins, someone arranges them in sorted order by their dates. If you search the sorted coins in Figure 16-4 sequentially for the date 1983, you would look at the coins dated 1972, 1979, and 1981 before arriving at 1983. If, instead, you look for the date 1984, you would look at the first four coins and then look at the one dated 1985. Should you keep looking? If the coins are sorted into ascending order and you have reached the one dated 1985, you will not find 1984 beyond it. If the coins were not sorted, you would have to examine all of them to determine that 1984 was not present.

Figure 16-4   Coins sorted by their mint dates

Note: A sequential search can be more efficient if the data is sorted.

If our array is sorted into either ascending or descending order, we can use the previous ideas to revise the sequential search. This modified search can determine that an item does not occur in an array faster than a sequential search of an unsorted array. The latter search always examines the entire array in this case. With a sorted array, however, a sequential search often makes far fewer comparisons to make the same determination. Exercise 1 at the end of this chapter asks you to implement a sequential search of a sorted array.

After expending the effort to sort an array, you often can search it much faster by using the method that we discuss next.

A Binary Search of a Sorted Array

16.9   Think of a number between 1 and 1 million. When I guess at your number, tell me whether my guess is correct, too high, or too low. At most, how many attempts will I need before I guess correctly? You should be able to answer this question by the time you reach the end of this section!

If you had to find a new friend's telephone number in a printed directory, what would you do? Typically you would open the book to a page near its middle, glance at the entries, and quickly see whether you were on the correct page. If you were not, you would decide whether you had to look at earlier pages—those in the left "half" of the book—or later pages—those in the right "half." What aspect of a telephone directory enables you to make this decision? The alphabetical order of the names.

If you decided to look in the left half, you could ignore the entire right half. In fact, you could tear off the right half and discard it, as Figure 16-5 illustrates. You have reduced the size of the search problem dramatically, as you have only half of the book left to search. You then would repeat the process on this half. Eventually you would either find the telephone number or discover that it is not there. This approach—called a **binary search**—sounds suspiciously recursive.

16.10   Let's adapt these ideas to searching an array a of n integers that are sorted into ascending order. (Descending order would also work with a simple change in our algorithm.) We know that

$$a[0] \leq a[1] \leq a[2] \leq \ldots \leq a[n-1]$$

Because the array is sorted, we can rule out whole sections of the array that could not possibly contain the number we are looking for—just as you ruled out an entire half of the telephone directory.

Figure 16-5   Ignoring one-half of the data when the data is sorted

I don't need this half of the book. I'll just throw it away.

For example, if we are looking for the number 7 and we know that a[5] is equal to 9, then, of course, we know that 7 is less than a[5]. But we also know that 7 cannot appear after a[5] in the array, because the array is sorted. That is,

$$7 < a[5] \leq a[6] \leq \ldots \leq a[n-1]$$

We know this without looking at the elements beyond a[5]. We therefore can ignore these elements as well as a[5]. Similarly, if the sought-after number were greater than a[5] (for example, if we were looking for 10), we could ignore a[5] and all the elements before it.

Replacing the index 5 in the preceding example with whatever index is in the middle of the array leads to a first draft of an algorithm:

> **Algorithm to search a[0] through a[n-1] for desiredItem**
> mid = *approximate midpoint between* 0 *and* n-1
> **if** (desiredItem *equals* a[mid])
>   **return true**
> **else if** (desiredItem < a[mid])
>   **return** *the result of searching* a[0] *through* a[mid-1]
> **else if** (desiredItem > a[mid])
>   **return** *the result of searching* a[mid+1] *through* a[n-1]

Notice that

> *Searching* a[0] *through* a[n-1]

involves either

> *Searching* a[0] *through* a[mid-1]

or

> *Searching* a[mid+1] *through* a[n-1]

These two searches of a portion of the array are smaller versions of the very task we are solving, and so can be accomplished with recursive calls to the algorithm itself.

16.11   There is, however, one complication with the previous pseudocode. The recursive calls search a subrange of the array. In the first case, it is the elements indexed by 0 through mid − 1. In the second case, it is the elements indexed by mid + 1 through n − 1. Thus, we need two extra parameters—first and last—to specify the first and last indices of the subrange of the array that is to be searched. Using these parameters, we can express the pseudocode more precisely as follows:

> **Algorithm to search a[first] through a[last] for desiredItem**
> mid = *approximate midpoint between* first *and* last
> **if** (desiredItem *equals* a[mid])
>   **return true**
> **else if** (desiredItem < a[mid])
>   **return** *the result of searching* a[first] *through* a[mid-1]
> **else if** (desiredItem > a[mid])
>   **return** *the result of searching* a[mid+1] *through* a[last]

To search the entire array, we initially set first to 0 and last to n − 1. Each recursive call will then use some other values for first and last. For example, the recursive call that appears first would set first to 0 and last to mid − 1.

When you write any recursive algorithm, you should always check that the recursion is not infinite. Let's check whether every possible invocation of the algorithm will lead to a base case. Consider the three cases in the nested if statement in the previous pseudocode. In the first case, the sought-after item is found in the array, so there is no recursive call, and the process terminates. In each of the other two cases, a smaller portion of the array is searched by a recursive call. If the sought-after item is in the array, the algorithm uses smaller and smaller portions of the array until it finds the item. But what if the item is not anywhere in the array? Will the resulting series of recursive calls eventually lead to a base case? Unfortunately not, but that is not hard to fix.

16.12   Note that in each recursive call, either the value of `first` is increased or the value of `last` is decreased. If they ever pass each other and `first` actually becomes larger than `last`, we will have run out of array elements to check. In that case, `desiredItem` is not in the array. If we add this test to our pseudocode, make the recursive calls look a bit more like Java, and refine the logic a bit, we get the following more complete algorithm:

> *Algorithm* **binarySearch(a, first, last, desiredItem)**
> mid = (first + last)/2 *// approximate midpoint*
> **if** (first > last)
>   **return false**
> **else if** (desiredItem *equals* a[mid])
>   **return true**
> **else if** (desiredItem < a[mid])
>   **return** binarySearch(a, first, mid-1, desiredItem)
> **else** // desiredItem > a[mid]
>   **return** binarySearch(a, mid+1, last, desiredItem)

Figure 16-6 provides an example of a binary search.

Question 5   Search the array in Figure 16-6 for 8 and for 16 by using a recursive sequential search. In each case, which algorithm—the recursive sequential search or the recursive binary search—requires fewer comparisons?

16.13   When implementing the method `contains` for the ADT sorted list, the algorithm `binarySearch` becomes a private method that `contains` invokes. The array `entry` in the sorted list's implementation takes the place of the array `a` in the algorithm, and `length` takes the place of n. Again, since `entry` and `length` are data fields, they are not parameters of `contains` and `binarySearch`.

Although the implementations of the sequential search that were given in Segments 16.3 and 16.6 use the method `equals` to make the necessary comparisons, the binary search requires more than a test for equality. To make the necessary comparisons, we need the method `compareTo`. Since all classes inherit `equals` from the class `Object` and can override it, all objects can invoke `equals`. But for an object to invoke `compareTo`, it must belong to a class that implements the interface `Comparable`. Thus, the method `binarySearch` has the following implementation:

```
private boolean binarySearch(int first, int last,
                             Comparable desiredItem)
{
  boolean found;
  int mid = (first + last)/2;
  if (first > last)
    found = false;
  else if (desiredItem.equals(entry[mid]))
    found = true;
  else if (desiredItem.compareTo(entry[mid]) < 0)
    found = binarySearch(first, mid-1, desiredItem);
  else
    found = binarySearch(mid+1, last, desiredItem);

  return found;
} // end binarySearch
```

Figure 16-6   A recursive binary search of a sorted array that (a) finds its target; (b) does not find its target

---

(a) A search for 8

Look at the middle entry, 10:

2	4	5	7	8	**10**	12	15	18	21	24	26
0	1	2	3	4	5	6	7	8	9	10	11

$8 < 10$, so search the left half of the array.

Look at the middle entry, 5:

2	4	**5**	7	8
0	1	2	3	4

$8 > 5$, so search the right half of the array.

Look at the middle entry, 7:

7	8
3	4

$8 > 7$, so search the right half of the array.

Look at the middle entry, 8:

8
4

$8 = 8$, so the search ends. 8 is in the array.

(b) A search for 16

Look at the middle entry, 10:

2	4	5	7	8	**10**	12	15	18	21	24	26
0	1	2	3	4	5	6	7	8	9	10	11

$16 > 10$, so search the right half of the array.

Look at the middle entry, 18:

12	15	**18**	21	24	26
6	7	8	9	10	11

$16 < 18$, so search the left half of the array.

Look at the middle entry, 12:

12	15
6	7

$16 > 12$, so search the right half of the array.

Look at the middle entry, 15:

15
7

$16 > 15$, so search the right half of the array.

The next subarray is empty, so the search ends. 16 is not in the array.

Since the parameter `desiredItem` of the method `contains` has type `Object`, we must cast it to `Comparable` before passing it to `binarySearch`. Thus, `contains` appears as follows:

```java
public boolean contains(Object desiredItem)
{
   return binarySearch(0, length-1, (Comparable)desiredItem);
} // end contains
```

Programming Tip: Classes that implement the `Comparable` interface must define a `compareTo` method. Such classes should also define an `equals` method that overrides the generic `equals` method inherited from `Object`. Both `compareTo` and `equals` should use the same test for equality. The previous method `binarySearch` uses both the methods `equals` and `compareTo`. If the objects in the array did not have an appropriate `equals` method, `binarySearch` would not execute correctly. Note, however, that you could use `compareTo` instead of `equals` to test for equality.

Question 6   During a binary search, which elements in the array

4 8 12 14 20 24

are compared to the target when the target is **a.** 2; **b.** 8; **c.** 15

Question 7   Modify the previous method `contains` so that it returns the index of the first array element that equals `desiredItem`. If the array does not contain such an element, return −1. You will have to modify `binarySearch` also.

Question 8   What changes to the binary search algorithm are necessary when the array is sorted in descending order (from largest down to smallest) instead of ascending order, as we have assumed during our discussion?

Java Class Library: The Method `binarySearch`

16.14   The class `Arrays` in the package `java.util` defines several versions of a static method `binarySearch` with the following specification:

```java
/** Task: Searches an entire array for a given item.
 *  @param array         an array sorted in ascending order
 *  @param desiredItem   the item to be found in the array
 *  @return index of the array element that equals desiredItem;
 *          otherwise returns -belongsAt-1, where belongsAt is
 *          the index of the array element that should contain
 *          desiredItem */
public static int binarySearch(type[] array, type desiredItem);
```

Here, both occurrences of *type* must be the same; *type* can be `Object` or any of the primitive types `byte`, `char`, `double`, `float`, `int`, `long`, or `short`.

The Efficiency of a Binary Search of an Array

16.15   The binary search algorithm eliminates about half of the array from consideration after only one comparison. It then eliminates another quarter of the array, and then another eighth, and so on.

Thus, most of the array is not searched at all, saving much time. Intuitively, the binary search algorithm is very fast.

But just how fast is it? Counting the comparisons that occur will provide a measure of the algorithm's efficiency. To see the algorithm's worst-case behavior, you count the maximum number of comparisons that can occur when searching an array of n items. A comparison occurs each time the algorithm divides the array in half. After each comparison, half of the items are left to search. That is, beginning with n items, we would be left with $n/2$ items, then $n/4$ items, and so on. In the worst case, the search would continue until only one item was left. That is, $n/2^k$ would equal 1 for some value of k. This value of k gives us the number of comparisons we seek.

If n is a power of 2, $n = 2^k$ for some positive k. By the definition of a logarithm, $k = \log_2 n$. Thus, the binary search performs at most $\log_2 n$ comparisons when n is a power of 2. If n is not a power of 2, you can find an integer $k \geq 1$ so that $2^{k-1} < n < 2^k$. For example, if n is 14, $2^3 < 14 < 2^4$. Thus, we have

$$2^{k-1} < n < 2^k$$
$$k - 1 < \log_2 n < k$$
$$k = 1 + \log_2 n \text{ rounded down}$$
$$= \log_2 n \text{ rounded up}$$

The binary search performs at most $\lceil \log_2 n \rceil$ comparisons when n is not a power of 2. Thus, the binary search is O(log n) in the worst case.

For example, to search an array of 1000 elements, the binary search will compare the target to about 10 array elements in the worst case. In contrast, a simple sequential search could compare the target to as many as all 1000 array elements, and on average will compare it to about 500 array elements.

Note: **The time efficiency of a binary search of an array**
Best case: O(1)
Worst case: O(log n)
Average case: O(log n)

While the binary search is O(log n) in both the average and worst cases, the actual running time in these cases is not the same. Remember that a Big Oh analysis ignores constant multipliers that affect the running time. In practice, an average-case binary search is about twice as fast as a worst-case search.

Question 9   Think of a number between 1 and 1 million. When I guess at your number, tell me whether my guess is correct, too high, or too low. At most, how many attempts will I need before I guess correctly?

16.16   **Another approach.** The binary search makes a comparison each time it locates the midpoint of the array. Thus, to search n items, the binary search looks at the middle item and then searches $n/2$ items. If we let $t(n)$ represent the time requirement for searching n items, we find that at worst

$$t(n) = 1 + t(n/2) \text{ for } n > 1$$
$$t(1) = 1$$

We encountered this recurrence relation in Segment 10.24. There, we showed that

$$t(n) = 1 + \log_2 n$$

Thus, the binary search is O(log n) in the worst case.

Searching an Unsorted Chain

16.17 Within a linked implementation of either the ADT list or the ADT sorted list, the method `contains` would search a chain of linked nodes for the target. As you will see, a sequential search is really the only practical choice. We begin with a chain whose data is unsorted, as typically would be the case for the ADT list.

Regardless of a list's implementation, a sequential search of the list looks at consecutive entries in the list, beginning with the first one, until either it finds the desired entry or it looks at all entries without success. When the implementation is linked, however, moving from node to node is not as simple as moving from one array location to another. Despite this fact, you can implement a sequential search of a chain of linked nodes either iteratively or recursively and with the same efficiency as that of a sequential search of an array.

An Iterative Sequential Search of an Unsorted Chain

16.18 Figure 16-7 illustrates a chain of linked nodes that contain the list's entries. Recall from Segment 6.23 that `firstNode` is a data field of the class that implements the list. While it is clear that a method can access the first node in this chain by using the reference `firstNode`, how can it access the subsequent nodes? Since `firstNode` is a data field that always references the first node in the chain, we would not want our search to alter it or any other aspect of the list. Thus, an iterative method `contains` should use a local reference variable `currentNode` that initially contains the same reference as `firstNode`. To make `currentNode` reference the next node, we would execute the statement

```
currentNode = currentNode.getNextNode();
```

Figure 16-7   A chain of linked nodes that contain the entries in a list

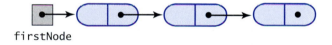

firstNode

The iterative sequential search has the following straightforward implementation:

```
public boolean contains(Object anEntry)
{
  boolean found = false;
  Node currentNode = firstNode;
  while (!found && (currentNode != null))
  {
    if (anEntry.equals(currentNode.getData()))
      found = true;
    else
      currentNode = currentNode.getNextNode();
  } // end for

  return found;
} // end contains
```

A Recursive Sequential Search of an Unsorted Chain

16.19 Recursively, a sequential search looks at the first entry in the list and, if it is not the desired entry, searches the rest of the list. This recursive approach is the same regardless of whether you implement the search at the client level by using only the list's ADT operations—as you did in Question 4—or as a public method of an array-based implementation of the list—as we did in Segment 16.6. We use the same approach for a linked implementation of the list, as follows.

How would you implement the step *search the rest of the list* when the list's entries are in a chain of linked nodes? The iterative method `contains` that you saw in the previous segment uses a local variable `currentNode` to move from node to node. A recursive method could not have `currentNode` as a local variable, since `currentNode` would get reset to an initial value at each recursive call. Instead, such a method needs `currentNode` as a formal parameter. But then we would have a method whose parameter depends on the list's implementation, making it unsuitable as a public method. Just as we did earlier in Segments 16.6 and 16.13, we would make this search method private and call it from the public method `contains`. Thus, we could write `contains` as follows:

```
public boolean contains(Object anEntry)
{
   return search(firstNode, anEntry);
} // end contains
```

Notice that the call to the method `search` initializes its parameter to `firstNode`, much as an iterative method initializes its local variable `currentNode` to `firstNode`.

The method `search` examines the list entry in the node that its parameter references. If the entry is not the desired one, the method recursively calls itself with an argument that references the next node in the chain. Thus, a recursive `search` has the following implementation:

```
/** Task: Recursively searches a chain of nodes for desiredItem,
 *        beginning with the node that current references. */
private boolean search(Node current, Object desiredItem)
{
   boolean found;

   if (current == null)
      found = false;
   else if (desiredItem.equals(current.getData()))
      found = true;
   else
      found = search(current.getNextNode(), desiredItem);

   return found;
} // end search
```

The Efficiency of a Sequential Search of a Chain

16.20 The efficiency of a sequential search of a chain is really the same as that of a sequential search of an array. In the best case, the desired item will be first in the chain. The search will be O(1), since you will have made only one comparison. In the worst case, you will search the entire chain, making n comparisons for a chain of n nodes. Therefore, the sequential search in the worst case is O(n). Typically, you will look at about one-half of the elements in the chain. Thus, the average-case search is O($n/2$), which is just O(n).

Note: **The time efficiency of a sequential search of a chain of linked nodes**

Best case: O(1)
Worst case: O(n)
Average case: O(n)

Searching a Sorted Chain

We now search a chain whose data is sorted. Such a chain would occur in a linked implementation of the ADT sorted list.

A Sequential Search of a Sorted Chain

16.21   Segment 16.8 described how to search an array of sorted data. Searching a chain of linked nodes whose data is sorted is similar to searching a sorted array. In fact, Segment 13.23 used the same idea in the linked implementation of the method getPosition for the ADT sorted list. As we noted then, the implementation of the sorted list method contains could invoke getPosition. Another option would be to incorporate the logic of getPosition into the implementation of contains, as follows:

```java
public boolean contains(Object anEntry)
{
  boolean found = false;
  Comparable entry = (Comparable)anEntry;

  Node currentNode = firstNode;

  while ( (currentNode != null) &&
          (entry.compareTo(currentNode.getData()) > 0) )
  {
    currentNode = currentNode.getNextNode();
  } // end while

  if ( (currentNode != null) &&
        entry.equals(currentNode.getData()) )
  {
    found = true;
  } // end if

  return found;
} // end contains
```

A Binary Search of a Sorted Chain

16.22   A binary search of an array looks first at the element that is at or near the middle of the array. It is easy to determine the index mid of this element by computing (first + last)/2, where first and last are the indices of the first and last elements, respectively, in the array. Accessing this middle element is also easy: For an array a, it is simply a[mid].

Now consider searching a chain of linked nodes, such as the one you saw earlier in Figure 16-7, whose nodes are sorted. How would you access the entry in the middle node? Since this chain has only three nodes, you can get to the middle node quickly, but what if the chain contained 1000 nodes? In general, you need to traverse the chain, beginning at the first node, until you reach the middle node. How will you know when you get there? If you know the length of the chain, you can divide it in half and count nodes as you traverse. The details are not as important as a realization that it takes a bit of work to access the middle node.

After looking at the entry in the middle node, you probably need to ignore half of the chain and search the other half. Can you ignore part of the chain without changing it? Not easily, but remember that you want to search the chain, not destroy it. Once you have determined the half that needs to be searched, you must find its middle node, again by traversing the chain. It should be clear to you that a binary search of a linked chain of nodes would be challenging to implement and extremely inefficient. In fact, such a search is impractical.

 Note: A binary search of a chain of linked nodes is impractical.

Choosing a Search Method

16.23   **Choosing between a sequential search and a binary search.** You just saw that you should use a sequential search to search a chain of linked nodes. But if you want to search an array of objects, you need to know which methods are applicable. To use a sequential search, the objects must have a method `equals` that determines whether two distinct objects are equal in some sense. Since all objects inherit `equals` from the class `Object`, you must ensure that the objects you search have overridden `equals` with a more appropriate version. To perform a binary search on an array of objects, on the other hand, the objects must have a `compareTo` method and the array must be sorted. If these conditions are not met, you must use a sequential search.

If both search algorithms are applicable to your array, what search should you use? If the array is small, you can simply use a sequential search. If the array is large and already sorted, a binary search is typically faster than a sequential search. But if the array is not sorted, should you sort it and then use a binary search? The answer depends on how often you plan to search the array. Sorting takes time, typically more time than a sequential search would. If you plan to search an unsorted array only a few times, sorting the array so that you can use a binary search likely will not save you time; use a sequential search instead.

Figure 16-8 summarizes the time efficiencies of the sequential search and the binary search. Only the sequential search is applicable to unsorted data. The efficiencies given for the binary search are for an array-based list. For a large, sorted list, the binary search is generally faster than a sequential search.

Figure 16-8   The time efficiency of searching, expressed in Big Oh notation

	Best Case	Average Case	Worst Case
Sequential search (unsorted data)	O(1)	O(n)	O(n)
Sequential search (sorted data)	O(1)	O(n)	O(n)
Binary search (sorted array)	O(1)	O($\log n$)	O($\log n$)

16.24   **Choosing between an iterative search and a recursive search.** Since the recursive sequential search is tail recursive, you can save some time and space by using the iterative version of the search. The binary search is fast, so using recursion will not require much additional space for the recursive calls. Also, coding the binary search recursively is usually easier than coding it iteratively. To convince yourself, try to code an iterative version of the binary search. (See Exercise 4 at the end of this chapter.)

CHAPTER SUMMARY

- A sequential search of either a list, an array, or a chain looks at the first item, the second item, and so on until it either finds a particular item or determines that the item does not occur in the group.

- The average-case performance of a sequential search is $O(n)$.

- Typically, you perform a sequential search iteratively, although a simple recursive form is possible.

- A binary search of an array requires that the array be sorted. It looks first at the middle of the array to determine in which half the desired item can occur. The search repeats this strategy on only this half of the array.

- A binary search is $O(\log n)$ in the worst case.

- Typically, you perform a binary search recursively, although an iterative form is possible.

- A binary search of a linked chain of nodes is impractical.

PROGRAMMING TIP

- Classes that implement the `Comparable` interface must define a `compareTo` method. Such classes should also define an `equals` method that overrides the generic `equals` method inherited from `Object`. Both `compareTo` and `equals` should use the same test for equality. The method `binarySearch` in Segment 16.13 uses both the methods `equals` and `compareTo`. If the objects in the array did not have an appropriate `equals` method, `binarySearch` would not execute correctly. Note, however, that you could use `compareTo` instead of `equals` to test for equality.

EXERCISES

1. When searching a sorted array sequentially, you can determine that a given item does not appear in the array without searching the entire array. For example, if you search the array

     2 5 7 9

for 6, you can use the approach described in Segment 16.8. That is, you compare 6 to 2, then to 5, and finally to 7. Since you did not find 6 after comparing it to 7, you do not have to look further, because the other elements in the array are greater than 7 and therefore cannot equal 6. Thus, you do not simply ask whether 6 equals an array element, you also ask whether it is greater than the element. Since 6 is greater than 2, you continue the search. Likewise for 5. Since 6 is less than 7, you have passed the point in the array where 6 would have had to occur, so 6 is not in the array.

   a. Write an iterative method `contains` to take advantage of these observations when searching a sorted array sequentially.

   b. Write a recursive method `search` that a method `contains` can call to take advantage of these observations when searching a sorted array sequentially.

   c. Repeat Part *b*, but search a sorted chain instead of an array.

2. Revise the recursive method `search`, as given in Segment 16.6, so that it looks at the last entry in the array instead of the first one.

3. Modify the method `binarySearch` in Segment 16.13 so that it returns the index of the first array element that equals `desiredItem`. If the array does not contain such an element, return `-(belongsAt + 1)`, where `belongsAt` is the index of the array location that should contain `desiredItem`. At the end of Segment 16.13, Question 7 asked you to return `-1` in this case. Notice that both versions of the method return a negative integer if and only if `desiredItem` is not found.

4. Implement a binary search of an array iteratively. Model your methods after the ones given in Segment 16.13.

5. Write a recursive method to find the largest object in an array-based list of `Comparable` objects. Like the binary search, your method should divide the array into halves. Unlike the binary search, your method should search both halves for the largest object. The largest object in the array will then be the larger of these two largest objects.

6. In Segment 16.13, the method `contains` calls a private method that performs a binary search of an array. Assuming a linked implementation of the ADT sorted list, revise this private method to perform a binary search of a chain of nodes. Do not alter the chain.

7. **a.** Write a recurrence relation for the number $f(n)$ of comparisons that a sequential search makes.
   b. Prove by induction on n that $f(n) = n$.

8. At the end of Segment 16.3, Question 2 asked you to write a method that performs an iterative sequential search of a list by using only operations of the ADT list. Compare the time efficiency of this method with the ADT operation `contains`.

PROJECTS

1. When an object does not occur in an array, a sequential search for it must examine the entire array. If the array is sorted, you can improve the search by using the approach described in Exercise 1. A **jump search** is an attempt to reduce the number of comparisons even further.

   Instead of examining the n objects in the array a sequentially, you look at the elements $a[j]$, $a[2j]$, $a[3j]$, and so on, for some positive $j < n$. If the target t is less than one of these objects, you only need to search the portion of the array between the current object and the previous object. For example, if t is less than $a[3j]$ but is greater than $a[2j]$, you search the elements $a[2j + 1]$, $a[2j + 2]$, ..., $a[3j - 1]$ by using the method in Exercise 1. What should you do when $t > a[k * j]$, but $(k + 1) * j > n$?

   Devise an algorithm for performing a jump search. Then, using $\lceil \sqrt{n} \rceil$ as the value of j, implement the jump search.

2. An **interpolation search** assumes that the data in an array is sorted and uniformly distributed. Whereas a binary search always looks at the middle item in an array, an interpolation search looks where the sought item is more likely to occur. For example, if you searched your telephone book for Victoria Appleseed, you probably would look near its beginning rather than its middle. And if you discovered many Appleseeds, you would look near the last Appleseed.

Instead of looking at the element a[mid] of an array a, as the binary search would, an interpolation search examines a[index], where

$$p = (desiredElement - a[first])/(a[last] - a[first])$$
$$index = \lceil (last - first) \cdot p \rceil$$

Implement an interpolation search of an array. For particular arrays, compare the outcomes of an interpolation search and a binary search. Consider arrays that have uniformly distributed elements and arrays that do not.

CHAPTER

17

Dictionaries

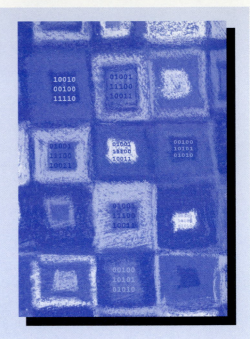

CONTENTS

Specifications for the ADT Dictionary
    A Java Interface
    Iterators
Using the ADT Dictionary
    A Directory of Telephone Numbers
    The Frequency of Words
    A Concordance of Words
Java Class Library: The Interface **Map**

PREREQUISITES

Chapter   4   Lists
Chapter   8   Java's Iterator Interfaces
Chapter 16   Searching

OBJECTIVES

After studying this chapter, you should be able to

- Describe the operations of the ADT dictionary
- Distinguish between a dictionary and a list
- Use a dictionary in a program

If you need to check the meaning of a word, you look it up in a dictionary. If you need a friend's address, you consult your address book. If you need someone's telephone number, you use a telephone directory—or call 411 to ask someone to look it up for you.

Each of these examples is actually a kind of dictionary. Each uses the concept of a two-part entry that consists of

- A keyword such as an English word or a person's name
- Other data such as a definition, an address, or a telephone number

The keyword enables you to locate the desired entry.

This chapter describes and uses an abstract data type that generalizes our everyday notion of a dictionary. The previous examples—finding a word's definition, a friend's address, or someone's telephone number—are all examples of searching a dictionary. The previous chapter examined how to search a list. You will see that a dictionary provides a more powerful way to organize data that will be searched.

Specifications for the ADT Dictionary

17.1   The ADT **dictionary**—also called a **map** or **table**—contains entries that each have two parts: a keyword, usually called a **search key,** and a value associated with that key. Figure 17-1 illustrates an everyday English dictionary. Each entry has a word as the search key and the word's definition as the value associated with the key.

The ADT dictionary organizes and identifies its entries by their search keys, rather than by another criterion such as position. Thus, you can retrieve or remove an entry from a dictionary given only the entry's search key. The fact that every entry in a dictionary has a search key distinguishes the dictionary from other ADTs such as a list. Although you certainly could put an entry that has a search key in a list, a list's data is organized by position, not by search key.

Figure 17-1   An English dictionary

computer An electronic device that computes...

Some dictionaries have distinct search keys, but others allow two or more entries to have the same search key. For example, a dictionary of student records organized by student identification numbers has distinct search keys, since those numbers are unique. On the other hand, an English-language dictionary has duplicate search keys since it often has several meanings for a word. For example, my dictionary has three entries for the word "book": One is a noun, one is a verb, and one is an adjective.

Printed versions of a natural-language dictionary, a telephone directory, a library catalog, and a thesaurus all have entries sorted by their search keys. These databases are dictionaries, but the ADT dictionary does not require sorted entries. Some dictionaries do sort their entries by search keys, while other dictionaries have unsorted entries. Why do our examples of printed dictionaries sort their entries? To make it easier for the reader to find a particular entry. In contrast, if you searched a computerized thesaurus for a word, you would not be aware of the order of its entries. Nor would you care, as long as you could retrieve a particular entry. Thus, whether a dictionary has sorted or unsorted search keys is more of an implementation detail than a necessary characteristic of the dictionary. But remember that the details of any implementation affect the efficiencies of the ADT operations in various ways.

17.2 The ADT dictionary has the same major operations—insert, delete, retrieve, search, and traverse—that are common to most databases, even if a particular implementation sorts its entries or allows duplicate search keys. In particular, these operations are

- Add a new entry to the dictionary, given a search key and associated value
- Remove an entry, given its associated search key
- Retrieve the value associated with a given search key
- Search for a given search key to determine whether it is in the dictionary
- Traverse all the keys in the dictionary
- Traverse all the values in the dictionary

In addition, the ADT dictionary has the following basic operations that are often associated with an ADT:

- Determine whether a dictionary is empty or full
- Get the number of entries in the dictionary
- Remove all entries from the dictionary

The following specifications define a set of operations for the ADT dictionary:

ABSTRACT DATA TYPE DICTIONARY

DATA

- A collection of pairs (k, v) of objects k and v, where k is the search key and v is the corresponding value
- The number of pairs in the collection

OPERATIONS

add(key, value)
Task: Adds the pair (key, value) to the dictionary.
Input: key is an object search key, value is an associated object.
Output: None.

remove(key)
Task: Removes from the dictionary the value that corresponds to a given search key.
Input: key is an object search key.
Output: Returns either the value that was associated with the search key, or null if no such object exists.

getValue(key)

Task: Retrieves the value that corresponds to a given search key.
Input: key is an object search key.
Output: Returns either the value associated with the search key, or null if no such object exists.

contains(key)

Task: Determines whether a specific entry is in the dictionary.
Input: key is an object's search key.
Output: Returns true if an entry in the dictionary has key as its search key.

getKeyIterator()

Task: Creates an iterator that traverses all search keys in the dictionary.
Input: None.
Output: Returns an iterator that provides sequential access to the search keys in the dictionary.

getValueIterator()

Task: Creates an iterator that traverses all values in the dictionary.
Input: None.
Output: Returns an iterator that provides sequential access to the values in the dictionary.

isEmpty()

Task: Determines whether the dictionary is empty.
Input: None.
Output: Returns true if the dictionary is empty.

isFull()

Task: Determines whether the dictionary is full.
Input: None.
Output: Returns true if the dictionary is full.

getSize()

Task: Gets the size of the dictionary.
Input: None.
Output: Returns the number of entries (key-value pairs) currently in the dictionary.

clear()

Task: Removes all entries from the dictionary.
Input: None.
Output: None.

Note: The ADT dictionary contains entries that are key-value pairs organized by their search keys. You can add a new entry, and you can locate, retrieve, or remove an entry given its search key. In addition, you can traverse a dictionary's search keys or values.

17.3   **Refining the specifications.** Even though all dictionaries can have this common set of operations, you do need to refine some of the specifications according to whether a dictionary's search keys are distinct:

- **Distinct search keys.** The method add can ensure that the search keys in a dictionary are distinct. If key is already in the dictionary, the operation add(key, value) could either refuse to add another key-value entry or change the existing value associated with key to value. In either case, the remaining methods can have simpler implementations if add takes on this responsibility. For example, the methods remove and getValue will either find the one value associated with a given search key or discover that no such value exists.

- **Duplicate search keys.** If the method add adds every given key-value entry to a dictionary, the methods remove and getValue must deal with multiple entries that have the same search key. Which entry should be removed or returned? The method remove could easily remove the first value it finds or remove all values associated with the given search key. If getValue returns an object, it could return the first value it finds. Or you could modify getValue to return an array of values, for example.

    Another possibility is to have a secondary search key that is used only when several entries have the same primary search key. For example, if you call directory assistance for a common name like John Smith, you most certainly will be asked for John's address.

For simplicity, we will assume distinct search keys and consider duplicate search keys in the exercises and projects at the end of this chapter.

A Java Interface

17.4   The following Java interface for the ADT dictionary specifies distinct search keys. The add method replaces the value associated with any search key that is already in the dictionary.

```java
/** A dictionary with distinct search keys. */
import java.util.Iterator;
public interface DictionaryInterface
{
  /** Task: Adds a new entry to the dictionary. If the given search
   *        key already exists in the dictionary, replaces the
   *        corresponding value.
   *  @param key    an object search key of the new entry
   *  @param value  an object associated with the search key
   *  @return either null if the new entry was added to the dictionary
   *          or the value that was associated with key if the value
   *          was replaced */
  public Object add(Object key, Object value);

  /** Task: Removes a specific entry from the dictionary.
   *  @param key  an object search key of the entry to be removed
   *  @return either the value that was associated with the search key
   *          or null if no such object exists */
  public Object remove(Object key);
```

```
/** Task: Retrieves the value associated with a given search key.
 *  @param key  an object search key of the entry to be retrieved
 *  @return either the value that is associated with the search key
 *          or null if no such object exists */
public Object getValue(Object key);

/** Task: Determines whether a specific entry is in the dictionary.
 *  @param key  an object search key of the desired entry
 *  @return true if key is associated with an entry in the
 *          dictionary */
public boolean contains(Object key);

/** Task: Creates an iterator that traverses all search keys in the
 *        dictionary.
 *  @return an iterator that provides sequential access to the search
 *          keys in the dictionary */
public Iterator getKeyIterator();

/** Task: Creates an iterator that traverses all values in the
 *        dictionary.
 *  @return an iterator that provides sequential access to the values
 *          in the dictionary */
public Iterator getValueIterator();

/** Task: Determines whether the dictionary is empty.
 *  @return true if the dictionary is empty */
public boolean isEmpty();

/** Task: Determines whether the dictionary is full.
 *  @return true if the dictionary is full */
public boolean isFull();

/** Task: Gets the size of the dictionary.
 *  @return the number of entries (key-value pairs) currently
 *          in the dictionary */
public int getSize();

/** Task: Removes all entries from the dictionary. */
public void clear();
} // end DictionaryInterface
```

Iterators

17.5 The methods getKeyIterator and getValueIterator each return an iterator that conforms to the interface java.util.Iterator that we discussed in Chapter 8. You can create iterators for the dictionary myTable, for example, by writing

```
Iterator keyIterator = myTable.getKeyIterator();
Iterator valueIterator = myTable.getValueIterator();
```

These two iterators enable you to traverse all the search keys and all the values in a dictionary in parallel. That is, the ith search key returned by keyIterator corresponds to the ith dictionary value returned by valueIterator, as Figure 17-2 illustrates. Clearly, the two iterations have the same length, since the number of search keys in a dictionary must be the same as the number of values. The following loop displays each entry in the dictionary as a key-value pair:

```
while (keyIterator.hasNext())
    System.out.println(keyIterator.next() + ", " + valueIterator.next());
```

For a sorted dictionary, keyIterator traverses the search keys in sorted order. For an unsorted dictionary, this traversal order is not specified. The examples in the next section demonstrate these iterators in several contexts.

Figure 17-2   Two iterators that traverse a dictionary's keys and values in parallel

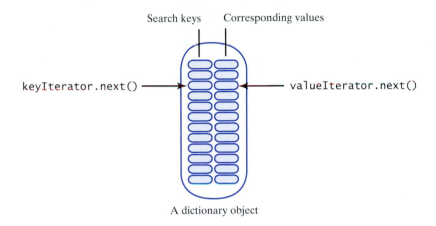

Search keys   Corresponding values

keyIterator.next() ⟶   ⟵ valueIterator.next()

A dictionary object

Note: An iteration of a dictionary's values corresponds to an iteration of its search keys. That is, the ith value in one iteration is associated in the dictionary with the ith search key in the second iteration.

Question 1   If the class Dictionary implements DictionaryInterface, write a Java statement that creates an empty dictionary myDictionary.

Question 2   If the dictionary that you created in Question 1 now contains the names and telephone numbers of your friends, write a Java statement that adds your name and telephone number to this dictionary. Assume that the names are the search keys and that both the names and telephone numbers are strings.

Question 3   Write Java statements that display either Brittany's telephone number, if she is in the dictionary described in Question 2, or an error message if she is not.

Using the ADT Dictionary

This section demonstrates how to use the ADT dictionary in a program by considering three different examples. We begin by creating a telephone directory.

A Directory of Telephone Numbers

17.6   A telephone directory contains the names and telephone numbers of the people who live in a given geographical region. The most frequent operation on a telephone directory is the retrieval of a telephone number, given a person's name. Thus, using the ADT dictionary to represent a telephone directory is a good choice. Clearly, the name should be the search key, and the telephone number should be the corresponding value. Often, but not always, retrieval is more efficient when the dictionary is sorted. Additionally, a sorted dictionary would make it easier to create a printed directory with entries alphabetized by name.

A major task, at least initially, is to create the directory from the available names and telephone numbers. Having this data in a text file will make this task convenient. After the telephone directory is created, operations on the directory, such as adding an entry, removing an entry, or changing a telephone number, will be used less often than searching for a given name. Traversing the directory is important to create either a hard copy or a backup file of the data, but this operation too is not done frequently. The next chapter discusses how to choose an efficient implementation of an ADT based on its expected use.

17.7   **Class design and use.** Our next step is to design a class to represent the telephone directory. A sorted dictionary will represent the data, which consists of name-number pairs. Each person's name can be an instance of the class Name that we encountered in Chapter 1, and the telephone number can be a string. Figure 17-3 shows a class diagram for our design. The class TelephoneDirectory contains an instance phoneBook of a dictionary. The class has the methods readFile and getPhoneNumber.

Figure 17-3   A class diagram for a telephone directory

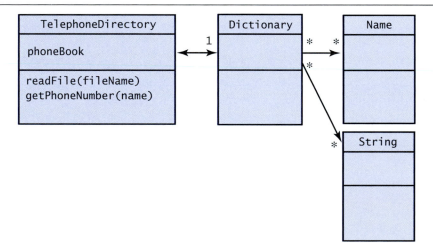

Before we implement the class TelephoneDirectory, let's consider its use. A client would create an instance of TelephoneDirectory and read the data file by invoking the method read-File. Given the text file data.txt, the client's main method could begin as follows:

```
public static void main(String[] args)
{
    TelephoneDirectory directory = new TelephoneDirectory();
```

```
String fileName = "data.txt";
try
{
  FileReader reader = new FileReader(fileName);
  BufferedReader dataFile = new BufferedReader(reader);

  directory.readFile(dataFile);
} // end try
catch (IOException e)
{
  System.err.println("I/O error " + e);
} // end catch
. . .
```

Most of the code involves reading the file, but you should focus on the highlighted lines that involve the class `TelephoneDirectory`.

17.8   **Implementation.** The implementation of `TelephoneDirectory` begins with its data fields and constructor, as follows:

```
import java.io.*;
import java.util.*;

public class TelephoneDirectory
{
  private DictionaryInterface phoneBook;
  private static final String DELIMITERS = " \n\r\t";

  public TelephoneDirectory()
  {
    phoneBook = new SortedDictionary();
  } // end default constructor
  . . .
```

We assume that the class `SortedDictionary` implements a sorted version of the ADT dictionary. We will explain the string `DELIMITERS` in a moment.

To implement the method `readFile`, you need to know what the data file looks like. Suppose that each line in the file contains three strings—a first name, a last name, and a telephone number—so that a typical line might appear as

Suzanne Nouveaux   401-555-1234

The method `readFile` must read each of these lines and extract the strings. If the method represents these strings as the variables `firstName`, `lastName`, and `phoneNumber`, the following Java statements will add the desired entry to the dictionary `phoneBook`:

```
Name fullName = new Name(firstName, lastName);
phoneBook.add(fullName, phoneNumber);
```

To simplify this example, we assume that the text file contains distinct names.

Here is the definition of `readFile`. Most of the code extracts the strings from each line.

```
/** Task: Reads a text file of names and telephone numbers.
 *  @param dataFile  a text file that is open for input */
public void readFile(BufferedReader dataFile) throws IOException
{
  String line = dataFile.readLine();
```

```
  while (line != null)
  {
    StringTokenizer tokenizer = new StringTokenizer(line, DELIMITERS);

    String firstName   = (String)tokenizer.nextToken();
    String lastName    = (String)tokenizer.nextToken();
    String phoneNumber = (String)tokenizer.nextToken();

    Name fullName = new Name(firstName, lastName);
    phoneBook.add(fullName, phoneNumber);

    line = dataFile.readLine();
  } // end while

  dataFile.close();
} // end readFile
```

The method begins by reading an entire line from the text file as a string. It then uses the class java.util.StringTokenizer to extract the three substrings, or **tokens,** that make up the name and telephone number. The string DELIMITERS contains the characters, or **delimiters,** that can end these substrings. The delimiters for this example are a space, a new-line character, a return, and a tab. Notice that DELIMITERS is defined as a constant data field that is available to other methods in the class.

Programming Tip: `java.util.StringTokenizer`

The class StringTokenizer enables you to break a string into substrings, or **tokens,** that are separated by characters called **delimiters.** Any character can be a delimiter, if it does not occur in any substring. You create a string of these delimiters and give it to the class's constructor.

The following methods in the class StringTokenizer enable you to extract the tokens from any string:

```
public String nextToken();
public boolean hasMoreTokens();
```

17.9   **A method that searches.** The class TelephoneDirectory has a method to find a person's telephone number. This method needs the person's name, and the user must supply it. If we assume that the client will interact with the user and provide the desired name, we could define the method as follows:

```
public String getPhoneNumber(String firstName, String lastName)
{
  Name fullName = new Name(firstName, lastName);
  return (String)phoneBook.getValue(fullName);
} // end getPhoneNumber
```

The method either returns a string that contains the desired telephone number or returns null if the number is not found.

We could define a similar method instead of or in addition to the previous method with the following signature:

```
public String getPhoneNumber(Name personName)
```

Or we could include the code that interacts with the user within our method. Such a method could begin as follows:

```
/** Task: Finds the telephone number of the person whose name is
 *          given by the user.
 *  @return the desired phone number as a string, or
 *              null if no phone number is found, or
 *              the string "quit" if the user enters quit instead of a name */
public String getPhoneNumber()
```

It would be a simple matter to provide all three versions of the method `getPhoneNumber` to provide flexibility for the client. With any version, the client could invoke the method within a loop to search the directory repeatedly.

Additional methods to add or remove a person or to change a person's telephone number are straightforward and are left as exercises.

Question 4   Implement a method for the class `TelephoneDirectory` that removes an entry from the directory. Given the person's name, the method should return either the person's telephone number or `null` if the person is not in the directory.

Question 5   Implement a method for the class `TelephoneDirectory` that changes a person's telephone number. Given the person's name, the method should return either the person's old telephone number or `null` if the person was not in the directory but has been added to it.

The Frequency of Words

17.10   Some word processors provide a count of the number of times each word occurs in a document. In this example, we will create a class `FrequencyCounter` that provides this capability. This class is somewhat like the one in the previous example, so we will omit some of the design details.

Basically, the class needs to count each occurrence of a word as it reads the document from a text file. It then needs to display the results. For example, if the text file contains

row, row, row your boat

the desired output would be

```
boat    1
row     3
your    1
```

Is the ADT dictionary the right one to use for this problem? A word and its frequency of occurrence in the document form a pair that is suitable as an entry in a dictionary. If we want to know a given word's frequency, the word should be the search key. Also, the words in the dictionary must be distinct, and if they are sorted, we can display them in alphabetical order. Thus, a sorted dictionary with distinct search keys is an appropriate choice for this problem. Clearly, the dictionary will be a data field of the class `FrequencyCounter`, so the class will begin much like the class `TelephoneDirectory` in the previous example. Let's call the dictionary for this example `wordTable`.

17.11   **Creating the dictionary.** Now let's look at the method `readFile`, which creates the dictionary from the text file. We invoke this method in exactly the same way that Segment 17.7 did. The method can process the text file in a manner similar to way `readFile` processed the file in

Segment 17.8. We use the class `StringTokenizer` to extract each word in the file. If the word is not in the dictionary, we add it with an associated value of 1. That is, this word has occurred once so far. However, if the word is in the dictionary already, we retrieve its associated value—its count—increment it, and store it back into the dictionary. Since the value portion of any dictionary entry is an object, we use the wrapper class `Integer` to represent each count.

The following implementation of the method changes all the strings it reads to lowercase and uses the string ".?!,;: \n\r\t" of possible word separators to isolate the words. This string, called `DELIMITERS`, is assumed to be a data field of the class.

```java
/** Task: Reads a text file of words and counts their frequencies
 *        of occurrence.
 *  @param dataFile  a text file open for input */
public void readFile(BufferedReader dataFile) throws IOException
{
  String line = dataFile.readLine();
  while (line != null)
  {
    line = line.toLowerCase();
    StringTokenizer tokenizer = new StringTokenizer(line, DELIMITERS);

    while (tokenizer.hasMoreTokens())
    {
      String word = (String)tokenizer.nextToken();
      Object value = wordTable.getValue(word);

      if (value == null)
      { // add new word to table
        wordTable.add(word, new Integer(1));
      }
      else
      { // increment counter of existing word
        Integer counter = (Integer) value;
        int wordFrequency = counter.intValue();
        wordFrequency++;

        // replace value (counter) associated with word
        wordTable.add(word, new Integer(wordFrequency));
      } // end if
    } // end while

    line = dataFile.readLine();
  } // end while

  dataFile.close();
} // end readFile
```

17.12 **Displaying the dictionary.** Now that we have created the dictionary, we need to display the results. An iteration of the search keys will produce the words in alphabetical order. A parallel iteration of the values provides the corresponding frequencies. The following method is a possible solution for this task:

```java
public void display()
{
```

```
        Iterator keyIterator = wordTable.getKeyIterator();
        Iterator valueIterator = wordTable.getValueIterator();
        while (keyIterator.hasNext())
          System.out.println(keyIterator.next() + " " +
                                  (Integer) valueIterator.next());
    } // end display
```

A Concordance of Words

17.13   An index provides a way to locate the occurrence of certain words within a larger document. For example, the index to this book is an alphabetical listing of words paired with the page numbers on which the words occur. The example in this section will create a simpler kind of index—called a **concordance**—to all the words in a text file. Instead of page numbers, a concordance provides the line numbers that contain a particular word.

For example, suppose that a text file contains only these lines:

Learning without thought is labor lost;
thought without learning is perilous.

The following concordance of all the words in the file indicates the line numbers in which the words occur:

is   1 2
labor   1
learning   1 2
lost   1
perilous   2
thought   1 2
without   1 2

Although a word can appear in several lines of the file, it appears only once in the concordance. Like the previous word-frequency example, this feature of the concordance suggests that we use a dictionary whose search keys are the words in the concordance. But unlike the word-frequency example, the value associated with each of these words is a list of line numbers. Since the line numbers are sorted, we could use the ADT sorted list. However, by processing the lines in the file in order, we can add the line numbers to the end of an ordinary unsorted list and achieve a sorted order.

17.14   **The method `readFile`.** The design and implementation of a class `Concordance` to represent the concordance are quite similar to those of the class `FrequencyCounter` from the previous example. The method `readFile` reads the text file and creates the concordance as a dictionary called `word-Table`. The values in the dictionary are instances of the class `LinkedListWithIterator`, which implements the ADT list. In the following definition of `readFile`, we highlight portions that differ from the analogous method that you just saw in Segment 17.11:

```
public void readFile(BufferedReader dataFile) throws IOException
{
  ListWithIteratorInterface numberList;
  int lineNumber = 1;
  String line = dataFile.readLine();
```

```java
while (line != null)
{
  line = line.toLowerCase();
  StringTokenizer tokenizer = new StringTokenizer(line, DELIMITERS);
  while (tokenizer.hasMoreTokens())
  {
    String word = (String)tokenizer.nextToken();
    Object value = wordTable.getValue(word);

    if (value == null)
    { // create list for new word; add list and word to index
      numberList = new LinkedListWithIterator();
      wordTable.add(word, numberList);
    }
    else
    { // retrieve list for existing word
      numberList = (LinkedListWithIterator)value;
    } // end if

    // add line number to end of list so list is sorted
    numberList.add(new Integer(lineNumber));
  } // end while

  lineNumber++;
  line = dataFile.readLine();
} // end while

dataFile.close();
} // end readFile
```

The most interesting part of this method is the list of line numbers as the value associated with a search key.

Since we have chosen a linked implementation of the list, we need to be concerned with the efficiency of adding to the end of the list. If the underlying chain of nodes had only a reference to the first node, each such addition would require a traversal to reach the end of the chain. Choosing a list implementation that maintains a reference to the last node in the chain makes the addition to the end of the list quite efficient. We discussed such tail references in Chapter 6.

17.15   **The method `display`.** The chosen list implementation should include an iterator so that the following method `display` can display the line numbers in the index efficiently. Notice that we use the dictionary iterators, just as we did in the analogous method `display` given in Segment 17.12 for the previous example.

```java
public void display()
{
  Iterator keyIterator = wordTable.getKeyIterator();
  Iterator valueIterator = wordTable.getValueIterator();

  while (keyIterator.hasNext())
  {
    // display the word
    System.out.print(keyIterator.next() + " ");
```

```
            // get line numbers and iterator
            ListWithIteratorInterface numberList =
                              (LinkedListWithIterator) valueIterator.next();
            Iterator listIterator = numberList.getListIterator();

            // display line numbers
            while (listIterator.hasNext())
              System.out.print(listIterator.next() + " ");

            System.out.println();
          } // end while
        } // end display
```

Java Class Library: The Interface Map

17.16   The standard package `java.util` contains the interface `Map` that is similar to our interface for the ADT dictionary. The following method signatures are for a selection of methods in `Map` that are similar to the ones you have seen in this chapter. We have used blue to indicate where they differ from our methods.

```
public Object put(Object key, Object value);
public Object remove(Object key);
public Object get(Object key);
public boolean containsKey(Object key);
public boolean containsValue(Object value);
public Set keySet();
public Collection values();
public boolean isEmpty();
public int size();
public void clear();
```

Notice the differences in the names of the methods. `Map` uses the method names `put`, `get`, `containsKey`, and `size` instead of our names `add`, `getValue`, `contains`, and `getSize`. `Map` also has the additional method `containsValue` that determines whether a dictionary contains a given value.

Instead of our methods `getKeyIterator` and `getValueIterator` that return iterators to a dictionary's keys and values, respectively, `Map` specifies the methods `keySet`, which returns a set of keys, and `values`, which returns a collection of values. The Java Class Library contains the interfaces `Set` and `Collection`, and each of these interfaces has a method `iterator` that returns an iterator to the values in the corresponding ADT.

Finally, note that duplicate keys are not permitted in a dictionary that conforms to the `Map` interface. Each key must correspond to only one value.

CHAPTER SUMMARY

- The entries in the ADT dictionary each contain two parts: a search key and a value associated with that key. The dictionary identifies its entries by their search keys.

- Dictionaries can organize their search keys in either sorted or unsorted order. The search keys can be either distinct or duplicate.

- You can add an entry to a dictionary given its search key and value. You can retrieve or remove an entry given only its search key. By using an iterator, you can traverse all the keys or all the values in a dictionary.

- An English dictionary, a directory of telephone numbers, an address book, and a library catalog are common examples of dictionaries.

- The Java Class Library contains the interface **Map**, which is similar to our **DictionaryInterface**.

PROGRAMMING TIP

- The class **java.util.StringTokenizer** enables you to break a string into substrings, or tokens, that are separated by characters called delimiters. Any character can be a delimiter, if it does not occur in any substring. You create a string of these delimiters and give it to the class's constructor. The following member methods enable you to extract the tokens from any string.

```java
public String nextToken();
public boolean hasMoreTokens();
```

EXERCISES

1. How does a dictionary differ from a sorted list?

2. Implement a method for the class **TelephoneDirectory**—described in Segment 17.8—that adds an entry to the directory, given the person's name and telephone number. The method should return true if the entry was added. If the person is already in the directory, the method should replace the person's telephone number and return false.

3. Implement a method for the telephone directory example in Segment 17.8 to display everyone's name and telephone number.

4. In the telephone directory example of Segment 17.8, the case of the letters in a name affects the name's order in the dictionary. What steps can you take so that case variations in the input file do not affect this order?

5. In the telephone directory example of Segment 17.8, suppose that the text file of names and telephone numbers is sorted by name.

   a. What impact would this aspect of the file have on the efficiency of the method **read-File** for various implementations of the dictionary?
   b. Would it matter whether the file was in reverse alphabetical order?

6. In the word-frequency example of Segment 17.10, the method **readFile** does not call **contains** to determine whether a word is already in the dictionary, but instead calls **getValue**. Why did we do this?

7. The word-frequency example in Segment 17.10 determines the frequency with which each distinct word occurs within some given text. Describe the changes that you could make to the class **FrequencyCounter** if you wanted to determine the words that occur for each frequency.

8. In the concordance example of Segment 17.13, if a word occurs more than once in a single line, the number of that line appears more than once in the concordance. Revise the Java code given in Segment 17.14 so that the line numbers associated with a given word are distinct.

9. The ADT dictionary that we discussed in this chapter assumes distinct search keys. Revise the specifications of the dictionary to remove this restriction. Consider each of the following possibilities:

a. The method add adds an entry whose search key is already in the dictionary but whose value is not. The remove method deletes all entries with a given search key. The method getValue retrieves all values associated with a given search key.

b. The methods behave as Part *a* describes, but a secondary search key enables remove and getValue to delete or retrieve a single entry.

PROJECTS

1. To simplify the telephone directory example in Segment 17.6, we assumed that the text file contained distinct names. Remove this assumption, with and without a secondary search key. (See Exercise 9.)

2. Determining the authorship of certain famous pieces of literature is an interesting problem. Comparisons must be made between pieces of disputed authorship and those of known authorship. One approach is to compare the frequency of pairs of letters. There are 26*26 different pairs of letters. Not all of them will appear in a piece of writing. For example, "qz" is unlikely to appear, while "th" is likely to appear often. Design a program, similar to the frequency counter of Segments 17.10 through 17.12, that counts all the pairs of letters that appear in a given piece of text.

3. A compiler must examine tokens in a program and determine whether or not they are reserved words or identifiers defined by the user. Design a program that reads a Java program and makes a list of all the identifiers. To do this, you should make use of two dictionaries. The first dictionary should hold all the Java reserved words. The second dictionary should hold all the identifiers that you find. Whenever you encounter a token, you first should search the dictionary of reserved words. If the token is not a reserved word, you then should search the dictionary of identifiers. If the token is not in either dictionary, you should add it to the dictionary of identifiers.

18

Dictionary Implementations

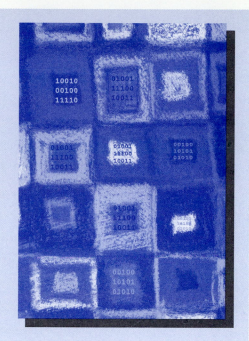

CONTENTS

Array-Based Implementations
> The Entries
> An Unsorted Array-Based Dictionary
> A Sorted Array-Based Dictionary
Vector-Based Implementations
Linked Implementations
> The Entries
> An Unsorted Linked Dictionary
> A Sorted Linked Dictionary

PREREQUISITES

Chapter   4   Lists
Chapter   5   List Implementations That Use Arrays
Chapter   6   List Implementations That Link Data
Chapter   8   Java's Iterator Interfaces
Chapter   9   The Efficiency of Algorithms
Chapter 16   Searching
Chapter 17   Dictionaries

OBJECTIVES

After studying this chapter, you should be able to

- Implement the ADT dictionary by using either an array, a vector, or a chain of linked nodes

The implementations of the ADT dictionary that we present in this chapter use techniques like the ones we used to implement the ADT list. We will use either an expandable array, an instance of Vector, or a chain of linked nodes to store the dictionary's entries. We will consider both sorted and unsorted dictionaries with distinct search keys. Later chapters will present more-sophisticated implementations for the ADT dictionary.

Array-Based Implementations

18.1 The ability to expand an array dynamically, as introduced in Segment 5.12, means that an array can provide as much storage as necessary for the entries in a dictionary. Remember that each entry consists of two parts—a search key and a value. You can encapsulate the two parts into an object, as Figure 18-1a illustrates. With this approach, you define a class Entry to represent the entries. A second approach uses two arrays, as shown in Figure 18-1b. One array represents the search keys and a second, **parallel array** represents the corresponding values. A third approach uses a two-dimensional array instead of two parallel arrays, as in Figure 18-1c. We will discuss the first approach and leave the exploration of the others as an exercise.

Figure 18-1 Three possible ways to use arrays to represent the entries in a dictionary: (a) an array of entry objects; (b) parallel arrays of search keys and values; (c) a two-dimensional array of search keys and values

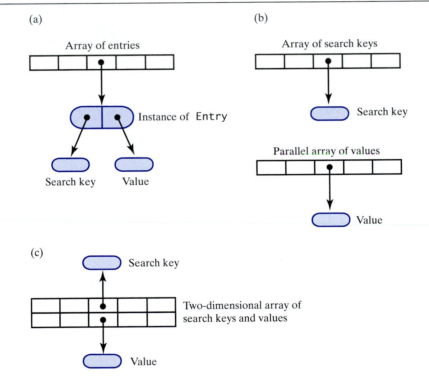

The Entries

18.2 When you use one array to represent the dictionary, as was illustrated in Figure 18-1a, you need a class to represent the dictionary's two-part entries. You can make this class either public, part of a package, or private and internal to the dictionary class. We chose the latter approach in defining the following private class Entry:

```
private class Entry implements java.io.Serializable
{
  private Object key;
  private Object value;
```

```
    private Entry(Object searchKey, Object dataValue)
    {
      key = searchKey;
      value = dataValue;
    } // end constructor

    private Object getKey()
    {
      return key;
    } // end getKey

    private Object getValue()
    {
      return value;
    } // end getValue

    private void setValue(Object dataValue)
    {
      value = dataValue;
    } // end setValue
  } // end Entry
```

Notice that the class has no method setKey to set or change the search key. Even though setValue can be useful in the implementation of add, you never need to change the search key. Without setKey, a default constructor would be useless, so none is defined.

The class Entry implements the interface Serializable so that instances of this class can be serialized. This aspect is necessary if we want to serialize instances of the dictionary.

Question 1   Figure 18-1 shows three ways to represent an array-based dictionary. How do the memory requirements for the three representations compare?

An Unsorted Array-Based Dictionary

18.3   One problem with array-based implementations of an ADT is the shifting of array elements that often occurs. When a dictionary's search keys are unsorted, you can add a new entry after the last entry in the array without shifting other entries, as Figure 18-2a illustrates. Removing an entry, however, does require you to shift other array elements to avoid a "hole" in the array. To remove an entry, you first locate it and then you shift the subsequent array elements toward the front of the array, as Figure 18-2b illustrates.

Removing or retrieving an entry requires a sequential search, since the search keys are not sorted. A sequential search must look at all the search keys in the array to determine that an entry is not present in the dictionary.

An iteration, or traversal, of the dictionary entries simply moves from location to location within the array. Since the search keys are not sorted, the order of the iteration is not specified. Whatever order is easy to implement is fine.

18.4   For this implementation, the worst-case efficiencies of the operations are as follows:

Addition   O(1)
Removal   O(n)
Retrieval O(n)
Traversal O(n)

Figure 18-2 An unsorted, array-based dictionary: (a) adding an entry; (b) removing an entry

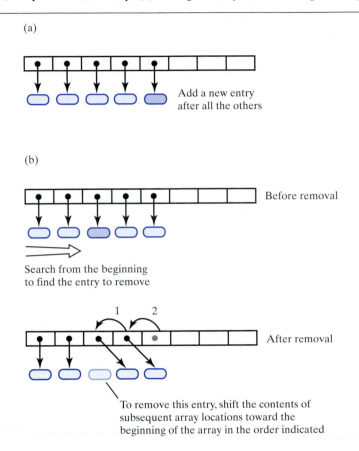

The implementation is suitable for an application that makes many additions to a dictionary and then displays the results. As we noted in Chapter 9, you should consider the operations that your application requires when choosing an implementation for an ADT. This tip from Chapter 9 bears repeating here:

 Programming Tip: If you use a particular ADT operation frequently, you want its implementation to be efficient. Conversely, if you rarely use an operation, you can afford to use a class that has an inefficient implementation of that operation.

 Programming Tip: Include comments in a class's implementation that advertise the efficiencies of its methods.

Realize that if you fill the array of dictionary entries, you must allocate a new, larger array and copy elements from the original array to the new array. This requirement adds overhead to any array-based implementation that the previous analysis does not reflect. In Java, the array elements are references to objects, so copying the array is fast. But for languages whose arrays contain objects instead of references, copying can be quite time-consuming. Ideally, you want to choose a sufficiently large dictionary, but not one that wastes space because it is overly large.

A Sorted Array-Based Dictionary

18.5   When the dictionary entries are sorted by their search keys, adding a new entry requires a search of the array of entries to see where the new entry belongs. After you determine the correct position for the new entry, you need to make room for it in the array. You do this by shifting subsequent array locations up by one position, beginning at the last entry, as Figure 18-3 shows.

Removing an entry can proceed in the manner shown in Figure 18-2b for an unsorted dictionary. The search for the entry to remove, however, can be done more efficiently, because the entries are sorted.

Retrieving an existing entry requires a search for the entry with the desired search key. Since the array is sorted, you can use a binary search and save time. An iteration, or traversal, of the entries in the dictionary starts with the first element in the array and moves sequentially through the remaining elements.

For this implementation, the worst-case efficiencies of the operations are as follows:

Addition $O(n)$
Removal $O(n)$
Retrieval $O(\log n)$
Traversal $O(n)$

The sorted array-based implementation is suitable for an application that creates a dictionary and then makes many retrievals.

Figure 18-3   Adding an entry to a sorted array-based dictionary: (a) search; (b) make room; (c) insert

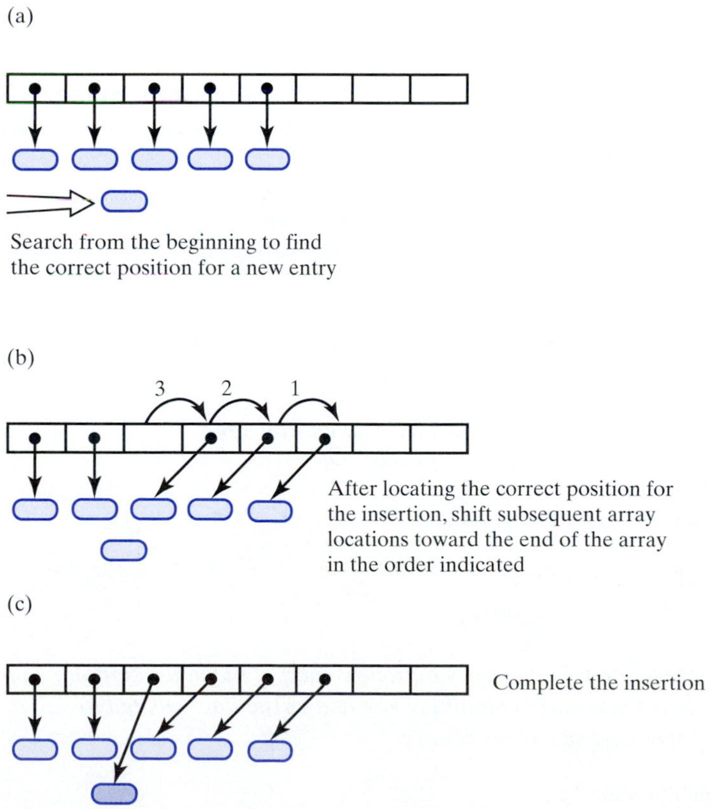

(a)

Search from the beginning to find
the correct position for a new entry

(b)

3   2   1

After locating the correct position for
the insertion, shift subsequent array
locations toward the end of the array
in the order indicated

(c)

Complete the insertion

18.6   **Beginning the implementation.** Our implementation uses one array, as pictured in Figure 18-1a. To avoid a full dictionary, we use an array that doubles in size as necessary. Each entry in the dictionary is an instance of the class `Entry` that you saw in Segment 18.2. The following code shows the beginning of the class `SortedArrayDictionary`:

```java
public class SortedArrayDictionary implements DictionaryInterface,
                                              java.io.Serializable
{
  private Entry[] entries; // array of sorted entries
  private int currentSize = 0; // number of entries
  private final static int DEFAULT_MAX_SIZE = 25;

  public SortedArrayDictionary()
  {
    entries = new Entry[DEFAULT_MAX_SIZE];
    currentSize = 0;
  } // end default constructor

  public SortedArrayDictionary(int maxSize)
  {
    entries = new Entry[maxSize];
    currentSize = 0;
  } // end constructor
  . . .
```

18.7   **Adding an entry.** A sorted dictionary's add method inserts a key-value entry into its proper order by search key. If key did not already exist in the dictionary, the method returns `null`. However, if key is in the dictionary when the method is called, key's corresponding value is replaced with value and the original value is returned. The following algorithm performs these steps:

> *Algorithm* add(key, value)
> // *Adds a new key-value entry to the dictionary and returns* `null`. *If* key *already exists*
> // *in the dictionary, returns the corresponding value and replaces it with* value.
>
> result = **null**
> *Search array until you either find an entry containing* key *or locate the point where it should be*
> **if** (key *is already in dictionary*)
> {
>   result = *value currently associated with* key
>   *Replace* key's *associated value with* value
> }
> **else** // *insert new entry*
> {
>   **if** (*array is full*)
>   *Double size of array*
>
>   *Make room in the array for a new entry at the index determined by the previous search*
>   *Insert new entry containing* key *and* value *into vacated location of the array*
>   *Increment size of dictionary*
> }
> **return** result

We can simplify the implementation of this algorithm by writing several private methods that we specify as follows:

```
/** Task: Returns either the index of the entry that contains key or
 *        the index where such an entry should occur */
private int locateIndex(Object key);

/** Task: Makes room for a new entry at a given index by shifting
 *        array locations. */
private void makeRoom(int index);

/** Task: Doubles the size of the array of entries. */
private void doubleArray();

/** Task: Determines whether the array of entries is full. */
private boolean isArrayFull();
```

The following implementation of the method add invokes these methods:

```
public Object add(Object key, Object value)
{
  Object result = null;

  int keyIndex = locateIndex(key);

  if ( (keyIndex < currentSize)
          && key.equals(entries[keyIndex].getKey()) )
  {
    // key found; return and replace old value
    result = entries[keyIndex].getValue();
    entries[keyIndex].setValue(value);
  }
  else
  {
    if (isArrayFull())
      doubleArray(); // expand array

    makeRoom(keyIndex);
    entries[keyIndex] = new Entry(key, value);
    currentSize++;
  } // end if

  return result;
} // end add
```

18.8   **The private method `locateIndex`.** We implement the private method `locateIndex` by using a sequential search that makes use of the array's sorted order. Recall from Segment 16.8 that a sequential search can determine when an entry is not in a sorted array without searching the entire array. We use that technique here.

```
private int locateIndex(Object key)
{
  // sequential search
  Comparable cKey = (Comparable) key;
  int index = 0;
```

```
    while ( (index < currentSize) &&
                cKey.compareTo(entries[index].getKey()) > 0 )
      index++;

    return index;
  } // end locateIndex
```

We must cast `key` to `Comparable` before it invokes `compareTo`. Making this cast a separate step at the beginning of the method is a way to reduce the number of parentheses in subsequent expressions.

A binary search would be faster, in general, than this modified sequential search—particularly when the dictionary is large. We leave such a revision of `locateIndex` as an exercise. We also leave the rest of the dictionary implementation as an exercise, since it is not difficult once you have reached this point.

 Programming Tip: Often a method's parameter has `Object` as its type and must be cast to another type. Performing this cast in a separate first step of the method can simplify later expressions.

 Question 2   Because the method `locateIndex` is private and so is not in `Dictionary-Interface`, you could change the data type of its parameter `key` to `Comparable`. If you make this change, what other changes would you make to the methods `locateIndex` and `add`?

Vector-Based Implementations

18.9   An implementation that uses an instance of Java's class `Vector` is similar in spirit to an array-based implementation. You can use one or two vectors, much like the one or two arrays pictured in Parts *a* and *b* of Figure 18-1. Since the underlying implementation of the class `Vector` is array based, the algorithms for the dictionary operations and their efficiencies are essentially the same whether you use an array or a vector.

With a vector, you do not need the private methods `makeRoom`, `doubleArray`, and `isArrayFull` that are in the array-based implementation. A vector accommodates the addition of a new entry without any extra effort by the client. A vector also expands as necessary. It automatically increases its size by creating a larger underlying array, just as we did manually in the previous sections with our array-based approach. By default, a vector doubles its size, but you can control the amount of this increase. Lastly, a vector counts its entries, so you do not have to. On the down side, using a vector requires some involved casts.

As an example of how to use a vector to implement a dictionary, we will consider a sorted implementation. The following code shows the beginning of the class `SortedVectorDictionary`:

```
public class SortedVectorDictionary implements DictionaryInterface,
                                                java.io.Serializable
{
  private Vector entries;

  public SortedVectorDictionary()
  {
    entries = new Vector(); // as needed, vector doubles its size
  } // end default constructor
```

```
        public SortedVectorDictionary(int maxSize)
        {
          entries = new Vector(maxSize);
        } // end constructor
        . . .
```

18.10   **The method add.** The implementation of the method add is similar to the one given earlier in Segment 18.7 for the array-based implementation. This version is shorter, since much of the busy work is handled for us by Vector, but we do have to write some casts that become somewhat confusing. You should compare this code with the code given earlier.

Assuming that we have already revised locateIndex from Segment 18.8 to work with vectors, we call it with the statement

```
        int keyIndex = locateIndex(key);
```

where key is the search key of the new entry. We then must see whether key is the same as the search key of the entry at keyIndex. Using Vector's method elementAt, we reference this entry by writing

```
        (Entry)entries.elementAt(keyIndex)
```

Since elementAt returns an instance of Object, a cast to Entry is necessary. To get this entry's search key, we write

```
        ((Entry)entries.elementAt(keyIndex)).getKey()
```

Notice the additional pair of parentheses that is required. This expression is now the argument of the method equals that is invoked by key, the new entry's search key:

```
        key.equals(((Entry)entries.elementAt(keyIndex)).getKey())
```

Ordinarily, we could simplify this expression by first assigning the argument of equals to a local variable, as follows:

```
        Entry currentEntry = (Entry)entries.elementAt(keyIndex);
```

We then could write the expression as

```
        key.equals(currentEntry.getKey())
```

But in our case, we also need to check the size of keyIndex. Thus, we are left with the choice of one messy, long if clause or several awkwardly nested but shorter if statements. We settle for the following implementation of add:

```
        public Object add(Object key, Object value)
        {
          Object result = null;
          int keyIndex = locateIndex(key);

          if ( (keyIndex < entries.size()) &&
               key.equals(((Entry)entries.elementAt(keyIndex)).getKey()))
          {
            // key found; return and replace old value
            Entry currentEntry = (Entry) entries.elementAt(keyIndex);
            result = currentEntry.getValue();
            currentEntry.setValue(value);
          }
          else // add new entry
          {
            Entry newEntry = new Entry(key, value);
            entries.insertElementAt(newEntry, keyIndex);
          } // end if
```

```
    return result;
} // end add
```

18.11   **The private method locateIndex.** To revise locateIndex, as given in Segment 18.8, to work with
a vector instead of an array, we modify the boolean expression in the while statement. This expression invokes compareTo and is similar to the expression we wrote in the previous segment that
involved equals. An additional cast is necessary here because, unlike equals, compareTo is not a
member of Object. Thus, we must cast key to Comparable before it invokes compareTo. As we
have done before, we make this cast in a separate step at the beginning of the method to simplify
expressions occurring later. Thus, the revised method appears as follows:

```
private int locateIndex(Object key)
{
  Comparable cKey = (Comparable)key;
  int currentSize = entries.size();
  int index = 0;

  while ( (index < currentSize) &&
           cKey.compareTo(((Entry)(entries.elementAt(index))).getKey())>0)
    index++;

  return index;
} // end locateIndex
```

You will see one other minor difference between this method and the array version in
Segment 18.8. In the previous version, currentSize is a data field of the dictionary class. Here it
is a local variable set to the vector's size entries.size().

Implementations for the methods remove and getValue are similar to the implementation for
add, and we leave them as exercises.

Linked Implementations

The third and final implementation of the ADT dictionary that we will consider in this chapter
stores the dictionary's entries in a chain of linked nodes.

The Entries

18.12   A chain of linked nodes, as introduced in Chapter 6, also can provide as much storage as necessary
for the entries in a dictionary. You can encapsulate the two parts of an entry into an object, as
Figure 18-4a illustrates, just as you did for an array or vector. If you choose this option, your dictionary class will use the classes Node from Segment 6.22 and Entry from Segment 18.2. Alternately,
you can use two chains, as shown in Figure 18-4b.

A simpler approach is to revise the definition of a node to include both parts of the entry, as
Figure 18-4c illustrates. The private class Node, which should be internal to the dictionary class,
would then contain the following data fields:

```
private Object entryKey;
private Object entryValue;
private Node   next;
```

Figure 18-4   Three possible ways to use linked nodes to represent the entries in a dictionary: (a) a chain of nodes that each reference an entry object; (b) parallel chains of search keys and values; (c) a chain of nodes that each reference a search key and a value

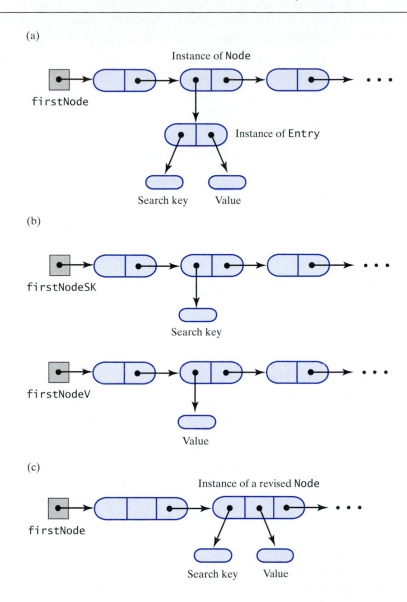

In addition to constructors, the class would contain the methods getKey, getValue, setValue, getNextNode, and setNextNode. Since changing the search key is not necessary and, in fact, could destroy the order of a sorted dictionary, no setKey method is provided.

An Unsorted Linked Dictionary

18.13   Since the entries in an unsorted dictionary are in no particular order, you add a new entry in the most efficient manner. When the entries are in a linked chain, the fastest addition is at the beginning of the chain, as Figure 18-5 shows. (If the class also maintains a tail reference to the last node of the chain, adding an entry after the last node would be equally fast.) Removing or retrieving an entry uses a sequential search from the beginning of the chain. Just as you would for an array, you would have to look at all the search keys in the chain to determine that a particular entry was not present. A traversal of either the search keys or the values in the chain is straightforward. For this implementation, the worst-case efficiencies of the operations are as follows:

Addition O(1)
Removal O(n)
Retrieval O(n)
Traversal O(n)

Like the unsorted array-based implementation, this implementation is suitable for an application that makes many additions to a dictionary and then displays the results.

Figure 18-5 Adding to an unsorted linked dictionary

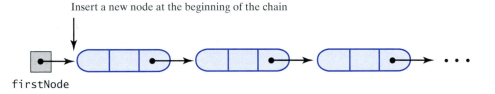

Insert a new node at the beginning of the chain

firstNode

A Sorted Linked Dictionary

18.14   When the nodes are sorted by their search keys, adding a new entry requires a sequential search from the beginning of the chain to determine the correct location for the new node. Removing or retrieving an entry also requires a sequential search of the chain that you use. Since the search keys are sorted, you can determine that a desired search key does not exist in the chain as soon as you pass the node that should have contained it. That is, you do not have to look at the entire chain, as you would if the search keys were unsorted. (Segments 16.8 and 16.21 described this variation of a sequential search.) Traversal of a sorted chain proceeds just as it would for an unsorted chain. Thus, the worst-case efficiencies of the operations are as follows:

Addition O(n)
Removal O(n)
Retrieval O(n)
Traversal O(n)

Although this implementation appears to be the least efficient of the implementations we have considered, it is not the worst implementation. The addition or removal of an entry is an O(n) operation regardless of whether you use an array, a vector, or a chain to implement a sorted dictionary. Realize, however, that an array requires you to shift its elements, whereas a linked chain does not. Also, this linked implementation does not require a good estimate of the dictionary's ultimate size. When you use an array that is too small, you can expand it by copying its elements to a new, larger array. If you use an array that is larger than necessary, you waste space. The same is true if you use a vector, but neither of these situations occur with a linked implementation.

18.15   **Adding an entry.** A sorted dictionary's add method inserts a key-value entry into its proper order by search key. If the key did not already exist in the dictionary, the method returns null. However, if the key is in the dictionary when the method is called, its corresponding value is replaced with value and its original value is returned. The following algorithm performs these steps:

> *Algorithm* add(key, value)
> *// Adds a new key-value entry to the dictionary and returns null. If key already exists*
> *// in the dictionary, returns the corresponding value and replaces it with* value.
>
> *Allocate a new node containing* key *and* value
> result = **null**
> *Search chain until either you find a node containing* key *or you pass the point where*
>   *it should be*
> **if** (key *is already in dictionary*)
> {
>   result = *value currently associated with* key
>   *Replace* key's *associated value with* value
> }
> **else if** (*chain is empty or new node belongs at beginning of chain*)
> {
>   *Add new node to beginning of chain*
>   *Increment length of dictionary*
> }
> **else**
> {
>   *Insert new node before the last node that was examined during the search*
>   *Increment length of dictionary*
> }
> **return** result

The following code shows the beginning of the class SortedLinkedDictionary and the implementation of the method add:

```java
public class SortedLinkedDictionary implements DictionaryInterface,
                                               java.io.Serializable
{
  private int  currentSize; // number of entries
  private Node firstNode;   // reference to first node of chain

  public SortedLinkedDictionary()
  {
    firstNode = null;
    currentSize = 0;
  } // end default constructor

  public Object add(Object key, Object value)
  {
    Object result = null;

    Node newNode = new Node(key, value);  // create new node

    Node currentNode = firstNode;
    Node nodeBefore = null;
```

```
        Comparable cKey = (Comparable) key;

        // search chain until you either find a node containing key
        // or pass the point where it should be
        while ( (currentNode != null)
               && cKey.compareTo(currentNode.getKey()) > 0 )
        {
          nodeBefore = currentNode;
          currentNode = currentNode.getNextNode();
        } // end while

        if ( (currentNode != null) && key.equals(currentNode.getKey()) )
        {
          result = currentNode.getKey();
          currentNode.setValue(value);  // replace value
        }
        // should insertion be at beginning of chain?
        else if (isEmpty() || (nodeBefore == null))
        {
          newNode.setNextNode(firstNode);
          firstNode = newNode;
          currentSize++;
        }
        else // add elsewhere in non-empty list
        {
          newNode.setNextNode(currentNode);
          nodeBefore.setNextNode(newNode);
          currentSize++;
        } // end if

        return result;
    } // end add
    . . .
```

Implementations for the methods remove and getValue are similar to the implementation for add, but are a bit simpler. We leave them as exercises.

18.16 **An iterator for search keys.** Our goal in providing iterators for the dictionary is to give the client an easy way to traverse the search keys and their corresponding values. The interface for the dictionary given in Segment 17.4 specifies two iterators, one for search keys and one for values. In that chapter we showed you how to use these iterators, and here we implement an iterator for the search keys.

Recall that the interface java.util.Iterator specifies the methods hasNext, next, and remove. We can define a class KeyIterator that implements this interface and make the class private and internal to the class SortedLinkedDictionary. We then implement the method getKeyIterator within SortedLinkedDictionary as follows:

```
public Iterator getKeyIterator()
{
  return new KeyIterator();
} // end getKeyIterator
```

The class KeyIterator has the following implementation:

```java
private class KeyIterator implements Iterator
{
  private Node currentNode; // marks current place in iteration

  private KeyIterator()
  {
    currentNode = firstNode;
  } // end default constructor

  public boolean hasNext()
  {
    return currentNode != null;
  } // end hasNext

  public Object next()
  {
    Object result;

    if (hasNext())
    {
      result = currentNode.getKey();
      currentNode = currentNode.getNextNode();
    }
    else
      throw new NoSuchElementException(); // in java.util

    return result;
  } // end next

  public void remove()
  {
    throw new UnsupportedOperationException(); // in java.lang
  } // end remove
} // end KeyIterator
```

Iterator's method remove is not relevant to the traversal of the search keys, so we do not support it. Instead we make remove throw an exception if it is invoked.

You can provide an iterator for the values by defining a second similar class. Exercise 7 at the end of this chapter suggests a way to avoid the redundancy in doing this.

Note: The add method for an unsorted dictionary is more efficient than the one for a sorted dictionary. Thus, an unsorted dictionary is suitable for applications that primarily add items to a dictionary. However, the methods remove and getValue typically are faster when the dictionary is sorted.

CHAPTER SUMMARY

- You can implement a dictionary by using either an array that you expand dynamically, a vector, or a chain of linked nodes. A linked implementation does not require a good estimate of the dictionary's ultimate size. When you use an array that is too small, you need to copy its elements to a new, larger array. If you use an array that is larger than necessary, you waste space. The same is true if you use a vector, but neither of these situations occur with a linked implementation.

- The worst-case efficiencies of the dictionary operations for array-based and linked implementations are as follows:

	Array-Based		Linked	
	Unsorted	Sorted	Unsorted	Sorted
Addition	O(1)	O(n)	O(1)	O(n)
Removal	O(n)	O(n)	O(n)	O(n)
Retrieval	O(n)	O(log n)	O(n)	O(n)
Traversal	O(n)	O(n)	O(n)	O(n)

- For a sorted dictionary, the addition or removal of an entry is an O(n) operation regardless of whether you use an array, a vector, or a chain to implement it. Realize, however, that an array or vector requires the shifting of its elements, whereas a linked chain does not.

- Using either an array or a vector to implement a sorted dictionary allows for an efficient retrieval operation because you can use a binary search.

- To implement the method `getKeyIterator` or `getValueIterator`, define a private class that is internal to the dictionary class. This private class should implement the interface **Iterator** in the package `java.util`.

- When choosing an implementation for an ADT, you should consider the operations that your application requires. If you frequently use a particular operation, you want its implementation to be efficient. Conversely, if you rarely use an operation, you can afford to use a class that has an inefficient implementation of that operation.

PROGRAMMING TIPS

- Include comments in a class's implementation that advertise the efficiencies of its methods.

- Often a method's parameter has **Object** as its type and must be cast to another type. Performing this cast in a separate first step of the method can simplify later expressions.

EXERCISES

1. Begin three array-based implementations of the ADT dictionary according to the three data structures that Figure 18-1 illustrates. Declare the data fields, define the constructors, and define the method add for unsorted data. Use arrays that you can expand during execution.

2. Begin three linked implementations of the ADT dictionary according to the three data structures that Figure 18-4 illustrates. Declare the data fields, define the constructors, and define the method add for unsorted data.

3. In the sorted, array-based implementation of a dictionary, replace the sequential search performed by the method `locateIndex` with a binary search. (See Segment 18.8.)

4. In the sorted, vector-based implementation of a dictionary, replace the sequential search performed by the method `locateIndex` with a binary search. (See Segment 18.11.)

5. For a linked implementation of a dictionary, write iterative versions of the methods `remove` and `getValue`.

6. For a linked implementation of a dictionary, write recursive versions of the methods `add`, `remove`, and `getValue`.

7. Segment 18.16 defines the class `KeyIterator`. An instance of this class is an iterator that traverses the search keys in the dictionary. In a similar fashion, you could define a class `ValueIterator` to provide a way to traverse the dictionary's values. Since these two classes are similar, replace them with one class whose constructor provides a choice of iterators.

8. Define an iterator for the ADT dictionary that returns entries containing both a search key and a value. Implement a method `getEntryIterator` that returns such an iterator.

PROJECTS

1. Implement an unsorted dictionary by using an array that can expand during execution.

2. Implement a sorted dictionary by using an array that can expand during execution.

3. Implement an unsorted dictionary by using an instance of `Vector`.

4. Implement a sorted dictionary by using an instance of `Vector`.

5. Implement an unsorted dictionary by using a chain of linked nodes.

6. Implement a sorted dictionary by using a chain of linked nodes.

7. The ADT dictionary that we discussed in this chapter assumes distinct search keys. Implement a dictionary that removes this restriction. Choose one of the following possibilities:

  a. The method `add` adds an entry whose search key is already in the dictionary but whose value is not. `Remove` deletes all occurrences of the search key. The method `getValue` retrieves all values associated with a search key.
  b. The methods behave as Part *a* describes, but a secondary search key enables `remove` and `getValue` to delete or retrieve a single entry.

8. Segment 17.6 began a discussion of a telephone directory. Use your dictionary implementation from Project 7 in a revision of the telephone directory that allows duplicate names.

9. Figure 18-1 illustrates how you can use either parallel arrays or a two-dimensional array to represent the entries in a dictionary. Implement the ADT dictionary by using one of these approaches.

10. Revise the class `Entry` given in Segment 18.2 so that it is public and implements the interface `Comparable`. You compare two `Entry` objects by comparing their search keys. Using this class and an implementation of the ADT sorted list, write an implementation for a sorted dictionary.

19

Hashing as a Dictionary Implementation

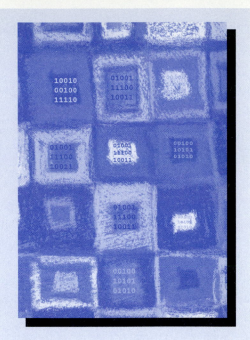

CONTENTS

What Is Hashing?
Hash Functions
    Computing Hash Codes
    Compressing a Hash Code into an Index for the Hash Table
Resolving Collisions
    Open Addressing with Linear Probing
    Open Addressing with Quadratic Probing
    Open Addressing with Double Hashing
    A Potential Problem with Open Addressing
    Separate Chaining
Efficiency
    The Load Factor
    The Cost of Open Addressing
    The Cost of Separate Chaining
Rehashing
Comparing Schemes for Collision Resolution
A Dictionary Implementation That Uses Hashing
    Entries in the Hash Table
    Data Fields and Constructors
    The Methods `getValue`, `remove`, and `add`
    Iterators
Java Class Library: The Class `HashMap`

PREREQUISITES

Chapter	5	List Implementations That Use Arrays
Chapter	6	List Implementations That Link Data
Chapter	8	Java's Iterator Interfaces
Chapter	9	The Efficiency of Algorithms
Chapter	17	Dictionaries
Chapter	18	Dictionary Implementations

OBJECTIVES

After studying this chapter, you should be able to

- Describe the basic idea of hashing
- Describe the purpose of a hash table, a hash function, and a perfect hash function
- Explain why you should override the method `hashCode` for objects that are search keys
- Describe how a hash function compresses a hash code into an index to the hash table
- Explain what collisions are and why they occur
- Describe open addressing as a method to resolve collisions
- Describe linear probing, quadratic probing, and double hashing as particular open addressing schemes
- Describe algorithms for the dictionary operations `getValue`, `add`, and `remove` when open addressing resolves collisions
- Describe separate chaining as a method to resolve collisions
- Describe algorithms for the dictionary operations `getValue`, `add`, and `remove` when separate chaining resolves collisions
- Describe clustering and the problems it causes
- Describe rehashing and why it is necessary
- Describe the relative efficiencies of the various collision resolution techniques
- Describe a hash table's load factor
- Use hashing to implement the ADT dictionary

Because searching databases is such a widespread application of computers, the dictionary is an important abstract data type. The implementations that we discussed in the previous chapter are fine for certain applications, but for others they are inadequate. For example, if locating data is critical, even an O(log n) search can be too slow. Such is the case for the emergency telephone (911) system. If you call 911, your telephone number is the key in a search of a dictionary of street addresses. Obviously, you want this search to find your address immediately!

This chapter explores a technique called hashing that ideally can result in O(1) search times. Hashing can be an excellent choice for implementing a dictionary when searching is the primary task. But as good as hashing can be, it is not always appropriate. For example, hashing cannot provide a traversal of the search keys in sorted order. Later in this book we will consider other implementations of the ADT dictionary.

What Is Hashing?

19.1 **A place for everything; everything in its place.** Do you spend time looking for your keys in the morning? Or do you know exactly where they are? Some of us spend too much time sequentially searching our unsorted possessions. Others have a special place for things and know just where to find each one.

An array can provide a place for a dictionary's entries. Admittedly, arrays have their disadvantages, but you can access any element in an array directly if you know its index. No other array element need be involved. **Hashing** is a technique that determines this index using only an entry's search key, without searching.

A **hash function** takes a search key and produces the integer index of an element in an array called the **hash table.** This array element is where you would either store or look for the search key's associated value. For example, the 911 emergency system can take your telephone number, convert it to a suitable integer *i*, and store a reference to your street address in the array element a[i]. The index that a hash function produces is called a **hash index.**

19.2   **Ideal hashing.** Consider an emergency system for a small town where everyone's telephone number begins with 555. Let the hash function *h* convert a telephone number to its last four digits. For example,

$$h(555\text{-}1214) = 1214$$

If hashTable is the hash table, we would place a reference to the street address associated with this telephone number in hashTable[1214], as Figure 19-1 illustrates. If the cost of evaluating the hash function is low, adding an entry to the array hashTable is an O(1) operation.

Figure 19-1   A hash function indexes its hash table

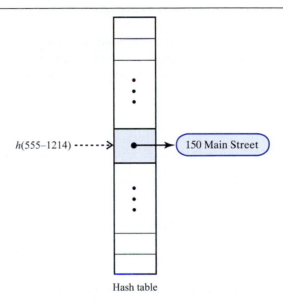

$h(555\text{-}1214)$ ------> • ——> 150 Main Street

Hash table

To later determine the street address associated with the number 555-1214, we once again compute $h(555\text{-}1214)$ and use the result to index hashTable. Thus, from hashTable[1214], we locate the desired street address. This operation also is O(1). Notice that we did not search the array hashTable.

Let's summarize what we know so far by writing simple algorithms for the dictionary operations that add or retrieve entries:

Algorithm **add(key, value)**
index = h(key)
hashTable[index] = value

Algorithm **getValue(key)**
index = h(key)
return hashTable[index]

Will these algorithms always work? We can make them work if we know all the possible search keys. In this example, the search keys range from 555-0000 to 555-9999, so the hash function will produce indices from 0 to 9999. If the array hashTable has 10,000 elements, each telephone number will correspond, or **map,** to one unique element in hashTable. That element references the appropriate street address. This scenario describes the ideal case for hashing, and the hash function here is a **perfect hash function.**

Note: A perfect hash function maps each search key into a different integer that is suitable as an index to the hash table.

19.3   **Typical hashing.** Because we need a database of all street addresses in the previous example, we must have one entry in the hash table for each telephone number. Our perfect hash function needs a hash table this large because it produces 10,000 different indices between 0 and 9999 from the 10,000 possible search keys. This hash table is always full if every telephone number in the 555 exchange is assigned. Although a full hash table is quite reasonable for this application, most hash tables are not full and can even be **sparse**—that is, have only a few of their elements actually in use.

For example, if our small town required only 700 telephone numbers, most of the 10,000-location hash table would be unused. We would waste most of the space allocated to the hash table. If the 700 numbers were not sequential, we would need a different hash function to use a smaller hash table.

We might develop this hash function as follows. Given a nonnegative integer i and a hash table with n locations, the value of i modulo n ranges from 0 to $n - 1$. Recall that i modulo n is the integer remainder after dividing i by n. This value is a valid index for the hash table. So a hash function h for a telephone number could have the following algorithm:

> *Algorithm* getHashIndex(phoneNumber)
> *// Returns an index to an array of* tableSize *locations.*
>
> i = *last four digits of* phoneNumber
> **return** i % tableSize

This hash function—like typical hash functions—performs two steps:

1. Convert the search key to an integer called the **hash code**.
2. **Compress** the hash code into the range of indices for the hash table.

Often the search key is not an integer, and frequently it is a string. So a hash function first converts the key to an integer hash code. Next, it transforms that integer into one that is suitable as an index to the particular hash table.

The hash function that the algorithm getHashIndex describes is not a perfect hash function when tableSize is less than 10,000. Since 10,000 telephone numbers map into tableSize indices, some telephone numbers will map into the same index. We call such an occurrence a **collision.** For example, if tableSize is 101, getHashIndex("555-1214") and getHashIndex("555-8132") each map into 52. If we have already stored the street address for 555-1214 in hashTable[52], as Figure 19-2 shows, what will we do with the address for 555-8132? Handling such collisions is called **collision resolution.** Before we look at collision resolution, we explore hash functions a bit further.

Note: Typical hash functions are not perfect because they can allow more than one search key to map into a single index, causing a collision in the hash table.

Figure 19-2   A collision caused by the hash function h

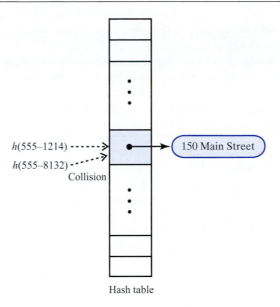

$h(555–1214)$ ┄┄┄→

$h(555–8132)$ ┄┄┄→

Collision

150 Main Street

Hash table

Hash Functions

19.4   **General characteristics.** Any function can be a hash function if it produces an integer that is suitable as an array index. But not every such function is a *good* hash function. Our previous discussions suggest that a good hash function should

- Minimize collisions
- Distribute entries uniformly throughout the hash table
- Be fast to compute

Recall that a typical hash function first converts a search key to an integer hash code. The hash function then compresses the hash code into an integer that is suitable as an index to the particular hash table.

First, consider how to convert a search key to an `int`. Realize that a search key can be either a primitive type or an instance of a class.

Computing Hash Codes

19.5   **The hash code for a class type.** Java's base class `Object` has a method `hashCode` that returns an integer hash code. Since every class is a subclass of `Object`, all classes inherit this method. But unless a class overrides `hashCode`, the method will return an `int` value derived from the invoking object's memory address. This default hash code usually is not appropriate for hashing, because equal but distinct objects will have different hash codes. To be useful as a dictionary implementation, hashing must map equal objects into the same location in a hash table. Thus, a class should define its own version of `hashCode` that adheres to the following guidelines.

Note: Guidelines for the method `hashCode`

- If a class overrides the method `equals`, it should override `hashCode`.
- If the method `equals` considers two objects equal, `hashCode` must return the same value for both objects.
- If an object invokes `hashCode` more than once during the execution of a program, and if the object's data remains the same during this time, `hashCode` must return the same hash code.
- An object's hash code during one execution of a program can differ from its hash code during another execution of the same program.

A perfect hash function would require that unequal objects have distinct hash codes. In general, however, unequal objects might have the same hash codes. Since duplicate hash codes lead to collisions, you want to avoid this situation when possible.

19.6   **The hash code for a string.** Search keys are often strings, so generating a good hash code from a string is important. Typically, you begin by assigning an integer to each character in the string. For example, you could assign the integers 1 through 26 to the letters "A" through "Z" and the integers 27 through 52 to the letters "a" through "z." However, using a character's Unicode integer is more common and actually easier to do.

Suppose that the search keys for a telephone directory are names such as *Brett*, *Carol*, *Gail*, and *Josh*. You can compute hash codes for these names in several ways. For example, you could take the Unicode value of the first letter in each name and get distinct hash codes. But if several names begin with the same letter, their hash codes will be the same if you use this scheme. Since the letters that occur in any one position of a name do not occur with equal probability, a hash function that uses any particular letter will not distribute the names uniformly throughout the hash table.

Suppose that you sum the Unicode values for each letter in the search key. In an application where two different search keys never contain the same letters, this approach can work. But if your search keys are airport codes, for example, *DUB* and *BUD* would have the same hash code. This approach also can restrict the range of the hash codes, since the Unicode values for letters lie between 65 and 122. Thus, three-letter words would map into values between 195 and 366 under this plan.

Note: Real-world data is not uniformly distributed.

19.7   A better approach to generating a hash code from a string multiplies the Unicode value of each character by a factor based on the character's position within the string. The hash code is then the sum of these products. Specifically, if the string s has n characters, and if u_i is the Unicode value for the ith character in s, the hash code can have the form

$$u_0 g^{n-1} + u_1 g^{n-2} + \ldots + u_{n-2} g + u_{n-1}$$

for some positive constant g. This expression is a polynomial in g. To minimize the number of arithmetic operations, write the polynomial in the following algebraically equivalent form:

$$(\ldots((u_0 g + u_1) g + u_2) g + \ldots + u_{n-2}) g + u_{n-1}$$

This way of evaluating a polynomial is called **Horner's method.**

The following Java statements perform this computation for the string s and the int constant g:

```
int hash = 0;
int n = s.length();
for (int i = 0; i < n; i++)
    hash = g * hash + s.charAt(i);
```

The ith character of the string is s.charAt(i). Adding this expression actually adds the character's Unicode value. An explicit cast of s.charAt(i) to int is not necessary and would not affect the result.

This computation can cause an overflow, particularly for long strings. Java ignores these overflows and, for an appropriate choice of g, the result will be a reasonable hash code. Current implementations of the method hashCode in Java's class String use this computation with 31 as the value of g. Realize, however, that the overflows can produce a negative result. You can deal with that when you compress the hash code into an appropriate index for the hash table.

19.8   **The hash code for a primitive type.** This segment contains Java operations that might be unfamiliar to you. However, they are not essential to the rest of this chapter.

If the search key's data type is int, you can use the key itself as the hash code. If the search key is an instance of either byte, short, or char, you can cast it to an int to get a hash code. Thus, casting to an int is one way to generate a hash code.

For other primitive types, you manipulate their internal binary representations. If the search key is an integer of type long, it contains 64 bits. An int has 32 bits. Simply casting the 64-bit search key to an int—or performing a modulo 2^{32}—would lose its first 32 bits. As a result, all keys that differ in only their first 32 bits will have the same hash code and collide. For this reason, ignoring part of a search key can be a problem.

> **Note:**   Derive the hash code from the *entire* search key. Do not ignore part of it.

Instead of ignoring a part of a long search key, divide it into several pieces. Then combine the pieces by using either addition or a bit-wise boolean operation such as **exclusive or.** This process is called **folding.**

For example, let's divide a long search key into two 32-bit halves. To get the left half, we can **shift** the search key to the right by a certain number of bits, or places. For example, if we shift the 8-bit binary number 10101100 to the right by 4 bits, we will get 00001010. We have isolated the number's left half and discarded its right half. If we now combine 00001010 with the original value and ignore the left half of the result, we will effectively have combined the left and right halves of the original key.

Now let's see how to do this in Java. The expression key >> 32 shifts the 64-bit key to the right by 32 bits, in effect eliminating its right half. Java's exclusive-or operator is ^ and has the following effect on one-bit quantities:

0 ∧ 0 is 0
1 ∧ 1 is 0
0 ∧ 1 is 1
1 ∧ 0 is 1

For two multibit quantities, the operator combines pairs of corresponding bits. So

1100 ∧ 1010 is 0110

Thus, the expression key ∧ (key >> 32) uses an exclusive-or operation to combine the halves of a 64-bit key. Although the result has 64 bits, the rightmost 32 bits contain the combined halves of key. We discard the leftmost 32 bits by casting the result to an int. Thus, the necessary computation is

```
(int)(key ^ (key >> 32))
```

We can perform a similar computation for a search key of type double. Since key is a real value, we cannot use it in the previous expression. Instead, we must get key's bit pattern by calling Double.doubleToLongBits(key). Thus, the following statements produce the desired hash code:

```
long bits = Double.doubleToLongBits(key);
int hashCode = (int)(bits ^ (bits >> 32));
```

Why not simply cast the search key from double to int? Since the search key is a real value, casting it to an int will simply give us the integral portion of the value. For example, if the key's value is 32.98, casting it to int results in the integer 32. While we could use 32 as the hash code, all search keys that have 32 as their integer portion also would have a hash code of 32. Unless you know that your real values have distinct integral portions, casting them to an int can cause many collisions.

The hash code of a search key of type float can be simply its 32 bits. You get these by calling Float.floatToIntBits(key).

These computations of hash codes for the primitives types are actually used by the corresponding wrapper classes in their implementations of the method hashCode.

Compressing a Hash Code into an Index for the Hash Table

19.9 The most common way to scale an integer so that it lies within a given range of values is to use modulo arithmetic—that is, Java's % operator. For a positive hash code c and a positive integer n, $c \% n$ divides c by n and takes the remainder as the result. This remainder lies between 0 and $n - 1$. Thus, $c \% n$ is ideal for the index of a hash table that has n locations.

So n should equal the size of the hash table, but not any n will do. For example, if n is even, $c \% n$ has the same parity as c—that is, if c is even, $c \% n$ is even; if c is odd, $c \% n$ is odd. If the hash codes are biased toward either even or odd values (and note that hash codes based on memory addresses are typically even), the indices to the hash table will have the same bias. Instead of a uniform distribution of indices, you will leave out the indices of many table locations if n is even. Thus, n—the size of the hash table—should always be an odd number.

When n is a prime number—one that is divisible only by 1 and itself—$c \% n$ provides values that are distributed throughout the index range 0 through $n - 1$. Prime numbers—with the exception of 2—are odd.

Note: The size of a hash table should be a prime number n. Then, if you compress a positive hash code c into an index for the table by using $c \% n$, the indices will be distributed uniformly between 0 and $n - 1$.

One final detail remains. You saw earlier that the method hashCode might return a negative integer, so you need to be a bit careful. If c is negative, $c \% n$ lies between $1 - n$ and 0. A zero result is fine, but if $c \% n$ is negative, add n to it so that it lies between 1 and $n - 1$.

19.10   We now can implement a hash function for the ADT dictionary. The following method computes the hash index for a given search key, where the data field hashTable is the array that serves as the hash table. Realize that hashTable.length is the size of the array, not the number of current entries in the hash table. We assume that this size is a prime number and that the method hashCode returns a hash code consistent with the previous discussion.

```
private int getHashIndex(Object key)
{
  int hashIndex = key.hashCode() % hashTable.length;
  if (hashIndex < 0)
    hashIndex = hashIndex + hashTable.length;

  return hashIndex;
} // end getHashIndex
```

Resolving Collisions

19.11   When adding to a dictionary, if your hash function maps a search key into a location in the hash table that is already in use, you need to find another spot for the search key's value. You have two fundamental choices:

● Use another location in the hash table
● Change the structure of the hash table so that each array location can represent more than one value

Finding an unused, or open, location in the hash table is called **open addressing.** This choice sounds simple, but it can lead to several complications. Changing the structure of the hash table usually is a better choice for resolving collisions than using an open addressing scheme, but it does require more memory. We will examine both approaches, beginning with several variations of open addressing.

Open Addressing with Linear Probing

19.12   When a collision occurs during the addition of an entry to a hash table, an open addressing scheme locates an alternate location in the hash table that is available, or open. You then use this location to reference the new entry.

Locating an open location in the hash table is called **probing,** and various probing techniques are possible. With **linear probing,** if a collision occurs at hashTable[k], we determine whether hashTable[k+1] is available. If not, we look at hashTable[k+2], and so on. The table locations that we consider in this search make up the **probe sequence.** If a probe sequence reaches the end of the hash table, it continues at the beginning of the table. Thus, we treat the hash table as if it were circular: The first location in the table comes immediately after the last location.

Note: **Linear probing** resolves a collision during hashing by examining consecutive locations in the hash table, beginning at the original hash index and locating the next available location.

19.13   **Additions that collide.** Recall the example illustrated in Figure 19-2. The search keys 555-1214 and 555-8132 both mapped into the index 52. Suppose that 555-4294 and 555-2072 also map into that same index, and we make the following additions to an empty dictionary addressBook:

```
addressBook.add("555-1214", "150 Main Street");
addressBook.add("555-8132", "75 Center Court");
addressBook.add("555-4294", "205 Ocean Road");
addressBook.add("555-2072", "82 Campus Way");
```

The first addition would use hashTable[52]. The second addition would find hashTable[52] occupied, and so it would probe ahead and use hashTable[53]. The third addition would find both hashTable[52] and hashTable[53] occupied, and so it would probe ahead and use hashTable[54]. Finally, the fourth addition would probe with indices 52, 53, and 54 before using hashTable[55] for the addition. Figure 19-3 shows the result of these additions to the hash table.

Figure 19-3   The effect of linear probing after adding four entries whose search keys hash to the same index

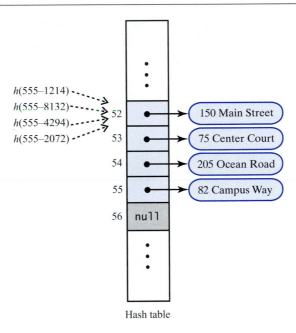

Hash table

Now how do we retrieve the street address associated with the search key 555-2072? That is, if the statement

```
String streetAddress = addressBook.getValue("555-2072");
```

is executed, what will getValue do? Since getHashIndex("555-2072") is 52, getValue will search consecutive locations in the array beginning at hashTable[52] until it finds the street address associated with the search key 555-2072. But wait! How can we tell which street address is the right one? We can't, unless we package a search key with its value. Segment 18.2 provided a class Entry that we could use for this purpose. Figure 19-4 shows the hash table given in Figure 19-3 after we make this revision.

Figure 19-4   A revision of the hash table shown in Figure 19-3 when linear probing resolves collisions;
each entry contains a search key and its associated value

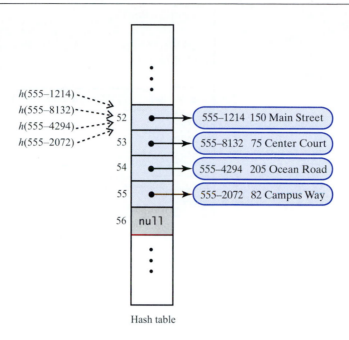

Hash table

Now the search for 555-2072 can follow the same probe sequence that was used to add this search key and its value to the hash table. This fact will be useful later when we assess the efficiency of hashing.

   Note: A successful search for an entry that corresponds to a given search key follows the same probe sequence used to add the entry to the hash table.

Now suppose that the search key is not in the hash table. The search of the probe sequence would encounter a `null` location, indicating an unsuccessful search. But before we can reach this conclusion, we need to know what the `remove` method does, because it has the potential to adversely affect subsequent retrievals.

19.14   **Removals.** Suppose that after the four additions illustrated in Figure 19-4, we removed two entries by executing

```
addressBook.remove("555-8132");
addressBook.remove("555-4294");
```

The simplest way to remove an entry from an array location is to place `null` in the location. Figure 19-5 shows the hash table after `remove` places `null` into `hashTable[53]` and `hash-Table[54]`. But now an attempt to find the search key 555-2072 will terminate unsuccessfully at `hashTable[53]`. Although a location in the hash table that was never used should end a search, a location that had been used and is now available again for use should not.

Figure 19-5   A hash table if `remove` used `null` to remove entries

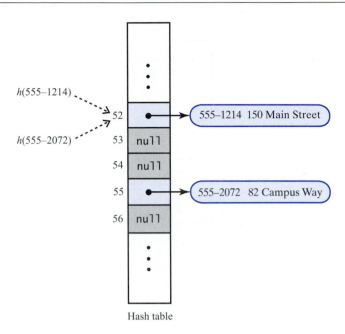

Thus, we need to distinguish among three kinds of locations in the hash table:

- Occupied—the location references an entry in the dictionary
- Empty—the location contains `null` and always did
- Available—the location's entry was removed from the dictionary

Accordingly, the method `remove` should not place `null` into the hash table, but instead should encode the location as available. The search of a probe sequence during a retrieval should then continue if it encounters an available location and should stop only if it is successful or reaches a `null` location. A search during a removal behaves in the same way.

Question 1   Suggest ways to implement the three states of a location in a hash table. Should this state be a responsibility of the location or of the dictionary entry that it references?

19.15   **Reusing locations in the hash table during an addition.** Recall the hash table pictured in Figure 19-4. The entry whose search key is 555-2072 mapped into `hashTable[52]` but was added to the hash table at `hashTable[55]` due to collisions. Figure 19-6a shows this hash table again, but in a simpler form. The four occupied locations constitute a probe sequence; the other locations contain `null`. Since the search key 555-2072 maps into the first location of the probe sequence but actually occurs in the fourth location, a brief sequential search will find it.

Now let's try removing the middle two entries of the probe sequence, as Figure 19-6b shows. A search for 555-2072 starts at the beginning of the probe sequence, must continue beyond the removed entries, and stops successfully at the last location in the probe sequence. If 555-2072 does not occur in this last location, the search will end unsuccessfully at the next location, since it contains `null`. Figure 19-6c illustrates these searches.

Finally, consider what happens when we add an entry that maps into this probe sequence. For example, the search key 555-1062 maps into hashTable[52]. The add operation first must determine whether this search key is in the hash table already. To do so, it searches the probe sequence. It has to search the entire probe sequence and reach a null location to discover that 555-1062 is not in the table. Figure 19-6d shows that this search ends at hashTable[56]. Should add place the new entry in this location? It could, but that would fill the hash table faster than if add reused a location that is presently in the available state. Two such locations are at the indices 53 and 54. We should place the new entry at hashTable[53]—that is, closest to the beginning of the probe sequence—so we can find it more quickly later. Figure 19-6e illustrates the hash table after this addition.

Figure 19-6   A linear probe sequence (a) after adding an entry; (b) after removing two entries; (c) after a search; (d) during the search while adding an entry; (e) after an addition to a formerly occupied location

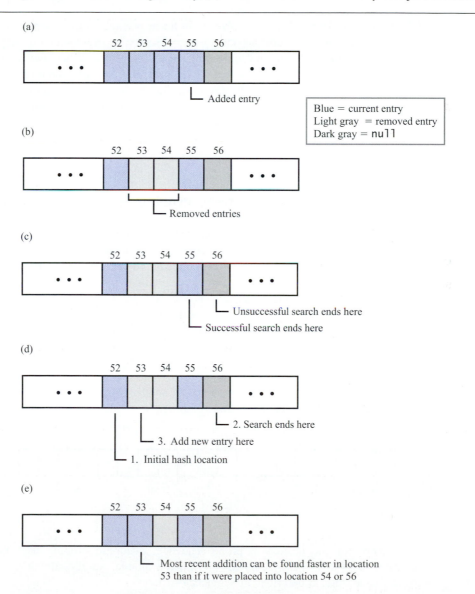

Note: **Searches that dictionary operations require when open addressing resolves collisions**

- To retrieve an entry, getValue(key) searches the probe sequence for key. It examines entries that are present and ignores locations that are in the available state. The search stops when either key is found or null is reached.
- The operation remove(key) searches the probe sequence using the same logic as a retrieval. If it finds key, it marks the location as available.
- The operation add(key, value) searches the probe sequence using logic like that of a retrieval, but it also notes the index of the first location encountered that is in the available state. The operation uses this location for a new entry if key is not found.

19.16   **Clustering.** Collisions that are resolved with linear probing cause groups of consecutive locations in the hash table to be occupied. Each group, or **cluster,** is actually a probe sequence that you must search when adding, removing, or retrieving a table entry. When few collisions occur, probe sequences remain short and can be searched rapidly. But any collision during an addition increases the size of the cluster. Larger clusters mean longer search times following a collision. As the clusters grow in size, they can merge into larger clusters, compounding the problem. This phenomenon can place many entries in one part of the hash table while another part is relatively empty. Clustering due to linear probing is called **primary clustering.**

Open Addressing with Quadratic Probing

19.17   You can avoid primary clustering by changing the probe sequence that you use to resolve a collision. As we discussed in the previous section, if a given search key hashes to index k, linear probing looks at the consecutive locations beginning at index k. **Quadratic probing,** on the other hand, considers the locations at indices $k + j^2$ for $j \geq 0$—that is, it uses the indices $k, k + 1, k + 4, k + 9$, and so on. As before, if the probe sequence reaches the end of the hash table, it wraps around to the beginning of the table. This open addressing scheme separates the entries in the probe sequence beyond the first two. In fact, this separation increases as the sequence grows in length. Figure 19-7 highlights the locations in a hash table that form one such probe sequence of five entries.

Figure 19-7   A probe sequence of length five using quadratic probing

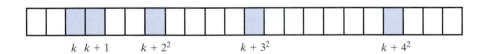

$$k \quad k + 1 \qquad k + 2^2 \qquad\qquad k + 3^2 \qquad\qquad\qquad k + 4^2$$

Except for the change in probe sequence, quadratic probing uses the three states that Segment 19.14 describes: occupied, empty, and available. Additionally, it reuses table locations in the available state, as described in Segment 19.15.

Although quadratic probing avoids primary clustering, it can lead to a different kind of clustering called **secondary clustering.** However, secondary clustering is usually not a serious problem.

An advantage of linear probing is that it can reach every location in the hash table. This property is important since it guarantees the success of the add operation when the hash table is not full. Quadratic probing can make the same guarantee for the add operation, if the hash table is at most half full and its size is a prime number. (See Exercise 8.)

Quadratic probing requires more effort to compute the indices for the probe sequence than does linear probing. Exercise 2 at the end of this chapter shows how to compute these indices without multiplications or divisions.

Note: **Quadratic probing**

- Resolves a collision during hashing by examining locations in the hash table at the original hash index plus j^2, for $j \geq 0$
- Reaches half of the locations in the hash table if the size of the table is a prime number
- Avoids primary clustering but can lead to secondary clustering

Open Addressing with Double Hashing

19.18   Beginning at the original hash index k, both linear probing and quadratic probing add increments to k to determine a probe sequence. These increments—1 for linear probing and j^2 for quadratic probing—are independent of the search key. **Double hashing** uses a second hash function to compute these increments in a key-dependent way. Thus, double hashing avoids both primary and secondary clustering.

Double hashing, like other open addressing schemes, should produce a probe sequence that reaches the entire table. Such will be the case if the size of the hash table is a prime number. (See Exercise 9 at the end of this chapter.) The second hash function must be different from the original hash function and must never have a zero value, since zero is not an appropriate increment.

19.19   **Example.** For example, consider the following pair of hash functions for a hash table whose size is 7:

$h_1(key) = key$ modulo 7

$h_2(key) = 5 - key$ modulo 5

This hash table is unusually small, but it allows us to study the behavior of the probe sequence. For a search key of 16, we have

$h_1(16) = 2$

$h_2(16) = 4$

The probe sequence begins at 2 and probes locations at increments of 4, as Figure 19-8 illustrates. Remember that when probing reaches the end of the table, it continues at the table's beginning. The table locations in the probe sequence then have the following indices: 2, 6, 3, 0, 4, 1, 5, 2, …. This sequence reaches all locations in the table and then repeats itself. Notice that the table size, 7, is a prime number.

Figure 19-8   The first three locations in a probe sequence generated by double hashing for the search key 16

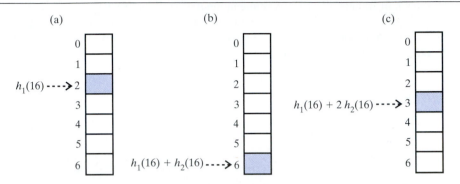

(a)   (b)   (c)

$h_1(16)$ ---→ 2

$h_1(16) + h_2(16)$ ---→ 6

$h_1(16) + 2\,h_2(16)$ ---→ 3

What happens if we change the size of the table to 6 and use the hash functions

$h_1(key) = key$ modulo 6
$h_2(key) = 5 - key$ modulo 5

For a search key of 16, we have

$h_1(16) = 4$
$h_2(16) = 4$

The probe sequence begins at 4 and probes locations at increments of 4. The sequence's indices are then 4, 2, 0, 4, 2, 0, …. The probe sequence does not reach all table locations before it begins to repeat. Notice that the table size, 6, is not prime.

Note: Double hashing

- Resolves a collision during hashing by examining locations in the hash table at the original hash index plus an increment determined by using a second hash function. The second hash function should
  - Differ from the first hash function
  - Depend on the search key
  - Have a nonzero value
- Reaches every location in the hash table, if the size of the table is a prime number
- Avoids both primary clustering and secondary clustering

A Potential Problem with Open Addressing

19.20   The previous three open addressing schemes for collision resolution assume that each table location is in one of three states: occupied, empty, or available. Recall that only empty locations contain null. Frequent additions and removals can cause every location in the hash table to reference either a current entry or a former entry. That is, a hash table might contain only a few dictionary entries yet have no location that contains null. If this happens, our approach to searching a probe sequence will not work. Instead, every unsuccessful search can end only after considering every location in the hash table. Also, detecting the end of the search will be somewhat more involved and costly than simply looking for null.

You should safeguard your implementation against this failure. Increasing the size of the hash table (see Segment 19.29) can correct the problem, if you detect it in time. Separate chaining—which we consider next—does not have this problem.

Separate Chaining

19.21   A second general approach to collision resolution alters the structure of the hash table so that each location can represent more than one value. Such a location is called a **bucket.** Anytime a new search key maps into a particular location, you simply place the key and its associated value in the bucket, much as we did with open addressing. To find a value, you hash the search key, locate the bucket, and look through the key-value pairs in it. In all likelihood, the bucket contains few values, so this mini-search will be fast. When you remove an entry, you find it in its bucket and delete it. Thus, the entry no longer exists in the hash table.

What can you use to represent a bucket? A list, a sorted list, a chain of linked nodes, an array, or a vector are some possibilities with which you are familiar. Anything that involves an array or vector will cause a substantial memory overhead, since each location in the hash table will have a fixed amount of memory allocated to it. Much of this memory will be unused. Either a linked implementation of a list or a chain of linked nodes is a reasonable choice for a bucket, since memory is allocated to the bucket only as needed. Figure 19-9 illustrates a hash table with linked chains as buckets. In this arrangement, each location in the hash table is a head reference to a chain of linked nodes that make up the bucket. Each node contains references to a search key, to the key's associated value, and to the next node in the chain. Notice that a node must reference the search key so that you can locate it later when you search the chain. Resolving collisions by using buckets that are linked chains is called **separate chaining.**

Figure 19-9   A hash table for use with separate chaining; each bucket is a chain of linked nodes

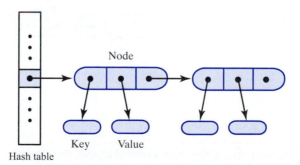

19.22   If your dictionary allows duplicate search keys, adding a new entry to the beginning of the appropriate chain is fastest, as Figure 19-10a indicates. However, if you want distinct search keys, adding a new entry requires you to search a chain for the search key. If you do not find it, you will be at the end of the chain, where you can add the new entry. Figure 19-10b illustrates this case. But since you have to search the chain anyway, you could maintain the chain in sorted order by search key, as Figure 19-10c shows. Subsequent searches would then be a little faster. As you will see, however, typical chains are short, so this refinement might not be worth the effort.

Figure 19-10 Where a new entry is inserted into a linked bucket when the integer search keys are
(a) duplicate and unsorted; (b) distinct and unsorted; (c) distinct and sorted

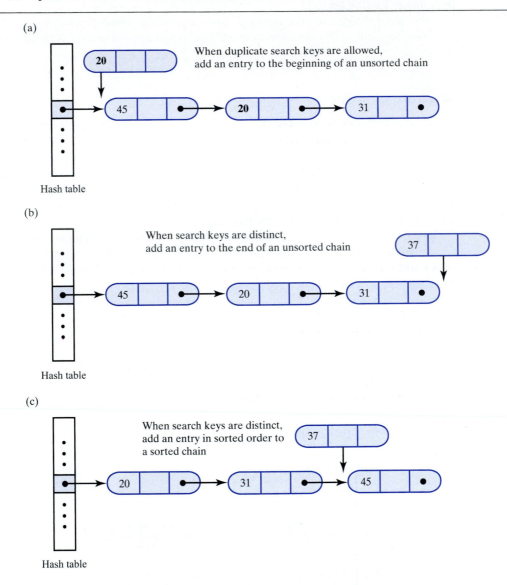

With distinct search keys and unsorted chains, the algorithms for the dictionary's add, remove, and getValue methods are as follows:

```
Algorithm add(key, value)
index = getHashIndex(key)
if (hashTable[index] == null)
{
    hashTable[index] = new Node(key, value)
    currentSize++
    return null
}
```

```
else
{
    Search chain that begins at hashTable[index] for a node that contains key
    if (key is found)
    { // assume currentNode references the node that contains key
        oldValue = currentNode.getValue()
        currentNode.setValue(value)
        return oldValue
    }
    else // add new node to end of chain
    { // assume nodeBefore references the last node
        newNode = new Node(key, value)
        nodeBefore.setNextNode(newNode)
        currentSize++
        return null
    }
```

***Algorithm* remove(key)**
```
index = getHashIndex(key)
```
Search chain that begins at hashTable[index] *for node that contains* key
```
if (key is found)
{
```
   Remove node that contains key *from chain*
```
    currentSize--
    return value in removed node
}
else
    return null
```

***Algorithm* getValue(key)**
```
index = getHashIndex(key)
```
Search chain that begins at hashTable[index] *for node that contains* key
```
if (key is found)
    return value in found node
else
    return null
```

All three operations search a chain of nodes. Each chain should contain only a few entries, if the hash table is sufficiently large and the hash function distributes the entries uniformly throughout the table. Thus, these operations should be time efficient. For a dictionary of n entries, the operations certainly are faster than O(n). In the worst case, however, all entries are in one chain, so the efficiency degenerates to O(n). We will discuss the efficiency of hashing in more detail later in this chapter.

Note: **Separate chaining** provides an efficient and simple way to resolve collisions. Because the structure of the hash table is altered, however, separate chaining requires more memory than open addressing.

Question 2 With distinct search keys and separate chaining with sorted chains, write an algorithm for the dictionary's add method.

Question 3 With distinct search keys and separate chaining with sorted chains, can you implement an iteration of the search keys in sorted order? Explain.

Efficiency

19.23   As you saw in the previous chapter, implementations of the ADT dictionary depend on whether the dictionary requires distinct search keys. In this section, we consider only dictionaries with distinct search keys. Recall that the add method for such a dictionary must ensure that duplicate search keys do not occur.

Each of the dictionary operations getValue, remove, and add search the hash table for a given search key. The success or failure of a search for a given key directly affects the success or failure of the retrieval and removal operations. The successful addition of a new entry occurs after a search for a given key fails. An unsuccessful addition replaces the value of an existing entry instead of adding a new entry. This operation occurs after a successful search for a given key. Thus, we have the following observations about the time efficiency of these operations:

- A successful retrieval or removal has the same efficiency as a successful search
- An unsuccessful retrieval or removal has the same efficiency as an unsuccessful search
- A successful addition has the same efficiency as an unsuccessful search
- An unsuccessful addition has the same efficiency as a successful search

So it is sufficient to analyze the time efficiency of searching the hash table for a given search key.

Note: The successful retrieval of an entry searches the same chain or probe sequence that was searched when the entry was first added to the hash table. Thus, the cost of a successful retrieval of an entry is the same as the cost of inserting that entry.

The Load Factor

19.24   We began this chapter with a perfect hash function that caused no collisions. If you can find a perfect hash function for your particular set of search keys, using it to implement the ADT dictionary will provide operations that are each O(1). Such an implementation is ideal. The good news is that finding a perfect hash function is quite feasible in certain situations. Unfortunately, using a perfect hash function is not always possible or practical. For those situations, collisions are likely to occur.

Resolving a collision takes time and thus causes the dictionary operations to be slower than an O(1) operation. As a hash table fills, collisions occur more often, so we expect performance to decrease even further. Since collision resolution takes considerably more time than evaluating the hash function, it is the prime contributor to the cost of hashing.

To help us express this cost, we define a measure of how full a hash table is. The **load factor** λ is the ratio of the size of the dictionary to the size of the hash table. That is,

$$\lambda = \frac{\textit{Number of entries in the dictionary}}{\textit{Number of locations in the hash table}}$$

Notice that λ is zero when the dictionary—and hence the hash table—is empty. The maximum value of λ depends on the type of collision resolution you use. For open addressing schemes, λ is 1 when the hash table is full, because each entry in the dictionary uses one location in the hash table. Notice that λ does not measure the number of locations in the available state. For separate chaining, the number of entries in the dictionary can exceed the size of the hash table, so λ has no maximum value.

The Cost of Open Addressing

19.25   Recall that all open addressing schemes use one location in the hash table per entry in the dictionary. The dictionary operations `getValue`, `remove`, and `add` each require a search of the probe sequence indicated by both the search key and the collision resolution scheme in effect. Analyzing the efficiency of these searches is sufficient.

For each open addressing scheme that we considered earlier, we will state the number of comparisons necessary to locate a search key in the hash table. We express these numbers in terms of the load factor λ. The derivations of these numbers are messy at best and in some cases difficult, so we omit them. Interpreting the results, however, is straightforward. Recall that for open addressing, λ ranges from 0, when the table is empty, to 1 when it is full.

19.26   **Linear probing.** When you use linear probing, more collisions will likely occur as the hash table fills. After a collision, you search a probe sequence that forms a cluster. If you add a new entry, the cluster grows in size. So you would expect the probe sequences to grow and, therefore, require longer search times. In fact, the average number of comparisons needed to search the probe sequence for a given search key is about

$$\frac{1}{2}\left\{1 + \frac{1}{(1-\lambda)^2}\right\} \quad \text{for an unsuccessful search and}$$

$$\frac{1}{2}\left\{1 + \frac{1}{(1-\lambda)}\right\} \quad \text{for a successful search}$$

After evaluating these expressions for a few values of λ, we get the results in Figure 19-11. As λ increases—that is, as the hash table fills—the number of comparisons for these searches increases. This result satisfies our initial intuition. For example, when the hash table is half full—that is, when λ is 0.5—an average unsuccessful search requires about 2.5 comparisons and an average successful search requires about 1.5 comparisons. As λ increases beyond 0.5, the number of comparisons for an unsuccessful search increases much more rapidly than for a successful search. Thus, performance degrades rapidly when the hash table is more than half full. Should this happen, you'd need to define a larger hash table, as we describe a bit later in this chapter in the section "Rehashing."

Note: The performance of hashing with linear probing degrades significantly as the load factor λ increases. To maintain reasonable efficiency, the hash table should be less than half full. That is, keep $\lambda < 0.5$.

Figure 19-11   The average number of comparisons required by a search of the hash table for given values of the load factor λ when using linear probing

λ	Unsuccessful Search	Successful Search
0.1	1.1	1.1
0.3	1.5	1.2
0.5	2.5	1.5
0.7	6.1	2.2
0.9	50.5	5.5

19.27 **Quadratic probing and double hashing.** Secondary clustering as a result of quadratic probing is not as serious as the primary clustering that occurs when you use linear probing. Here, the average number of comparisons needed to search the probe sequence for a given search key is about

$$\frac{1}{(1-\lambda)} \quad \text{for an unsuccessful search and}$$

$$\frac{1}{\lambda} \log\left(\frac{1}{1-\lambda}\right) \quad \text{for a successful search}$$

Figure 19-12 evaluates these expressions for the same values of λ that we used for linear probing. Notice that the number of comparisons for an unsuccessful search grows with λ more rapidly than for a successful search. The degradation in performance as λ increases is not as severe as with linear probing. Even so, you still want $\lambda < 0.5$ to maintain efficiency.

Even though double hashing avoids the clustering of linear probing and quadratic probing, the estimate of its efficiency is the same as for quadratic probing.

 Note: If you use quadratic probing or double hashing, the hash table should be less than half full. That is, λ should be less than 0.5.

Figure 19-12 The average number of comparisons required by a search of the hash table for given values of the load factor λ when using either quadratic probing or double hashing

λ	Unsuccessful Search	Successful Search
0.1	1.1	1.1
0.3	1.4	1.2
0.5	2.0	1.4
0.7	3.3	1.7
0.9	10.0	2.6

The Cost of Separate Chaining

19.28 With separate chaining as the collision resolution strategy, each entry in the hash table can reference a chain of linked nodes. The number of such chains, including empty ones, is then the size of the hash table. Thus, the load factor λ is the number of dictionary entries divided by the number of chains. That is, λ is the average number of dictionary entries per chain. Since this number is an average, we expect some chains to contain fewer than λ entries—or even none—and some to have more. We assume that the chains are not sorted; remember that we are considering only dictionaries with distinct search keys.

The dictionary operations getValue, remove, and add each require a search of the chain indicated by the search key. As was the case for open addressing, analyzing the efficiency of these searches is sufficient. Again, we will state the number of comparisons necessary to locate a search key in the hash table in terms of the load factor λ.

An unsuccessful search of a hash table sometimes will encounter an empty chain, so that operation is O(1) and would be the best case. But for the average case when the chains are not sorted, searching for an entry in the hash table without success examines λ nodes. In contrast, a successful search always inspects a chain that is not empty. In addition to seeing that the table location at the hash index is not `null`, an average successful search considers a chain of λ nodes and locates the desired entry after looking at $\lambda/2$ of them. Thus, the average number of comparisons during a search when separate chaining is used is about

λ for an unsuccessful search

$1 + \lambda/2$ for a successful search

After evaluating these expressions for a few values of λ, we get the results in Figure 19-13. The number of comparisons for these searches increases only slightly as λ increases—that is, as the hash table fills. A typical upper bound for λ is 1, as smaller values do not provide significantly better performance. Notice the unusual result: Successful searches take more time than unsuccessful searches when $\lambda < 2$.

Remember that these results are for the average case. In the worst case, all search keys map into the same table location. Thus, all entries occur in the same chain of nodes. The worst-case search time, then, is O(n), where n is the number of entries.

 Note: The average performance of hashing with separate chaining does not degrade significantly as the load factor λ increases. To maintain reasonable efficiency, you should keep $\lambda < 1$.

Figure 19-13 The average number of comparisons required by a search of the hash table for given values of the load factor λ when using separate chaining

λ	Unsuccessful Search	Successful Search
0.1	0.1	1.1
0.3	0.3	1.2
0.5	0.5	1.3
0.7	0.7	1.4
0.9	0.9	1.5
1.1	1.1	1.6
1.3	1.3	1.7
1.5	1.5	1.8
1.7	1.7	1.9
1.9	1.9	2.0
2.0	2.0	2.0

 Note: The load factor

Collisions and their resolution typically cause the load factor λ to increase and the efficiency of the dictionary operations to decrease. To maintain efficiency, you should restrict the size of λ as follows:

$\lambda < 0.5$ for open addressing

$\lambda < 1.0$ for separate chaining

Should the load factor exceed these bounds, you must increase the size of the hash table, as the next section describes.

Rehashing

19.29   The previous section discussed the efficiency of hashing as a dictionary implementation when using various ways of resolving collisions. As you saw, to ensure an efficient implementation, you must not let the load factor λ get too large. You can readily compute λ and determine whether it exceeds a certain upper limit as indicated by the particular collision resolution scheme. In particular, λ should be less than 0.5 for open addressing schemes or 1.0 for separate chaining.

So what do you do when λ reaches its limit? First, you can expand the array that serves as the hash table, as described in Chapter 5. Typically, you double the size of an ordinary array, but here you need to ensure that the array's size is a prime number. Expanding the array's size to a prime number that is at least twice its previous size is not too difficult.

Ordinarily, when you expand an array, the next step is to copy the contents of the original array into corresponding locations of the new array. This is not the case for a hash table, however. Since you have changed the size of the hash table, the compression function $c \% n$ will compute different indices than it did for the original hash table. For example, if the hash table originally contained 101 locations, the hash code 505 would have compressed to the index 0. The new hash table will contain 211 locations, since 211 is the smallest prime number greater than 2 times 101. But now 505 compresses to the index 83. You cannot simply copy the location at index 0 from the original table to the location at index 0 in the new table. And you cannot copy it to the location at index 83 in the new table, because you also need to consider collisions.

After creating a new larger hash table of an appropriate size, you use the method add to add each item in the original hash table to the new table. The method computes the hash index using the size of the new table and handles any collisions. This process of enlarging a hash table and computing new hash indices for its contents is called **rehashing.** You can see that increasing the size of a hash table requires considerably more work than increasing the size of an ordinary array. Rehashing is a task that you should not do often.

Note: Rehashing

When the load factor λ becomes too large, expand the hash table. To determine the table's new size, first double its present size and then increase the result to the next prime number. Use the method add to add the current entries in the dictionary to the new hash table.

Comparing Schemes for Collision Resolution

19.30   In previous segments, you saw how the load factor λ affects the average number of comparisons required by a search of a hash table for various ways to resolve collisions. The graphs in Figure 19-14 illustrate this effect for various collision resolution schemes. When λ is less than 0.5, the average number of comparisons for a successful search is about the same regardless of the process used to resolve collisions. For unsuccessful searches, the three open addressing schemes have about the same efficiency when λ is less than 0.5. However, separate chaining is somewhat more efficient in this case.

As λ exceeds 0.5, the efficiency of open addressing degrades rapidly, with linear probing the least efficient. Separate chaining, on the other hand, remains efficient for values of λ up to 1. In fact, the tabulated data in Figure 19-13 shows that its efficiency degrades only slightly for λ between 1 and 2.

Separate chaining certainly appears to be the fastest approach. But separate chaining can require more memory than open addressing, since each location in the hash table can reference a chain of linked nodes. On the other hand, the hash table itself can be smaller than when you use an open addressing scheme, since λ can be larger.

If all of these collision resolution schemes used hash tables of equal size, open addressing would be more likely to lead to rehashing than separate chaining would. To reduce the likelihood of rehashing, an open addressing strategy could use a large hash table. Remember that in Java, the table contains references that do not require much memory. So even though at least half of the table must remain unused, the actual space allocation would not be excessive.

Among open addressing schemes, double hashing is a good choice. It uses fewer comparisons than linear probing. Additionally, its probe sequence can reach the entire table, whereas quadratic probing cannot.

Figure 19-14 The average number of comparisons required by a search of the hash table versus the load factor λ for four collision resolution techniques when the search is (a) successful; (b) unsuccessful

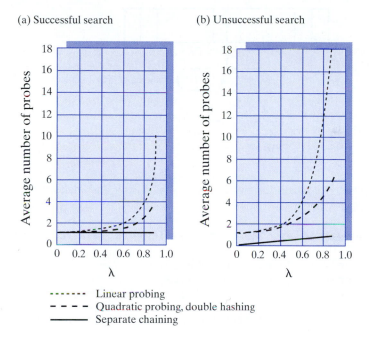

(a) Successful search   (b) Unsuccessful search

- - - - - - Linear probing
- - - - Quadratic probing, double hashing
———— Separate chaining

A Dictionary Implementation That Uses Hashing

The efficiency of separate chaining makes it a desirable method for resolving collisions that occur during hashing. Because it has a straightforward implementation, we leave it to you to implement. Instead, we will implement the linear probing method of open addressing. Most of this dictionary implementation is independent of the particular open addressing technique that you use. Adapting it to use quadratic probing or double hashing involves few changes.

Entries in the Hash Table

19.31   Our hash table will be like the array in Figure 18-1a that we used to implement the dictionary in the previous chapter. Each array location can reference an object that contains a search key and an associated value. The class `TableEntry` of these objects is similar to the class `Entry` that you saw in Segment 18.2 of the previous chapter.

However, with open addressing, each location in the hash table is in one of three states: occupied, empty, or available. (See Segment 19.14.) An empty location contains `null`. Rather than altering the structure of the hash table to indicate the other states, we make the entry objects indicate whether they are currently in the table or have been removed from it. Hence, we add another data field to the class of entry objects. This field is a boolean flag; it is true if the entry is in the dictionary or false if it has been removed. Figure 19-15 illustrates the hash table and one dictionary entry.

Figure 19-15 A hash table and one of its entry objects

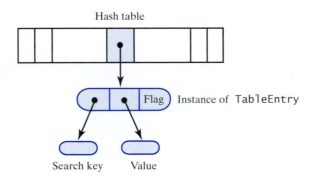

Thus, we create the private class `TableEntry` and make it internal to the dictionary class. `TableEntry` begins as follows:

```
private class TableEntry implements java.io.Serializable
{
  private Object  entryKey;
  private Object  entryValue;
  private boolean inTable; // true if entry is in hash table

  private TableEntry(Object key, Object value)
  {
    entryKey = key;
    entryValue = value;
    inTable = true;
  } // end constructor
  . . .
```

In addition to the methods `getKey`, `getValue`, and `setValue`, this class has the methods `isIn`, `isRemoved`, `setToIn`, and `setToRemoved` to interrogate or set the value of the boolean flag `inTable`.

Data Fields and Constructors

19.32   If you do not use a perfect hash function, you must expect collisions. All open addressing methods to resolve collisions become less efficient as the hash table fills, so you need to increase the size of the table. We use an array for this purpose and will expand it as necessary during execution. Thus, the class begins as follows:

```java
public class HashedMapOpenAddressing implements DictionaryInterface,
                                                java.io.Serializable
{
  private TableEntry[] hashTable;  // dictionary entries
  private int currentSize;          // current number of entries
  private static final int DEFAULT_SIZE = 101; // must be prime

  // fraction of hash table that can be filled
  private static final double MAX_LOAD_FACTOR = 0.5;

  public HashedMapOpenAddressing()
  {
    hashTable = new TableEntry[DEFAULT_SIZE];
    currentSize = 0;
  } // end default constructor
  . . .
```

The default constructor allocates an array for the hash table; the array has a predetermined size.

19.33 You can provide an additional constructor that lets the client specify the size of the hash table. However, this constructor should ensure that the table's size is prime and at least as big as the client wants. The following constructor uses the private method getNextPrime to find the prime number greater than or equal to a given integer:

```java
public HashedMapOpenAddressing(int tableSize)
{
  int primeSize = getNextPrime(tableSize);

  hashTable = new TableEntry[primeSize];
  currentSize = 0;
} // end constructor
```

Note: To implement getNextPrime(anInteger), first see whether anInteger is even. If it is, it cannot be prime, so add 1 to make it odd. Then use a private method isPrime to find the first prime number among the parameter anInteger and subsequent odd integers.

To implement isPrime, note that 2 and 3 are prime but 1 and even integers are not. An odd integer 5 or greater is prime if it is not divisible by every odd integer up to its square root.

The Methods getValue, remove, and add

We consider next the major operations of the dictionary: getValue, remove, and add. The note at the end of Segment 19.15 summarized just what these operations need to do.

19.34 **The method getValue.** We begin with an algorithm for the retrieval method getValue:

Algorithm getValue(key)
// Returns the value associated with the given search key, if it is in the dictionary.
// Otherwise, returns null*.*

index = getHashIndex(key)
Search the probe sequence that begins at hashTable[index] *for* key
if (key *is found*)
  return hashTable[index].getValue()
else
  return null

In addition to the private method getHashIndex, which you have seen already in Segment 19.10, this algorithm suggests another private method that searches the probe sequence. We name this method locate and specify it informally as follows:

locate(index, key)   Task: Follows the probe sequence that begins at index (the key's hash index) and returns either the index of the entry containing key or –1, if no such entry exists.

The method getValue then has the following implementation:

```
public Object getValue(Object key)
{
  Object result = null;

  int index = getHashIndex(key);
  index = locate(index, key);

  if (index != -1)
    result = hashTable[index].getValue(); // key found; get value

  // else key not found; result is null

  return result;
} // end getValue
```

19.35   **The method remove.** Removing an entry from the hash table is similar to retrieving an entry, since both methods must locate the search key. As the following implementation shows, you use the methods getHashIndex and locate to locate the desired entry. If you find it, you change its state to removed and return its value. Otherwise, you return null.

```
public Object remove(Object key)
{
  Object result = null;

  int index = getHashIndex(key);
  index = locate(index, key);

  if (index != -1)
  { // key found; flag entry as removed and return its value
    hashTable[index].setToRemoved();
    result = hashTable[index].getValue();
    currentSize--;
  } // end if
  // else key not found; result is null

  return result;
} // end remove
```

19.36   **The private method locate.** Before we look at add, let's implement the method locate(index, key) that both getValue and remove invoke. The method, given the search key and its hash index, looks for the search key along the probe sequence that begins at hashTable[index]. Recall that this search must ignore entries that are in the removed state. The search continues until it locates either key or null.

To follow the probe sequence, this method must implement the particular open addressing scheme you choose to resolve collisions. For simplicity, we will implement linear probing. The following algorithm summarizes our approach:

Algorithm `locate(index, key)`
// Returns either the index of the entry containing key *or –1 if no such entry is found.*

while (key *is not found and* hashTable[index] *is not* null)
{
  if (hashTable[index] *references an entry that is in the dictionary and contains* key)
    Exit loop
  else
    index = *next probe index*
}

if (key *is found*)
  return index
else
  return -1

The implementation of locate now follows from a refinement of this pseudocode:

```
/** @return either the index of the table location that references
            the entry containing key or -1 if no such entry is found */
private int locate(int index, Object key)
{
  boolean found = false;
  boolean repeatedIndex = false;
  int firstIndex = index; // first index in probe sequence
  while ( !found && !repeatedIndex && (hashTable[index] != null) )
  {
    if ( hashTable[index].isIn() &&
        key.equals(hashTable[index].getKey()) )
      found = true; // key found
    else // follow probe sequence
    if ( index == firstIndex)
    repeatedIndex = true; // probe sequence is repeating
      index = (index + 1) % hashTable.length; // linear probing
  } // end while
  // Assertion: either key is found or a null location is reached

  int result = -1;
  if (found)
    result = index;

  return result;
} // end locate
```

You can change from linear probing to another open addressing scheme for collision resolution by replacing the highlighted assignment statement in the previous method.

19.37 **The method add.** We begin with the algorithm for adding a new entry:

Algorithm `add(key, value)`
// Adds a new key-value entry to the dictionary. If key *is already in the dictionary,*
// returns its corresponding value and replaces it in the dictionary with value*.*
if (*hash table is too full*)
  rehash()

```
index = getHashIndex(key)
Check for collision and resolve it (this step can alter index)
if (key is not found )
{ // add entry to hash table
  hashTable[index] = new TableEntry(key, value)
  currentSize++
  return null
}
else // search key is in table; return and replace entry's value
{
  oldValue = hashTable[index].getValue()
  hashTable[index].setValue(value)
  return oldValue
}
```

This algorithm suggests that you write several more private methods. We specify them infor-mally as follows:

isHashTableTooFull()	Task: Returns true if the hash table's load factor is ≥ MAX_LOAD_FACTOR. Recall that the load factor is the ratio currentSize/hashTable.length.
rehash()	Task: Expands the hash table to a size that is both prime and at least double its current size, and then adds the current entries in the dictionary to the new hash table.
probe(index, key)	Task: Detects whether key collides with hashTable[index] and resolves it by following a probe sequence. Returns the index of either an available location along the probe sequence or the entry containing key. This index is always legal, since the probe sequence stays within the hash table.

Using these private methods, we implement the method add as follows:

```
public Object add(Object key, Object value)
{
  Object oldValue; // value to return

  if (isHashTableTooFull())
    rehash();

  int index = getHashIndex(key);
  index = probe(index, key); // check for and resolve collision
  // Assertion: index is within legal range for hashTable

  if ( (hashTable[index] == null) || hashTable[index].isRemoved())
  { // key not found, so insert new entry
    hashTable[index] = new TableEntry(key, value);
    currentSize++;
    oldValue = null;
  }
```

```
else
{ // key found; get old value for return and then replace it
  oldValue = hashTable[index].getValue();
  hashTable[index].setValue(value);
} // end if

return oldValue;
} // end add
```

19.38   **The private method probe.** The method probe(key, index) is similar to the method locate in that it looks for key along the probe sequence that begins at hashTable[index]. The search ignores entries that are in the removed state and continues until it locates either key or null. During this search, the method records the index of the first location, if any, that references an entry that has been removed from the table. This additional task is what distinguishes probe from locate. Thus, probe returns the index of a table location that either references an entry containing key or is available for an addition to the table.

Notice that probe returns the index of the removed entry that it *first* encounters along the probe sequence. Since add will insert a new entry into this location, a subsequent search for this entry will encounter it sooner than if add had inserted it in a location further along the probe sequence.

The following pseudocode summarizes the logic of probe:

Algorithm probe(index, key)
// Searches the probe sequence that begins at index. *Returns either the index of the entry*
// containing key *or the index of an available location in the hash table.*

```
while (key is not found and hashTable[index] is not null)
{
  if (hashTable[index] references a removed entry)
  {
    if (this is the first removed entry encountered)
      removedStateIndex = index
  }
  else if (the entry in hashTable[index] contains key)
    Exit loop
  else
    index = next probe index
}
if (key is found or a removed entry was not encountered)
  return index
else
  return removedStateIndex // index of first entry removed
```

The following method implements this algorithm:

```
private int probe(int index, Object key)
{
  boolean found = false;
  boolean repeatedIndex = false;
  int firstIndex = index; // first index in probe sequence
  int removedStateIndex = -1; // index of first location in
                              // removed state
  while ( !found && !repeatedIndex && (hashTable[index] != null) )
  {
    if (hashTable[index].isRemoved())
    {
      // save index of first not-in-use location found
```

```
         if (removedStateIndex == -1)
            removedStateIndex = index;
         index = (index + 1) % hashTable.length; // linear probing
      }
      else if (key.equals(hashTable[index].getKey()))
         found = true; // key found
      else // follow probe sequence
         index = (index + 1) % hashTable.length; // linear probing
      if (index == firstIndex)
            repeatedIndex = true; // probe sequence is repeating
   } // end while
   // Assertion: either key or null is found at hashTable[index]

   if (found || (removedStateIndex == -1) )
      return index; // index of either key or null
   else
      return removedStateIndex;
} // end probe
```

The methods probe and locate are so similar that you can omit locate and use probe instead. To do so, you must change the implementations of remove and getValue slightly. The following question asks you to make this change.

Question 4   What changes to the methods remove and getValue are necessary so they can call probe instead of locate?

19.39   **The private method rehash.** Recall that the method rehash expands the hash table to a size that is both prime and at least double its current size. Since the hash function depends on the size of the table, you cannot copy elements from the old array and put them into the same positions in the new array. You need to apply the revised hash function to each entry to determine its proper position in the new table. But doing so can lead to collisions that need to be resolved. Thus, you should use the method add to add the existing entries to the new and larger hash table. Since add increments the data field currentSize, you must remember to set this field to zero before adding the entries.

The method has the following implementation:

```
private void rehash()
{
   TableEntry[] oldTable = hashTable;
   int oldSize = hashTable.length;
   int newSize = getNextPrime(oldSize + oldSize);
   hashTable = new TableEntry[newSize]; // increase size of array
   currentSize = 0; // reset size of dictionary, since it will be
                    //    incremented by add during rehash

   // rehash dictionary entries from old array to the new and bigger
   // array; skip both null locations and removed entries
   for (int index = 0; index < oldSize; index++)
   {
      if ( (oldTable[index] != null) && oldTable[index].isIn() )
         add(oldTable[index].getKey(), oldTable[index].getValue());
   } // end for
} // end rehash
```

As we traverse the old hash table, notice that we skip both the null locations and the entries that have been removed from the dictionary but are still in the hash table.

This method does not retain the instances of `TableEntry` that were in the old hash table. Instead, it uses an entry's key and value to create a new entry. You can avoid this reallocation of entries; Exercise 12 at the end of this chapter asks you to investigate this possibility.

Question 5   When the method add calls rehash, rehash calls add. But when rehash calls add, does add call `rehash`? Explain.

Iterators

19.40   Finally, we provide iterators for the dictionary, much as we did in Chapter 18. For example, we can implement an internal class `KeyIterator` to define an iteration of the search keys. The iteration must traverse the hash table, ignoring cells that either contain `null` or reference removed entries. Figure 19-16 shows a sample hash table. Cells in blue reference the dictionary entries, light gray cells reference removed entries, and dark gray cells contain `null`. As we traverse this table, we skip cells that are gray. The only real concern in this implementation is determining when the method `hasNext` should return false. The occurrence of a gray cell and the size of the hash table are not the proper criteria for this determination. Instead, you simply count backward from `currentSize` each time the method `next` returns the next search key.

Figure 19-16 A hash table containing dictionary entries, removed entries, and `null` values

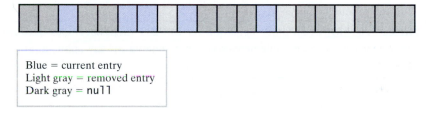

Blue = current entry
Light gray = removed entry
Dark gray = `null`

The implementation of `KeyIterator` follows. A class that defines an iteration of values would have a similar implementation.

```
private class KeyIterator implements Iterator
{
  private int currentIndex; // current position in hash table
  private int numberLeft;   // number of entries left in iteration

  private KeyIterator()
  {
    currentIndex = 0;
    numberLeft = currentSize;
  } // end default constructor

  public boolean hasNext()
  {
    return numberLeft > 0;
  } // end hasNext

  public Object next()
  {
    Object result = null;
```

```
        if (hasNext())
        {
          // find index of next entry
          while ( (hashTable[currentIndex] == null) ||
                    hashTable[currentIndex].isRemoved() )
          {
            currentIndex++;
          } // end while

          result = hashTable[currentIndex].getKey();
          numberLeft--;
          currentIndex++;
        }
        else
          throw new NoSuchElementException();

        return result;
      } // end next

    public void remove()
    {
      throw new UnsupportedOperationException();
    } // end remove
  } // end KeyIterator
```

Note: Hashing as an implementation of the ADT dictionary does not provide the ability to sort its entries. Such an implementation is not suitable for any application that requires a sorted iteration of the entries.

Java Class Library: The Class HashMap

19.41   The standard package `java.util` contains the class `HashMap`. This class implements the interface `java.util.Map` that we mentioned in Segment 17.16. Recall that this interface is similar to our `DictionaryInterface`. `HashMap` assumes that the search-key objects belong to a class that overrides the methods `hashCode` and `equals`.

The hash table is a collection of buckets, where each bucket can contain several entries. As you know, a hash table's load factor λ is a measure of how full the table is. The constructors for `HashMap` enable you to specify the initial number of buckets and the maximum load factor λ_{max}. These constructors are as follows:

public HashMap()
Creates an empty hash table with a default size and a default maximum load factor of 0.75.

public HashMap(**int** initialSize)
Creates an empty hash table with a given initial size and a default maximum load factor of 0.75.

public HashMap(**int** initialSize, **float** maxLoadFactor)
Creates an empty hash table with a given initial size and a given maximum load factor.

public HashMap(Map table)
Creates a hash table with the same entries as table.

The authors of `HashMap` chose a default maximum load factor of 0.75 to provide a balance between time and memory requirements. Even though higher values of the load factor permit smaller hash tables, they cause higher search times, which in turn reduce the efficiency of the `get`, `put`, and `remove` methods.

When the number of entries in the hash table exceeds λ_{max} times the number of buckets, the size of the hash table is increased by using rehashing. But rehashing takes time. You can avoid rehashing if you choose

$$\text{Number of buckets} > \frac{\text{Maximum number of entries in the dictionary}}{\lambda_{max}}$$

Of course, too large a hash table wastes space.

CHAPTER SUMMARY

- Hashing is a dictionary implementation that stores entries into an array called the hash table. A hash function transforms an entry's search key into the index of the array location that will contain the entry.

- All classes have a method **hashCode** that returns an integer hash code. If a class's instances are to be search keys, you should override **hashCode** to produce suitable hash codes. A hash code should depend on the entire search key.

- A hash function uses **hashCode** to compute a hash code from a search key and then compresses that hash code into an index to the hash table. A typical way to compress the hash code c is to compute c modulo n, where n is a prime number and the size of the hash table. This computation produces an index whose magnitude lies between 0 and $n - 1$.

- A perfect hash function maps each search key into a distinct location in the hash table. You can find such a function if you know all possible search keys. Using a perfect hash function makes possible $O(1)$ implementations of the dictionary operations.

- With a typical hash function, more than one search key can map into the same location in the hash table. This occurrence is called a collision.

- Various methods are available to deal with collisions. Among them are open addressing and separate chaining.

- With open addressing, all entries that map into the same location are ultimately stored within the hash table. These entries are in a sequence of locations called the probe sequence. Several different versions of open addressing determine a probe sequence. Linear probing uses consecutive locations. Quadratic probing spaces the locations in a probe sequence at increasing increments. These increments are 1, 4, 9, and so on—that is, the squares of the integers 1, 2, 3, . . . Double hashing uses a fixed increment that depends on the search key. A second hash function determines this increment.

- With open addressing, you remove an entry by placing it into a removed state. You do not set its table location to **null** because that would terminate subsequent searches prematurely. You retrieve an entry by searching its probe sequence, ignoring removed entries, until you either find the desired entry or encounter **null**. You perform the same search when you add a new entry, but while searching, you note the first location—if any—that references a removed entry. You use this location for the added entry. If no such location exists, the addition extends the probe sequence by using the **null** location encountered after searching the entire sequence.

- A disadvantage of linear probing and quadratic probing is clustering. Clustering lengthens a probe sequence and so increases the time to search it.

- With separate chaining, the hash table is an array of chains of linked nodes. That is, each location in the hash table references the beginning of a chain. All entries that map into the same location are stored in the chain that the location references.

- You add new entries to a chain either in sorted search-key order or at the end of the chain. Although sorted chains can improve search time somewhat, an iteration of the entire hash table will not be in sorted order.

- With separate chaining, you retrieve or remove an entry by mapping its search key into a table location. You then search the chain that the location references.

- Hashing is efficient as long as the ratio of dictionary size to hash-table size remains small. This ratio is called the load factor. The load factor should be less than 1 for separate chaining and less than 0.5 for open addressing. If the load factor exceeds these bounds, you must rehash the table.

- Rehashing is the process that increases the size of a hash table to a prime number that is greater than twice the table's current size. Since the hash function depends on the table size, you cannot simply copy entries from the old table to the new one. Instead, you use the method **add** to add all current entries to the new table.

- Separate chaining, as compared to open addressing, provides faster dictionary operations on average, can use a smaller hash table, and needs rehashing less frequently. If both approaches have the same size array for a hash table, separate chaining uses more memory due to its linked chains.

- Hashing as a dictionary implementation does not support operations that involve sorted search keys. For example, you cannot easily traverse the keys in sorted order, determine keys that lie within a given range, or identify the largest or smallest search key.

- The package `java.util` contains the class **HashMap**, which implements the interface **Map**.

EXERCISES

1. Define a `hashCode` method for the class Name, as given in Segment 1.16.

2. Quadratic probing uses the following indices to define a probe sequence:
$$(k + j^2) \text{ modulo } n \text{ for } j \geq 0$$
where k is the hash index and n is the size of the hash table.

   a. If the hash table contains 17 locations and the hash index is 3, what are the first six indices of the array locations in the probe sequence that quadratic probing defines?
   b. You can compute the indices for the probe sequence more efficiently by using the recurrence relation
   $$k_{i+1} = (k_i + 2i + 1) \text{ modulo } n \text{ for } i \geq 0 \text{ and } k_0 = k$$
   Derive this recurrence relation.
   c. Demonstrate that you can replace the modulo operation in Part b with one comparison and an occasional subtraction.

3. Suppose that you use open addressing to resolve collisions. Now imagine that your hash table is getting full. To avoid the bad performance that results from a nearly full hash table, you should create a new, larger hash table.

   a. What steps should you take to move all of your entries to this new table?
   b. What happens to the hash function?

4. Suppose that the size of your hash table is 31, that you use the hash code described in Segment 19.7, and that you use separate chaining to resolve collisions. List five different names that would hash to the same location in the table.

5. Assume the hash table and hash function described in Exercise 4, but use open addressing with linear probing to resolve collisions. List five different names that do not all hash to the same location in the table yet would nonetheless result in collisions and clustering.

6. Repeat Exercise 5, but instead use open addressing with quadratic probing to resolve collisions.

7. Given an example of a probe sequence produced by quadratic probing that does not reach the entire hash table, even if the size of the table is a prime number.

8. Demonstrate that quadratic probing will guarantee a successful addition, if the hash table is at most half full and its size is a prime number.

9. Demonstrate that double hashing will produce a probe sequence that reaches the entire table, if the size of the hash table is a prime number. *Hint*: Show that this is true if the increment and the table size are relatively prime. Then, if the table size is prime, all increments will be relatively prime to it.

10. Imagine that you alter the linear probing scheme of Segment 19.12 as follows. When a collision occurs at `hashTable[k]`, you check `hashTable[k+c]`, `hashTable[k+2c]`, `hashTable[k+3c]`, and so on, where c is a constant. Does this scheme eliminate primary clustering?

11. Revise the method `add` given in Segment 19.37 when duplicate search keys are allowed in the dictionary.

12. The method `rehash` does not retain the instances of `TableEntry` that were in the old hash table. It could if the method `add` had an entry as its parameter instead of the search key and value. Write such a method as an additional `add` method and then revise `rehash` so it retains the instances of `TableEntry` that were in the old hash table.

13. Imagine a collection of names that are instances of the class `Name`, as modified in Exercise 1. For each name, imagine a string that represents a nickname. Suppose that each nickname is a search key, and you plan to add nickname-name pairs to a dictionary that is an instance of the class `HashMap`, as described in Segment 19.41.

   a. Suppose that you plan to add 1000 entries to this dictionary. Create an instance of the class `HashMap` that can accommodate the 1000 entries without rehashing.
   b. Write statements that add four nickname-name pairs to your dictionary. Then write statements that retrieve and display the name that corresponds to a nickname of your choice.

14. You have approximately 1000 thumbnail images that you want to store in a dictionary that uses hashing in its implementation. Each image is 20 pixels wide by 20 pixels high, and each pixel is one of 256 colors. Suggest some possible hash functions that you could use.

PROJECTS

1. Implement the ADT dictionary by using hashing and separate chaining. Use an array of chains of linked nodes as the hash table. The dictionary's entries should have distinct search keys.

2. Repeat Project 1, but use the ADT list for the buckets instead of a chain of linked nodes. What implementation of the list would be reasonable?

3. The following experiment compares the performance of linear probing and quadratic probing. You will need a list of 500 names or user names that can be obtained from your instructor or from a system administrator. Implement a hash table of size 1000, and use the hash code described in Segment 19.7. Count the number of collisions that occur for both linear probing and quadratic probing when 500 names are added to the table. Repeat the experiment for tables of size 950, 900, 850, 800, 750, 700, 650, and 600.

4. Design an experiment similar to the one in Project 3, but instead of comparing linear probing and quadratic probing, compare two different hash functions.

20

Stacks

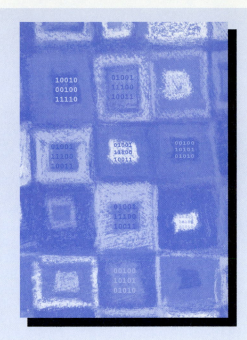

CONTENTS

Specifications of the ADT Stack
Using a Stack to Process Algebraic Expressions
    Checking for Balanced Parentheses, Brackets, and Braces in an Infix Algebraic Expression
    Transforming an Infix Expression to a Postfix Expression
    Evaluating Postfix Expressions
    Evaluating Infix Expressions
The Program Stack
    Recursive Methods
Using a Stack Instead of Recursion
    An Iterative Binary Search
Java Class Library: The Class **Stack**

PREREQUISITES

Chapter   3   Designing Classes
Chapter 10   Recursion
Chapter 13   Sorted Lists
Chapter 16   Searching

OBJECTIVES

After studying this chapter, you should be able to

- Describe the operations of the ADT stack
- Use a stack to determine whether the parentheses, brackets, and braces in an algebraic expression are paired correctly
- Use a stack to convert an infix expression to a postfix expression
- Use a stack to evaluate a postfix expression
- Use a stack to evaluate an infix expression
- Use a stack in a program
- Describe how the Java run-time environment uses a stack to track the execution of methods
- Use a stack to implement a recursive algorithm iteratively

In everyday life, a stack is a familiar thing. You might see a stack of books on your desk, a stack of dishes in the cafeteria, a stack of towels in the linen closet, or a stack of boxes in the attic. When you add an item to a stack, you place it on top of the stack. When you remove an item, you take the topmost one. This topmost item is the last one that was added to the stack. So when you remove an item, you remove the item added most recently. That is, the last item added to the stack is the first one removed.

In spite of our examples of a stack, everyday life usually does not follow this **last-in, first-out**, or **LIFO,** behavior. Although the employee hired most recently is often the first one fired, we live in a first-come, first-served society. In the computer science world, however, last-in, first-out is exactly the behavior required by many important algorithms. These algorithms often use the abstract data type stack, which is an ADT that exhibits a last-in, first-out behavior. For example, a compiler uses a stack to interpret the meaning of an algebraic expression, and a run-time environment uses a stack when executing a recursive method.

This chapter describes the ADT stack and provides several examples of its use.

Specifications of the ADT Stack

20.1   The ADT **stack** organizes its entries according to the order in which they were added. All additions are to one end of the stack called the **top.** The top, then, is the newest item among the items currently in a stack. Figure 20-1 shows some stacks that should be familiar to you.

Figure 20-1   Some familiar stacks

 Note: Among the items in a stack, the one added most recently is the top of the stack. (Other items might have been added to the stack more recently and then removed.)

The stack is the first of our ADTs that restricts access to its entries. A client can look at or remove only the top of the stack. The only way to look at an entry that is not the top of the stack is to repeatedly remove items from the stack until the desired item reaches the top. If you were to remove all of a stack's entries, one by one, you would get them in chronological order, beginning with the most recent and ending with the first item added to the stack.

20.2   Typically, a stack has no search operation.[1] An entry can have a search key, but the key is not relevant to the stack or to the entry's position within the stack. The operation that adds an entry to a stack is traditionally called push. The remove operation is pop. The operation that retrieves the top of the stack without removing it is named peek. The following specifications define a set of operations for the ADT stack.

ABSTRACT DATA TYPE STACK

DATA

- A collection of objects in a specific order

OPERATIONS

push(newEntry)	Task: Adds a new entry to the top of the stack. Input: newEntry is the new entry. Output: None.
pop()	Task: Removes and returns the top of the stack. Input: None. Output: Returns either the top of the stack or, if the stack was empty, null.
peek()	Task: Retrieves the top of the stack without changing the stack in any way. Input: None. Output: Returns either the top of the stack or, if the stack is empty, null.
isEmpty()	Task: Determines whether the stack is empty. Input: None. Output: Returns true if the stack is empty.
clear()	Task: Removes all entries from the stack. Input: None. Output: None.

Note: Alternate names for methods

It is not unusual for a class designer to include aliases for certain methods. For example, you could include the additional methods add and remove (or insert and delete) in the ADT stack to mean push and pop. Moreover, pull is sometimes used to mean pop, and getTop can mean peek, so including them as aliases is reasonable.

---

1. However, the stack within the Java Class Library does have a search method, as you will see later in this chapter.

20.3   The following Java interface specifies a stack of objects. Remember that Object is the superclass, or base class, of all other classes. Thus, by specifying Object as the data type of the items in a stack, you can place any object in the stack.

```java
public interface StackInterface
{
  /** Task: Adds a new entry to the top of the stack.
   *  @param newEntry  an object to be added to the stack */
  public void push(Object newEntry);

  /** Task: Removes and returns the top of the stack.
   *  @return either the object at the top of the stack or null if
   *          the stack was empty */
  public Object pop();

  /** Task: Retrieves the top of the stack.
   *  @return either the object at the top of the stack or null if
   *          the stack is empty */
  public Object peek();

  /** Task: Determines whether the stack is empty.
   *  @return true if the stack is empty */
  public boolean isEmpty();

  /** Task: Removes all entries from the stack */
  public void clear();
} // end StackInterface
```

20.4   **Example: Demonstrating the stack methods.** The following statements add, retrieve, and remove strings from a stack. We assume that the class LinkedStack implements StackInterface and is available for our use.

```java
StackInterface myStack = new LinkedStack();
myStack.push("Jim");
myStack.push("Jess");
myStack.push("Jill");
myStack.push("Jane");
myStack.push("Joe");

String top = (String) myStack.peek();
System.out.println(top + " is at the top of the stack.");

top = (String) myStack.pop();
System.out.println(top + " is removed from the stack.");

top = (String) myStack.peek();
System.out.println(top + " is at the top of the stack.");

top = (String) myStack.pop();
System.out.println(top + " is removed from the stack.");
```

Parts *a* through *e* of Figure 20-2 show five additions to the stack. At this point, the stack contains—from top to bottom—the strings *Joe*, *Jane*, *Jill*, *Jess*, and *Jim*. The string at the top of the stack is *Joe*; peek retrieves it. The method pop retrieves *Joe* again and then removes it (Figure 20-2f). A subsequent call to peek retrieves *Jane*. Then pop retrieves *Jane* and removes it (Figure 20-2g).

Three more calls to pop would remove *Jill*, *Jess*, and *Jim*, leaving the stack empty. A subsequent call to either pop or peek would return null.

Figure 20-2   A stack of strings after (a) push adds *Jim*; (b) push adds *Jess*; (c) push adds *Jill*; (d) push adds *Jane*; (e) push adds *Joe*; (f) pop retrieves and removes *Joe*; (g) pop retrieves and removes *Jane*

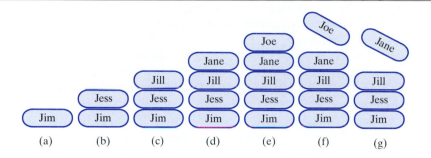

Question 1   After the following statements execute, what string is at the top of the stack and what string is at the bottom?

```
StackInterface myStack = new LinkedStack();
myStack.push("Jim");
myStack.push("Jess");
myStack.pop();
myStack.push("Jill");
myStack.push("Jane");
myStack.pop();
```

Question 2   Consider the stack that was created in Question 1 and define a new empty stack yourStack.

a.   Write a loop that pops the strings from myStack and pushes them onto yourStack.
b.   Describe the contents of the stacks myStack and yourStack when the loop that you just wrote completes its execution.

Programming Tip: Methods such as peek and pop must behave reasonably when the stack is empty. Here, we specify that they return null. Another possibility is to have them throw an exception.

Using a Stack to Process Algebraic Expressions

20.5   In mathematics, an algebraic expression is composed of operands that are variables or constants and operators, such as + and *. We will use the Java notation +, -, *, and / to indicate addition, subtraction, multiplication, and division. We will use $\wedge$ to indicate exponentiation, with the warning that Java has no operator for exponentiation; in Java $\wedge$ is the exclusive-or operator.[2]

Operators generally have two operands, and so are called **binary operators.** For example, the + in $a + b$ is a binary operator. The operators + and – can also be **unary operators** when they have one operand. For example, the minus sign in –5 is a unary operator.

When an algebraic expression has no parentheses, operations occur in a certain order. Exponentiations occur first; they take **precedence** over the other operations. Next, multiplications and divisions occur, and then additions and subtractions. For example, the expression

$$20 - 2 * 2 \wedge 3$$

evaluates as 20 – 2 * 8, then as 20 – 16, and finally as 4.

But what happens when two or more adjacent operators have the same precedence? Exponentiations, such as those in $a \wedge b \wedge c$, occur right to left. Thus, $2 \wedge 2 \wedge 3$ means $2 \wedge (2 \wedge 3)$, or 2^8, instead of $(2 \wedge 2) \wedge 3$, which is 4^3. Other operations occur left to right, such as the multiplication and division in $a * b / c$ or the addition and subtraction in $a - b + c$. Therefore, 8 – 4 + 2 means (8 – 4) + 2, or 6, instead of 8 – (4 + 2), which is 2. Parentheses in an expression override the normal operator precedence.

Ordinarily, a binary operator occurs between its operands, as in $a + b$. An expression in this familiar notation is called an **infix expression.** Other notations are possible. For example, you could write a binary operator before its two operands. Thus, $a + b$ becomes $+ a b$. This expression is called a **prefix expression.** Or you could write a binary operator after its two operands, so $a + b$ becomes $a b +$. This expression is a **postfix expression.** Although infix expressions are more familiar to us, both prefix and postfix expressions are simpler to process because they do not use precedence rules or parentheses. The precedence of an operator in either a prefix expression or a postfix expression is implied by the order in which the operators and operands occur in the expression. We will say more about these expressions later in this chapter.

Our first example looks at ordinary infix expressions.

Note: **Algebraic expressions**
In an infix expression, each binary operator appears between its operands, as in $a + b$.
In a prefix expression, each binary operator appears before its operands, as in $+ a b$.
In a postfix expression, each binary operator appears after its operands, as in $a b +$.

Checking for Balanced Parentheses, Brackets, and Braces in an Infix Algebraic Expression

20.6   Although programmers use parentheses when writing an arithmetic expression in Java, mathematicians use parentheses, square brackets, and braces for the same purpose. These delimiters must be paired correctly. For example, an open parenthesis must correspond to a close parenthesis. In addition, pairs of delimiters must not intersect. Thus, an expression can contain a sequence of delimiters such as

$$\{ [( ) ( )] ( ) \}$$

---

2.   Chapter 19 used the Java operator $\wedge$ in a hash function in Segment 19.8.

but not

> [( ])

For convenience, we will say that a **balanced expression** contains delimiters that are paired correctly, or are **balanced.**

We want an algorithm that determines whether an expression is balanced.

20.7   **Example: A balanced expression.** Let's determine whether the expression

$$a \,\{b \,[c \,(d \,+ e)/2 - f] + 1\}$$

is balanced. We scan the expression from left to right for delimiters, ignoring any characters that are not delimiters. When we encounter an open delimiter, we must save it. When we find a close delimiter, we must determine whether it corresponds to the most recently encountered open delimiter. If it does, we discard the open delimiter and continue scanning the expression. If we are able to scan the entire expression without a mismatch, the delimiters in the expression are balanced.

The ADT that enables us to store objects and then retrieve or remove the most recent one is a stack. Figure 20-3 shows the contents of a stack as we scan the previous expression. Since we ignore all characters that are not delimiters, it is sufficient for us to represent the expression as

> { [( )] }

After pushing the first three open delimiters onto the stack, the open parenthesis is at the top of the stack. The next delimiter, the close parenthesis, pairs with the open parenthesis at the top of the stack. We pop the stack and continue by comparing the close bracket with the delimiter now at the top of the stack. They correspond, so we pop the stack again and continue by comparing the close brace with the top of the stack. These delimiters correspond and we reach the end of the expression. The stack is empty. Each open delimiter correctly corresponds to a close delimiter, so the delimiters are balanced.

Figure 20-3   The contents of a stack during the scan of an expression that contains the balanced delimiters { [( )] }

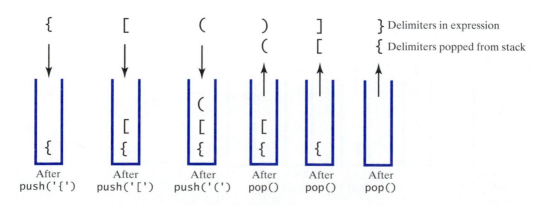

20.8

Example: Unbalanced expressions. Let's examine some expressions that contain unbalanced delimiters. Figure 20-4 shows a stack during the scan of an expression that contains the delimiters { [( ]) }. This is an example of intersecting pairs of delimiters. After we push the first three open delimiters onto the stack, the open parenthesis at the top of the stack does not correspond to the close bracket that comes next in the expression.

Figure 20-5 shows a stack during the scan of an expression that contains the unbalanced delimiters [( )] }. The close brace does not have a corresponding open brace. When we finally reach the close brace, the stack is empty. Since the stack does not contain an open brace, the delimiters are unbalanced.

Figure 20-4   The contents of a stack during the scan of an expression that contains the unbalanced delimiters { [( ]) }

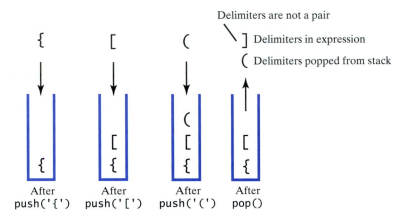

Figure 20-5   The contents of a stack during the scan of an expression that contains the unbalanced delimiters [( )] }

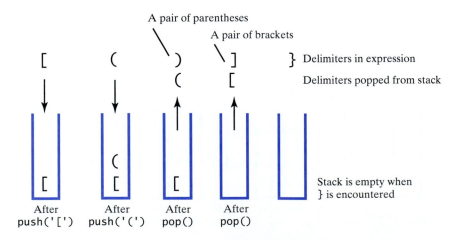

Figure 20-6 shows a stack during the scan of an expression that contains the unbalanced delimiters { [( )]. The open brace does not have a corresponding close brace. When you reach the end of the expression, having processed the brackets and parentheses, the stack contains the open brace. Since this delimiter is left over, the expression contains unbalanced delimiters.

20.9   **The algorithm.** The previous discussion and figures reveal the possible paths that our algorithm must take. We formalize these observations in the following pseudocode:

Figure 20-6   The contents of a stack during the scan of an expression that contains the unbalanced delimiters { [( )]

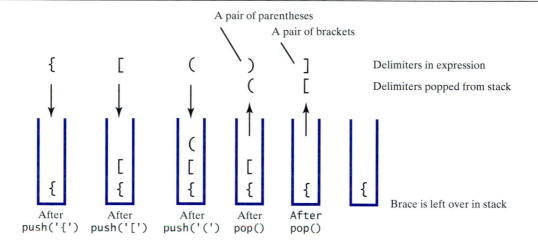

Algorithm checkBalance(expression)
// Returns true if the parentheses, brackets, and braces in an expression are paired
// correctly.

```
isBalanced = true
while ( (isBalanced == true) and not at end of expression)
{
   nextCharacter = next character in expression
   switch (nextCharacter)
   {
      case '(': case '[': case '{':
        Push nextCharacter onto stack
        break

      case ')': case ']': case '}':
        if (stack is empty)
           isBalanced = false
        else
        {
           openDelimiter = top of stack
           Pop stack
           isBalanced = true or false according to whether openDelimiter and
                        nextCharacter are a pair of delimiters
        }
        break
   }
}
```

```
    if (stack is not empty)
       isBalanced = false

    return isBalanced
```

20.10   Let's examine this algorithm for each of the examples given in the previous figures. For the balanced expression in Figure 20-3, the while loop ends with an empty stack and isBalanced set to true. For the expression in Figure 20-4, the loop ends when it finds that the close bracket does not correspond to the open parenthesis. The flag isBalanced is false; the fact that the stack is not empty does not affect the outcome of the algorithm.

With the expression in Figure 20-5, the loop ends at the close brace because the stack is empty at that point. Retrieving or popping the top of the empty stack results in null, so the flag isBalanced is set to false. Finally, with the expression in Figure 20-6, the loop ends at the end of the expression with isBalanced set to true. But the stack is not empty—it contains an open brace—so after the loop, isBalanced becomes false.

Question 3   Show the contents of the stack as you trace the algorithm checkBalance, as given in Segment 20.9, for each of the following expressions.

a. $[a \{b \, / \, (c - d) + e \, / \, (f + g)\} - h]$
b. $\{a \, [b + (c + 2)/d] + e) + f\}$
c. $[a \{b + [c \, (d+e) - f] + g\}$

20.11   **Java implementation.** The following class implements our algorithm as the static method checkBalance. The method has one parameter, the expression as a string. We assume that the class LinkedStack implements StackInterface and is available. Since StackInterface specifies a stack of objects, but the previous algorithm uses a stack of characters, the implementation uses the wrapper class Character to create objects suitable for the stack.

```java
public class BalanceChecker
{
  /** Task: Determines whether the parentheses, brackets, and braces
   *        in a string occur in left/right pairs.
   *  @param expression  a string to be checked
   *  @return true if the delimiters are paired correctly */
  public static boolean checkBalance(String expression)
  {
    StackInterface openDelimiterStack = new LinkedStack();
    int characterCount = expression.length();

    boolean isBalanced = true;
    int index = 0;
    char nextCharacter = ' ';

    for (; isBalanced && (index < characterCount); index++)
    {
      nextCharacter = expression.charAt(index);
      switch (nextCharacter)
      {
        case '(': case '[': case '{':
          openDelimiterStack.push(new Character(nextCharacter));
          break;
```

```
      case ')': case ']': case '}':
        if (openDelimiterStack.isEmpty())
          isBalanced = false;
        else
        {
          Character open = (Character) openDelimiterStack.pop();
          char openDelimiter = open.charValue();
          isBalanced = isPaired(openDelimiter, nextCharacter);
        } // end if
        break;

      default: break;
    } // end switch
  } // end for

  if (!openDelimiterStack.isEmpty())
    isBalanced = false;

  return isBalanced;
} // end checkBalance

/** Task: Determines whether two delimiters are a pair of
 *         parentheses, brackets, or braces.
 *  @param open    a character
 *  @param close   a character
 *  @return true if open/close form a pair of parentheses, brackets,
 *                or braces */
private static boolean isPaired(char open, char close)
{
  return (open == '(' && close == ')') ||
         (open == '[' && close == ']') ||
         (open == '{' && close == '}');
} // end isPaired
} // end BalanceChecker
```

The following statements provide an example of how you might use this class:

```
String expression = "a {b [c (d + e)/2 - f] + 1}";
boolean isBalanced = BalanceChecker.checkBalance(expression);
if (isBalanced)
  System.out.println(expression + " is balanced");
else
  System.out.println(expression + " is not balanced");
```

Transforming an Infix Expression to a Postfix Expression

20.12   Our ultimate goal is to show you how to evaluate infix algebraic expressions, but evaluating postfix expressions is easier. So we first look at how to represent an infix expression by using postfix notation.

Recall that in a postfix expression, a binary operator follows its two operands. Here are a few examples of infix expressions and their corresponding postfix forms:

Infix	Postfix
$a + b$	$a\ b\ +$
$(a + b) * c$	$a\ b + c\ *$
$a + b * c$	$a\ b\ c\ * +$

Notice that the order of the operands *a*, *b*, and *c* in an infix expression is the same in the corresponding postfix expression. However, the order of the operators might change. This order depends on the precedence of the operators.

20.13   **A pencil and paper scheme.** One way to deduce the order in which operators should appear in a postfix expression begins with a fully parenthesized infix expression. For example, we write (*a* + *b*) * *c* as ((*a* + *b*) * *c*). This step removes the expression's dependence on the rules of operator precedence. Each operator is now associated with a pair of parentheses. We now move each operator to the right so that it appears immediately before its associated close parenthesis to get ((*a b* +) *c* *). Finally, we remove the parentheses to obtain the postfix expression *a b* + *c* *.

This scheme should give you some understanding of the order of the operators in a postfix expression. It also can be useful when checking the results of a conversion algorithm. However, the algorithm that we will develop next is not based on this approach.

Question 4   Using the previous scheme, convert each of the following infix expressions to postfix expressions:

a.   *a* + *b* * *c*
b.   *a* * *b* / (*c* – *d*)
c.   *a* / *b* + (*c* – *d*)
d.   *a* / *b* + *c* – *d*

20.14   **The basics of a conversion algorithm.** To convert an infix expression to postfix form, we scan the infix expression from left to right. When we encounter an operand, we place it at the end of the new expression that we are creating. Recall that operands in an infix expression remain in the same order in the corresponding postfix expression. When we encounter an operator, we must save it until we determine where in the output expression it belongs. For example, to convert the infix expression *a* + *b*, we append *a* to the initially empty output expression, save +, and append *b* to the output expression. We now need to retrieve the + and put it at the end of the output expression to get the postfix expression *a b* +. Retrieving the operator saved most recently is easy if we have saved it in a stack.

In this example, we saved the operator until we processed its second operand. In general, we hold the operator in a stack at least until we compare its precedence with that of the next operator. For example, to convert the expression *a* + *b* * *c*, we append *a* to the output expression, push + onto a stack, and then append *b* to the output. What we do now depends on the relative precedences of the next operator, *, and the + at the top of the stack. Since * has a greater precedence than +, *b* is not the addition's second operand. Instead, the addition waits for the result of the multiplication. Thus, we push * onto the stack and append *c* to the output expression. Having reached the end of the input expression, we now pop each operator from the stack and append it to the end of the output expression, getting the postfix expression *a b c* * +. Figure 20-7 illustrates these steps.

20.15   **Successive operators with the same precedence.** What if two successive operators have the same precedence? We need to distinguish between operators that have a left-to-right association—namely +, –, *, and /—and exponentiation, which has a right-to-left association. For example, consider the expression *a* – *b* + *c*. When we encounter the +, the stack will contain the operator – and the incomplete postfix expression will be *ab*. The subtraction operator belongs to the operands *a* and *b*, so we pop the stack and append – to the end of the expression *ab*. Since the stack is empty, we push the + onto the stack. We then append *c* to the result, and finally we pop the stack and append the +. The result is *a b* – *c* +. Figure 20-8a illustrates these steps.

Now consider the expression $a \wedge b \wedge c$. By the time we encounter the second $\wedge$ operator, the stack contains $\wedge$, and the result so far is ab. As before, the current operator has the same precedence as the top of the stack. But since $a \wedge b \wedge c$ means $a \wedge (b \wedge c)$, we must push the second $\wedge$ onto the stack.

Figure 20-7   Converting the infix expression $a + b * c$ to postfix form

Next Character	Postfix	Operator Stack (bottom to top)
a	a	
+	a	+
b	a b	+
*	a b	+ *
c	a b c	+ *
	a b c *	+
	a b c * +	

Figure 20-8   Converting an infix expression to postfix form: (a) $a - b + c$; (b) $a \wedge b \wedge c$

(a)

Next Character	Postfix	Operator Stack (bottom to top)
a	a	
−	a	−
b	a b	−
+	a b −	
	a b −	+
c	a b − c	+
	a b − c +	

(b)

Next Character	Postfix	Operator Stack (bottom to top)
a	a	
∧	a	∧
b	a b	∧
∧	a b	∧ ∧
c	a b c	∧ ∧
	a b c ∧	∧
	a b c ∧ ∧	

Question 5   In general, when should you push an exponentiation operator $\wedge$ onto the stack?

Note:
- If an operator other than $\wedge$ has the same precedence as the operator at the top of the stack, you pop the stack.
- If an operator is $\wedge$, you push it onto the stack regardless of what is at the top of the stack.

20.16 **Parentheses.** Parentheses override the rules of operator precedence. We always push an open parenthesis onto the stack. Once it is in the stack, we treat an open parenthesis as an operator with the lowest precedence. That is, any subsequent operator will get pushed onto the stack. When we encounter a close parenthesis, we pop operators from the stack and append them to the result until we pop an open parenthesis. The algorithm continues with no parentheses added to the postfix expression.

20.17 **The infix-to-postfix algorithm.** To summarize, we take the following actions, according to the symbols we encounter, as we process the infix expression from left to right:

Operand	Append each operand to the end of the output expression.
Operator ^	Push ^ onto the stack.
Operator +, -, *, or /	Pop operators from the stack, appending them to the output expression, until the stack is empty or its top has a lower precedence than the new operator. Then push the new operator onto the stack.
Open parenthesis	Push (onto the stack.
Close parenthesis	Pop operators from the stack and append them to the output expression until we pop an open parenthesis. Discard both parentheses.

The following algorithm encompasses these observations. For simplicity, all operands in our expression are single-letter variables.

> *Algorithm* `convertToPostfix(infix)`
> *// Converts an infix expression to an equivalent postfix expression.*
>
> `operatorStack` = *a new empty stack*
> `postfix` = *a new empty string*
> **while** (`infix` *has characters left to parse*)
> {
>   `nextCharacter` = *next nonblank character of* `infix`
>   **switch** (`nextCharacter`)
>   {
>   **case** *variable*:
>   *Append* `nextCharacter` *to* `postfix`
>   **break**
>
>   **case** `'^'`:
>   `operatorStack.push(nextCharacter)`
>   **break**
>
>   **case** `'+'`: **case** `'-'`: **case** `'*'`: **case** `'/'`:
>   **while** (`!operatorStack.isEmpty()` *and*
>   *precedence of* `nextCharacter` `<=` *precedence of* `operatorStack.peek()`)
>   {
>   *Append* `operatorStack.peek()` *to* `postfix`

```
            operatorStack.pop()
      }

      operatorStack.push(nextCharacter)
      break

   case '(':
      operatorStack.push(nextCharacter)
      break

   case ')':  // stack is not empty if infix expression is valid
      topOperator = operatorStack.pop()
      while (topOperator != '(')
      {
         Append topOperator to postfix
         topOperator = operatorStack.pop()
      }
      break

   default: break
   } // end switch
} // end while

while (!operatorStack.isEmpty())
{
   topOperator = operatorStack.pop()
   Append topOperator to postfix
}
return postfix
```

Figure 20-9 traces this algorithm for the infix expression $a / b * (c + (d - e))$. The resulting postfix expression is $a\,b\,/\,c\,d\,e\,-\,+\,*$.

Figure 20-9   The steps in converting the infix expression $a / b * (c + (d - e))$ to postfix form

Next Character	Postfix	Operator Stack (bottom to top)
a	a	
$/$	a	$/$
b	$a\,b$	$/$
$*$	$a\,b\,/$	
	$a\,b\,/$	$*$
$($	$a\,b\,/$	$*\,($
c	$a\,b\,/\,c$	$*\,($
$+$	$a\,b\,/\,c$	$*\,(+$
$($	$a\,b\,/\,c$	$*\,(+\,($
d	$a\,b\,/\,c\,d$	$*\,(+\,($
$-$	$a\,b\,/\,c\,d$	$*\,(+\,(-$
e	$a\,b\,/\,c\,d\,e$	$*\,(+\,(-$
$)$	$a\,b\,/\,c\,d\,e\,-$	$*\,(+\,($
	$a\,b\,/\,c\,d\,e\,-$	$*\,(+$
$)$	$a\,b\,/\,c\,d\,e\,-\,+$	$*\,($
	$a\,b\,/\,c\,d\,e\,-\,+$	$*$
	$a\,b\,/\,c\,d\,e\,-\,+\,*$	

Question 6   Using the previous algorithm, represent each of the following infix expressions as a postfix expression.

a. $(a + b) / (c - d)$
b. $(a - b * c) / (d * e * f + g)$

20.18   **The Java implementation.** The following class implements this algorithm as the static method convertToPostfix. The method has one parameter, the expression as a string. Note the use of the class java.lang.StringBuffer in forming the postfix expression. StringBuffer is like String, but its instances are mutable—that is, they can change in value.

```java
public class Postfix
{
  /** Task: Creates a postfix expression that represents a given infix
   *        expression.
   *  @param infix  a string that is a valid infix expression
   *  @return a string that is the postfix expression equivalent of
   *          infix */
  public static String convertToPostfix(String infix)
  {
    StringBuffer postfix = new StringBuffer();
    StackInterface operatorStack = new LinkedStack();
    int characterCount = infix.length();
    Character top;
    char topOperator;

    for (int index = 0; index < characterCount; index++)
    {
      boolean done = false;
      char nextCharacter = infix.charAt(index);

      if (isVariable(nextCharacter))
        postfix = postfix.append(nextCharacter);
      else
      {
        switch (nextCharacter)
        {
          case '^':
            operatorStack.push(new Character(nextCharacter));
            break;

          case '+': case '-': case '*': case '/':
            while (!done && !operatorStack.isEmpty())
            {
              top = (Character) operatorStack.peek();
              topOperator = top.charValue();

              if (getPrecedence(nextCharacter) <=
                  getPrecedence(topOperator))
              {
                postfix = postfix.append(topOperator);
                operatorStack.pop();
              }
```

```java
        else
          done = true;
      } // end while

      operatorStack.push(new Character(nextCharacter));
      break;

    case '(':
      operatorStack.push(new Character(nextCharacter));
      break;

    case ')': // stack is not empty if infix expression is valid
      top = (Character) operatorStack.pop();
      topOperator = top.charValue();
      while (topOperator != '(')
      {
        postfix = postfix.append(topOperator);
        top = (Character) operatorStack.pop();
        topOperator = top.charValue();
      } // end while
      break;

      default: break;
    } // end switch
  } // end if
} // end for

while (!operatorStack.isEmpty())
{
  top = (Character) operatorStack.pop();
  postfix = postfix.append(top.charValue());
} // end while

return postfix.toString();
} // end convertToPostfix

/** Task: Determines the precedence of a given operator.
 *  @param operator  a character that is (, ), +, -, *, /, or ^
 *  @return an integer that indicates the precedence of operator:
 *          0 if ( or ), 1 if + or -, 2 if * or /, 3 if ^, -1 if
 *          anything else */
private static int getPrecedence(char operator)
{
  switch (operator)
  {
    case '(': case ')': return 0;
    case '+': case '-': return 1;
    case '*': case '/': return 2;
    case '^':           return 3;
  } // end switch

  return -1;
} // end getPrecedence

private static boolean isVariable(char character)
{
```

```
        return Character.isLetter(character);
    } // end isVariable
} // end Postfix
```

Evaluating Postfix Expressions

20.19   Evaluating a postfix expression requires no rules of operator precedence, since the order of its operators and operands dictates the order of the operations. Additionally, a postfix expression contains no parentheses to complicate the evaluation.

As we scan the postfix expression, we must save operands until we find the operators that apply to them. For example, to evaluate the postfix expression *a b /*, we locate the variables *a* and *b* and save their values.[3] When we identify the operator */*, its second operand is the most recently saved value—that is, *b*'s value. The value saved before that—*a*'s value—is the operator's first operand. Storing values in a stack enables us to access the necessary operands for an operator. Figure 20-10 traces the evaluation of *a b /* when *a* is 2 and *b* is 4.

Figure 20-10 The stack during the evaluation of the postfix expression *a b /* when *a* is 2 and *b* is 4

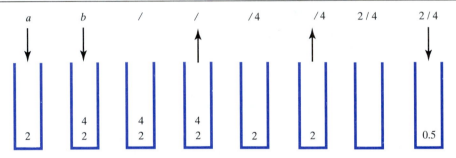

Now consider the postfix expression *a b + c /*, where *a* is 2, *b* is 4, and *c* is 3. The expression corresponds to the infix expression (*a* + *b*) / *c*, so its value should be 2. After finding the variable *a*, we push its value 2 onto a stack. Likewise, we push *b*'s value 4 onto the stack. The + operator is next, so we pop two values from the stack, add them, and push their sum 6 onto the stack. Notice that this sum will be the first operand of the / operator. The variable *c* is next in the postfix expression so we push its value 3 onto the stack. Finally, we encounter the operator /, so we pop two values from the stack and form their quotient 6/3. We push this result onto the stack. We are at the end of the expression, and one value, 2, is in the stack. This value is the value of the expression. Figure 20-11 traces the evaluation of this postfix expression.

Figure 20-11 The stack during the evaluation of the postfix expression *a b + c /* when *a* is 2, *b* is 4, and *c* is 3

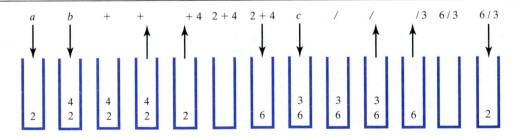

---

3. Finding the value of a variable is not an easy task, but we will not explore this detail in this book.

20.20   The evaluation algorithm follows directly from these examples:

> ***Algorithm*** `evaluatePostfix(postfix)`
> *// Evaluates a postfix expression.*
>
> `valueStack` = *a new empty stack*
> **while** (`postfix` *has characters left to parse*)
> {
>   `nextCharacter` = *next nonblank character of* `postfix`
>   **switch** (`nextCharacter`)
>   {
>   **case** *variable*:
>   `valueStack.push(`*value of the variable* `nextCharacter)`
>   **break**
>
>   **case '+': case '-': case '*': case '/': case '^':**
>   `operandTwo = valueStack.pop()`
>   `operandOne = valueStack.pop()`
>   `result` = *the result of the operation in* `nextCharacter` *and its operands*
>   `operandOne` *and* `operandTwo`
>   `valueStack.push(result)`
>   **break**
>
>   **default: break**
>   }
> }
>
> **return** `valueStack.peek()`

We can implement this algorithm as a static method of the class `Postfix` that was given in Segment 20.18. The implementation is left as an exercise.

Question 7   Using the previous algorithm, evaluate each of the following postfix expressions. Assume that $a = 2$, $b = 3$, $c = 4$, $d = 5$, and $e = 6$.

a. $a\ e + b\ d - /$
b. $a\ b\ c * d * -$

Evaluating Infix Expressions

Using the two algorithms in Segments 20.17 and 20.20, we could evaluate an infix expression by converting it to an equivalent postfix expression and then evaluating it. We can save some intermediate work by combining the two algorithms into one that evaluates an infix expression directly by using two stacks. A stack of operators is maintained according to the algorithm that converts an infix expression to postfix form. But instead of appending operands to the end of an expression, the combined algorithm pushes the value of an operand onto a second stack according to the algorithm that evaluates a postfix expression.

20.21   **Example.** Consider the infix expression $a + b * c$. When a is 2, b is 3, and c is 4, the expression's value is 14. To compute this result, we push the value of the variable a onto a stack of values, push the + onto a stack of operators, and push the value of b onto the stack of values. Since * has a higher precedence than the + at the top of the operator stack, we push it onto the stack. Finally, we push the value of c onto the stack of values. Figure 20-12a shows the state of the two stacks at this point.

Figure 20-12   Two stacks during the evaluation of $a + b * c$ when a is 2, b is 3, and c is 4: (a) after reaching the end of the expression; (b) while performing the multiplication; (c) while performing the addition

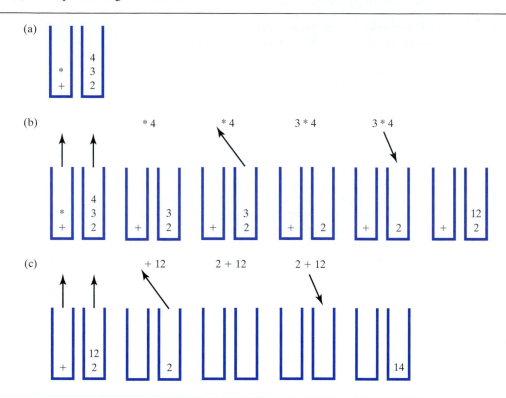

We now pop the operator stack and get the *. We get this operator's second and first operands, respectively, by popping the stack of values twice. After computing the product 3 * 4, we push the result 12 onto the stack of values, as Figure 20-12b shows. In a similar fashion, we pop the operator stack once and the value stack twice, compute 2 + 12, and push the result, 14, onto the stack of values. Since the operator stack is now empty, the value of the expression—14—is at the top of the stack of values. Figure 20-12c shows these final steps.

20.22   **The algorithm.** The algorithm to evaluate an infix expression follows. You should recognize aspects of its logic from the previous algorithms.

> *Algorithm* `evaluateInfix(infix)`
> *// Evaluates an infix expression.*
>
> `operatorStack` = *a new empty stack*
> `valueStack` = *a new empty stack*
> **while** (`infix` *has characters left to process*)
> {
>   `nextCharacter` = *next nonblank character of* `infix`
>   **switch** (`nextCharacter`)
>   {
>   **case** *variable*:
>   `valueStack.push(`*value of the variable* `nextCharacter)`
>   **break**

```
  case '^':
    operatorStack.push(nextCharacter)
    break

  case '+': case '-': case '*': case '/':
    while (!operatorStack.isEmpty() and
        precedence of nextCharacter <= precedence of operatorStack.peek())
    {
      // Execute operator at top of operatorStack
      topOperator = operatorStack.pop()
      operandTwo = valueStack.pop()
      operandOne = valueStack.pop()
      result = the result of the operation in topOperator and its operands
               operandOne and operandTwo
      valueStack.push(result)
    }

    operatorStack.push(nextCharacter)
    break

  case '(':
    operatorStack.push(nextCharacter)
    break

  case ')': // stack is not empty if infix expression is valid
    topOperator = operatorStack.pop()
    while (topOperator != '(')
    {
      operandTwo = valueStack.pop()
      operandOne = valueStack.pop()
      result = the result of the operation in topOperator and its operands
               operandOne and operandTwo
      valueStack.push(result)
      topOperator = operatorStack.pop()
    }
    break

  default: break
  } // end switch
} // end while

while (!operatorStack.isEmpty())
{
  topOperator = operatorStack.pop()
  operandTwo = valueStack.pop()
  operandOne = valueStack.pop()
  result = the result of the operation in topOperator and its operands
           operandOne and operandTwo
  valueStack.push(result)
}
return valueStack.peek()
```

 Question 8   Using the previous algorithm, evaluate each of the following infix expressions. Assume that $a = 2$, $b = 3$, $c = 4$, $d = 5$, and $e = 6$.

a. $a + b * c - 9$

b. $(a + e) / (b - d)$

c. $a + (b + c * d) - e / 2$

The Program Stack

20.23   When a program executes, a special location called the **program counter** references the current instruction. The program counter might be part of an actual computer or, in the case of Java, part of a virtual computer.[4]

When a method is called, the program's run-time environment creates an object called an **activation record,** or **frame,** for the method. The activation record shows the method's state during its execution. In particular, the activation record contains the method's arguments, local variables, and a reference to the current instruction—that is, a copy of the program counter. At the time the method is called, the activation record is pushed onto a stack called the **program stack** or, in Java, the **Java stack.** Since one method can call another, the program stack often contains more than one activation record. The record at the top of the stack belongs to the method that is currently executing. The record just beneath the top record belongs to the method that called the current method.

Figure 20-13 illustrates a program stack for a main method that calls methodA, which then calls methodB. When main begins execution, its activation record is at the top of the program stack (Figure 20-13a). When main calls methodA, a new record is pushed onto the stack. Suppose that the program counter is 50 at that time. Figure 20-13b shows the updated record for main and the new record for methodA just as the method begins execution. When methodA calls methodB, the program counter is 120. A new activation record is pushed onto the stack. Figure 20-13c shows the unchanged record for main, the updated record for methodA, and the new record for methodB just as it begins execution.

As methodB executes, its activation record is updated, but the records for main and methodA remain unchanged. The record for methodA, for example, represents the method's state at the time it called methodB. When methodB completes its execution, its record is popped from the stack. The program counter is reset to 120 and then advanced to the next instruction. Thus, methodA resumes execution with the values of its argument and local variable as given in its activation record.

Recursive Methods

20.24   Figure 20-13 illustrates an example in which methodA and methodB are distinct methods. However, they need not be. That is, the program stack enables a run-time environment to execute recursive methods. Each invocation of a method produces an activation record that is pushed onto the program stack. The activation record of a recursive method is not special in any way.

Chapter 10 traced the execution of two recursive methods in Figures 10-4 and 10-5. The activation records in those figures show less detail than the records just illustrated in Figure 20-13. Exercise 10 at the end of this chapter asks you to provide such detail.

A recursive method that makes many recursive calls will place many activation records in the program stack. You now should see why a recursive method can use more memory than an iterative method. You also should appreciate that too many recursive calls can use all the memory available for the program stack and cause an error message.

One way to replace recursion with iteration is to simulate the program stack. In fact, we can implement a recursive algorithm by using a stack instead of recursion. The next section provides an example of such an implementation.

---

4. To maintain computer independence, Java runs on a virtual computer called the **Java Virtual Machine (JVM).**

Figure 20-13 The program stack at three points in time: (a) when main begins execution;
(b) when methodA begins execution; (c) when methodB begins execution

```
1     public static
      void main(string[] arg)
      {
        . . .
        int x = 5;
50      int y = methodA(x);
        . . .
      } // end main

100   public static
      int methodA(int a)
      {
        . . .
        int z = 2;
120     methodB(z);
        . . .
        return z;
      } // end methodA

150   public static
      void methodB(int b)
      {
        . . .
      } // end methodB
```

```
                                                     methodB
                                                      PC = 150
                                                      b = 2

                                   methodA           methodA
                                    PC = 100           PC = 120
                                    a = 5              a = 5
                                                       z = 2

         main            main               main
          PC = 1          PC = 50             PC = 50
          arg = 800       arg = 800           arg = 800
                          x = 5               x = 5
                          y = 0               y = 0

           (a)             (b)                 (c)
```

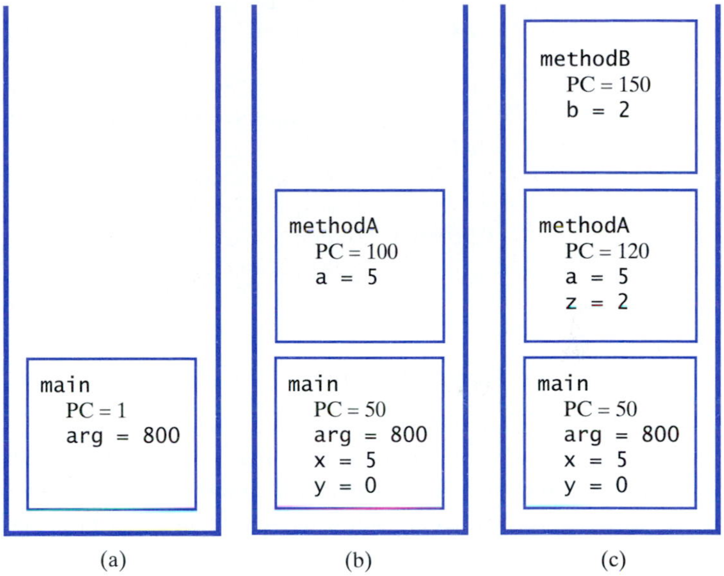

Program   Program stack at three points in time (PC is the program counter)

Using a Stack Instead of Recursion

20.25   Chapter 13 introduced the ADT sorted list. Like the ADT list, the sorted list has a search operation contains. When the implementation of the sorted list is array based, we can perform a binary search of the array of list items to implement contains. The array is a data field of the class that implements the sorted list. Since we are searching for a particular item in the list, the list items must be Comparable.

To hide the detail of array indices, contains invokes a private method binarySearch that actually does the binary search. The methods contains and a recursive version of binarySearch appear here as they did in Chapter 16:

```
public boolean contains(Object desiredItem)
{
  return binarySearch(0, length-1, (Comparable)desiredItem);
} // end contains

/** Task: Searches entry[first] through entry[last] for
 *        desiredItem, where the array entry is a data field.
 * @param first  an integer index >= 0 and < length of list
```

```
 *   @param last    an integer index >= 0 and < length of list
 *   @param desiredItem   the object to be found in the array
 *   @return true if desiredItem is found */
private boolean binarySearch(int first, int last, Comparable desiredItem)
{
  boolean found;
  int mid = (first + last)/2;
  if (first > last)
    found = false;
  else if (desiredItem.equals(entry[mid]))
    found = true;
  else if (desiredItem.compareTo(entry[mid]) < 0)
    found = binarySearch(first, mid-1, desiredItem);
  else
    found = binarySearch(mid+1, last, desiredItem);

  return found;
} // end binarySearch
```

An Iterative Binary Search

20.26   We can replace the recursive method `binarySearch` given in the previous segment with an iterative version by using a stack that mimics the program stack. We create a stack that is local to the method. We push objects onto this stack that are like the activation records described in Segment 20.23. An activation record in a Java stack contains the method's arguments, local variables, and a reference to the current instruction. Our objects need not contain all of this. In `binary-Search`, for example, the third argument `desiredItem` stays the same in each recursive call, so we can omit it from our record. Only the first two arguments change, so they must be saved in a record. Since both recursive calls to `binarySearch` occur right before the method's `return` statement, there is no need to distinguish between them by storing a representation of the program counter in the record. This simplification is not true in general, however.

To represent a record, we define a class that, in this case, has data fields for the method's arguments `first` and `last`. The following simple class is sufficient if we make it internal to the list class:

```
private class Record
{
  private int first, last;

  private Record(int firstIndex, int lastIndex)
  {
    first =firstIndex;
    last = lastIndex;
  } // end constructor
} // end Record
```

20.27   In general, when a method begins execution, it pushes an activation record onto a program stack. At its return, a record is popped from this stack. We want an iterative `binarySearch` to maintain its own stack. When the method begins execution, it should push a record onto this stack. Each recursive call should do likewise. As long as the stack is not empty, the method should remove a record from the stack and act according to the contents of the record. The method ends its execution when the stack becomes empty.

Here is an iterative version of binarySearch that uses a stack as we just described:

```java
private boolean binarySearch(int first, int last, Comparable desiredItem)
{
  StackInterface programStack = new ArrayStack();
  boolean found = false;
  boolean done = false;

  programStack.push(new Record(first, last));

  while (!done && !programStack.isEmpty())
  {
    Record topRecord = (Record)programStack.pop();
    first = topRecord.first;
    last = topRecord.last;
    int mid = (first + last)/2;
    if (first > last)
    {
      found = false;
      done = true;
    }
    else if (desiredItem.equals(entry[mid]))
    {
      found = true;
      done = true;
    }
    else
    {
      if (desiredItem.compareTo(entry[mid]) < 0)
        programStack.push(new Record(first, mid-1));
      else
        programStack.push(new Record(mid+1, last));
    } // end if
  } // end while

  return found;
} // end binarySearch
```

This approach does not always produce an elegant solution. We certainly can write an iterative version of binarySearch that is easier to understand than this version and does not require a stack. But sometimes, a simple iterative solution is not apparent; the stack approach offers a possible solution. You will see a more useful example of a stack-based iteration in Segment 25.14 of Chapter 25.

Java Class Library: The Class Stack

20.28   The package java.util contains the class Stack. The following four methods in this class are similar to methods in our StackInterface. We have used blue to indicate where they differ from our methods.

```java
public Object push(Object item);
public Object pop();
```

```
public Object peek();
public boolean empty();
```

In addition, Stack has the following methods that enable you to either search or traverse the stack:

```
/** Task: Searches for a given object in the stack.
 *  @param desiredItem  the object to be found
 *  @return either the position of desiredItem if it is in the stack
 *          or -1 if it is not; the top of the stack is at position 1 */
public int search(Object desiredItem);

/** @return an iterator for the stack that conforms to Java's
 *          interface Iterator */
public Iterator iterator();

/** @return an iterator for the stack that conforms to Java's
 *          interface ListIterator */
public ListIterator listIterator();
```

Finally, Stack has methods from the class Vector, since Stack extends Vector.

CHAPTER SUMMARY

- The ADT stack organizes its entries on a last-in, first-out basis. The top of the stack is the entry added most recently.

- A stack's major operations—**push**, **pop**, and **peek**—deal only with the top of the stack. The method **push** adds an entry to the top of the stack; **pop** removes and returns the top of the stack, and **peek** just returns it.

- Arithmetic operators that have two operands are binary operators. When an operator such as + or − has one operand, it is a unary operator.

- An algebraic expression often contains parentheses, square brackets, and braces. You can use a stack to determine whether these delimiters are paired correctly.

- Ordinary algebraic expressions are called infix expressions, because each binary operator appears between its two operands. An infix expression requires rules of operator precedence and can use parentheses to override these rules.

- In a postfix expression, each binary operator appears after its two operands. In a prefix expression, each binary operator appears before its two operands. Postfix and prefix expressions use no parentheses and have no rules of operator precedence.

- You can use a stack of operators to form a postfix expression that is equivalent to a given infix expression.

- You can use a stack of values to evaluate a postfix expression.

- You can use two stacks—one for operators and one for values—to evaluate an infix expression.

- When a method is called, the Java run-time environment creates an activation record, or frame, to record the status of the method. The record contains the method's arguments and local variables, along with the address of the current instruction. The record is placed in a stack called the program stack.

- You can use a stack instead of recursion to implement a recursive algorithm. This stack mimics the behavior of the program stack.

PROGRAMMING TIP

● Methods such as **peek** and **pop** must behave reasonably when the stack is empty. For example, they could return **null** or throw an exception.

EXERCISES

1. If you push the objects x, y, and z onto an initially empty stack, in what order will three pop operations remove them from the stack?

2. Suppose that s and t are empty stacks and a, b, c, and d are objects. What do the stacks contain after the following sequence of operations executes?

```
s.push(a);
s.push(b);
s.push(c);
t.push(d);
t.push(s.pop());
t.push(s.peek());
s.push(t.pop());
t.pop();
```

3. Consider the following Java statements:

```
int n = 4;
StackInterface myStack = new ArrayStack();
while (n > 0)
{
   myStack.push(new Integer(n));
   n--;
} // end while
int result = 1;
while (!myStack.isEmpty())
{
   Integer integer = (Integer)myStack.pop();
   result = result * integer.intValue();
} // end while
System.out.println("result = " + result);
```

a. What value is displayed when this code executes?
b. What mathematical function does the code evaluate?

4. Show the contents of the stack as you trace the algorithm checkBalance, given in Segment 20.9, for each of the following expressions:

a. $a \{b [c * (d + e)] - f\}$
b. $\{a (b * c) / [d + e] / f) - g\}$
c. $a\{b [c - d] e]) f$

5. Using the algorithm in Segment 20.17, convert each of the following infix expressions to postfix expressions:

a. $(a + b) / (c - d)$
b. $(a - b * c) / (d * e * f + g)$
c. $a / b * (c + (d - e))$
d. $(a \wedge b * c - d) \wedge e + f \wedge g \wedge h$

6. Using the algorithm in Segment 20.20, evaluate each of the following postfix expressions. Assume that $a = 2$, $b = 3$, $c = 4$, $d = 5$, and $e = 6$.

   a. $a\ b + c * d -$
   b. $a\ b * c\ a - / d\ e * +$
   c. $a\ c - b \wedge d +$

7. Implement the algorithm `evaluatePostfix` given in Segment 20.20 as a static method of the class `Postfix`.

8. Show the contents of the two stacks as you trace the algorithm given in Segment 20.22 to evaluate each of the following infix expressions. Assume that $a = 2$, $b = 3$, $c = 4$, $d = 5$, $e = 6$, and $f = 7$.

   a. $(a + b) / (c - d) - 5$
   b. $(d * f + 1) * e / (a \wedge b - b * c + 1) - 72$
   c. $(a \wedge c - f) \wedge a - a \wedge b \wedge a$

9. A **palindrome** is a string of characters (a word, phrase, or sentence) that is the same regardless of whether you read it forward or backward—assuming that you ignore spaces, punctuation, and case. For example, *Race car* is a palindrome. So is *A man, a plan, a canal: Panama*. Describe how you could use a stack to determine whether a string is a palindrome.

10. Chapter 10 traced the execution of two recursive methods in Figures 10-4 and 10-5. Revise those figures to provide the detail in the activation records that Figure 20-13 provides.

PROJECTS

1. Consider the following algorithm to sort the entries in a stack S_1. First create two empty stacks, S_2 and S_3. Move the top of S_1 to S_2. Now, at any given time, stack S_2 holds the entries in sorted order, with the smallest at the top of the stack. Consider the top t of S_1. Pop entries of stack S_2 and push them onto stack S_3 until you reach the correct place to put t. Then push t onto S_2. Next move all the entries from S_3 to S_2.

   a. Implement this algorithm both recursively and iteratively.
   b. Consider the following revision of this algorithm. After pushing t onto S_2, do not move the entries in S_3 back to S_2. Instead, compare the new top t_1 of S_1 with the top of S_2. Then either move entries from S_2 to S_3 or from S_3 to S_2 until you locate the correction position for t_1. Push t_1 onto S_2. Implement this revised algorithm.

21

Stack Implementations

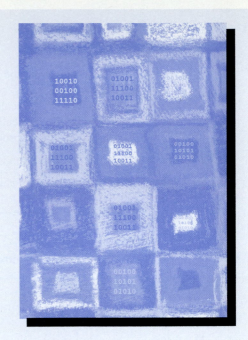

CONTENTS

A Linked Implementation
An Array-Based Implementation
A Vector-Based Implementation

PREREQUISITES

Chapter   5   List Implementations That Use Arrays
Chapter   6   List Implementations That Link Data
Chapter   20   Stacks

OBJECTIVES

After studying this chapter, you should be able to

- Implement the ADT stack by using either a linked chain, an array, or a vector
- Compare and contrast the various implementations and their performance

The implementations of the ADT stack described in this chapter use techniques like the ones we used to implement the ADT list. We will use, in turn, a chain of linked nodes, an array, and an instance of Vector to store the stack's entries. You should be pleasantly surprised by the simplicity and efficiency of these implementations.

A Linked Implementation

21.1   Each of the operations push, pop, and peek of the ADT stack involve the top of the stack. If we use a chain of linked nodes to implement a stack, where in the chain should the top of the stack be? Recall that when a chain has only a head reference, we can add, remove, or retrieve its first node faster than any other node. Thus, the stack operations will execute fastest if the first node in the chain references the top of the stack, as Figure 21-1 illustrates.

Also note from the figure that each node in the chain references one entry in the stack. Nodes are allocated—that is, created—only when needed for a new entry. They are deallocated when an entry is removed. Recall from the note on page 140 that the Java run-time environment automatically reclaims, or deallocates, memory that a program no longer references, without explicit instruction from the programmer.

Note: If you use a chain of linked nodes to implement a stack, the first node should reference the stack's top.

Figure 21-1   A chain of linked nodes that implements a stack

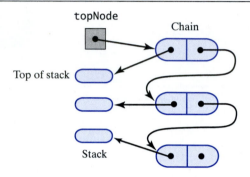

21.2   **Data field and constructor.** The linked implementation of the stack begins like the analogous implementation of the list in Segment 6.23. A data field `topNode` is the head reference of the chain of nodes, and the default constructor sets this field to `null`:

```java
public class LinkedStack implements StackInterface, java.io.Serializable
{
   private Node topNode; // references first node in chain

   public LinkedStack()
   {
      topNode = null;
   } // end default constructor
   . . .
```

Each node is an instance of the private class `Node` that is defined within the class `LinkedStack`:

```java
private class Node implements java.io.Serializable
{
   private Object data; // entry in stack
   private Node   next; // link to next node

   < Constructors and the methods getData, setData, getNextNode, and setNextNode
      are here. >
   . . .
} // end Node
```

This class is like the one you first saw in Segment 6.21, but it implements `Serializable`. Although we did not actually define or use set and get methods in Chapter 6, we will use them here.

21.3   Adding to the top. We push an entry onto the stack by first allocating a new node that references the stack's existing chain, as Figure 21-2a illustrates. This reference is in `topNode`, the head reference to the chain. We then set `topNode` to reference the new node, as in Figure 21-2b. Thus, the method push has the following definition:

```java
public void push(Object newEntry)
{
  Node newNode = new Node(newEntry, topNode);
  topNode = newNode;
} // end push
```

This operation requires no search and is independent of the other entries in the stack. Its performance is thus O(1).

Figure 21-2   (a) A new node that references the top of the stack; (b) the new node is now at the top of the stack

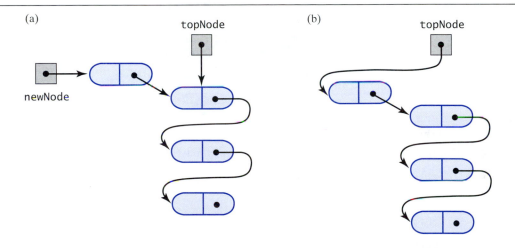

21.4   Retrieving the top. We get the top of the stack by accessing the data portion of the first node in the chain. Thus peek, like push, is an O(1) operation. Note that if the stack is empty, peek returns `null`.

```java
public Object peek()
{
  Object top = null;

  if (topNode != null)
    top = topNode.getData();

  return top;
} // end peek
```

21.5   Removing the top. We pop, or remove, the top of the stack by setting `topNode` to the reference in the first node. Thus, `topNode` will reference what was the second node in the chain, as Figure 21-3 shows.

```
public Object pop()
{
   Object top = null;

   if (topNode != null)
   {
      top = topNode.getData();
      topNode = topNode.getNextNode();
   } // end if

   return top;
} // end pop
```

This operation also is O(1).

Figure 21-3   The stack after the first node in the chain is deleted

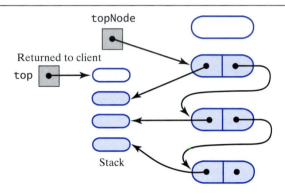

21.6   **The rest of the class.** The remaining public methods isEmpty and clear involve only topNode:

```
public boolean isEmpty()
{
   return topNode == null;
} // end isEmpty
```

```
public void clear()
{
   topNode = null;
} // end clear
```

Question 1   Is an implementation of the ADT stack reasonable if you place the top of the stack at the end of a chain of linked nodes? Explain.

An Array-Based Implementation

21.7   If we use an array to implement the stack, where should we place the top of the stack? If the first location of the array references the stack's top, as shown in Figure 21-4a, we must move all the elements in the array any time we add or remove a stack entry. We can have more efficient stack operations if the first array location is the bottom of the stack. The top of the stack is then the last occupied location in the array, as Figure 21-4b shows. This configuration allows us to add or remove stack entries without moving other array elements. Thus, one disadvantage of a typical array-based implementation does not apply here. The exercises at the end of this chapter consider other ways to place a stack's entries in an array.

Using dynamic array expansion avoids a stack that is too full to accept another entry. However, unlike the linked chain in the previous section, the array in Figure 21-4 contains locations that are unused. If we eventually fill the array with additional stack entries, we can expand the size of the array—but then we will have more unused locations. The chain has its downside as well, in that it uses additional memory for the link portions of its nodes.

Note: If you use an array to implement a stack, the array's first element should represent the bottom of the stack. The last occupied location in the array, then, represents the stack's top.

Figure 21-4   An array that implements a stack; its first location references (a) the top of the stack; (b) the bottom of the stack

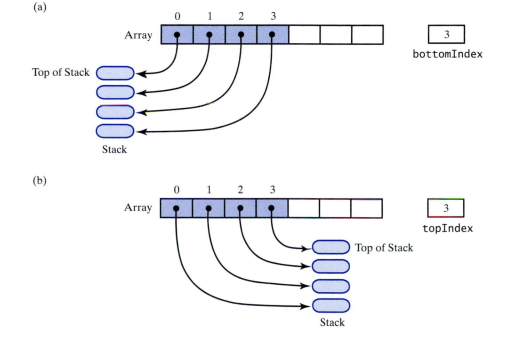

21.8   **Data fields and constructors.** The array-based implementation of the stack begins like the analogous implementation of the ADT list in Segment 5.5. Two data fields are an array of stack entries and an index to the top entry. The default constructor allocates an array with a default size; another constructor lets the client choose the array size.

```
public class ArrayStack implements StackInterface, java.io.Serializable
{
    private Object[] stack;   // array of stack entries
    private int topIndex;     // index of top entry
    private static final int DEFAULT_MAX_SIZE = 50;
```

```java
public ArrayStack()
{
  stack = new Object[DEFAULT_MAX_SIZE];
  topIndex = -1;
} // end default constructor

public ArrayStack(int maxSize)
{
  stack = new Object[maxSize];
  topIndex = -1;
} // end constructor
. . .
```

21.9 **Adding to the top.** The push operation first checks whether the array has room for a new entry. If it does not, push doubles the size of the array. It then places the new entry immediately after the last occupied location in the array:

```java
public void push(Object newEntry)
{
  topIndex++;

  if (topIndex >= stack.length) // if array is full
    doubleArray(); // expand array

  stack[topIndex] = newEntry;
} // end push
```

When push does not invoke doubleArray, it is an O(1) operation, since its performance is independent of the size of the stack. However, doubleArray is an O(n) operation, so when the array is full, the performance of push degrades to O(n). If this happens, however, the very next push is O(1) again. To be fair, all push operations should share the cost of the occasional execution of doubleArray. That is, we **amortize** the cost of doubling the array over all additions to the stack. Unless we must double the array many times, each push is almost O(1).

21.10 **Retrieving the top.** The operation peek returns either the array element at topIndex or null if the stack is empty:

```java
public Object peek()
{
  Object top = null;

  if (!isEmpty())
    top = stack[topIndex];

  return top;
} // end peek
```

This operation is O(1).

21.11 **Removing the top.** The pop operation, like peek, retrieves the top of the stack, but then removes it. To remove the top of the stack in Figure 21-4b, we simply could decrement topIndex, as Figure 21-5a illustrates. This simple step would be sufficient, since the other methods would behave correctly. For example, peek would return the item that stack[2] references in Figure 21-5a. However, the object that previously was the top of the stack and is returned to the client would still be referenced by the array. No harm will come from this situation if our implementation is correct. To be safe, pop can set stack[topIndex] to null before decrementing topIndex. Figure 21-5b illustrates the stack in this case.

Figure 21-5 An array-based stack after its top is removed by (a) decrementing `topIndex`;
(b) setting `stack[topIndex]` to `null` and then decrementing `topIndex`

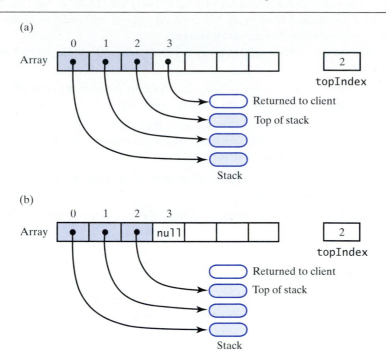

The following implementation of pop reflects these comments:

```
public Object pop()
{
   Object top = null;

   if (!isEmpty())
   {
      top = stack[topIndex];
      stack[topIndex] = null;
      topIndex--;
   } // end if

   return top;
} // end pop
```

Like peek, pop is an O(1) operation.

Question 2   If we implemented a stack of primitives instead of a stack of objects, what changes should we make to the method pop?

21.12   **The rest of the class.** The method `isEmpty` involves only `topIndex`:

```
public boolean isEmpty()
{
   return topIndex < 0;
} // end isEmpty
```

If the method `clear` simply sets `topIndex` to –1, the stack methods would behave correctly as though the stack were empty. However, the objects that were in the stack would remain allocated. Just as `pop` sets `stack[topIndex]` to `null`, `clear` should set to `null` each array location that was used for the stack. Alternatively, `clear` could call `pop` repeatedly until the stack is empty. We leave the implementation of `clear` as an exercise.

The private method `doubleArray` is like `doubleArray` in Segment 5.16, except for the name of the array.

Question 3   If `stack` is an array that contains the entries in a stack, what is a disadvantage of maintaining the top of the stack in `stack[0]`?

Question 4   If you use the locations at the end of an array `stack` for a stack's entries before you use the array's first locations, which stack entry—the top or the bottom—should be in `stack[stack.length-1]`? Why?

Question 5   Write an implementation of `clear` that sets to `null` each array location that was used for the stack.

Question 6   Write an implementation of `clear` that repeatedly calls `pop` until the stack is empty.

A Vector-Based Implementation

21.13   Using a vector is like using an array to implement the stack, but easier. We let the first element of the vector represent the bottom of the stack. Thus, the vector looks like the array in Figure 21-4b. We do not need to maintain an index to the top of the stack, however, as we can determine this index from the vector's size, which is readily available. Also, the vector expands as necessary, so we do not have to worry about this detail.

Since the implementation of `Vector` is based on an array that can be expanded dynamically, the performance of this implementation of the stack is like that of the array-based implementation given in the previous section.

Note: If you use a vector to implement a stack, the vector's first element should represent the bottom of the stack. Then the last occupied location in the vector represents the stack's top.

21.14   **Data fields and constructors.** The class that implements the stack begins by declaring a vector as a data field and allocating the vector in its constructors:

```
import java.util.Vector;
public class VectorStack implements StackInterface,
java.io.Serializable
{
   private Vector stack; // top of stack is last element

   public VectorStack()
   {
      stack = new Vector(); // vector doubles in size if necessary
   } // end default constructor

   public VectorStack(int maxSize)
   {
      stack = new Vector(maxSize);
   } // end constructor
   . . .
```

21.15   **Adding to the top.** We use Vector's method addElement to add an entry to the end of the vector, that is, to the top of the stack.

```java
public void push(Object newEntry)
{
  stack.addElement(newEntry);
} // end push
```

21.16   **Retrieving the top.** We retrieve the top of the stack by using Vector's method lastElement.

```java
public Object peek()
{
  Object top = null;

  if (!isEmpty())
    top = stack.lastElement();

  return top;
} // end peek
```

21.17   **Removing the top.** We can remove the top of the stack by using Vector's method removeElementAt. The argument to this method is the index of the last entry in the vector, since that entry is the top of the stack. This index is 1 less than the vector's current size stack.size().

```java
public Object pop()
{
  Object top = null;

  if (!isEmpty())
  {
    top = stack.lastElement();
    stack.removeElementAt(stack.size()-1);
  } // end if

  return top;
} // end pop
```

21.18   **The rest of the class.** The remaining public methods isEmpty and clear invoke analogous Vector methods:

```java
public boolean isEmpty()
{
  return stack.isEmpty();
} // end isEmpty

public void clear()
{
  stack.removeAllElements();
} // end clear
```

We also can use an instance of the ADT list to represent a stack. Such an implementation is similar to the vector implementation, and we leave it to you as a programming project.

    Question 7   If stack is a vector that contains the entries in a stack, is it reasonable to maintain the top of the stack in the vector's first element?

CHAPTER SUMMARY

- You can implement a stack by using a chain of linked nodes that has only a head reference. The stack operations execute fastest if the first node in the chain references the top of the stack. This is true because you can add, remove, or access a chain's first node faster than any other node.

- The stack operations are O(1) for a linked implementation.

- You can implement a stack by using an array. If you make the bottom of the stack the first entry in the array, no array elements will be moved when you add or remove stack entries.

- Using dynamic array expansion avoids a stack that is too full to accept another entry. However, the array generally contains locations that are unused.

- The stack operations are O(1) for an array-based implementation. However, when the array is full, **push** doubles the size of the array. In that case, **push** is O(n). If you spread this extra cost over all other pushes, and if doubling the array is not frequent, **push** is almost O(1).

- You can implement a stack by using a vector. You maintain the bottom of the stack at the beginning of the vector.

- Since the implementation of **Vector** is based on an array that can be expanded dynamically, the performance of a vector-based implementation is like that of the array-based implementation.

EXERCISES

1. Discuss the advantages and disadvantages of an array-based implementation of the ADT stack as compared to a linked implementation.

2. Imagine a linked implementation of the ADT stack that places the top of the stack at the end of a chain of linked nodes. Describe how you can define the stack operations push, pop, and peek so that they do not traverse the chain.

3. Segment 21.9 noted that an array-based push method is normally O(1), but when a stack needs to be doubled in size, push is O(n). This observation is not as bad as it seems, however. Suppose that you double the size of a stack from n elements to $2n$ elements.

   a. How many calls to push can you make before the stack must double in size again?
   b. Remembering that each of these calls to push is O(1), what is the average cost of all the push operations? (The average cost is the total cost of all calls to push divided by the number of calls to push.)

PROJECTS

1. Implement the ADT stack by using an array stack to contain its entries. Expand the array dynamically, as necessary. Choose one of the following possibilities:

   a. Maintain the bottom of the stack in stack[stack.length-1].
   b. Maintain the top of the stack in stack[stack.length-1].

2. Write the implementation of the ADT stack that Exercise 2 describes.

3. Implement the ADT stack by using an ADT list to contain its entries. Discuss the efficiency of your implementation as it relates to the implementation of the list.

4. Implement the ADT stack by extending the class `java.util.Vector`. Compare your implementation with the one given in this chapter, and discuss the trade-offs.

5. Write a Java program that uses a stack to determine whether an input string is a palindrome. Exercise 9 in Chapter 20 defines "palindrome" and asks you to describe a solution to this problem.

6. The ADT stack lets you peek at its top element without removing it. For some applications of stacks, you also need to peek at the element beneath the top element without removing it. We will call such an operation `peek2`. If the stack has more than one element, `peek2` returns the second element from top without altering the stack. If the stack has fewer than two elements, `peek2` returns `null`. Write a linked implementation of a stack that includes a method `peek2`.

22

Queues, Deques, and Priority Queues

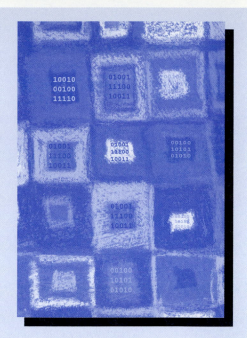

CONTENTS

Specifications of the ADT Queue
Using a Queue to Simulate a Waiting Line
  The Classes `WaitLine` and `Customer`
Using a Queue to Compute the Capital Gain in a Sale of Stock
  The Classes `StockLedger` and `StockPurchase`
Specifications of the ADT Deque
Using a Deque to Compute the Capital Gain in a Sale of Stock
Specifications of the ADT Priority Queue
Using a Priority Queue to Compute the Capital Gain in a Sale of Stock

PREREQUISITES

Chapter   3   Designing Classes
Chapter   20   Stacks

OBJECTIVES

After studying this chapter, you should be able to

- Describe the operations of the ADT queue
- Use a queue to simulate a waiting line
- Use a queue in a program that organizes data in a first-in, first-out manner
- Describe the operations of the ADT deque
- Use a deque in a program that organizes data chronologically and can operate on both the oldest and newest entries
- Describe the operations of the ADT priority queue
- Use a priority queue in a program that organizes data objects according to their priorities

Waiting for your turn is a fact of life. Most people have spent much time standing in lines at stores, banks, or movie theaters. You have probably waited on the telephone for an airline representative or a technical support person, and you may have waited for your printed output to finally reach the printer in the computer lab. In each of these examples, people wait with the expectation that they will be served before everyone who has come after them. That is, first come, first served.

A **queue** is another name for a waiting line, and it is the name of an ADT that we will investigate in this chapter. Queues are used within operating systems and to simulate real-world events—that is, they come into play whenever processes or events must wait.

Sometimes you need more flexibility than a queue permits. A **double-ended queue**, or **deque**, organizes data like a queue but enables you to operate on both its oldest and newest entries. And when the importance of an object depends on criteria other than its arrival time, you can assign it a priority. You can organize such objects within a **priority queue** according to their priorities instead of chronologically.

The queue, deque, and priority queue are three ADTs that this chapter will explore.

Specifications of the ADT Queue

22.1   Like a stack, the ADT **queue** organizes its entries according to the order in which they were added. But while a stack has a last-in, first-out behavior, a queue exhibits a **first-in, first-out,** or **FIFO,** behavior. To achieve this behavior, all additions to a queue are at its **back.** The back of a queue, then, is the item added most recently. The **front** of a queue is the item that was added earliest. Figure 22-1 provides some examples of common queues.

Figure 22-1   Some everyday queues

 Note: Among the items in a queue, the one added first, or earliest, is the **front of the queue,** and the one added most recently is the **back of the queue.**

A queue, like a stack, restricts access to its entries. Although someone might cut into a line of people, additions to a software queue must occur at its back. A client can look at or remove only the front of the queue. The only way to look at an entry that is not the front of a queue is to repeatedly remove items from the queue until the desired item reaches the front. If you were to remove all of a queue's entries one by one, you would get them in chronological order, beginning with the first item added to the queue.

The queue has no search operation. An entry can have a search key, but the key is not relevant to the queue or to the entry's position within the queue.

22.2   The operation that adds an entry to a queue is traditionally called enqueue (pronounced "N-Q"). The operation to remove an entry is dequeue (pronounced "D-Q"). The operation that retrieves the front of the queue is called getFront. The following specifications define a set of operations for the ADT queue:

ABSTRACT DATA TYPE QUEUE

DATA

- A collection of objects in a specific order

OPERATIONS

enqueue(newEntry)

    Task: Adds a new entry to the back of the queue.
    Input: newEntry is the new entry.
    Output: None.

dequeue()

    Task: Removes and returns the front of the queue.
    Input: None.
    Output: Returns either the front of the queue or null if
           the queue was empty.

getFront()

    Task: Retrieves the front of the queue without
          changing the queue in any way.
    Input: None.
    Output: Returns either the front of the queue or null if
           the queue is empty.

isEmpty()

    Task: Determines whether the queue is empty.
    Input: None.
    Output: Returns true if the queue is empty.

clear()

    Task: Removes all entries from the queue.
    Input: None.
    Output: None.

Note: Alternate names for methods

As we mentioned in Chapter 20, class designers often include aliases for certain methods. For a queue, you could include the additional methods put and get to mean enqueue and dequeue. The names add, insert, remove, and delete are also reasonable aliases. Likewise, you could provide a method peek to mean getFront.

22.3   The following Java interface specifies a queue of objects. Since `Object` is the superclass, or base class, of all other classes, we can specify `Object` as the data type of the items in the queue. Doing so allows us to place any object in the queue.

```java
public interface QueueInterface
{
  /** Task: Adds a new entry to the back of the queue.
   *  @param newEntry  an object to be added */
  public void enqueue(Object newEntry);

  /** Task: Removes and returns the front of the queue.
   *  @return either the object at the front of the queue or null
   *          if the queue was empty */
  public Object dequeue();

  /** Task: Retrieves the front of the queue.
   *  @return either the object at the front of the queue or null
   *          if the queue is empty */
  public Object getFront();

  /** Task: Determines whether the queue is empty.
   * @return true if the queue is empty */
  public boolean isEmpty();

  /** Task: Removes all entries from the queue. */
  public void clear();
} // end QueueInterface
```

22.4   **Example: Demonstrating the queue methods.** The following statements add, retrieve, and remove strings from a queue. We assume that the class `LinkedQueue` implements `QueueInterface` and is available.

```java
QueueInterface myQueue = new LinkedQueue();
myQueue.enqueue("Jim");
myQueue.enqueue("Jess");
myQueue.enqueue("Jill");
myQueue.enqueue("Jane");
myQueue.enqueue("Joe");

String front = (String) myQueue.getFront();
System.out.println(front + " is at the front of the queue.");

front = (String) myQueue.dequeue();
System.out.println(front + " is removed from the queue.");

myQueue.enqueue("Jerry");

front = (String) myQueue.getFront();
System.out.println(front + " is at the front of the queue.");

front = (String) myQueue.dequeue();
System.out.println(front + " is removed from the queue.");
```

Parts *a* through *e* of Figure 22-2 illustrate the five additions to the queue. It contains—from front to back—the strings *Jim, Jess, Jill, Jane,* and *Joe.* The string at the front of the queue is *Jim*; `getFront` retrieves it. The method dequeue retrieves *Jim* again and then removes it from the queue

(Figure 22-2f). A subsequent call to enqueue adds *Jerry* to the back of the queue but does not affect the front (Figure 22-2g). Thus, getFront retrieves *Jess*, and dequeue retrieves *Jess* and then removes it (Figure 22-2h).

If we now were to execute dequeue repeatedly until the queue was empty, an additional call to either dequeue or getFront would return null.

Figure 22-2   A queue of strings after (a) enqueue adds *Jim*; (b) enqueue adds *Jess*; (c) enqueue adds *Jill*; (d) enqueue adds *Jane*; (e) enqueue adds *Joe*; (f) dequeue retrieves and removes *Jim*; (g) enqueue adds *Jerry*; (h) dequeue retrieves and removes *Jess*

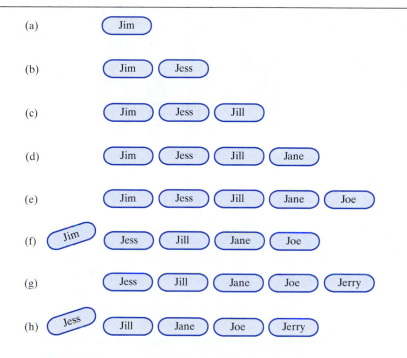

 Question 1   After the following statements execute, what string is at the front of the queue and what string is at the back?

```
QueueInterface myQueue = new LinkedQueue();
myQueue.enqueue("Jim");
myQueue.enqueue("Jess");
myQueue.enqueue("Jill");
myQueue.enqueue("Jane");
String name = myQueue.dequeue();
myQueue.enqueue(name);
myQueue.enqueue(myQueue.getFront());
name = myQueue.dequeue();
```

 Programming Tip: Methods such as getFront and dequeue must behave reasonably when the queue is empty. Here, we specify that they return null. Another possibility is to have them throw an exception.

Using a Queue to Simulate a Waiting Line

22.5   In many everyday situations, you will wait in a line. Whether the line is at a store, a ticket window, or a car wash, a line behaves like the ADT queue. The person at the front of the line is served first; newcomers go to the back of the line, as Figure 22-3 shows.

Figure 22-3   A line, or queue, of people

Most businesses are concerned with the time that their customers must wait for service. A short wait time enables an organization to increase customer satisfaction, serve more people, and make more money. If two agents serve one line, you will wait less time than if only one agent is on duty. A business, however, does not want to employ more people than necessary. And a car wash certainly would not build an additional service bay to test its effect on its customer's wait time.

Computer simulation of a real-world situation is a common way to test various business scenarios. In this example, we will simulate a single line of people waiting for service from one agent. Customers arrive at different intervals and require various times to complete their transactions. One way to achieve this variety is to assume that the events are random.

In a **time-driven simulation,** a counter enumerates simulated units of time—minutes, for example. Customers arrive at random times during the simulation and enter the queue. Each customer is assigned a random transaction time that does not exceed some arbitrary upper bound. During the simulation, the time that each customer waits in the queue is recorded. At the conclusion of the simulation, summary statistics are generated, including the number of customers served and the average time that each waited.

The Classes `WaitLine` and `Customer`

22.6   **Design.** Two kinds of objects occur in the description of this problem: the waiting line and the customers. We can design a class for each of these.

The class `WaitLine` simulates the waiting line for a given period of time. During this time, customers enter the line at random intervals and leave it after being served. At the conclusion of the simulation, the class computes the summary statistics. Figure 22-4 shows a CRC card for this class.

The class `Customer` records and makes available the customer's arrival time, transaction time, and customer number. Figure 22-5 contains a class diagram for `WaitLine` and `Customer`.

Figure 22-4   A CRC card for the class `WaitLine`

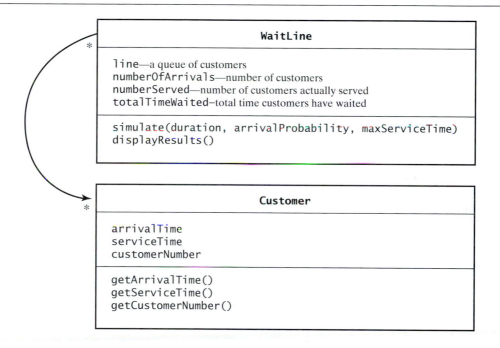

WaitLine

Responsibilities
Simulate customers entering and leaving a
waiting line
Display number served, total wait time,
average wait time, amd number left in line

Collaborations
Customer

Figure 22-5   A diagram of the classes `WaitLine` and `Customer`

WaitLine

`line`—a queue of customers
`numberOfArrivals`—number of customers
`numberServed`—number of customers actually served
`totalTimeWaited`—total time customers have waited

`simulate(duration, arrivalProbability, maxServiceTime)`
`displayResults()`

Customer

`arrivalTime`
`serviceTime`
`customerNumber`

`getArrivalTime()`
`getServiceTime()`
`getCustomerNumber()`

22.7   **The method `simulate`.** The method `simulate` is the heart of this example and of the class `Wait-Line`. To maintain the clock for this time-driven simulation, `simulate` contains a loop that counts up to a given duration. For example, the clock could simulate one hour by counting minutes, beginning at 0 and continuing until 60.

At each value of the clock, the method determines whether the current customer is still being served and whether a new customer has arrived. If a new customer arrives, the method creates a new customer object, assigns it a random service time—that is, the amount of time required for the customer's transaction—and places the customer into the queue. If a customer is still being served, the clock advances; if not, a customer leaves the front of the queue and begins service. At this point, the time the customer waited is noted. Figure 22-6 provides an example of the queue for a portion of the simulation.

Figure 22-6   A simulated waiting line

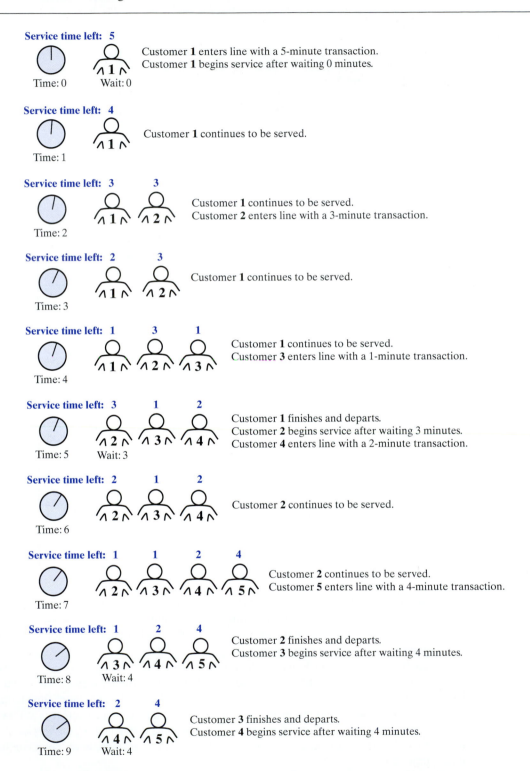

The following pseudocode describes the method `simulate`. It assumes that the class `WaitLine` has initialized its data fields as follows: `line` is an empty queue, and `numberOfArrivals`, `numberServed`, and `totalTimeWaited` are each zero.

> *Algorithm* `simulate(duration, arrivalProbability, maxServiceTime)`
> `serviceTimeLeft = 0`
> **`for`** `(clock = 0; clock < duration; clock++)`
> `{`
>   **`if`** (*a new customer arrives*)
>   `{`
>   `numberOfArrivals++`
>   `serviceTime =` *a random time that does not exceed* `maxServiceTime`
>   `nextArrival =` *a new customer containing* `clock`, `serviceTime`, *and*
>   *a customer number that is* `numberOfArrivals`
>   `line.enqueue(nextArrival)`
>   `}`
>
>   **`if`** `(serviceTimeLeft > 0)` // *if present customer is still being served*
>   `serviceTimeLeft--`
>   **`else if`** `(!line.isEmpty())`
>   `{`
>   `nextCustomer = line.dequeue()`
>   `serviceTimeLeft = nextCustomer.getServiceTime() - 1`
>   `timeWaited = clock - nextCustomer.getArrivalTime()`
>   `totalTimeWaited = totalTimeWaited + timeWaited`
>   `numberServed++`
>   `}`
> `}`

22.8   **Implementation details for `simulate`.** At each value of the clock, `simulate` must determine whether a new customer has arrived. To do so, it needs the probability that a customer will arrive. This arrival probability is a parameter of the method and has a value between 0 and 1. For example, if there is a 65 percent chance that a customer will arrive at any given time, the arrival probability is 0.65. We then generate a random number between 0 and 1 by using the method `random` in Java's class `Math`. If `Math.random()` is less than the given arrival probability, `simulate` creates a new customer and places it into the queue.

The method assigns to each new customer a random service time, that is, the amount of time required for the customer's transaction. If we provide a maximum value for this time, we can multiply it by `Math.random()` to get a random service time. Adding 1 to the result ensures that the service time is never 0 but allows a small chance that the service time will exceed the given maximum value by 1. For simplicity, we will tolerate this small imprecision.

In the following implementation of the class `WaitList`, the definition of `simulate` contains print statements to help you follow the simulation. The other methods in the class are straightforward.

```
/** Simulates a waiting line. */
public class WaitLine
{
  private QueueInterface line;
  private int numberOfArrivals;
  private int numberServed;
  private int totalTimeWaited;
```

```java
public WaitLine()
{
  line = new LinkedQueue();
  reset();
} // end default constructor

/** Task: Simulates a waiting line with one serving agent.
 *  @param duration  the number of simulated minutes
 *  @param arrivalProbability  a real number between 0 and 1 that is
 *          the probability of a customer arriving at a given time
 *  @param maxServiceTime  the longest service time for a customer */
public void simulate(int duration, double arrivalProbability,
                         int maxServiceTime)
{
  int serviceTimeLeft = 0;

  for (int clock = 0; clock < duration; clock++)
  {
    if (Math.random() < arrivalProbability)
    {
      numberOfArrivals++;
      int serviceTime = (int)(Math.random() * maxServiceTime + 1);
      Customer nextArrival = new Customer(clock, serviceTime,
                                          numberOfArrivals);
      line.enqueue(nextArrival);
      System.out.println("Customer " + numberOfArrivals
                      + " enters line at time " + clock
                      + ". Service time is " + serviceTime);
    } // end if

    if (serviceTimeLeft > 0)
      serviceTimeLeft--;
    else if (!line.isEmpty())
    {
      Customer nextCustomer = (Customer)line.dequeue();
      serviceTimeLeft = nextCustomer.getServiceTime() - 1;
      int timeWaited = clock - nextCustomer.getArrivalTime();
      totalTimeWaited = totalTimeWaited + timeWaited;
      numberServed++;
      System.out.println("Customer "
                      + nextCustomer.getCustomerNumber()
                      + " begins service at time " + clock
                      + ". Time waited is " + timeWaited);
    } // end if
  } // end for
} // end simulate

/** Task: Displays summary results of the simulation. */
public void displayResults()
{
  System.out.println();
  System.out.println("Number served = " + numberServed);
  System.out.println("Total time waited = " + totalTimeWaited);
  double averageTimeWaited = ((double)totalTimeWaited)/numberServed;
```

```
        System.out.println("Average time waited = " + averageTimeWaited);
        int leftInLine = numberOfArrivals - numberServed;
        System.out.println("Number left in line = " + leftInLine);
    } // end displayResults

    /** Task: Initializes the simulation. */
    public final void reset()
    {
        line.clear();
        numberOfArrivals = 0;
        numberServed = 0;
        totalTimeWaited = 0;
    } // end reset
} // end WaitLine
```

22.9   **Sample output.** The Java statements

```
        WaitLine customerLine = new WaitLine();
        customerLine.simulate(20, 0.5, 5);
        customerLine.displayResults();
```

simulate the line for 20 minutes with a 50 percent arrival probability and a 5-minute maximum service time. They produce the following results:

> Customer 1 enters line at time 0. Service time is 4
>
> Customer 1 begins service at time 0. Time waited is 0
>
> Customer 2 enters line at time 2. Service time is 2
>
> Customer 3 enters line at time 4. Service time is 1
>
> Customer 2 begins service at time 4. Time waited is 2
>
> Customer 4 enters line at time 6. Service time is 4
>
> Customer 3 begins service at time 6. Time waited is 2
>
> Customer 4 begins service at time 7. Time waited is 1
>
> Customer 5 enters line at time 9. Service time is 1
>
> Customer 6 enters line at time 10. Service time is 3
>
> Customer 5 begins service at time 11. Time waited is 2
>
> Customer 7 enters line at time 12. Service time is 4
>
> Customer 6 begins service at time 12. Time waited is 2
>
> Customer 8 enters line at time 15. Service time is 3
>
> Customer 7 begins service at time 15. Time waited is 3
>
> Customer 9 enters line at time 16. Service time is 3
>
> Customer 10 enters line at time 19. Service time is 5
>
> Customer 8 begins service at time 19. Time waited is 4
>
> Number served = 8
> Total time waited = 16
> Average time waited = 2.0
> Number left in line = 2

Since this example uses random numbers, another execution of the Java statements likely will have different results.

> **Note: Pseudo-random numbers**
> Java's method `Math.random()` generates numbers that are uniformly distributed over the interval from 0 to 1. Actual times for processing customer transactions, however, are not uniformly distributed. They are close together, and few times are far from the average transaction time. One such distribution is called a **Poisson distribution.** Ideally, this simulation should use a different pseudo-random number generator. Since our maximum transaction time is small, however, using `Math.random()` probably has little effect on the average wait time.

Using a Queue to Compute the Capital Gain in a Sale of Stock

22.10   Suppose that you buy n shares of a stock or mutual fund for d dollars each. Later you sell some of these shares. If the sale price exceeds the purchase price, you have made a profit—a **capital gain.** On the other hand, if the sale price is lower than the purchase price, you experience a loss. We will designate a loss as a negative capital gain.

Typically, investors buy shares in a particular company or fund over a period of time. For example, suppose that last year you bought 20 shares of Presto Pizza at $45 per share. Last month, you bought 20 additional shares at $75 per share, and today you sold 30 shares at $65 per share. What is your capital gain? Well, which of your 40 shares did you actually sell? Unfortunately, you cannot pick and choose. When computing capital gain, you must assume that you sell shares in the order in which you purchased them (meaning that stock sales are a first-in, first-out application). So in our example, you sold the 20 shares that you bought at $45 each and 10 of the shares that you bought at $75 each. Your cost for the 30 shares is $1650. You sold them for $1950, a profit of $300.

The Classes StockLedger and StockPurchase

22.11   **Design.** Let's design a way to record our investment transactions chronologically and to compute the capital gain of any stock sale. To simplify the example, we assume that all transactions are for stocks of a single company and that there is no commission charge for the transactions. The class `StockPurchase` records the cost of a single share of stock.

Figure 22-7 shows a CRC card for the class `StockLedger`. The class enables us to record stock purchases in chronological order. At the time of sale, the class computes the capital gain and updates the record of stocks owned. These last two steps are related, so we combine them into one method. Thus, the class has two methods, buy and sell, as Figure 22-8 illustrates.

Figure 22-7   A CRC card for the class `StockLedger`

StockLedger
Responsibilities
Record the shares of a stock purchased, in chronological order
Remove the shares of a stock sold, beginning with the ones held the longest
Compute the capital gain (loss) on shares of a stock sold
Collaborations
Share of stock

Figure 22-8   A diagram of the classes `StockLedger` and `StockPurchase`

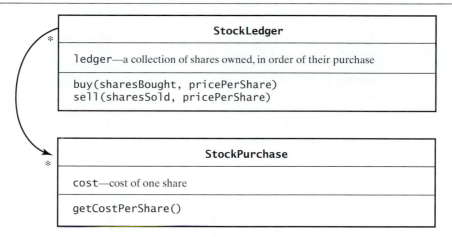

The following statements demonstrate how we could use `StockLedger` to record the transactions given in Segment 22.10:

```
StockLedger myStocks = new StockLedger();
myStocks.buy(20, 45); // buy 20 shares at $45
myStocks.buy(20, 75); // buy 20 shares at $75
double capGain = myStocks.sell(30, 65)); // sell 30 shares at $65
```

22.12   **Implementation.** In this example, `StockLedger` records instances of `StockPurchase`—which represent the shares we own—in a queue. A queue orders the shares chronologically, so we can sell them in the order in which we purchased them. The method buy then just enqueues each share bought.

The method `sell` removes from the queue as many shares as are sold. As it does this, it computes the total capital gain from the sale and returns it. The class `StockLedger` then appears as follows:

```
public class StockLedger
{
   private QueueInterface ledger;

   public StockLedger()
   {
      ledger = new LinkedQueue();
   } // end default constructor

   /** Task: Records a stock purchase in the ledger.
    *   @param sharesBought   the number of shares purchased
    *   @param pricePerShare  the price per share */
   public void buy(int sharesBought, double pricePerShare)
   {
      for (; sharesBought > 0; sharesBought--)
      {
         StockPurchase purchase = new StockPurchase(pricePerShare);
         ledger.enqueue(purchase);
      } // end for
   } // end buy

   /** Task: Removes from the ledger any shares that were sold
    *         and computes the capital gain or loss.
    *   @param sharesSold     the number of shares sold
```

```
      *    @param pricePerShare   the price per share
      *    @return the capital gain (loss) */
     public double sell(int sharesSold, double pricePerShare)
     {
        double saleAmount = sharesSold * pricePerShare;
        double totalCost = 0;

        while (sharesSold > 0)
        {
           StockPurchase share = (StockPurchase) ledger.dequeue();
           double shareCost = share.getCostPerShare();
           totalCost = totalCost + shareCost;
           sharesSold--;
        } // end while

        return saleAmount - totalCost; // gain or loss
     } // end sell
  } // end StockLedger
```

22.13   **An observation about this solution.** A typical stock transaction involves multiple shares, and the methods buy and sell reflect this reality in their parameters. For example, the invocation myStocks.buy(30, 45) indicates a purchase of 30 shares at $45 per share. However, notice that the implementation of buy adds each of the 30 shares to a queue. Figure 22-9a shows such a queue. The advantage of this approach is that sell can remove as many or as few shares as necessary.

Suppose that we instead encapsulate the purchase of 30 shares into one object and add it to the queue, as Figure 22-9b illustrates. If we then sell 20 of those shares, we would remove the object from the queue to determine the purchase price. But we would have 10 shares that must remain in the queue. Since these are the oldest shares, we could not simply add them to the back of the queue; they must remain at the front. The ADT queue has no operation that modifies its front, nor does it have one to add an object to its front. As you can see, if each entry represents more than one share of stock and is immutable, the queue is not the right ADT to use. The next section explores another ADT that you can use for this purpose. If each entry is mutable, however, Java will allow the client to modify it by using the reference that getFront returns. In this case, you can use a queue.

Figure 22-9   A queue of (a) individual shares of stock; (b) grouped shares

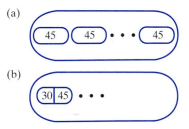

Specifications of the ADT Deque

22.14   Imagine that you are in a line at the post office. When it is finally your turn, the postal agent asks you to fill out a form. You step aside to do so and let the agent serve the next person in the line. After you complete the form, the agent will serve you next. Essentially, you go to front of the line.

Sometimes you might join a line at its end but then decide it is too long, so you leave it. To simulate both of these examples, you want an ADT whose operations enable you to add, remove, or retrieve entries at both the front and back of a queue. Such an ADT is called a **double-ended queue,** or **deque** (pronounced "deck").

A deque has both queue like operations and stack like operations. For example, the deque operations addToBack and removeFront are like the queue operations enqueue and dequeue, respectively. And addToFront and removeFront are like the stack operations push and pop, respectively. In addition, a deque has the operations getFront, getBack, and removeBack. Figure 22-10 illustrates a deque and these methods. From this diagram, you can see that a deque also behaves like a double-ended stack: You can push, pop, or get items at either of its ends.

Figure 22-10 An instance d of a deque

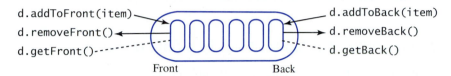

Since the specifications for the deque operations are like those that you have already seen for a queue and a stack, we provide the following brief Java interface without comments:

```java
public interface DequeInterface
{
    public void addToFront(Object newEntry);
    public void addToBack(Object newEntry);
    public Object removeFront();
    public Object removeBack();
    public Object getFront();
    public Object getBack();
    public boolean isEmpty();
    public void clear();
} // end DequeInterface
```

A comparison of the operations that add, remove, and retrieve the entries of a stack, queue, and deque is provided in Figure 22-11.

Figure 22-11 A comparison of operations for a stack s, a queue q, and a deque d: (a) add; (b) remove; (c) retrieve

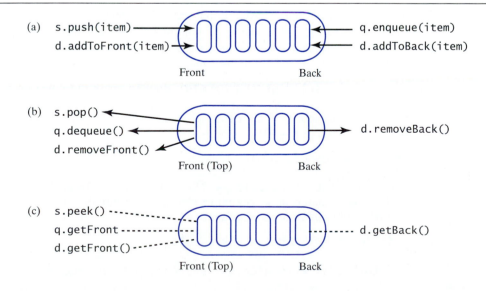

Question 2   After the following statements execute, what string is at the front of the deque and what string is at the back?

```
DequeInterface myDeque = new LinkedDeque();
myDeque.addToFront("Jim");
myDeque.addToBack("Jess");
myDeque.addToFront("Jill");
myDeque.addToBack("Jane");
String name = myDeque.getFront();
myDeque.addToBack(name);
myDeque.removeFront();
myDeque.addToFront(myDeque.removeBack());
```

Using a Deque to Compute the Capital Gain in a Sale of Stock

22.15   When we concluded the capital gain example in Segment 22.13, we saw that our queue contained individual shares of stock. Since a typical stock transaction involves more than one share, representing a transaction as one object is more natural. But you saw that if we do so, and the object is immutable, the queue is not the right ADT to use.

In this section, we revise the implementation, but not the design, of the class StockLedger that was introduced in Segment 22.11. We also revise the class StockPurchase so that it represents the purchase of *n* shares of stock at *d* dollars per share, as Segment 22.13 suggests. The revised class has the data fields shares and cost, a constructor, and the accessor methods getNumberOfShares and getCostPerShare.

We can revise the implementation of the class StockLedger given in Segment 22.12 as follows. The data field ledger is now an instance of a deque instead of a queue. The method buy creates an instance of StockPurchase and places it at the back of the deque, as follows:

```
public void buy(int sharesBought, double pricePerShare)
{
    StockPurchase purchase = new StockPurchase(sharesBought, pricePerShare);
    ledger.addToBack(purchase);
} // end buy
```

The method sell is more involved. It must remove a StockPurchase object from the front of the deque and decide whether that object represents more shares than the number sold. If it does, the method creates a new instance of StockPurchase to represent the shares that remain in the portfolio. It then adds that instance to the front of the deque, since it is these shares that would be sold next.

```
public double sell(int sharesSold, double pricePerShare)
{
    double saleAmount = sharesSold * pricePerShare;
    double totalCost = 0;

    while (sharesSold > 0)
    {
    StockPurchase transaction = (StockPurchase) ledger.removeFront();
        double shareCost = transaction.getCostPerShare();
        int numberOfShares = transaction.getNumberOfShares();

        if (numberOfShares > sharesSold)
        {
            totalCost = totalCost + sharesSold * shareCost;
```

```
      int numberToPutBack = numberOfShares - sharesSold;
      StockPurchase leftOver = new StockPurchase(numberToPutBack,
                                                 shareCost);
      ledger.addToFront(leftOver); // return leftover shares
      // Assertion: loop will exit since sharesSold will be <= 0 later
    }
    else
      totalCost = totalCost + numberOfShares * shareCost;

    sharesSold = sharesSold - numberOfShares;
  } // end while

  return saleAmount - totalCost; // gain or loss
} // end sell
```

Specifications of the ADT Priority Queue

22.16   Although a bank serves its customers in the order in which they arrive, an emergency room treats patients according to the urgency of their malady. The bank organizes its customers into chronological order by using a queue. A hospital assigns a **priority** to each patient that overrides the time at which the patient arrived.

The ADT **priority queue** organizes objects according to their priorities. Exactly what form a priority takes depends on the nature of the object. Priorities can be integers, for example. A priority of 1 can be the highest priority, or it can be the lowest. By making the objects Comparable, we can hide this detail in the method compareTo. The priority queue then can use compareTo to compare objects by their priorities. Thus, the priority queue can have the following Java interface:

```
public interface PriorityQueueInterface
{
  /** Task: Adds a new entry to the priority queue.
   *  @param newEntry  an object */
  public void add(Comparable newEntry);

  /** Task: Removes and returns the item with the highest priority.
   *  @return the object with the highest priority, or null
   *          if the priority queue was empty */
  public Comparable remove();

  /** Task: Retrieves the item with the highest priority.
   *  @return the object with the highest priority, or null
   *          if the priority queue is empty */
  public Comparable get();

  /** Task: Determines whether the priority queue is empty.
   *  @return true if the priority queue is empty */
  public boolean isEmpty();

  /** Task: Gets the size of the priority queue.
   *  @return the number of entries currently in the priority queue */
  public int getSize();

  /** Task: Removes all entries from the priority queue */
  public void clear();
} // end PriorityQueueInterface
```

Using a Priority Queue to Compute the Capital Gain in a Sale of Stock

22.17   Considering our capital gain example one more time, we begin by revising the class `StockPurchase` described in Segment 22.15 to include a data field `date` that represents the purchase date of the stock. We assume that `date` is an instance of a `Comparable` class that represents the date. Thus, `date.compareTo(otherDate)` is negative, for example, if `date` occurs before `otherDate`. Since we will use a stock's purchase date as its priority, the earliest date should represent the highest priority. Thus, the `compareTo` method for `StockPurchase` is simply

```java
public int compareTo(Object other)
{
  StockPurchase otherPurchase = (StockPurchase)other;
  return -date.compareTo(otherPurchase.date);
} // end compareTo
```

22.18   We now revise the implementation of the class `StockLedger` given in Segment 22.12 by making the data field `ledger` an instance of a priority queue. The method `buy` creates an instance of `StockPurchase` and adds it to the priority queue, as follows:

```java
public void buy(int sharesBought, double pricePerShare,
                Date purchaseDate)
{
  StockPurchase purchase =
    new StockPurchase(sharesBought, pricePerShare, purchaseDate);
  ledger.add(purchase);
} // end buy
```

The method `sell` is similar to the one given in Segment 22.15. Recall that the sale of *n* shares of stock that were bought on a given date might leave us still holding *m* shares bought on the same date. Since we would have removed the *n* + *m* shares from `ledger`, we need to put *m* shares back. When `ledger` was a deque, `sell` contained the following statements:

```java
StockPurchase transaction = (StockPurchase) ledger.removeFront();
double shareCost = transaction.getCostPerShare();
int numberOfShares = transaction.getNumberOfShares();

if (numberOfShares > sharesSold)
{
  totalCost = totalCost + sharesSold * shareCost;
  int numberToPutBack = numberOfShares - sharesSold;
  StockPurchase leftOver = new StockPurchase(numberToPutBack,
                                             shareCost);
  ledger.addToFront(leftOver); // return leftover shares to deque
}
```

Now that `ledger` is a priority queue, we revise these statements as follows:

```java
StockPurchase transaction = (StockPurchase) ledger.remove();
double shareCost = transaction.getCostPerShare();
int numberOfShares = transaction.getNumberOfShares();

if (numberOfShares > sharesSold)
{
  totalCost = totalCost + sharesSold * shareCost;
  int numberToPutBack = numberOfShares - sharesSold;
```

```
        Date dateBought = transaction.getDate();
        StockPurchase leftOver = new StockPurchase(numberToPutBack,
                                              shareCost, dateBought);
        ledger.add(leftOver); // return leftover shares to priority queue
}
```

CHAPTER SUMMARY

- The ADT queue organizes its entries on a first-in, first-out basis. The front of the queue is the entry added first; the back is the entry added most recently.

- A queue's major operations—**enqueue**, **dequeue**, and **getFront**—deal only with the ends of the queue. The method **enqueue** adds an entry to the back of the queue; **dequeue** removes and returns the front of the queue, and **getFront** just returns it.

- You can use a queue to simulate a waiting line. A time-driven simulation counts simulated units of time. Customers arrive at random times, are assigned a random transaction time, and enter a queue.

- When computing the capital gain from a sale of stock, you must sell shares in the order in which you purchased them. If you record your purchases of individual shares in a queue, they will be in the order that they must be sold.

- A double-ended queue, or deque, has operations that add, remove, or retrieve entries at both its front and back. As such, it combines and expands the operations of a queue and stack. The deque's major operations are **addToFront**, **removeFront**, **getFront**, **addToBack**, **removeBack**, and **getBack**.

- A priority queue organizes its entries according to their priorities, as determined by the entries' **compareTo** method. Besides adding entries to a priority queue, you can retrieve and remove the entry with the highest priority.

PROGRAMMING TIP

- Methods such as **getFront** and **dequeue** must behave reasonably when the queue is empty. Here, we specify that they return **null**. Another possibility is to have them throw an exception.

EXERCISES

1. If you add the objects x, y, and z to an initially empty queue, in what order will three dequeue operations remove them from the queue?

2. If you add the objects x, y, and z to an initially empty deque, in what order will three removeBack operations remove them from the deque?

3. After the following statements execute, what are the contents of the queue?

```
        QueueInterface myQueue = new LinkedQueue();
        myQueue.enqueue("Jane");
        myQueue.enqueue("Jess");
        myQueue.enqueue("Jill");
        myQueue.enqueue(myQueue.dequeue());
        myQueue.enqueue(myQueue.getFront());
        myQueue.enqueue("Jim");
        String name = myQueue.dequeue();
        myQueue.enqueue(myQueue.getFront());
```

4. After the following statements execute, what are the contents of the deque?

```
DequeInterface myDeque = new LinkedDeque();
myDeque.addToFront("Jim");
myDeque.addToFront("Jess");
myDeque.addToBack("Jill");
myDeque.addToBack("Jane");
String name = myDeque.removeFront();
myDeque.addToBack(name);
myDeque.addToBack(myDeque.getFront());
myDeque.addToFront(myDeque.removeBack());
myDeque.addToFront(myDeque.getBack());
```

5. Complete the simulation begun in Figure 22-6.

6. Assume that `customerLine` is an instance of the class `WaitLine` given in Segment 22.8. The call `customerLine.simulate(15, 0.5, 5)` produces the following random events:

    Customer 1 enters the line at time 6 with a service time of 3.
    Customer 2 enters the line at time 8 with a service time of 3.
    Customer 3 enters the line at time 10 with a service time of 1.
    Customer 4 enters the line at time 11 with a service time of 5.

During the simulation, how many customers are served, and what is their average waiting time?

7. Repeat Exercise 6, but instead use the following random events:

    Customer 1 enters the line at time 0 with a service time of 4.
    Customer 2 enters the line at time 1 with a service time of 4.
    Customer 3 enters the line at time 3 with a service time of 1.
    Customer 4 enters the line at time 4 with a service time of 4.
    Customer 5 enters the line at time 9 with a service time of 3.
    Customer 6 enters the line at time 12 with a service time of 2.
    Customer 7 enters the line at time 13 with a service time of 1.

8. When using a queue for the capital gains example, Segment 22.13 observed that the queue's entries could not represent more than one share of stock and be immutable. Discuss the possibility of making these entries mutable.

9. Segment 12.20 provided the pseudocode for a radix sort of an array. Each bucket in that algorithm is actually a queue. Describe why you can use a queue but not a stack for a radix sort.

10. Exercise 9 of Chapter 20 describes a palindrome. Can you use one of the ADTs described in this chapter instead of a stack to determine whether a string is a palindrome? If so, develop an algorithm to do so for each applicable ADT.

PROJECTS

1. Implement the radix sort, as given in Segment 12.20, by using a queue for each bucket.

2. Expand the capital gains example described in this chapter to allow more than one type of stock in the portfolio. Identify different stocks by using a string for the stock's symbol. Record the shares of each company in a separate queue, deque, or priority queue. Maintain the collection of these ADTs in a list or dictionary.

3. Simulate a small airport with one runway. Airplanes waiting to take off join a queue on the ground. Planes waiting to land join a queue in the air. Only one plane can use the runway at any given time. All planes in the air must land before any plane can take off.

4. Repeat Project 3, but use a priority queue for the planes waiting to land. Develop a priority schedule for situations such as low fuel or mechanical problems.

5. When each object in a collection has a priority, how should you organize several objects that have the same priority? One way is to order the objects with the same priority in chronological order. Thus, you can create a priority queue of queues. Design such an ADT.

23

Queue, Deque, and Priority Queue Implementations

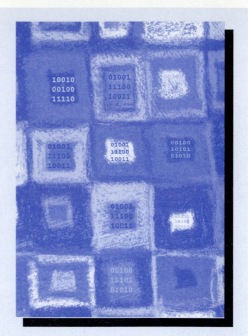

CONTENTS

A Linked Implementation of a Queue
An Array-Based Implementation of a Queue
    A Circular Array
    A Circular Array with One Unused Location
A Vector-Based Implementation of a Queue
Circular Linked Implementations of a Queue
    A Two-Part Circular Linked Chain
A Doubly Linked Implementation of a Deque
Possible Implementations of a Priority Queue

PREREQUISITES

Chapter   5   List Implementations That Use Arrays
Chapter   6   List Implementations That Link Data
Chapter 22   Queues, Deques, and Priority Queues

OBJECTIVES

After studying this chapter, you should be able to

- Implement the ADT queue by using either a chain of linked nodes, an array, or a vector
- Add nodes to or delete nodes from a chain of doubly linked nodes
- Implement the ADT deque by using a chain of doubly linked nodes
- Implement the ADT priority queue by using either an array or a chain of linked nodes

The implementations of the ADT queue that are in this chapter use techniques like the ones we used to implement the ADT list and the ADT stack. We will use either a chain of linked nodes, an array, or an instance of Vector to store the queue's entries. Although the stack implementations were quite simple, the implementations of a queue are a bit more involved.

511

We also present a linked implementation of the double-ended queue, or deque. Since the deque allows access to both its front and back, an ordinary chain of linked nodes is not sufficient. For example, deleting the last node in a chain is not possible without a reference to the preceding node. Thus, we use a new kind of chain, one that links its nodes in both directions. That is, a node in this chain references both its next and preceding nodes. Such a chain provides an efficient implementation of the deque.

A Linked Implementation of a Queue

23.1   If we use a chain of linked nodes to implement a queue, the two ends of the queue will be at opposite ends of the chain. If we have only a head reference to the chain, accessing the chain's last node will be inefficient. Using a tail reference, as described in Segment 6.44, is one approach to this problem and is the one we will take here.

With both head and tail references, which node should be the front of the queue and which node should be the back? We must be able to remove the front of the queue. If it is at the beginning of the chain, we will be able to remove it easily. If it is at the end of the chain, we will not have a reference to the preceding node unless we traverse the chain. Without such a reference, we cannot remove the chain's last node.

Placing the front of the queue at the beginning of the chain obviously forces the back of the queue to the chain's end. Since we add entries only to the back of the queue, and since we have a tail reference for the chain, this arrangement will work.

Figure 23-1 illustrates a chain of linked nodes with both head and tail references. The chain contains one node for each entry in the queue. Nodes are allocated only when needed for a new entry and are deallocated when an entry is removed.

Figure 23-1   A chain of linked nodes that implements a queue

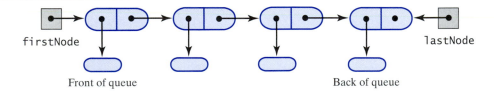

firstNode

lastNode

Front of queue

Back of queue

23.2   **Data fields and constructor.** The linked implementation of the queue has two data fields. The field firstNode references the chain's first node, which contains the front of the queue. And lastNode references the chain's last node, which contains the back of the queue. Since both of these fields are null when the queue is empty, the default constructor sets them to null.

```
public class LinkedQueue implements QueueInterface, java.io.Serializable
{
   private Node firstNode; // references node for front of queue
   private Node lastNode;  // references node for back of queue

   public LinkedQueue()
   {
      firstNode = null;
      lastNode = null;
   } // end default constructor
   . . .
```

23.3 **Adding to the back.** To add an entry to the back of the queue, we allocate a new node and add it to the end of the chain. If the queue—and therefore the chain—is empty, both data fields, `firstNode` and `lastNode`, must reference the new node, as Figure 23-2 illustrates. Otherwise, both the last node in the chain and the data field `lastNode` reference the new node, as shown in Figure 23-3. Thus, the definition of enqueue appears as follows:

```
public void enqueue(Object newEntry)
{
   Node newNode = new Node(newEntry, null);
   if (isEmpty())
      firstNode = newNode;
   else
      lastNode.setNextNode(newNode);

   lastNode = newNode;
} // end enqueue
```

This operation requires no search and is independent of the other entries in the queue. Its performance is thus O(1).

Figure 23-2   (a) Before adding a new node to an empty chain; (b) after adding it

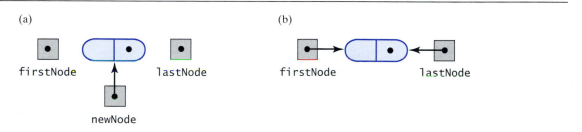

Figure 23-3   (a) Before adding a new node to the end of a chain; (b) after adding it

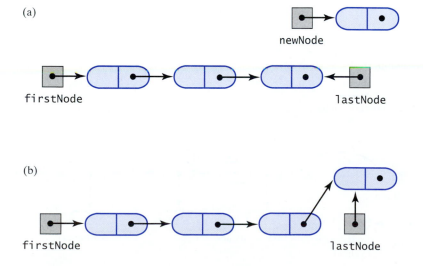

23.4   **Retrieving the front.** We get the front of the queue by accessing the data portion of the first node in the chain. Like enqueue, `getFront` is an O(1) operation.

```java
public Object getFront()
{
   Object front = null;

   if (!isEmpty())
      front = firstNode.getData();

   return front;
} // end getFront
```

23.5   **Removing the front.** After retrieving the front of the queue, the method `dequeue` removes the chain's first node by making `firstNode` reference the second node in the chain, as shown in Figure 23-4. If the chain had only one node, `dequeue` would make the chain empty by setting both `firstNode` and `lastNode` to `null`, as Figure 23-5 illustrates.

```java
public Object dequeue()
{
   Object front = null;

   if (!isEmpty())
   {
      front = firstNode.getData();
      firstNode = firstNode.getNextNode();

      if (firstNode == null)
         lastNode = null;
   } // end if

   return front;
} // end dequeue
```

Like enqueue, dequeue requires no search and is independent of the other entries in the queue. Its performance is thus O(1).

Figure 23-4   (a) A queue of more than one entry; (b) after removing the queue's front

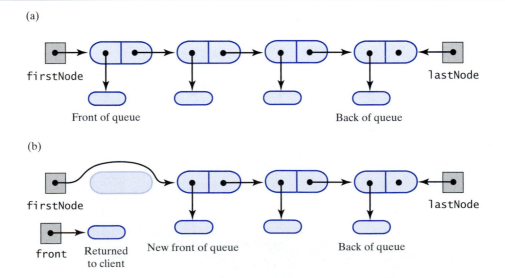

Figure 23-5   (a) A queue of one entry; (b) after removing the queue's front

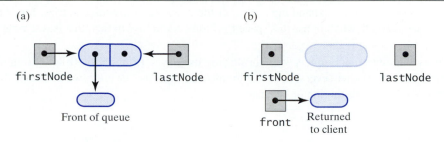

(a)   (b)

firstNode   lastNode   firstNode   lastNode

Front of queue   front   Returned
                                                            to client

23.6   **The rest of the class.** The remaining public methods isEmpty and clear are straightforward:

```
public boolean isEmpty()
{
   return firstNode == null;
} // end isEmpty

public void clear()
{
   firstNode = null;
   lastNode = null;
} // end clear
```

The class also contains the private class Node, like the one you first saw in Segment 6.21. We also used this class in Chapter 21 for an implementation of the ADT stack:

```
private class Node implements java.io.Serializable
{
   private Object data; // data portion
   private Node   next; // link to next node

   < Constructors and the methods getData, setData, getNextNode, and setNextNode
     are here. >
   . . .
} // end Node
```

Question 1   Why is a tail reference desirable when you use a chain of linked nodes to implement a queue?

An Array-Based Implementation of a Queue

23.7   If we use an array queue to contain the entries in a queue, we could let queue[0] be the queue's front, as Figure 23-6a shows. Here, frontIndex and backIndex are the indices of the queue's front and back, respectively. But what happens when we remove the front? If we insist that the new front be in queue[0], we would need to shift each array element by one position toward the beginning of the array. This arrangement would make the operation dequeue inefficient.

Instead, we can leave other array entries in their current positions when we remove the front. For example, if we begin with the array in Figure 23-6a and execute dequeue twice, the array will be as shown in Figure 23-6b. Not moving array elements is attractive, but after several additions and removals, the array can look like the one pictured in Figure 23-6c. The queue entries have migrated to the end of the array. The last available array location is allocated to the last entry added to the queue. We could expand the array, but the queue has only three entries. Since most of the array is unoccupied, why not use this space for future additions? In fact, that is just what we will do next.

Figure 23-6 An array that represents a queue without shifting its entries: (a) initially; (b) after removing the front twice; (c) after several more additions and removals; (d) after two additions that wrap around to the beginning of the array

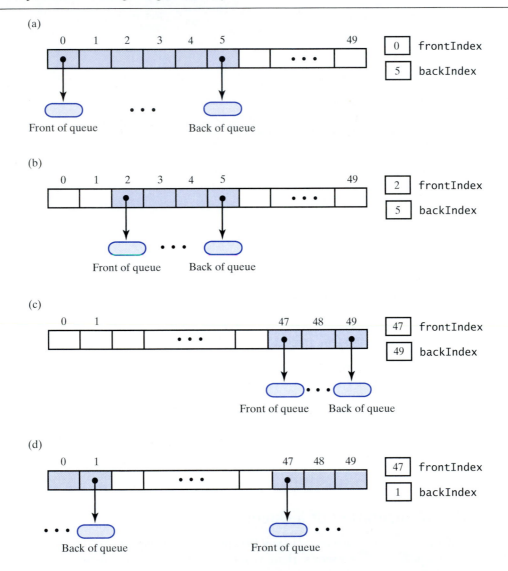

A Circular Array

23.8 Once the queue reaches the end of the array, as in Figure 23-6c, we can add subsequent entries to the beginning of the array. Figure 23-6d shows the array after two such additions to the queue. We make the array behave as though it were **circular,** so that its first location follows its last one. To do this, we use modulo arithmetic on the indices. Specifically, when we add an entry to the queue, we first increment backIndex modulo the size of the array. For example, if queue is the name of the array, we increment backIndex with the statement

```
backIndex = (backIndex + 1) % queue.length;
```

To remove an entry, we increment frontIndex modulo the size of the array in a similar fashion.

Question 2   When we used an array to implement the ADT list, as we did in Chapter 5, we shifted entries in the array. Yet the implementation of the queue just described does not do so. Explain why this difference in implementations is possible.

23.9   **Complications.** Using a circular array complicates the implementation somewhat. For example, how can we detect when the array is full? Clearly the array in Figure 23-7a is full. This array is the result of several additions to the queue pictured in Figure 23-6d. So it appears that the queue is full when frontIndex is backIndex + 1.

Figure 23-7   A circular array that represents a queue: (a) when full; (b) after removing two entries; (c) after removing three more entries; (d) after removing all but one entry; (e) after removing the remaining entry

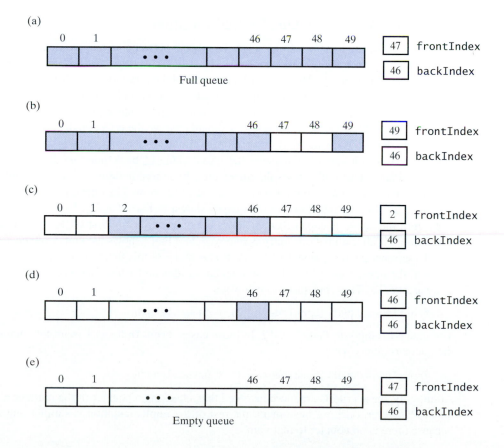

Now remove some entries from the queue. Figure 23-7b shows the array after executing dequeue twice. Notice that `frontIndex` advances to 49. If we continue to remove items from the queue, `frontIndex` will wrap around to zero and beyond. Figure 23-7c shows the array after three more items are removed. As we remove more items from the queue, `frontIndex` advances. Figure 23-7d shows the array after all but one item is removed from the queue. Now remove that one item. In Figure 23-7e, we see that `frontIndex` has advanced so that it is 1 more than `backIndex`. The queue is empty, and `frontIndex` is `backIndex + 1`. This is exactly the same condition we encountered in Figure 23-7a when the queue was full.

> **Note:** With a circular array, `frontIndex` equals `backIndex + 1` both when the queue is empty and when it is full.

As you can see, we cannot determine whether the queue is empty or full by using `frontIndex` and `backIndex`. One solution is to maintain a count of queue items. If the count is zero, the queue is empty; if the count equals the array's capacity, the queue is full. When the queue is full, the next enqueue operation can double the array's size before adding a new entry.

Having a counter as a data field leads to a reasonable implementation, but each enqueue and dequeue must update the count. We can avoid this extra work by leaving one array location unused. We develop this approach next.

A Circular Array with One Unused Location

23.10   Not using one array location allows us to distinguish between an empty queue and a full queue by examining only `frontIndex` and `backIndex`. In Java, each array location contains only a reference, so we waste little memory. Here we will leave unused the array location that follows the back of the queue. Project 2 at the end of this chapter considers a different location.

Figure 23-8 illustrates a seven-element circular array that represents a queue of at most six entries. As we add and remove entries, you should observe the effect on the indices `frontIndex` and `backIndex`. Part *a* of the figure shows the array initially when the queue is empty. Notice that adding an entry to this queue increments the initial value of `backIndex` so that it becomes zero, as shown in Part *b*. Part *c* illustrates the queue after five more additions, making it full. Now remove the front and add an entry to the back, as Parts *d* and *e* show. The queue is full once again. Repeating this pair of operations leads to the queues shown in Parts *f* and *g*. Now repeatedly remove the front until the queue is empty. Part *h* shows the queue after the first of these dequeue operations, Part *i* shows it after all but one entry is removed, and Part *j* shows the empty queue.

To summarize, the queue is full in Parts *c*, *e*, and *g* of this figure. In each of these examples, the index of the unused location is 1 more than `backIndex` and 1 less than `frontIndex`, if we treat the array as circular. Thus, the queue is full when

    frontIndex equals (backIndex + 2) % queue.length

The queue is empty in Parts *a* and *j*. In those cases, `frontIndex` is 1 more than `backIndex`. Thus, the queue is empty when

    frontIndex equals (backIndex + 1) % queue.length

Admittedly, these criteria are more involved than checking a counter of the number of entries in the queue. However, once we have them, the rest of the implementation is simpler and more efficient because there is no counter to maintain.

Figure 23-8   A seven-location circular array that contains at most six entries of a queue

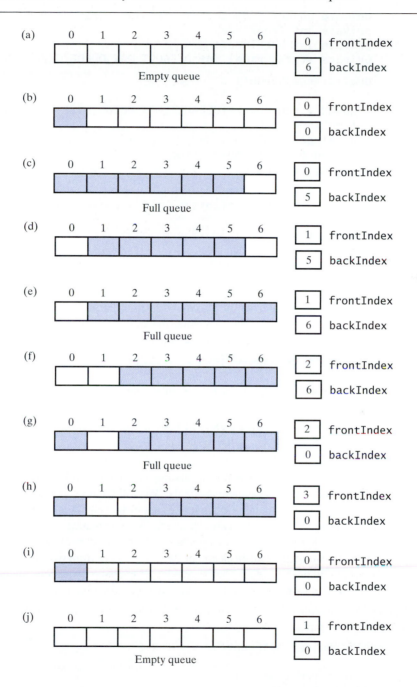

23.11   **Data fields and constructors.** This array-based implementation of the queue begins with four data fields and two constructors. The fields are the array of queue entries, indices to the front and back of the queue, and a maximum size for the queue that the default constructor creates. Another constructor lets the client choose the initial queue size.

```java
public class ArrayQueue implements QueueInterface, java.io.Serializable
{
  private Object[] queue; // circular array of queue entries
  private int frontIndex;
  private int backIndex;
  private static final int DEFAULT_MAX_QUEUE_SIZE = 50;

  public ArrayQueue()
  {
    queue = new Object[DEFAULT_MAX_QUEUE_SIZE + 1];
    frontIndex = 0;
    backIndex = DEFAULT_MAX_QUEUE_SIZE;
  } // end default constructor

  public ArrayQueue(int initialMaxQueueSize)
  {
    queue = new Object[initialMaxQueueSize + 1];
    frontIndex = 0;
    backIndex = initialMaxQueueSize;
  } // end constructor
  . . .
```

23.12   **Adding to the back.** The method enqueue doubles the size of the array if it is full and places the new entry immediately after the last occupied location in the array. To determine the index of this location, we increment backIndex. But since the array is circular, we use the modulo (%) operator to make backIndex zero after reaching its maximum value.

```java
public void enqueue(Object newEntry)
{
  if (isFull()) // isFull is private
    doubleArray();

  backIndex = (backIndex + 1) % queue.length;
  queue[backIndex] = newEntry;
} // end enqueue
```

The method doubleArray is private. Its implementation differs from the doubleArray given in Segment 5.16 because the array here is circular. We will see how to implement it shortly.

The performance of enqueue when it does not invoke doubleArray is independent of the size of the queue. Thus, it is O(1) in this case. However, its performance degrades to O(n) when the array is full, because doubleArray is an O(n) operation. If this happens, however, the very next enqueue is O(1) again. As we mentioned in Segment 21.9, we could **amortize** the cost of doubling the array over all additions to the queue. That is, we let all enqueue operations share the cost of executing doubleArray. Unless the array is doubled many times, each enqueue is almost O(1).

23.13   **Retrieving the front.** The method getFront returns either the array element at frontIndex or null if the queue is empty:

```java
public Object getFront()
{
  Object front = null;
  if (!isEmpty())
    front = queue[frontIndex];
  return front;
} // end getFront
```

This operation is O(1).

23.14   **Removing the front.** The method dequeue, like getFront, retrieves the front of the queue, but then it removes it. To remove the front of the queue in Figure 23-9a, we could simply increment frontIndex, as Figure 23-9b illustrates. This step would suffice because the other methods would behave correctly. For example, getFront would return the item that queue[6] references. However, the object that previously was the front of the queue and is returned to the client would still be referenced by the array. This fact is of no real concern if our implementation is correct. To be safe, dequeue can set queue[frontIndex] to null before incrementing frontIndex. Figure 23-9c illustrates the queue in this case.

Figure 23-9   An array-based queue: (a) initially; (b) after removing its front by incrementing frontIndex; (c) after removing its front by setting queue[frontIndex] to null and then incrementing frontIndex

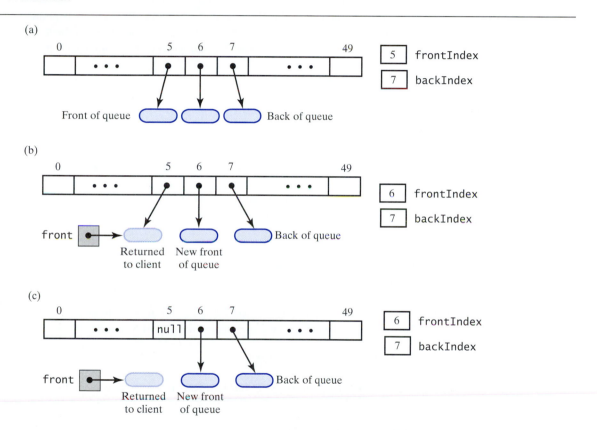

The following implementation of dequeue reflects these comments:

```java
public Object dequeue()
{
  Object front = null;

  if (!isEmpty())
  {
    front = queue[frontIndex];
    queue[frontIndex] = null;
```

```
        frontIndex = (frontIndex + 1) % queue.length;
    } // end if

    return front;
} // end dequeue
```

Like `getFront`, dequeue is an O(1) operation.

23.15 **The private method `doubleArray`.** As you saw in Segment 5.16, when we expand the size of an array, we must copy its entries into the newly allocated space. We need to be careful, though, because here the array is circular. We must copy entries in the order in which they appear in the queue.

For example, the seven-element array in Figure 23-8g is full. Call this array `oldQueue`. After allocating a new array queue of 14 locations, we copy the front of the queue from `oldQueue[frontIndex]` to `queue[0]`. We continue copying elements from the old array to the new array, proceeding to the end of the old array and wrapping around to its beginning.

In addition, `doubleArray` must set `frontIndex` and `backIndex` to reflect the reorganized array. The differences between this method and the analogous method in Chapter 5 appear in color:

```
private void doubleArray()
{
    Object[] oldQueue = queue;
    int oldSize = oldQueue.length;
    queue = new Object[2*oldSize];

    for (int index = 0; index < oldSize - 1; index++)
    {
        queue[index] = oldQueue[frontIndex];
        frontIndex = (frontIndex + 1) % oldSize;
    } // end for

    frontIndex = 0;
    backIndex = oldSize - 2;
} // end doubleArray
```

23.16 **The rest of the class.** The public method `isEmpty` and the private method `isFull` have the following implementations, based on our comments at the end of Segment 23.10:

```
public boolean isEmpty()
{
    return frontIndex == ((backIndex + 1) % queue.length);
} // end isEmpty

private boolean isFull()
{
    return frontIndex == ((backIndex + 2) % queue.length);
} // end isFull
```

The method `clear` could simply set `frontIndex` to 0 and `backIndex` to `queue.length` − 1. The other queue methods would behave as expected for an empty queue. However, the objects that were in the queue will remain allocated. To deallocate them, `clear` should set to `null` each array location that was used for the queue. Alternatively, `clear` could call dequeue repeatedly until the queue is empty, if dequeue sets `queue[frontIndex]` to `null`. We leave the implementation of `clear` as an exercise.

Question 3   If queue is an array that contains the entries in a queue, and queue is not treated as a circular array, what is a disadvantage of maintaining the bottom of the queue in queue[0]?

Question 4   Write an implementation of clear that sets to null each array location that was used for the queue.

Question 5   Write an implementation of clear that repeatedly calls dequeue until the queue is empty. How does this implementation compare to the one you wrote for Question 4?

A Vector-Based Implementation of a Queue

23.17   Using a vector to represent a queue's entries is relatively easy. We maintain the front of the queue at the beginning of the vector, as Figure 23-10 illustrates. We can use Vector's method addElement to add an entry to the back of the queue. When we remove the front of the queue from the vector, the vector's elements move so that the new front will be at the beginning of the vector. Thus, we do not need to maintain indices to the front and back of the queue. Also, the vector expands as necessary, so we do not have to worry about this detail.

Figure 23-10   A vector that represents a queue

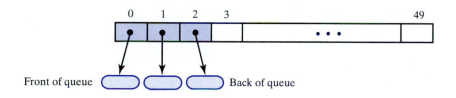

23.18   **Data fields and constructors.** The class that implements the queue begins by declaring a vector as a data field and allocating the vector in its constructors:

```java
import java.util.Vector;
public class VectorQueue implements queueInterface, java.io.Serializable
{
  private Vector queue;   // queue front is first in the vector

  public VectorQueue()
  {
    queue = new Vector(); // vector doubles in size if necessary
  } // end default constructor

  public VectorQueue(int maxSize)
  {
    queue = new Vector(maxSize);
  } // end constructor
  . . .
```

23.19   **Adding to the back.** We use `Vector`'s method `addElement` to add an entry to the end of the vector— that is, to the back of the queue.

```java
public void enqueue(Object newEntry)
{
   queue.addElement(newEntry);
} // end enqueue
```

23.20   **Retrieving the front.** We retrieve the front of the queue by using `Vector`'s method `firstElement`:

```java
public Object getFront()
{
   Object front = null;

   if (!isEmpty())
      front = queue.firstElement();

   return front;
} // end getFront
```

23.21   **Removing the front.** We can remove the front of the queue by using `Vector`'s method `removeEle-mentAt` with an argument of zero:

```java
public Object dequeue()
{
   Object front = null;

   if (!isEmpty())
   {
      front = queue.firstElement();
      queue.removeElementAt(0);
   } // end if

   return front;
} // end dequeue
```

23.22   **The rest of the class.** The remaining public methods `isEmpty` and `clear` invoke analogous `Vector` methods:

```java
public boolean isEmpty()
{
   return queue.isEmpty();
} // end isEmpty

public void clear()
{
   queue.removeAllElements();
} // end clear
```

23.23   **Efficiency.** The implementation of `Vector` is based on an array that expands dynamically, but not one that is circular. Since we add entries to one end of a queue and remove them from the other end, the vector implementation inherently moves its entries after each removal. Thus, dequeue is $O(n)$, while the other operations are $O(1)$. The performance of this implementation is not as good as the one that uses a circular array.

23.24   We can also use an instance of the ADT list to represent a queue. Such an implementation is similar to the vector implementation, and we leave it to you as an exercise.

Circular Linked Implementations of a Queue

23.25   Figure 23-1 in Segment 23.1 shows a chain of linked nodes that implements the ADT queue. This chain has two external references—one to the first node and one to the last node in the chain. Recall that these references are particularly useful for a queue implementation, since a queue's operations affect both of its ends. Like the chains you have seen before, the last node in this chain contains null. Such chains are sometimes called **linear linked chains,** regardless of whether they have a tail reference in addition to a head reference.

In a **circular linked chain,** the last node references the first node, so no node contains null. Despite the fact that each node references the next node, a circular linked chain has a beginning and an end. We could have an external reference to the chain's first node, but then a traversal of the chain would be necessary to locate the last node. Having both a reference to the first node and a reference to the last node is usually more than is necessary. Since the chain's last node references its first node, we can have a solitary reference to the last node and still locate the first node quickly. Figure 23-11 illustrates such a chain.

When a class uses a circular linked chain to represent a queue, its only data field is the reference lastNode to the chain's last node. The implementation therefore does not have the overhead of maintaining a data field that references the first node. Any time such a reference is needed, lastNode.getNextNode() provides it. Despite this simplification, this approach is not necessarily better than the one used in the first section of this chapter. It is mostly just different, as you will see if you complete Project 3 at the end of this chapter.

We now investigate another way to use a circular linked chain to represent a queue.

Figure 23-11   A circular linked chain with an external reference to its last node that (a) has more than one node; (b) has one node; (c) is empty

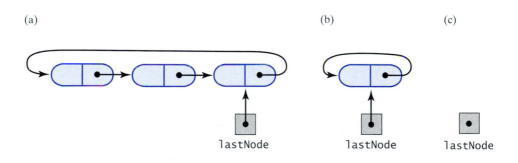

(a)   (b)   (c)

lastNode   lastNode   lastNode

A Two-Part Circular Linked Chain

23.26   When a linked chain—whether it is linear or circular—represents a queue, it has one node for each entry in the queue. When we add an entry to the queue, we allocate a new node for the chain. When we remove an entry from the queue, a node is deallocated.

In the circular array implementation, the queue uses a subset of the fixed number of array locations available. When we add an entry to the queue, we use the next unused location in the array. When we remove an entry from the queue, we make its array location available for the queue's later use. Since additions and removals are at the ends of a queue, the queue occupies contiguous locations in the circular array. The unused locations also are contiguous, again because the array is circular. Thus, the circular array has two parts: One part contains the queue and the other part is available for the queue.

Suppose that we had two parts in a circular linked chain. The linked nodes that form the queue are followed by linked nodes that are available for use in the queue, as Figure 23-12 illustrates. Here `queueNode` references the node assigned to the front of the queue; `freeNode` references the first available node that follows the end of the queue. You could think of this configuration as two chains—one for the queue and one for the available nodes—that are joined at their ends to form a circle.

Figure 23-12   A two-part circular linked chain that represents both a queue and the nodes available to the queue

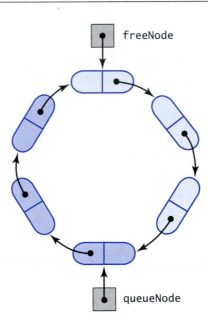

The available nodes are not allocated all at once the way locations are allocated for an array. Initially there are no available nodes; we allocate a node each time we add a new entry to the queue. However, when we remove an entry from the queue, we keep its node in the circle of nodes rather than deallocating it. Thus, a subsequent addition to the queue uses a node from the chain of available nodes. But if no such node is available, we allocate a new one and link it into the chain.

23.27   Detecting an empty queue or an absence of available nodes is easier if one node in the circular linked chain is unused. The situation is analogous to the circular array that we used in Segment 23.10. Figure 23-13a shows the queue when it is empty. Both `queueNode` and `freeNode` reference the same unused node. Notice that the node references itself. We can tell that the queue is empty because `queueNode` equals `freeNode`.

To add an entry to this empty queue, we allocate a new node and link it into the circular chain. Figure 23-13b shows the resulting chain for a queue of one entry. To simplify the figure, the actual object in the queue is not illustrated. Although a node in the chain references an object in the queue, we will sometimes say that the node is in the queue.

Figure 23-13 A two-part circular linked chain that represents a queue: (a) when it is empty; (b) after adding one entry; (c) after adding three more entries; (d) after removing the front; (e) after adding one more entry

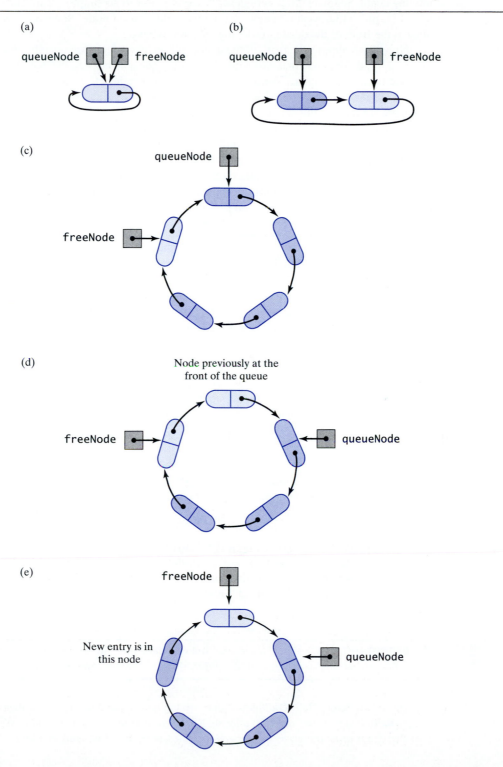

While `queueNode` references the node assigned to the queue, `freeNode` still references the unused node. After three more additions to the queue, three more nodes are allocated and linked into the chain. Segment 23.29 will describe exactly how to accomplish this. The chain now appears as in Figure 23-13c. Again, `freeNode` references the unused node. Since `queueNode` references the node at the front of the queue, retrieving the front is easy.

Now if we remove the front of the queue, we advance `queueNode` so the chain is as pictured in Figure 23-13d. The node that was at the front of the queue is not deallocated. A subsequent addition is at the back of the queue. We use the node that `freeNode` references for the new entry and then advance `freeNode`. Figure 23-13e shows the chain at this point. Notice that we did not allocate a new node for the additional entry in this case.

How can we tell whether we must allocate a new node when we add to the queue? We must do so if we want to add to the queue in Figure 23-13e. At this point, `queueNode` equals `freeNode.getNextNode()`. That was not the case when we added an entry to the queue in Figure 23-13d; a node was available without allocating a new one. But notice in Figure 23-13a that `queueNode` also equals `freeNode.getNextNode()` when the queue is empty. To add to an empty queue, we need to allocate a new node.

Note: For a two-part circular linked implementation of a queue, one node is unused. Two external references partition the chain into two parts: `queueNode` references the front node of the queue and `freeNode` references the node that follows the queue. This node is either the first available node or the unused node. The queue is empty if `queueNode` equals `freeNode`. You must allocate a new node for a new queue entry if `queueNode` equals `freeNode.getNextNode()`. Otherwise, you use the available node at `freeNode` for the new entry.

23.28   **Data fields and constructor.** The class that implements the queue by using a two-part circular linked chain has the references `queueNode` and `freeNode` as data fields. Since the chain must always contain at least one node, the default constructor allocates a node, makes the node reference itself, and sets `queueNode` and `freeNode` to reference this new node. Thus, the class begins as follows:

```
public class TwoPartCircularLinkedQueue implements QueueInterface,
                                                   java.io.Serializable
{
  private Node queueNode; // references first node in queue
  private Node freeNode;  // references node after back of queue

  public TwoPartCircularLinkedQueue()
  {
    freeNode = new Node(null, null);
    freeNode.setNextNode(freeNode);
    queueNode = freeNode;
  } // end default constructor
  . . .
```

Programming Tip: When a circular linked chain has one node, the node must reference itself. Forgetting this step is easy to do and leads to an error during execution.

23.29   **Adding to the back.** Before adding an entry to the queue, we determine whether a node is available in the chain. If one is not, we must allocate a new one and link it into the chain. We insert a new node into the chain *after* the node that `freeNode` references, as illustrated in Figure 23-14a. We do not insert it before this node because we would need a reference to the previous node to do so. Getting such a reference would take time. The node that freeNode references joins the queue, and the new node becomes either the next available node or the unused node, as is the case here. Figure 23-14b shows the chain after the new node is added to it. Notice that freeNode now references the new node, which becomes the unused node.

Figure 23-14 A chain that requires a new node for an addition to a queue: (a) before the addition; (b) after the addition

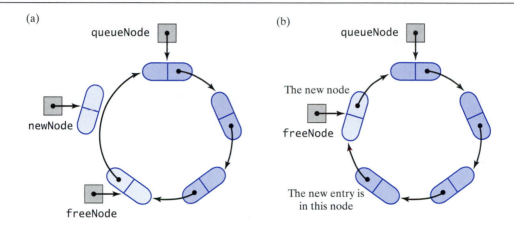

If a node is available in the chain, we use the node that freeNode references for the new entry. Figure 23-15 shows the chain before and after an existing node becomes part of the queue. After the addition, freeNode references the node that follows the back of the queue. In this example, that node is unused.

The method enqueue is easier to write and to understand if we hide the detail of determining whether to allocate a new node within a private method. Here, that private method is isChainFull; it returns true if the chain has no nodes available for use in the queue. The implementation of isChainFull is not difficult and appears later in Segment 23.32.

Figure 23-15 A chain with a node available for an addition to a queue: (a) before the addition; (b) after the addition

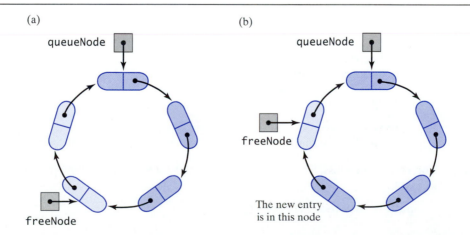

The following implementation of enqueue is an O(1) operation:

```
public void enqueue(Object newEntry)
{
  if (isChainFull())
  {
    // allocate a new node and insert it after node that freeNode
    // references
    Node newNode = new Node(null, freeNode.getNextNode());
    freeNode.setNextNode(newNode);
  } // end if

  freeNode.setData(newEntry);
  freeNode = freeNode.getNextNode();
} // end enqueue
```

23.30   **Retrieving the front.** If the queue is not empty, queueNode references its front node. The method getFront is therefore straightforward:

```
public Object getFront()
{
  Object front = null;

  if (!isEmpty())
    front = queueNode.getData();

  return front;
} // end getFront
```

This method is O(1).

23.31   **Removing the front.** The method dequeue returns the front of the queue. It then moves the front's node from the queue's part of the chain to the available part simply by advancing queueNode. Parts *c* and *d* of Figure 23-13 show a chain before and after this step. Since the node that contained the removed entry is not deallocated, the removed entry is not deallocated unless you set the node's data portion to null.

Like getFront, dequeue is an O(1) operation:

```
public Object dequeue()
{
  Object front = null;

  if (!isEmpty())
  {
    front = queueNode.getData();
    queueNode.setData(null);
    queueNode = queueNode.getNextNode();
  } // end if

  return front;
} // end dequeue
```

23.32   **The rest of the class.** The methods isEmpty and isChainFull follow from the discussion in Segment 23.27:

```
public boolean isEmpty()
{
```

```
    return queueNode == freeNode;
} // end isEmpty

private boolean isChainFull()
{
    return queueNode == freeNode.getNextNode();
} // end isChainFull
```

The method clear sets queueNode equal to freeNode to make the queue appear empty. It retains all nodes currently in the chain. However, unless you set the data portions of these nodes to null, the objects in the queue are not deallocated. We leave the implementation of clear as an exercise.

 Question 6   Describe two different ways in which you could implement the method clear.

23.33   **Choosing a linked implementation.** So far, we have discussed several possible linked implementations of the ADT queue. You can use a linear chain with both head and tail references, as shown in Figure 23-1, or an equivalent circular chain with one external reference, as shown in Figure 23-11. In both of these implementations, removing an entry from the queue disconnects and deallocates a node in the chain. If, after removing entries from the queue, you seldom add entries, these implementations are fine. But if you frequently add an entry after removing one, the two-part circular chain saves the time of deallocating and reallocating nodes.

A Doubly Linked Implementation of a Deque

23.34   Earlier, in Segment 23.1, while planning the linked implementation of the queue, we noticed that the front of the queue should not be at the tail of the chain of linked nodes. If it were, we would have to traverse the chain to get a reference to the preceding node so that we could remove the queue's front.

Although placing the front of the queue at the head of the chain solved our problem, such is not the case for a deque. We must be able to remove both the front *and* the back of a deque. So even if the deque's front is at the head of the chain, the deque's back will be at the chain's tail—and therein lies the problem.

Each node in a chain can reference only the next node. Thus, a chain, with its head reference, permits us to begin at the first node and move ahead from node to node. Having a tail reference lets us access the last node in the chain, but not the next-to-last node. That is, we cannot move backward from a node, and this is just what we need to do to remove the back of a deque.

23.35   What we need is a node that can reference the previous node as well as the next node in a chain. We call a chain of such nodes a **doubly linked chain.** We sometimes will call an ordinary chain a **singly linked chain** when a distinction is necessary. Figure 23-16 illustrates a doubly linked chain with its head and tail references. While an interior node references both the next node and the previous node, the first and last nodes each contain one null reference. Thus, when traversing the chain from the first node to the last, we will encounter null when we reach the last node. Likewise, when traversing the chain from the last node to the first, we will encounter null when we reach the first node.

Figure 23-16 A doubly linked chain with head and tail references

firstNode   lastNode

The node in a doubly linked chain is an instance of the class `DLNode`, which is similar to the class `Node`. This class has three data fields: `next` and `previous` are references to two other nodes, and `data` is a reference to the node's data. The class also has the methods `getData`, `setData`, `getNextNode`, `setNextNode`, `getPreviousNode`, and `setPreviousNode`.

23.36   **Data fields and constructor.** The doubly linked implementation of the deque begins like the linked implementation of the queue given in Segment 23.2. The class has two data fields— `firstNode` and `lastNode`—that the default constructor sets to `null`.

```
public class LinkedDeque implements DequeInterface, java.io.Serializable
{
    private DLNode firstNode; // references node for front of deque
    private DLNode lastNode;  // references node for back of deque

    public LinkedDeque()
    {
        firstNode = null;
        lastNode = null;
    } // end default constructor
    . . .
```

23.37   **Adding an entry.** The implementation of the method `addToBack` is like the implementation of `enqueue` given in Segment 23.3. Both methods add a node to the end of a chain so that the chain's current last node references the new node. Here, we also make the new node reference the current last node by passing the deque's data field `lastNode` to the node's constructor. The addition to the back of a chain that is not empty is illustrated in Figure 23-17. An implementation of the method follows.

```
public void addToBack(Object newEntry)
{
    DLNode newNode = new DLNode(lastNode, newEntry, null);

    if (isEmpty())
        firstNode = newNode;
    else
        lastNode.setNextNode(newNode);

    lastNode = newNode;
} // end addToBack
```

Figure 23-17   Adding to the back of a nonempty deque: (a) after the new node is allocated; (b) after the addition is complete

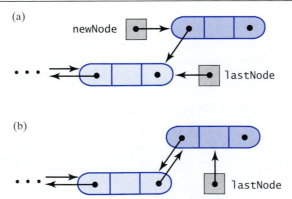

This method differs from enqueue only in the statement that allocates a new node.

The method addToFront has an analogous implementation. When adding a node to the beginning of a doubly linked chain, we must make the chain's current first node reference the new node by passing the deque's data field firstNode to the node's constructor. Compare the following definition for addToFront with the one just given for addToBack:

```java
public void addToFront(Object newEntry)
{
   DLNode newNode = new DLNode(null, newEntry, firstNode);

   if (isEmpty())
     lastNode = newNode;
   else
     firstNode.setPreviousNode(newNode);

   firstNode = newNode;
} // end addToFront
```

Both addToFront and addToBack are O(1) operations, as given here.

23.38   **Removing an entry.** The method removeFront has an implementation much like that of dequeue, but it has one other concern. After detaching the first node, if the deque is not empty, removeFront must set the field previous to null in the new front node. This step occurs in the else clause of the following definition:

```java
public Object removeFront()
{
   Object front = null;

   if (!isEmpty())
   {
     front = firstNode.getData();
     firstNode = firstNode.getNextNode();

     if (firstNode == null)
       lastNode = null;
     else
       firstNode.setPreviousNode(null);
   } // end if

   return front;
} // end removeFront
```

Figure 23-18 illustrates the effect of this method for a deque of at least two entries.

The method removeBack has an analogous definition:

```java
public Object removeBack()
{
   Object back = null;

   if (!isEmpty())
   {
     back = lastNode.getData();
     lastNode = lastNode.getPreviousNode();

     if (lastNode == null)
       firstNode = null;
```

```
        else
            lastNode.setNextNode(null);
    } // end if

    return back;
} // end removeBack
```

The implementations of removeFront and removeBack are each O(1).

Figure 23-18 (a) A deque containing at least two entries; (b) after removing the first node and obtaining a reference to the deque's first entry

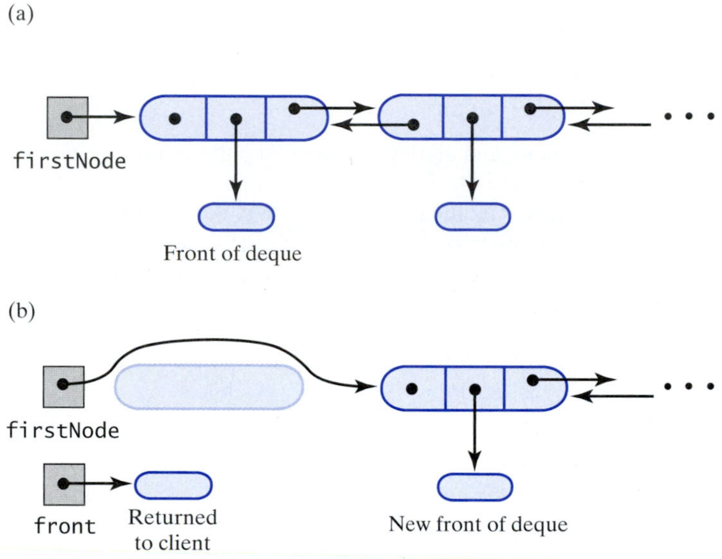

(a)

(b)

23.39   **Retrieving an entry.** The method getFront has the same implementation as given in Segment 23.4 for a queue. The method getBack is analogous to getFront and is left as an exercise. Both getFront and getBack are O(1) operations.

Question 7   Implement the method getBack for the ADT deque when a doubly linked chain contains the deque's entries.

23.40   **Reusing this implementation.** Once you have implemented the ADT deque, you can use it to implement other ADTs such as the queue and the stack. These implementations are straightforward and are left as exercises.

Possible Implementations of a Priority Queue

23.41   We can use either an array or a linked chain to implement the ADT priority queue. In both cases, we would maintain the entries in sorted order by their priorities. With an array, the entry with the highest priority should occur at the end of the array, so removing it would leave the other entries in their present places. Figure 23-19a illustrates this implementation.

If a linked chain contains the entries in a priority queue, the entry with the highest priority should occur at the beginning of the chain, where it is easy to remove. Figure 23-19b shows such a chain.

Chapter 24 describes a more efficient implementation of a priority queue that uses an ADT called a **heap.**

Figure 23-19 Two possible implementations of a priority queue using (a) an array; (b) a chain of linked nodes

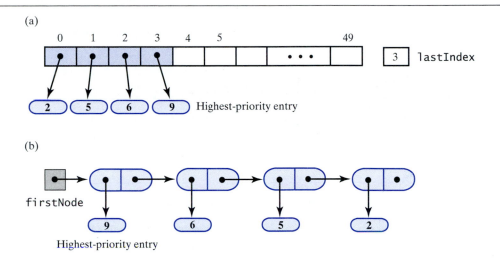

- You can implement a queue by using a chain of linked nodes that has both a head reference and a tail reference. The first node in the chain references the front of the queue, because you can remove or access a chain's first node faster than any other node. The tail reference allows you to quickly add a node to the end of the chain, which is the queue's back.

- The queue operations are O(1) for a linked implementation.

- You can implement a queue by using an array. Once a queue entry is added to the array, it does not move. After many additions, the last array location will be allocated. Removals, however, will free locations at the beginning of the array. Thus, the array can appear full even when it is not. To solve this problem, you treat the array as if it were circular.

- The queue operations are O(1) for an array-based implementation. However, when the array is full, **enqueue** doubles the size of the array. In that case, **enqueue** is O(n). Typically, we amortize the cost of doubling the array over all additions to the queue. If the array is doubled occasionally, each **enqueue** is almost O(1).

- You can implement a queue by using a vector. Since the front of the queue is always first in the vector, and since the implementation of **Vector** is based on an array that is expanded as necessary, entries in the vector move. Thus, the vector-based implementation is less efficient than our array-based implementation.

- In a circular linked chain, every node references the next node in the chain. No node contains **null**. A circular linked chain can have a beginning and an end. Since the last node references the first node in the chain, one external reference to the last node provides convenient access to both the chain's last node and its first node.

● You can use a circular linked chain to implement a queue in much the same way that you use a linear linked chain that has both head and tail references. With both kinds of chain, **dequeue** removes a node and deallocates it.

● Another implementation of a queue uses a circular linked chain that has two parts. One part is used for the queue and the other part contains one unused node and any nodes that are available for use. In this implementation, **dequeue** removes an entry from the queue but does not remove a node from the chain. Instead, the node joins the available part of the chain.

● Since a deque has operations that add and remove entries at both ends, you can use a doubly linked chain whose nodes reference both the next and the previous nodes. A doubly linked chain with head and tail references provides O(1) implementations of the deque operations.

● You can use either an array or a chain to implement a priority queue, but a more efficient implementation is possible by using a heap.

PROGRAMMING TIP

● When a circular linked chain has one node, the node must reference itself. Forgetting this step is easy to do and leads to an error during execution.

EXERCISES

1. Implement the ADT queue by using an ADT list to contain its entries.

2. Segment 23.32 describes an implementation of the queue's method `clear` when a two-part circular linked chain represents the queue. Write two different implementations of `clear`. One version should repeatedly invoke `dequeue`. The other version should set the data portion of each node in the queue to `null`.

3. Implement the ADT queue by using an ADT deque to contain its entries.

4. Implement the ADT stack by using an ADT deque to contain its entries.

5. Describe an implementation of a queue that uses two stacks, and comment on its efficiency.

6. Implement the ADT deque by using a vector to contain its entries.

7. Can you use a hash table to implement a priority queue? Explain.

PROJECTS

1. Use a circular array, as described in Segments 23.8 and 23.9, to implement the queue. Count entries to determine whether the queue is empty or full.

2. The implementation of the ADT queue that was introduced in Segment 23.10 uses a circular array with one unused location. Revise that implementation so that the unused location is always before the front of the queue, with `frontIndex` as the index of this unused location. Let `backIndex` be the index of the back of the queue. Initially, both `frontIndex` and `backIndex` are set to the maximum size of the queue (the array will be 1 larger than this number). You can distinguish an empty queue from a full queue by examining these indices. What tests should you perform to do so?

3. Implement the ADT queue by using a circular linked chain, as shown in Figure 23-11. Recall that this chain has only an external reference to its last node.

4. Implement the ADT deque by using an array to contain its entries. Expand the array dynamically when necessary.

5. One difficulty with the implementation of the doubly linked chain described in Segment 23.35 is the number of special cases that occur at the beginning and end of the chain. You can eliminate these cases if the chain is never empty. Thus, you begin each chain with a **dummy node** that you do not use for data.

   Revise the implementation of the deque given in this chapter by using a dummy node.

6. In a **circular doubly linked chain,** the first node references the last node, and the last node references the first. Only one external reference is necessary—a reference to the first node—since you can quickly get to the last node from the first node. Use a circular doubly linked chain to implement the ADT deque.

7. Implement the ADT priority queue by using an array, as pictured in Figure 23-19a.

8. Implement the ADT priority queue by using a chain of linked nodes, as pictured in Figure 23-19b.

9. Implement the ADT priority queue by using an instance of a sorted list.

10. Revise the interface for the ADT priority queue, as given in Segment 22.16, by replacing the method add with the following method:

    ```
    public void add(Object newEntry, Comparable priorityValue);
    ```

    Implement this version of the priority queue.

11. Implement a priority queue of queues, as described in Project 5 of Chapter 22.

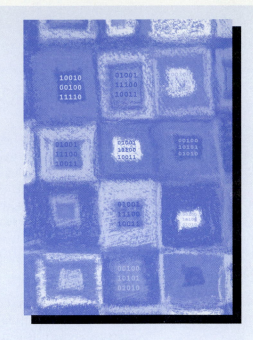

CONTENTS

Tree Concepts
    Hierarchical Organizations
    Tree Terminology
Traversals of a Tree
    Traversals of a Binary Tree
    Traversals of a General Tree
Java Interfaces for Trees
    Interfaces for All Trees
    An Interface for Binary Trees
Examples of Binary Trees
    Expression Trees
    Decision Trees
    Binary Search Trees
    Heaps
Examples of General Trees
    Parse Trees
    Game Trees

PREREQUISITES

Chapter   6   List Implementations That Link Data
Chapter   8   Java's Iterator Interfaces
Chapter 10   Recursion
Chapter 16   Searching
Chapter 20   Stacks

OBJECTIVES

After studying this chapter, you should be able to

- Describe binary trees and general trees using standard terminology
- Traverse a tree in one of four ways: preorder, postorder, inorder, and level order

- Give examples of binary trees, including expression trees, decision trees, binary search trees, and heaps
- Give examples of general trees, including parse trees and game trees

As a plant, a tree is well known. As a way to organize data, the tree is more familiar than you might think. A family tree or a chart of players in a tournament are two common examples of a tree. A tree provides a hierarchical organization in which data items have ancestors and descendants. The organization is richer and more varied than any you have seen previously.

This chapter explores the ADT tree in its two forms—binary and general—and provides several examples of how such trees are used.

Tree Concepts

24.1   The data organizations that you have seen so far have placed data in a linear order. Objects in a list, dictionary, stack, or queue appear one after the other. As useful as these organizations are, you often must categorize data into groups and subgroups. Such a classification is **hierarchical,** or **nonlinear,** since the data items appear at various levels within the organization.

We begin by looking at several familiar examples of hierarchical data. Each example will be illustrated by a diagram that represents a tree.

Hierarchical Organizations

24.2   **Example: File directories.** Typically, you organize the files on your computer into **folders,** or **directories**. Each folder contains several other folders and/or files. Figure 24-1 shows the organization of the folders and files on Paul's computer. This organization is hierarchical. That is, all of Paul's files are organized within folders that are ultimately within the folder myStuff. For example, to look at his budget, Paul would start with the folder myStuff, find the folder home, and finally locate the file budget.txt.

Figure 24-1   Computer files organized into folders

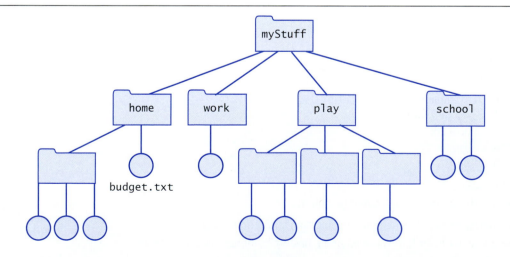

24.3 **Example: A university's organization.** Corporations, schools, churches, and governments all organize their staff hierarchically. For example, Figure 24-2 shows the administrative structure of a typical university. All offices ultimately report to the president. Immediately beneath the president are three vice presidents. The Vice President for Academic Affairs, for example, oversees the deans of the colleges. The deans in turn manage the chairs of the various academic departments like computer science and accounting.

Figure 24-2   A university's administrative structure

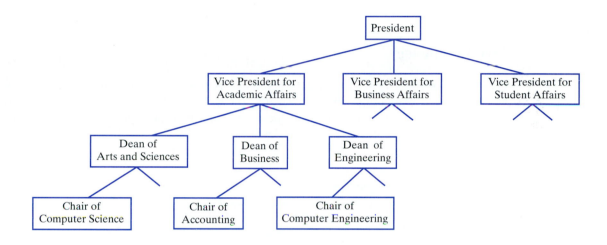

24.4 **Example: Family trees.** Your relatives can be arranged hierarchically in more than one way. Figure 24-3 shows Carole's children and grandchildren. Her son Brett has one daughter, Susan. Carole's daughter, Jennifer, has two children—Jared and Jamie.

Figure 24-4 shows Jared's parents and grandparents. Jared's father is John and his mother is Jennifer. John's father and mother are James and Mary; Jennifer's parents are Robert and Carole.

Figure 24-3   Carole's children and grandchildren

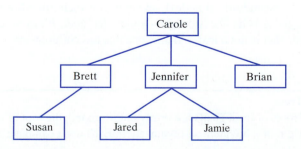

Figure 24-4   Jared's parents and grandparents

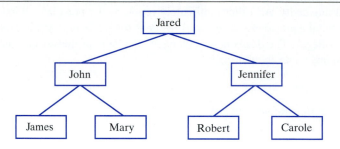

Tree Terminology

24.5   Each of the previous figures is an example of a tree. A **tree** is a set of **nodes** connected by **edges** that indicate the relationships among the nodes. The nodes are arranged in **levels** that indicate the nodes' hierarchy. At the top level is a single node called the **root**. Figure 24-5 shows a tree that, except for the names of the nodes, is identical to the tree in Figure 24-1. In Figure 24-1, the root of the tree is the folder myStuff; in Figure 24-5, the root is node *A*.

Figure 24-5   A tree equivalent to the tree in Figure 24-1

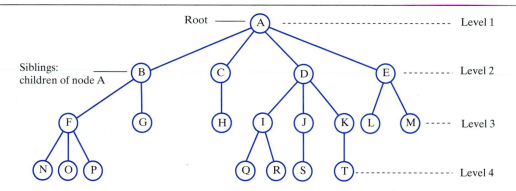

The nodes at each successive level of a tree are the **children** of the nodes at the previous level. A node that has children is the **parent** of those children. In Figure 24-5, node *A* is the parent of nodes *B*, *C*, *D*, and *E*. Since these children have the same parent, they are called **siblings.** They also are the **descendants** of node *A*, and node *A* is their **ancestor.** Furthermore, node *P* is a descendant of *A*, and *A* is an ancestor of *P*. Notice that node *P* has no children. Such a node is called a **leaf.** A node that is not a leaf—that is, one that has children—is called either an **interior node** or a **nonleaf.**

Note: Trees

While the roots of most plants are firmly in the ground, the root of an ADT tree is at the tree's top; it is the origin of a hierarchical organization. Each node can have children. A node with children is a parent; a node without children is a leaf. The root is the only node that has no parent; all other nodes have one parent each.

Question 1   Consider the tree in Figure 24-5.

   a.   Which nodes are the leaves?
   b.   Which nodes are the siblings of node K?
   c.   Which nodes are the children of node B?
   d.   Which nodes are the descendants of node B?
   e.   Which nodes are the ancestors of node N?

24.6   In general, each node in a tree can have an arbitrary number of children. We sometimes call such a tree a **general tree.** If each node has no more than n children, the tree is called an **n-ary tree.** Realize that not every general tree is an n-ary tree. If each node has at most two children, the tree is called a **binary tree.** The tree in Figure 24-4 is a binary tree, but the trees in the other previous figures are general trees.

Note: **Can a tree be empty?**
We allow any of our trees to be empty. Some people allow empty binary trees but require that general trees contain at least one node. While the reasons for doing so are quite valid, we will avoid confusion here by not making this subtle distinction between binary and general trees.

Any node and its descendants form a **subtree** of the original tree. A **subtree of a node** is a tree rooted at a child of that node. For example, one subtree of node B in Figure 24-5 is the tree rooted at F. A **subtree of a tree** is a subtree of the tree's root.

Question 2   This book has a hierarchical organization that you can represent by using a tree. Sketch a portion of this tree and indicate whether it is a general tree or a binary tree.

24.7   The **height** of a tree is the number of levels in the tree. We number the levels in a tree beginning with the root at level 1. The tree in Figure 24-5 has four levels, and so has height 4. The height of a one-node tree is 1, and the height of an empty tree is 0.

We can express the height of a nonempty tree recursively by considering its subtrees:

Height of tree T = 1 + height of the tallest subtree of T

The root of the tree in Figure 24-5 has four subtrees of heights 3, 2, 3, and 2. Since the tallest of these subtrees has height 3, the tree has height 4.

We can reach any node in a tree by following a **path** that begins at the root and goes from node to node along the edges that join them. The path between the root and any other node is unique. The **length of a path** is the number of edges that compose it. For example, in Figure 24-5, the path that passes through the nodes A, B, F, and N has length 3. No other path from the root to a leaf is longer than this particular path. This tree has height 4, which is 1 more than the length of this longest path. In general, the height of a tree is 1 more than the length of the longest of the paths between its root and leaves. Alternatively, the height of a tree is the number of nodes along the longest path between the root and a leaf.

Note: The **height of a tree** is the number of levels in the tree. The height also equals the number of nodes along the longest path between the root and a leaf.

Note: **Alternate definitions of level and height**

Some people define both the levels and the height of a tree to be 1 less than those we will use in this book. For example, the root of a tree would be at level 0 instead of 1. Also, a one-node tree would have height 0 instead of 1.

Question 3 What are the heights of the trees in Figures 24-1, 24-3, and 24-4?

24.8 **Binary trees.** As we mentioned earlier, each node in a binary tree has at most two children. They are called the **left child** and the **right child.** For example, each tree in Figure 24-6 is a binary tree. In Figure 24-6a, nodes B, D, and F are left children, and nodes C, E, and G are right children. The root of this binary tree has two subtrees. The **left subtree** is rooted at B and the **right subtree** is rooted at C. Thus, the left subtree of a binary tree is the left subtree of its root; likewise for the right subtree.

Figure 24-6 Three binary trees

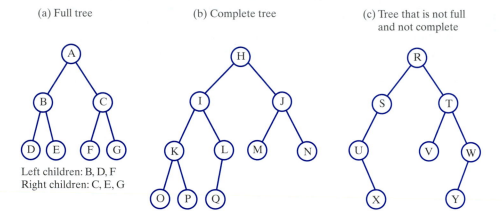

(a) Full tree

Left children: B, D, F
Right children: C, E, G

(b) Complete tree

(c) Tree that is not full and not complete

Every subtree in a binary tree is also a binary tree. In fact, we can define a binary tree recursively as follows:

Note: A binary tree is either empty or has the following form:

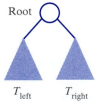

where T_{left} and T_{right} are binary trees.

When every nonleaf in a binary tree has exactly two children, the tree is said to be **full.** Figure 24-6a shows a full binary tree. If all levels of a binary tree but the last contain as many nodes as possible, and the nodes on the last level are filled in from left to right—as in Figure 24-6b—the tree is **complete.** The binary tree in Figure 24-6c is neither full nor complete. In this case, a node can have a left child but no right child (for example, node S), or a right child but no left child (for example, node U).

> **Note:** Every nonleaf in a **full binary tree** has exactly two children. A **complete binary tree** is full to its next-to-last level, and its leaves on the last level are filled from left to right. Binary trees are used extensively, and these special trees will be important to our later discussions.

24.9   **The height of full or complete trees.** In later chapters, the height of full or complete trees will be important in our discussions of efficiency. Figure 24-7 shows some full trees that get progressively taller. We can compute the number of nodes that each tree contains as a function of its height. Beginning at the root of the tallest tree in the figure, we can see that the number of nodes at each level doubles as we move toward the leaves. The total number of nodes in this tallest tree is 1 + 2 + 4 + 8 + 16, or, 31. In general, the number of nodes in a full binary tree is

$$\sum_{i=0}^{h-1} 2^i$$

Figure 24-7   The number of nodes in a full binary tree as a function of the tree's height

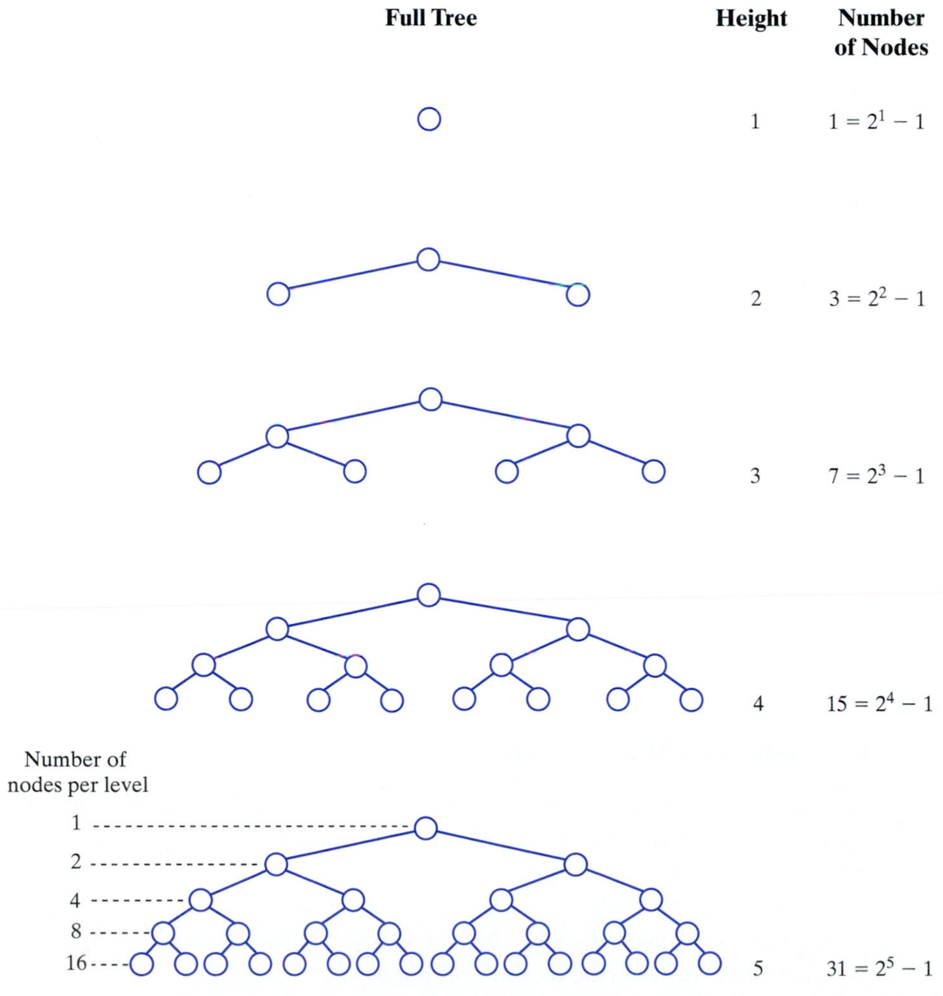

Full Tree	Height	Number of Nodes
	1	$1 = 2^1 - 1$
	2	$3 = 2^2 - 1$
	3	$7 = 2^3 - 1$
	4	$15 = 2^4 - 1$
	5	$31 = 2^5 - 1$

Number of nodes per level
1
2
4
8
16

where h is the tree's height. This sum is equal to $2^h - 1$. You can convince yourself that this result is true by examining Figure 24-7, and you can prove it as an exercise by using mathematical induction.

Now, if n is the number of nodes in a full tree, we have the following results:

$$n = 2^h - 1$$
$$2^h = n + 1$$
$$h = \log_2 (n + 1)$$

That is, the height of a full tree that has n nodes is $\log_2 (n + 1)$.

We leave it to you as an exercise to prove that the height of a complete tree having n nodes is $\log_2 (n + 1)$ rounded up.

Note: The height of a binary tree with n nodes that is either complete or full is $\log_2 (n + 1)$ rounded up.

Question 4   Show that the relationship between a tree's height and its number of nodes is true for the binary trees in Parts a and b of Figure 24-6.

Question 5   How many nodes are in a full binary tree of height 6?

Question 6   What is the height of a complete tree that contains 14 nodes?

Traversals of a Tree

24.10   Until now, we treated the contents of the nodes in a tree simply as labels for identification. As an ADT, however, a tree's nodes contain data that we process. We now consider the nodes in this way.

Traversing the items in a data collection is a common operation that we have seen in previous chapters. In those cases, data was arranged linearly, so the sequence of the items in the traversal was clear. Such is not the case for a tree.

In defining a traversal, or iteration, of a tree, we must **visit,** or process, each data item exactly once. However, the order in which we visit items is not unique. We can choose an order suitable to our application. Because traversals of a binary tree are somewhat easier to understand than traversals of a general tree, we begin there. To simplify our discussion, we will use the phrase "visit a node" to mean "process the data within a node."

Note: "Visiting a node" means "processing the data within a node." It is an action that we perform during a traversal of a tree. A traversal can pass through a node without visiting it at that moment.

Traversals of a Binary Tree

24.11   We know that the subtrees of the root of a binary tree are themselves binary trees. Using this recursive nature of a binary tree in the definition of its traversal is natural. To visit all the nodes in a binary tree, we must

Visit the root
Visit all the nodes in the root's left subtree
Visit all the nodes in the root's right subtree

Whether we visit the root before, between, or after visiting the subtrees determines three common orders for a traversal.

In a **preorder traversal,** we visit the root *before* we visit the root's subtrees. We then visit all the nodes in the root's left subtree before we visit the nodes in the right subtree. Figure 24-8 labels the nodes in a binary tree in the order in which a preorder traversal visits them. After first visiting the root, we visit the nodes in the root's left subtree. Since this subtree is a binary tree, visiting its nodes in preorder means to visit its root before visiting its left subtree. The traversal continues in this recursive manner until all nodes are visited.

Figure 24-8   The visitation order of a preorder traversal

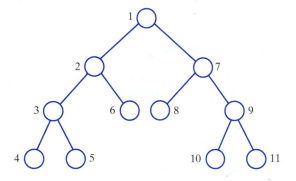

24.12   An **inorder traversal** visits the root of a binary tree *between* visiting the nodes in the root's subtrees. In particular, it visits nodes in the following order:

> Visit all the nodes in the root's left subtree
> Visit the root
> Visit all the nodes in the root's right subtree

Figure 24-9 labels the nodes in a binary tree in the order in which an inorder traversal visits them. Recursively visiting the nodes in the left subtree results in visiting the leftmost leaf first. We visit that leaf's parent next and then the parent's right child. We visit the tree's root after we have visited all of the nodes in the root's left subtree. Finally, we visit the nodes in the root's right subtree in this recursive manner.

Figure 24-9   The visitation order of an inorder traversal

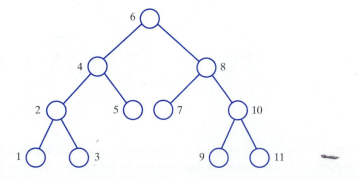

24.13   A **postorder traversal** visits the root of a binary tree *after* visiting the nodes in the root's subtrees. In particular, it visits nodes in the following order:

> Visit all the nodes in the root's left subtree
> Visit all the nodes in the root's right subtree
> Visit the root

Figure 24-10 labels the nodes in a binary tree in the order in which a postorder traversal visits them. Recursively visiting the nodes in the left subtree results in visiting the leftmost leaf first. We then visit that leaf's sibling and then their parent. After visiting all the nodes in the root's left subtree, we visit the nodes in the root's right subtree in this recursive manner. Finally we visit the root.

Figure 24-10   The visitation order of a postorder traversal

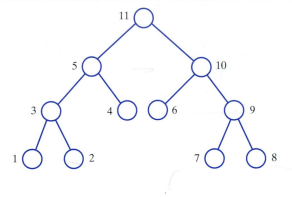

24.14   We will consider only one more traversal order. A **level-order traversal** begins at the root and visits nodes one level at a time. Within a level, it visits nodes from left to right. Figure 24-11 labels the nodes in a binary tree in the order in which a level-order traversal visits them.

Figure 24-11   The visitation order of a level-order traversal

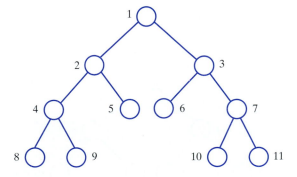

The level-order traversal is an example of a **breadth-first traversal.** It follows a path that explores an entire level before moving to the next level. The preorder, inorder, and postorder

traversals are examples of a **depth-first traversal.** This kind of traversal fully explores one subtree before exploring another. That is, the traversal follows a path that descends the levels of a tree as deeply as possible until it reaches a leaf.

Note: **Traversals of a binary tree**
A preorder traversal visits the root of a binary tree before visiting the nodes in its two subtrees.
An inorder traversal visits the root between visiting the nodes in its two subtrees.
A postorder traversal visits the root after visiting the nodes in its two subtrees.
A level-order traversal visits nodes from left to right within each level of the tree, beginning with the root.

Question 7   Suppose that visiting a node means simply displaying the data in the node. What are the results of each of the following traversals of the binary tree in Figure 24-4? Preorder, postorder, inorder, and level order.

Traversals of a General Tree

24.15   A general tree has traversals that are in level order, preorder, and postorder. An inorder traversal is not well defined for a general tree.

A level-order traversal visits nodes level by level, beginning at the root. This traversal is just like a level-order traversal of a binary tree, except that nodes in a general tree can have more than two children each.

A preorder traversal visits the root and then visits the nodes in each of the root's subtrees. A postorder traversal first visits the nodes in each of the root's subtrees and then visits the root last. Figure 24-12 gives an example of a preorder traversal and a postorder traversal for a general tree.

Figure 24-12 The visitation order of two traversals of a general tree: (a) preorder; (b) postorder

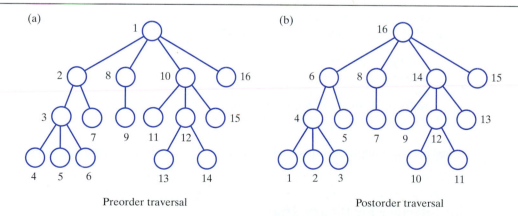

Question 8   In what order will a level-order traversal visit the nodes of the tree in Figure 24-12?

Java Interfaces for Trees

Trees come in many shapes and have varied applications. Writing one Java interface for an ADT tree that satisfies every use would be an unwieldy task. Instead we write several interfaces that we can combine as needed for a particular application.

Interfaces for All Trees

24.16   **Fundamental operations.** We begin with an interface that specifies operations common to all trees:

```java
public interface TreeInterface
{
  public Object getRootData();
  public int getHeight();
  public int getNumberOfNodes();
  public boolean isEmpty();
  public void clear();
} // end TreeInterface
```

This interface is quite basic. It does not include operations to add or remove nodes, as even the specification of these operations depends on the kind of tree. We also did not include traversal operations in this interface, since not every application uses them. Instead we will provide a separate interface for traversals.

24.17   **Traversals.** One way to traverse a tree is to use an iterator that has the methods hasNext and next, as given in the interface java.util.Iterator. As in previous chapters, we can define a method that returns such an iterator. Since we can have several kinds of traversals, a tree class could have several methods that each return a different kind of iterator. We can define an interface for these methods as follows:

```java
import java.util.Iterator;
public interface TreeIteratorInterface
{
  public Iterator getPreorderIterator();
  public Iterator getPostorderIterator();
  public Iterator getInorderIterator();
  public Iterator getLevelOrderIterator();
} // end TreeIteratorInterface
```

A tree class can implement this interface and define as many of the methods as are needed.

An Interface for Binary Trees

24.18   Many applications of trees in fact use binary trees. We could use a Java class of general trees for such an application, but using a special class of binary trees is more convenient and efficient. Because binary trees occur so frequently, developing special Java classes for them is worthwhile.

We can define an interface for a basic binary tree by adding methods to those already in the interfaces `TreeInterface` and `TreeIteratorInterface`. Since a Java interface can extend more than one interface, we can write the following interface for a class of binary trees:

```java
public interface BinaryTreeInterface extends TreeInterface,
                                             TreeIteratorInterface
{
  /** Task: Sets an existing binary tree to a new one-node binary tree.
   *  @param rootData   an object that is the data in the new
   *                    tree's root */
  public void setTree(Object rootData);

  /** Task: Sets an existing binary tree to a new binary tree.
   *  @param rootData   an object that is the data in the new
   *                    tree's root
   *  @param leftTree   the left subtree of the new tree
   *  @param rightTree  the right subtree of the new tree */
  public void setTree(Object rootData,
                      BinaryTreeInterface leftTree,
                      BinaryTreeInterface rightTree);
} // end BinaryTreeInterface
```

The two `setTree` methods transform an existing binary tree object into a new tree formed from given arguments. The first method forms a one-node tree from a given data object. The second method forms a tree whose root node contains a given data object and has as its subtrees the two given binary trees. A class that implements this interface certainly could have constructors that perform the same tasks as these two methods. However, since an interface cannot contain constructors, we have no way to force an implementor to provide them.

24.19   **Example.** Suppose that the class `BinaryTree` implements the interface `BinaryTreeInterface`. To construct the binary tree in Figure 24-13, we first represent each of its leaves as a one-node tree. Notice that each node in this tree contains a one-letter string. Moving up the tree from its leaves, we use `setTree` to form larger and larger subtrees until we have the desired tree. Here are some Java statements that build the tree and then display some of its characteristics:

```java
// represent each leaf as a one-node tree
BinaryTreeInterface dTree = new BinaryTree();
dTree.setTree("D");
BinaryTreeInterface fTree = new BinaryTree();
fTree.setTree("F");
BinaryTreeInterface gTree = new BinaryTree();
gTree.setTree("G");
BinaryTreeInterface hTree = new BinaryTree();
hTree.setTree("H");
BinaryTreeInterface emptyTree = new BinaryTree();

// form larger subtrees
BinaryTreeInterface eTree = new BinaryTree();
eTree.setTree("E", fTree, gTree); // subtree rooted at E

BinaryTreeInterface bTree = new BinaryTree();
bTree.setTree("B", dTree, eTree); // subtree rooted at B

BinaryTreeInterface cTree = new BinaryTree();
cTree.setTree("C", emptyTree, hTree); // subtree rooted at C
```

```
BinaryTreeInterface aTree = new BinaryTree();
aTree.setTree("A", bTree, cTree); // desired tree rooted at A

// display root, height, number of nodes
System.out.println("Root of tree is " + aTree.getRootData());
System.out.println("Height of tree is " + aTree.getHeight());
System.out.println("Tree has " + aTree.getNumberOfNodes() +
                   " nodes");

// display nodes in preorder
Iterator preorder = aTree.getPreorderIterator();
while (preorder.hasNext())
  System.out.print(preorder.next() + " ");
System.out.println();
```

Figure 24-13 A binary tree whose nodes contain one-letter strings

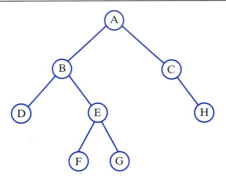

Examples of Binary Trees

We now look at some examples that use trees to organize data. We leave implementation details for a later chapter. Our first example includes a demonstration of some of the traversals introduced earlier in this chapter.

Expression Trees

24.20   We can use a binary tree to represent an algebraic expression whose operators are binary. Recall from Segment 20.5 that a binary operator has two operands. For example, we can represent the expression *a / b* as the binary tree in Figure 24-14a. The root of the tree contains the operator / and the root's children contain the operands for the operator. Notice that the order of the children matches the order of the operands. Such a binary tree is called an **expression tree.** Figure 24-14 contains other examples of expression trees. Notice that any parentheses in an expression do not appear in its tree. The tree in fact captures the order of the expression's operations without the need for parentheses.

24.21   Segment 20.5 mentioned that we can write an algebraic expression in several ways. The expressions that we normally write are called infix expressions. Each binary operator appears between its two operands. A prefix expression places each operator before its two operands, and a postfix expression places each operator after its two operands. Various traversals of an expression tree are related to these forms of an expression.

Figure 24-14 Expression trees for four algebraic expressions

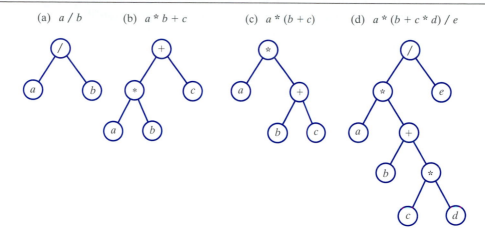

(a) a / b (b) $a * b + c$ (c) $a * (b + c)$ (d) $a * (b + c * d) / e$

An inorder traversal of an expression tree visits the variables and operators in the tree in the order in which they appear in the original infix expression. If we were to write each node's contents when we visited it, we would get the infix expression, but without any parentheses.

A preorder traversal produces a prefix expression that is equivalent to the original infix expression. For example, a preorder traversal of the tree in Figure 24-14b visits nodes in this order: $+ * a b c$. This result is the prefix form of the infix expression $a * b + c$. Recall that, like an expression tree, a prefix expression never contains parentheses.

A postorder traversal produces a postfix expression that is equivalent to the original expression. A postfix expression also has no parentheses, so the traversal produces the correct result. For example, a postorder traversal of the tree in Figure 24-14b visits nodes in the following order: $a b * c +$. This result is the postfix form of the infix expression $a * b + c$.

Question 9   Write an expression tree for each of these algebraic expressions.

a. $a + b * c$
b. $(a + b) * c$

Question 10   In what order are nodes visited by a preorder, inorder, and postorder traversal of the trees in Parts a, c, and d of Figure 24-14?

Question 11   Which trees, if any, in Figure 24-14 are full? Which are complete?

24.22   **Evaluating an algebraic expression.** Since an expression tree represents the order of an expression's operations, we can use it to evaluate the expression. The root of an expression tree is always an operator whose operands are represented by the root's left and right subtrees. If we can evaluate the subexpressions that these subtrees represent, we can evaluate the entire expression. Notice that such is the case for each expression tree in Figure 24-14, if we know the values of the variables a, b, and c.

A postorder traversal of an expression tree visits the root's left subtree, then the root's right subtree, and finally the root. If during the visits of the subtrees we evaluate their expressions, we can combine the results with the operator in the root and get the value of the original expression. Thus, the value of an expression tree is given by the following recursive algorithm:

Algorithm `evaluate(expressionTree)`
`if` (expressionTree *is empty*)
    `return` 0
`else`
`{`
    `firstOperand` = evaluate(*left subtree of* `expressionTree`)
    `secondOperand` = evaluate(*right subtree of* `expressionTree`)
    `operator` = *the root of* `expressionTree`
    `return` *the result of the operation* `operator` *and its operands*
            `firstOperand` *and* `secondOperand`
`}`

We will implement an expression tree in the next chapter.

Question 12 What value does the previous algorithm return for the expression tree in Figure 24-14b? Assume that *a* is 3, *b* is 4, and *c* is 5.

Decision Trees

24.23   **Example: Expert systems.** An **expert system** helps its users solve problems or make decisions. Such a program might help you pick a major or apply for financial aid. It reaches a conclusion based upon your answers to a series of questions.

A **decision tree** can be the basis of an expert system. Each nonleaf of a decision tree is a question that has a finite number of responses. For example, we might use questions whose answers are true or false, yes or no, or multiple choice. Each possible answer to the question corresponds to a child of that node. Each child might be an additional question or a conclusion. Nodes that are conclusions would have no children, and so would be leaves.

In general, a decision tree is an *n*-ary tree so that it can accommodate multiple-choice questions. Often, however, a decision tree is a binary tree. For example, the decision tree in Figure 24-15 is a binary tree of yes-or-no questions that diagnose a problem with a television. To use this decision tree, we first would display the question in the root. According to the user's answer, we would move to the appropriate child and display its contents. Thus, we move along a path in a decision tree from the root to a leaf according to responses made by the user. At each nonleaf, we display a question. When we reach a leaf, we provide a conclusion. Notice that each node in a binary decision tree either has two children or is a leaf.

Figure 24-15 A binary decision tree

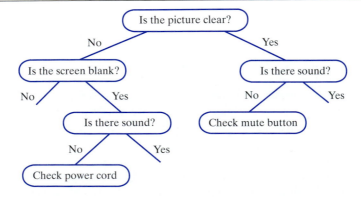

A decision tree provides operations that move us along a path through the tree and access the current node. Here is a possible Java interface for a binary decision tree:

```java
public interface DecisionTreeInterface extends BinaryTreeInterface
{
  /** Task: Gets the data in the current node.
   *  @return the data object in the current node */
  public Object getCurrentData();

  /** Task: Determines whether current node contains an answer.
   *  @return true if the current node is a leaf */
  public boolean isAnswer();

  /** Task: Sets the current node to the left (right) child of
   *        the current node. */
  public void advanceToNo();
  public void advanceToYes();

  /** Task: Sets the current node to the root of the tree.*/
  public void reset();
} // end DecisionTreeInterface
```

24.24

E

Example: Guessing game. In a guessing game, you think of something and I have to guess what it is by asking you questions that have a yes or no answer. Suppose that a program asks the questions for me. This program uses a binary decision tree that grows as the game progresses. Instead of creating the tree before it is used, the program acquires facts from the user and adds them to the decision tree. Thus, the program learns by playing the game and becomes more proficient over time.

To simplify the problem, let's restrict your choice of things. For example, suppose that you think of a country. The program could begin with the simple three-node tree pictured in Figure 24-16. With this tree, the program asks the question in the root and makes one of two guesses. Depending on the answer to the question. Here is one possible exchange between the program and the user (user replies are bold):

Is it in North America?
Yes
My guess is U. S. A. Am I right?
Yes
I win.
Play again?

The program has guessed correctly; the tree remains unchanged.

Figure 24-16 An initial decision tree for a guessing game

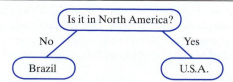

24.25   Suppose the user is thinking of something else. The exchange might go like this:

> Is it in North America?
> **No**
> My guess is Brazil. Am I right?
> **No**
> I give up; what are you thinking of?
> **England**
> Give me a question whose answer is yes for England and no for Brazil.
> Is it in Europe?
> Play again?

With this new information, we augment the tree, as in Figure 24-17. We replace the contents of the leaf that contained the wrong answer—Brazil in this case—with the new question provided by the user. We then give the leaf two children. One child contains the guess that was in the former leaf (Brazil), and the other contains the user's answer (England) as a new guess. The program now can distinguish between Brazil and England.

Figure 24-17 The decision tree for a guessing game after acquiring another fact

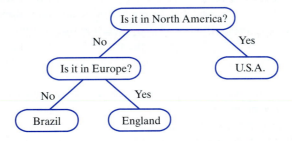

24.26   We demonstrate some of the methods declared in the interface `DecisionTreeInterface` by implementing part of a class `GuessingGame`. This class begins with a decision tree as a data field and a constructor that creates an initial tree. The tree has one yes-or-no question as its root and two guesses as children, one guess for each possible answer to the question.

```
public class GuessingGame
{
  private DecisionTree tree;

  public GuessingGame(String question, String noAnswer,
                      String yesAnswer)
  {
    DecisionTree no  = new DecisionTree(noAnswer);
    DecisionTree yes = new DecisionTree(yesAnswer);
    tree = new DecisionTree(question, no, yes);
  } // end default constructor
```

We assume that `DecisionTree` will have the constructors that we used here.

GuessingGame has one other public method, play, that uses methods of DecisionTree to maintain the tree. Since the game requires user interaction, we assume that the client of GuessingGame provides methods that communicate with the user. In particular, we assume that a class Client has a static method isUserResponseYes that returns true if the user responds "yes" to a question.

```java
public void play()
{
  tree.reset();

  while (!tree.isAnswer())
  {
    // ask current question
    System.out.println(tree.getCurrentData());

    if (Client.isUserResponseYes())
      tree.advanceToYes();
    else
      tree.advanceToNo();
  } // end while

  // Assertion: leaf is reached; make guess
  System.out.println("My guess is " + tree.getCurrentData() +
                         ". Am I right?");

  if (Client.isUserResponseYes())
    System.out.println("I win.");
  else
    learn();
} // end play
```

The private method learn asks the user for a question that distinguishes two guesses. Using this information, the method adds nodes to the decision tree, as described earlier in Segment 24.25.

 Question 13   Why should the method learn be private within the class GuessingGame?

Binary Search Trees

24.27   Earlier chapters have already discussed the importance of searching for data. Since we can traverse the nodes in any tree, searching a tree for a specific piece of data is certainly feasible. Searching a tree in this way, however, can be as inefficient as performing a sequential search of an array. A **search tree,** however, organizes its data so that a search can be more efficient. In this chapter, we present the simplest kind of search tree, the binary search tree. Chapter 28 will look at other search trees.

A **binary search tree** is a binary tree whose nodes contain Comparable objects and are organized as follows:

Note: For each node in a binary search tree,

- The node's data is greater than the data in the node's left subtree
- The node's data is less than the data in the node's right subtree

For example, Figure 24-18 shows a binary search tree of names. *Jared* is greater than all the names in *Jared*'s left subtree but less than all names in *Jared*'s right subtree. These characteristics are true for every node in the tree, not only for the root. Notice that each of *Jared*'s subtrees is itself a binary search tree.

The previous definition implies that the entries in a binary search tree are distinct. We have imposed this restriction to make our discussion simpler, but we could revise our definition to allow duplicate entries. Chapter 26 considers this possibility.

Figure 24-18 A binary search tree of names

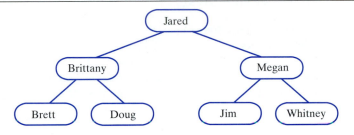

24.28   The configuration of a binary search tree is not unique. That is, we can form several different binary search trees from the same set of data. For example, Figure 24-19 shows two binary search trees containing the same names that are in Figure 24-18; other binary search trees are possible.

Question 14 How many different binary search trees can you form from the strings *a*, *b*, and *c*?

Question 15 What are the heights of the shortest and tallest trees that you formed in Question 14?

24.29   **Searching a binary search tree.** The organization of the nodes in a binary search tree enables us to search the tree for a particular data object, given its search key. For example, suppose that we search the tree in Figure 24-18 for the string *Jim*. Beginning at the root of the tree, we compare *Jim* with *Jared*. Since the string *Jim* is greater than the string *Jared*, we search the right subtree of the root. Comparing *Jim* to *Megan*, we find that *Jim* is less than *Megan*. We search *Megan*'s left subtree next and find *Jim*.

To search for *Laura*, we would compare *Laura* with *Jared*, then with *Megan*, and then with *Jim*. Since *Laura* is greater than *Jim*, we would search *Jim*'s right subtree. But this subtree is empty, so we conclude that *Laura* does not occur in the tree.

We can express our search algorithm recursively: To search a binary search tree, we search one of its two subtrees. The search ends when either we find the item we seek or we encounter an empty subtree. We can formalize this search by writing the following pseudocode:

Algorithm `bstSearch(binarySearchTree, desiredObject)`
// Searches a binary search tree for a given object.
// Returns true if the object is found.

if (binarySearchTree *is empty*)
  return false
else if (desiredObject `==` *object in the root of* binarySearchTree)
  return true
else if (desiredObject `<` *object in the root of* binarySearchTree)
  return bstSearch(*left subtree of* binarySearchTree, desiredObject)
else
  return bstSearch(*right subtree of* binarySearchTree, desiredObject)

Figure 24-19 Two binary search trees containing the same data as the tree in Figure 24-18

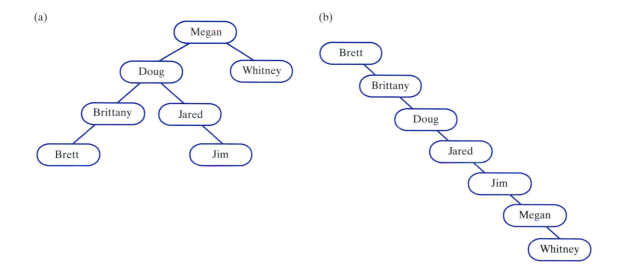

(a)

(b)

This algorithm is somewhat like a binary search of an array. Here we search one of two subtrees; a binary search searches one half of an array. You will see how to implement this algorithm in Chapter 26.

If you think that you could implement the ADT dictionary by using a binary search tree, you would be right. Chapter 26 will show you how.

24.30   **The efficiency of a search.** The algorithm `bstSearch` examines nodes along a path through a binary search tree, beginning at the tree's root. The path ends at either the node that contains the desired search key or some other node that is a leaf. In the previous segment, the search for *Jim* in Figure 24-18 examined the three nodes containing *Jared*, *Megan*, and *Jim*. In general, the number of comparisons that a successful search requires is the number of nodes along the path from the root to the node that contains the desired name.

Searching for *Jim* in Figure 24-19a requires four comparisons; searching Figure 24-19b for *Jim* requires five comparisons. Both trees in Figure 24-19 are taller than the tree in Figure 24-18.

The height of a tree directly affects the length of the longest path from the root to a leaf and hence affects the efficiency of a worst-case search. Thus, searching a binary search tree of height h is $O(h)$.

Note that the tree in Figure 24-19b is the tallest among trees containing seven nodes. A search of this tree has the performance of a sequential search of either a sorted array or a sorted linked chain. Each of these searches has an efficiency of $O(n)$.

To make searching a binary search tree as efficient as possible, the tree must be as short as possible. The tree in Figure 24-18 is full and is the shortest possible binary search tree that we can form with this data. As you will see in Chapter 26, inserting or deleting nodes can turn a full binary search tree into a much taller tree. Thus, such operations can decrease the time efficiency of a search. Chapter 28 will show you strategies for maintaining the search's efficiency.

Heaps

24.31   **Definitions.** A **heap** is a complete binary tree whose nodes contain `Comparable` objects and are organized as follows. Each node contains an object that is no smaller (or no larger) than the objects in its descendants. In a **maxheap,** the object in a node is greater than or equal to its descendant objects. In a **minheap,** the relation is less than or equal to. Figure 24-20 gives an example of a maxheap and a minheap. For simplicity, we use integers instead of objects in our illustrations.

Figure 24-20   (a) A maxheap and (b) a minheap that contain the same values

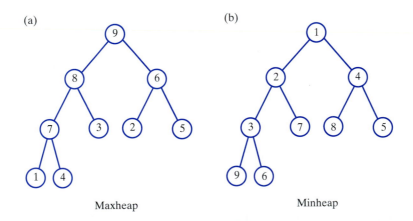

The root of a maxheap contains the largest object in the heap. Notice that the subtrees of any node in a maxheap are also maxheaps. Although we will focus on maxheaps, minheaps behave in an analogous fashion.

 Note: A maxheap is a complete binary tree such that each node in the tree contains a `Comparable` object that is greater than or equal to the objects in the node's descendants.

24.32   **Operations.** In addition to typical ADT operations such as `add`, `isEmpty`, `getSize`, and `clear`, a heap has operations that retrieve and remove the object in its root. This object is either the largest or the smallest object in the heap, depending on whether we have a maxheap or a minheap. This characteristic enables us to use a heap to implement the ADT priority queue, as you will see in the next segment.

The following Java interface specifies operations for a maxheap:

```java
public interface MaxHeapInterface
{
  /** Task: Adds a new entry to the heap. */
  public void add(Comparable newEntry);

  /** Task: Removes and returns the largest item in the heap,
   *        or returns null if the heap was empty. */
  public Comparable removeMax();

  /** Task: Returns either the largest item in the heap,
   *        or null if the heap is empty. */
  public Comparable getMax();

  /** Task: Determines whether the heap is empty. */
  public boolean isEmpty();

  /** Task: Gets the size of the heap. */
  public int getSize();

  /** Task: Removes all entries from the heap. */
  public void clear();
} // end MaxHeapInterface
```

If you place items into a maxheap and then remove them, you will get the items in descending order. Thus, we can use a heap to sort an array, as you will see in Chapter 27.

Question 16 Does a maxheap that contains a given set of objects have a unique root? Justify your answer by using the maxheap in Figure 24-20a as an example.

Question 17 Is a maxheap that contains a given set of objects unique? Justify your answer by using the maxheap in Figure 24-20a as an example.

24.33   **Priority queues.** We can use a heap to implement the ADT priority queue. Assuming that the class `MaxHeap` implements `MaxHeapInterface`, a class that implements the priority queue as an adapter class begins as follows:

```java
public class PriorityQueue implements PriorityQueueInterface
{
  private MaxHeapInterface pq;

  public PriorityQueue()
  {
    pq = new MaxHeap();
  } // end default constructor
```

```
        public void add(Comparable newEntry)
        {
          pq.add(newEntry);
        } // end add
        . . .
    } // end PriorityQueue
```

Alternatively, the class `MaxHeap` could implement `PriorityQueueInterface`. We then could define an instance of a priority queue as follows:

```
    PriorityQueueInterface pq = new MaxHeap();
```

Examples of General Trees

We conclude this chapter with two examples of general trees. A parse tree is useful in the construction of a compiler; a game tree is a generalization of the decision tree that Segment 24.23 described.

Parse Trees

24.34   Segment 10.42 mentioned the following rules to describe strings that are valid algebraic expressions:

- An algebraic expression is either a term or two terms separated by a + or – operator.
- A term is either a factor or two factors separated by a * or / operator.
- A factor is either a variable or an algebraic expression enclosed in parentheses.
- A variable is a single letter.

These rules form a **grammar** for algebraic expressions, much like the grammar that describes the English language. In fact, any programming language has a grammar.

Typically, computer scientists use a notation to write the rules of a grammar. For example, the previous rules for algebraic expressions could appear as follows, where the symbol | means "or":

<expression> ::= *<term>* | *<term>* + *<term>* | *<term>* – *<term>*
<term> ::= *<factor>* | *<factor>* * *<factor>* | *<factor>* / *<factor>*
<factor> ::= *<variable>* | (*<expression>*)
<variable> ::= a | b | ... | z | A | B ... | Z

To see whether a string is a valid algebraic expression—that is, to check its syntax—we must see whether we can derive the string from *<expression>* by applying these rules. If we can, the derivation will be a **parse tree** with *<expression>* as its root and the variables and operators of the algebraic expression as its leaves. A parse tree for the expression *a* * (*b* + *c*) is shown in Figure 24-21. Beginning at the tree's root, we see that an expression is a term. A term is the product of two factors. The first factor is a variable, in particular, *a*. The second factor is an expression enclosed in parentheses. That expression is the sum of two terms. Each of those terms is a factor; each of those factors is a variable. The first variable is *b*; the second is *c*. Since we are able to form this parse tree, the string *a* * (*b* + *c*) is a valid algebraic expression.

A parse tree must be a general tree so that it can accommodate any expression. In fact, we are not restricted to algebraic expressions. We can use a parse tree to check the validity of any string according to any grammar. Since programming languages have grammars, compilers use parse trees both to check the syntax of a program and to produce executable code.

Figure 24-21 A parse tree for the algebraic expression *a* * (*b* + *c*)

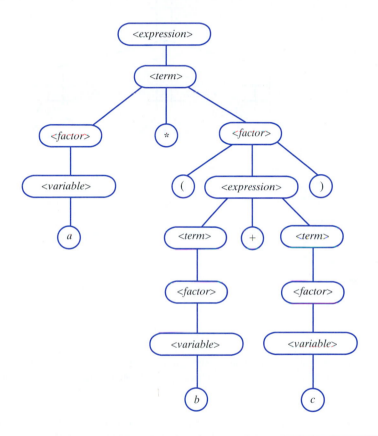

Question 18 Draw a parse tree for the algebraic expression *a* * *b* + *c*.

Game Trees

24.35   For a two-person game such a tic-tac-toe, we can use a general decision tree to represent the possible moves in any situation. Such a decision tree is called a **game tree.** If a given node in the tree represents the state of the game after one player has made a move, the node's children represent the states possible after the second player makes a move. Figure 24-22 shows a portion of a game tree for tic-tac-toe.

We can use a game tree in a program that plays tic-tac-toe. We could create the tree ahead of time or have the program build the tree as it plays. In either case, the program could ensure that poor moves do not remain in the tree. In this way, the program could use a game tree to improve its play.

Figure 24-22 A portion of a game tree for tic-tac-toe

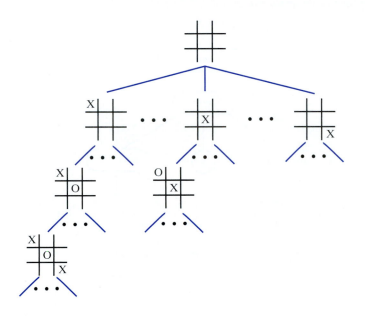

CHAPTER SUMMARY

● A tree is a set of nodes connected by edges that indicate the relationships among the nodes. The nodes are arranged in levels that denote the nodes' hierarchy. At the top level is a single node called the root.

● At each successive level of a tree are nodes that are the children of the nodes at the previous level. A node with no children is called a leaf. A node that has children is the parent of those children. The root is the only node with no parent.

● In a general tree, a node can have any number of children. A node in a binary tree has at most two children.

● The height of a tree is the number of levels in the tree. The height also equals the number of nodes along the longest path between the root and a leaf.

● Every nonleaf in a full binary tree has exactly two children.

● A complete binary tree is full to its next-to-last level. Its leaves on the last level are filled from left to right.

- You can traverse the nodes in a tree by visiting each node exactly once. Several traversal orders are possible. A level-order traversal begins at the root and visits nodes from left to right, one level at a time. In a preorder traversal, you visit the root before you visit the root's subtrees. In a postorder traversal, you visit the root after you visit the root's subtrees. For a binary tree, an inorder traversal visits the nodes in the left subtree, then the root, and finally the nodes in the right subtree.

- An expression tree is a binary tree that represents an algebraic expression whose operators are binary. The operands of the expression appear in the tree's leaves. Any parentheses in an expression do not appear in the tree. You can use an expression tree to evaluate an algebraic expression.

- A decision tree contains a question in each nonleaf. Each child of the nonleaf corresponds to one possible answer to the question. Within each of these children is either an additional question or a conclusion. Nodes that are conclusions have no children and so are leaves. You can use a decision tree to create an expert system.

- A binary search tree is a binary tree whose nodes contain `Comparable` objects that are organized as follows:

    The data in a node is greater than the data in the node's left subtree.

    The data in a node is less than the data in the node's right subtree.

- A search of a binary search tree can be as fast as O(log n) or as slow as O(n). The performance of the search depends on the shape of the tree.

- A heap is a complete binary tree whose nodes contain `Comparable` objects. The data in each node is no smaller (or no larger) than the data in the node's descendants.

- You can use a heap to implement a priority queue.

- Certain rules form a grammar that describes an algebraic expression. A parse tree is a general tree that pictures how these rules apply to a specific expression. You can use a parse tree to check the syntax of a given expression.

- A game tree is a general decision tree that contains the possible moves for a game such as tic-tac-toe.

EXERCISES

1. In Chapter 10, Figure 10-10a shows the recursive computation of the term F_6 in the Fibonacci sequence. Recall that this sequence is defined as follows:

    $$F_0 = 1, \ F_1 = 1, \ F_n = F_{n-1} + F_{n-2} \text{ when } n \geq 2$$

    The root of the tree is the value for F_6. The children of F_6 are F_5 and F_4, the two values necessary to compute F_6. Notice that the leaves of the tree contain the base-case values F_0 and F_1.

      Using Figure 10-10a as an example, draw a binary tree that represents the recursive calls in the algorithm mergeSort, as given in Segment 12.3. Assume an array of 20 elements.

2. What is the height of the shortest binary tree that contains 21 nodes? Is this tree full?

3. Suppose that you draw a binary tree so that no two nodes align vertically. Demonstrate that a vertical line moving from left to right across the tree crosses the nodes in the same order that an inorder traversal visits nodes.

Figure 24-23   Two trees for Exercises 4, 5, and 6

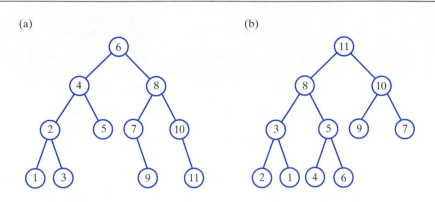

4. Consider a traversal of a binary tree. Suppose that visiting a node means to simply display the data in the node. What are the results of each of the following traversals of the tree in Figure 24-23a?

   a. Preorder
   b. Postorder
   c. Inorder
   d. Level order

5. Repeat Exercise 4, but instead traverse the tree in Figure 24-23b.

6. The two trees in Figure 24-23 contain integer data.

   a. Is the tree in Part *a* a binary search tree? Why?
   b. Is the tree in Part *b* a maxheap? Why?

7. Draw the shortest possible binary search tree from the following strings: *Ann, Ben, Chad, Drew, Ella, Jenn, Jess, Kip, Luis, Pat, Rico, Scott, Tracy, Zak*. Is your tree unique?

8. Draw a maxheap from the strings given in Exercise 7. Is your maxheap unique?

9. Can a binary search tree ever be a maxheap? Explain.

10. Prove that the sum

$$\sum_{i=0}^{h-1} 2^i$$

   is equal to $2^h - 1$. Use mathematical induction.

11. At most, how many nodes can a binary tree have at level *n*? Use induction to prove your answer.

12. Prove that the height of a complete tree having *n* nodes is $\log_2 (n + 1)$ rounded up.

13. Suppose that you number the nodes of a complete binary tree in the order in which a level-order traversal would visit them. The tree's root would then be node 1. Figure 24-24 shows an example of such a tree. What number is node i's

a. Sibling, if any
b. Left child, if any
c. Right child, if any
d. Parent, if any

Figure 24-24 A complete binary tree with its nodes numbered in level order (Exercise 13)

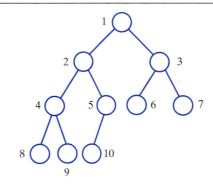

14. Draw an expression tree for the algebraic expression $(a + b) * (c - d)$.

15. What value does the algorithm given in Segment 24.22 return for the expression tree in Figure 24-14c? Assume that a is 3, b is 4, and c is 5.

16. Draw a parse tree for each of the following algebraic expressions:

a. $a + b * c$
b. $(a + b) * (c - d)$

PROJECTS

1. Draw a class diagram for the guessing game described in Segments 24.24 through 24.26.

For each of the following projects, assume that you have a class that implements `BinaryTreeInterface`, *given in Segment 24.18. The next chapter will discuss such implementations.*

2. Write Java code like the code in Segment 24.19 that creates a tree whose nodes contain the strings $A, B, \ldots, H$, such that the inorder traversal of the tree visits the nodes in alphabetical order. Write one version that creates a full tree and one version that creates a tree of maximum height. The inorder traversals of both trees should produce the same result.

3. Given an array `wordList` of 15 strings in any order, write Java code that creates a full tree whose inorder traversal returns the strings in alphabetical order. *Hint*: Sort the list of strings and then use the eighth string as the root.

4. Write a program that takes a postfix expression and produces a binary expression tree. You can assume that you have only binary operators and that the postfix expression is given as a list.

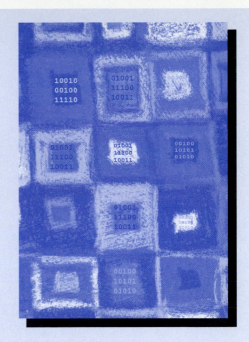

CONTENTS

The Nodes in a Binary Tree
    An Interface for a Node
    An Implementation of `BinaryNode`
An Implementation of the ADT Binary Tree
    Creating a Basic Binary Tree
    The Method `privateSetTree`
    Accessor and Mutator Methods
    Computing the Height and Counting Nodes
    Traversals
An Implementation of an Expression Tree
General Trees
    A Node for a General Tree
    Using a Binary Tree to Represent a General Tree

PREREQUISITES

Chapter   2   Creating Classes from Other Classes
Chapter 24   Trees

OBJECTIVES

After studying this chapter, you should be able to

- Describe the necessary operations on a node within a binary tree
- Implement a class of nodes for a binary tree
- Implement a class of binary trees
- Implement an expression tree by extending the class of binary trees
- Describe the necessary operations on a node within a general tree
- Use a binary tree to represent a general tree

The most common implementation of a tree is linked. Nodes, analogous to the nodes we used in a linked chain, represent each element in the tree. Each node can reference its children, which are other nodes in the tree. Although we could use either an array or a vector to implement a tree, we will not do so in this chapter. Such implementations are attractive only when the tree is complete. In Chapter 27, we will encounter a use for a complete tree, so we will postpone until then any other implementation of the tree.

This chapter emphasizes binary trees, although it concludes with a brief discussion of general trees. We do not cover binary search trees here, as the entire next chapter is devoted to them.

The Nodes in a Binary Tree

25.1   The elements in a tree are called nodes, as are the Java objects in a linked chain. We will use similar objects to represent a tree's nodes and call them nodes as well. The distinction between a node in a tree that you draw and the Java node that represents it usually is not essential.

A node object that represents a node in a tree references both data and the node's children. We could define one class of nodes for all trees, regardless of how many children a node has. But such a class would not be convenient or efficient for a node in a binary tree, since it has at most two children. Figure 25-1 illustrates a node for a binary tree. It contains a reference to a data object and references to its left child and right child, which are other nodes in the tree. Either reference to a child could be null. If both of them are null, the node is a leaf node.

Figure 25-1   A node in a binary tree

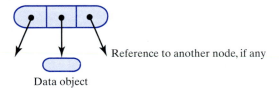

Reference to another node, if any

Data object

While the nodes in a linked chain belong to a private class Node that is internal to classes such as LList and LinkedStack, our class of tree nodes will not be internal to the class of binary trees. Since any class that extends our fundamental class of binary trees might need to manipulate nodes, we will define our class of tree nodes outside of our binary tree class. Typically, we can include this class of nodes within a package that contains the classes of the various trees. In this way the node remains an implementation detail that is not available to any of the tree's clients.

An Interface for a Node

25.2   Here is a Java interface for a class of nodes suitable for a binary tree. These nodes have more responsibilities than the nodes in a linked chain.

```java
public interface BinaryNodeInterface
{
   /** Task: Retrieves the data portion of the node.
    *  @return the object in the data portion of the node */
   public Object getData();
```

```
/** Task: Sets the data portion of the node.
 *  @param newData  an object */
public void setData(Object newData);

/** Task: Retrieves the left (right) child of the node.
 *  @return the node that is this node's left (right) child */
public BinaryNodeInterface getLeftChild();
public BinaryNodeInterface getRightChild();

/** Task: Sets the node's left child to a given node.
 *  @param leftChild  a node that will be the left child */
public void setLeftChild(BinaryNodeInterface leftChild);

/** Task: Sets the node's right child to a given node.
 *  @param rightChild  a node that will be the right child */
public void setRightChild(BinaryNodeInterface rightChild);

/** Task: Determines whether the node has a left (right) child.
 *  @return true if the node has a left (right) child */
public boolean hasLeftChild();
public boolean hasRightChild();

/** Task: Determines whether the node is a leaf.
 *  @return true if the node is a leaf */
public boolean isLeaf();
} // end BinaryNodeInterface
```

Soon we will make the tree node do more than we have specified here to simplify the implementation of the binary tree. But first, we implement this interface as the class BinaryNode.

An Implementation of BinaryNode

25.3   Since we want to hide the node from clients of the binary tree, we place BinaryNode within a package and make it available only to other classes within that package. The implementation of BinaryNode is straightforward, so we present only a portion of it.

```
package TreePackage;
class BinaryNode implements BinaryNodeInterface,
                            java.io.Serializable
{
  private Object     data;
  private BinaryNode left;
  private BinaryNode right;

  public BinaryNode()
  {
    this(null); // call next constructor
  } // end default constructor

  public BinaryNode(Object dataPortion)
  {
    this(dataPortion, null, null); // call next constructor
  } // end constructor
```

```java
public BinaryNode(Object dataPortion, BinaryNode leftChild,
                                      BinaryNode rightChild)
{
  data = dataPortion;
  left = leftChild;
  right = rightChild;
} // end constructor

public Object getData()
{
  return data;
} // end getData

public void setData(Object newData)
{
  data = newData;
} // end setData

public BinaryNodeInterface getLeftChild()
{
  return left;
} // end getLeftChild

public void setLeftChild(BinaryNodeInterface leftChild)
{
  left = (BinaryNode)leftChild;
} // end setLeftChild

public boolean hasLeftChild()
{
  return left != null;
} // end hasLeftChild

public boolean isLeaf()
{
  return (left == null) && (right == null);
} // end isLeaf
```

< *Implementations of* getRightChild, setRightChild, *and* hasRightChild *are analogous to their left-child counterparts.* >

```
    . . .
} // end BinaryNode
```

Note: Typically, the class that represents a node in a tree is a detail that you hide from the client. Placing it within a package makes it available to all classes involved in the implementation of a tree.

An Implementation of the ADT Binary Tree

The previous chapter described several variations of a binary tree. The expression tree and decision tree, for example, each include operations that augment the basic operations of a binary tree. We will define a class of binary trees that can be the superclass of other classes like the class of expression trees.

Creating a Basic Binary Tree

25.4   Recall from the previous chapter that we defined the following interface for a class of binary trees:

```java
public interface BinaryTreeInterface extends TreeInterface,
                                             TreeIteratorInterface
{
  public void setTree(Object rootData);

  public void setTree(Object rootData,
                      BinaryTreeInterface leftTree,
                      BinaryTreeInterface rightTree);
} // end BinaryTreeInterface
```

Notice that `TreeInterface` specifies basic operations common to all trees, and `TreeIteratorInterface` specifies operations for traversals of a tree.

We begin our implementation of a binary tree with constructors and the `setTree` methods.

```java
package TreePackage;
import java.util.*;
public class BinaryTree implements BinaryTreeInterface,
                                   java.io.Serializable
{
  private BinaryNode root;

  public BinaryTree()
  {
    root = null;
  } // end default constructor

  public BinaryTree(Object rootData)
  {
    root = new BinaryNode(rootData);
  } // end constructor

  public BinaryTree(Object rootData, BinaryTree leftTree,
                                     BinaryTree rightTree)
  {
    privateSetTree(rootData, leftTree, rightTree);
  } // end constructor

  public void setTree(Object rootData)
  {
    root = new BinaryNode(rootData);
  } // end setTree

  public void setTree(Object rootData, BinaryTreeInterface leftTree,
                                       BinaryTreeInterface rightTree)
  {
    privateSetTree(rootData, (BinaryTree)leftTree, (BinaryTree)rightTree);
  } // end setTree
```

```
    private void privateSetTree(Object rootData, BinaryTree leftTree,
                                                  BinaryTree rightTree)
    {
       < FIRST DRAFT - See Segments 25.5 - 25.8 for improvements. >
       root = new BinaryNode(rootData);

       if (leftTree != null)
         root.setLeftChild(leftTree.root);

       if (rightTree != null)
         root.setRightChild(rightTree.root);
    } // end privateSetTree
    . . .
```

The private method `privateSetTree` has parameters of type `BinaryTree`, whereas the public `setTree` that the interface specifies has parameters of type `BinaryTreeInterface`. We use this private method in the implementation of `setTree` to simplify the casts from `BinaryTreeInterface` to `BinaryTree`.

The third constructor—which has parameters of type `BinaryTree`—also calls `privateSetTree`. If it called `setTree`, we would declare `setTree` as a `final` method so that no subclass could override it and thereby change the effect of the constructor. Finally, note that the private method could have been named `setTree` instead of `privateSetTree`.

Programming Tip: No cast is needed when you pass an instance of `BinaryTree` to a method whose parameter has the type `BinaryTreeInterface`. The converse, however, requires a cast.

The Method `privateSetTree`

25.5   **A problem.** The implementation of `privateSetTree` given previously is really not sufficient to handle all possible uses of the method. Suppose that the client defines three distinct instances of `BinaryTree`—treeA, treeB, and treeC—and executes the statement

    treeA.setTree(a, treeB, treeC);

Since `setTree` calls `privateSetTree`, treeA shares nodes with treeB and treeC, as Figure 25-2 illustrates. If the client now changes treeB, for example, treeA also changes. This result generally is undesirable.

Figure 25-2   The binary tree `treeA` shares nodes with `treeB` and `treeC`

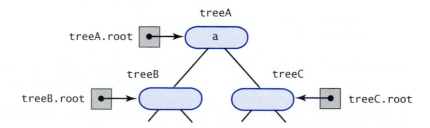

25.6   **One solution.** One solution is for `privateSetTree` to copy the nodes in `treeB` and `treeC`. Then `treeA` will be separate and distinct from `treeB` and `treeC`. Any subsequent changes to either `treeB` or `treeC` will not affect `treeA`. Let's explore this approach.

Since we are copying nodes, we add a method `copy` to the class `BinaryNode` that returns a copy of a node. To copy a node, we actually must copy the subtree rooted at the node. Beginning with the node, we copy it and then copy the nodes in its left and right subtrees. Thus, we perform a preorder traversal of the subtree. For simplicity, we will not copy the data in the nodes.

The method `copy` appears as follows:

```
public BinaryNode copy()
{
   BinaryNode newRoot = new BinaryNode(data);

   if (left != null)
     newRoot.left = left.copy();

   if (right != null)
     newRoot.right = right.copy();

   return newRoot;
} // end copy
```

Now `privateSetTree` can invoke `copy` to copy the nodes from the two given subtrees:

```
private void privateSetTree(Object rootData, BinaryTree leftTree,
                                              BinaryTree rightTree)
{
   root = new BinaryNode(rootData);

   if ((leftTree != null) && !leftTree.isEmpty())
     root.setLeftChild(leftTree.root.copy());

   if ((rightTree != null) && !rightTree.isEmpty())
     root.setRightChild(rightTree.root.copy());
} // end privateSetTree
```

Since copying nodes is expensive, we could consider other implementations of `privateSetTree`. As you will see next, we must copy at least some nodes in certain situations.

25.7   **Another approach, more problems.** Instead of always copying nodes, `privateSetTree` could behave as follows. Returning to our earlier example,

```
treeA.setTree(a, treeB, treeC);
```

`privateSetTree` first could link the root node of `treeA` to the root nodes of `treeB` and `treeC`. It then could set `treeB.root` and `treeC.root` to `null`. This approach solves the problem of a node appearing in more than one tree, but it makes the trees that the client passed as arguments empty. Other difficulties also exist.

Suppose that the client executes

```
treeA.setTree(a, treeA, treeB);
```

If `privateSetTree` makes the subtrees empty, `setTree` will destroy the new `treeA`!

Another problem occurs if the client executes

```
treeA.setTree(a, treeB, treeB);
```

The left and right subtrees of treeA's root will be identical, as Figure 25-3 illustrates. The solution to this dilemma is to copy the nodes of treeB so that the subtrees are distinct. The general case cannot avoid copying nodes, but such copying will be infrequent.

We now implement a solution to these difficulties.

Figure 25-3   treeA has identical subtrees

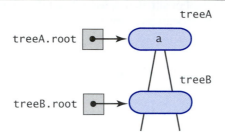

25.8   **The second solution.** To summarize, privateSetTree should take the following steps:

1. Create a root node *r* containing the given data.
2. If the left subtree exists and is not empty, attach its root node to *r* as a left child.
3. If the right subtree exists, is not empty, and is distinct from the left subtree, attach its root node to *r* as a right child. But if the right and left subtrees are the same, attach a copy of the right subtree to *r* instead.
4. If the left (right) subtree exists and differs from the invoking tree object, set its data field root to null.

An implementation of privateSetTree follows:

```
private void privateSetTree(Object rootData,
                            BinaryTree leftTree, BinaryTree rightTree)
{
   root = new BinaryNode(rootData);

   if ((leftTree != null) && !leftTree.isEmpty())
     root.setLeftChild(leftTree.root);

   if ((rightTree != null) && !rightTree.isEmpty())
   {
     if (rightTree != leftTree)
       root.setRightChild(rightTree.root);
     else
       root.setRightChild(rightTree.root.copy());
   } // end if

   if ((leftTree != null) && (this != leftTree))
     leftTree.clear();

   if ((rightTree != null) && (this != rightTree))
     rightTree.clear();
} // end privateSetTree
```

Question 1   At the end of the implementation of privateSetTree, can you set rightTree to null instead of invoking clear?

Accessor and Mutator Methods

25.9 The public methods `getRootData`, `isEmpty`, and `clear` are easy to implement. In addition to these methods, we define several protected methods—`setRootData`, `setRootNode`, and `getRootNode`—that will be useful in the implementation of a subclass. The implementations of these methods follow:

```java
public Object getRootData()
{
  Object rootData = null;

  if (root != null)
    rootData = root.getData();

  return rootData;
} // end getRootData

public boolean isEmpty()
{
  return root == null;
} // end isEmpty

public void clear()
{
  root = null;
} // end clear

protected void setRootData(Object rootData)
{
  root.setData(rootData);
} // end setRootData

protected void setRootNode(BinaryNode rootNode)
{
  root = rootNode;
} // end setRootNode

protected BinaryNode getRootNode()
{
  return root;
} // end getRootNode
```

Computing the Height and Counting Nodes

25.10 **Methods within `BinaryTree`.** The methods `getHeight` and `getNumberOfNodes` are more interesting than the previous ones. Although we could perform the necessary computations within the class `BinaryTree`, performing them within the class `BinaryNode` is easier. Thus, the following methods of `BinaryTree` invoke analogous methods of `BinaryNode`:

```java
public int getHeight()
{
  return root.getHeight();
} // end getHeight
```

```
public int getNumberOfNodes()
{
   return root.getNumberOfNodes();
} // end getNumberOfNodes
```

We now complete the methods `getHeight` and `getNumberOfNodes` within `BinaryNode`.

25.11   Methods within BinaryNode. Within `BinaryNode`, the method `getHeight` returns the height of the subtree rooted at the node that invokes the method. Likewise, `getNumberOfNodes` returns the number of nodes within that same subtree.

The public method `getHeight` can call a private recursive method `getHeight` that has a node as its parameter. The height of the tree rooted at a node is 1—for the node itself—plus the height of the node's tallest subtree. Thus, we have the following implementation:

```
public int getHeight()
{
   return getHeight(this); // call private getHeight
} // end getHeight

private int getHeight(BinaryNode node)
{
   int height = 0;

   if (node != null)
      height = 1 + Math.max(getHeight(node.left),
                            getHeight(node.right));

   return height;
} // end getHeight
```

We could implement `getNumberOfNodes` by using the same approach, but instead we will show you another way. The number of nodes in a tree rooted at a given node is 1—for the node itself—plus the number of nodes in both the left and right subtrees. Thus, we have the following recursive implementation:

```
public int getNumberOfNodes()
{
   int leftNumber = 0;
   int rightNumber = 0;

   if (left != null)
      leftNumber = left.getNumberOfNodes();

   if (right != null)
      rightNumber = right.getNumberOfNodes();

   return 1 + leftNumber + rightNumber;
} // end getNumberOfNodes
```

Traversals

25.12   Traversing a binary tree recursively. The previous chapter described four orders in which we could traverse all the nodes in a binary tree: inorder, preorder, postorder, and level order. An inorder traversal, for example, visits all nodes in the root's left subtree, then visits the root, and finally visits all nodes in the root's right subtree. Since an inorder traversal visits the nodes in the subtrees by using an inorder traversal, its description is recursive.

We could add a recursive method to the class `BinaryTree` to perform an inorder traversal. Such a method, however, must do something specific to or with the data in each node that it visits. For simplicity, we will display the data even though a class that implements an ADT generally should not perform input or output.

So that the method can process the subtrees recursively, it needs the root of a subtree as a parameter. To hide this detail from the client, we make the recursive method private and call it from a public method that has no parameters. Thus, we have the following result:

```java
public void inorderTraverse()
{
   inorderTraverse(root);
} // end inorderTraverse

private void inorderTraverse(BinaryNode node)
{
   if (node != null)
   {

      inorderTraverse((BinaryNode)node.getLeftChild());
      System.out.println(node.getData());
      inorderTraverse((BinaryNode)node.getRightChild());
   } // end if
} // end inorderTraverse
```

We could implement similar methods for preorder and postorder traversals.

Question 2   Trace the method `inorderTraverse` with the binary tree in Figure 25-4. What data is displayed?

Question 3   Implement a recursive method `preorderTraverse` that displays the data in a binary tree in preorder.

Figure 25-4   A binary tree

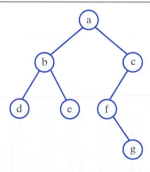

Note: Generally, the methods in a class that implements an ADT should not perform input and output. We are doing so here to simplify the discussion that follows. Instead of actually displaying the data in the tree, a method like `inorderTraverse` could return a string composed of the data. The client that uses the tree could display this string by using a statement such as

```java
System.out.println(myTree.inorderTraverse());
```

25.13   **Traversals that use an iterator.** A method such as `inorderTraverse` is not hard to implement, but this method only displays the data during the traversal. Once the method is invoked, the entire traversal takes place. To provide the client with more flexibility, we should define the traversals as iterators. Recall that Java's interface `Iterator` declares the methods `hasNext` and `next`. These methods enable a client to retrieve the data from the current node in the traversal at any time. That is, the client can retrieve a node's data, do something with it, and then retrieve the data in the next node in the iteration.

If we look at `BinaryTreeInterface` in Segment 25.4, we will see that the class `BinaryTree` must implement the methods in the interface `TreeIteratorInterface`. For example, the method `getInorderIterator` has the following implementation:

```
public Iterator getInorderIterator()
{
   return new InorderIterator();
} // end getInorderIterator
```

As we did in earlier chapters, we define the class `InorderIterator` as a private inner class of `BinaryTree`.

An iterator must be able to pause during a traversal. This suggests that we not use recursion in its implementation. Chapter 20 showed how to use a stack instead of recursion. That is what we will do here.

25.14   **An iterative version of `inorderTraverse`.** Before we define an iterator, let's consider an iterative version of the method `inorderTraverse`. This method will be a little easier to construct than the iterator, yet it will take similar steps.

Figure 25-5 shows the result of using a stack to perform an inorder traversal of the tree in Figure 25-4. We begin by pushing the root, *a*, onto the stack. We then traverse to the left as far as possible, pushing each node onto the stack. We then pop the *d* from the stack and display it. Since *d* has no right child, we pop the stack again and display *b*. Now *b* has a right child, *e*, which we push onto the stack. Since *e* has no children, we pop it from the stack and display it. The process continues until we have visited all the nodes—that is, until both the stack is empty and the current node is `null`.

Figure 25-5   Using a stack to perform an inorder traversal of the binary tree in Figure 25-4

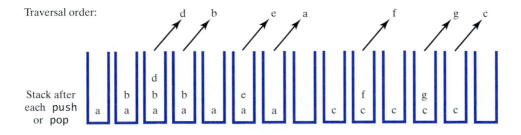

Here is an iterative implementation of `inorderTraverse`:

```
public void inorderTraverse()
{
   StackInterface nodeStack = new LinkedStack();
   BinaryNode currentNode = root;
```

```
      while (!nodeStack.isEmpty() || (currentNode != null))
      {
        // find leftmost node with no left child
        while (currentNode != null)
        {
          nodeStack.push(currentNode);
          currentNode = (BinaryNode)currentNode.getLeftChild();
        } // end while

        // visit leftmost node, then traverse its right subtree
        if (!nodeStack.isEmpty())
        {
          BinaryNode nextNode = (BinaryNode) nodeStack.pop();
          // Assertion: nextNode != null since nodeStack was
          //            not empty before the pop
          System.out.println(nextNode.getData());
          currentNode = (BinaryNode)nextNode.getRightChild();
        } // end if
      } // end while
  } // end inorderTraverse
```

25.15   **The private class `InorderIterator`.** To implement an iterator, we distribute the logic of `inorder-Traverse` among the iterator's constructor and the methods `hasNext` and `next`. The stack and the variable `currentNode` are data fields in the iterator class. The method `next` advances `currentNode`, adds to the stack as necessary, and eventually pops the stack to return the data in the node that is next in the iteration. Thus, the implementation of the class `InorderIterator` appears as follows:

```
private class InorderIterator implements Iterator
{
  private StackInterface nodeStack;
  private BinaryNode     currentNode;

  public InorderIterator()
  {
    nodeStack = new LinkedStack();
    currentNode = root;
  } // end default constructor

  public boolean hasNext()
  {
    return !nodeStack.isEmpty() || (currentNode != null);
  } // end hasNext

  public Object next()
  {
    BinaryNode nextNode = null;

    while (currentNode != null)
    {
      nodeStack.push(currentNode);
      currentNode = (BinaryNode)currentNode.getLeftChild();
    } // end while
```

```
            if (!nodeStack.isEmpty())
            {
               nextNode = (BinaryNode) nodeStack.pop();
               currentNode = (BinaryNode)nextNode.getRightChild();
            }
            else
               throw new NoSuchElementException();

            return nextNode.getData();
         } // end next

         public void remove()
         {
            throw new UnsupportedOperationException();
         } // end remove
      } // end InorderIterator
```

25.16 **Preorder and postorder traversals.** Figure 25-6 shows the result of using a stack to perform a preorder traversal and a postorder traversal of the tree in Figure 25-4. A level-order traversal has logic similar to that of a preorder traversal, but we use a queue instead of a stack. Figure 25-7 shows the result of using a queue to perform a level-order traversal of the tree in Figure 25-4. We leave the implementation of the necessary iterator classes for you as an exercise.

 Programming Tip: An iterator object that has not traversed the entire binary tree can be adversely affected by changes to the tree.

Figure 25-6 Using a stack to traverse the binary tree in Figure 25-4 in (a) preorder; (b) postorder

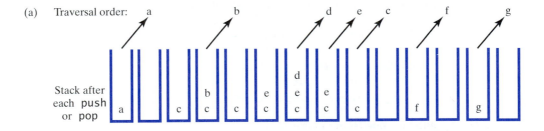

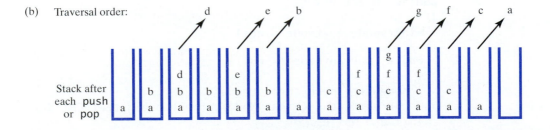

Figure 25-7   Using a queue to traverse the binary tree in Figure 25-4 in level order

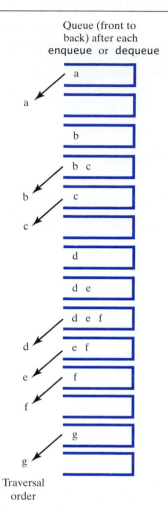

An Implementation of an Expression Tree

25.17   In the previous chapter, you saw that an expression tree is a binary tree that represents an algebraic expression. Figure 24-14 provided some examples of these trees. By using the algorithm given in Segment 24.22, we can evaluate the expression in the tree.

We can define an interface for an expression tree by extending the interface for a binary tree and adding a declaration for the method `evaluate`, as follows:

```
public interface ExpressionTreeInterface extends BinaryTreeInterface
{
   /** Task: Computes the value of the expression in the tree.
    *  @return the value of the expression */
   public double evaluate();
} // end ExpressionTreeInterface
```

Since an expression tree is a binary tree, we can derive a class of expression trees from `Binary-Tree`. We implement the method `evaluate` as a part of the derived class. A portion of the class `ExpressionTree` follows:

```java
public class ExpressionTree extends BinaryTree
{
  public ExpressionTree()
  {
  } // end default constructor

  public double evaluate()
  {
    return evaluate(getRootNode());
  } // end evaluate

  private double evaluate(BinaryNodeInterface rootNode)
  {
    double result;

    if (rootNode == null)
      result = 0;
    else if (rootNode.isLeaf())
    {
      String variable = (String) rootNode.getData();
      result = getValueOf(variable);
    }
    else
    {
      double firstOperand = evaluate(rootNode.getLeftChild());
      double secondOperand = evaluate(rootNode.getRightChild());
      String operator = (String) rootNode.getData();
      result = compute(operator, firstOperand, secondOperand);
    } // end if

    return result;
  } // end evaluate
  . . .
```

The public method `evaluate` calls a private method `evaluate` that is recursive. This private method uses methods declared in `BinaryNodeInterface` and the private methods `getValueOf` and `compute`. The method `getValueOf` returns the numeric value of a given variable in the expression, and `compute` returns the result of a given arithmetic operation and two given operands.

Notice how important the methods of the class `BinaryNode` are to the implementation of `evaluate`. For this reason, we do not want `BinaryNode` to be internal to `BinaryTree`. Rather, it should be part of a package.

Note: The class `ExpressionTree` is serializable because its base class `BinaryTree` is serializable.

Question 4   Trace the method `evaluate` for the expression tree in Figure 24-14c. What value is returned? Assume that *a* is 3, *b* is 4, and *c* is 5.

General Trees

To wrap up our discussion of tree implementations, we will consider one way to represent a node for a general tree. Rather than developing an implementation of a general tree that uses this node, we will see that we can use a binary tree to represent a general tree.

A Node for a General Tree

25.18   Since a node in a binary tree can have only two children, it is reasonable for each node to contain two references to these children. In addition, the number of node operations that test for, set, or get each child is reasonable. But dealing with more children per node in this way quickly becomes unwieldy.

We can define a node for a general tree that accommodates any number of children by referencing an object, such as a list or a vector, that contains the children. For example, the node in Figure 25-8 contains two references. One reference is to the data object, and the other is to a list of child nodes. An iterator for the list enables us to access these children.

Figure 25-8   A node for a general tree

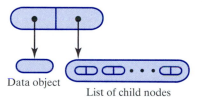

Data object

List of child nodes

In the following interface for a general node, `getChildrenIterator` returns an iterator to the node's children. A separate operation adds a child, assuming that the children are in no particular order. If the order of the children is important, the iterator could provide an operation to insert a new child at the current position within the iteration.

```
public interface GeneralNodeInterface
{
   public Object getData();
   public void setData(Object newData);
   public boolean isLeaf();
   public Iterator getChildrenIterator();
   public void addChild(GeneralNodeInterface newChild);
} // end GeneralNodeInterface
```

Using a Binary Tree to Represent a General Tree

25.19   Instead of the implementation just suggested, we can use a binary tree to represent any general tree. For example, let's represent the general tree in Figure 25-9a with a binary tree. As an intermediate step, we connect the nodes with new edges, as in Figure 25-9b. The root *A* has one of its original children—*B* in this case—as a left child. We then draw an edge from *B* to its sibling *C* and from *C* to another sibling *D*. Likewise, each parent in the general tree has one of its children as a left child in the binary tree, and these children are linked by edges.

Figure 25-9   (a) A general tree; (b) an equivalent binary tree; (c) a more conventional view of the same binary tree

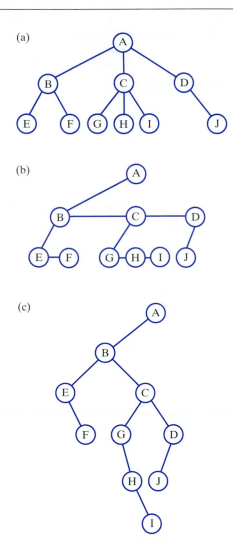

(a)

(b)

(c)

If we consider each node in Figure 25-9b that is to the right of its sibling as the right child of that sibling, we will have a binary tree that has an unorthodox form. We can move the nodes in the drawing without disconnecting them to get the familiar look of a binary tree, as Figure 25-9c shows.

25.20   **Traversals.** Let's examine the various traversals of the general tree in Figure 25-9a and compare them with traversals of the equivalent binary tree pictured in Figure 25-9c. The general tree has the following traversals:

Preorder: A B E F C G H I D J
Postorder: E F B G H I C J D A
Level order: A B C D E F G H I J

The traversals of the binary tree are as follows:

Preorder: A B E F C G H I D J
Postorder: F E I H G J D C B A
Level order: A B E C F G D H J I
Inorder: E F B G H I C J D A

The preorder traversals of the two trees are the same. The postorder traversal of the general tree is the same as the inorder traversal of the binary tree. We must invent a new kind of traversal of the binary tree to get the same results as a level-order traversal of the general tree. We leave that task to you as an exercise.

 Question 5   What binary tree can represent the general tree in Figure 24-3?

CHAPTER SUMMARY

- A node in a binary tree is an object that references a data object and two child nodes in the tree.

- A basic class of binary trees contains methods common to all trees: `getRootData`, `getHeight`, `getNumberOfNodes`, `isEmpty`, `clear`, and various traversals. The basic class also has a method that sets the root and subtrees of an existing binary tree to given values.

- The implementation of `getHeight` and `getNumberOfNodes` is easier if the class of nodes has similar methods.

- Preorder, postorder, and inorder traversals have simple recursive implementations. But to implement a traversal as an iterator, you must use an iterative approach, since an iterator needs to be able to pause during the traversal. You use a stack for preorder, postorder, and inorder traversals; you use a queue for a level-order traversal.

- You can derive a particular binary tree, such as an expression tree, from the class of basic binary trees.

- A node in a general tree is an object that references its children and a data object. To accommodate any number of children, the node can reference a list or a vector, for example. An iterator can provide access to the children. In this way, the node contains only two references.

- Instead of creating a general node for a general tree, you can use a binary tree to represent a general tree.

PROGRAMMING TIPS

- No cast is needed when you pass an instance of `BinaryTree` to a method whose parameter has the type `BinaryTreeInterface`. The converse, however, requires a cast.

- An iterator object that has not traversed the entire binary tree can be adversely affected by changes to the tree.

EXERCISES

1. Implement `getHeight` in the class `BinaryNode`, using the approach that Segment 25.11 uses for `getNumberOfNodes`.

2. Implement a recursive method `postorderTraverse` that displays the data in a binary tree in postorder.

3. Trace the iterative method `inorderTraverse` given in Segment 25.14 with the binary tree in Figure 25-10. Show the contents of the stack after each push and pop.

Figure 25-10 A binary tree for Exercises 3, 4, and 5

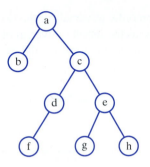

4. Show the contents of the stack after each push and pop during a preorder traversal of the binary tree in Figure 25-10. Repeat for a postorder traversal.

5. Show the contents of the queue after each enqueue and dequeue during a level-order traversal of the binary tree in Figure 25-10.

6. Trace the method `evaluate` given in Segment 25.17 for the expression tree in Figure 24-14d. What value is returned? Assume that *a* is 2, *b* is 4, *c* is 5, *d* is 6, and *e* is 4.

7. Replace the method `copy`, as discussed in Segment 25.6, with a method `clone`. That is, make `BinaryNode` `Cloneable`. Cloning a node should also clone the node's data object.

8. What binary tree represents the general tree in each of the following figures?

   a. Figure 24-5
   b. Figure 24-21

9. Define a traversal of the binary tree that represents a general tree that is equivalent to a level-order traversal of the general tree.

10. The preorder and inorder traversals of a binary tree always uniquely define the tree. The same is true for the postorder and inorder traversals.

   a. Draw the unique binary tree with the following preorder and inorder traversals:

   Preorder: A, B, D, E, C, F, G, H
   Inorder: E, D, B, A, G, F, H, C

   b. Draw the unique binary tree with the following postorder and inorder traversals:

   Postorder: B, D, F, G, E, C, A
   Inorder: B, A, D, C, F, E, G

11. Although you can uniquely determine a binary tree from either its preorder and inorder traversals, or its postorder and inorder traversals, more than one binary tree can have the same preorder and postorder traversals. Give an example of two different binary trees with the same preorder and postorder traversals.

12. In a tree, it is sometimes useful to be able to move from a node to its parent. To do this, a binary tree node would need a reference to its parent also. You then would be able to traverse a path from a leaf to the root. Redesign the node used in a binary tree so that each one has a reference to its parent as well as to its left child and right child. What methods will need to be changed?

PROJECTS

1. Using the results in Figures 25-6 and 25-7, implement iterator classes for preorder, postorder, and level-order traversals of a binary tree.

2. Write a Java program that distinguishes among 10 different animals. The program should play a guessing game similar to the one described in Segment 24.24. The user thinks of one of the 10 animals, and the program asks a sequence of questions until it can guess the animal.

As a bonus, expand your program so that it learns from the user. If your program makes an incorrect guess, it asks the user to enter a new question that can distinguish between the correct animal and the program's incorrect guess. The decision tree should be updated with this new question.

3. Complete the implementation of an expression tree that was begun in Segment 25.17.

4. Consider the redesigned node for a binary tree that Exercise 12 describes. Add an additional data field to the node to record the height of the subtree tree rooted at the node. Modify all the methods in the implementation of the binary tree so that the height field is updated anytime the structure of the tree changes.

A Binary Search Tree Implementation

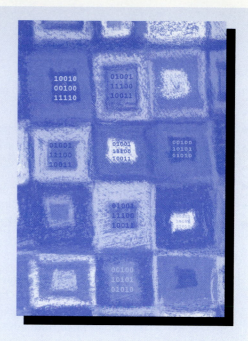

CONTENTS

Getting Started
    An Interface for the Binary Search Tree
    Duplicate Entries
    Beginning the Class Definition
Searching and Retrieving
Traversing
Adding an Entry
    An Iterative Implementation
    A Recursive Implementation
Removing an Entry
    Removing an Entry Whose Node Is a Leaf
    Removing an Entry Whose Node Has One Child
    Removing an Entry Whose Node Has Two Children
    Removing an Entry in the Root
    An Iterative Implementation
    A Recursive Implementation
The Efficiency of Operations
    The Importance of Balance
    The Order in Which Nodes Are Added
An Implementation of the ADT Dictionary

PREREQUISITES

Chapter   2   Creating Classes from Other Classes
Chapter   17   Dictionaries
Chapter   24   Trees
Chapter   25   Tree Implementations

OBJECTIVES

After studying this chapter, you should be able to

- Determine whether a binary tree is a binary search tree
- Locate a given entry in a binary search tree using the fewest comparisons
- Traverse the entries in a binary search tree in sorted order
- Add a new entry to a binary search tree
- Remove an entry from a binary search tree
- Describe the efficiency of operations on a binary search tree
- Use a binary search tree to implement the ADT dictionary

Recall from Chapter 24 that a search tree stores data in a way that facilitates searching it. In particular, we saw the binary search tree, which is both a binary tree and a search tree. The nature of a binary search tree enables us to search it by using a simple recursive algorithm. This algorithm is similar in spirit to a binary search of an array and can be just as efficient. However, the shape of a binary search tree affects the efficiency of this algorithm. Since we can create several different binary search trees from the same data, we want to pick the tree whose shape provides the most efficient search.

For a database that remains stable, a binary search tree provides a relatively simple way to achieve an efficient search. Most databases, however, change to remain current. Thus, we must add nodes to and remove nodes from the binary search tree. Unfortunately, these operations change the shape of the tree, often making a search less efficient.

This chapter implements the binary search tree and, in doing so, describes the algorithms for adding and removing entries. Chapter 28 looks at ways that a search tree can provide an efficient search despite additions and removals.

Getting Started

26.1   A **binary search tree** is a binary tree whose nodes contain Comparable objects and are organized as follows. For each node in the tree,

- The data in a node is greater than the data in the node's left subtree
- The data in a node is less than the data in the node's right subtree

Figure 26-1 shows the binary search tree that you saw in Chapter 24.

Figure 26-1   A binary search tree of names

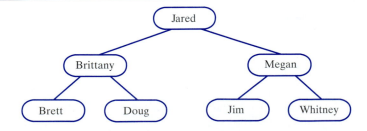

Recall that a Comparable object belongs to a class that implements the interface Comparable. Such objects have a method compareTo that we use to compare them. The basis for this comparison is varied and depends upon the composition of the object.

An Interface for the Binary Search Tree

26.2 **The operations.** In addition to the common operations of a tree, as given in the interface Tree-Interface, a binary search tree has basic database operations that search, retrieve, add, remove, and traverse its entries. We can design the following interface for a binary search tree, as well as for other search trees that you will see in Chapter 28:

```java
import java.util.Iterator;
public interface SearchTreeInterface extends TreeInterface
{
  /** Task: Searches for a specific entry in the tree.
   *  @param entry  an object to be found
   *  @return true if the object was found in the tree */
  public boolean contains(Comparable entry);

  /** Task: Retrieves a specific entry in the tree.
   *  @param entry  an object to be found
   *  @return either the object that was found in the tree or
   *          null if no such object exists */
  public Comparable getEntry(Comparable entry);

  /** Task: Adds a new entry to the tree. If the entry matches
   *        an object that exists in the tree already, replaces
   *        the object with the new entry.
   *  @param newEntry  an object to add to the tree
   *  @return either null if newEntry was not in the tree already,
   *          or an existing entry that matched the parameter
   *          newEntry and has been replaced in the tree */
  public Comparable add(Comparable newEntry);

  /** Task: Removes a specific entry from the tree.
   *  @param entry  an object to be removed
   *  @return either the object that was removed from the tree or
   *          null if no such object exists */
  public Comparable remove(Comparable entry);

  /** Task: Creates an iterator that traverses all entries in the
   *        tree.
   * @return an iterator that provides sequential access to the
   *         entries in the tree */
  public Iterator getInorderIterator();
} // end SearchTreeInterface
```

26.3 **Understanding the specifications.** These specifications allow us to use a binary search tree in the implementation of the ADT dictionary, as you will see later in this chapter. The methods use return values instead of exceptions to indicate whether an operation has failed. The return value for a successful retrieve, add, or remove operation, however, might seem strange at first. For example, it appears that the retrieve operation, getEntry, returns the same entry it is given to find. In fact, getEntry returns an object that is in the tree and that matches the given entry according to the compareTo method. Let's look at an example that adds entries and then retrieves them.

Imagine a class Person that has two strings as data fields representing the person's name and identification number. The class implements the Comparable interface, and so has a compareTo method. Suppose that compareTo bases its comparison only on the name field. Consider the following operations on a binary search tree:

```
BinarySearchTree myTree = new BinarySearchTree();
Person whitney = new Person("Whitney", "111223333");
Person returnValue = (Person)myTree.add(whitney);
```

Following the add operation, returnValue is null, since whitney was not in the tree already. Now suppose we try to add another *Whitney*:

```
Person whitney2 = new Person("Whitney", "444556666");
returnValue = (Person)myTree.add(whitney2);
```

Since whitney and whitney2 have the same names, whitney.compareTo(whitney2) is zero. Therefore, the add method will not add whitney2 to the tree. Instead it replaces whitney with whitney2 and returns whitney, the original object in the tree, as Figure 26-2 illustrates. We can think of this as a way to change the identification number of a person named *Whitney*.

Figure 26-2   Adding an entry that matches an entry already in a binary search tree

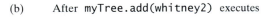

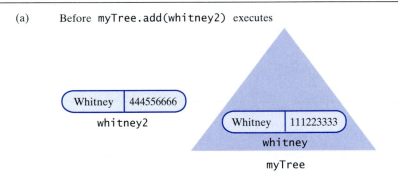

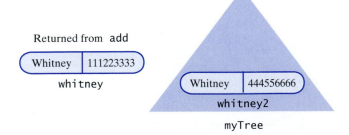

Now the statement

```
returnValue = (Person)myTree.getEntry(whitney);
```

sets `returnValue` to `whitney2`, since it is in the tree and matches `whitney`. Similarly,

> `returnValue = (Person)myTree.remove(whitney);`

returns and removes `whitney2`.

Now imagine that the method `compareTo` uses both the name and identification fields of a `Person` object to make a comparison. Since `whitney` and `whitney2` would not be equal according to this `compareTo`, we could add both objects to the tree. Then `getEntry(whitney)` would return `whitney`, and `remove(whitney)` would remove and return `whitney`.

Duplicate Entries

26.4   To make our discussion a bit simpler, we insist that a binary search tree contain distinct entries. Notice that the add method in `SearchTreeInterface` ensures that duplicates are never added to the tree. In practice, this restriction can be desirable, but sometimes it is not. By making a small change to our definition of a binary search tree, we can have entries in a binary search tree that occur elsewhere in the tree.

Figure 26-3 shows a binary search tree in which *Jared* occurs twice. If we are at the root of this tree and want to know whether *Jared* occurs again, it would help to know in which subtree we should look. Thus, if any entry *e* has a duplicate entry *d*, we arbitrarily require that *d* occur in the right subtree of *e*'s node. Accordingly, we modify our definition as follows:

For each node in a binary search tree,

● The data in a node is greater than the data in the node's left subtree
● The data in a node is less than *or equal to* the data in the node's right subtree

Figure 26-3   A binary search tree with duplicate entries

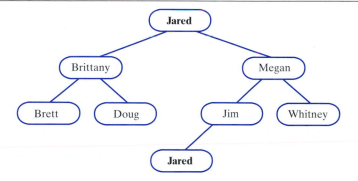

Note: Duplicate entries
If you permit duplicate entries in a binary search tree, place the duplicate of an entry in the entry's right subtree. Although our choice of the right subtree is arbitrary, you must be consistent.

With duplicate entries, the add method has less to do. But which entry will `getEntry` retrieve? Will `remove` delete the first occurrence of an entry or all occurrences? Exactly what happens is up to the class designer, but these questions should indicate the complications that duplicate entries cause. We will not consider duplicate entries any further, and will leave this issue to you as a programming project.

Question 1   If you add *Megan* to the binary search tree in Figure 26-3 as a leaf, where should you place the new node?

Beginning the Class Definition

26.5   Let's begin the definition of a class of binary search trees. Since a binary search tree is a binary tree, we derive our new class from the class `BinaryTree` that we defined in Chapter 25. Thus, we begin our class as follows:

```
import java.util.Iterator;
public class BinarySearchTree extends BinaryTree
                              implements SearchTreeInterface
{
  public BinarySearchTree()
  {
    super();
  } // end default constructor

  public BinarySearchTree(Comparable rootEntry)
  {
    super();
    setRootNode(new BinaryNode(rootEntry));
  } // end constructor
  . . .
```

Note: The class `BinarySearchTree` is serializable because its base class `BinaryTree` is serializable.

26.6   **Disallow `setTree`.** Before we go any further, consider the two `setTree` methods that our class inherits from `BinaryTree`. The client could use these methods to create a tree that is not a binary search tree. This outcome would be impossible if the client uses `SearchTreeInterface` to declare an instance of the database. For example, if we write

```
SearchTreeInterface dataBase = new BinarySearchTree();
```

dataBase would not have the method `setTree`, since the method is not in `SearchTreeInterface`. But if we wrote

```
BinarySearchTree dataBase = new BinarySearchTree();
```

dataBase would have the method `setTree`.

To prevent a client from using either version of `setTree`, we should override these methods so that they throw an exception if called. For example, we could define the following method in `BinarySearchTree`:

```
public void setTree(Object rootData)
{
  throw new UnsupportedOperationException();
} // end setTree
```

Question 2   Is it necessary to define the methods `isEmpty` and `clear` within `BinarySearchTree`? Explain.

Searching and Retrieving

26.7   **The search algorithm.** Segment 24.29 presented the following recursive algorithm to search a binary search tree:

> *Algorithm* `bstSearch(binarySearchTree, desiredObject)`
> *// Searches a binary search tree for a given object.*
> *// Returns true if the object is found.*
>
> **if** (binarySearchTree *is empty*)
>   **return false**
> **else if** (desiredObject `==` *object in the root of* binarySearchTree)
>   **return true**
> **else if** (desiredObject `<` *object in the root of* binarySearchTree)
>   **return** bstSearch(*left subtree of* binarySearchTree, desiredObject)
> **else**
>   **return** bstSearch(*right subtree of* binarySearchTree, desiredObject)

This algorithm is the basis of the method `getEntry`. Although the algorithm returns a boolean value, our implementation will return the located data object.

Note: Searching a binary search tree is like performing a binary search of an array: You search one of two subtrees of the binary search tree. For a binary search, you search one of two halves of an array.

26.8   **The method getEntry.** As is often the case with recursive algorithms, we implement the actual search as a private method `findEntry` that `getEntry` invokes. Thus, we have the following methods:

```
public Comparable getEntry(Comparable entry)
{
  return findEntry(getRootNode(), entry);
} // end getEntry

private Comparable findEntry(BinaryNode rootNode, Comparable entry)
{
  Comparable result = null;

  if (rootNode != null)
  {
    Object rootEntry = rootNode.getData();

    if (entry.equals(rootEntry))
      result = (Comparable)rootEntry;
    else if (entry.compareTo(rootEntry) < 0)
      result = findEntry((BinaryNode)rootNode.getLeftChild(), entry);
```

```
        else
            result = findEntry((BinaryNode)rootNode.getRightChild(), entry);
      } // end if

      return result;
   } // end findEntry
```

We use the methods `compareTo` and `equals` to compare the given entry with the existing entries in the tree. Also, notice our use of methods from the class `BinaryNode`. We assume that we have at least package access to this class.

You can implement `getEntry` iteratively as well, with or without the use of a private method such as `findEntry`. We leave this implementation as an exercise.

26.9   **The method `contains`.** The method `contains` can simply call `getEntry` to determine whether a given entry is in the tree:

```
      public boolean contains(Comparable entry)
      {
         return getEntry(entry) != null;
      } // end contains
```

Traversing

26.10   `SearchTreeInterface` provides the method `getInorderIterator`, which returns an inorder iterator. Since our class is a subclass of `BinaryTree`, it inherits `getInorderIterator`. For a binary search tree, this iterator traverses the entries in ascending order, as defined by the entries' method `compareTo`.

Adding an Entry

26.11   Adding entries to a binary search tree is an essential operation, since that is how we build one initially. So suppose that we have a binary search tree and we want to add a new entry to it. We cannot add it just anywhere in the tree, because we must retain the relationships among the nodes. That is, the tree must still be a binary search tree after the addition. Also, the method `getEntry` must be able to locate the new entry. For example, if we want to add the entry *Chad* to the tree in Figure 26-4a, we could not add the new node to *Jared*'s right subtree. Since *Chad* comes before *Jared*, *Chad* must be in *Jared*'s left subtree. Since *Brittany* is the root of this left subtree, we compare *Chad* with *Brittany* and find that *Chad* is larger. Thus, *Chad* belongs in *Brittany*'s right subtree. Continuing, we compare *Chad* with *Doug* and find that *Chad* belongs in *Doug*'s left subtree. But this subtree is empty. That is, *Doug* has no left child.

If we make *Chad* the left child of *Doug*, we will get the binary search tree in Figure 26-4b. Now `getEntry` will be able to locate *Chad* by making the same comparisons we just described. That is, `getEntry` will compare *Chad* with *Jared*, *Brittany*, and *Doug* before locating *Chad*. Notice that the new node is a leaf.

Note: Every addition to a binary search tree adds a new leaf to the tree.

Figure 26-4   (a) A binary search tree; (b) the same tree after adding *Chad*

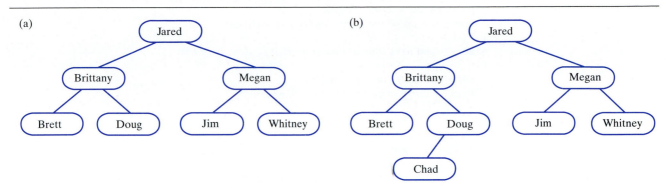

Question 3   Add the names *Chris*, *Jason*, and *Kelley* to the binary search tree in Figure 26-4b.

Question 4   Add the name *Miguel* to the binary search tree in Figure 26-4a, and then add *Nancy*. Beginning with the original tree, add *Nancy* and then add *Miguel*. Does the order in which you add the two names affect the tree that results?

An Iterative Implementation

26.12   **An iterative algorithm for adding a new entry.** The following iterative algorithm formalizes our previous discussion, in accordance with the specifications of the method `add` in `SearchTreeInterface`. Recall that we decided to have only distinct entries in the binary search tree. If we try to add an entry to a tree that matches an entry already in the tree, we replace that entry with the new entry and return the old entry.

> *Algorithm* `add(binarySearchTree, newEntry)`
> *// Adds a new entry to a binary search tree.*
> *// Returns* `null` *if* `newEntry` *did not exist already in the tree. Otherwise, returns the entry*
> *// presently in the tree that matched* `newEntry` *and replaces it with* `newEntry`*.*
>
> `result` = **null**
> **if** (`binarySearchTree` *is empty*)
>   *Create a new root node and place* `newEntry` *into it*
> **else**
> {
>   `currentNode` = *root node*
>   **while** (`newEntry` *is not found and* `currentNode` *is not* **null**)
>   {
>   **if** (`newEntry` < *entry in* `currentNode`)
>   {
>   `parentNode` = `currentNode`
>   `currentNode` = *the left child of* `parentNode`
>   }

```
        else if (newEntry > entry in currentNode)
        {
          parentNode = currentNode
          currentNode = the right child of parentNode
        }
        else // newEntry matches an entry that is already in tree
        {
          result = entry in currentNode
          Replace entry in currentNode with newEntry
        }
      }

    if (newEntry is not found in tree)
    {
      Create a new node and place newEntry into it
      if (newEntry < entry in parentNode)
        Make the new node the left child of parentNode
      else
        Make the new node the right child of parentNode
    }
  }

  return result
```

26.13 **An iterative implementation of the method add.** The Java implementation of the previous algorithm closely follows the algorithm's logic, but it contains some details that make the code simpler to read.

```java
public Comparable add(Comparable newEntry)
{
  Comparable result = null;

  if (isEmpty())
    setRootNode(new BinaryNode(newEntry)); // method is protected
                                           // in BinaryTree
  else // look for newEntry in tree
  {
    BinaryNode currentNode = getRootNode(); // currentNode != null
    BinaryNode parentNode = null;
    boolean found = false;
    char direction = ' ';

    while (!found && (currentNode != null) )
    {
      Object currentEntry = currentNode.getData();
      int comparison = newEntry.compareTo(currentEntry);

      if (comparison < 0)
      { // search left
        direction = 'L';
        parentNode = currentNode;
        currentNode = (BinaryNode)currentNode.getLeftChild();
      }
```

```
      else if (comparison > 0)
      { // search right
        direction = 'R';
        parentNode = currentNode;
        currentNode = (BinaryNode)currentNode.getRightChild();
      }
      else
      { // newEntry matches currentEntry: return and replace
        // currentEntry
        result = (Comparable) currentEntry;
        currentNode.setData(newEntry);
        found = true;
      } // end if
    } // end while

    if (!found)
    { // add new entry as a leaf child of parentNode
      if (direction == 'L')
        parentNode.setLeftChild(new BinaryNode(newEntry));
      else
        parentNode.setRightChild(new BinaryNode(newEntry));
    } // end if
  } // end if

  return result;
} // end add
```

A Recursive Implementation

26.14   The method add has an elegant recursive implementation that is much shorter than the iterative implementation just given. However, it is a bit hard to understand, particularly at first.

For instance, consider again the example given earlier in Segment 26.11. If we want to add *Chad* to the binary search tree in Figure 26-4a, we take the following steps:

To add *Chad* to the binary search tree whose root is *Jared*:
  Observe that *Chad* is less than *Jared*.
  Add *Chad* to *Jared*'s left subtree, whose root is *Brittany*.

To add *Chad* to the binary search tree whose root is *Brittany*:
  Observe that *Chad* is greater than *Brittany*.
  Add *Chad* to *Brittany*'s right subtree, whose root is *Doug*.

To add *Chad* to the binary search tree whose root is *Doug*:
  Observe that *Chad* is less than *Doug*.
  Add *Chad* to *Doug*'s left subtree, which is empty.

Make *Chad* the left child of *Doug*.

We can see that adding an entry to the tree rooted at *Jared* depends upon adding to progressively smaller subtrees, as Figure 26-5 shows.

Figure 26-5   Recursively adding *Chad* to smaller subtrees of a binary search tree

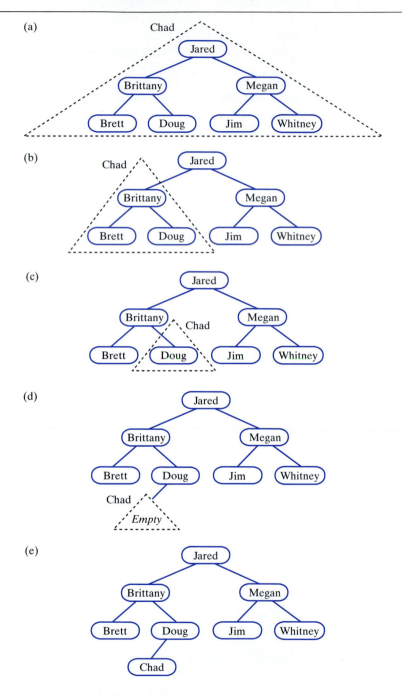

26.15   **A recursive algorithm for adding a new entry.** The following recursive algorithm formalizes this approach:

> *Algorithm* **add(binarySearchTree, newEntry)**
> *// Adds a new entry to a binary search tree.*

// Returns null *if* newEntry *did not exist already in the tree. Otherwise, returns the entry*
// presently in the tree that matched newEntry *and replaces it with* newEntry.

```
result = null
if (binarySearchTree is empty)
    Create a new root node and place newEntry into it
else if (newEntry < entry in root of binarySearchTree)
    result = add(left subtree of binarySearchTree, newEntry)
else if (newEntry > entry in root of binarySearchTree)
    result = add(right subtree of binarySearchTree, newEntry)
else // key is already in tree
{
    result = entry in root node
    Replace entry in root node with newEntry
}
return result
```

26.16   **A recursive implementation of the method add.** Recall the recursive search algorithm given in
Segment 26.7. The public method getEntry in Segment 26.8 invokes a private recursive method
findEntry that implements the search algorithm. The recursive method has a node as a parameter
that is initially the root node of the tree. When called recursively, this parameter is either the left
child or the right child of the current root.

Our implementation of add here needs a similar organization to handle the recursion. So
suppose that the public method add calls a private recursive method addNode. Like findEntry,
addNode has a node as a parameter that is initially the root node of the tree and later is the left
child or the right child of the current root. The difficulty here is that we need to alter the tree by
inserting a new node. If we are not careful, the new node will not be linked to the rest of the tree.

Remember where we place a new node into a binary search tree. As Figures 26-4 and 26-5
illustrate, a new node always becomes a leaf in the tree. Now imagine the recursive calls to addNode
when adding *Chad* to the tree in Figure 26-5a. Eventually, the node containing *Doug* is passed to
addNode as its argument (Figure 26-5c). Since *Chad* is less than *Doug*, *Doug*'s left child is passed
to addNode (Figure 26-5d). This child is null. But when a node is passed to addNode, its reference
is copied into the parameter rootNode, as Figure 26-6a shows. Since this reference is null, a new
node is created that rootNode references (Figure 26-6b).

Figure 26-6   (a) The method addNode copies its argument (null) to its local parameter rootNode;
(b) rootNode references a new node that contains *Chad*

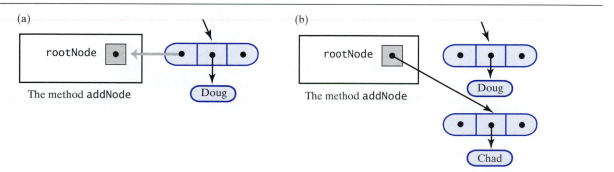

(a)   rootNode   The method addNode   Doug

(b)   rootNode   The method addNode   Doug   Chad

The problem is that the new node needs to be *Doug*'s left child. How do we make *Doug*'s node
reference the new node? If addNode returns the reference to the new node, we can place the reference

into *Doug*'s node, as Figure 26-7 illustrates. In general, `addNode` returns the reference to the altered subtree whose root it was given as an argument.

Figure 26-7   After adding a node to the subtree passed to it, `addNode` returns a reference to the subtree so it can be attached to the rest of the original tree

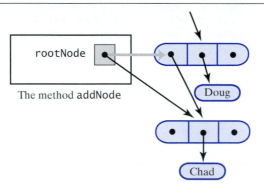

26.17   For the moment, ignore the possibility that the new entry is in the tree already. It is always a good idea to simplify a difficult problem temporarily while drafting a solution. So suppose that `addNode` has the following signature:

```
private BinaryNode addNode(BinaryNode rootNode, Entry newEntry)
```

The first step in this method's implementation asks whether the given subtree is empty. If it is, we create a new node for the subtree. Thus, we have

```
if (rootNode == null)
    rootNode = new BinaryNode(newEntry);
```

If the subtree is not empty, we determine into which of its subtrees we must add the new node. Here is the case that adds to the left subtree:

```
else if (newEntry.compareTo(rootNode.getData()) < 0)
{
    BinaryNode leftChild = (BinaryNode)rootNode.getLeftChild();
    BinaryNode subtreeRoot = addNode(leftChild, newEntry);
    rootNode.setLeftChild(subtreeRoot);
}
```

We begin by comparing the new entry and the entry in the root. If the comparison is "less than," we get the root's left child and pass it to `addNode`. Remember that when we are coding a recursive method such as `addNode`, we assume that it works when we write the recursive call. Thus, `addNode` places a new node containing `newEntry` into this left subtree, and it returns a reference to the augmented subtree. We store this reference in `subtreeRoot`. We set the left child reference in the given tree's root to `subtreeRoot` to complete the addition. If you prefer, you can condense the previous code by combining the last two statements, as follows:

```
rootNode.setLeftChild(addNode(leftChild, newEntry));
```

You would write analogous code for inserting into the right subtree.

26.18   Now we must deal with the case in which the given entry is in the tree already. In that event, the add method returns and replaces the entry in the tree that matches `newEntry`. Since `addNode` is the method that actually does the work, it needs to return this entry. But it already must return a reference to the altered tree. Certainly it cannot return two objects.

A solution is to pass another parameter to addNode and have the method alter its value if necessary. Thus, the signature for addNode becomes

```
private BinaryNode addNode(BinaryNode rootNode, Comparable newEntry,
                           ReturnObject oldEntry)
```

ReturnObject is an internal class that has a single Comparable data field and simple methods set and get to manipulate it. Initially, oldEntry's data field is null, since that is what add returns if newEntry is not in the tree. If newEntry matches an entry in the tree, addNode must execute the following statements:

```
Comparable rootEntry = (Comparable)rootNode.getData();
oldEntry.set(rootEntry);
rootNode.setData(newEntry);
```

The method add then can return the value of oldEntry's data field. Thus, we have the following implementation for the method add:

```
public Comparable add(Comparable newEntry)
{
  ReturnObject oldEntry = new ReturnObject(null);
  BinaryNode newRoot =
      (BinaryNode)addNode(getRootNode(), newEntry, oldEntry);
  setRootNode(newRoot);

  return oldEntry.get();
} // end add
```

Finally, the implementation of addNode follows:

```
/** Task: Adds a new entry to the subtree rooted at a given node.
 *  @param rootNode   a reference to the root of a subtree
 *  @param newEntry   an object that is the new entry
 *  @param oldEntry   an object whose data field is null
 *  @return the root node of the resulting tree; if newEntry
 *          matched an entry that was already in the tree,
 *          oldEntry's data field is that current entry;
 *          otherwise it is null */
private BinaryNode addNode(BinaryNode rootNode, Comparable newEntry,
                           ReturnObject oldEntry)
{
  if (rootNode == null)
    rootNode = new BinaryNode(newEntry);
  else if (newEntry.compareTo(rootNode.getData()) < 0)
  {
    BinaryNode leftChild = (BinaryNode)rootNode.getLeftChild();
    BinaryNode subtreeRoot = addNode(leftChild, newEntry, oldEntry);
    rootNode.setLeftChild(subtreeRoot);
  }
  else if (newEntry.compareTo(rootNode.getData()) > 0)
  {
    BinaryNode rightChild = (BinaryNode)rootNode.getRightChild();
```

```
            rootNode.setRightChild(addNode(rightChild, newEntry, oldEntry));
         }
         else // newEntry matches entry in root
         {
           Comparable rootEntry = (Comparable)rootNode.getData();
           oldEntry.set(rootEntry);
           rootNode.setData(newEntry);
         } // end if
         return rootNode;
      } // end addNode
```

Removing an Entry

26.19   To remove an entry from a binary search tree, we pass a matching entry to the method `remove`. The desired entry is then removed from the tree and returned to the client. If no such entry exists, the method returns `null`.

Removing an entry is somewhat more involved than adding an entry, as the required logic depends upon the number of children that belong to the node containing the entry. We consider now three cases:

- The node has no children—it is a leaf
- The node has one child
- The node has two children

Removing an Entry Whose Node Is a Leaf

26.20   The simplest case is when the node is a leaf, that is, has no children. For example, suppose that node *N* contains the entry to be removed from the binary search tree. Figure 26-8a shows two possibilities for node *N*: It could be either the left child or the right child of its parent node *P*. Since *N* is a leaf, we can delete it by setting the appropriate child reference in node *P* to `null`. Figure 26-8b shows the result of this operation.

Figure 26-8   (a) Two possible configurations of a leaf node *N*; (b) the resulting two possible configurations after removing node *N*

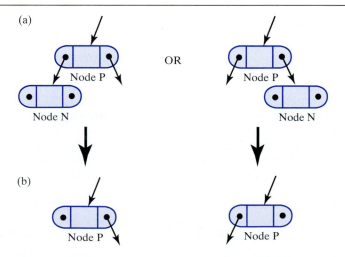

Removing an Entry Whose Node Has One Child

26.21   Now imagine that the entry to be removed is in a node *N* that has exactly one child *C*. Figure 26-9a shows the four possibilities for node *N* and its parent *P*. To remove the entry in *N*, we remove *N* from the tree. We do this by making *C* a child of *P* instead of *N*. As Figure 26-9b shows, if *N* was a left child of *P*, we make *C* be the left child of *P*. Likewise, if *N* was a right child of *P*, we make *C* be the right child of *P*.

Figure 26-9   (a) Four possible configurations of a node *N* that has one child; (b) the resulting two possible configurations after removing node *N*

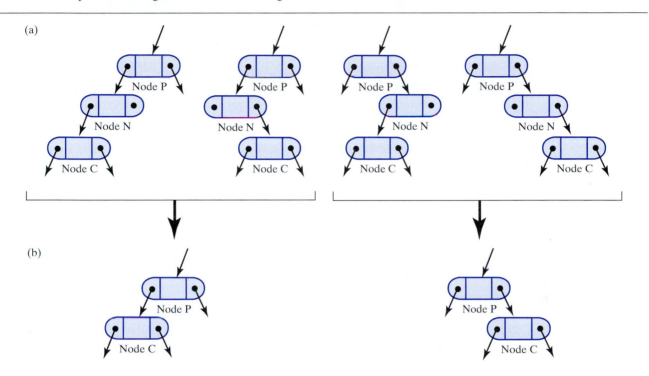

Removing an Entry Whose Node Has Two Children

26.22   The previous two cases are really not too difficult, conceptually or in practice. But this last case is a bit tricky. Once again, suppose that the entry to be removed is in a node *N*, but now *N* has two children. Figure 26-10 shows two possible configurations for *N*. If we try to remove node *N*, we will leave its two children without a parent. Although node *P* could reference one of them, it hasn't room for both. Removing node *N* is not an option.

We do not actually have to remove node *N* to remove its entry. Let's find a node *A* that is easy to remove—it would have no more than one child—and replace *N*'s entry with the entry now in *A*. We then can remove node *A* and still have the correct entries in the tree. But will the tree still be a binary search tree? Clearly, node *A* cannot be just any node; it must contain an entry in the tree that legally can be in node *N*.

Figure 26-10 Two possible configurations of a node N that has two children

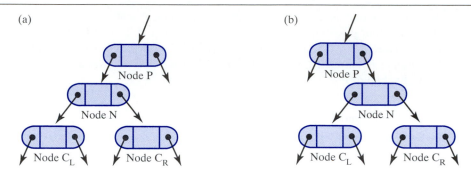

Let e be the entry in node N. Since node N has two children, e cannot be the smallest entry in the tree, nor can it be the largest. We also know that the entries in the tree are distinct. Thus, if we imagine the tree's entries in ascending order, we can write

... $a < e < b$ ...

Here, a is the entry that is immediately before e, and b is the one that is immediately after. An inorder traversal of the tree would visit these entries in this same order. Thus, a is called the **inorder predecessor** of e, and b is the **inorder successor** of e.

Now the entry a must occur in a node in N's left subtree; b is in a node in N's right subtree, as Figure 26-11a illustrates. Moreover, a is the largest entry in N's left subtree, since a is the entry that is immediately before e. Suppose that we delete the node that contains a and replace e with a, as Figure 26-11b shows. Now all of the remaining entries in N's left subtree are less than a, as needed. All of the entries in N's right subtree are greater than e and so are greater than a. Thus, we still have a binary search tree.

26.23   **Locating the entry a.** The previous segment assumed that we could find the appropriate entry a. So let's locate the node that contains a and verify that it does not have two children. Consider again the original tree in Figure 26-11a. We already know that a must be in N's left subtree, and that a is the largest entry in that subtree. To find an entry larger than the one in any given node, we look at the node's right child. Thus, a occurs in the subtree's rightmost node R, as Figure 26-12 illustrates. Node R cannot have a right child, because if it did, the child's entry would be greater than a. Thus, node R has no more than one child and can be removed from the tree easily.

Figure 26-11 Node N and its subtrees: (a) the entry a is immediately before the entry e, and b is immediately after e; (b) after deleting the node that contained a and replacing e with a

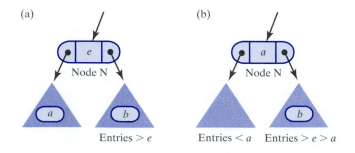

Figure 26-12 The largest entry *a* in node *N*'s left subtree occurs in the subtree's rightmost node *R*

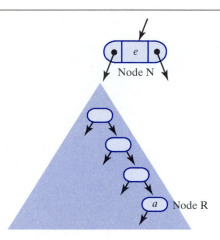

26.24   The following pseudocode summarizes this discussion:

> ***Algorithm Delete the entry e that occurs in a node N that has two children***
> *Find the rightmost node R in N's left subtree*
> *Replace the entry in node N with the entry that is in node R*
> *Delete node R*

An alternate approach involves *b*, the entry that is immediately after *e* in sorted order. We already have noted that *b* occurs in *N*'s right subtree. It would have to be the smallest entry in that subtree, so it would occur in the leftmost node in the subtree. Thus, we have the following alternate pseudocode:

> ***Algorithm Delete the entry e that occurs in a node N that has two children***
> *Find the leftmost node L in N's right subtree*
> *Replace the entry in node N with the entry that is in node L*
> *Delete node L*

Both approaches work equally well.

Note: To remove an entry whose node has two children, you first replace the entry with another whose node has no more than one child. You then remove the second node from the binary search tree.

26.25

Example. Figure 26-13 shows several consecutive removals from a binary search tree of names. The first algorithm given in the previous segment is used. To remove *Chad* from the tree in Figure 26-13a, we replace it with its inorder predecessor *Brittany*. We then remove the node that contained *Brittany* to get the tree in Figure 26-13b. To remove *Sean* from this new tree, we replace it with its inorder predecessor *Reba* and remove *Reba*'s original node. This gives us the tree in Figure 26-13c. Finally, to remove *Kathy* from this tree, we replace it with its inorder predecessor *Doug* and remove *Doug*'s original node, to get the tree in Figure 26-13d.

Figure 26-13   (a) A binary search tree; (b) after removing *Chad*; (c) after removing *Sean*; (d) after removing *Kathy*

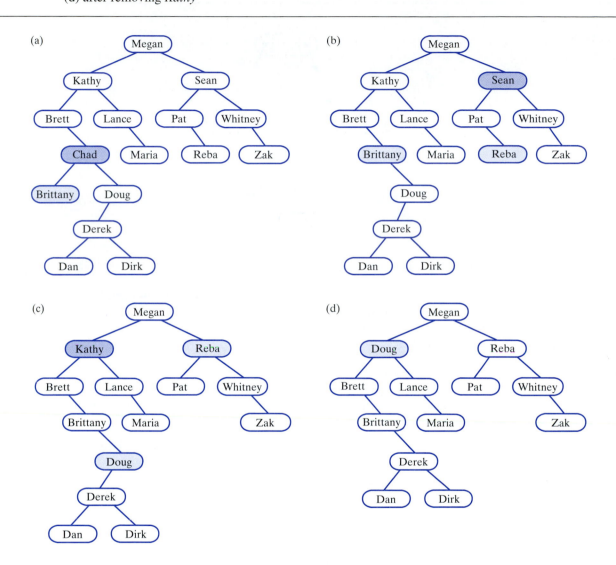

 Question 5   The second algorithm described in Segment 26.24 involves the inorder successor. Using this algorithm, remove *Chad* and *Sean* from the tree in Figure 26-13a.

Question 6   Remove *Megan* from the tree in Figure 26-13a in two different ways.

Removing an Entry in the Root

26.26   Removing an entry that is in the root of the tree is a special case only if we actually remove the root node. That will occur when the root has at most one child. If the root has two children, the previous segment shows that we would replace the root's entry and delete a different node.

If the root is a leaf, the tree has only one node. Deleting it results in an empty tree. If the root has one child, as Figure 26-14 illustrates, the child is either a right child or a left child. In either case, we simply delete the root node by making the child node *C* the root of the tree.

Figure 26-14 (a) Two possible configurations of a root that has one child; (b) after removing the root

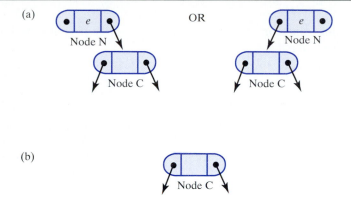

An Iterative Implementation

26.27   **Locating the desired entry.** Recall that the method `remove` is given an entry that matches the entry to be removed from the tree. If `remove` finds such an entry in the tree, it returns the entry. If no such entry occurs, the method returns `null`.

So `remove`'s first step is to search the tree. We use the `compareTo` method to compare the given entry with the other entries in the tree. The code for this first step is similar to code that we have seen earlier in this chapter. Here, as we consider each node, we keep track of the node's parent. If we find the desired entry, we save a reference to it. Thus, `remove` begins as follows:

```java
public Comparable remove(Comparable entry)
{
   Comparable result = null;
   boolean found = false;

   // locate the node that contains a match for entry
   BinaryNode currentNode = getRootNode();
   BinaryNode parentNode = null;
   while (!found && (currentNode != null) )
   {
      Object currentEntry = currentNode.getData();
      int comparison = entry.compareTo(currentEntry);

      if (comparison == 0)
      {
         found = true;
         result = (Comparable)currentEntry;
      }
      else
      {
         parentNode = currentNode;
```

```
            if (comparison < 0)
              currentNode = (BinaryNode)currentNode.getLeftChild();
            else
              currentNode = (BinaryNode)currentNode.getRightChild();
        } // end if
      } // end while
    . . .
```

At this point, `currentNode` is node *N* in our discussion; it is the node that contains the entry to be removed from the tree.

26.28 **Case 1: The node has two children.** Having located the node that contains the entry to be removed from the tree, we proceed according the node's number of children. If the node has two children, we will remove another node that has no more than one child. Thus, we should consider the case for two children first, so our code can sequence into the other cases that actually delete a node.

Assuming that node *N* has two children, we take the following steps. To make this pseudocode closer to the actual Java code, we use `currentNode` to denote node *N* and `rightChild` to denote node *R*.

```
// find inorder predecessor by searching the left subtree; it will be the node
// with the largest entry in the subtree, occurring as far right as possible
leftSubtreeRoot = left child of currentNode
rightChild = leftSubtreeRoot
priorNode = currentNode
while (rightChild has a right child)
{
  priorNode = rightChild
  rightChild = right child of rightChild
}
// Assertion: rightChild is the node to be removed and has no more than one child

Copy entry from rightChild to currentNode
Remove rightChild
```

The following Java code implements these previous steps and should immediately follow the code given in Segment 26.27. The actual removal of the node `rightChild` will be done by the code that handles the cases when node *N* has no more than one child. We still need to write that code, but notice how the following code eventually renames `rightChild` to `currentNode` so that the subsequent code can make the deletion.

```
    if (found)
    {
      if (currentNode.hasLeftChild() && currentNode.hasRightChild())
      {
        // find node with largest entry in left subtree by
        // moving as far right in the subtree as possible
        BinaryNode leftSubtreeRoot = (BinaryNode)currentNode.getLeftChild();
        BinaryNode rightChild = leftSubtreeRoot;
        BinaryNode priorNode = currentNode;
        while (rightChild.hasRightChild())
        {
          priorNode = rightChild;
          rightChild = (BinaryNode)rightChild.getRightChild();
        } // end while
```

```
        // copy entry from rightmost node to current node
        currentNode.setData(rightChild.getData());

        // need to remove the rightmost node, so rename it as currentNode
        currentNode = rightChild;
        parentNode = priorNode; // parent of currentNode
    } // end if
    // Assertion: current node is the node to be removed;
    //            it has at most one child

    < More code to come >
    . . .

  } // end if

  return result;
} // end remove
```

26.29   **Case 2: The node has at most one child.** At the ellipses in the code in the previous segment, currentNode is the node to remove. It has at most one child. If currentNode is not the root, parentNode is its parent. We handle all of these cases here.

The following pseudocode sets childNode to the child, if any, of currentNode:

```
if (currentNode has a left child)
   childNode = left child of currentNode
else
   childNode = right child of currentNode
// Assertion: if currentNode is a leaf, childNode is null
```

Notice that if currentNode is a leaf, childNode is set to null, since currentNode has no right child.

We now remove the current node, accounting for the case when the node is the root:

```
if (currentNode is the root of the tree)
   Set the root of the tree to childNode
else
   Link the parent of currentNode to childNode, thereby deleting current node
```

If we set the root of the tree to childNode, realize that we will correctly set the root to null if currentNode is a leaf.

The following Java code implements these steps and replaces the ellipses in the previous segment:

```
BinaryNode childNode;
if (currentNode.hasLeftChild())
   childNode = (BinaryNode)currentNode.getLeftChild();
else
   childNode = (BinaryNode)currentNode.getRightChild();
// Assertion: if currentNode is a leaf, childNode is null

// remove current node
if (currentNode == getRootNode())
   setRootNode(childNode);
```

```
                  // else link the parent of the current node to childNode,
                  // thereby deleting the current node
                  else if (parentNode.getLeftChild() == currentNode)
                    parentNode.setLeftChild(childNode);
                  else
                    parentNode.setRightChild(childNode);
```

For your reference, here is the complete iterative implementation of the method remove:

```
public Comparable remove(Comparable entry)
{
  Comparable result = null;
  boolean found = false;

  // locate node that contains a match for entry
  BinaryNode currentNode = getRootNode();
  BinaryNode parentNode = null;
  while (!found && (currentNode != null) )
  {
    Object currentEntry = currentNode.getData();
    int comparison = entry.compareTo(currentEntry);

    if (comparison == 0)
    {
      found = true;
      result = (Comparable)currentEntry;
    }
    else
    {
      parentNode = currentNode;
      if (comparison < 0)
        currentNode = (BinaryNode)currentNode.getLeftChild();
      else
        currentNode = (BinaryNode)currentNode.getRightChild();
    } // end if
  } // end while

  if (found)
  {
    // Case 1: current node has two children
    if (currentNode.hasLeftChild() && currentNode.hasRightChild())
    {
      // find node with largest entry in left subtree by
      // moving as far right in the subtree as possible
      BinaryNode leftSubtreeRoot = (BinaryNode)currentNode.getLeftChild();
      BinaryNode rightChild = leftSubtreeRoot;
      BinaryNode priorNode = currentNode;
      while (rightChild.hasRightChild())
      {
        priorNode = rightChild;
        rightChild = (BinaryNode)rightChild.getRightChild();
      } // end while

      // copy entry from rightmost node to current node
      currentNode.setData(rightChild.getData());
```

```
                    // need to remove the rightmost node, so rename it as currentNode
                    currentNode = rightChild;
                    parentNode = priorNode; // parent of currentNode
                } // end if
                // Assertion: current node is the node to be removed; it has at most
                //            one child; case 1 has been transformed to case 2

                // Case 2: current node has at most one child
                BinaryNode childNode;
                if (currentNode.hasLeftChild())
                    childNode = (BinaryNode)currentNode.getLeftChild();
                else
                    childNode = (BinaryNode)currentNode.getRightChild();
                // Assertion: if currentNode is a leaf, childNode is null

                // remove current node
                if (currentNode == getRootNode())
                    setRootNode(childNode);

                // else link the parent of the current node to childNode,
                // thereby deleting the current node
                else if (parentNode.getLeftChild() == currentNode)
                    parentNode.setLeftChild(childNode);
                else
                    parentNode.setRightChild(childNode);
            } // end if

            return result;
        } // end remove
```

A Recursive Implementation

26.30   **The public method remove.** Removing an entry recursively from a binary search tree shares some implementation details with the recursive methods for adding an entry that you saw in Segment 26.18. The public method remove calls a private recursive method remove. Recall that the public remove returns the removed entry. Since the private method must return the root of the revised tree, we use a parameter that is an instance of ReturnObject to return the value that remove needs. We used this technique for the recursive add method earlier in this chapter. Initially, this parameter's data field is null, since remove returns null when the entry is not found in the tree.

Thus, the public remove has the following implementation:

```
public Comparable remove(Comparable entry)
{
    ReturnObject oldEntry = new ReturnObject(null);
    BinaryNode newRoot = remove(getRootNode(), entry, oldEntry);
    setRootNode(newRoot);
    return oldEntry.get();
} // end remove
```

26.31   **The private method** remove. If the entry to be removed is in the root of the given tree, the following private method remove calls the private method removeEntry to remove it. If the entry is in either of the root's subtrees, a recursive call removes the entry.

```java
/** Task: Removes an entry from the tree rooted at a given node.
 *  @param rootNode  a reference to the root of a tree
 *  @param entry     the object to be removed
 *  @param oldEntry  an object whose data field is null
 *  @return the root node of the resulting tree; if entry matches
 *          an entry in the tree, oldEntry's data field is the
 *          entry that was removed from the tree; otherwise it is
 *          null */
private BinaryNode remove(BinaryNode rootNode, Comparable entry,
                          ReturnObject oldEntry)
{
  boolean found = false;

  if (rootNode != null)
  {
    Comparable rootData = (Comparable)rootNode.getData();
    int comparison = entry.compareTo(rootData);

    if (comparison == 0)        // entry == root entry
    {
      oldEntry.set(rootData);
      rootNode = (BinaryNode)removeEntry(rootNode);
    }

    else if (comparison < 0) // entry < root entry
    {
      BinaryNode leftChild = (BinaryNode)rootNode.getLeftChild();
      BinaryNode subtreeRoot = remove(leftChild, entry, oldEntry);
      rootNode.setLeftChild(subtreeRoot);
    }
    else                        // entry > root entry
    {
      BinaryNode rightChild = (BinaryNode)rootNode.getRightChild();
      rootNode.setRightChild(remove(rightChild, entry, oldEntry));
    } // end if
  } // end if

  return rootNode;
} // end remove
```

26.32   **The private method** removeEntry. This method removes the entry in a given node. We consider whether the node has zero, one, or two children, much as we did earlier for the iterative version of remove. If the given node has at most one child, we delete the node and its entry. To remove the entry in a node having two children, we must find the largest entry in the node's left subtree. We remove the node containing this largest entry. The largest entry then replaces the entry to be removed. As you will see, the method uses the private methods findLargest and removeLargest to perform these tasks.

Notice that `removeEntry` treats the given node as the root of a subtree. The method returns the root of the subtree after a node is removed.

```
/** Task: Removes the entry in a given root node of a subtree.
 *  @param rootNode  the root node of the subtree
 *  @return the root node of the revised subtree */
private BinaryNode removeEntry(BinaryNode rootNode)
{
  // Case 1: rootNode has two children
  if (rootNode.hasLeftChild() && rootNode.hasRightChild())
  {
    // find node with largest entry in left subtree
    BinaryNode leftSubtreeRoot = (BinaryNode)rootNode.getLeftChild();
    BinaryNode largestNode = findLargest(leftSubtreeRoot);

    // replace entry in root
    rootNode.setData(largestNode.getData());

    // remove node with largest entry in left subtree
    rootNode.setLeftChild(removeLargest(leftSubtreeRoot));
  } // end if

  // Case 2: rootNode has at most one child
  else if (rootNode.getLeftChild() == null)
    rootNode = (BinaryNode)rootNode.getRightChild();
  else
    rootNode = (BinaryNode)rootNode.getLeftChild();

  // Assertion: if rootNode was a leaf, it is now null

  return rootNode;
} // end removeEntry
```

26.33   **The private method `findLargest`.** The node with the largest entry will occur in the rightmost node of a binary search tree. Thus, as long as a node has a right child, we search the subtree rooted at that child. The following recursive method performs this search, given the tree:

```
/** Task: Finds the node containing the largest entry in a
 *          given tree
 *  @param rootNode  the root node of the tree
 *  @return the node with the largest entry */
private BinaryNode findLargest(BinaryNode rootNode)
{
  if (rootNode.hasRightChild())
    rootNode = findLargest((BinaryNode)rootNode.getRightChild());

  return rootNode;
} // end findLargest
```

26.34   **The private method `removeLargest`.** To remove the node with the largest entry, we cannot simply call `findLargest` and then remove the returned node. We cannot remove a node from a tree knowing only its reference. We must have a reference to its parent as well. The following recursive method removes the node with the largest entry—that is, the rightmost node—but unfortunately it must repeat the search that `findLargest` just performed.

```
/** Task: Removes the node containing the largest entry in a
 *          given tree.
 *  @param rootNode   the root node of the tree
 *  @return the root node of the revised tree */
private BinaryNode removeLargest(BinaryNode rootNode)
{
   if (rootNode.hasRightChild())
   {
      BinaryNode rightChild = (BinaryNode)rootNode.getRightChild();
      BinaryNode root = removeLargest(rightChild);
      rootNode.setRightChild(root);
   }
   else
      rootNode = (BinaryNode)rootNode.getLeftChild();

   return rootNode;
} // end removeLargest
```

The method begins much like findLargest. To remove the rightmost node from the given tree, we remove the rightmost node from tree's right subtree. The recursive call returns the root of the revised subtree. This root must become the right child of the original tree's root.

When a tree's root has no right child, the left child is returned, effectively deleting the root. Notice that this recursive method does not explicitly keep track of the parent of the current right child. Rather, a reference to this parent is retained in the implicit stack of the recursion.

The Efficiency of Operations

26.35   Each of the operations add, remove, and getEntry requires a search that begins at the root of the tree. When adding an entry, the search ends at a leaf if the entry is not already in the tree; otherwise, the search can end sooner. When removing or retrieving an entry, the search ends at a leaf if it is unsuccessful; a successful search can end sooner. So in the worst case, these searches begin at the root and examine each node on a path that ends at a leaf. The longest path from the root to a leaf has a length that equals the height of the tree. Thus, the maximum number of comparisons that each operation requires is directly proportional to the height h of the tree. That is, the operations add, remove, and getEntry are O(h).

Recall that several different binary search trees can contain the same data. Figure 26-15 contains two such trees. Figure 26-15a is the shortest binary search tree that we can form from this data; Figure 26-15b is the tallest such tree.

The tallest tree has height n if it contains n nodes. In fact, this tree looks like a linked chain, and searching it is like searching a linked chain. It is an O(n) operation. Thus, add, remove, and getEntry for this tree are also O(n) operations.

In contrast, the shortest tree is full. Searching this tree will be as efficient as possible. In Chapter 24, we saw that the height of a full tree containing n nodes is $\log_2 (n + 1)$. Thus, in the worst case, searching a full binary search tree is an O($\log n$) operation. So add, remove, and getEntry are O($\log n$) operations in this case.

Question 7   What is the worst-case efficiency of the method contains?

Question 8   What is the worst-case efficiency of the method isEmpty?

Figure 26-15 Two binary search trees that contain the same data

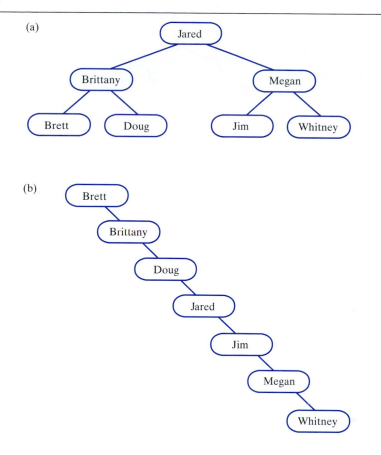

The Importance of Balance

26.36   We do not need a full binary search tree to get O(log n) performance from the addition, removal, and retrieval operations. For example, if we remove some of the leaves from a full tree, we will not change the performance of these operations. In particular, a complete tree will give us O(log n) performance.

The notion of *balance* affects the performance of a particular search tree. In a **completely balanced** tree, the subtrees of each node have exactly the same height. The only completely balanced binary trees are full. Other trees are said to be **height balanced,** or simply **balanced,** if the subtrees of each node in the tree differ in height by no more than 1. A complete binary tree is height balanced, for example, but so are some trees that are not complete, as Figure 26-16 shows. Notice that the concept of balance applies to all trees, not just binary trees or binary search trees.

It happens that the addition, removal, and retrieval operations of a binary search tree will have O(log n) performance if the tree is height balanced. Certainly when we create a binary search tree, we want it to be height balanced. Unfortunately, we can disturb the balance of a binary search tree by adding or removing entries, since these operations affect the shape of the tree.

Figure 26-16 Some binary trees that are height balanced

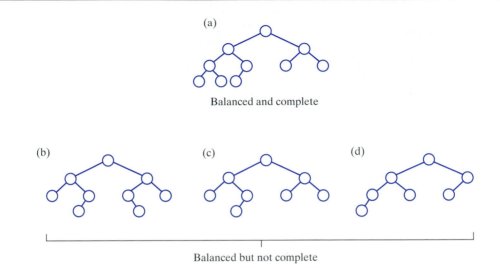

The Order in Which Nodes Are Added

26.37   If you answered Question 4 correctly earlier, you realized that the order in which you add entries to a binary search tree affects the shape of the tree. This observation is most important when you create a binary search tree by making additions into an initially empty tree.

   For example, suppose that we want to create the full binary search tree in Figure 26-15a from a given set of data. Often such data sets are sorted, so it is reasonable that we have the names in alphabetical order. Now imagine that we define an empty binary search tree and then add the names to it in the following order: *Brett, Brittany, Doug, Jared, Jim, Megan, Whitney*. Figure 26-15b shows the tree that results from these additions. It is as tall as possible and has the least efficient operations among the trees that we could build.

> **Note:**   If you add entries into an initially empty binary search tree, do not add them in sorted order.

26.38   In what order should we add the entries? *Jared* is the root of the tree in Figure 26-15a, so let's add *Jared* first. Next add *Brittany* and then *Brett* and *Doug*. Finally, add *Megan, Jim,* and *Whitney*. While it should be clear that by using this order we get the tree in Figure 26-15a, how do we determine the order ahead of time? Looking at our alphabetical set of names, notice that *Jared* is exactly in the middle. We add *Jared* first. *Brittany* is in the middle of the left half of the data set, so we add *Brittany* next. The halves that *Brittany* defines each contain only one name, so we add them next. We repeat this process with the names that occur after *Jared*—that is, the right half of the data set.

   We shouldn't have to do this much work! In fact, if we add data to a binary search tree in random order, we can expect a tree whose operations are O(log *n*). It probably will not be the shortest tree we could create, but it will be close.

The operations of a binary search tree ensure that the tree remains a binary search tree. Unfortunately, they do not ensure that the tree remains balanced. Chapter 28 looks at search trees that are responsible for maintaining their balance, and hence their efficiency.

An Implementation of the ADT Dictionary

26.39   We can use the ideas developed thus far in this chapter to implement the ADT dictionary. Recall from Chapter 17 that a dictionary stores search keys and their associated values. For example, suppose that you want a dictionary of names and telephone numbers. In terms of the ADT dictionary, the name could be the search key and the telephone number could be the corresponding value. To retrieve a telephone number, we would provide a name, and the dictionary would return its value.

Here is the interface for a dictionary as given in Segment 17.4, but without the comments:

```java
import java.util.Iterator;
public interface DictionaryInterface
{
  public Object add(Object key, Object value);
  public Object remove(Object key);
  public Object getValue(Object key);
  public boolean contains(Object key);
  public Iterator getKeyIterator();
  public Iterator getValueIterator();
  public boolean isEmpty();
  public int getSize();
  public void clear();
} // end DictionaryInterface
```

Earlier in this book we saw several implementations of the ADT dictionary. A dictionary implementation that uses a balanced search tree to store its entries can be an attractive alternative. As an example of such an implementation, we will use a binary search tree here even though it might not remain balanced after additions or removals. Chapter 28 presents search trees that are always balanced and could also be used to implement the dictionary.

26.40   **The data entries.** We need a class of data objects that will contain both a search key and an associated value. The following class Entry is suitable for our purpose and is similar to the class we used in the array-based implementation of the ADT dictionary in Chapter 18. Here, we make the class Comparable by defining the method compareTo. This method compares two instances of Entry by comparing their search keys.

The class can be private and internal to the class Dictionary:

```java
private class Entry implements Comparable, java.io.Serializable
{
  private Object key;
  private Object value;

  private Entry(Object searchKey, Object dataValue)
  {
    key = searchKey;
    value = dataValue;
  } // end constructor
```

```
  public int compareTo(Object other)
  {
    Comparable cKey = (Comparable)key;
    return cKey.compareTo(((Entry)other).key);
  } // end compareTo
```

> *The class also defines the methods equals,* getKey, getValue, *and* setValue*;
>   no* setKey *method is provided.* >

```
    . . .
  } // end Entry
```

26.41   **The class `Dictionary`.** The class `Dictionary` contains a binary search tree as its data field, which the constructor allocates. The class begins as follows:

```
import java.util.Iterator;
public class Dictionary implements DictionaryInterface,
                                   java.io.Serializable
{
  private SearchTreeInterface bst;

  public Dictionary()
  {
    bst = new BinarySearchTree();
  } // end default constructor
    . . .
} // end Dictionary
```

The method add encapsulates the given search key and value into an instance of Entry that it passes to BinarySearchTree's add method. It then uses the entry that this method returns to form its own return value. Dictionary's add method has the following implementation:

```
public Object add(Object key, Object value)
{
  Entry newEntry = new Entry(key, value);
  Entry returnedEntry = (Entry)bst.add(newEntry);

  Object result = null;
  if (returnedEntry != null)
    result = returnedEntry.getValue();

  return result;
} // end add
```

Both remove and getValue have implementations that are similar to add's. Since these methods have only a search key as a parameter, the instances of Entry that they form encapsulate the key and a null value. For example, remove begins as

```
public Object remove(Object key)
{
  Entry findEntry = new Entry(key, null);
  Entry returnedEntry = (Entry)bst.remove(findEntry);
```

and ends just like the method add. The implementation of the method getValue is identical to that of remove, except that it calls getEntry from BinarySearchTree instead of remove.

We can implement the methods getSize, isEmpty, contains, and clear by calling appropriate methods of BinarySearchTree. We leave these to you as exercises.

Question 9   Implement each of the Dictionary methods getSize, isEmpty, contains, and clear by calling methods of BinarySearchTree.

Question 10   Write another implementation of the method contains by invoking Dictionary's method getValue.

26.42   **The iterators.** DictionaryInterface specifies two methods that return iterators. The method get-KeyIterator returns an iterator that accesses the search keys in sorted order; getValueIterator returns an iterator that provides the values belonging to these search keys.

For example, getKeyIterator has the following implementation:

```
public Iterator getKeyIterator()
{
   return new KeyIterator();
} // end getKeyIterator
```

The class KeyIterator is internal to Dictionary and uses the method getInorderIterator from BinarySearchTree. It has the following implementation:

```
private class KeyIterator implements Iterator
{
   Iterator localIterator;

   public KeyIterator()
   {
      localIterator = bst.getInorderIterator();
   } // end default constructor

   public boolean hasNext()
   {
      return localIterator.hasNext();
   } // end hasNext

   public Object next()
   {
      return ((Entry)localIterator.next()).getKey();
   } // end next

   public void remove()
   {
      throw new UnsupportedOperationException();
   } // end remove
} // end KeyIterator
```

You implement getValueIterator in a similar manner.

26.43   **Comments.** This implementation of the ADT dictionary is as time efficient as the underlying search tree. When the binary search tree is balanced, the operations are O(log n). But a binary search tree can lose its balance, so the efficiency of the dictionary operations can degrade to O(n) as entries are added or removed. A search tree that stays balanced, such as those you will see in Chapter 28, would provide a better implementation of the dictionary than the one shown here.

Also, notice that a binary search tree maintains the dictionary entries in sorted order by their search keys. As a result, getKeyIterator enables us to traverse the search keys in sorted order. In contrast, other dictionary implementations—hashing, for example—traverse the search keys in unsorted order.

CHAPTER SUMMARY

- A binary search tree is a binary tree whose nodes contain **Comparable** objects. For each node in the tree,
  - The data in a node is greater than the data in the node's left subtree
  - The data in a node is less than (or equal to) the data in the node's right subtree

- A search tree has the operations **getEntry**, **add**, **remove**, and **contains**, in addition to the operations common to all trees.

- The class **BinarySearchTree** can be a subclass of **BinaryTree**, but it must disallow **setTree**. A client must create a binary search tree by using only the **add** method, to avoid changing the order of the nodes in the tree.

- The search algorithm to locate an entry in a binary search tree forms the basis of the methods **getEntry**, **add**, and **remove**. These methods each have reasonable iterative and recursive implementations.

- Each addition of an entry to a binary search tree adds a leaf to the tree. The new entry is placed where the search algorithm will find it.

- Removing an entry from a binary search tree depends on the number of children that belong to the node containing the entry. When the node is a leaf or has one child, you remove the node itself. The node's parent can adopt a solitary child when it exists. However, when the node N has two children, you replace the node's entry with another one r whose node is easy to remove. To maintain the order of the binary search tree, this entry r can be either the largest entry in N's left subtree or the smallest entry in N's right subtree. It follows that r's node is a leaf or a node with one child.

- In a completely balanced binary tree, the subtrees of each node have exactly the same height. Such trees must be full. Other binary trees are said to be height balanced if the subtrees of each node in the tree differ in height by no more than 1.

- The retrieve, add, and remove operations on a binary search tree can be as fast as $O(\log n)$ or as slow as $O(n)$. The performance of the search depends on the shape of the tree. When the tree is height balanced, the operations on a binary search tree are $O(\log n)$.

- The order in which you add entries to a binary search tree affects the tree's shape and hence its balance. Random additions tend to result in a balanced tree.

- You can implement the ADT dictionary by using a binary search tree. Although the implementation is not difficult to write, its efficiency can suffer if additions and removals destroy the balance of the tree.

EXERCISES

1. Show the results of adding the following search keys into an initially empty binary search tree: 10, 5, 6, 13, 15, 8, 14, 7, 12, 4.

2. Why does an inorder traversal of a binary search tree visit the nodes in sorted search-key order? Use the definition of a binary search tree given in Segment 26.1.

3. What ordering of the search keys 10, 5, 6, 13, 15, 8, 14, 7, 12, 4 would result in the most balanced tree if they were added to an initially empty binary search tree?

4. Give four different orderings of the search keys 10, 5, 6, 13, 15, 8, 14, 7, 12, 4 that would result in the least balanced tree if they were added to an initially empty binary search tree.

5. In Chapter 10, Figure 10-10a shows the recursive computation of the term F_6 in the Fibonacci sequence. Is this tree height balanced?

6. Implement the method getEntry iteratively.

7. Remove *Doug* from the binary search tree pictured in Figure 26-13a. Then remove *Chad* in two different ways.

8. Remove *Doug* from the binary search tree pictured in Figure 26-13d in two different ways.

9. Suppose that a node with two children contains an entry *e*, as Figure 26-11a illustrates. Show that you will have a binary search tree if you replace *e* with its inorder successor *b* and remove the node that contains *b*.

10. Consider a full binary search tree such as the one pictured in Figure 26-15a. Now imagine that you traverse the tree and save its data in a file. If you now read the file and add the data to an initially empty binary search tree, what tree will you get if the traversal was
    a. Preorder   **b.** inorder   **c.** level order   **d.** postorder

11. Imagine that you traverse a binary search tree and save its data in a file. If you then read the file and add the data to an initially empty binary search tree, what traversal should you use when writing the file so that the new tree is

    a. As tall as possible
    b. Identical to the original binary search tree

12. Segment 26.38 builds a balanced binary search tree from one particular set of search keys. Generalize this approach, and write a recursive algorithm that creates a balanced binary search tree from a sorted collection of *n* items.

13. Write an algorithm that returns the smallest search key in a binary search tree.

14. Beginning with Segment 26.22, you saw how to find the inorder predecessor or the inorder successor of a node with two children. Unfortunately, this approach will not work for a leaf node. Discuss how the node data structure might be modified so that the inorder predecessor or the inorder successor can be found for any node.

15. Why might a binary search tree work poorly as an implementation of a priority queue?

PROJECTS

1. Specify and implement a class of binary search trees in which duplicate entries are allowed.

2. Implement the ADT sorted list by using a binary search tree.

3. Devise an algorithm that uses a binary search tree to sort an array of objects. Such a sort is called **treesort.** Implement and test your algorithm. Discuss the time efficiency of your treesort in both the average and worst cases.

4. Implement a binary search tree that includes the following methods based on Exercises 13 and 14:

```
/** @return the entry with the smallest search key */
public Comparable getMin();

/** @return the entry with the largest search key */
public Comparable getMax();

/** @return either the inorder predecessor of entry,
 *          null if entry is not in the tree, or
 *          entry if it is the smallest element in the tree */
public Comparable getPredecessor(Comparable entry);

/** @return either the inorder successor of entry,
 *          null if entry is not in the tree, or
 *          entry if it is the largest element in the tree */
public Comparable getSuccessor(Comparable entry);
```

5. Write Java code that creates a binary search tree from n random integer values and returns the height of the search tree. Run the code for $n = 2^h - 1$, where h ranges from 4 to 12. Compare the height of the randomly built search tree with h, the height of the shortest binary search tree.

6. Write Java code that will create a balanced binary search tree of the reserved words in the Java language. Use this tree to implement Project 3 of Chapter 17 with binary search trees. (Why is it important that the search tree containing Java reserved words be balanced? Can you guarantee that the search tree of user-defined identifiers is also balanced?)

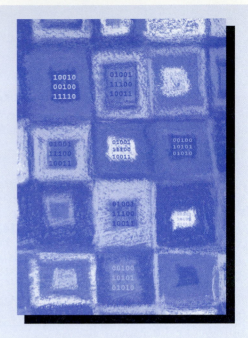

CONTENTS

Reprise: The ADT Heap
Using an Array to Represent a Heap
Adding an Entry
Removing the Root
Creating a Heap
Heapsort

PREREQUISITES

Chapter   5   List Implementations That Use Arrays
Chapter   24   Trees

OBJECTIVES

After studying this chapter, you should be able to

- Use an array to represent a heap
- Add an entry to an array-based heap
- Remove the root of an array-based heap
- Create a heap from given entries
- Sort an array by using a heapsort

Recall from Chapter 24 that a heap is a complete binary tree whose nodes are ordered in a certain manner. When a binary tree is complete, you can use an array to represent it in an efficient and elegant way. An array-based implementation of a heap is the most common one and is the implementation that we will describe in this chapter.

As you saw in Chapter 24, you can use a heap as an efficient implementation of the ADT priority queue.

Reprise: The ADT Heap

27.1   A heap is a complete binary tree whose nodes contain `Comparable` objects. In a maxheap, the object in each node is greater than or equal to the objects in the node's descendants. Segment 24.32 provided the following interface for the maxheap:

```
public interface MaxHeapInterface
{
   public void add(Comparable newEntry);
   public Comparable removeMax();
   public Comparable getMax();
   public boolean isEmpty();
   public int getSize();
   public void clear();
} // end MaxHeapInterface
```

We will use this interface in our implementation of a maxheap.

 Note: You may also have heard the word "heap" used to refer to the collection of memory cells that are available for allocation to your program when the `new` operator executes. But that heap is not an instance of the ADT heap that we will discuss in this chapter. It would be considered, however, in a book about programming languages.

Using an Array to Represent a Heap

27.2   We begin by using an array to represent a complete binary tree. A complete tree is full to its next-to-last level, and its leaves on the last level are filled in from left to right. Thus, until we get to the last leaf, a complete tree has no holes.

Suppose that we number the nodes in a complete binary tree in the order in which a level-order traversal would visit them, beginning with 1. Figure 27-1a shows such a tree numbered in this way. Now suppose that we place the result of this tree's level-order traversal into consecutive array locations beginning at index 1, as Figure 27-1b shows. This representation of the data in the tree enables us to implement any needed tree operations. By beginning at index 1 instead of 0, we can simplify the implementation somewhat, as you will see.

Figure 27-1   (a) A complete binary tree with its nodes numbered in level order; (b) its representation as an array

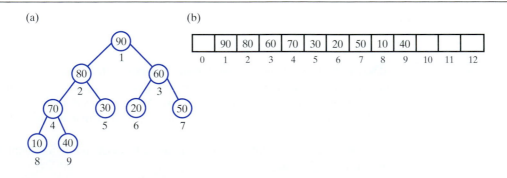

27.3   Since the tree is complete, we can locate either the children or the parent of any node by performing a simple computation on the node's number. This number is the same as the node's corresponding array index. Thus, the children of the node i—if they exist—are stored in the array at indices $2i$ and $2i + 1$. The parent of this node is at array index $i/2$, unless of course the node is the root. In that case, $i/2$ is 0, since the root is at index 1. To detect the root, we can watch for either this index or a special value—called a **sentinel**—that we place at index 0.

Note: When a binary tree is complete, you can use a level-order traversal to store the tree's data into consecutive locations of an array. This representation enables you to easily locate the data in a node's parent or children. If you begin storing the tree at index 1 of the array—that is, if you skip the array's first element—the node at array index i

- Has a parent at index $i/2$, unless the node is the root (i is 1)
- Has any children at indices $2i$ and $2i + 1$

Exercise 1 at the end of this chapter asks you to begin storing the tree's entries at index 0. There you will see that the index computations involve an additional operation.

The complete binary tree in Figure 27-1 is actually a maxheap. We will now use the previous array representation of a complete tree in our implementation of a maxheap.

27.4   **Beginning the class `MaxHeap`.** Our class begins with the following data fields: an array of `Comparable` heap entries, a constant for the default size of this array, and the index of the last entry in the array. If this index is less than 1, the heap is empty, since we begin the heap at index 1.

```java
public class MaxHeap implements MaxHeapInterface, java.io.Serializable
{
  private Comparable[] heap;  // array of heap entries
  private static final int DEFAULT_MAX_SIZE = 25;
  private int lastIndex;       // index of last entry
  . . .
```

Two simple constructors are similar to constructors we have seen before in array-based implementations:

```java
public MaxHeap()
{
  heap = new Comparable[DEFAULT_MAX_SIZE];
  lastIndex = 0;
} // end default constructor
```

```java
public MaxHeap(int maxSize)
{
  heap = new Comparable[maxSize];
  lastIndex = 0;
} // end constructor
```

The methods `getMax`, `isEmpty`, `getSize`, and `clear` have simple implementations:

```java
public Comparable getMax()
{
  Comparable root = null;
```

```
       if (!isEmpty())
          root = heap[1];

       return root;
   } // end getMax

   public boolean isEmpty()
   {
       return lastIndex < 1;
   } // end isEmpty

   public int getSize()
   {
       return lastIndex;
   } // end getSize

   public void clear()
   {
       for (; lastIndex > -1; lastIndex--)
          heap[lastIndex] = null;
       lastIndex = 0;
   } // end clear
```

Adding an Entry

27.5   **The basic algorithm.** The algorithm to add an entry to a heap is not difficult. Recall that in a max-heap, the object in a node is greater than or equal to its descendant objects. Suppose that we want to add 85 to the maxheap in Figure 27-1. We first would place the new entry as the next leaf in the tree. Figure 27-2a shows that we add 85 as a left child of the 30. Notice that we actually would place 85 at index 10 of the array in Figure 27-1b.

Figure 27-2a is no longer a heap, since 85 is out of place. To transform the tree into a heap, we let 85 *float up* to its correct location. Since 85 is larger than its parent, 30, we swap it with the parent, as Figure 27-2b shows. The 85 is still larger than its new parent, 80, so we swap again (Figure 27-2c). Now 85 is less than its parent, so we have transformed the tree in Figure 27-2a into a maxheap.

Figure 27-2   The steps in adding 85 to the maxheap of Figure 27-1a

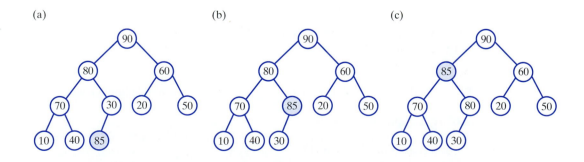

Question 1   What steps are necessary to add 100 to the heap in Figure 27-2c?

27.6   **Avoiding swaps.** Although the swaps mentioned in the previous segment make the algorithm easier to understand and to describe, they require more work than is actually necessary. Instead of placing the new entry in the next available position within the tree, as we did in Figure 27-2a, we need only reserve space for it. In an array-based implementation, we simply check that the array is not full. Figure 27-3a shows the new child as an empty circle.

   We then compare the new entry—the 85 in this example—with the parent of the new child. Since 85 is larger than 30, we move the 30 to the new child, as Figure 27-3b shows. We treat the node that originally contained 30 as if it were empty. We now compare 85 with the parent, 80, of the empty node. Since 85 is larger than 80, we move the 80 to the empty node, as Figure 27-3c shows. Since 85 is not larger than the next parent, 90, we place the new entry into the empty node, as Figure 27-3d shows.

Note: To add a new entry to a heap, you begin at the next available position for a leaf. You follow a path from this leaf toward the root until you find the correct position for the new entry. As you do, you move entries from parent to child to ultimately make room for the new entry.

Figure 27-3   A revision of the steps shown in Figure 27-2 to avoid swaps

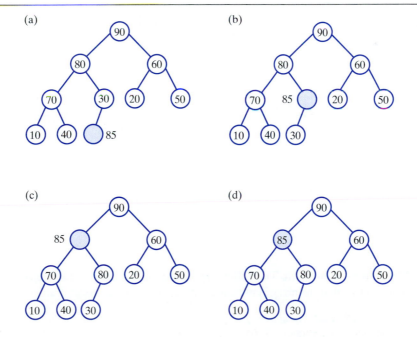

   Figure 27-4 shows these same steps from the viewpoint of the array that represents the heap. In Part *a*, which is analogous to Figure 27-3a, we note that we have room for a new entry at index 10.

The parent of this location is at location 10/2, or 5. We thus compare the new entry 85 to 30, the contents of the location at index 5. Since 85 > 30, we move 30 to the location at index 10 (Figures 27-4b and 27-3b.) The remaining steps proceed in a similar fashion. Note that Figure 27-3c corresponds to Figure 27-4d, and Figure 27-3d corresponds to Figure 27-4f.

Figure 27-4   An array representation of the steps in Figure 27-3

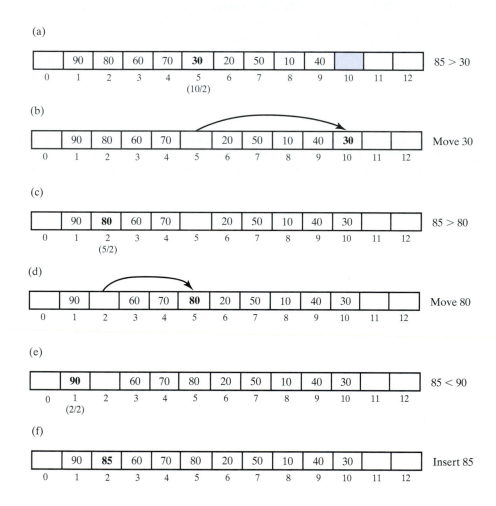

27.7

The refined algorithm. The following algorithm summarizes the steps that add a new entry to a heap. Notice that the array is expanded dynamically as necessary.

Algorithm `add(newEntry)`
if (*the array* heap *is full*)
    Double the size of the array

`newIndex` = *index of next available array location*
`parentIndex` = `newIndex/2`   *// index of parent of available location*

```
while (newEntry > heap[parentIndex])
{
  heap[newIndex] = heap[parentIndex]   // move parent to available location

  // update indices
  newIndex = parentIndex
  parentIndex = newIndex/2
}

heap[newIndex] = newEntry   // place new entry in correct location
```

Question 2   Repeat Question 1 using the previous algorithm without swaps. Show the heap at each step as a tree and as an array.

27.8   **The method add.** We now implement the previous algorithm. The add method begins by incrementing the index `lastIndex` of the last array entry and then checks that the array is large enough to hold a new entry. If it is not, we double the size of the array, as we have done in previous chapters. (See Segment 5.16, for example.) The rest of the implementation closely follows the pseudocode. We do need to protect the `while` statement from an illegal array index. In the following implementation, we simply ensure that `newIndex` is greater than 1.

```
public void add(Comparable newEntry)
{
  lastIndex++;

  if (lastIndex >= heap.length)
    doubleArray(); // expand array

  int newIndex = lastIndex;
  int parentIndex = newIndex/2;
  while ( (newIndex > 1) &&
          newEntry.compareTo(heap[parentIndex]) > 0)
  {
    heap[newIndex] = heap[parentIndex];

    newIndex = parentIndex;
    parentIndex = newIndex/2;
  } // end while

  heap[newIndex] = newEntry;
} // end add
```

We can omit the test of `newIndex` in the `while` statement if we place a sentinel value in the unused array location at index 0. We can use `newEntry` as this sentinel. You should convince yourself that this change will work.

In the worst case, this method follows a path from a leaf to the root. In Segment 24.9, we saw that the height of a complete tree is $\log_2 (n + 1)$ rounded up. Thus, the add method is an $O(\log n)$ operation in the worst case.

Question 3   Revise the previous method add by placing `newEntry` as a sentinel value in the unused array location at index 0. You then can omit the test of `newIndex` in the `while` statement.

Removing the Root

27.9   **The basic algorithm.** The `removeMax` method for a maxheap removes and returns the heap's largest object. This object is in the root of the maxheap. Let's remove the entry in the root of the heap in Figure 27-3d. Figure 27-5a shows this heap as if its root was empty.

We do not want to rip the root node out of the heap, as this will leave two disjoint subtrees. Instead we remove a leaf, namely the last one in the heap. To do so, we copy the leaf's data—30—to the root and then remove the leaf from the tree, as Figure 27-5b illustrates. Of course, in the array-based implementation, removing the leaf simply means adjusting `lastIndex`.

The 30 is out of place, so we no longer have a heap. We let the 30 *sink down* to its correct location. As long as 30 is less than its children, we swap it with its larger child. Thus, in Figure 27-5c, we have swapped 30 and 85. Continuing, we swap 30 and 80, as Figure 27-5d shows. In this case the 30 has settled at a leaf. In general, the out-of-place entry would settle at a node whose children are not greater than the entry.

Figure 27-5   The steps to remove the entry in the root of the maxheap of Figure 27-3d

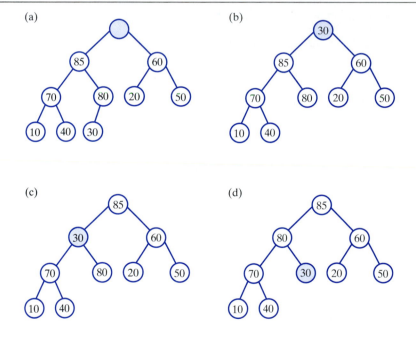

   Question 4   What steps are necessary to remove the root from the heap in Figure 27-5d?

27.10   **Transforming a semiheap into a heap.** The tree in Figure 27-5b is called a **semiheap**. Except for the root, the objects in a semiheap are ordered as they are in a heap. In removing the root of the heap, we formed a semiheap and then transformed it back into a heap. As in the method add, we can save time by not swapping entries. Figure 27-6 shows the semiheap from Figure 27-5b and the steps that transform it into a heap without the swaps.

Figure 27-6   The steps that transform a semiheap into a heap without swaps

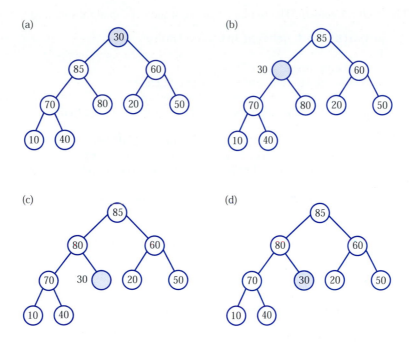

The following algorithm transforms a semiheap to a heap. To make the algorithm more general, we assume that the root of the semiheap is at a given index instead of at index 1.

Algorithm `reheap(rootIndex)`
// Transforms the semiheap rooted at `rootIndex` *into a heap*

```
done = false
orphan = heap[rootIndex]
largerChildIndex = index of the larger of the root's children, if any

while (!done)
{
  if (orphan < heap[largerChildIndex])
  {
    heap[rootIndex] = heap[largerChildIndex]

    rootIndex = largerChildIndex
    largerChildIndex = index of the larger child, if any, of heap[rootIndex]
  }
  else
    done = true
}

heap[rootIndex] = orphan
```

As you will see, this algorithm has several uses.

Question 5   Show the contents of the array `heap` as you trace the steps of the algorithm reheap that correspond to those pictured in Figure 27-6.

27.11   **The method `reheap`.** The implementation of the `reheap` algorithm as a private method follows:

```
private void reheap(int rootIndex)
{
   boolean done = false;
   Comparable orphan = heap[rootIndex];
   int largerChildIndex = 2*rootIndex; // index of left child, if any
   while (!done && (largerChildIndex <= lastIndex) )
   {
      int rightChildIndex = largerChildIndex + 1;
      if ( (rightChildIndex <= lastIndex) &&
            heap[rightChildIndex].compareTo(heap[largerChildIndex]) > 0)
      {
         largerChildIndex = rightChildIndex;
      }

      if (orphan.compareTo(heap[largerChildIndex]) < 0)
      {
         heap[rootIndex] = heap[largerChildIndex];

         rootIndex = largerChildIndex;
         largerChildIndex = 2*rootIndex; // index of next left child
      }
      else
         done = true;
   } // end while

   heap[rootIndex] = orphan;
} // end reheap
```

27.12   **The method `removeMax`.** The method `removeMax` replaces the heap's root with its last leaf to form a semiheap like the one in Figure 27-6a. The method then calls `reheap` to transform the semiheap back into a heap. Thus, `removeMax` has the following implementation:

```
public Comparable removeMax()
{
   Comparable root = null;

   if (!isEmpty())
   {
      root = heap[1];              // return value
      heap[1] = heap[lastIndex];  // form a semiheap
      lastIndex--;                // decrease size
      reheap(1);                  // transform to a heap
   } // end if

   return root;
} // end removeMax
```

In the worst case, `reheap` follows a path from the root to a leaf. Recall that the height of a complete tree is $\log_2 (n + 1)$ rounded up, so the `removeMax` method is an O(log n) operation.

Note: To remove a heap's root, you first replace the root with the heap's last child. This step forms a semiheap, so you use the method `reheap` to transform the semiheap to a heap.

Creating a Heap

27.13   **Using add.** We could create a heap from a collection of objects by using the add method to add each object to an initially empty heap. Figure 27-7 shows the steps that this approach would take to add 20, 40, 30, 10, 90, and 70 to a heap. Since add is an O(log *n*) operation, creating the heap in this manner would be O(*n* log *n*).

Figure 27-7   The steps in adding 20, 40, 30, 10, 90, and 70 to a heap

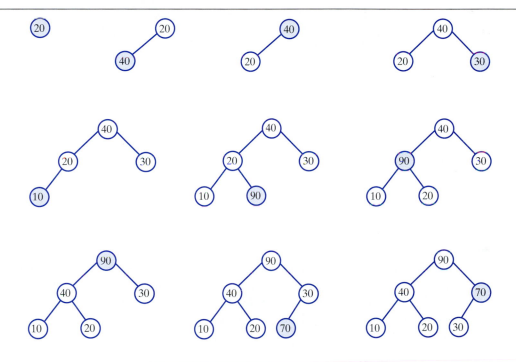

27.14   **Using reheap.** A more efficient way to create a heap uses the method `reheap`. We begin by placing the entries for the heap into an array beginning at index 1. Figure 27-8a provides an example of one such array. This array can represent the complete tree shown in Figure 27-8b. Does this tree contain any semiheaps that we can transform into heaps? The leaves are semiheaps, but they are also heaps. Thus, we can ignore the entries 70, 90, and 10. These entries are at the end of the array.

Moving toward the beginning of the array, we encounter 30, which is the root of a semiheap within the tree pictured in Figure 27-8b. If we apply `reheap` to this semiheap, we get the tree in Figure 27-8c. Continuing in this manner, we apply `reheap` to the semiheaps rooted at 40 and then 20. Parts *d*, *e*, and *f* of Figure 27-8 show the results of these steps. Figure 27-8f is the desired heap. We can transform an array of entries into a heap by using `reheap` with less work than if we used add to add the entries to the heap.

Figure 27-8 The steps in creating a heap by using `reheap`

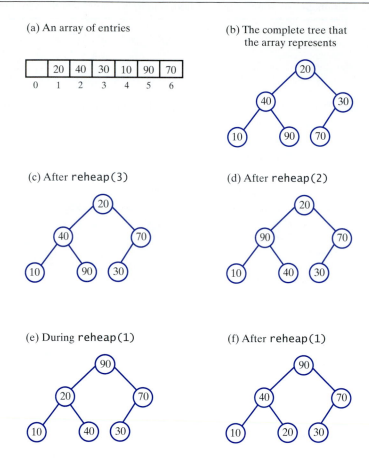

(a) An array of entries

(b) The complete tree that the array represents

(c) After `reheap(3)`

(d) After `reheap(2)`

(e) During `reheap(1)`

(f) After `reheap(1)`

27.15　Another constructor. We can use the technique just described to implement another constructor for the class `MaxHeap`. Suppose that n entries for our heap are given in an array of exactly n locations. The following constructor takes this array, copies it into the data field `heap`, and uses `reheap` to create a heap. Remember that although the entries in the given array begin at index 0, we place them into the array `heap` beginning at index 1.

```
public MaxHeap(Comparable[] entries)
{
   lastIndex = entries.length;
   heap = new Comparable[lastIndex + 1];

   // copy given array to data field
   for (int index = 0; index < entries.length; index++)
      heap[index+1] = entries[index];

   // create heap
   for (int index = heap.length/2; index > 0; index--)
      reheap(index);
} // end constructor
```

In applying reheap, we begin at the first nonleaf closest to the end of the array and work toward heap[1]. This nonleaf is at index heap.length/2.

Note: You can create a heap more efficiently by using the method reheap instead of the method add.

Heapsort

27.16   We can use a heap to sort an array. If we place the array items into a maxheap and then remove them, we will get the items in descending order. We saw in Segments 27.13 and 27.14 that using reheap instead of add is a more efficient way to create a heap from an array of items. In fact, we wrote a constructor in Segment 27.15 that invoked reheap for this purpose. So if a is the array of items, we could use this constructor to create the heap, as follows:

```
MaxHeapInterface myHeap = new MaxHeap(a);
```

As we remove the items from myHeap, we could place them in order back into the array a. The problem with this approach is the additional memory required, since the heap uses an array besides the given array. However, by mimicking the heap's array-based implementation, we can make this approach more efficient without using the class MaxHeap. The resulting algorithm is called a **heapsort.**

We begin by revising the method reheap so that it is suitable for our sorting algorithm. The major change is to the method's signature, which we write as

```
private static void reheap(Comparable[] heap, int first, int last)
```

The portion of the array heap that represents the heap ranges from the index first to the index last. To reflect this, we make the following changes to the identifiers in the body of the method reheap given in Segment 27.11:

- Change rootIndex to first.
- Change lastIndex to last.

27.17   To create an initial heap from the given array, we call reheap repeatedly, as we did in the constructor given in Segment 27.15. However, in the constructor the heap begins at index 1, whereas the array to be sorted begins at index 0. The following loop reflects this change, assuming *n* elements in the array:

```
for (int index = n/2; index >= 0; index--)
    reheap(heap, index, n-1);
```

Parts *a* and *b* of Figure 27-9 show an array and the heap that results by executing the previous statements.

The largest item in the array is now in heap[0] (Figure 27-9b), so we swap it with the last item in the array, as Figure 27-9c shows. The array is now partitioned into a tree region and a sorted region.

Following this swap, we call reheap on the tree portion—transforming it into a heap—and perform another swap, as Figures 27-9d and 27-9e illustrate. We repeat these operations until the tree region consists of one item (Figure 27-9k). Notice that the array actually is sorted in Figure 27-9g, but the algorithm does not detect this fact.

Figure 27-9   A trace of heapsort

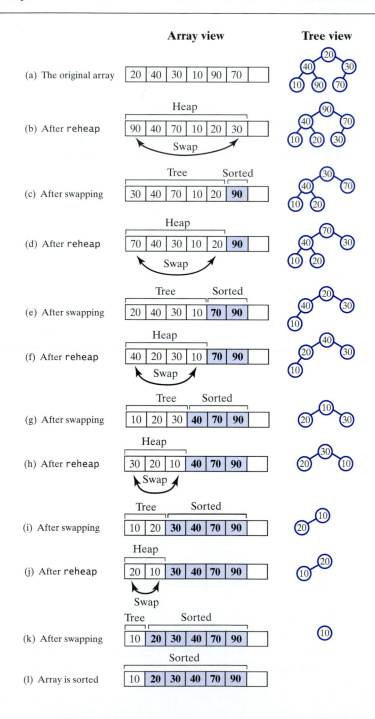

27.18   The implementation of heapsort follows:

```
public static void heapSort(Comparable[] array, int n)
{
  // create first heap
  for (int index = n/2; index >= 0; index--)
    reheap(array, index, n-1);

  swap(array, 0, n-1);

  for (int last = n-2; last > 0; last--)
  {
    reheap(array, 0, last);
    swap(array, 0, last);
  } // end for
} // end heapSort

private static void reheap(Comparable[] heap, int first, int last)
{
  < Statements from Segment 27.11, replacing rootIndex with first and
    lastIndex with last. >
  . . .
} // end reheap
```

Like mergesort and quicksort, heapsort is an O(*n* log *n*) algorithm. As implemented here, heapsort does not require a second array, but mergesort does. Recall that quicksort is O(*n* log *n*) most of the time, but is O(n^2) in its worst case. Since we usually can avoid quicksort's worst case by choosing appropriate pivots, it generally is the preferred sorting method.

Note: The time efficiency of heapsort

Although heapsort is O(*n* log *n*) in the average case, quicksort usually is the sorting method of choice.

Question 6   Trace the steps that the method `heapSort` takes when sorting the following array into ascending order: 9 6 2 4 8 7 5 3.

CHAPTER SUMMARY

- Since a heap is a complete binary tree, it has an efficient array-based implementation.

- You add a new entry to a heap as the next leaf in a complete binary tree. You then make the entry float up to its proper location within the heap.

- You begin to remove the root entry of a heap by replacing it with the entry in the last leaf and then removing the leaf. The result is a semiheap. You transform the semiheap into a heap by making the new root entry sink down to its proper location within the heap.

- You could create a heap from a given array of entries by adding each entry to the heap. A more efficient approach treats each nonleaf as a semiheap. You transform each such semiheap into a heap by using the same technique that you use when removing the root of the heap.

- A heapsort uses a heap to sort the entries in a given array.

EXERCISES

1. If the array heap contains the entries of a heap beginning at index 0, what array entries represent a node's parent, left child, and right child?

2. Trace the formation of a maxheap by the constructor given in Segment 27.15 for each of the following arrays:

   a. 10 20 30 40 50
   b. 10 20 30 40 50 60 70 80 90 100

3. Trace the addition of each of the following values to an initially empty maxheap:

   10 20 30 40 50

   Compare your trace with the results of Exercise 2a.

4. Trace the steps of a heapsort on each of the following arrays:

   a. 10 20 30 40 50 60
   b. 60 50 40 30 20 10
   c. 20 50 40 10 60 30

5. If you do not swap entries during a heapsort, you will sort the array into descending order. If you use a minheap instead of a maxheap and do not swap entries, you can sort the array into ascending order. Make each of these changes to the method heapSort given in Segment 27.18.

PROJECTS

1. Recall from Segment 24.31 that in a minheap, the object in each node is less than or equal to the objects in the node's descendants. While a maxheap has the method getMax, a minheap has the method getMin instead. Use an array to implement a minheap.

2. Complete the implementation of heapsort. Compare the execution times of heapsort, mergesort, and quicksort on various arrays chosen at random. The "Projects" section of Chapter 9 described one way to time the execution of code.

3. Use a binary search tree to implement a maxheap. Where in the tree will the largest entry occur? How efficient is this implementation?

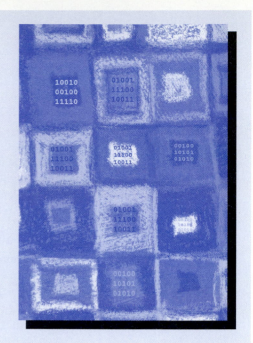

C H A P T E R

28

Balanced Search Trees

CONTENTS

AVL Trees
  Single Rotations
  Double Rotations
  Implementation Details
2-3 Trees
  Searching a 2-3 Tree
  Adding Entries to a 2-3 Tree
  Splitting Nodes During Addition
2-4 Trees
  Adding Entries to a 2-4 Tree
  Comparing AVL, 2-3, and 2-4 Trees
Red-Black Trees
  Properties of a Red-Black Tree
  Adding Entries to a Red-Black Tree
  Java Class Library: The Class `TreeMap`
B-Trees

PREREQUISITES

Chapter 24   Trees
Chapter 25   Tree Implementations
Chapter 26   A Binary Search Tree Implementation

OBJECTIVES

After studying this chapter, you should be able to

- Perform a rotation to restore the balance of an AVL tree after an addition
- Search for or add an entry to a 2-3 tree
- Search for or add an entry to a 2-4 tree
- Form a red-black tree from a given 2-4 tree

- Search for or add an entry to a red-black tree
- Describe the purpose of a B-tree

In Chapter 26, you saw that the operations on a binary search tree are O(log *n*) if the tree is balanced. Although the add and remove operations ensure that the tree remains a binary search tree, unfortunately they do not ensure that it remains balanced. This chapter will consider search trees that maintain their balance, and hence their efficiency.

Our goal is to introduce you to several types of balanced search trees and compare them. So that you can build these trees, we will discuss the algorithms that add entries to a search tree while retaining its balance. We also will show you how to search the trees. We will not, however, cover the algorithms that remove entries, leaving this topic for a future course.

The entries in a tree are usually objects, but to make the pictures of trees clear and concise, we will show the entries as integers.

AVL Trees

28.1   Segment 24.28 showed that you can form several differently shaped binary search trees from the same collection of data. Some of these trees will be balanced and some will not. Recall that every node in a balanced binary tree has subtrees whose heights differ by no more than 1. Thus, you could take an unbalanced binary search tree and rearrange its nodes to get a balanced binary search tree. This idea was first developed by two mathematicians, Adel'son-Vel'skii and Landis. Named after them, the **AVL tree** is a binary search tree that rearranges its nodes whenever it becomes unbalanced. The balance of a binary search tree is upset only when you add or remove a node. Thus, during these operations, the AVL tree rearranges nodes as necessary to maintain its balance.

For example, Parts *a*, *b*, and *c* of Figure 28-1 show a binary search tree as we add 60, 50, and 20 to it. After the third addition, the tree is not balanced. An AVL tree would rearrange its nodes to restore balance, as shown in Figure 28-1d. This particular reorganization is called a **right rotation.** If we now add 80 to the tree, it remains balanced, as Figure 28-2a shows. Adding 90 disrupts the balance (Figure 28-2b), but a **left rotation** restores it (Figure 28-2c). Notice that after each rotation, the tree is still a binary search tree.

Figure 28-1   After inserting (a) 60; (b) 50; and (c) 20 into an initially empty binary search tree, the tree is not balanced; (d) a corresponding AVL tree rotates its nodes to restore balance

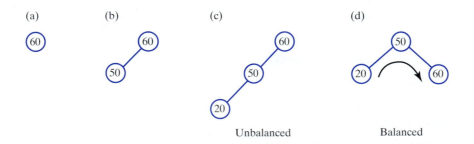

Figure 28-2 (a) Adding 80 to the tree in Figure 28-1d does not change the balance of the tree; (b) a subsequent addition of 90 makes the tree unbalanced; (c) a left rotation restores its balance

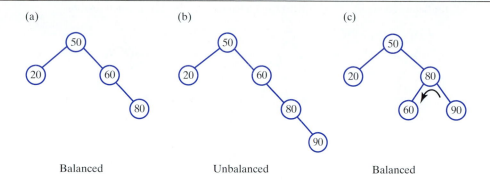

In discussing balance, we sometimes will mention a **balanced node.** A node is balanced if it is the root of a balanced tree, that is, if its two subtrees differ in height by no more than 1.

Single Rotations

28.2 Let's examine the previous rotations in more detail. Figure 28-3a shows a subtree of an AVL tree that is balanced. An addition that occurs in the left subtree T_1 of node C will add a leaf to T_1. Suppose that such an addition increases the height of T_1 from h to $h + 1$, as Figure 28-3b shows. The subtree rooted at node N is now unbalanced. N is the first node that is unbalanced along the path between the inserted leaf and N. A right rotation about node C restores the balance of the tree, as Figure 28-3c shows. Notice that after the rotation, the tree has the same height as it did before the addition of a node.

Figure 28-4 shows a left rotation in a mirror image of Figure 28-3.

Figure 28-3 Before and after an addition to an AVL subtree that requires a right rotation to maintain its balance

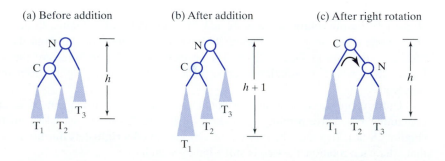

Figure 28-4 Before and after an addition to an AVL subtree that requires a left rotation to maintain its balance

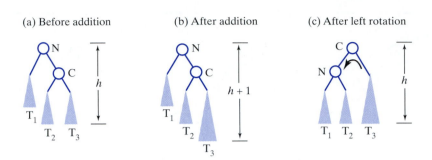

(a) Before addition

(b) After addition

(c) After left rotation

Note: An imbalance at node N of an AVL tree can be corrected by a single rotation if

- The addition occurred in the left subtree of N's left child (right rotation), or
- The addition occurred in the right subtree of N's right child (left rotation)

28.3   The following steps perform the right rotation illustrated in Figure 28-3:

> *Algorithm* `rotateRight(nodeN)`
> nodeC = *left child of* nodeN
> *Set* nodeN*'s left child to* nodeC*'s right child*
> *Set* nodeC*'s right child to* nodeN

The following steps perform the left rotation illustrated in Figure 28-4:

> *Algorithm* `rotateLeft(nodeN)`
> nodeC = *right child of* nodeN
> *Set* nodeN*'s right child to* nodeC*'s left child*
> *Set* nodeC*'s left child to* nodeN

Double Rotations

28.4   **Right-left double rotations.** Now we add 70 to the AVL tree in Figure 28-2c. An imbalance occurs at the node containing 50, as Figure 28-5a shows. A right rotation about the node containing 60 results in the tree in Figure 28-5b. The mechanics of this rotation are the same as the one in Figure 28-3, where the rotation is about node C. The subtree heights differ in these two figures, however.

Unfortunately, this rotation does not balance the tree. A subsequent left rotation about the node containing 60—corresponding to node C in Figure 28-4b—is necessary to restore the balance (Figure 28-5c). Together, these two rotations are called a **right-left double rotation.** Again, notice that after each rotation, the tree is still a binary search tree.

Figure 28-5   (a) Adding 70 to the tree in Figure 28-2c destroys its balance; to restore the balance, perform both (b) a right rotation and (c) a left rotation

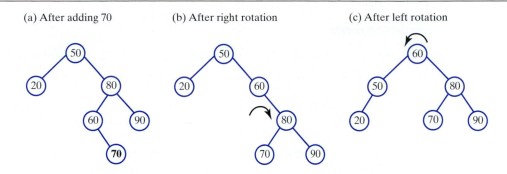

(a) After adding 70   (b) After right rotation   (c) After left rotation

Let's look at the general case. Figure 28-6a shows a subtree of an AVL tree that is height balanced. An addition that occurs in the right subtree T_3 of node G adds a leaf to T_3. When such an addition increases the height of T_3, as Figure 28-6b shows, the subtree rooted at N becomes unbalanced. Notice that nodes N, C, and G correspond to the nodes in Figure 28-5a that contain 50, 80, and 60, respectively.

Node N is the first node that is unbalanced along the path between the inserted leaf and N. After a right rotation about node G, the subtree rooted at G is unbalanced, as Figure 28-6c shows. A left rotation about G restores the balance of the tree, as you can see in Figure 28-6d.

Figure 28-6   Before and after an addition to an AVL subtree that requires both a right rotation and a left rotation to maintain its balance

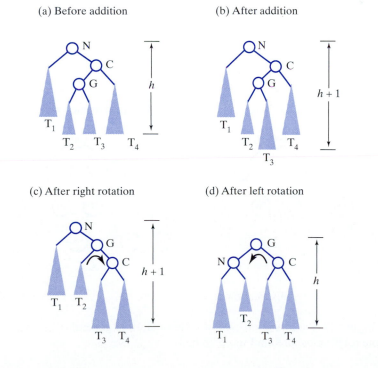

(a) Before addition   (b) After addition

(c) After right rotation   (d) After left rotation

The following steps perform the right-left double rotation illustrated in Figure 28-6:

***Algorithm* `rotateRightLeft(nodeN)`**
`nodeC` = *right child of* `nodeN`
Set `nodeN`*'s right child to the subtree produced by* `rotateRight(nodeC)`
`rotateLeft(nodeN)`

The second step applies to Figure 28-6b and results in Figure 28-6c. The third step then transforms Figure 28-6c to Figure 28-6d.

28.5   **Left-right double rotations.** Now we add 55, 10, and 40 to the tree in Figure 28-5c to get the tree in Figure 28-7a. As long as we add 55 first, these additions maintain the tree's balance without rotations. After we add 35, as Figure 28-7b shows, the tree is unbalanced at the node containing 50. To restore the balance, we perform a left rotation about the node containing 40 to get the tree in Figure 28-7c. Then we perform a right rotation about the node containing 40 to get the balanced tree in Figure 28-7d.

Figure 28-7   (a) The AVL tree in Figure 28-5c after additions that maintain its balance; (b) after an addition that destroys the balance; (c) after a left rotation; (d) after a right rotation

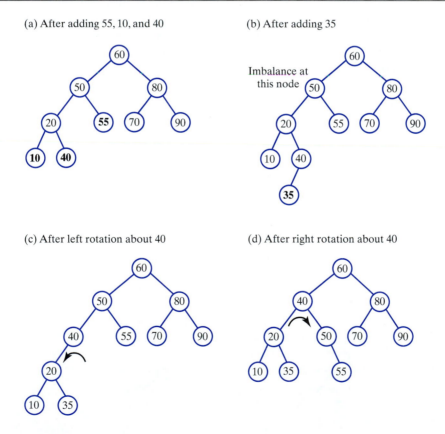

Figure 28-8 shows a left-right double rotation in general. It is a mirror image of the right-left double rotation pictured in Figure 28-6.

Figure 28-8 Before and after an addition to an AVL subtree that requires both a left rotation and a right rotation to maintain its balance

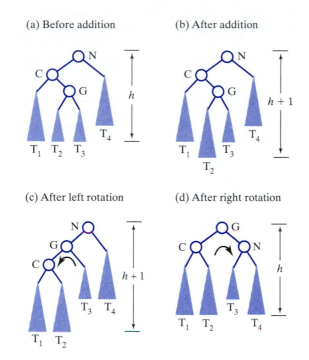

(a) Before addition

(b) After addition

(c) After left rotation

(d) After right rotation

The following steps perform the left-right double rotation illustrated in Figure 28-8:

Algorithm `rotateLeftRight(nodeN)`
`nodeC` = *left child of* `nodeN`
Set `nodeN`*'s left child to the subtree produced by* `rotateLeft(nodeC)`
`rotateRight(nodeN)`

Note: An imbalance at node N of an AVL tree can be corrected by a double rotation if

- The addition occurred in the left subtree of N's right child (right-left rotation), or
- The addition occurred in the right subtree of N's left child (left-right rotation)

Note: A double rotation is accomplished by performing two single rotations:

1. A rotation about node N's grandchild (its child's child)
2. A rotation about node N's new child

28.6 **Summary comments about rotation.** Following an addition to an AVL tree, a temporary imbalance might occur. Let N be an unbalanced node that is closest to the new leaf. Either a single or double rotation will restore the tree's balance. No other rotations are necessary. To see this, remember that before the addition, the tree was balanced; after all, it is an AVL tree. After an addition that causes a rotation, the tree has the same height as it did before the addition. Therefore, no node above *N* can be unbalanced now if it was balanced before the addition.

Removing an entry from a binary search tree results in the removal of a node, but not necessarily the node that contained the entry. Thus, removing an entry from an AVL tree can lead to a temporary imbalance. We restore the tree's balance by using one single or double rotation as described previously for addition. We leave the details for you as an exercise.

> **Note:** One single or double rotation during the addition or removal of an entry will restore the balance of an AVL tree.

Question 1 What AVL tree results when you make the following additions to an initially empty AVL tree? 70, 80, 90, 20, 10, 50, 60, 40, 30

Question 2 If you make the same additions given in Question 1 to an initially empty binary search tree, how does the resulting tree compare to the AVL tree you created in Question 1?

28.7 **An AVL tree versus a binary search tree.** We created the AVL tree in Figure 28-7d by adding 60, 50, 20, 80, 90, 70, 55, 10, 40, and 35 to an initially empty AVL tree. Figure 28-9a shows that tree again. If we make the same additions to an initially empty binary search tree, we get the tree in Figure 28-9b. This tree is unbalanced and is taller than the AVL tree.

Figure 28-9 The result of adding 60, 50, 20, 80, 90, 70, 55, 10, 40, and 35 to an initially empty (a) AVL tree; (b) binary search tree

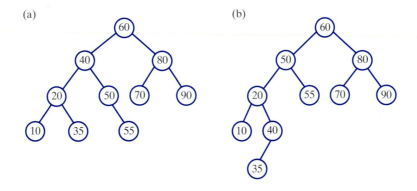

Implementation Details

28.8 **Rotations.** Since an AVL tree is simply a balanced binary search tree, we add or remove an entry by using the same algorithms that we discussed in Chapter 26. However, we need to detect and correct any imbalance that might occur.

We begin by looking at the methods that perform rotations. They closely follow the steps given in the previous segments. As these rotations are useful for other balanced search trees, we encapsulate them into a class as static methods. Since a double rotation is equivalent to two single rotations, the methods that perform double rotations each call the methods that perform single rotations.

```
package TreePackage;
class TreeRotations
{
  public static BinaryNode rotateRight(BinaryNode nodeN)
  {
    BinaryNode nodeC = (BinaryNode)nodeN.getLeftChild();
    nodeN.setLeftChild(nodeC.getRightChild());
    nodeC.setRightChild(nodeN);

    return nodeC;
  } // end rotateRight

  public static BinaryNode rotateLeft(BinaryNode nodeN)
  {
    BinaryNode nodeC = (BinaryNode)nodeN.getRightChild();
    nodeN.setRightChild(nodeC.getLeftChild());
    nodeC.setLeftChild(nodeN);

    return nodeC;
  } // end rotateLeft

  public static BinaryNode rotateRightLeft(BinaryNode nodeN)
  {
    BinaryNode nodeC = (BinaryNode)nodeN.getRightChild();
    nodeN.setRightChild(rotateRight(nodeC));

    return rotateLeft(nodeN);
  } // end rotateRightLeft

  public static BinaryNode rotateLeftRight(BinaryNode nodeN)
  {
    BinaryNode nodeC = (BinaryNode)nodeN.getLeftChild();
    nodeN.setLeftChild(rotateLeft(nodeC));

    return rotateRight(nodeN);
  } // end rotateLeftRight
} // end TreeRotations
```

28.9   **Rebalancing.** Previously, you saw that you can correct an imbalance at node N of an AVL tree by performing only one of the following rotations:

- Right rotation if the addition occurred in the left subtree of N's left child
- Left rotation if the addition occurred in the right subtree of N's right child
- Right-left rotation if the addition occurred in the left subtree of N's right child
- Left-right rotation if the addition occurred in the right subtree of N's left child

The following pseudocode uses these criteria to rebalance the tree:

Algorithm **rebalance(nodeN)**
if (nodeN's *left subtree is taller than its right subtree by more than 1*)
{ // *insertion was in* nodeN's *left subtree*
   if (*the left child of* nodeN *has a left subtree that is taller than its right subtree*)
      rotateRight(nodeN)   // *addition was in left subtree of left child*
   else
      rotateLeftRight(nodeN)   // *addition was in right subtree of left child*
}

```
else if (nodeN's right subtree is taller than its left subtree by more than 1)
{ // insertion was in nodeN's right subtree
  if (the right child of nodeN has a right subtree that is taller than its left subtree)
    rotateLeft(nodeN)          // addition was in right subtree of right child
  else
    rotateRightLeft(nodeN)    // addition was in left subtree of right child
}
```

No rebalancing is needed if the heights of node *N*'s two subtrees either are the same or differ by 1.

28.10   A method `getHeightDifference` that returns the difference in the heights of a node's left and right subtrees would help us to implement the previous algorithm. From the signed return value, we can determine whether the subtrees differ in height and if so, which one is taller. This method can be private within the class `AVLTree` or public within the class `BinaryNode`. The latter choice would be more efficient if each node maintained height information as one or more data fields instead of recomputing it each time the method is called.

A node is unbalanced if its two subtrees differ in height by more than 1, that is, if `getHeight-Difference` returns a value either greater than 1 or less than -1. If this return value is greater than 1, the left subtree is taller; if it is less than -1, the right subtree is taller.

Using the method `getHeightDifference`, we can implement the previous pseudocode within the class `AVLTree`, as follows:

```
private BinaryNode rebalance(BinaryNode nodeN)
{
  int heightDifference = getHeightDifference(nodeN);

  if (heightDifference > 1)
  { // left subtree is taller by more than 1,
    // so addition was in left subtree
    if (getHeightDifference((BinaryNode)nodeN.getLeftChild()) > 0)
      // addition was in left subtree of left child
      nodeN = TreeRotations.rotateRight(nodeN);
    else
      nodeN = TreeRotations.rotateLeftRight(nodeN);
  }
  else if (heightDifference < -1)
  { // right subtree is taller by more than 1,
    // so addition was in right subtree
    if (getHeightDifference((BinaryNode)nodeN.getRightChild()) < 0)
      // insertion was in right subtree of right child
      nodeN = TreeRotations.rotateLeft(nodeN);
    else
      nodeN = TreeRotations.rotateRightLeft(nodeN);
  } // end if
  // else nodeN is balanced

  return nodeN;
} // end rebalance
```

28.11   The method `add` for an AVL tree is like `add` for a binary search tree, but with a rebalancing step. For example, in a recursive implementation, we call `rebalance` from one of two places within the method `addNode`:

```
private BinaryNode addNode(BinaryNode rootNode, Comparable newEntry,
                            ReturnObject oldEntry)
{
  if (rootNode == null)
    rootNode = new BinaryNode(newEntry);
  else if (newEntry.compareTo(rootNode.getData()) < 0)
  {
    BinaryNode leftChild = (BinaryNode)rootNode.getLeftChild();
    BinaryNode subtreeRoot = addNode(leftChild, newEntry, oldEntry);
    rootNode.setLeftChild(subtreeRoot);
    rootNode = rebalance(rootNode);
  }
  else if (newEntry.compareTo(rootNode.getData()) > 0)
  {
    BinaryNode rightChild = (BinaryNode)rootNode.getRightChild();
    rootNode.setRightChild(addNode(rightChild, newEntry, oldEntry));
    rootNode = rebalance(rootNode);
  }
  else // newEntry matches entry in root
  {
    Comparable rootEntry = (Comparable)rootNode.getData();
    oldEntry.set(rootEntry);
    rootNode.setData(newEntry);
  } // end if

  return rootNode;
} // end addNode
```

This recursive implementation is not as efficient as possible, since `addNode` continues execution after a rotation occurs. An iterative approach would enable the method to exit after the one necessary rotation takes place. Also, the implementation would be less tedious if we used inheritance. We will not make these improvements, however. As attractive as an AVL tree might seem, better search trees have been developed.

2-3 Trees

28.12   A **2-3 tree** is a general search tree whose interior nodes must have either two or three children. A **2-node** contains one data item *s* and has two children, like the nodes in a binary search tree. This data *s* is greater than any data in the node's left subtree and less than any data in the right subtree. That is, the data in the node's left subtree is less than *s*, and any data in the right subtree is greater than *s*, as Figure 28-10a shows.

A **3-node** contains two data items, *s* and *l*, and has three children. Data that is less than the smaller data item *s* occurs in the node's left subtree. Data that is greater than the larger data item *l* occurs in the node's right subtree. Data that is between *s* and *l* occurs in the node's middle subtree. Figure 28-10b shows a typical 3-node.

Because it can contain 3-nodes, a 2-3 tree tends to be shorter than a binary search tree. To make the 2-3 tree balanced, we require that all leaves occur on the same level. Thus, a 2-3 tree is completely balanced.

Note: A 2-3 tree is a general search tree whose interior nodes must have either two or three children and whose leaves occur on the same level. A 2-3 tree is completely balanced.

Figure 28-10 (a) A 2-node; (b) a 3-node

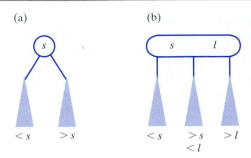

Searching a 2-3 Tree

28.13   If we had a 2-3 tree, such as the one in Figure 28-11, how would we search it? Notice that each 2-node adheres to the ordering of a binary search tree. The 3-node leaf <35 40> contains values that are between the values in its parent. Knowing this, we can search for the 40, for example, by first comparing 40 with the root value 60. We then move to 60's left subtree and compare 40 with the values in the root of this subtree. Since 40 lies between the 20 and 50, it would occur in the middle subtree, if it appears at all. While searching the middle subtree, we compare 40 with 35 and then finally with 40.

Figure 28-11 A 2-3 tree

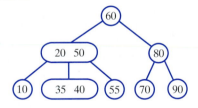

The search algorithm is an extension of the search algorithm for a binary search tree:

Algorithm `search23Tree(23Tree, desiredObject)`
// Searches a 2-3 tree for a given object.
// Returns true if the object is found.

```
if (23Tree is empty)
   return false
else if (desiredObject is in the root of 23Tree)
   return true
else if (the root of 23Tree contains two entries)
{
   if (desiredObject < smaller object in the root)
      return search23Tree(left subtree of 23Tree, desiredObject)
   else if (desiredObject > larger object in the root)
      return search23Tree(right subtree of 23Tree, desiredObject)
   else
      return search23Tree(middle subtree of 23Tree, desiredObject)
}
```

```
    else if (desiredObject < object in the root)
        return search23Tree(left subtree of 23Tree, desiredObject)
    else
        return search23Tree(right subtree of 23Tree, desiredObject)
```

Question 3   What comparisons are made while searching the 2-3 tree in Figure 28-11 for each of the following values?
a. 5 **b.** 55 **c.** 41 **d.** 30

Adding Entries to a 2-3 Tree

28.14   Using an example, we will describe how to add an entry to a 2-3 tree. So that we can compare our results with an AVL tree, we will make the same sequence of additions to an initially empty 2-3 tree that we made when forming the AVL tree in Figure 28-9a.

As we did when adding to a binary search tree, we add an entry to a 2-3 tree at a leaf. We locate this leaf by using the search algorithm that we described in the previous segment. Thus, once we make the addition, the search algorithm will be able to locate the new entry.

We will now add the following entries: 60, 50, 20, 80, 90, 70, 55, 10, 40, and 35.

28.15   **Adding 60, 50, and 20.** After we add 60, the 2-3 tree consists of a single 2-node. After we add 50, the tree is a single 3-node. Figures 28-12a and 28-12b show the tree after each of these additions.

Now we add 20. To facilitate our description of this addition, we show the 20 in Figure 28-12c within the only node in the tree. This is an imaginary placement, since a 3-node can contain only two data items. We would not actually place more data in this node. Since the node cannot accommodate the 20, we **split** it into three nodes, moving the middle value 50 up one level. In this case we are splitting a leaf that is also the tree's root. Moving the 50 up requires that we create a new node that becomes the new root of the tree. This step increases the height of the tree by 1, as Figure 28-12d shows.

Figure 28-12   An initially empty 2-3 tree after adding (a) 60 and (b) 50; (c), (d) adding 20 causes the 3-node to split

28.16   **Adding 80, 90, and 70.** To add 80, we note that the search algorithm would look for 80 in the tree's rightmost leaf. Since this leaf has room for another data entry, that is where we should add 80. Figure 28-13a shows the result of this addition.

The search algorithm would look for 90 in the leaf to which we just added 80. Although the leaf has no room for another entry, we imagine that we have added 90 there. We then move the middle value—the 80—up a level and split the leaf into two nodes for the 60 and 90, as Figure 28-13b shows. Since the root can accept the 80, the addition is complete.

The entry 70 belongs in the root's middle subtree, and since this leaf can accept another entry, we add 70 there. Figure 28-13c shows the tree after this addition.

Figure 28-13 The 2-3 tree after adding (a) 80; (b) 90; (c) 70

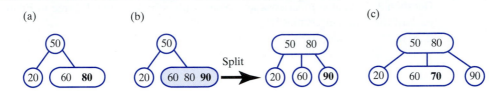

28.17   **Adding 55.** When we add 55 to the tree in Figure 28-13c, the search algorithm terminates at the root's middle subtree, which is a leaf. As Figure 28-14a indicates, this leaf cannot accommodate another entry. The leaf splits and 60 moves up a level to the root, as shown in Figure 28-14b. Moving the 60 causes the root to split, and 60 moves up another level to a new node that becomes the new root. Figure 28-14c shows the result of this addition.

Figure 28-14 Adding 55 to the 2-3 tree causes a leaf and then the root to split

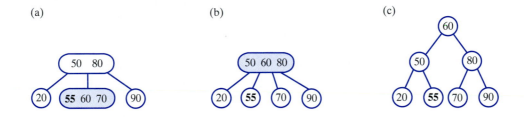

28.18   **Adding 10, 40, and 35.** The leaf that contains 20 has room for 10 as an additional entry, as Figure 28-15a shows. An additional entry, 40, belongs in the same leaf. Since the leaf already contains two entries, we split it and move 20 up a level to the node that contains 50. Figures 28-15b and 28-15c show this result. Finally, Figure 28-16 shows the result of adding 35 to the tree. The leaf that contains 40 accommodates this new entry.

Figure 28-15 The 2-3 tree after adding (a) 10; (b), (c) 40

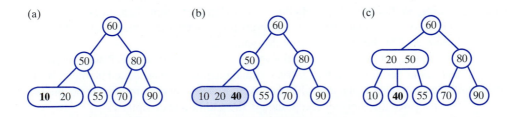

Figure 28-16   The 2-3 tree after adding 35

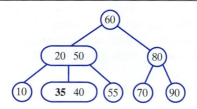

Compare the final 2-3 tree in Figure 28-16 with the AVL tree in Figure 28-9a. We used the same sequence of additions to form both trees. The 2-3 tree is shorter than the balanced AVL tree. Later, we will compare these trees with the 2-4 tree in the next section and draw some conclusions.

Splitting Nodes During Addition

28.19   **Splitting a leaf.** During the addition of a new entry to a 2-3 tree, the first node that splits is a leaf that already contains two entries. Figure 28-17a shows a leaf that would need to accommodate three entries. These entries are shown in ascending order as s, m, and l. The node splits into two nodes that contain s and l, respectively, and the middle entry m moves up a level. If the parent of the leaf has room for m, no further action is necessary. This is the case in Figure 28-17a. But in Figure 28-17b, the parent already contains two entries, so we must split it as well. We consider that case next.

Although Figure 28-17 shows the leaf as a right child of its parent, other analogous configurations are possible.

Figure 28-17   Splitting a leaf to accommodate a new entry when the leaf's parent contains (a) one entry; (b) two entries

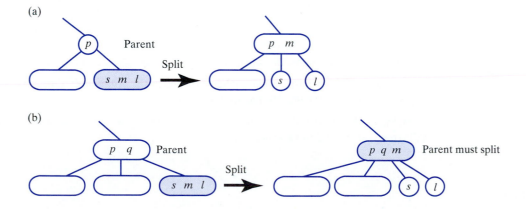

28.20   **Splitting an internal node.** You just saw that splitting a leaf can cause the leaf's parent to have too many entries. This parent also has too many children, as illustrated in Figure 28-17b. Figure 28-18

shows such an internal node in general. This node must accommodate three entries s, m, and l, given in ascending order, and four children that are the roots of the subtrees T_1 through T_4. Thus, we split the node, move the middle entry m up to the node's parent, place s and l into their own nodes, and distribute the original node's subtrees between s and l. If the parent has room for m, no further splitting is necessary. If not, we split the parent as just described.

Other analogous configurations for an internal node are possible.

Figure 28-18 Splitting an internal node to accommodate a new entry

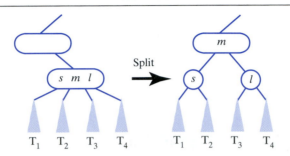

28.21   **Splitting the root.** Splitting a root proceeds just like the previous cases, except that when we move an entry up a level, we allocate a new node for the entry. This new node becomes the root of the tree, as Figure 28-19 illustrates. Notice that only this case increases the height of a 2-3 tree.

Figure 28-19 Splitting the root to accommodate a new entry

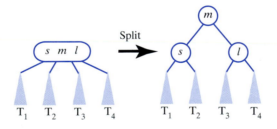

Question 4   What tree results when you add 30 to the 2-3 tree in Figure 28-16?

Question 5   What 2-3 tree results when you make the following additions to an initially empty 2-3 tree? 70, 80, 90, 20, 10, 50, 60, 40, 30

Question 6   How does the tree that you created in the previous question compare to the AVL tree you created in Question 1?

2-4 Trees

28.22   A **2-4 tree,** sometimes called a **2-3-4 tree,** is a general search tree whose interior nodes must have either two, three, or four children. In addition to 2-nodes and 3-nodes, as we described in the previous section, this tree also contains 4-nodes. A **4-node** contains three data items s, m, and l and has four children. Data that is less than the smaller data item s occurs in the node's left subtree.

Data that is greater than the larger data item *l* occurs in the node's right subtree. Data that is between *s* and *m* or between *m* and *l* occurs in the node's middle subtrees. Figure 28-20 illustrates a typical 4-node.

Searching a 2-4 tree is like searching a 2-3 tree, but with additional logic to handle the 4-nodes. This search forms the basis of an algorithm to add entries to a 2-4 tree.

Figure 28-20   A 4-node

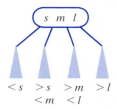

 Note: A 2-4 tree is a general search tree whose interior nodes must have either two, three, or four children and whose leaves occur on the same level. A 2-4 tree is completely balanced.

Adding Entries to a 2-4 Tree

28.23   Recall how we add a new entry to a 2-3 tree. We make comparisons along a path that begins at the root and ends at a leaf. At this point, if the leaf is a 3-node, it already contains two data entries, and so we must split it. Since an entry would now move up a level, this split could require splits in nodes above the leaf. Thus, adding to a 2-3 tree can require us to retrace the path from the leaf back to the root.

In a 2-4 tree, we avoid this retrace by splitting each 4-node as soon as we first consider it during the search from root to leaf. After a split, we will be at the parent of the next node along the comparison path. This parent is not a 4-node, since it is the result of a split. If the next child considered is a 4-node, the parent has room for the entry that moves up from this child. No other splits occur, as would happen in a 2-3 tree. You will see an example of this shortly.

As in the previous section, we will use an example to show you how to add an entry to a 2-4 tree. So that we can compare our results with previous trees, we use the same sequence of additions—namely, 60, 50, 20, 80, 90, 70, 55, 10, 40, and 35—that we used earlier.

28.24   **Adding 60, 50, and 20.** Figure 28-21 shows an initially empty 2-4 tree after adding 60, 50, and 20. The resulting tree consists of a single 4-node.

Figure 28-21   An initially empty 2-4 tree after adding (a) 60; (b) 50; (c) 20

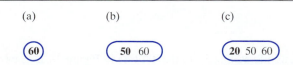

28.25   **Adding 80 and 90.** To add an entry to the 2-4 tree in Figure 28-21c, we find that the root is a 4-node. We split it by moving the middle entry 50 up. Since we are at a root, we create a new node for the 50. That node becomes the new root of the tree, as shown in Figure 28-22a. We now can add 80 and 90 to the root's right leaf, as Figures 28-22b and 28-22c illustrate.

Figure 28-22   The 2-4 tree after (a) splitting the root; (b) adding 80; (c) adding 90

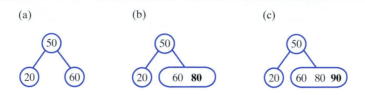

28.26   **Adding 70.** While searching the 2-4 tree in Figure 28-22c for a place to add 70, we encounter the 4-node that is the root's right child. We split this node into two nodes and move the middle entry 80 up to the root. The result of this split in shown in Figure 28-23a. We now have room to add 70 to the root's middle child, as Figure 28-23b shows.

Figure 28-23   The 2-4 tree after (a) splitting a 4-node; (b) adding 70

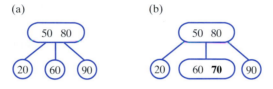

28.27   **Adding 55, 10, and 40.** The 2-4 tree in Figure 28-23b can accommodate the addition of 55, 10, and 40 without splitting nodes. Figure 28-24 shows the results of these additions.

Figure 28-24   The 2-4 tree after adding (a) 55; (b) 10; (c) 40

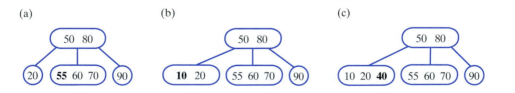

28.28   **Adding 35.** While adding 35 to the 2-4 tree in Figure 28-24c, our search encounters the root's left child, which is a 4-node. We split this node into two nodes and move the middle entry 20 up to the root, as shown in Figure 28-25a. We now can add 35 to the root's middle left child, as Figure 28-25b shows. This is the final addition that we will make.

Figure 28-25 The 2-4 tree after (a) splitting the leftmost 4-node; (b) adding 35

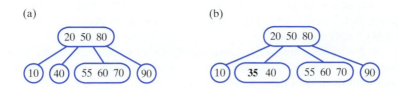

Note: When adding a new entry to a 2-4 tree, you split any 4-node as soon as you encounter it during the search for the new entry's position in the tree. The addition is complete right after this search ends. Thus, adding to a 2-4 tree is more efficient than adding to a 2-3 tree.

Question 7   What comparisons are made while searching the 2-4 tree in Figure 28-25b for each of the following values?
a. 5   **b.** 56   **c.** 41   **d.** 30

Question 8   What tree results when you add 30 to the 2-4 tree in Figure 28-25b?

Question 9   What 2-4 tree results when you make the following additions to an initially empty 2-4 tree? 70, 80, 90, 20, 10, 50, 60, 40, 30

Question 10   How does the tree that you created in the previous question compare to the 2-3 tree you created in Question 5?

Comparing AVL, 2-3, and 2-4 Trees

28.29   Earlier we asked you to compare the final 2-3 tree in Figure 28-16 with the AVL tree in Figure 28-9a. We also want to compare those results with the 2-4 tree that we just constructed. Figure 28-26 shows these trees again. The AVL tree is a balanced binary search tree of height 4. The other trees are completely balanced general trees. The height of the 2-3 tree is 3; the height of the 2-4 tree is 2. In general 2-4 trees are shorter than 2-3 trees, which are shorter than AVL trees.

Figure 28-26 Three balanced search trees obtained by adding 60, 50, 20, 80, 90, 70, 55, 10, 40, and 35: (a) AVL; (b) 2-3; (c) 2-4

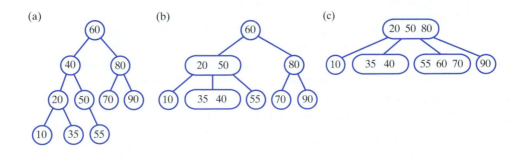

You saw in segment 26.36 that searching a balanced binary search tree, such as an AVL tree, is an O(log n) operation. Since 2-3 and 2-4 trees are no taller than a corresponding AVL tree, we usually can search them by examining fewer nodes. However, 3-nodes and 4-nodes contain more entries than 2-nodes, so require a longer search time. In general, searching an AVL, 2-3, or 2-4 tree is an O(log n) operation.

A 2-3 tree is attractive because maintaining its balance is easier than for an AVL tree. Maintaining the balance of a 2-4 tree is even easier. But considering search trees whose nodes contain more than three data items is usually counterproductive, because the number of comparisons per node increases. As you will see later in this chapter, such a search tree is attractive when it is maintained in external storage, such as a disk, instead of internal memory.

Red–Black Trees

28.30   You just saw that a 2-4 tree is attractive because maintaining its balance is easier than maintaining either an AVL tree or a 2-3 tree. A **red-black tree** is a binary tree that is equivalent to a 2-4 tree. Adding an entry to a red-black tree is like adding an entry to a 2-4 tree, in that only one pass from root to leaf is necessary. But a red-black tree is a binary tree, so it uses simpler operations to maintain its balance than does a 2-4 tree. Additionally, the implementation of a red-black tree uses only 2-nodes, whereas a 2-4 tree requires 2-nodes, 3-nodes, and 4-nodes. This added requirement of a 2-4 tree makes it less desirable than a red-black tree.

Note: A red-black tree is a binary tree that is equivalent to a 2-4 tree. Conceptually, a red-black tree is more involved than a 2-4 tree, but its implementation uses only 2-nodes and so is more efficient.

28.31   When designing a node for the 2-4 tree, you need to decide how to represent the entries that are in the node. Since you must order these entries, you could use an ADT such as the sorted list for the entries. You might also use a binary search tree. For example, consider the 2-4 tree in Figure 28-26c. The entries in the root of this tree are 20, 50, and 80. We can represent these entries as a binary search tree whose root is 50 and whose subtrees are 20 and 80. Likewise, the entries in the 3-node leaf of this 2-4 tree are 35 and 40. We can represent these entries as one of two binary search trees: One has 35 as its root and 40 as its right subtree; the other has 40 as its root and 35 as its left subtree. Thus, we can convert all 3-nodes and 4-nodes to 2-nodes. The result is a binary search tree instead of a 2-4 tree.

Each time we convert a 3-node or a 4-node to a 2-node, we increase the height of the tree. We use color to highlight the new nodes that cause this increase in height. First, we use black for all the nodes in the original 2-4 tree. Since we do not change the 2-nodes, they remain black in the new tree.

Figure 28-27a shows how to represent a 4-node by using 2-nodes. The root of the resulting subtree remains black, but we color its children. The traditional color is red. Our figures use blue since that is our book's second color. Similarly, Figure 28-27b shows how to represent a 3-node by using one of two different subtrees, each having a black root and a red child.

With this notation, we can draw the 2-4 tree in Figure 28-26c as the balanced binary search tree in Figure 28-28. This binary search tree is called a **red-black tree.**

Question 11   What comparisons are made while searching the 2-4 tree in Figure 28-26c and the equivalent red-black tree in Figure 28-28 for

a. 60   **b.** 55

Figure 28-27 Using 2-nodes to represent (a) a 4-node; (b) a 3-node

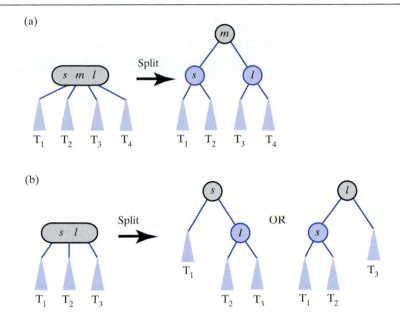

Figure 28-28 A red-black tree that is equivalent to the 2-4 tree in Figure 28-26c

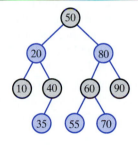

Properties of a Red-Black Tree

28.32   The root of every red-black tree is black. If the original 2-4 tree had a 2-node as its root, the 2-node would be black. And if its root was either a 3-node or a 4-node, we would replace it with a subtree whose root is black, as shown in Figure 28-27.

Since we create red nodes only when we convert 3-nodes and 4-nodes to 2-nodes, every red node has a black parent, as you can see in Figure 28-27. It follows that a red node cannot have red children. If it did, the red child would have a red parent, and this contradicts our previous conclusion that every red node has a black parent.

When we form a red-black tree from a 2-4 tree, 2-nodes stay black and the representation of any other node contains one black node. Thus, every node in a 2-4 tree produces exactly one black node in the equivalent red-black tree. Since a 2-4 tree is completely balanced, all paths from the root to a leaf connect the same number of nodes. So every path from the root to a leaf in a red-black tree must contain the same number of black nodes.

Note: **Properties of a red-black tree**

1. The root is black.
2. Every red node has a black parent.
3. Any children of a red node are black; that is, a red node cannot have red children.
4. Every path from the root to a leaf contains the same number of black nodes.

Question 12 Show that the red-black tree in Figure 28-28 satisfies the four properties just given.

Question 13 What red-black tree is equivalent to the 2-4 tree in Figure 28-24c?

Question 14 Show that the red-black tree that answers Question 13 satisfies the four properties given previously.

Note: Searching a red-black tree

A red-black tree is really a binary search tree whose nodes are either red or black. If you ignore these colors, you can search a red-black tree by using the same algorithm that you use to search a binary search tree.

Adding Entries to a Red-Black Tree

28.33 **Adding a leaf.** What color should we assign to a new node that we add to the tree? An addition to a binary search tree always occurs at a leaf, so the same is true for a red-black tree. If we use black for a new leaf, we will increase the number of black nodes on the paths to that leaf. This increase violates the fourth property of a red-black tree. Thus, any new node must be red. However, do not assume that all the leaves in a red-black tree are red. Adding or removing entries can change the color of various nodes, including that of leaves added earlier.

Consider some simple cases. Figure 28-29 shows two possibilities when we add a new entry e to a one-node red-black tree. In each case, the new red node is legal: It maintains the properties of a red-black tree.

Figure 28-29 The result of adding a new entry e to a one-node red-black tree

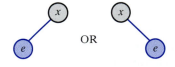

Now suppose that the red-black tree had two nodes before we added the new entry e. Figure 28-30a shows this original tree when it consists of a root x and right child y. Also pictured is the 2-4 tree that is equivalent to the original red-black tree. The rest of the figure shows the possible outcomes of the addition, depending on how e compares with x and y. In Part b, e is the left child of the root and we are done. In Part c, a red node has a red child. These two consecutive red nodes are illegal in a red-black tree. To understand what further action is necessary, consider the equivalent 2-4 tree. The original 2-node red-black tree is equivalent to the 2-4 tree that contains the one node $<x\ y>$ (Figure 28-30a). If we add an entry e that is larger than y, the 2-4 tree becomes the single node $<x\ y\ e>$ (Figure 28-30c). Notice the red-black tree that is equivalent to this 3-node. This tree is the one we need as the result of adding e. We can get it from the first red-black tree shown in Part c by first performing a single left rotation about the node containing y. You have seen this rotation before when we talked about AVL trees. After the rotation, we need to reverse the colors of the nodes containing x and y—that is, the parent and grandparent of the new node. We call this step a **color flip.**

Figure 28-30d shows the last possible result of adding e to the two-node red-black tree. Here, a right-left double rotation followed by a color flip of the new node and its grandparent are necessary to avoid two consecutive red nodes. Figure 28-6b, c, and d show the rotation in general in the context of an AVL tree.

Figure 28-31 shows mirror images of the cases in Figure 28-30.

Figure 28-30   The possible results of adding a new entry e to a two-node red-black tree

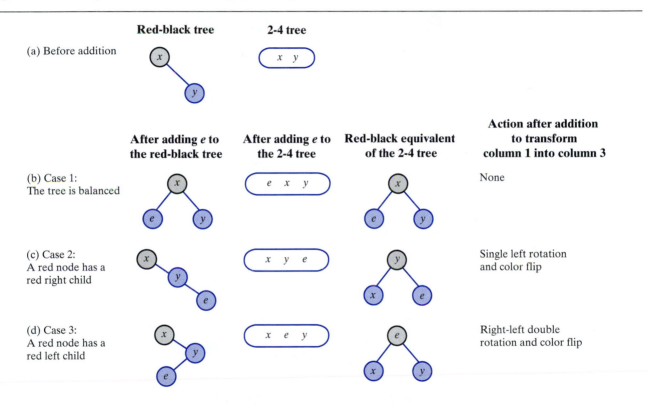

28.34   **Splitting a 4-node whose parent is black.** During an addition to a 2-4 tree, we split any 4-nodes that we encounter as we move along the path from the root to the eventual insertion point. We must perform an equivalent action during an addition to a red-black tree. Figure 28-27a shows that when a black node has two red children, we have encountered the red-black representation of a 4-node. We will call this configuration a red-black 4-node, or simply a 4-node.

Figure 28-32a recalls how to split a 4-node when its parent in the 2-4 tree is a 2-node. The middle entry m moves up to the node's parent, and the other entries s and l are given their own nodes as replacement children of the parent. Figure 28-32b shows the corresponding red-black trees. Notice that the three nodes in the subtree rooted at m reverse colors. Thus, we split the red-black representation of a 4-node by performing a color flip.

Figure 28-31 The possible results of adding a new entry *e* to a two-node red-black tree: Mirror images of Figure 28-30

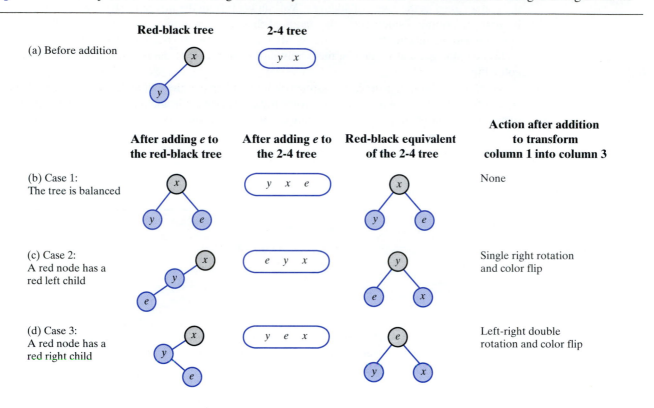

Figure 28-32 Splitting a 4-node whose parent is a 2-node in (a) a 2-4 tree; (b) a red-black tree

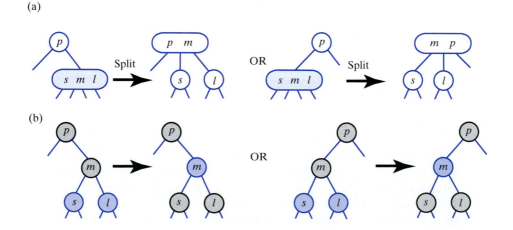

A color flip is all that is necessary when a red-black 4-node has a black parent. As you can see from Figure 28-32, a black parent corresponds to a 2-node in the 2-4 tree. If a 4-node in a 2-4 tree has a 3-node as its parent, the red-black 4-node will have a red parent. We examine this situation in the next segment.

28.35   **Splitting a 4-node whose parent is red: Case 1.** Figure 28-33a shows the splitting of a 4-node that has a 3-node parent within a 2-4 tree. Figure 28-33b shows the red-black representations of the two trees in Part *a*. How can we transform the first red-black tree into the second? Figure 28-34 shows the necessary steps. In Part *a*, we detect a 4-node at *m*, since this node has two red children. A color flip results in two adjacent red nodes, as shown in Figure 28-34b. Earlier, in Figure 28-30c, we saw this configuration of a black node and two consecutive right descendants that are red. As we did then, we perform a left rotation about *p*, as Figure 28-34c shows, and then we reverse the colors of the nodes containing *p* and *g*. This color flip, together with the rotation, resolves the illegal red nodes. The result in Figure 28-34d is the desired red-black tree that we saw in Figure 28-33b.

Figure 28-33 Splitting a 4-node that has a 3-node parent within (a) a 2-4 tree; (b) a red-black tree

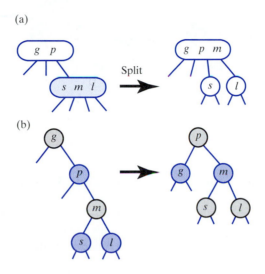

Figure 28-34 Splitting a 4-node that has a red parent within a red-black tree: Case 1

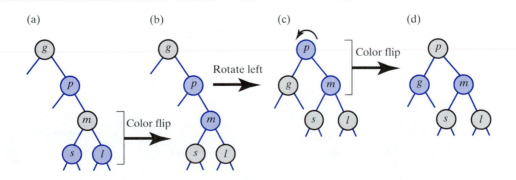

Since a 3-node has two different red-black representations, we can replace Figure 28-34a with a different red-black tree. We leave it to you to show that the final result will be the same, but with less work.

28.36 **Splitting a 4-node whose parent is red: Case 2.** The 4-node in Figure 28-33a is a right child of its parent. If it were a left child, the red-black representation would be as in Figure 28-35a. The rest of this figure shows that both color flips and a right rotation are necessary to split the 4-node.

As before, we can replace Figure 28-35a with a different red-black tree and get the same final result. Again we leave the details to you as an exercise.

Figure 28-35 Splitting a 4-node that has a red parent within a red-black tree: Case 2

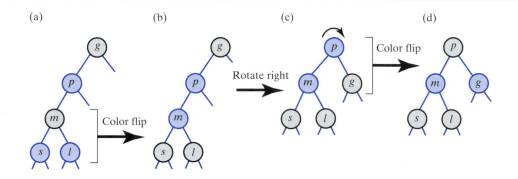

28.37 **Splitting a 4-node whose parent is red: Cases 3 and 4.** Now consider the case in which the 4-node is the middle child of its 3-node parent. This time, we look at both red-black representations that the 3-node parent produces. Figure 28-36a shows one possible red-black tree. After the color flip in Part *b*, we resolve the consecutive red nodes as we did in Figure 28-30d. A right-left double rotation followed by a color flip produces the desired results, as you can see in the rest of Figure 28-36.

Figure 28-37a shows the second possible red-black tree. After the color flip in Part *b*, we resolve the consecutive red nodes as we did in Figure 28-31d. A left-right double rotation followed by a color flip is necessary, as Figure 28-37 shows.

Figure 28-36 Splitting a 4-node that has a red parent within a red-black tree: Case 3

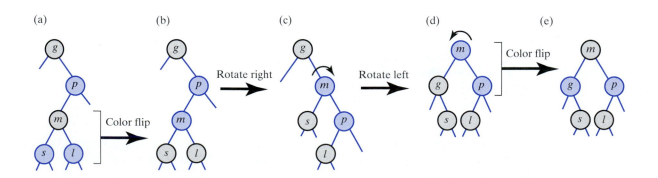

Figure 28-37 Splitting a 4-node that has a red parent within a red-black tree: Case 4

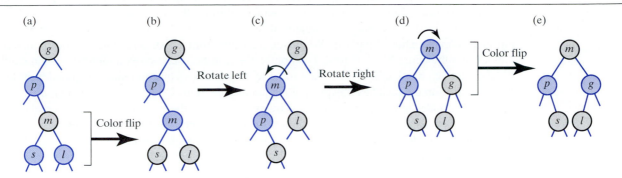

Java Class Library: The Class `TreeMap`

28.38   The package `java.util` contains the class `TreeMap`. This class uses a red-black tree to implement the methods in the interface `java.util.SortedMap`. `SortedMap` extends the interface `Map`, which we described in Segment 17.16. Recall that the interface `Map` is similar to our interface for the ADT dictionary. `SortedMap`, however, specifies that search keys be maintained in ascending order. Because a red-black tree is used, methods such as `get`, `put`, `remove`, and `containsKey` are all O(log *n*) operations.

B-Trees

28.39   A **multiway search tree of order *m***—or sometimes an **_m_-way search tree**—is a general tree whose nodes have up to *m* children each. A node that has *k* − 1 data items and *k* children is called a **_k_-node.** An order *m* multiway search tree can contain *k*-nodes for values of *k* ranging from 2 to *m*.

A binary search tree is a multiway search tree of order 2. You know that not all binary search trees are balanced; likewise, not all multiway search trees are balanced. However, 2-3 trees and 2-4 trees are balanced multiway search trees of orders 3 and 4, respectively. We maintained the balance of a 2-3 tree, for example, by insisting that every interior node have two or three children and that all leaves occur on the same level.

A **B-tree of order *m*** is a balanced multiway search tree of order *m* that has the following additional properties to maintain its balance:

- The root has either no children or between 2 and *m* children.
- Other interior nodes (nonleaves) have between $\lceil m/2 \rceil$ and *m* children.
- All leaves are on the same level.

2-3 and 2-4 trees satisfy these constraints, and so are examples of B-trees.

28.40   The search trees that you have seen so far maintain their data within the main memory of a computer. At some point, we probably will save this data in external memory, such as a disk. As long as we can read the data back into internal memory, we can use any of the previous search trees. But what happens when your database becomes too large to be retained entirely within internal memory? Typically, you use a B-tree.

Since external memory has a mechanical component, accessing its data is much slower than accessing data in main memory. When reading external data, the major cost is that of positioning a read head. You therefore want to reduce the number of times that the read head must move.

Data on a disk, for example, is organized sequentially into **blocks,** whose size depends on the physical characteristics of the disk. When you read data from a disk, a read head is positioned over a block and the entire block is read. Positioning the read head takes much more time than reading the data. If each block contains the data for at least one node, you can reduce the number of times that you position the read head by placing numerous data items in each node. Although many comparisons per node are possible, their cost is overshadowed by the cost of accessing external data.

Since increasing the number of data items per node decreases the tree's height, you decrease the number of nodes that you must search and hence the number of disk accesses. A high-order B-tree fits these requirements. You would choose the order m so that $m - 1$ data items fit into a block on the disk.

Note: Although a high order B-tree is usually counterproductive for an internal database because the number of comparisons per node increases, it is attractive when it is maintained in external storage such as a disk.

EXERCISES

1. Add 62 and 65 to the AVL tree in Figure 28-26a.

2. Add 62 and 65 to the 2-3 tree in Figure 28-26b.

3. Add 62 and 65 to the 2-4 tree in Figure 28-26c.

4. Add 62 and 65 to the red-black tree in Figure 28-28.

5. Each of the trees in Figures 28-26 and 28-28 contains the same values. Exercises 1 through 4 asked you to add 62 and 65 to each of them. Describe the effect that these additions had on each tree.

6. What red-black tree is equivalent to the 2-4 tree in Figure 28-24b?

7. What tree results when you add the values 10, 20, 30, 40, 50, 60, 70, 80, 90, and 100 to each of the following initially empty trees?
   a. An AVL tree   **b.** A 2-3 tree   **c.** A 2-4 tree   **d.** A red-black tree

8. Add the values given in Exercise 7 to an initially empty binary search tree. Compare the resulting tree with the trees you created in Exercise 7. Which tree could you search most efficiently?

9. Using pseudocode, describe an inorder traversal of
   a. A 2-3 tree   **b.** A 2-4 tree

10. Figure 28-33a shows a 4-node within a 2-4 tree that is the right child of a 3-node parent containing data items *g* and *p*. When converting these nodes to red-black notation, make *p* be the parent of *g*. Revise Figure 28-34 to show that a color flip is all that is necessary to get the desired red-black tree.

11. Repeat Exercise 10, but this time assume that the 4-node is a left child.

12. Color the nodes in each tree in Figure 28-38 so that it is a red-black tree.

13. Which of the data structures that you studied in this chapter could be used to implement a priority queue? Recall that we discussed the priority queue in Chapter 22.

14. How efficiently could a red-black tree or an AVL tree implement the add and remove methods of a priority queue?

Figure 28-38 Three binary trees for Exercise 12

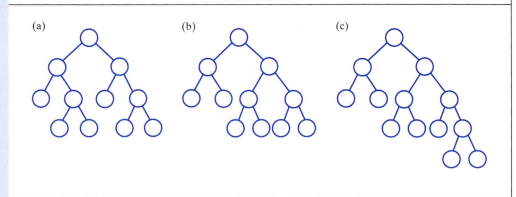

(a)   (b)   (c)

PROJECTS

1. You remove an entry from an AVL tree in the same way that you remove an entry from a binary search tree. However, after you remove the appropriate node from the tree, an imbalance can occur that you must correct by performing a single or double rotation. Develop an algorithm that removes a node from an AVL tree.

2. Implement a class of AVL trees.

3. Design a class of nodes that you can use in the implementation of a 2-4 tree. Is one class enough, or will you need several?

4. Implement a class of 2-4 trees in which only additions and retrievals are permitted.

5. Implement a class of red-black trees that permit only additions and retrievals.

6. Design and carry out an experiment to compare the heights of ordinary binary search trees with either AVL trees or red-black trees. You first will need to complete either Project 2 or Project 5.

7. Implement a priority queue by using one of the balanced search trees in this chapter.

29

Graphs

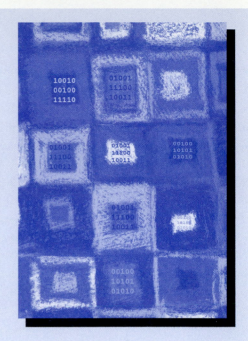

CONTENTS

Some Examples and Terminology
    Road Maps
    Airline Routes
    Mazes
    Course Prerequisites
    Trees
Traversals
    Breadth-First Traversal
    Depth-First Traversal
Topological Order
Paths
    Finding a Path
    The Shortest Path in an Unweighted Graph
    The Shortest Path in a Weighted Graph
Java Interfaces for the ADT Graph

PREREQUISITES

Chapter 20   Stacks
Chapter 22   Queues, Deques, and Priority Queues
Chapter 24   Trees

OBJECTIVES

After studying this chapter, you should be able to

- Describe the characteristics of a graph, including its vertices, edges, and paths
- Give examples of graphs, including those that are undirected, directed, unweighted, and weighted
- Give examples of vertices that are adjacent and those that are not adjacent for both directed and undirected graphs
- Give examples of paths, simple paths, cycles, and simple cycles
- Give examples of connected graphs, disconnected graphs, and complete graphs

- Perform a depth-first traversal and a breadth-first traversal on a given graph
- List a topological order for the vertices of a directed graph without cycles
- Determine whether a path exists between two given vertices of a graph
- Determine the path with the fewest edges that joins one vertex to another
- Determine the path with the lowest cost that joins one vertex to another in a weighted graph
- Describe the operations for the ADT graph

The news media often use line graphs, pie charts, and bar graphs to help us visualize certain statistics. But these common graphs are *not* examples of the kind of graph that we will study in this chapter. The graphs that computer scientists and mathematicians use include the trees that you saw in Chapter 24. In fact, a tree is a special kind of graph. These graphs represent the relationships among data elements. This chapter will present the terminology we use when discussing graphs, the operations on them, and some typical applications.

Some Examples and Terminology

Although the graphs that you have drawn in the past likely are not the kind of graph that we will discuss here, the examples in this section will be familiar. But you probably have never called them graphs!

Road Maps

29.1   Figure 29-1 contains a portion of a road map for Cape Cod, Massachusetts. Small circles represent the towns, and the lines that join them represent the roads. A road map is a graph. In a graph, the circles are called **vertices,** or **nodes,** and the lines are called **edges.** A **graph,** then, is a collection of distinct vertices and distinct edges. A **subgraph** is a portion of a graph that is itself a graph, just as the road map in Figure 29-1 actually is a part of a larger map.

Figure 29-1   A portion of a road map

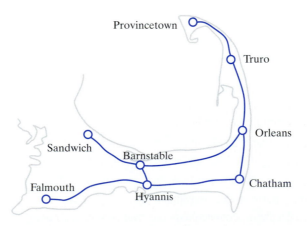

Since you can travel in both directions along the roads in Figure 29-1, the corresponding graph and its edges are said to be **undirected.** But cities often have one-way streets. The graph in Figure 29-2 has a vertex for each intersection in a city's street map. The edges each have a direction and are called **directed edges.** A graph with directed edges is called a **directed graph,** or **digraph.** You can transform an undirected graph into a directed graph by replacing each undirected edge with two directed edges that have opposite directions.

Figure 29-2   A directed graph representing a portion of a city's street map

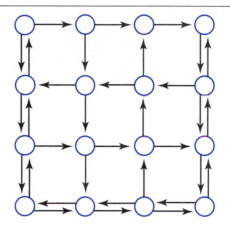

29.2   **Paths.** A **path** is a sequence of edges that connect two vertices in a graph. A path in a directed graph must consider the direction of the edges, and is called a **directed path.** The **length** of a path is the number of edges that it comprises. If the path does not pass through any vertex more than once, it is a **simple path.** Figure 29-1 contains a simple path from Provincetown to Orleans of length 2.

A **cycle** is a path that begins and ends at the same vertex. A **simple cycle** passes through other vertices only once each. In Figure 29-1, the cycle Chatham-Hyannis-Barnstable-Orleans-Chatham is a simple cycle. A graph that has no cycles is **acyclic.**

You use a road or street map to determine how to get from point A to point B. That is, you find a path from A to B that usually is a simple path. In doing so, you avoid retracing your steps or going around in circles. People who take a ride to view the autumn leaves, however, would follow a cycle that begins and ends at home.

29.3   **Weights.** You might be happy just to get from one place to another, but you often have a choice of several paths. You could choose the shortest, the fastest, or the cheapest path, for example. To do so, you use a **weighted graph,** which has values on its edges. These values are called either **weights** or **costs.** For example, Figure 29-3 shows the road map from Figure 29-1 as a weighted graph. In this version, each weight represents the distance in miles between two towns. Other types of weights you might use could represent the driving time or the cost of traveling by taxi.

A path in a weighted graph also has a weight, or cost, that is the sum of its edge weights. For example, the weight of the path from Provincetown to Orleans in Figure 29-3 is 27.

Figure 29-3   A weighted graph

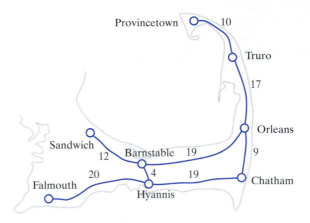

Provincetown   10

Truro

17

Orleans

Sandwich
12   Barnstable   19   9

20   4   19   Chatham

Falmouth
Hyannis

Question 1   Consider the graph in Figure 29-3.

a.   What is the length of the path that begins in Provincetown, passes through Truro and Orleans, and ends in Chatham?

b.   What is the weight of the path just described?

c.   Consider all paths from Truro to Sandwich that do not have cycles. Which path has the shortest length?

d.   Of the paths you considered in Part *c*, which one has the smallest weight?

29.4   **Connected graphs.** The towns on a road map are connected by roads in a way that enables you to go from any town to any other town. That is, you can get from here to there. A graph that has a path between every pair of distinct vertices is **connected.** A **complete graph** goes even further; it has an edge between every pair of distinct vertices. Figure 29-4 provides examples of undirected graphs that are connected, complete, or **disconnected**—that is, not connected. Notice the simple path in Part *a* and the simple cycle in Part *c*.

Figure 29-4   Undirected graphs

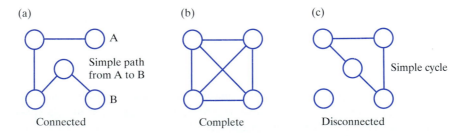

(a)

A

Simple path from A to B

B

Connected

(b)

Complete

(c)

Simple cycle

Disconnected

29.5   **Adjacent vertices.** Two vertices are **adjacent** in an undirected graph if they are joined by an edge. In Figure 29-3, Orleans and Chatham are adjacent, but Orleans and Sandwich are not. We sometimes say that adjacent vertices are **neighbors.** In a directed graph, vertex *i* is adjacent to vertex *j* if a directed edge begins at *j* and ends at *i*. In Figure 29-5, vertex *A* is adjacent to vertex *B*, but vertex *B* is not adjacent to vertex *A*. That is, vertex *A* is vertex *B*'s neighbor, but the converse is not true.

Figure 29-5   Vertex *A* is adjacent to *B*, but *B* is not adjacent to *A*

Airline Routes

29.6   A graph that represents the routes that an airline flies is similar to one that represents a road map. They are different, however, because not every city has an airport, and not every airline flies to or from every airport. For example, the graph in Figure 29-6 shows the flights for a small airline on the East Coast of the United States. The graph is undirected and consists of two **subgraphs** that are each connected. The entire graph, however, is disconnected.

Notice that you can fly from Boston to Provincetown, but not from Boston to Key West. Algorithms exist that make these determinations.

Note: Figure 29-6 contains one graph that consists of two distinct subgraphs. Although each subgraph is connected, the entire graph is disconnected.

Figure 29-6   Airline routes

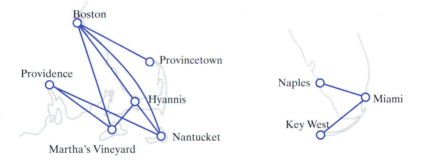

Mazes

29.7   Mazes have been constructed in Victorian English gardens and modern-day cornfields. A typical maze, like the one in Figure 29-7a, has a path from its entrance to its exit. Other paths begin at the entrance, but some lead to dead ends, rather than to the exit. Can you find your way through the maze?

We can represent this maze as a graph by placing a vertex at the entrance and exit, at each turn in the path, and at each dead end, as Figure 29-7b shows. This graph, like the road map in Figure 29-1, is connected. For such graphs, we can determine whether a path exists between any two vertices, as you will see later in this chapter.

Figure 29-7   (a) A maze; (b) its representation as a graph

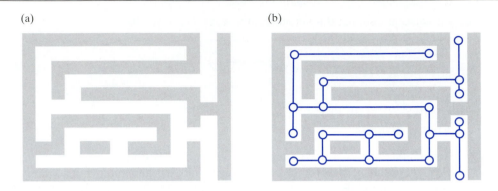

(a)   (b)

Course Prerequisites

29.8   As a college student, you must take a sequence of courses in your major. Each course has certain prerequisite courses that you must complete first. In what order can you take the required courses and satisfy the prerequisites?

To answer this question, we first create a directed graph to represent the courses and their prerequisites. Figure 29-8 is an example of such a graph. Each vertex represents a course, and each directed edge begins at a course that is a prerequisite to another. Notice, for example, that you must complete cs1, cs2, cs4, cs7, cs9, *and* cs5 before you can take cs10.

This graph has no cycles. In a directed graph without cycles, we can arrange the vertices so that vertex *a* precedes vertex *b* whenever a directed edge exists from *a* to *b*. The order of the vertices in this arrangement is called a **topological order.** Later in this chapter, you will see how to discover this order, and so to learn the order in which you should complete your course requirements.

Figure 29-8   The prerequisite structure for a selection of courses as a directed graph without cycles

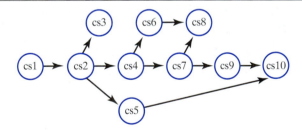

Trees

29.9   The ADT tree is a kind of graph that uses parent-child relationships to organize its nodes in a hierarchical fashion. One particular node, the root, is the ancestor of all other nodes in the tree. But not all graphs have a hierarchical organization, so not all graphs are trees.

 Note: All trees are graphs, but not all graphs are trees. A tree is a connected graph without cycles.

Question 2 What physical systems in a typical house could you represent as a graph?

Question 3 Is the graph in Figure 29-1 connected? Is it complete?

Question 4 Is the graph in Figure 29-8 a tree? Explain.

Question 5 For the graph in Figure 29-8,

       a. Is cs1 adjacent to cs2?   **c.** Is cs1 adjacent to cs4?
       b. Is cs2 adjacent to cs1?   **d.** Is cs4 adjacent to cs1?

Traversals

29.10 As you learned in earlier chapters, you usually search a tree for a node that contains a particular value. Graph applications, however, focus on the connections between vertices, rather than the contents of vertices. These applications often are based on a traversal of the graph's vertices.

    In Chapter 24, we examined several orders in which we could visit the nodes of a tree. The preorder, inorder, and postorder traversals are examples of a **depth-first traversal.** This kind of traversal follows a path that descends the levels of a tree as deeply as possible until it reaches a leaf, as Figure 29-9a shows. More generally, a depth-first traversal of a graph follows a path that goes as deeply into the graph as possible before following other paths.

    The level-order traversal of a tree is an example of a **breadth-first traversal.** It follows a path that explores an entire level before moving to the next level, as Figure 29-9b shows. In a graph, a breadth-first traversal visits all neighbors of a node before visiting the neighbors' neighbors.

Figure 29-9 The visitation order of two traversals: (a) depth first; (b) breadth first

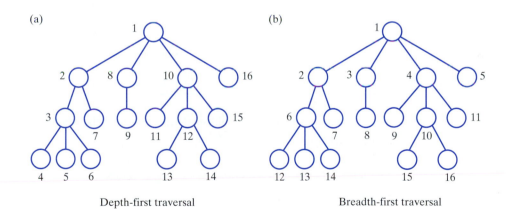

Depth-first traversal   Breadth-first traversal

Note: Visiting a node in either a tree or a graph is an action that we perform during a traversal. In a tree, "visit a node" means to "process the node's data." In a graph, "visit a node" means simply to "mark the node as visited."

    A traversal of a tree visits all of the tree's nodes. However, a graph traversal that begins at a fixed vertex—called the **origin vertex**—visits only the vertices that it can reach. Only when a graph is connected can such a traversal visit all the vertices.

Breadth-First Traversal

29.11   Given an origin vertex, a breadth-first traversal visits the origin and the origin's neighbors. It then considers each of these neighbors and visits their neighbors. The traversal uses a queue to hold the unvisited neighbors of a vertex. When we remove a vertex from this queue, we enqueue the vertex's unvisited neighbors. The traversal order is then the order in which vertices are added to the queue. We can maintain this traversal order in a second queue.

The following algorithm performs a breadth-first traversal of a nonempty graph beginning at a given vertex.

> *Algorithm* `getBreadthFirstTraversal(originVertex)`
> `vertexQueue` = *a new queue to hold neighbors*
> `traversalOrder` = *a new queue for the resulting traversal order*
>
> *Mark* `originVertex` *as visited*
> `traversalOrder.enqueue(originVertex)`
> `vertexQueue.enqueue(originVertex)`
> **while** `(!vertexQueue.isEmpty())`
> {
>   `frontVertex = vertexQueue.dequeue()`
>   **while** `(frontVertex` *has an unvisited neighbor)*
>   {
>   `nextNeighbor` = *next unvisited neighbor of* `frontVertex`
>   *Mark* `nextNeighbor` *as visited*
>   `traversalOrder.enqueue(nextNeighbor)`
>   `vertexQueue.enqueue(nextNeighbor)`
>   }
> }
> **return** `traversalOrder`

Figure 29-10 traces this algorithm for a directed graph. For convenience, we place the vertex labels within the circles that represent the vertices.

Note: Breadth-first traversal

A breadth-first traversal visits a vertex and then each of the vertex's neighbors before advancing.

Question 6   In what order does a breadth-first traversal visit the vertices in the graph in Figure 29-10a when you begin at vertex *E*?

Figure 29-10 A trace of a breadth-first traversal for a directed graph, beginning at vertex *A*

(a)

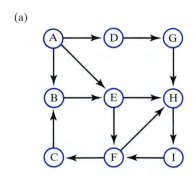

Figure 29-10 A trace of a breadth-first traversal for a directed graph, beginning at vertex *A* **(CONTINUED)**

(b)

frontVertex	nextNeighbor	Visited vertex	vertexQueue (front to back)	traversalOrder (front to back)
		A	A	A
A			*empty*	
	B	B	B	AB
	D	D	BD	ABD
	E	E	BDE	ABDE
B			DE	
D			E	
	G	G	EG	ABDEG
E			G	
	F	F	GF	ABDEGF
	H	H	GFH	ABDEGFH
G			FH	
F			H	
	C	C	HC	ABDEGFHC
H			C	
	I	I	CI	ABDEGFHCI
C			I	
I			*empty*	

Depth-First Traversal

29.12   Given an origin vertex, a depth-first traversal visits the origin, then a neighbor of the origin, and a neighbor of the neighbor. It continues in this fashion until it finds no unvisited neighbor. Backing up by one vertex, it considers another neighbor. This traversal has a recursive feel, since traversing from the origin leads to a traversal from the origin's neighbor. It should not surprise you, then, that we use a stack in the iterative description of this traversal.

Note: Depth-first traversal
A depth-first traversal visits a vertex, then a neighbor of the vertex, a neighbor of the neighbor, and so on, advancing as far as possible from the original vertex. It then backs up by one vertex and considers another neighbor.

We begin by pushing the origin vertex into the stack. When the vertex at the top of the stack has an unvisited neighbor, we push that neighbor onto the stack. If no such neighbor exists, we pop the stack. The traversal order is the order in which vertices are added to the stack. We can maintain this traversal order in a queue.

The following algorithm performs a depth-first traversal of a nonempty graph beginning at a given vertex:

Algorithm `getDepthFirstTraversal(originVertex)`
`vertexStack` = *a new stack to hold vertices as they are visited*
`traversalOrder` = *a new queue for the resulting traversal order*

Mark `originVertex` *as visited*
`traversalOrder.enqueue(originVertex)`
`vertexStack.push(originVertex)`

```
while (!vertexStack.isEmpty())
{
    topVertex = vertexStack.peek()

    if (topVertex has an unvisited neighbor)
    {
        nextNeighbor = next unvisited neighbor of topVertex
        Mark nextNeighbor as visited
        traversalOrder.enqueue(nextNeighbor)
        vertexStack.push(nextNeighbor)
    }
    else // all neighbors are visited
        vertexStack.pop()
}
return traversalOrder
```

Figure 29-11 traces this algorithm for the directed graph given in Figure 29-10a.

Question 7   In what order does a depth-first traversal visit the vertices in the graph in Figure 29-10a when you begin at vertex *E*?

Figure 29-11   A trace of a depth-first traversal beginning at vertex *A* of the directed graph in Figure 29-10a

topVertex	nextNeighbor	Visited vertex	vertexStack (top to bottom)	traversalOrder (front to back)
		A	A	A
A			A	
	B	B	BA	AB
B			BA	
	E	E	EBA	ABE
E			EBA	
	F	F	FEBA	ABEF
F			FEBA	
	C	C	CFEBA	ABEFC
C			FEBA	
F			FEBA	
	H	H	HFEBA	ABEFCH
H			HFEBA	
	I	I	IHFEBA	ABEFCHI
I			HFEBA	
H			FEBA	
F			EBA	
E			BA	
B			A	
A			A	
	D	D	DA	ABEFCHID
D			DA	
	G	G	GDA	ABEFCHIDG
G			DA	
D			A	
A			*empty*	ABEFCHIDG

Topological Order

29.13   Figure 29-8 shows a graph that represents the prerequisite structure of a group of computer science courses. This graph is a directed graph without cycles. Recall that you can place the vertices in such a graph in a topological order.

Note: In a topological order of the vertices in a directed graph without cycles, vertex a precedes vertex b whenever a directed edge exists from a to b.

A graph can have several different topological orders. For example, one such order for the graph in Figure 29-8 is cs1, cs2, cs5, cs4, cs7, cs9, cs10, cs6, cs8, cs3. That is, if you complete the courses in this order, you will satisfy all prerequisites. Suppose that you can move the vertices in the graph so that they align in this order, stretching the edges as needed. The result will be like the graph in Figure 29-12a. Notice that each edge points toward a node that comes after it. You will be able to find at least one such arrangement for every directed graph, if the graph has no cycles. Figure 29-12 shows two other topological orders for this graph. As is true for this example, any one topological order is usually sufficient to solve a given problem.

Figure 29-12   Three topological orders for the graph in Figure 29-8

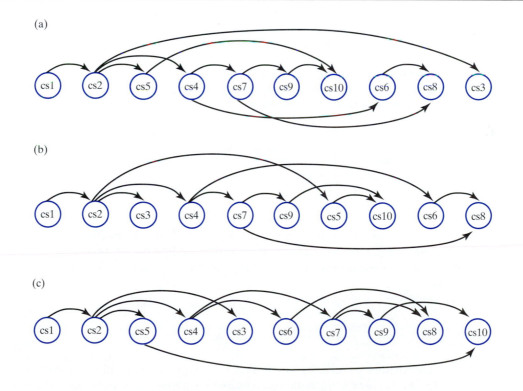

A topological order is not possible for a graph that has a cycle. If vertices a and b are on the cycle, a path exists from a to b and from b to a. One of these paths will contradict any order that we choose for *a* and *b*. For example, the graph in Figure 29-13 contains a cycle. You need to complete cs15 and cs20 before taking cs30. But you need to complete cs30 before taking cs20. This circular logic is caused by the cycle and creates an impossible situation.

Figure 29-13 An impossible prerequisite structure for three courses, as a directed graph with a cycle

Question 8   What is another topological order for the graph in Figure 29-8?

29.14   The process that discovers a graph's topological order is called a **topological sort.** Several algorithms for this process are possible. We can begin a topological sort by locating a vertex that has no successor, that is, no adjacent vertex. Finding this vertex is possible because the graph has no cycles. We mark the vertex as visited and push it onto a stack. We continue by finding another vertex *u* that is unvisited and whose neighbors, if any, are visited. We mark *u* as visited and push it onto the stack. We proceed in this way until we have visited all the vertices. At that time, the stack contains the vertices in topological order, beginning at the top of the stack.

The following algorithm describes this topological sort:

Algorithm `getTopologicalSort()`
vertexStack = *a new stack to hold vertices as they are visited*
n = *number of vertices in the graph*
for (counter = 1 *to* n)
{
   nextVertex = *an unvisited vertex whose neighbors, if any, are all visited*
   Mark nextVertex *as visited*
   stack.push(nextVertex)
}
return stack

Figure 29-14 traces this algorithm for the graph in Figure 29-8. At each iteration of the algorithm's loop, `nextVertex` becomes shaded in the figure. The topological order is the opposite of the order in which this occurs. In this example, the topological order is the one pictured in Figure 29-12a.

Paths

Learning whether a particular airline flies between two given cities is important to the average traveler. We can obtain this information by using a graph—such as the one in Figure 29-6—to represent the airline's routes and testing whether a path exists from vertex *a* to vertex *b*. If a path exists, we can also find out what it is. If not any path will do, we can find the one that is shortest or cheapest.

Figure 29-14 Finding a topological order for the graph in Figure 29-8

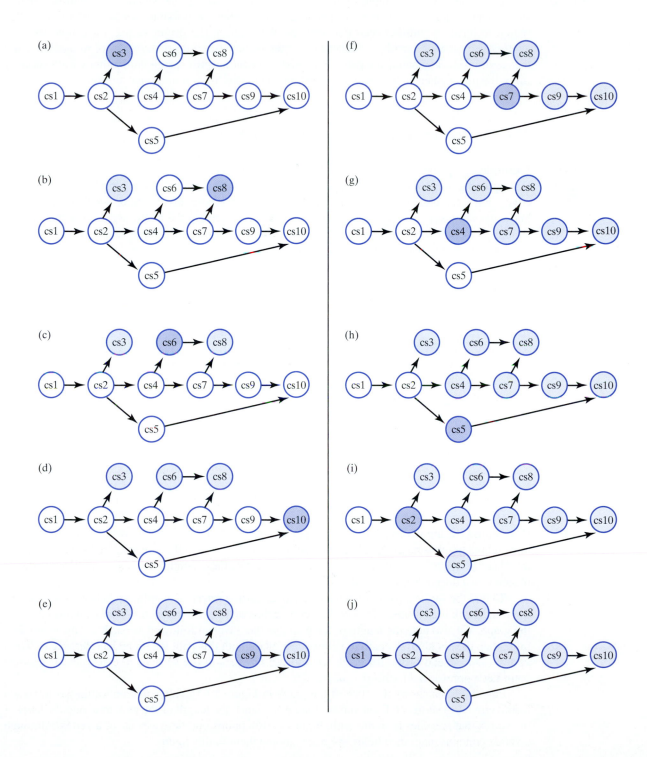

Finding a Path

29.15 For the moment we are content to find any path, not necessarily the best one. A depth-first search stays on a path through the graph as it visits as many vertices as possible. We can easily modify this search to locate a path between two vertices. We begin at the origin vertex. Each time we visit another vertex, we determine whether that vertex is the desired destination. If so, we are done and the resulting stack contains the path. Otherwise, we continue our search until either we are successful or the traversal ends. We leave the development of this algorithm as an exercise.

The Shortest Path in an Unweighted Graph

29.16 **Example.** A graph can have several different paths between the same two vertices. In an unweighted graph, we can find the path with the shortest length, that is, the path that has the fewest edges. For example, consider the unweighted graph in Figure 29-15a. Suppose that we want to know the shortest path from vertex *A* to vertex *H*. By inspecting the graph, we can see that several simple paths—shown in Part *b* of the figure—are possible between these two vertices. The path from *A* to *E* to *H* has length 2 and is the shortest.

Figure 29-15 (a) An unweighted graph and (b) the possible paths from vertex *A* to vertex *H*

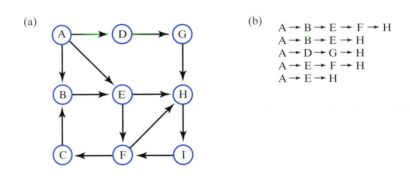

29.17 **Developing the algorithm.** The algorithm to find the shortest path between two given vertices in an unweighted graph is based on a breadth-first traversal. Recall that this traversal visits the origin vertex, then the origin's neighbors, the neighbors of each of these neighbors, and so on. Each vertex is placed into a queue as it is visited.

To find the shortest path, we enhance the breadth-first traversal as follows. When we visit a vertex *v* and mark it as visited, we note the vertex *p* that we just left to reach *v*. That is, *p* precedes *v* in the graph. We also note the length of the path that the traversal followed to reach *v*. This length is 1 more than the length of the path to vertex *p*. We place both this path length and a reference to *p* into vertex *v*. At the end of the traversal, we will use this data in the vertices to construct the shortest path. Let's jump ahead to this part of the algorithm.

Figure 29-16a shows the state of the graph in Figure 29-15a after the algorithm has traversed from vertex *A* to vertex *H*. Each vertex contains its label, the length of the path to it, and the label of the vertex that precedes it on this path. Figure 29-16b points out these aspects of a vertex. Although a vertex contains other data fields, we have ignored them in this figure.

Figure 29-16 The graph in Figure 29-15a after the shortest-path algorithm has traversed from vertex *A* to vertex *H*

(a)

(b)

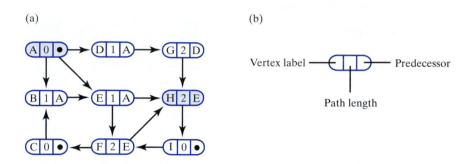

Vertex label ——— ⊂ ▯ ⊃ ——— Predecessor

Path length

Now, by examining the destination vertex—*H*—we determine that its predecessor along the shortest path is vertex *E*. From vertex *E* we find that its predecessor is vertex *A*. Thus, the desired shortest path from vertex *A* to vertex *H* is *A* → *E* → *H*. Our algorithm has discovered what we of course knew to be true by inspecting this simple graph.

Note: In an unweighted graph, the shortest path between two given vertices has the shortest length—that is, it has the fewest edges. The algorithm to find this path is based on a breadth-first traversal. If several paths have the same shortest length, the algorithm will find only one of them.

29.18   The pseudocode for the algorithm is as follows:

Algorithm getShortestPath(originVertex, endVertex)
done = **false**
vertexQueue = *a new queue to hold neighbors*
Mark originVertex *as visited*
vertexQueue.enqueue(originVertex)

while (!done && !vertexQueue.isEmpty())
{
  frontVertex = vertexQueue.dequeue()

  while (!done && frontVertex *has an unvisited neighbor*)
  {
    nextNeighbor = *next unvisited neighbor of* frontVertex
    Mark nextNeighbor *as visited*
    Set the length of the path to nextNeighbor *to 1 + length of path to* frontVertex
    Set the predecessor of nextNeighbor *to* frontVertex
    vertexQueue.enqueue(nextNeighbor)

    if (nextNeighbor *equals* endVertex)
      done = **true**
  }
}

// traversal ends - construct shortest path
path = *a new stack of vertices*

```
        path.push(endVertex)
        while (endVertex has a predecessor)
        {
            endVertex = predecessor of endVertex
            path.push(endVertex)
        }
        return path
```

29.19   Tracing the algorithm. Figure 29-17 traces the steps that the algorithm takes to produce the path information shown in Figure 29-16a. After adding the origin—vertex A—to the queue, we enqueue the origin's three neighbors. Notice that the path length for these neighbors is 1. Since vertex A has no more neighbors, we remove vertex B from the queue. This vertex has vertex E as a neighbor, but E has been visited already. This implies that we can get to E from A without first going through B. That is, B is not on any shortest path that begins at A and goes through E. Indeed, the path $A \rightarrow B \rightarrow E$ is longer than the path $A \rightarrow E$. We do not know whether our final path involves E, but if it does, it will not pass through B.

The algorithm now removes vertex D from the queue. Its neighbor G is unvisited, so we set G's path-length field to 2 and its predecessor to D. We then enqueue G. The algorithm continues in this manner and eventually encounters the destination vertex, H. After H is updated, the outer loop ends. We then construct the path by working back from H, as we did earlier in Segment 29.17.

Figure 29-17   Finding the shortest path from vertex A to vertex H in the unweighted graph in Figure 29-15a

frontVertex	nextNeighbor	Visited vertex	vertexQueue (front to back)
		A	(A│0│●)
(A│0│●)			empty
	B	B	(B│1│A)
	D	D	(B│1│A) (D│1│A)
	E	E	(B│1│A) (D│1│A) (E│1│A)
(B│1│A)			(D│1│A) (E│1│A)
(D│1│A)			(E│1│A)
	G	G	(E│1│A) (G│2│D)
(E│1│A)			(G│2│D)
	F	F	(G│2│D) (F│2│E)
	H	H	(G│2│D) (F│2│E) (H│2│E)

Question 9   What is the shortest path from vertex A to vertex C in the graph in Figure 29-15a? *Hint*: Continue the trace begun in Figure 29-17.

The Shortest Path in a Weighted Graph

29.20

Example. In a weighted graph, the shortest path is not necessarily the one with the fewest edges. Rather, it is the one with the smallest edge-weight sum. Figure 29-18a shows a weighted graph obtained by adding weights to the graph in Figure 29-15a. The possible paths from vertex *A* to vertex *H* are the same as you saw in Figure 29-15b. This time, we list each path with its weight—that is, the sum of the weights of its edges—in Figure 29-18b.

We can see that the smallest path weight is 8, so the shortest path is $A \to D \to G \to H$. When the weights are distances, the term "shortest" is appropriate. When the weights represent costs, we might think of this path as the "cheapest" path.

Figure 29-18 (a) A weighted graph and (b) the possible paths from vertex *A* to vertex *H*

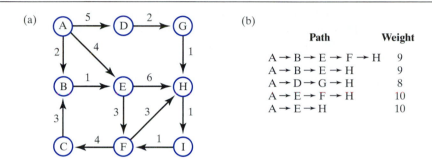

Path	Weight
A → B → E → F → H	9
A → B → E → H	9
A → D → G → H	8
A → E → F → H	10
A → E → H	10

29.21   **The algorithm.** The algorithm to find the shortest, or cheapest, path between two given vertices in a weighted graph is based on a breadth-first traversal. It is similar to the algorithm we developed for an unweighted graph. In that algorithm, we noted the number of edges in the path that led to the vertex under consideration. Here, we compute the sum of the edge weights in the path leading to a vertex. In addition, we must record the cheapest of the possible paths. Whereas before we used a queue to order vertices, this algorithm uses a priority queue.

Note: In a weighted graph, the shortest path between two given vertices has the smallest edge-weight sum. The algorithm to find this path is based on a breadth-first traversal. Several paths in a weighted graph might share the same minimum edge-weight sum. Our algorithm will find only one of these paths.

Each entry in the priority queue is an object that contains a vertex, the cost of the path to that vertex from the origin vertex, and the previous vertex on that path. The priority value is the cost of the path, with the smallest value having the highest priority. Thus, the cheapest path is at the front of the priority queue, and it is thus the first one removed.

At the conclusion of the algorithm, the vertices in the graph contain predecessors and weights that enable us to construct the cheapest path, much as we constructed the path with the fewest edges from Figure 29-16a.

Figure 29-19 traces the steps that the algorithm takes when vertex *A* is the origin. Initially, an object containing *A*, zero, and null is placed in the priority queue. We begin a cycle in the algorithm by removing the front entry from the priority queue. We use the contents of this entry to change the state of the indicated vertex—*A* in this case—in the graph. We mark *A* as visited.

Vertex *A* has three unvisited neighbors, *B*, *D*, and *E*. The cost of the paths from *A* to each of these neighbors is 2, 5, and 4, respectively. These costs, along with *A* as the previous vertex, are used to create objects that are placed into the priority queue. Notice how the priority queue orders these objects so that the cheapest path is first.

We remove the front entry from the priority queue. The entry contains B, so we visit vertex B and record the path length 2 and its predecessor A within the vertex. Now B has vertex E as its sole unvisited neighbor. The cost of the path $A \rightarrow B \rightarrow E$ is the cost of the path $A \rightarrow B$ plus the weight of the edge from B to E. This total cost is 3. We encapsulate E, the cost 3, and the predecessor B into an object that we place into the priority queue. Notice that two objects in the priority queue involve vertex E, but the most recent one has the cheapest path.

We again remove the front entry from the priority queue. Now we visit vertex E and record the path length 3 and its predecessor B. Vertex E has two unvisited neighbors, F and H. The cost of the paths to these neighbors is the cost of the path to E plus the weight of the edge to the neighbor. Two new objects are added to the priority queue.

The next object removed from the priority queue represents the vertex E, but since E has been visited, we ignore it. We then remove the next object from the priority queue. The algorithm continues until the destination vertex H is visited.

Figure 29-19 Finding the cheapest path from vertex A to vertex H in the weighted graph in Figure 29-18a

frontEntry	Visited vertex	nextNeighbor	Priority queue (front to back)
			(A|0|•)
(A|0|•)	A		*empty*
		B	(B|2|A)
		D	(B|2|A) (D|5|A)
		E	(B|2|A) (E|4|A) (D|5|A)
(B|2|A)	B		(E|4|A) (D|5|A)
		E	(E|3|B) (E|4|A) (D|5|A)
(E|3|B)	E		(E|4|A) (D|5|A)
		F	(E|4|A) (D|5|A) (F|6|E)
		H	(E|4|A) (D|5|A) (F|6|E) (H|9|E)
(E|4|A)			(D|5|A) (F|6|E) (H|9|E)
(D|5|A)	D		(F|6|E) (H|9|E)
		G	(F|6|E) (G|7|D) (H|9|E)
(F|6|E)	F		(G|7|D) (H|9|E)
		H	(G|7|D) (H|9|E) (H|9|F)
		C	(G|7|D) (H|9|E) (H|9|F) (C|10|F)
(G|7|D)	G		(H|9|E) (H|9|F) (C|10|F)
		H	(H|8|G) (H|9|E) (H|9|F) (C|10|F)
(H|8|G)	H		(H|9|E) (H|9|F) (C|10|F)

29.22   Figure 29-20 shows the state of the graph at the conclusion of the trace given in Figure 29-19. By looking at the destination vertex *H*, we can see that the weight of the cheapest path from *A* to *H* is 8. Tracing back from *H* to *A*, we see that this path is $A \rightarrow D \rightarrow G \rightarrow H$, as we noted in Segment 29.20.

Figure 29-20 The graph in Figure 29-18a after finding the cheapest path from vertex *A* to vertex *H*

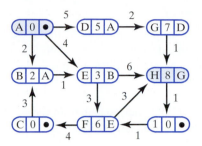

29.23   **Pseudocode.** The pseudocode for the algorithm we just described follows. We assume that objects for the priority queue are instances of a class `PathEntry`.

```
Algorithm getCheapestPath(originVertex, endVertex)
done = false
vertexQueue = a new priority queue

vertexQueue.add(new PathEntry(originVertex, 0, null))

while (!done && !vertexQueue.isEmpty())
{
    frontEntry = vertexQueue.remove()
    frontVertex = vertex in frontEntry

    if (frontVertex is unvisited)
    {
        Mark frontVertex as visited
        Set cost of path to frontVertex to cost in frontEntry
        Set the predecessor of frontVertex to the predecessor in frontEntry

        if (frontVertex equals endVertex)
            done = true
        else
        {
            while (frontVertex has an unvisited neighbor)
            {
                nextNeighbor = next unvisited neighbor of frontVertex
                edgeWeight = weight of edge to nextNeighbor
                nextCost = edgeWeight + cost of path to frontVertex
                vertexQueue.add(new PathEntry(nextNeighbor, nextCost,
                                              frontVertex))
            }
        }
    }
}
```

```
// traversal ends; construct cheapest path
path = a new stack of vertices
path.push(endVertex)
while (endVertex has a predecessor)
{
  endVertex = predecessor of endVertex
  path.push(endVertex)
}
return path
```

The origin of the cheapest path will be at the top of the stack that `getCheapestPath` returns. At the bottom of the stack is the destination vertex. The cost of the path is in this vertex.

This algorithm is based on Dijkstra's algorithm, which finds the shortest paths from an origin to all other vertices.

Question 10   What is the shortest path from vertex *A* to vertex *C* in the graph in Figure 29-18a? *Hint*: Continue the trace begun in Figure 29-19.

Java Interfaces for the ADT Graph

29.24   The ADT graph is a bit different from other ADTs in that you usually do not alter it once you have created it. Instead, you use it to answer questions based on the relationships among its vertices. Therefore, we divide the graph operations into two Java interfaces. The operations in the first interface create the graph and report basic information such as the number of vertices. The second interface specifies operations such as the traversals and path searches that we discussed earlier in this chapter. For convenience, we define a third interface, `GraphInterface`, that combines the first two interfaces.

To make these interfaces as general as possible, we have them specify graphs that are either directed or undirected, and weighted or unweighted. The first interface appears as follows:

```java
public interface BasicGraphInterface
{
  /** Task: Adds a given vertex to the graph.
   *  @param vertexLabel  an object that labels the new vertex */
  public void addVertex(Object vertexLabel);

  /** Task: Adds an edge between two given vertices that are already
   *        in the graph. In a directed graph, the edge begins at the
   *        first vertex given.
   *  @param begin  an object that labels the origin vertex of the edge
   *  @param end    an object that labels the end vertex of the edge
   *  @param edgeWeight  the real value of the edge's weight, if any */
  public void addEdge(Object begin, Object end);
  public void addEdge(Object begin, Object end, double edgeWeight);

  /** Task: Determines whether an edge exists between two given
   *        vertices.
   *  @param begin  an object that labels the origin vertex of the edge
   *  @param end    an object that labels the end vertex of the edge
   *  @return true if an edge exists */
  public boolean hasEdge(Object begin, Object end);
```

```
/** Task: Determines whether the graph is empty.
 *   @return true if the graph is empty */
public boolean isEmpty();

/** Task: Gets the number of vertices in the graph.
 *   @return the number of vertices in the graph */
public int getNumberOfVertices();

/** Task: Gets the number of edges in the graph.
 *   @return the number of edges in the graph */
public int getNumberOfEdges();

/** Task: Removes all vertices and edges from the graph. */
public void clear();
} // end BasicGraphInterface
```

29.25

Example. The following statements create the graph shown in Figure 29-21, which is a portion of the graph in Figure 29-6:

```
BasicGraphInterface airRoutes = new UndirectedGraph();
airRoutes.addVertex("Boston");
airRoutes.addVertex("Provincetown");
airRoutes.addVertex("Nantucket");
airRoutes.addEdge("Boston", "Provincetown");
airRoutes.addEdge("Boston", "Nantucket");
```

At this point,

```
airRoutes.getNumberOfVertices()
```

returns 3, and

```
airRoutes.getNumberOfEdges()
```

returns 2.

Question 11   What revisions to the previous Java statements are necessary to make air-Routes a weighted graph?

Figure 29-21 A portion of the flight map in Figure 29-6

29.26   If you look closely at the algorithms discussed earlier in this chapter, you will see many operations on a graph that are not specified in the previous interface. Although we could make these operations public so the client could implement various algorithms, such as the topological sort, we choose not to do so. Instead, the methods that implement the graph algorithms will be a part of the graph class. The following interface specifies these methods:

```java
public interface GraphAlgorithmsInterface
{
  /** Task: Performs a depth-first traversal of a graph.
   *  @param origin  an object that labels the origin vertex of the
   *                 traversal
   *  @return a queue of labels of the vertices in the traversal, with
   *          the label of the origin vertex at the queue's front */
  public QueueInterface getDepthFirstTraversal(Object origin);

  /** Task: Performs a breadth-first traversal of a graph.
   *  @param origin  an object that labels the origin vertex of the
   *                 traversal
   *  @return a queue of labels of the vertices in the traversal, with
   *          the label of the origin vertex at the queue's front */
  public QueueInterface getBreadthFirstTraversal(Object origin);

  /** Task: Performs a topological sort of the vertices in a graph
   *        without cycles.
   *  @return a stack of vertex labels in topological order, beginning
   *          with the stack's top */
  public StackInterface getTopologicalSort();

  /** Task: Finds the path between two given vertices that has the
   *        shortest length.
   *  @param begin  an object that labels the path's origin vertex
   *  @param end    an object that labels the path's destination vertex
   *  @return a stack of labels of the vertices along the path, with
   *          the label of the origin vertex at the top and
   *          the label of the destination at the bottom */
  public StackInterface getShortestPath(Object begin, Object end);

  /** Task: Finds the path between two given vertices that has the
   *        least cost.
   *  @param begin  an object that labels the path's origin vertex
   *  @param end    an object that labels the path's destination vertex
   *  @return a stack of labels of the vertices along the path, with
   *          the label of the origin vertex at the top and
   *          the label of the destination at the bottom */
  public StackInterface getCheapestPath(Object begin, Object end);
} // end GraphAlgorithmsInterface
```

The following interface combines BasicGraphInterface and GraphAlgorithmsInterface:

```java
public interface GraphInterface extends BasicGraphInterface,
                                        GraphAlgorithmsInterface
{ }
```

29.27

Example. Imagine that we want to find the shortest route between the towns of Truro and Falmouth. By "shortest route" we mean the route with the least number of miles, not the path with the fewest edges. We first could create the graph in Figure 29-3, much as we created a graph in Segment 29.25. We then could use the method `getCheapestPath` to answer our question. The following statements indicate how to perform these steps and to display the names of the cities along the shortest route:

```
GraphInterface roadMap = new UndirectedGraph();
roadMap.addVertex("Provincetown");
roadMap.addVertex("Truro");
. . .
roadMap.addVertex("Falmouth");
roadMap.addEdge("Provincetown", "Truro", 10);
. . .
roadMap.addEdge("Hyannis", "Falmouth", 20);
StackInterface bestRoute = roadMap.getCheapestPath("Truro", "Falmouth");
while (!bestRoute.isEmpty())
    System.out.println(bestRoute.pop());
```

Note: The operations of the ADT graph enable you to create a graph and answer questions based on the relationships among its vertices.

Question 12   The previous example finds the shortest route between two towns. Why did we invoke the method `getCheapestPath` instead of `getShortestPath`?

CHAPTER SUMMARY

- A graph is a collection of distinct vertices and distinct edges. A subgraph is a portion of a graph that is itself a graph.

- A tree is a special graph that has a hierarchical order and a root that is the ancestor of all other nodes in tree.

- Each edge in a directed graph has a direction from one vertex to another. The edges in an undirected graph are bidirectional.

- A path is a sequence of edges that connect two vertices. The length of the path is the number of these edges. A simple path passes through a vertex once. A cycle is a path that begins and ends at the same vertex. A simple cycle passes through its other vertices once.

- The edges in a weighted graph have values called weights or costs. A path in a weighted graph has a weight, or cost, that is the sum of its edge weights.

- A graph that has a path between every pair of distinct vertices is connected. A complete graph has an edge between every pair of distinct vertices.

- Two vertices in an undirected graph are adjacent if they are joined by an edge. In a directed graph, vertex *i* is adjacent to vertex *j* if a directed edge begins at *j* and ends at *i*. Adjacent vertices are called neighbors.

- You can traverse the vertices in a graph by using either a depth-first traversal or a breadth-first traversal. A depth-first traversal follows a path that goes as deeply into the graph as possible before following other paths. A breadth-first traversal visits all neighbors of a vertex before visiting the neighbors' neighbors.

- A directed graph without cycles imposes an order on its vertices called a topological order. This order is not unique. You use a topological sort to discover these orders.

- You can use a depth-first traversal to determine whether a path exists between two given vertices of a graph.

- You can modify the breadth-first traversal to find the path that joins one vertex to another and has the fewest edges.

- You can modify the breadth-first traversal to determine the path that joins one vertex to another in a weighted graph and has the lowest cost.

EXERCISES

1. Suppose that five vertices are arranged at the corners of a pentagon. Draw a connected graph that contains these vertices.

2. Describe each graph in Figure 29-22, using the terms introduced in Segments 29.1 through 29.4.

Figure 29-22 Graphs for Exercise 2

(a)   (b)   (c)

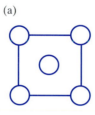   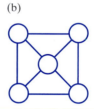   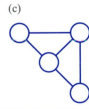

3. In what order does a breadth-first traversal visit the vertices in the graph in Figure 29-10a when you begin at

   a. Vertex *G*
   b. Vertex *F*

4. In what order does a depth-first traversal visit the vertices in the graph in Figure 29-10a when you begin at

   a. Vertex *G*
   b. Vertex *F*

5. Consider the directed graph in Figure 29-10a and remove the edges between vertices *E* and *F*, and vertices *F* and *H*.

   a. In what order will a breadth-first traversal visit the vertices when you begin at vertex *A*?
   b. Repeat Part *a*, but perform a depth-first traversal instead.

6. Draw a directed graph that depicts the prerequisite structure of the courses required for your major. Find a topological order for these courses.

7. A computer network such as the World Wide Web or a local area network can be represented as a graph. Each computer is a node (vertex) in the graph. An edge between two vertices represents a direct connection between two computers. Explain when and why you would be interested in each of the following tasks:

   a. Finding a path in this graph
   b. Finding multiple paths from one particular vertex to another
   c. Finding the shortest path from one particular vertex to another
   d. Determining whether the graph is connected

8. Write an algorithm that finds a path from vertex *a* to vertex *b* in a directed graph by using a slightly modified depth-first traversal. Segment 29.15 outlines an approach to this problem.

9. A tree is a connected graph without cycles.

   a. What is the smallest number of edges that could be removed from the graph of Figure 29-1 to make it a tree?
   b. Give one example of such a set of edges.

10. Figure 29-7b shows a graph that represents a maze. Label the vertices of this graph, with the uppermost vertex labeled *s* (the entrance to the maze) and the lowest vertex labeled *t* (the exit from the maze).

   a. Is this graph a tree?
   b. What is the shortest path from *s* to *t*?
   c. What is the longest simple path in this graph?

11. Revise the unweighted, directed graph in Figure 29-15a by adding a directed edge from *D* to *H*. The resulting graph has two paths from *A* to *H* that are shortest among all paths between these two vertices. Which of these two paths will the algorithm in Segment 29.18 find?

12. Revise the unweighted, directed graph in Figure 29-15a by removing the directed edge from *E* to *H*. The resulting graph has two paths from *A* to *H* that are shortest among all paths between these two vertices. Which of these two paths will the algorithm in Segment 29.18 find?

13. Revise the weighted, directed graph in Figure 29-18a by adding a directed edge from *D* to *H*. Let the weight of this new edge be 3. The resulting graph has two paths from *A* to *H* that are cheapest among all paths between these two vertices. Which of these two paths will the algorithm in Segment 29.23 find?

14. Find a map of the routes of a major U. S. airline. Such maps are usually printed at the back of in-flight magazines. You could also search the Internet for one. The map is a graph like the one in Figure 29-6. Consider the following pairs of cities:

   Providence (RI) and San Diego (CA)
   Albany (NY) and Phoenix (AZ)
   Boston (MA) and Baltimore (MD)
   Dallas (TX) and Detroit (MI)
   Charlotte (NC) and Chicago (IL)
   Portland (ME) and Portland (OR)

a. Which pairs of cities in this list have edges (nonstop flights) between them?

b. Which pairs are not connected by any path?

c. For each of the remaining pairs, find the path with the fewest edges.

15. Find the trail map of a cross-country ski center. Represent the trail map as an undirected graph, where each intersection of trails is a vertex, and each section of trail between intersections is an edge. Consider a cross-country skier who wishes to take the longest tour possible, but does not want to ski on any trail more than once. What is the longest path that starts and ends at the ski center and does not traverse any section of trail more than once? (Intersections may be passed through more than once, and some sections of trail may be left unskied.)

16. Find the trail map of a downhill ski center. Represent the trail map as a graph, where each intersection of trails is a vertex, and each section of trail between intersections is an edge.

a. Is the graph directed or undirected?

b. Does the graph have cycles?

c. Find the longest path possible that begins at the top of the mountain and ends at the ski center.

17. Write statements appropriate for the client of the class `UndirectedGraph` that create the graph in Figure 29-3. Assume that `UndirectedGraph` implements `GraphInterface`.

18. Write statements appropriate for the client of the class `DirectedGraph` that create the graph in Figure 29-8. Assume that `DirectedGraph` implements `GraphInterface`. Then write statements to find and display a topological order for this graph.

PROJECTS

1. In a search tree, it is easy to search for any value. For other trees in which the children of a node are not ordered in any particular way, you can use a breadth-first search, as described for graphs, to find a path from the root to some other node (vertex) *v*. Implement such a method for a general tree.

2. Write Java code that creates the graph given in Figure 29-1. Find the shortest path from Sandwich to Falmouth. Do the same for the weighted graph in Figure 29-3. (See Exercise 17.)

3. Write Java code that creates the graph in Figure 29-10a. Perform a breadth-first traversal of the graph beginning at the node labeled *A*.

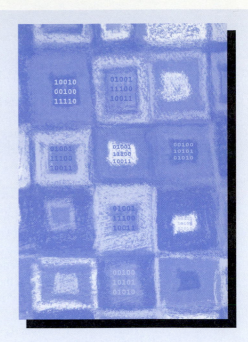

CONTENTS

An Overview of Two Implementations
    The Adjacency Matrix
    The Adjacency List
Vertices and Edges
    Specifying the Class **Vertex**
    The Class **Edge**
    Implementing the Class **Vertex**
An Implementation of the ADT Graph
    Basic Operations
    Graph Algorithms

PREREQUISITES

Chapter   4   Lists
Chapter 17   Dictionaries
Chapter 24   Trees
Chapter 29   Graphs

OBJECTIVES

After studying this chapter, you should be able to

- Describe an adjacency matrix
- Describe an adjacency list
- Specify and implement the classes that represent the vertices and edges of a graph
- Implement the ADT graph by using an adjacency list

Like the ADTs you have seen previously, graphs have several implementations. Each implementation must represent the vertices in the graph and the edges between the vertices. In general, you use either a list or a dictionary to hold the vertices, and an array or a list to represent the edges. Each representation of the edges has its own advantage, but the list representation is most typical.

An Overview of Two Implementations

Two common implementations of the ADT graph use either an array or a list to represent the graph's edges. The array is typically a two-dimensional array called an **adjacency matrix.** The list is called an **adjacency list.** Each of these constructs represents the connections—that is, the edges—among the vertices in the graph.

The Adjacency Matrix

30.1   The adjacency matrix for a graph of n vertices has n rows and n columns. Each row and each column corresponds to a vertex in the graph. You number the vertices from 0 through $n - 1$ to match the row indices and the column indices. If a_{ij} is the element in row i and column j of the matrix, a_{ij} indicates whether an edge exists between vertex i and vertex j. For an unweighted graph, you can use boolean values in the matrix. For a weighted graph, you can use edge weights when edges exist and a representation of infinity otherwise.

Figure 30-1 provides an example of an unweighted, directed graph and its adjacency matrix. Let's consider vertex A, which we have numbered as vertex 0. Since directed edges exist from vertex A to each of the vertices B, D, and E, the matrix elements a_{01}, a_{03}, and a_{04} are true. We have used a "T" in the figure to represent true. The other entries in the first row are false (blank in the figure).

Although a directed edge exists from vertex A to vertex B, the converse is not true. Therefore, a_{10} is false, even though a_{01} is true. The adjacency matrix for an undirected graph, however, is **symmetric;** that is, a_{ij} and a_{ji} have the same value.

Figure 30-1   (a) A directed graph and (b) its adjacency matrix

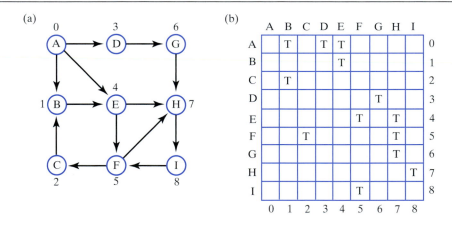

	A	B	C	D	E	F	G	H	I	
A		T		T	T					0
B					T					1
C		T								2
D							T			3
E						T		T		4
F			T					T		5
G								T		6
H									T	7
I						T				8
	0	1	2	3	4	5	6	7	8	

30.2   From an adjacency matrix, you quickly determine whether an edge exists between any two given vertices. But if you want to know all the neighbors of a particular vertex, you need to scan an entire row of the matrix. Additionally, the matrix occupies a considerable, fixed amount of space that depends on the number of vertices but not on the number of edges. In fact, an adjacency matrix represents every possible edge in a graph, regardless of whether the edges actually exist. However, most graphs have relatively few of the many edges possible—that is, they are **sparse.** For such graphs, an adjacency list uses less space, as you will now see.

Note: An adjacency matrix uses a fixed amount of space that depends on the number of vertices, but not the number of edges, in a graph. The adjacency matrix for a typical graph is

sparse, because the graph has relatively few edges. Using an adjacency matrix, you quickly can determine whether an edge exists between any two given vertices. But if you want to know all the neighbors of a particular vertex, you need to scan an entire row of the matrix.

Question 1   Consider the graph in Figure 29-4b of the previous chapter. Number the vertices from 0 through 3, starting at the vertex in the upper left corner and moving in a clockwise direction. What adjacency matrix represents this graph?

The Adjacency List

30.3   An adjacency list for a given vertex represents only those edges that originate from the vertex. In Figure 30-2, each vertex of the graph in Figure 30-1a references a list of adjacent vertices. Space is not reserved for edges that do not exist. Thus, the adjacency lists, taken together, use less memory in general than a corresponding adjacency matrix. For this reason, typical graph implementations use adjacency lists. The implementation that we present in this chapter will do so also.

Figure 30-2   Adjacency lists for the directed graph in Figure 30-1a

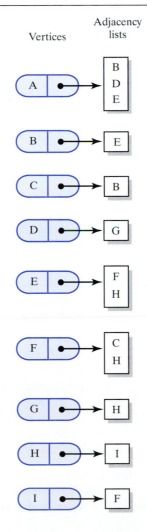

Although the adjacency lists in our diagram contain vertices, they will actually contain edges in our implementation. Each of these edges, however, will contain the illustrated vertex as its terminal vertex.

Note: An adjacency list for a given vertex represents only those edges that originate from the vertex. An adjacency list uses less memory in general than a corresponding adjacency matrix. Using an adjacency list, you quickly can determine all the neighbors of a particular vertex. But if you want to know whether an edge exists between any two given vertices, you need to search a list.

Question 2   What adjacency lists represent the graph described in Question 1?

Vertices and Edges

30.4   While designing a class that implements the ADT graph, we encounter two other types of objects, the vertex and the edge. These objects are interrelated: A vertex has edges that leave it, and an edge is defined by the vertices at its ends.

A vertex in a graph is like a node in a tree. In Segment 25.3, we used a package-friendly class `BinaryNode` for a binary tree. We then realized that we could simplify the implementation of a binary tree if the binary node had more than simple accessor and mutator operations. The same is true now for the implementation of the ADT graph. In fact, the specifications of the ADT graph that you saw in the previous chapter (Segment 29.24) omit the operations necessary to implement various graph algorithms. We assign these operations to the vertices.

Specifying the Class `Vertex`

30.5   **Identifying vertices.** First, we need a way to identify the vertices in a graph. One simple way is to use either integers or strings. A more general approach—the one we will use—labels each vertex with an object. This label will be a data field of the class `Vertex`. One operation of `Vertex`, then, is to retrieve a vertex's label.

30.6   **Visiting vertices.** The algorithms that we discussed in the previous chapter required us to mark certain vertices when they were visited. We therefore give operations to `Vertex` that mark a vertex, test whether a vertex is marked, and remove the mark.

30.7   **The adjacency list.** As we mentioned earlier in this chapter, a vertex's adjacency list indicates its neighbors. Rather than placing this list within the class of graphs, it is more convenient to make it a part of the class `Vertex`. Soon we will define a simple class `Edge` whose instances we will place in these adjacency lists. Thus, a particular vertex's adjacency list contains the edges that leave the vertex. Each edge references the vertex that ends the edge and indicates its weight, if any. `Vertex` then needs methods to add edges to the adjacency list.

In addition, we need an iterator that provides access to the adjacency list for a given vertex. For convenience, we also include a method to test whether a vertex has at least one neighbor.

30.8   **Path operations.** While finding a path through a graph, we must be able to locate the vertex that comes before a given vertex on the path—in other words, the vertex's predecessor. Thus, we need set, get, and test operations for a vertex's predecessor. Certain algorithms find the path with the shortest length or the path that has the smallest weight, or cost. A vertex can record either the length or the weight of the path from the origin to itself. Thus, we have operations that set and get this recorded value.

30.9   **The Java interface.** The following interface specifies the vertex operations that we have just introduced:

```java
import java.util.Iterator;
public interface VertexInterface
{
  /** Task: Gets the vertex's label.
   *  @return the object that labels the vertex */
  public Object getLabel();

  /** Task: Marks the vertex as visited */
  public void visit();

  /** Task: Marks the vertex as unvisited */
  public void unVisit();

  /** Task: Determines whether the vertex is marked as visited.
   *  @return true if the vertex is visited */
  public boolean isVisited();

  /** Task: Connects this vertex and the given vertex with an edge.
   *  @param endVertex  a vertex in the graph that ends the edge
   *  @param edgeWeight  a real-valued edge weight, if any */
  public void addEdge(Vertex endVertex); // for unweighted graph
  public void addEdge(Vertex endVertex, double edgeWeight);

  /** Task: Creates an iterator that traverses all edges that begin at
   *        the vertex.
   *  @return an iterator of the edge objects that begin at this
   *          vertex */
  public Iterator getNeighborIterator();

  /** Task: Determines whether the vertex has an unvisited neighbor.
   *  @return true if the vertex has an unvisited neighbor */
  public boolean hasUnvisitedNeighbor();

  /** Task: Gets an unvisited neighbor, if any, of the vertex.
   *  @return either a vertex that is an unvisited neighbor or null
   *          if no such neighbor exists */
  public Vertex getUnvisitedNeighbor();

  /** Task: Records the previous vertex on a path to this vertex.
   *  @param predecessor  the vertex previous to this one */
  public void setPredecessor(Vertex predecessor);

  /** Task: Gets the vertex recorded as the previous vertex.
   *  @return either the previous vertex or null if no vertex was recorded */
  public Vertex getPredecessor();

  /** Task: Determines whether a previous vertex was recorded.
   *  @return true if a previous vertex was recorded for this vertex */
  public boolean hasPredecessor();
```

```
/** Task: Records the cost of a path to this vertex.
 *  @param newCost  the cost of the path */
public void setCost(double newCost);

/** Task: Gets the recorded cost of the path to this vertex.
 *  @return the cost of the path */
public double getCost();
} // end VertexInterface
```

The Class Edge

30.10   Since Vertex and Edge are intertwined, we look at Edge before we implement Vertex. We will place instances of Edge in a vertex's adjacency list to indicate the edges that originate at the vertex. Thus, each edge must record both the vertex that ends it and the edge's weight, if any. Recording an edge weight is the only reason we need a class of edges. For unweighted graphs, we could simply place vertices in the adjacency list. Using edge objects, however, allows us to use one class for both weighted and unweighted graphs.

Choosing an edge with the smallest weight is easier if we can compare edges based on their weights. Thus, the class Edge implements the interface Comparable and defines the method compareTo based on edge weights. The class also should define the method equals. Two edges are equal if they have identical weights.

To make Edge an implementation detail that is not available to any of the graph's clients, we place it within a package that contains the other classes of this implementation. The class Edge appears next.

```java
package GraphPackage;

class Edge implements Comparable, java.io.Serializable
{
  private Vertex vertex; // end vertex
  private double weight;

  public Edge(Vertex endVertex, double edgeWeight)
  {
    vertex = endVertex;
    weight = edgeWeight;
  } // end constructor

  public Vertex getEndVertex()
  {
    return vertex;
  } // end getEndVertex

  public double getWeight()
  {
    return weight;
  } // end getWeight

  public int compareTo(Object other)
  {
    Edge otherEdge = (Edge)other;
```

```
      return (int) (weight - otherEdge.weight);
   } // end compareTo

   public boolean equals(Object other)
   {
      Edge otherEdge = (Edge)other;
      return weight == otherEdge.weight;
   } // end equals
} // end Edge
```

Note that the method `equals` is consistent with the method `compareTo`; that is, they reach the same conclusion for two edges that have the same weight.

Note: An instance of the class `Edge` contains both the vertex that ends it and the edge's weight, if any. Although not necessary for unweighted graphs, `Edge` allows us to use one class for both weighted and unweighted graphs.

Implementing the Class `Vertex`

30.11   **Beginning the class.** To hide `Vertex` from the clients of the graph, we place it within the package that contains `Edge` and the other classes of this implementation. Most of the implementation of `Vertex` is straightforward, so we present only a portion of it.

We begin with the class's data fields and constructor. We have chosen a linked implementation of the ADT list as the adjacency list.

```
package GraphPackage;
import java.util.Iterator;
class Vertex implements VertexInterface, java.io.Serializable
{
   private Object label;
   private LList edgeList;        // edges to adjacent vertices
   private boolean visited;       // true if visited
   private Vertex previousVertex; // on path to this vertex
   private double cost;           // of path to this vertex

   public Vertex(Object vertexLabel)
   {
      label = vertexLabel;
      edgeList = new LList();
      visited = false;
      previousVertex = null;
      cost = 0;
   } // end constructor
   . . .
```

Note: The data fields in the class `Vertex` facilitate the implementation of the algorithms presented in the previous chapter. For example, the fields `previousVertex` and `cost` are useful in a breadth-first search for the cheapest path from one vertex to another.

30.12 **The addEdge methods.** The two addEdge methods place an edge into a vertex's adjacency list. We first implement the method for weighted graphs and then use it to implement the method for unweighted graphs. Notice that addEdge calls the list's add method.

```java
public void addEdge(Vertex endVertex, double edgeWeight)
{
    edgeList.add(new Edge(endVertex, edgeWeight));
    endVertex.setPredecessor(this);
} // end addEdge

public void addEdge(Vertex endVertex)
{
    addEdge(endVertex, 0);
} // end addEdge
```

30.13 **Accessing the adjacency list.** The method getNeighborIterator simply returns the iterator defined in the class LList. That is, it returns edgeList.getIterator(). The method hasNeighbor uses the isEmpty method of LList to determine whether edgeList is empty. We leave the implementation of these methods as an exercise.

Finding an unvisited neighbor of a vertex is a necessary task in a topological sort. The method getUnvisitedNeighbor returns an adjacent vertex that is unvisited:

```java
public Vertex getUnvisitedNeighbor()
{
    Vertex result = null;

    Iterator edges = getNeighborIterator();
    while (edges.hasNext() && (result == null) )
    {
        Edge edgeToNextNeighbor = (Edge)edges.next();
        Vertex nextNeighbor = edgeToNextNeighbor.getEndVertex();
        if (!nextNeighbor.isVisited())
            result = nextNeighbor;
    } // end while

    return result;
} // end getUnvisitedNeighbor
```

30.14 **The remaining methods.** Vertex should override the method equals. Two vertices are equal if they have labels that are equal.

```java
public boolean equals(Object other)
{
    return label.equals(((Vertex)other).label);
} // end equals
```

The remaining methods of Vertex have uncomplicated implementations and are left as exercises.

Question 3 Given the classes Vertex and Edge, where Vertex implements Vertex-Interface, write Java statements that create the vertices and edges for the following directed, weighted graph. This graph contains three vertices—*A*, *B*, and *C*—and the following four edges: $A \rightarrow B$, $B \rightarrow C$, $C \rightarrow A$, $A \rightarrow C$. These edges have the weights 2, 3, 4, and 5, respectively.

An Implementation of the ADT Graph

We now consider how to put these pieces together in an implementation of a directed graph.

Basic Operations

30.15   **Beginning the class.** We will use an adjacency list to implement a directed graph that can be either weighted or unweighted. Whether we use an adjacency list or an adjacency matrix in our implementation, we must have a container for the graph's vertices. If we use integers to identify the vertices, a list would be a natural choice for this container, since each integer could correspond to a position within the list. If we use an object such as a string to identify them, a dictionary is a better choice. That is what we will do here.

Note: Regardless of the kind of graph or how you implement it, you need a container such as a dictionary for the graph's vertices.

Figure 30-3 illustrates a dictionary of vertices for a small directed graph. Each of the vertices *A* and *D* has an adjacency list of the edges that originate at that vertex. The letters within these edges represent references to corresponding vertices within the dictionary.

Figure 30-3   (a) A directed graph and (b) its implementation using adjacency lists

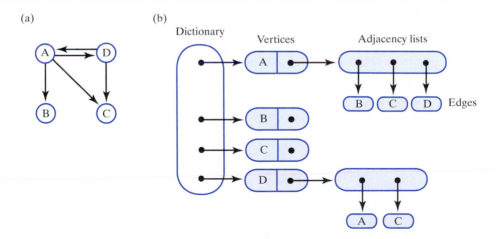

The dictionary of vertices is a data field of our class. Since the class Vertex, in conjunction with the class Edge, enables each vertex to maintain its own adjacency list, we have no need to define those lists within the graph class. As a result, the edges are not easily counted. Thus, we should maintain an edge count as a data field within the graph class. A similar count of vertices is not necessary, since the dictionary will count the vertices for us. Thus, our class begins as follows:

```
package GraphPackage;
import java.util.Iterator;
public class DirectedGraph implements GraphInterface,
                                      java.io.Serializable
{
  private DictionaryInterface vertices;
  private int edgeCount;

  public DirectedGraph()
  {
    vertices = new SortedLinkedDictionary();
    edgeCount = 0;
  } // end default constructor
  . . .
```

30.16 **Adding vertices.** Much of the work that the methods addVertex and addEdge must do is actually accomplished by methods in other classes. For example, addVertex uses Vertex's constructor to create a new vertex and then invokes the dictionary's method add to add it to the dictionary of vertices:

```
public void addVertex(Object vertexLabel)
{
  vertices.add(vertexLabel, new Vertex(vertexLabel));
} // end addVertex
```

Notice that vertexLabel is the search key for the dictionary entry, and the vertex is the associated value. This organization allows us to quickly locate a particular vertex, given its label.

30.17 **Adding edges.** Methods such as addEdge that identify vertices by their labels must locate the actual vertex within the dictionary vertices. To do this, they invoke the dictionary method getValue, using the vertex label as the search key. Having located the two vertices that delineate the edge to be added, addEdge adds an edge to the adjacency list of the origin vertex. It does this by invoking Vertex's addEdge method. Thus, addEdge has the following two definitions, one for weighted graphs and one for unweighted graphs:

```
public void addEdge(Object begin, Object end, double edgeWeight)
{
  Vertex beginVertex = (Vertex)vertices.getValue(begin);
  Vertex endVertex = (Vertex)vertices.getValue(end);
  beginVertex.addEdge(endVertex, edgeWeight);
  edgeCount++;
} // end addEdge

public void addEdge(Object begin, Object end)
{
  addEdge(begin, end, 0);
} // end addEdge
```

Notice that addEdge increments the count of edges. Also, recall that the addEdge methods assume that the given vertices are in the graph.

30.18 **Testing for an edge.** The method hasEdge begins like addEdge, by locating the two vertices that define the desired edge. With the origin vertex in hand, addEdge invokes Vertex's method getNeighborIterator and searches the origin's adjacency list for the desired edge. In the following implementation, you can see why overloading the equals method in Vertex is important.

```java
public boolean hasEdge(Object begin, Object end)
{
  boolean found = false;
  Vertex beginVertex = (Vertex)vertices.getValue(begin);
  Vertex endVertex = (Vertex)vertices.getValue(end);

  Iterator edges = beginVertex.getNeighborIterator();
  while (!found && edges.hasNext())
  {
    Edge nextEdge = (Edge)(edges.next());
    if (endVertex.equals(nextEdge.getEndVertex()))
      found = true;
  } // end while

  return found;
} // end hasEdge
```

30.19   **Miscellaneous methods.** The methods isEmpty, clear, getNumberOfVertices, and getNumber-OfEdges have the following simple implementations:

```java
public boolean isEmpty()
{
  return vertices.isEmpty();
} // end isEmpty

public void clear()
{
  vertices.clear();
  edgeCount = 0;
} // end clear

public int getNumberOfVertices()
{
  return vertices.getSize();
} // end getNumberOfVertices

public int getNumberOfEdges()
{
  return edgeCount;
} // end getNumberOfEdges
```

30.20   **Resetting vertices.** You saw in Segment 30.11 that the class Vertex has the data fields visited, previousVertex, and cost. These fields are necessary for the implementation of the graph algorithms that we introduced in the previous chapter. Once you have searched a graph for a shortest path, for example, many of the vertices will have been marked visited. Before you could perform a topological sort on the same graph, you would have to reset the field visited for each vertex in the graph.

The following method resetVertices sets the fields visited, previousVertex, and cost to their initial values. To do so, the method uses one of the iterators defined in the class Dictionary.

```java
protected void resetVertices()
{
  Iterator vertexIterator = vertices.getValueIterator();
  while (vertexIterator.hasNext())
  {
    Vertex nextVertex = (Vertex)vertexIterator.next();
```

```
      nextVertex.unVisit();
      nextVertex.setCost(0);
      nextVertex.setPredecessor(null);
    } // end while
  } // end resetVertices
```

 Question 4   Create an instance of the class `DirectedGraph` for the graph described in Question 3.

Graph Algorithms

30.21   **Breadth-first traversal.** Segment 29.11 of the previous chapter presented an algorithm for a breadth-first traversal of a nonempty graph that begins at a given origin vertex. Recall that the traversal first visits the origin and the origin's neighbors. It then visits each neighbor of the origin's neighbors. The traversal uses a queue to hold the unvisited vertices. The traversal order is the order in which vertices are added to this queue. But since the algorithm must remove vertices from this queue, we maintain the traversal order in a second queue.

The following implementation of the method `getBreadthFirstTraversal` closely follows the pseudocode given in the previous chapter. The parameter `origin` is an object that labels the origin vertex of the traversal.

```
public QueueInterface getBreadthFirstTraversal(Object origin)
{
  resetVertices();
  QueueInterface vertexQueue = new LinkedQueue();
  QueueInterface traversalOrder = new LinkedQueue();

  Vertex originVertex = (Vertex)vertices.getValue(origin);
  originVertex.visit();
  traversalOrder.enqueue(originVertex);
  vertexQueue.enqueue(originVertex);

  while (!vertexQueue.isEmpty())
  {
    Vertex frontVertex = (Vertex)vertexQueue.dequeue();

    Iterator edges = frontVertex.getNeighborIterator();
    while (edges.hasNext())
    {
      Edge edgeToNextNeighbor = (Edge)edges.next();
      Vertex nextNeighbor = edgeToNextNeighbor.getEndVertex();
      if (!nextNeighbor.isVisited())
      {
        nextNeighbor.visit();
        traversalOrder.enqueue(nextNeighbor);
        vertexQueue.enqueue(nextNeighbor);
      } // end if
    } // end while
  } // end while

  return traversalOrder;
} // end getBreadthFirstTraversal
```

The implementation of a similar method to perform a depth-first traversal is left as an exercise.

Question 5   Write Java statements that display the vertices in a breadth-first traversal of the graph that you created in Question 4, beginning with vertex *A*.

30.22   **Shortest path.** The shortest path of all paths from one vertex to another in an unweighted graph is the path that has the fewest edges. The algorithm that finds this path—as you saw in Segment 29.18 of the previous chapter—is based on a breadth-first traversal. When we visit a vertex *v*, we mark it as visited, note the vertex *p* that precedes *v* in the graph, and note the length of the path that the traversal followed to reach *v*. We place both this path length and a reference to *p* into the vertex *v*. When the traversal reaches the desired destination, we construct the shortest path from this data in the vertices.

The implementation of the method `getShortestPath` closely follows the pseudocode given in the previous chapter. The parameters `begin` and `end` are objects that label the origin and destination vertices of the path.

```java
public StackInterface getShortestPath(Object begin, Object end)
{
  resetVertices();
  boolean done = false;
  QueueInterface vertexQueue = new LinkedQueue();

  Vertex originVertex = (Vertex)vertices.getValue(begin);
  Vertex endVertex = (Vertex)vertices.getValue(end);

  originVertex.visit();
  // Assertion: resetVertices() has executed setCost(0)
  // and setPredecessor(null) for originVertex

  vertexQueue.enqueue(originVertex);

  while (!done && !vertexQueue.isEmpty())
  {
    Vertex frontVertex = (Vertex)vertexQueue.dequeue();

    Iterator edges = frontVertex.getNeighborIterator();
    while (!done && edges.hasNext())
    {
      Edge edgeToNextNeighbor = (Edge)edges.next();
      Vertex nextNeighbor = edgeToNextNeighbor.getEndVertex();

      if (!nextNeighbor.isVisited())
      {
        nextNeighbor.visit();
        nextNeighbor.setCost(1 + frontVertex.getCost());
        nextNeighbor.setPredecessor(frontVertex);

        vertexQueue.enqueue(nextNeighbor);
      } // end if

      if (nextNeighbor.equals(endVertex))
        done = true;
    } // end while
  } // end while
```

```
// traversal ends; construct shortest path
StackInterface path = new LinkedStack();
path.push(endVertex);

while (endVertex.hasPredecessor())
{
  endVertex = endVertex.getPredecessor();
  path.push(endVertex);
} // end while

return path;
} // end getShortestPath
```

The implementation of the method getCheapestPath for a weighted graph is left as an exercise.

 Question 6   Write statements that display the vertices in the shortest path from vertex *A* to vertex *C* for the graph that you created in Question 4.

CHAPTER SUMMARY

- An adjacency matrix represents the edges in a graph. If you number the vertices from 0 through $n - 1$, the element in row i and column j of the matrix indicates whether an edge exists between vertex i and vertex j. For an unweighted graph, you can use boolean values in the matrix. For a weighted graph, you can use edge weights when edges exist and a representation of infinity otherwise.

- Using an adjacency matrix, you quickly can determine whether an edge exists between any two given vertices. But if you want to know all the neighbors of a particular vertex, you need to scan an entire row of the matrix.

- An adjacency list for a given vertex references a list of adjacent vertices.

- Using an adjacency list, you quickly can determine all the neighbors of a particular vertex. But if you want to know whether an edge exists between any two given vertices, you need to search a list.

- An adjacency list represents only those edges that originate from a vertex, but an adjacency matrix reserves space for every possible edge in a graph. Thus, an adjacency list uses less memory in general than a corresponding adjacency matrix. For this reason, typical graph implementations use adjacency lists.

- One way to implement an adjacency list is to make it a data field of a class **Vertex**. So that you can represent weighted graphs as well as unweighted graphs, you place instances of a class **Edge** in the adjacency list. **Edge**'s data fields include the terminal vertex of an edge and the edge weight. Both **Vertex** and **Edge** are accessed from within their package instead of publicly.

- To facilitate the implementation of various graph algorithms, an instance of the class **Vertex** can indicate whether it has been visited. It also can record data about a path to it, such as the previous vertex and the cost.

EXERCISES

1. What adjacency matrix represents the graph in Figure 29-15a of the previous chapter?

2. What adjacency matrix represents the graph in Figure 29-18a of the previous chapter?

3. What adjacency lists represent the graph in Figure 29-15a of the previous chapter?

4. What adjacency lists represent the graph in Figure 29-18a of the previous chapter?

5. When are adjacency matrices just as space-efficient as adjacency lists?

6. Suppose that you want only to test whether some particular pair of vertices is connected by an edge. Does an adjacency matrix or an adjacency list provide a more efficient way of doing this?

7. Suppose that you want only to find all vertices that are adjacent to some particular vertex. Does an adjacency matrix or an adjacency list provide a more efficient way of doing this?

8. Complete the implementation of the class `Vertex` that was begun in Segment 30.11 of this chapter.

9. Implement the method `getDepthFirstTraversal`. Segment 29.12 of the previous chapter presents the pseudocode for this method.

10. Implement the method `getCheapestPath` for a weighted graph. The pseudocode for this method appears in Segment 29.23 of the previous chapter.

11. The **out degree** of a vertex is the number of edges that originate at the vertex. The **in degree** of a vertex is the number of edges that terminate at the vertex. Modify the class `DirectedGraph` so that it can compute the in degree and out degree of any of its vertices.

12. Draw a class diagram that shows the relationships among the classes `DirectedGraph`, `Vertex`, `Edge`, and any other supporting classes such as `Dictionary`.

13. A graph is said to be **bipartite** if the vertices can be divided into two groups such that every edge goes from a vertex in one group to a vertex in the other group. The graph of Figure 29-1 is a bipartite graph. We could put Sandwich, Hyannis, Orleans, and Provincetown in group A, and Barnstable, Falmouth, Chatham, and Truro in group B. Every edge goes from a vertex of group A to a vertex of group B.

   a. Which of the graphs in Figures 29-4, 29-6, and 29-7b are bipartite?
   b. How might the implementation of a bipartite graph differ from that of a regular graph to take advantage of its bipartite nature?

14. A graph is said to be **biconnected** if two paths that do not share edges or vertices exist between every pair of vertices.

   a. Which graphs of Figures 29-1 and 29-4 are biconnected?
   b. What are some applications that would use a biconnected graph?

PROJECTS

1. Complete the implementation of the class `DirectedGraph` that was begun in Segment 30.15 of this chapter. Revise the `addEdge` methods to remove the assumption that their parameter vertices are in the graph.

2. Implement the classes `Vertex`, `Edge`, and `DirectedGraph` by using an adjacency matrix.

3. Implement a class of undirected graphs by extending the class `DirectedGraph`.

4. Assuming an implementation of a class of undirected graphs, implement a method that determines whether an undirected graph is acyclic. You can look for cycles during either a breadth-first traversal or a depth-first traversal by discovering an edge to a vertex that is not the parent and has already been visited.

5. Implement a method that determines whether a graph is connected.

Java Essentials

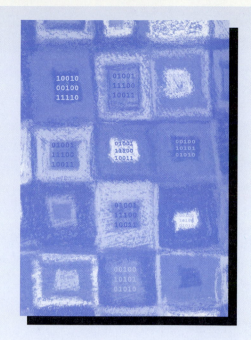

CONTENTS

Introduction
    Applications and Applets
    Objects and Classes
    A First Java Application Program
Java Basics
    Identifiers
    Reserved Words
    Variables
    Primitive Types
    Constants
    Assignment Statements
    Assignment Compatibilities
    Type Casting
    Arithmetic Operators and Expressions
    Parentheses and Precedence Rules
    Increment and Decrement Operators
    Special Assignment Operators
    Named Constants
    The `Math` Class
Simple Input and Output Using the Keyboard and Screen
    Screen Output
    Keyboard Input Using `SavitchIn`
The `if-else` Statement
    Boolean Expressions
    Nested Statements
    Multiway `if-else` Statements
    The Conditional Operator *(Optional)*
The `switch` Statement

Scope
Loops
    The **while** Statement
    The **for** Statement
    The **do-while** Statement
    Additional Loop Information
The Class **String**
    Characters Within Strings
    Concatenation of Strings
    String Methods
The Class **StringBuffer**
The Class **StringTokenizer**
Arrays
    Array Parameters and Returned Values
    Initializing Arrays
    Array Index Out of Bounds
    Use of = and == with Arrays
    Multidimensional Arrays
    Wrapper Classes

PREREQUISITE

Knowledge of a programming language

T his book assumes that you know how to write programs in Java. If you know some other programming language, this appendix will help you to learn Java. We review the essential elements of Java here. Chapters 1 and 2 supplement the coverage of Java that is presented here by discussing methods, classes, and inheritance. Appendices B, C, and D cover exceptions, file I/O, and comments.

    If you already know Java, note that this book uses applications, not applets. If you know only about applets, you should read at least the first few pages of this appendix.

Introduction

Applications and Applets

A.1   There are two kinds of Java programs, applications and applets. An **application** is simply a program that runs on your computer like any other program. It is a **stand-alone** program. In contrast, an **applet** is a program that cannot run without the support of a browser or a viewer. Typically, an applet is sent to another location on the Internet and run there. The term "applet" is meant to suggest a little application.

    Applets and applications are almost identical. Once you know how to design and write one, it is easy to learn to write the other. This book uses applications rather than applets.

Objects and Classes

A.2   An **object** is a program construct that contains data and can perform certain actions. When a Java program is run, the objects interact with one another to accomplish a particular task. The actions performed by objects are called **methods.** When you ask an object to perform an action, you **invoke,** or **call**, a method. Java has two kinds of methods. A **valued method** returns a result, but a **void method** does not.

All objects of the same kind are said to be in the same class. So a **class** is a category or kind or type of object. All objects in the same class have the same types of data and the same methods.

You will see some objects and methods in the next section and again when we discuss the classes Math, SavitchIn, and String later in this appendix. Chapter 1 reviews classes, objects, and methods in more detail. If you are not familiar with these concepts, you should read at least Segment 1.1 in Chapter 1 now and the rest of Chapter 1 and Chapter 2 later.

A First Java Application Program

A.3   We want to give you a feel for the Java language by giving you a brief, informal description of the following sample Java application program:

```java
public class FirstProgram
{
  public static void main(String[] args)
  {
    System.out.println("Hello out there.");
    System.out.println("Want to talk some more?");
    System.out.println("Answer y for yes or n for no.");

    char answerLetter = SavitchIn.readLineNonwhiteChar();
    if (answerLetter == 'y')
      System.out.println("Nice weather we are having.");
    System.out.println("Good-bye.");

    System.out.println("Press Enter key to end program.");
    String junk = SavitchIn.readLine();
  } // end main
} // end FirstProgram
```

Figure A-1 shows two screen displays that might be produced when a user runs and interacts with this program. The text typed by the user is shown in boldface.

A.4   For now, ignore the first four lines of the program. You can think of these opening lines as being Java's way of writing "Begin the program named FirstProgram." You need not worry about them yet.

Figure A-1   Two possible results when running the sample program

```
Hello out there.
Want to talk some more?
Answer y for yes or n for no.
y
Nice weather we are having.
Good-bye.
Press Enter key to end program.
```

```
Hello out there.
Want to talk some more?
Answer y for yes or n for no.
n
Good-bye.
Press Enter key to end program.
```

The next three lines are the first things the program does:

```
System.out.println("Hello out there.");
System.out.println("Want to talk some more?");
System.out.println("Answer y for yes or n for no.");
```

Each of these lines causes the quoted string given within the parentheses to be displayed on the screen. `System.out` is an object that can send output to the screen; `println` is the method—that is, the action that this object carries out when sending the string in parentheses to the screen. You invoke an object's method by writing the object followed by a period, or **dot,** followed by the method name and some parentheses that may or may not have something inside them. The text inside of the parentheses is called an **argument** and provides the information the method needs to can carry out its action. In each of these first three lines, the method `println` writes its argument—the characters inside the quotes—to the screen.

The next line of the program reads a character that is typed at the keyboard and stores this character in the variable `answerLetter`:

```
char answerLetter = SavitchIn.readLineNonwhiteChar();
```

`SavitchIn` is a class designed for you that reads data from the keyboard, and `readLineNonwhite-Char` is a method of this class that reads a single nonblank character from the keyboard. If the user types some input on a single line and presses the Enter key (also called the Return key), this method will read the first nonblank character on that line and discard everything else on the line. You will learn more about `SavitchIn` later in this appendix.

The expression

```
SavitchIn.readLineNonwhiteChar();
```

is a different way of invoking a method. Notice that `SavitchIn` is a class, not an object. For some special methods, you use the name of a class rather than the name of an object when you invoke the method. You will see this type of method call again when we discuss the class `Math` later in this appendix.

A.5   The next two lines of the program make a decision to do or not do something based on the value of the variable `answerLetter`. The first line asks whether the character stored in the variable `answerLetter` is the character *y*. If it is, a message is displayed on the screen. Otherwise, the message is not displayed.

Notice that the first sample dialogue in Figure A-1 displays the string *Nice weather we are having,* and the second one does not. That is because, in the first run of the program, the character *y* is stored in the variable `answerLetter`, and in the second run of the program, the character *n* is stored in `answerLetter`.

The following two lines at the end of the program prevent the screen output from disappearing before you can read it. Some systems will erase the screen as soon as the program ends. These two lines make the program, and the screen, wait for us to press the Enter (Return) key:

```
System.out.println("Press Enter key to end program.");
String junk = SavitchIn.readLine();
```

If pressing the Enter key one time does not end the program, just press it a second time. This detail can vary a little from one system to another.

The type `String` means that `junk` can hold an entire string of characters. If the user simply presses the Enter (Return) key, `readLine` will read the blank line of input. We named the variable junk because the value stored in the variable is not used for anything. The method `readLine` is similar to the method `readLineNonwhiteChar`, except that `readLine` reads in an entire line of input rather than a single character.

A final semicolon ends each Java statement. The semicolon acts as ending punctuation, just as a period ends an English sentence. The braces at the end simply end the program.

Of course, there are very precise rules for how you write each part of a Java program. These rules form the **grammar** for the Java language, just as there are rules for the grammar of the English language. The grammar rules for a programming language (or any language) are called the **syntax** of the language. We now look at the elements of Java in more detail.

Java Basics

In this section, we examine how to use Java to perform arithmetic computations.

Identifiers

A.6   You use **identifiers** to name certain parts of a program. An identifier in Java consists entirely of letters, digits, and the underscore character _. An identifier cannot start with a digit and must not contain a space or any other character such as a period or an asterisk. There is no official limit to the length of a name, though in practice, there is always a limit. Although Java allows identifiers to contain the symbol $, it is reserved for special purposes, and so you should not use $ in a Java identifier.

Java is **case sensitive.** This means that it treats uppercase letters and lowercase letters as different characters. For example, `mystuff`, `myStuff`, and `MyStuff` are three different identifiers. Having these identifiers in the same program could be confusing to human readers, and therefore doing so is a poor programming practice. But the Java compiler would be happy with them.

Java uses a character set, called **Unicode,** that includes characters from languages other than English. Java allows you to use these extra letters in identifiers, but you are not likely to find them on most keyboards.

A.7   Although it is not required by the Java language, the common practice, and the one followed in this book, is to start the names of classes with uppercase letters and to start the names of objects, methods, and variables (which you are about to see) with lowercase letters. These names are usually spelled using only letters and digits. We separate multiword names by using uppercase letters, since we cannot use spaces. For example, the following are all legal identifiers that follow this well-established convention:

```
inputStream    YourClass    CarWash    hotCar    theTimeOfDay
```

Some people use an underscore to separate the words in an identifier, but typically we will not.

The following are all illegal identifiers in Java, and the compiler will complain if you use any of them:

```
My.Class    go-team    7eleven
```

The first two contain illegal characters, either a dot or a dash. The last name is illegal because it starts with a digit.

Reserved Words

A.8   Some words, such as the word `if`, have a special predefined meaning in the Java language. You cannot use these words, called **reserved words** or **keywords,** for anything other than their intended meaning. A full list of reserved words for Java is given on the inside cover of this book. Within a programming environment, the names of reserved words are often highlighted in some way. In this book, they will appear in boldface.

Some other words, such as String, name classes that are supplied with Java. They have a predefined meaning but are not reserved words. This means that you can change their meaning, but doing so could easily confuse you or somebody else reading your program.

Variables

A.9   A **variable** in a program represents a memory location that stores data such as numbers and letters. The number, letter, or other data item in a variable is called its **value.** This value can be changed, so that at one time the variable contains, say, 6, and at another time after the program has run for a while, the variable contains a different value, such as 4.

You use an identifier to name a variable. Besides following the rules and conventions for identifiers, you should choose variable names that suggest their use or the kind of data they will hold. For example, if a variable is used to count something, you might name the variable count. If the variable is used to hold the speed of an automobile, you might call the variable speed. You should almost never use single-letter variable names like x and y.

A.10   A variable's **type** determines what kind of value the variable can hold. If the type is int, the variable can hold integers. If the type is double, the variable can hold numbers with a decimal point and a fractional part after the decimal point. If the type is char, the variable can hold any one character from the computer keyboard.

Java has two kinds of types, primitive types and reference types. A **reference type**—also called a **class type**—is a type that represents a class, that is, a type for objects of a class. For example, String is a class type. A **primitive type** is a simpler type. Values of a primitive type are not complex items but simple, indecomposable values, such as a single number or a single letter. The types int, double, and char are primitive types. The names of primitive types begin with a lowercase letter. By convention, the names of class types begin with an uppercase letter. Also by convention, variable names of either class types or primitive types begin with a lowercase letter.

Note: Naming conventions help you to distinguish among identifiers when reading a program.

A.11   A **variable declaration** tells the type of data the variable will hold. Different types of data are stored in the computer's memory in different ways. Variable declarations are necessary so that the value of a variable can be correctly stored in or retrieved from the computer's memory. Even though there are different mechanisms for storing values in the variables of class types and those of primitive types, you declare variables for class types and primitive types in the same way.

You declare a variable by writing a type name followed by a list of variable names separated by commas and ending with a semicolon. All the variables named in the list will have the same type given at the start of the declaration. For example,

```
int numberOfBaskets, eggsPerBasket, totalEggs;
String myName;
```

The first line declares that the three variables numberOfBaskets, eggsPerBasket, and totalEggs will contain values of type int. The second line declares that myName will store a String object.

You must declare a variable in a Java program before you use it. Normally, you declare a variable either just before it is used or at the start of a method definition.

Primitive Types

A.12   A whole number without a decimal point, such as 0, 1, or −2, is called an **integer.** A number with a decimal point, such as 3.14159, −8.63, or 5.0 is called a **floating-point number.** Notice that 5.0 is a floating-point number, not an integer. If a number has a fractional part, even if the fractional part is zero, it is a floating-point number.

All the Java primitive types appear inside the front cover of this book. Notice that there are four types for integers—namely `byte`, `short`, `int`, and `long`. The only difference among the various integer types is the range of integers they can store and the amount of computer memory they use. If you cannot decide which integer type to use, use the type `int`. It has a large enough range for most purposes and does not use as much memory as the type `long`.

Java has two types for floating-point numbers, `float` and `double`. If you cannot decide between the types `float` and `double`, use `double`. It allows a wider range of values and is used as a default type for floating-point numbers.

You use the primitive type `char` for single characters, such as letters, digits, or punctuation. For example, the following declares the variable `symbol` to be of type `char`, stores the character for uppercase *A* in `symbol`, and then displays that value—the *A*—on the screen:

```
char symbol;
symbol = 'A';
System.out.println(symbol);
```

Notice that we enclose the character *A* in single quotes. Again note that uppercase letters and lowercase letters are different characters. For example, `'a'` and `'A'` represent two different characters.

Finally, the primitive type `boolean` has two values, true and false. You can use a variable of type `boolean` to store the answer to a true/false question such as "Is `myTime` less than `your-Time`?"

Constants

A.13   A variable can have its value changed; its value *varies*. A literal number like 2 cannot change. It is always 2. It is never 3. Values like 2 or 3.7 are called **constants,** or **literals,** because their values do not change.

You write constants of integer types with an optional plus sign or a minus sign, but without commas or decimal points. Floating-point constants have an optional plus sign or a minus sign and no commas. You can write a floating-point constant in one of two ways. One way looks like the everyday way of writing numbers. For example, 9.8, −3.14, and 5.0 are floating-point constants, because they contain a decimal point. The second way is to include a multiplier that is a power of 10. You use the letter `e` to represent both the multiplication sign and the 10. For example, you would write 8.65×10^8 in Java as `8.65e8` (or in the less convenient form `865000000.0`). The two forms, `8.65e8` and `865000000.0`, are equivalent in a Java program.

Similarly, the number 4.83×10^{-4}, which is equal to 0.000483, can be written as `4.83e-4` in Java. The e stands for "exponent," since it is followed by a number that is thought of as an exponent of 10. The number before the e can be a number with or without a decimal point. The number after the e cannot contain a decimal point.

Other types of literal expressions are also called constants. You write constants of type `char` by placing the character in single quotes. For example, `'Y'` is a constant of type `char`. A string constant is a sequence of characters enclosed in double quotes, as in `"Java"`.

Assignment Statements

A.14 You can use an **assignment statement** to give a value to a variable. For example, if answer is a variable of type int and we want to give it the value 42, we could use the following assignment statement:

```
answer = 42;
```

An assignment statement always consists of a single variable on the left-hand side of an equal sign and an expression on the right-hand side followed by a semicolon. The expression can be another variable, a constant, or a more complicated expression made up by combining operators, such as + and *, with variables and constants. The value of the expression is assigned to the variable on the left of the equal sign.

For example, the following are all examples of assignment statements:

```
amount = 3.99;
firstInitial = 'B';
score = numberOfCards + handicap;
```

Here we assume that amount is a variable of type double, firstInitial is of type char, and the rest of the variables are of type int. If the variable numberOfCards has the value 7 and handicap has the value 2, the value of the variable score is 9.

The equal sign, =, which is called the **assignment operator,** does not mean equality. You can think of the assignment operator as saying, "Make the value of the variable equal to what follows." For example, in the statement

```
eggsPerBasket = eggsPerBasket - 2;
```

the variable eggsPerBasket occurs on both sides of the assignment operator. This statement subtracts 2 from the present value of eggsPerBasket and assigns the new value to eggsPerBasket. In effect, the statement decreases the value of eggsPerBasket by 2.

A.15 A variable that has been declared but that has not yet been given a value by the program is **uninitialized.** If the variable has a class type, it literally has no value. If the variable has a primitive type, it may have some default value. However, your program will be clearer if you explicitly give the variable a value, even if you are simply reassigning it the default value. (The exact details on default values have been known to change and should not be counted on.)

One easy way to ensure that you do not have an uninitialized variable is to initialize it within the declaration. Simply combine the declaration and an assignment statement, as in the following examples:

```
int count = 0;
double taxRate = 0.075;
char grade = 'A';
int balance = 1000, newBalance;
```

Note that a single declaration, such as the last statement above, can initialize some variables and not others.

Sometimes the compiler may complain that you have failed to initialize a variable. In most cases, this is indeed true. Occasionally, the compiler is mistaken about this. However, the compiler will not compile your program until you convince it that the variable in question is initialized. To make the compiler happy, initialize the variable when it is declared, even if the variable will be given a different value before you use it for anything. In such cases, you cannot argue with the compiler.

Assignment Compatibilities

A.16   You cannot put a square peg in a round hole, and similarly you cannot put a value of one type in a variable of another type. You cannot put an `int` value like 42 in a variable of type `char`. You cannot put a `double` value like 3.5 in a variable of type `int`. You cannot even put the `double` value 3.0 in a variable of type `int`. You cannot store a value of one type in a variable of another type unless the value is somehow converted to match the type of the variable.

When dealing with numbers, however, this conversion will sometimes—but not always—be performed automatically for you. For example, you can always assign a value of an integer type to a variable of a floating-point type, such as when you write either

```
double interestRate = 7;
```

or

```
int wholeRate = 7;
double interestRate = wholeRate;
```

More generally, you can assign a value of any type on the following list to a variable of any type that appears further down on the list:

byte → short → int → long → float → double

For example, you can assign a value of type `long` to a variable whose type is either `long`, `float`, or `double`. Notice that you can assign a value of any integer type to a variable of any floating-point type. This is not an arbitrary ordering of the types. As you move down the list from left to right, the types become more complex, or **wider,** either because they allow larger values or because they allow decimal points in the numbers. Thus, you can assign a value of one type to a variable of a wider type.

In addition, you can assign a value of type `char` to a variable of type `int` or to any of the numeric types that follow `int` in the previous list of types. However, we do not advise doing so, because the result could be confusing.[1]

If you want to assign a value of type `double` to a variable of type `int`, you must change the type of the value explicitly by using a type cast, as we explain next.

Type Casting

A.17   A **type cast** is the changing of the type of a value to some other type, such as changing the type of 2.0 from `double` to `int`. The previous segment described when a change in type is done for you automatically. In all other cases, if you want to assign a value of one type to a variable of another type, you must perform a type cast. For example, you cannot simply assign a value of type `double` to a variable of type `int`, even if the value of type `double` happens to have all zeros after the decimal point and so is conceptually a whole number. Thus, the second of the following statements is illegal:

```
double distance = 9.0;
int points = distance; // ILLEGAL
```

---

1. Readers who have used certain other languages, such as C or C++, may be surprised to learn that we cannot assign a value of type `char` to a variable of type `byte`. This is because Java uses the Unicode character set rather than the ASCII character set, and so Java reserves two bytes of memory for each value of type `char`, but naturally reserves only one byte of memory for values of type `byte`. This is one of the few cases where we might notice that Java uses the Unicode character set. Indeed, if we convert from an `int` to a `char` or vice versa, we can expect to get the usual correspondence of ASCII numbers and characters.

To cast the type of distance to int, you enclose int within parentheses and place it in front of distance. For example, we would replace the preceding illegal assignment with

int points = (**int**)distance; // casting from double to int

Note that when you type-cast from any floating-point type to any integer type, the value is not rounded. The part after the decimal point is simply discarded, or **truncated.** For example, if the variable distance contains 25.86, (int)distance has an int value of 25. A type cast does not really change the value of a variable; distance is still 25.86, but points is 25.

Recall that when you assign an integer value to a variable of a floating-point type, the type cast is done automatically for you.

Arithmetic Operators and Expressions

A.18   In Java, you perform arithmetic by using the **arithmetic operators** +, -, *, /, and %. You combine variables and constants with these operators and parentheses to form an **arithmetic expression.** The variables and constants in an expression are called **operands.** Spaces around the operators, operands, and parentheses within an expression are ignored.

A **unary operator** is one that has only one operand, like the operator - in the assignment statement

bankBalance = -cost;

A **binary operator** has two operands, like the operators + and * in

total = cost + (tax * discount);

Note that the operators - and + can be used as both unary and binary operators.

The meaning of an expression is basically what you expect it to be, but there are some subtleties about the type of the result and occasionally even about the value of the result. The type of the value produced when an expression is evaluated depends on the types of the values being combined. Consider an expression with only two operands, such as

amount - adjustment

If both amount and adjustment are of type int, the result of the subtraction has type int. If either amount or adjustment, or both, is of type double, the result is of type double. If we replace the operator - with any of the operators +, *, /, or % , the type of the result is determined in the same way. The operator % is used typically with integers, as you will see soon.

Larger expressions using more than two operands are viewed as a series of steps, each of which involves only two operands. For example, to evaluate the expression

balance + (balance * rate)

we evaluate balance * rate and obtain a number, and then we add that number to balance. Thus, if balance is int and rate is double, balance * rate is double and so is the entire expression.

Note: If all the items in an arithmetic expression have the same type, the result has that type. If at least one of the items have a floating-point type, the result has a floating-point type.

Knowing whether the value produced has an integer type or a floating-point type is typically all that you need. However, if you need to know the exact type of the value produced by an arithmetic expression, you can use the following rule:

> **Note:** The type of the value of an arithmetic expression is the type of the value within the expression that appears rightmost in the following list:
>
> byte → short → int → long → float → double
>
> For example, if sum is float and more is int, sum + more is float.

A.19   The division operator / deserves special attention, because the type of its operands can affect the value produced in a dramatic way. When you combine two numbers with the division operator / and at least one of the numbers has a floating-point type, the result has a floating-point type. For example, 9.0/2 has one operand of type double, namely 9.0. Hence, the result is the type double number 4.5. However, when both operands have an integer type, the result can be surprising. For example 9/2 has two operands of type int, and so it yields the result 4 of type int, not 4.5. The fraction after the decimal point is simply lost. Be sure to notice that when you divide two integers, the result is truncated, *not* rounded. The part after the decimal point is discarded no matter how large it is. So, 11/3 is 3, not 3.6666…. If nothing but a zero is after the decimal point, that decimal point and zero are still lost. Even this seemingly trivial difference can be of some significance. For example, 8.0/2 has the value 4.0 of type double, which technically is only an approximate quantity. However, 8/2 has the int value 4, which is an exact quantity. The approximate nature of 4.0 can affect the accuracy of any further calculation that is performed with this result.

Often the % operator has operands only of integer types. You use it to recover something equivalent to the fraction after the decimal point. When you divide one integer by another, you get a result (which some call a quotient) and a remainder. For example, 14 divided by 4 yields 3 with a remainder of 2 (or with 2 left over). The % operation gives the remainder—that is, the amount left over after doing the division. So 14/4 is 3 and 14%4 is 2, because 14 divided by 4 is 3 with 2 left over. The % operator is called the **modulo, or mod, operator.**

The % operator has more applications than you might at first suspect. It allows your program to count by 2s, 3s, or any other number. For example, if you want to do something to every other integer, you need to know whether the integer is even or odd. An integer n is even if n%2 is zero, and it is odd if n%2 is not zero. Similarly, if you want your program to do something to every third integer, you test whether the integer n is divisible by 3. It will be if n%3 is zero.

Parentheses and Precedence Rules

A.20   You can use parentheses to group portions of an arithmetic expression in the same way that you use parentheses in algebra and arithmetic. With the aid of parentheses, you can indicate which operations are performed first, second, and so forth. For example, consider the following two expressions that differ only in the positioning of their parentheses:

```
(cost + tax) * discount
cost + (tax * discount)
```

To evaluate the first expression, the computer first adds cost and tax and then multiplies the result by discount. To evaluate the second expression, it multiplies tax and discount and then adds the result to cost. If you use some numbers for the values of the variables and carry out the two evaluations, you will see that they produce different results.

If you omit parentheses, as in the assignment statement

```
total = cost + tax * discount;
```

multiplication occurs before addition. Thus, the previous statement is equivalent to

```
total = cost + (tax * discount);
```

More generally, when the order of operations is not determined by parentheses, the operations occur in an order determined by the following **precedence rules:**

Note: **Precedence of arithmetic operators**
Arithmetic operators execute in the following order:
The unary operators +, –
The binary operators *, /, %
The binary operators +, –

Operators that are listed higher on the list are said to have **higher precedence.** Operators of higher precedence execute before operators of lower precedence, unless parentheses override this order. Operators at the same level have the same precedence. When two operators have equal precedence, you follow this convention:

Note: Binary operators of equal precedence are performed in left-to-right order.

Increment and Decrement Operators

A.21   The increment and decrement operators increase or decrease the value of a variable by 1. The **increment operator** is written as two plus signs ++. For example, the following Java statement will increase the value of the variable count by 1:

```
count++;
```

If the variable count has the value 5 before this statement is executed, it will have the value 6 after this statement is executed. Thus, this statement is equivalent to

```
count = count + 1;
```

You can use the increment operator with variables of any numeric type, but it is used most often with variables of an integer type such as int.

The **decrement operator** is similar, except that it subtracts 1 rather than adds 1 to the value of the variable. The decrement operator is written as two minus signs – –. For example, the following will decrease the value of the variable count by 1:

```
count--;
```

If the variable count has the value 5 before this statement is executed, it will have the value 4 after this statement is executed. This statement is equivalent to

```
count = count - 1;
```

A.22   You can use the increment and decrement operators within expressions, but when you do, the increment operator or the decrement operator changes the value of the variable it is applied to and returns a value. Although we do not recommend using the increment and decrement operators in expressions, you should be familiar with them used in this way, because you are likely to see this use in other people's code.

In expressions, you can place the ++ or -- either before or after a variable, but your choice affects the result. For example, consider the code

```java
int n = 3;
int m = 4;
int result = n * (++m);
```

After this code executes, the value of n is unchanged at 3, the value of m is 5, and the value of result is 15. Thus, ++m changes the value of m and returns that changed value to the multiply operator.

In the previous example, we placed the increment operator before the variable m. If we place it after the variable m, something slightly different happens. Consider the code

```java
int n = 3;
int m = 4;
int result = n * (m++);
```

Now, after the code executes, the value of n is 3 and the value of m is 5, just as in the previous example. However, the value of result is 12, not 15. What happened?

The two expressions n * (++m) and n * (m++) both increase the value of m by 1, but the first expression increases the value of m *before* it does the multiplication, whereas the second expression increases the value of m *after* it does the multiplication. Both ++m and m++ have the same effect on the final value of m, but when we use them as part of an arithmetic expression, they give a different value to the expression.

Similarly, both --m and m-- have the same effect on the final value of m, but when we use them as part of an arithmetic expression, they give a different value to the expression. If the -- is *before* the m, the value of m is decreased *before* its value is used in the expression. If the -- is *after* the m, the value of m is decreased *after* its value is used in the expression.

The increment and decrement operators can be applied only to variables. They cannot be applied to constants or to entire, more complicated arithmetic expressions.

Programming Tip: To avoid errors and confusing code, use the operator ++ or -- only in an expression that involves one operand.

Special Assignment Operators

A.23   You can combine the simple assignment operator (=) with an arithmetic operator, such as +, to produce a kind of special-purpose assignment operator. For example, the following will increase the value of the variable amount by 5:

```java
amount += 5;
```

This is really just a shorthand for

```java
amount = amount + 5;
```

You can do the same thing with any of the other arithmetic operators -, *, /, and %. For example, the statement

```java
amount *= 25;
```

is equivalent to

```java
amount = amount * 25;
```

Named Constants

A.24   You probably recognize the number 3.14159 as the approximate value of *pi*, the number that is used in many circle calculations and that is often written as π. However, when you see 3.14159, you might not be sure that it is π and not some other number; somebody other than you might have no idea of where the number 3.14159 came from. To avoid such confusion, you should always give a name to constants, such as 3.14159, and use the name instead of writing out the number. For example, we might give the number 3.14159 the name `PI`. Then the assignment statement

```
area = 3.14159 * radius * radius;
```

could be written more clearly as

```
area = PI * radius * radius;
```

How do you give a number, or other constant, a name like `PI`? You could use a variable named `PI` and initialize it to the desired value 3.14159. But then you might inadvertently change the value of this variable. However, Java provides a mechanism that allows you to define and initialize a variable and moreover fix the variable's value so it cannot be changed. The syntax is

public static final *type   name* = *constant*;

For example, the statement

public static final double `PI = 3.14159;`

gives the name `PI` to the constant 3.14159. The part

double `PI = 3.14159;`

simply declares `PI` as a variable and initializes it to 3.14159. The word `public` says that there are no restrictions on where we can use the name `PI`. The word `static` defines one copy of `PI` that every object of the class can access instead of having its own copy of `PI`. The word `final` means that the value 3.14159 is the *final* value assigned to `PI` or, to phrase it another way, it means that the program cannot change the value of `PI`. Chapter 1 provides more details about `static` and `final`.

Place this declaration of `PI` within the class definition but outside of the `main` method and outside of any other method definitions. It is a good practice to place named constants near the beginning of the class. This is handy in case you need to change the definition of a named constant. We might, for example, want to change the number of digits we provide for `PI`.

Note: Programmers typically use all uppercase letters when naming constants, and use an underscore as a separator in multiword names. This convention helps distinguish constants from ordinary variables.

The `Math` Class

A.25   The predefined class `Math` provides a number of the standard mathematical methods. These methods are **static methods.** (Segment 1.23 of Chapter 1 discusses static methods in more detail.) When you invoke a static method, you write the class name—`Math`, in this case—a dot, the name of the method, and a pair of parentheses. Most `Math` methods require that you specify items within these parentheses. These items are called **arguments** to the method. In other words, a typical method invocation has the form `Math`.*method_name* (*arguments*).

You can invoke the method in an assignment statement, such as

variable = `Math`.*method_name* (*arguments*) ;

or embed it within an arithmetic expression. That is, you can use `Math.`*method_name* (*arguments*) anyplace that you can use a variable of a primitive data type. Figure A-2 describes some of the available methods in this class.

The class `Math` also has two predefined named constants. `E` is the base of the natural logarithm system—often written *e* in mathematical formulas—and is approximately 2.72. `PI` is used in calculations involving circular geometric figures—often written π in mathematical formulas—and is approximately 3.14159. Because these constants are defined in the class `Math`, you use them by writing `Math.E` and `Math.PI`.

Figure A-2   Some methods in the class `Math`

In each of the following methods, the argument and the return value are `double`:

`Math.pow(x, y)`	Returns x^y.
`Math.exp(x)`	Returns e^x.
`Math.log(x)`	Returns the natural logarithm (base e) of x.
`Math.sqrt(x)`	Returns the square root of x.
`Math.sin(x)`	Returns the trigonometric sine of the angle x in radians.
`Math.cos(x)`	Returns the trigonometric cosine of the angle x in radians.
`Math.tan(x)`	Returns the trigonometric tangent of the angle x in radians.
`Math.ceil(x)`	Returns the nearest whole number that is $\geq x$.
`Math.floor(x)`	Returns the nearest whole number that is $\leq x$.

`Math round(x)`	Returns the nearest whole number to x. If x is `float`, returns an `int`; if x is `double`, returns a `long`.

In each of the following methods, the argument and the return value have the same type—either `int`, `long`, `float`, or `double`:

`Math.abs(x)`	Returns the absolute value of x.
`Math.max(x, y)`	Returns the larger of x and y.
`Math.min(x, y)`	Returns the smaller of x and y.

Simple Input and Output Using the Keyboard and Screen

A.26   The input and output of data is usually referred to as **I/O.** A Java program can perform I/O in many different ways. In this section, we present some ways to handle simple text input that we type at the keyboard and simple text output displayed on the screen.

To perform I/O in Java conveniently, you almost always need to add some classes to the language. Sometimes these classes are provided with all implementations of Java, even though they are not part of the language proper. Other times, you must either write these classes yourself or obtain them from someone else. In this section, we will display output by using a class provided with the Java language. However, Java does not provide a class to conveniently handle simple keyboard input, so we will use the class `SavitchIn`. This class was written for readers of this and other texts.

Screen Output

A.27   Statements like

```
System.out.println("Enter a whole number from 1 to 99.");
```

and

```
System.out.println(quarters + " quarters");
```

send output to the display screen. `System.out` is an object that is part of the Java language. This object has `println` as one of its methods. So the preceding output statements are calls to the method `println` of the object `System.out`. You simply follow `System.out.println` with a pair of parentheses that contain what you want to display. You end the statement with a semicolon.

Within the parentheses can be strings of text in double quotes, like `"Enter a whole number from 1 to 99."`, variables like `quarters`, numbers like `5` or `7.3`, and almost any other object or value. To display more than one thing, simply place a plus sign between them. For example,

```
System.out.println("Lucky number = " + 13 +
                   "Secret number = " + number);
```

If the value of `number` is 7, the output will be

Lucky number = 13Secret number = 7

Notice also that no spaces are added. If we want a space between the 13 and the word "Secret" in the preceding output—and we probably do—we should add a space to the beginning of the string `"Secret number = "` so that it becomes `" Secret number = "`.

Notice that you use double quotes, not single quotes, and that the left and right quotes are the same symbol. Finally, notice that you can place the statement on two lines if it is too long. However, you should break the line before or after a + sign, not in the middle of a quoted string or a variable name. You also should indent the second line to make the entire statement easier to read.

Later, in the section about the class `String`, you will see that the + operator joins, or concatenates, two strings. In the preceding `System.out.println` statement, Java converts the number 13 to the string `"13"`. Likewise, it converts the integer 7 in the variable `number` to the string `"7"`. Then the + operator joins the strings and the `System.out.println` statement displays the result. You do need to be a bit careful, however. If you write a + between two numeric values or variables, they will be added rather than concatenated.

You can also use the `println` method to display the value of a `String` variable, as illustrated by the following:

```
String greeting = "Hello Programmers!";
System.out.println(greeting);
```

This will cause the following to be written on the screen.

Hello Programmers!

A.28   Every invocation of `println` ends a line of output. If you want the output from two or more output statements to appear on a single line, use `print` instead of `println`. For example,

```
System.out.print("One, two,");
System.out.print(" buckle my shoe.");
System.out.println(" Three, four,");
System.out.println("shut the door.");
```

will produce the following output:

One, two, buckle my shoe. Three, four,
shut the door.

Notice that a new line is not started until you use `println`, rather than `print`. Also notice that the new line starts *after* displaying the items specified in the `println` statement. This is the only difference between `print` and `println`.

Keyboard Input Using `SavitchIn`

A.29   The Java language does not provide a convenient way to perform input from the keyboard. To accept keyboard input, you must use some class that is defined either for you or by you. In this section, we will read input by using the class `SavitchIn`. The class `SavitchIn` was written by one of the authors for readers of this book. It is not part of the Java language and does not come with the Java language. However, the class `SavitchIn` is provided on this book's companion website at

www.prenhall.com/carrano

`SavitchIn` is a simple class, and once you know Java, you will have no problem understanding the code for this class definition. However, in this section, we will explain only how to use the class `SavitchIn`.

The class `SavitchIn` has static methods that read a piece of data from the keyboard and return that data. When you invoke one of these methods, you use the class name `SavitchIn` as if it were the calling object. In other words, a typical method invocation has the form

variable = `SavitchIn.`*method_name*`();`

For example, the statement

`int amount = SavitchIn.readLineInt();`

reads one integer and assigns its value to the variable `amount`. The user must type a single number on a line by itself. The read operation occurs only after the user presses the Enter key (also called the Return key).

The number that the user types may have whitespace characters before and/or after it but should not have other characters on the line. **Whitespace characters** are the characters that appear as spaces when printed on paper or displayed on the screen. The blank-space character is likely the only whitespace character that will concern us at first, but the start of a new line and the tab symbol are also whitespace characters. If the user types anything else as input to `readLineInt`, an error message will appear on the screen and the user will be asked to enter the data again.

A.30   `SavitchIn` has a different method for each type of value you want to read from the keyboard. The methods `readLineLong`, `readLineFloat`, and `readLineDouble` work like `readLineInt`, except that they read in values of type `long`, `float`, and `double`, respectively. You can use the method `readLineNonwhiteChar` to read the first character on a line that is not whitespace, as follows:

`char symbol = SavitchIn.readLineNonwhiteChar();`

If more than one nonwhitespace character is on the line, `readLineNonwhiteChar` will read the first such character and discard the rest of the input line.

If you want to read in an entire line, use the method `readLine`. For example,

`String sentence = SavitchIn.readLine();`

reads in one line of input as a string and places it in the `String` variable `sentence`.

None of the previous methods have to be invoked in a simple assignment statement, although that is their most common usage. Since each method returns a value, you can call it within an arithmetic expression, for example.

A.31 **More input methods.** All the methods in the class SavitchIn that begin with readLine, such as readLine and readLineInt, always read an entire line of text. Sometimes, however, you do not want to read a whole line. For example, given the input

2 4 6

we might want to read these three numbers by using three statements that put the numbers into three different variables. We can do this by using the method readInt, as follows:

```
int first = SavitchIn.readInt();
int second = SavitchIn.readInt();
int third = SavitchIn.readInt();
```

After an integer is read with readInt, reading continues on the same line (unless it happens to have reached the end of the line). So in the previous example, first is 2, second is 4, and third is 6. If the user enters

10 20 30

then the statements

```
int count = SavitchIn.readInt();
String theRest = SavitchIn.readLine();
```

assign 10 to count and the string *20 30* to theRest.

Two other similar methods in SavitchIn read less than a whole line. They are readDouble and readNonwhiteChar. The only difference between these methods and readInt is that readDouble reads a value of type double and readNonwhiteChar reads a nonwhitespace character.

The methods readInt, readDouble, and readNonwhiteChar each require that the input items be separated by one or more blank spaces. Moreover, these methods do not prompt the user if the input format is incorrect. When using these methods, you need to be certain that the input will be entered correctly the first time.

The last method from the class SavitchIn that we will consider here is readChar. This method reads whatever single character is next in the input stream. For example, if the user enters

a b c d e f g h i

the statements

```
char c1 = SavitchIn.readChar();
char c2 = SavitchIn.readChar();
char c3 = SavitchIn.readChar();
```

assign *a* to c1, the blank character to c2, and *b* to c3. Any further reading would begin with the blank after the letter *b*.

The documentation and source code for the class SavitchIn are on the book's companion website at www.prenhall.com/carrano.

Note: To be safe, use the methods in the class SavitchIn that begin with readLine and that read a whole line. You should use the other methods sparingly and with caution. Methods such as readLineInt and readLineDouble prompt the user to enter the input again if the user enters it in an incorrect format. In contrast, the methods readInt and readDouble have no such recovery mechanisms, so you should use them only when you are certain that the input will be in the correct format. For most of our applications, you cannot be sure that the user will enter the input in the correct format.

The methods `readChar` and `readNonwhiteChar` also do not check the format of the input, but they are less dangerous to use because they will process almost any kind of input the user enters.

The `if-else` Statement

A.32   In programs, as in everyday life, things can sometimes go in one of two different ways. If you have money in your checking account, some banks will pay you a little interest. On the other hand, if you have overdrawn your checking account, you will be charged a penalty. This might be reflected in the bank's accounting program by the following Java statement, known as an `if-else` statement:

```java
if (balance >= 0)
    balance = balance + (INTEREST_RATE * balance)/12;
else
    balance = balance - OVERDRAWN_PENALTY;
```

The two-symbol operator `>=` means "greater than or equal to" in Java, because the one-character symbol $\geq$ is not on the keyboard.

The meaning of an `if-else` statement is really just the meaning it would have if read as an English sentence. When your program executes an `if-else` statement, it first checks the expression in parentheses after the `if`. This expression must be evaluate to either true or false. If it is true, the statement after the `if` is executed. If the expression is false, the statement after the `else` is executed. In the preceding example, if `balance` is positive or zero, the following action occurs:

```java
balance = balance + (INTEREST_RATE * balance)/12;
```

(We divide by 12 because the interest is for only 1 of 12 months.) On the other hand, if the value of `balance` is negative, the following is executed instead:

```java
balance = balance - OVERDRAWN_PENALTY;
```

The indentation in the `if-else` statement is conventional as an aid in reading the statement; it does not affect the statement's meaning.

A.33   If you want to include more than one statement in either of the two portions of the `if-else` statement, you simply enclose the statements in braces, as in the following example:

```java
if (balance >= 0)
{
    System.out.println("Good for you. You earned interest.");
    balance = balance + (INTEREST_RATE * balance)/12;
}
else
{
    System.out.println("You will be charged a penalty.");
    balance = balance - OVERDRAWN_PENALTY;
}
```

When you enclose several statements within braces, you get one larger statement called a **compound statement.** Compound statements are seldom used by themselves but often are used as substatements of larger statements such as `if-else` statements.

Programming Tip: Some programmers always use compound statements within other statements such as if-else, even when the compound statement contains a single statement between braces. Doing so makes it easier to add another statement to the compound statement, but more importantly, it avoids the error that would occur if you did not remember to add the braces.

A.34   You can omit the else part. If you do, nothing happens when the tested expression is false. For example, if your bank does not charge an overdraft penalty, the statement in its program would be the following, instead of the previous one:

```
if (balance >= 0)
{
   System.out.println("Good for you. You earned interest.");
   balance = balance + (INTEREST_RATE * balance)/12;
}
```

If balance is negative, the statement after the closing brace executes next.

Boolean Expressions

A.35   A **boolean expression** is an expression that is either true or false. The expression

```
balance >= 0
```

that we used in the previous if-else statement is an example of a simple boolean expression. Such expressions compare two things, like numbers, variables, or other expressions. Figure A-3 shows the various Java comparison operators you can use to compare two expressions.

Figure A-3   Java comparison operators

Math Notation	Name	Java Operator	Java Examples
=	Equal to	==	balance == 0 answer == 'y'
≠	Not equal to	!=	income != tax answer != 'y'
>	Greater than	>	expenses > income
≥	Greater than or equal to	>=	points >= 60
<	Less than	<	pressure < max
≤	Less than or equal to	<=	expenses <= income

A.36   Often, when you write an if-else statement, you will want to use a boolean expression that is more complicated than a simple comparison. You can form more complicated boolean expressions from simpler ones by joining expressions with either the Java version of "and," which is **&&,** or the Java version of "or," which is **||.** For example, consider the following:

```
if ((pressure > min) && (pressure < max))
    System.out.println("Pressure is OK.");
else
    System.out.println("Warning: Pressure is out of range.");
```

If the value of pressure is greater than min, *and* the value of pressure is less than max, the output will be

Pressure is OK.

Otherwise, the output is

Warning: Pressure is out of range.

Note that you *cannot* use a string of inequalities in Java, like the following:

min < pressure < max ◄——Illegal!

Instead, you must express each inequality separately and connect them with **&&**, as follows:

(pressure > min) && (pressure < max)

The parentheses in the previous expression are not necessary, but we typically include them. The parentheses that surround the entire expression in an if-else statement are required, however.

A.37   When you form a larger boolean expression by connecting two smaller expressions with **&&**, the entire larger expression is true provided that both of the smaller expressions are true. Thus, if at least one of pressure > min and pressure < max is false, the larger expression is false. Moreover, if the first part of the larger expression is false, the second part is ignored, since the larger expression must be false regardless of the value of the second part. For example, if pressure is less than min, we know that

(pressure > min) && (pressure < max)

is false without looking at pressure < max.

A.38   You also can use **||** to form a larger boolean expression from smaller ones in the same way that you use **&&**, but with different results. The meaning is essentially the same as the English word "or." For example, consider

```
if ((salary > expenses) || (savings > expenses))
    System.out.println("Solvent");
else
    System.out.println("Bankrupt");
```

If the value of salary is greater than the value of expenses *or* the value of savings is greater than the value of expenses—or both—the output will be

Solvent

Otherwise, the output will be

Bankrupt

The entire larger expression is true if either of the smaller expressions is true. Moreover, if the first part of the larger expression is true, the second part is ignored, since the larger expression must be true regardless of the value of the second part. For example, if salary is greater than expenses, we know that

(salary > expenses) || (savings > expenses)

is true without looking at savings > expenses.

You use parentheses in expressions containing the || operator in the same way that you use them with &&.

A.39   You can negate a boolean expression by preceding it with the operator !. For example, the expression

```
!(number >= min)
```

has the same meaning as the expression

```
number < min
```

In this case, you can and should avoid using !.

Sometimes, however, the use of ! makes perfect sense. For example, if you have two strings that should be the same for normal processing to continue, you would compare them and issue a warning if they are not equal. Later, in the section about the class String, you will see that you use the equals method to compare two strings. For example,

```
stringOne.equals(stringTwo)
```

is true if the strings stringOne and stringTwo are equal. But if we care only about when these strings are not equal, we could write

```
if (!stringOne.equals(stringTwo))
   System.out.println("Warning: The strings are not the same.");
```

The precedence of the boolean operators in relation to each other and to the arithmetic operators follows:

Note: **Precedence of boolean operators and arithmetic operators**
Operators execute in the following order:
The unary operators +, -, !
The binary arithmetic operators *, /, %
The binary arithmetic operators +, -
The boolean operators <, >, <=, >=
The boolean operators ==, !=
The boolean operator &
The boolean operator ∧
The boolean operator |
The boolean operator &&
The boolean operator ||

Nested Statements

A.40   Notice that an if-else statement contains smaller statements within it. These smaller statements can be any sort of Java statements. In particular, you can use one if-else statement within another if-else statement to get **nested** if-else statements, as illustrated by the following:

```
if (balance >= 0)
   if (INTEREST_RATE >= 0)
      balance = balance + (INTEREST_RATE * balance)/12;
   else
      System.out.println("Cannot have a negative interest.");
else
   balance = balance - OVERDRAWN_PENALTY;
```

If the value of balance is greater than or equal to zero, the entire following if-else statement is executed:

```
if (INTEREST_RATE >= 0)
  balance = balance + (INTEREST_RATE * balance)/12;
else
  System.out.println("Cannot have a negative interest.");
```

When writing nested if-else statements, you may sometimes become confused about which if goes with which else. To eliminate this confusion, you can add braces as follows:

```
if (balance >= 0)
{
  if (INTEREST_RATE >= 0)
    balance = balance + (INTEREST_RATE * balance)/12;
  else
    System.out.println("Cannot have a negative interest.");
}
else
  balance = balance - OVERDRAWN_PENALTY;
```

Here, the braces are an aid to clarity but are not, strictly speaking, needed. In other cases, they are needed.

A.41   If you omit an else, things get a bit trickier. The following two if-else statements differ only in that one has a pair of braces, but they do not have the same meaning:

```
// First Version
if (balance >= 0)
{
  if (INTEREST_RATE >= 0)
    balance = balance + (INTEREST_RATE * balance)/12;
}
else
  balance = balance - OVERDRAWN_PENALTY;

// Second Version
if (balance >= 0)
  if (INTEREST_RATE >= 0)
    balance = balance + (INTEREST_RATE * balance)/12;
else
  balance = balance - OVERDRAWN_PENALTY;
```

In the second version, without braces, the else is paired with the second if, not the first one, as the indentation leads us to believe. Thus, the meaning is

```
// Equivalent to Second Version
if (balance >= 0)
{
  if (INTEREST_RATE >= 0)
    balance = balance + (INTEREST_RATE * balance)/12;
  else
    balance = balance - OVERDRAWN_PENALTY;
}
```

To clarify the difference a bit more, consider what happens when `balance` is less than zero. The first version causes the following action:

```
balance = balance - OVERDRAWN_PENALTY;
```

However, the second version takes no action.

Note: In an `if-else` statement, each `else` is paired with the nearest previous unmatched `if`.

Programming Tip: Indentation within an `if-else` statement does not affect the action of the statement. For clarity, you should use indentation that matches the logic of the statement.

Multiway `if-else` Statements

A.42   Since you can branch two ways, you can branch four ways. You simply branch two ways and have each of those two outcomes branch two ways. Using this trick, you can use nested `if-else` statements to produce **multiway branches** that branch into any number of possibilities. There is a standard way of doing this. In fact, it has become so standard that it is treated as if it were a new kind of branching statement rather than just a nested statement made up of several nested `if-else` statements. Let's start with an example.

Suppose `balance` is a variable that holds your checking account balance and you want to know whether your balance is positive, negative (overdrawn), or zero. To avoid any questions about accuracy, let's assume that `balance` is of type `int`—that is, `balance` is the number of dollars in your account, with the cents ignored. To find out if your balance is positive, negative, or zero, you could use the following nested `if-else` statement:

```java
if (balance > 0)
   System.out.println("Positive balance");
else if (balance < 0)
   System.out.println("Negative balance");
else if (balance == 0)
   System.out.println("Zero balance");
```

This is really an ordinary nested `if-else` statement, but it is indented differently than before. The indentation reflects the way we think about these multiway `if-else` statements and is the preferred way of indenting them.

When a multiway `if-else` statement is executed, the computer tests the boolean expressions one after the other, starting from the top. When it finds the first true boolean expression, it executes the statement after the expression. The rest of the `if-else` statement is ignored. For example, if `balance` is greater than zero, the preceding statements will display

Positive balance

Exactly one of the three possible outputs will be produced, depending on the value of the variable `balance`.

A.43   The previous example has three possibilities, but you can have any number of possibilities by adding more `else-if` parts. In this example, the possibilities are mutually exclusive. That is, only one of the three possibilities can actually occur for any given value of `balance`. However, you can use any boolean expressions, even if they are not mutually exclusive. If more than one boolean expression is true, only the action associated with the first true boolean expression is executed. A multiway if-else statement never performs more than one action.

If none of the boolean expressions is true, nothing happens. However, it is a good practice to add an else clause—without any if—at the end, so that the else clause will execute in case none of the boolean expressions is true. In fact, we can rewrite our previous example in this way. We know that if balance is neither positive nor negative, it must be zero. So we do not need the test

```
if (balance == 0)
```

Thus, we can and should write the previous if-else statement as

```
if (balance > 0)
    System.out.println("Positive balance");
else if (balance < 0)
    System.out.println("Negative balance");
else
    System.out.println("Zero balance");
```

The Conditional Operator (Optional)

A.44   To allow compatibility with older programming styles, Java includes an operator that is a notational variant on certain forms of the if-else statement. A **conditional operator expression** consists of a boolean expression followed by a question mark and two expressions separated by a colon. For example, the expression on the right side of the assignment operator in the following statement is a conditional operator expression:

```
max = (n1 > n2) ? n1 : n2;
```

The ? and : together form a **ternary operator** that has three operands and is known as the **conditional operator.** If the boolean expression is true, the value of the first of the two expressions is returned; otherwise, the value of the second of the two expression is returned. Thus, the logic of this example is equivalent to

```
if (n1 > n2)
    max = n1;
else
    max = n2;
```

We feel that an if-else statement is much clearer than an equivalent conditional operator expression. Thus, we will not use conditional operator expressions in this book. If you decide to use them in your program, realize that not everyone will know their meaning.

The switch Statement

A.45   Multiway if-else statements can become unwieldy when you must choose from among many possible courses of action. If the choice is based on the value of an integer or character expression, the **switch statement** can make your code easier to read.

The switch statement begins with the word switch followed by an expression in parentheses. This expression is called the **controlling expression.** Its value must be of type int, char, byte, or short. The switch statement in the following example determines the price of a ticket according to the location of the seat in a theater. An integer code that indicates the seat location is the controlling expression:

```java
int seatLocationCode;
double price;
< Code here assigns a value to seatLocationCode. >
. . .
switch (seatLocationCode)
{
  case 1:
    System.out.println("Balcony.");
    price = 15.00;
    break;
  case 2:
    System.out.println("Mezzanine.");
    price = 30.00;
    break;
  case 3:
    System.out.println("Orchestra.");
    price = 40.00;
    break;
  default:
    System.out.println("Unknown ticket code.");
    break;
} // end switch
```

The switch statement contains a list of cases, each consisting of the reserved word case, a constant, a colon, and a list of statements that are the actions for the case. The constant after the word case is called a **case label.** When the switch statement executes, the controlling expression—in this example, seatLocationCode—is evaluated. The list of alternative cases is searched until a case label that matches the current value of the controlling expression is found. Then the action associated with that label is executed. You are not allowed to have duplicate case labels, as that would be ambiguous.

If no match is found, the case labeled default is executed. The default case is optional. If there is no default case and no match is found to any of the cases, no action takes place. Although the default case is optional, we encourage you to always use it. If you think your cases cover all the possibilities without a default case, you can insert an error message as the default case. You never know when you might have missed some obscure case.

Notice that the action for each case in the previous example ends with a **break statement.** If you omit the break statement, the action just continues with the statements in the next case until it reaches either a break statement or the end of the switch statement. Sometimes this feature is desirable, but sometimes omitting the break statement causes unwanted results.

Note: The controlling expression in a switch statement provides an entry point to a case within the statement. Execution continues from this point until it reaches either a break statement or the end of the switch.

A.46   At times, you will want to take the same action in more than one case. You can list cases one after the other so that they all apply to the same action. In the following example, we have changed the seat location code to a character instead of an integer. A code of *B* or *b*, for example, indicates a balcony seat:

```
char seatLocationCode;
double price;
... // code here assigns a value to seatLocationCode
switch (seatLocationCode)
{
  case 'B':
  case 'b':
    System.out.println("Balcony.");
    price = 15.00;
    break;
  case 'M': case 'm':
    System.out.println("Mezzanine.");
    price = 30.00;
    break;
  case 'O': case 'o':
    System.out.println("Orchestra.");
    price = 40.00;
    break;
  default:
    System.out.println("Unknown ticket code.");
    break;
} // end switch
```

The first case, *B*, has no break statement; in fact, the case has no action statements at all. Execution continues with the case for *b*, as desired. Note that we have written the cases in two ways to show two common programming styles.

The controlling expression in a switch statement need not be a single variable. It can be a more complicated expression, but it must evaluate to a single value. The expression cannot indicate a range of values. That is, the expression cannot be a boolean expression like the ones you use in an if-else statement. Thus, if you want to take one action when the controlling expression has values from 1 to 10 and a second action for values from 11 to 20, you would need a case label for each value. For this example, a switch statement would be harder to write than an if-else statement.

Programming Tip: Omitting a break statement

If you test a program that contains a switch statement and it executes two cases when you expect it to execute only one case, you probably have forgotten to include a break statement where one is needed.

Scope

A.47   The **scope** of a variable (or a named constant) is the portion of a program in which the variable is available. That is, a variable does not exist outside of its scope. A variable's scope begins at its declaration and ends at the closing brace of the pair of braces that enclose the variable's declaration.

For example, consider the following statements that involve two variables, counter and greeting:

```
{
  // counter and greeting are not available here
  . . .
  int counter = 1;
  // counter is available here
  . . .
  {
    String greeting = "Hello!";
    // both greeting and counter are available here
    . . .
  } // end scope of greeting
  . . .
  // only counter is available here
  . . .
} // end scope of counter
```

The variable `counter` is available anywhere after its declaration. The variable `greeting` is available only within the inner pair of braces.

The concept of scope applies to every pair of braces within a Java program, regardless of whether they delineate the definition of a class or a method, appear within an `if-else` statement or `switch` statement, or appear within the loops described in the next section.

Loops

A.48   Programs often need to repeat some action. For example, a grading program would contain some code that assigns a letter grade to a student based on the student's scores on assignments and exams. To assign grades to the entire class, the program would repeat this action for each student in the class. A portion of a program that repeats a statement or group of statements is called a **loop.** The statement (or group of statements) to be repeated in a loop is called the **body** of the loop. Each repetition of the loop body is called an **iteration** of the loop.

When you design a loop, you need to determine what action the body of the loop will take, and you need to determine a mechanism for deciding when the loop should stop repeating the loop body. Once you have made these choices, you can choose from among three Java statements to implement the loop: the `while` statement, the `for` statement, or the `do-while` statement.

The `while` Statement

A.49   One way to construct a loop in Java is with a **while statement,** which is also known as a **while loop.** A `while` statement repeats its action again and again until a controlling boolean expression becomes false. That is, the loop is repeated *while* the controlling boolean expression is true. The general form of a `while` statement is

```
while (expression)
   statement;
```

The `while` loop starts with the reserved word `while` followed by a boolean expression in parentheses. The loop body is a statement, typically a compound statement enclosed in braces {}. The loop body is repeated while the boolean expression is true. The loop body normally contains some action that can change the value of the boolean expression from true to false and so ends the loop.

For example, the following `while` statement displays the integers from 1 to a given integer `number`:

```
int number;
. . . // assign a value to number here
int count = 1;
while (count <= number)
{
   System.out.println(count);
   count++;
} // end while
```

Let's suppose that number is 2. The variable count begins at 1. Since the boolean expression count <= number is true at this point, the body of the loop executes. Thus, 1 is displayed and then count becomes 2. The expression count <= number is still true, so the loop's body executes a second time, displaying 2 and incrementing count to 3. Now count <= number is false, so the while loop ends. Execution continues with any statement that follows the loop.

Notice that if number is zero or negative in the previous example, nothing is displayed. The body of the loop would not execute at all, since count, which is 1, would be greater than number.

Programming Tip: **A while loop can perform zero iterations**
The body of a while loop can execute zero times. When a while loop executes, its first action is to check the value of the boolean expression. If the boolean expression is false, the loop body is not executed even one time. Perhaps the loop adds up the sum of all your expenses for the day. If you did not go shopping on a given day, you do not want the loop body to execute at all.

A.50   **Infinite loops.** A common program bug is a loop that does not end but simply repeats its loop body again and again. A loop that iterates its body repeatedly without ever ending is called an **infinite loop.** Normally, a statement in the body of the loop will change some variables so that the controlling boolean expression becomes false. If this variable does not change in the right way, you can get an infinite loop.

For instance, let's consider a slight variation to the previous example of a while loop. If we forget to increment count, the boolean expression will never change and the loop will be infinite:

```
int count = 1;
while (count <= number)
{
   System.out.println(count);
} // end while
```

Some infinite loops will not really run forever but will instead end your program in an abnormal state when a system resource is exhausted. However, some infinite loops will run forever if left alone. To end a program that is in an infinite loop, you should learn how to force a program to stop running. The way to do this depends on your particular operating system. For example, in a Unix operating system, you would press Ctrl-C.

Sometimes a programmer might intentionally write an infinite loop. For example, an ATM machine would typically be controlled by a program with an infinite loop that handles deposits and withdrawals indefinitely. However, at this point in your programming, an infinite loop is likely to be an error.

The for Statement

A.51   When a counter controls the number of iterations in a while loop, you can replace the while statement with a **for statement,** or **for loop.** The for statement has the following general form:

```
for (initialize; test; update)
   statement;
```

Here *initialize* is an optional assignment of a value to a variable, *test* is a boolean expression, and *update* is an optional assignment that can change the value of *test*.

For example, the following for statement is exactly equivalent to the while statement in Segment A.49:

```
int count, number;
. . . // assign a value to number here
for (count = 1; count <= number; count++)
   System.out.println(count);
```

The first of the three expressions in parentheses, count = 1, initializes the counter before the loop body is executed for the first time. The second expression, count <= number, is a boolean expression that determines whether the loop should continue execution. This boolean expression is tested immediately after the first expression executes and again after each execution of the third expression. The third expression, count++, executes after each iteration of the loop body. Thus, the loop body is executed while count <= number is true.

In the previous example, we declared count before the for statement. After the loop completes its execution, count is still available as a variable. We could instead declare count within the for statement, as follows:

```
int number;
. . . // assign a value to number here
for (int count = 1; count <= number; count++)
   System.out.println(count);
```

In this case, count is defined only within the for loop and is not available after the loop completes its execution.

Programming Tip: Although declaring a variable within a for statement is convenient, realize that the variable's scope is then the for loop. The variable is not available after the loop completes its execution.

The counter in a for statement is not restricted to an integer type. It can have any primitive type. You can omit any of the expressions *initialize*, *test*, and *update* from a for statement, but you cannot omit their semicolons. Sometimes it is more convenient to write the *initialize* part before the for statement or the *update* part within the body of the loop. This is especially true when these parts are lengthy. Although you technically can omit the *test* from a for loop, you will get an infinite loop if you do.

Java programmers tend to favor the for statement over the while statement because in the for statement the initialization, testing, and incrementing of the counter all appear at the beginning of the loop. A for statement is basically another notation for a kind of while loop, however. Thus, like a while loop, a for statement might not execute its loop body at all.

A.52   **The comma in for statements.** A for loop can perform more than one initialization. To use a list of initialization actions, separate the actions with commas, as in the following example:

```
int n, product;
for (n = 1, product = 1; n <= 10; n++)
   product = product*n;
```

This `for` loop initializes n to 1 and `product` to 1. Note that you use a comma, not a semicolon, to separate the initialization actions.

You cannot have multiple boolean expressions to test for ending a `for` loop. However, you can string together multiple tests by using the `&&` and `||` operators to form one larger boolean expression.

You can have multiple update actions that are separated by commas. This can sometimes lead to a situation in which the `for` statement has an empty body and still does something useful. For example, we can rewrite the previous `for` statement in the following equivalent way:

```
for (n = 1, product = 1; n <= 10; product = product*n, n++);
```

In effect, we have made the loop body part of the update action. Notice the semicolon at the end of the statement. We do not advocate `for` loops with no body, because such loops are often the result of a programming error.

We could write this loop as follows so that the empty body is explicit:

```
for (n = 1, product = 1; n <= 10; product = product*n, n++)
{
}
```

However, a more readable style is to use the update action only for variables that control the loop, as in the original version of this `for` loop.

Programming Tip: If you have used other programming languages that have a general-purpose comma operator, be warned that the comma operator in Java can appear only in `for` statements.

The **do-while** Statement

A.53   The **do-while statement,** or **do-while loop,** is similar to the `while` statement, but the body of a do-while statement always executes at least once. As you just saw, the body of a `while` loop might not execute at all.

The general form of a do-while statement is

do
   statement;
while (*expression*);

The do-while loop starts with the reserved word do. The loop body is a statement, typically a compound statement enclosed in braces {}. The loop ends with the reserved word `while` followed by a boolean expression in parentheses and a semicolon.

Programming Tip: Be sure to include a semicolon at the end of a do-while statement.

The loop body executes and is repeated while the boolean expression is true. The loop body normally contains some action that can change the value of the boolean expression from true to false and so end the loop. The boolean expression is tested at the end of the loop, not at its beginning, as it is in a `while` statement. Thus, the loop body executes at least once even if the boolean expression starts out false.

The following do-while statement displays the integers from 1 to a given integer number:

```java
int number;
. . . // assign a value to number here
int count = 1;
do
{
   System.out.println(count);
   count++;
} while (count <= number);
```

Again, let's suppose that number is 2. The variable count begins at 1 and is displayed. Next, count is incremented to 2. Since the expression count <= number is true at this point, the body of the loop executes again. The value of count (2) is displayed, and then count becomes 3. The expression count <= number is now false, so the do-while loop ends. Execution continues with any statement that follows the loop.

If number is zero or negative in the previous example, 1 is displayed, since the body of the loop executes at least once. If number can possibly be zero or negative, we probably should use either a while loop or a for loop here instead of a do-while loop.

Notice that we placed the ending brace and the while on the same line. Some programmers prefer to place them on different lines. Either form is fine, but be consistent.

You might understand a do-while loop better if you see the previous example rewritten in the following way:

```java
int number;
. . . // assign a value to number here
int count = 1;
{
   System.out.println(count);
   count++;
}
while (count <= number)
{
   System.out.println(count);
   count++;
}
```

When we look at the example this way, it is obvious that a do-while loop differs from a while loop in only one detail. With a do-while loop, the loop body is always executed at least once. With a while loop, the loop body might not execute at all.

Additional Loop Information

A.54   **Choosing a loop statement.** Suppose you decide that your program needs a loop. How do you decide whether to use a while statement, a for statement, or a do-while statement? You *cannot* use a do-while statement unless you are certain that the loop body should execute at least one time. If you are certain of this, a do-while statement is likely to be a good choice. However, more often than you might think, a loop requires the possibility that the body will not execute at all. In those cases, you must use either a while statement or a for statement. If it is a computation that changes some numeric quantity by some equal amount on each iteration, consider a for statement. If the for statement does not work well, use a while statement. The while statement is always a safe choice, since you can use it for any sort of loop. But sometimes one of the other alternatives is easier or clearer.

Programming Tip: A while loop can do anything that another loop can do.

A.55   **The break and continue statements in loops.** You can use the break statement in a switch statement or in any kind of loop statement. When the break statement executes in a loop, the immediately enclosing loop ends, and the remainder of the loop body is not executed. Execution continues with the statement after the loop.

Adding a break statement to a loop can make the loop more difficult to understand. Without a break statement, a loop has a simple, easy-to-understand structure. There is a test for ending the loop at the top (or bottom) of the loop, and every iteration will go to the end of the loop body. When you add a break statement, the loop might end because either the condition given at the top (or bottom) of the loop is false or the break statement has executed. Some loop iterations may go to the end of the loop body, but one loop iteration might end prematurely. Because of the complications they introduce, you should avoid break statements in loops. Some authorities contend that a break statement should never be used to end a loop, but virtually all programming authorities agree that they should be used at most sparingly.

The continue statement ends the current iteration of a loop. The loop continues with the next iteration. Using a continue statement in this way has the same problems as using a break statement. However, replacing an empty loop body with a continue statement is acceptable. For example, you can revise the loop at the end of Segment A.52, as follows:

```
for (n = 1, product = 1; n <= 10; product = product*n, n++)
   continue;
```

A.56   **The exit method.** Sometimes your program can encounter a situation that makes continuing with the program pointless. In these cases, you can end your program by calling the exit method, as follows:

```
System.exit(0);
```

The number 0 given as the argument to System.exit is returned to the operating system. Most operating systems use zero to indicate a normal termination of the program and nonzero to indicate an abnormal termination of the program. In this case, "normal" means the program did not violate any system or other important constraints. It does not mean that the program did what you wanted it to do. So you would almost always use 0 as the argument.

The Class String

A.57   Strings of characters, such as "Enter the amount:", do not have a primitive type in Java. However, Java does provide a class, called String, that you use to create and process strings of characters. The string constant "Enter the amount:", in fact, is a value of type String. The class String is part of the package java.lang.

A variable of type String can name one of these string values. The statement

```
String greeting;
```

declares greeting to be the name of a String variable, and the following statement sets the value of greeting to the String value "Hello!":

```
greeting = "Hello!";
```

These two statements are often combined into one, as follows:

```
String greeting = "Hello!";
```

We now can display greeting on the screen by writing

```
System.out.println(greeting);
```

The screen will show

Hello!

Characters Within Strings

A.58   Most programming languages use the **ASCII** character set, which assigns a standard number to each of the characters normally used on an English-language keyboard. Java, however, uses the **Unicode** character set instead. The Unicode character set includes all the ASCII characters plus many of the characters used in languages that have an alphabet different from English. As it turns out, this is not likely to be a big issue if you are using an English-language keyboard. Normally, you can just program as if Java were using the ASCII character set, since the codes for the ASCII characters are the same in Unicode. The advantage of the Unicode character set is that it allows you to easily handle languages other than English. The disadvantage of the Unicode character set is that it requires more computer memory to store each character than the ASCII character set does.

A.59   **Escape characters.** Suppose we want to display the following line on the screen:

The word "Java" names a language and a drink!

This string contains quotes, so the statement

```
System.out.println("The word "Java" names a language and a drink!");
```

will not work: It produces a compiler error message. The problem is that the compiler sees

```
"The word "
```

as a perfectly valid quoted string. Then the compiler sees

```
Java"
```

which is not valid in the Java language. The compiler does not know that we mean to include the quote character as part of the string unless we tell it that we want to do so. We tell the compiler this by placing a backslash \ before the troublesome character, like so:

```
System.out.println("The word \"Java\" names a language and a drink!");
```

Some other special characters also need a backslash in order to be included in strings. They are listed in Figure A-4. These are often called **escape characters** because they escape from the usual meaning of a character in Java, such as the usual meaning of the double quote character.

It is important to note that each escape sequence is a single character, even though it is spelled with two symbols. So the string "Say \"Hi\"!" contains 9 characters, not 11.

To include a backslash in a string, you must write two backslashes. Displaying the string "abc\\def" on the screen would produce

abc\def

Figure A-4   Escape characters

```
\"      Double quote.
\'      Single quote (apostrophe).
\\      Backslash.
\n      New line. (Go to the beginning of the next line.)
\r      Carriage return. (Go to the beginning of the current line.)
\t      Tab. (Insert whitespace up to the next tab stop.)
```

Writing the string with only one backslash, as in "abc\def", is likely to produce the error message "Invalid escape character."

The escape sequence \n indicates that the string starts a new line at the \n. For example, the statement

```
System.out.println("The motto is\nGo for it!");
```

will write the following to the screen

The motto is

Go for it!

It is perfectly valid to include a single quote (apostrophe) inside a quoted string, such as "How's this?" But you cannot write a single quote within single quotes. Thus, to define a single-quote character, you use the escape sequence \', as follows:

```
char singleQuote = '\'';
```

Concatenation of Strings

A.60   You can join two strings by using the + operator. Joining two strings together, end to end, to obtain a larger string is called **concatenation.** When + is used with strings, it is sometimes called the **concatenation operator.** For example, the statements

```
String greeting = "Hello";
String sentence = greeting + "my friend.";
System.out.println(sentence);
```

set the variable sentence to "Hellomy friend." and will write the following on the screen:

Hellomy friend.

No space separates the first two words, because no spaces are added when you concatenate two strings. If we want sentence to contain "Hello my friend.", we could change the assignment statement to

```
sentence = greeting + " my friend.";
```

Notice the space before the word "my."

You can concatenate any number of String objects by using the + operator. You can even concatenate a String object to any other type of object and get a String object as a result. Java can express any object as a string when you concatenate it to a string. For simple objects like numbers, Java does the obvious thing. For example,

```
String solution = "The answer is " + 42;
```

will set the `String` variable `solution` to "The answer is 42". This is so natural that it may seem as though nothing special is happening, but it does require a real conversion from one type to another. The Java constant 42 is a number, whereas "42" is a string consisting of the two characters 4 and 2. Java converts the number constant 42 to the string constant "42" and then concatenates the two strings "The answer is " and "42" to obtain the longer string "The answer is 42".

Note: Every class has a method `toString` that Java uses to get a string representation of any object. If you do not define `toString` for a class that you write, the default `toString` will return a representation of an object's location in memory. Thus, you generally should provide your own `toString` method when you define a class. Chapters 1 and 2 discuss this method in more detail.

You can also concatenate a single character to a string by using +. For example,

```
String label = "mile";
String pluralLabel = label + 's';
```

sets `pluralLabel` to the string "miles".

Segment A.63 will show you another way to concatenate strings.

String Methods

A.61   A `String` object has methods as well as a value. You use these methods to manipulate string values. A few of these `String` methods are described here. You invoke, or call, a method for a `String` object by writing the object name, a dot, and the name of the method, followed by a pair of parentheses. Some methods require nothing within the parentheses, while others require that you specify arguments. Let's look at some examples.

A.62   **The method `length`.** The method `length` gets the number of characters in a string. For example, suppose we declare two `String` variables as follows:

```
String command = "Sit Fido!";  // 9 characters
String answer = "bow-wow";     // 7 characters
```

Now `command.length()` has the value 9 (it returns 9), and `answer.length()` returns 7. Notice that you must include a pair of parentheses, even though there are no arguments to the method `length`. Also notice that spaces, special symbols, and repeated characters are all counted in computing the length of a string. All characters are counted.

You can use a call to the method `length` anywhere that you can use a value of type `int`. For example, all of the following are legal Java statements:

```
int count = command.length();
System.out.println("Length is " + command.length());
count = answer.length() + 3;
```

A.63   **The method `concat`.** You can use the method `concat` instead of the + operator to concatenate two strings. For example, if we declare the `String` variables

```
String one = "sail";
String two = "boat";
```

the expressions

```
one + two
```

and

```
one.concat(two);
```

are the same string, *sailboat*.

A.64   **Indices.** Many of the methods for the class `String` depend on counting **positions** in the string. Positions in a string start with 0, not with 1. Thus, in the string `"Hi Mom"`, *H* is in position 0, *i* is in position 1, the blank character is in position 2, and so forth. A position is usually referred to as an **index.** So it would be more normal to say that *H* is at index 0, *i* is at index 1, and so on. Figure A-5 illustrates how index positions are numbered in a string.

Figure A-5   Indices 0 through 11 for the string `"Java is fun."`

```
  0   1   2   3   4   5   6   7   8   9   10  11
┌───┬───┬───┬───┬───┬───┬───┬───┬───┬───┬───┬───┐
│ J │ a │ v │ a │   │ i │ s │   │ f │ u │ n │ . │
└───┴───┴───┴───┴───┴───┴───┴───┴───┴───┴───┴───┘
```

A.65   **The methods `charAt` and `indexOf`.** The method `charAt` returns the character at the index given as its one argument. For example, the statements

```
String phrase = "Time flies like an arrow.";
char sixthCharacter = phrase.charAt(5);
```

assign the character *f* to the variable `sixthCharacter`, since the *f* in *flies* is at index 5. (Remember, the first index is 0, not 1.)

    The method `indexOf` determines whether a string contains a given substring and, if it does, returns the index at which the substring begins. Thus, `phrase.indexOf("flies")` will return 5 because the substring *flies* begins at index 5 within `phrase`.

A.66   **Changing case.** The method `toLowerCase` returns a string obtained from its argument string by replacing any uppercase letters with their lowercase counterparts. Thus, if `greeting` is defined by

```
String greeting = "Hi Mary!";
```

the expression

```
greeting.toLowerCase()
```

returns the string `"hi mary!"`. An analogous method `toUpperCase` converts any letters in a string to uppercase.

A.67   **The method `trim`.** The method `trim` trims off any leading and trailing whitespace, such as blanks. So the statements

```
String command = "   Sit Fido!   ";
String trimmedCommand = command.trim();
```

set `trimmedCommand` to the string `"Sit Fido!"`.

A.68   **Comparing strings.** You use the method `compareTo` to compare two strings. Strings are ordered according to the Unicode values of their characters. This ordering—called **lexicographic ordering**—is analogous to alphabetical ordering. The expression

    stringOne.compareTo(stringTwo)

returns a negative integer or a positive integer according to whether `stringOne` occurs before or after `stringTwo`. The expression returns zero if the two strings are equal.

Programming Tip: Do not use the operators <=, >=, !=, or == to compare the contents of two strings.

If you want only to determine whether two strings are equal—that is, contain the same values—you can use the method `equals`. Thus,

    stringOne.equals(stringTwo)

is true if `stringOne` equals `stringTwo` and is false if they are not equal. The method `equalsIgnoreCase` behaves similarly to `equals`, except that the uppercase and lowercase versions of the same letter are equal. For example, the method `equals` finds the strings `"Hello"` and `"hello"` unequal, but the method `equalsIgnoreCase` finds them equal.

Programming Tip: When applied to two strings (or any two objects), the operator == tests whether they are stored in the same memory location. Sometimes that is sufficient, but if you want to know whether two strings that are in different memory locations contain the same sequence of characters, use the method `equals`.

The Class `StringBuffer`

A.69   Once you create a string object of the class `String`, you cannot alter it. But sometimes you would like to. For example, we might define the string

    String name = "rover";

and then decide that we want to capitalize its first letter. We cannot. We could, of course, write

    name = "Rover";

but this statement creates a new string *Rover* and discards *rover*.

The class `String` has no method that modifies a `String` object. The class `StringBuffer` in the package `java.lang` does have such a method, however. `StringBuffer` contains methods such as the following:

```
/** Task: Sets the character at the given index of this string to a
 *   given character.
 *   Throws StringIndexOutOfBoundsException if the index is invalid. */
public void setCharAt(int index, char character);

/** Task: Concatenates the string s to the end of this string. */
public StringBuffer append(String s);

/** Task: Inserts the string s into this string at the given index.
 *   Throws StringIndexOutOfBoundsException if the index is invalid.*/
public StringBuffer insert(int index, String s);
```

```
/** Task: Removes the characters in a substring of this string
 *   beginning at the index start and ending at either the index
 *   end-1 or the end of the string, whichever occurs first.
 *   Throws StringIndexOutOfBoundsException if start is invalid. */
public StringBuffer delete(int start, int end);

/** Task: Replaces the characters in a substring of this string with
 *   characters of the string s. The substring to be replaced begins
 *   at the index start and ends at either the index end-1 or the end
 *   of the string, whichever occurs first.
 *   Throws StringIndexOutOfBoundsException if start is invalid. */
public StringBuffer replace(int start, int end, String s);
```

If you are not familiar with exceptions, think of them as error messages for now. The next appendix will explain them to you.

A.70   **Examples.** If we have the following instance of `StringBuffer`

```
StringBuffer message = new StringBuffer("rover");
```

we can capitalize its first letter by writing

```
message.setCharAt(0, 'R');
```

Now the statement

```
message.append(", roll over!");
```

changes `message` to the string *Rover, roll over!*, and

```
message.insert(7, "Rover, ");
```

changes it to *Rover, Rover, roll over!* Next,

```
message.delete(0, 7);
```

changes `message` to *Rover, roll over!*, and

```
message.replace(7, 16, "come here");
```

changes `message` to *Rover, come here!*

The Class StringTokenizer

A.71   The class `StringTokenizer` in the package `java.util` enables you to locate pieces—called **tokens**—of a string. Each token must be followed by a character known as a **delimiter.** You can specify the delimiters and indicate whether they themselves are treated as tokens.

`StringTokenizer` contains constructors and methods such as the following:

```
/** Task: Creates a string tokenizer for the specified string s, assuming
 *   the following default delimiters: space, tab, newline, and carriage
 *   return. Delimiters separate tokens, but are not returned as tokens. */
public StringTokenizer(String s);

/** Task: Creates a string tokenizer for the specified string s,
 *   using the characters in the string delimiters as the delimiters.
```

```
                   *  Delimiters separate tokens, but are not returned as tokens. */
                   public StringTokenizer(String s, String delimiters);

                   /** Task: Creates a string tokenizer for the specified string s,
                    *  using the characters in the string delimiters as the delimiters.
                    *  If the argument tokens is true, delimiters are returned as tokens;
                    *  otherwise they separate tokens and are skipped. */
                   public StringTokenizer(String s, String delimiters, boolean tokens);

                   /** Task: Returns true if the string contains more tokens. */
                   public boolean hasMoreTokens();

                   /** Task: Returns the next token in the string.
                    *  Throws NoSuchElementException if no more tokens are in the string.*/
                   public String nextToken();
```

A.72   **Example.** We can use the class StringTokenizer to extract the separate words in a string, as follows:

```
        StringTokenizer wordFinder =
                    new StringTokenizer("Happy birthday, Chris.");
        while (wordFinder.hasMoreTokens())
          System.out.println(wordFinder.nextToken());
```

The default constructor specifies that the delimiters are whitespace characters, and so the comma and period are part of the tokens. These statements produce the following output:

Happy
birthday,
Chris.

Notice that NoSuchElementException is an unchecked exception, so we do not need to catch it. (The next appendix discusses exceptions.)

A.73   **Example.** The previous example uses the whitespace characters as delimiters by default. Thus, the punctuation in our string is included as part of the words. If you want to specify your own set of separator characters, you use a different constructor. For example, the string of delimiters is the second argument to the constructor in the following statements:

```
        String delimiters = " .,\n";
        StringTokenizer secondWordFinder =
                new StringTokenizer("Happy birthday, Chris.", delimiters);
        while (secondWordFinder.hasMoreTokens())
          System.out.println(secondWordFinder.nextToken());
```

They produce this output:

Happy
birthday
Chris

Since the period and comma are delimiters, they are not part of the tokens produced.

Arrays

A.74 In Java, an array is a special kind of object that stores a finite collection of elements having the same data type. For example, you can create an array of seven elements of type `double` as follows:

```java
double[] temperature = new double[7];
```

The left side of the assignment operator declares `temperature` as an array whose elements are of type `double`. The right side uses the `new` operator to request seven memory locations for the array. This is like declaring the following strangely named variables to have type `double`:

```java
temperature[0], temperature[1], temperature[2], temperature[3],
temperature[4], temperature[5], temperature[6]
```

Note that the numbering starts with 0, not 1. Each of these seven variables can be used just like any other variable of type `double`. For example, we can write

```java
temperature[3] = 32;
temperature[6] = temperature[3] + 5;
System.out.println(temperature[6]);
```

But these seven variables are more than just seven plain old variables of type `double`. The number in square brackets—called an **index,** or **subscript**—can be any arithmetic expression whose value is an integer. In this example, the index value must be between 0 and 6, because we declared that the array `temperature` should have seven elements. A variable such as `temperature[3]` is called either an **indexed variable,** a **subscripted variable,** or simply an **element** of the array.

For example, the following statements read seven temperatures into an array and compare them with their average:

```java
public static final int DAYS_IN_WEEK = 7;
. . .
double[] temperature = new double[DAYS_IN_WEEK];

System.out.println("Enter " + DAYS_IN_WEEK + " temperatures:");
double sum = 0;
for (int index = 0; index < DAYS_IN_WEEK; index++)
{
  temperature[index] = SavitchIn.readLineDouble();
  sum = sum + temperature[index];
} // end for

double average = sum/DAYS_IN_WEEK;

System.out.println("The average temperature is " + average);
System.out.println("The temperatures are");
for (int index = 0; index < DAYS_IN_WEEK; index++)
{
  if (temperature[index] < average)
    System.out.println(temperature[index] + " below average.");
  else if (temperature[index] > average)
    System.out.println(temperature[index] + " above average.");
  else // temperature[index] == average
    System.out.println(temperature[index] + " average.");
} // end for
```

Figure A-6 illustrates the array `temperature` after seven values have been read into it.

Figure A-6   An array of seven temperatures

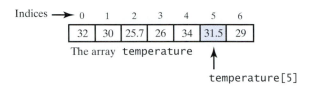

temperature[5]

Each location in the array `temperature` contains a temperature. That is, the array is full. But arrays are not always full. You need to distinguish between the number of locations in an array—its **length**—and the number of items currently stored in the array.

An array has a data field `length` that contains the declared maximum number of elements in the array. For example, if we create an array by writing

```
int[] age = new int[50];
```

then `age.length` is 50. Notice that `length` is not a method, so no parentheses follow it. If we place only 10 values into the first 10 locations of this array, `age.length` is still 50. If we need to know how many values we place into an array, we will need to keep track of that ourselves.

Array Parameters and Returned Values

Readers who need to review methods should consult Chapter 1 before reading this section.

A.75 **Array parameters.** You can pass an indexed variable as an argument to a method anyplace that you can pass an ordinary variable of the array's base type. For example, if a method has the signature

```
public double compute(double value)
```

and `temperature` is the array of `double` values that we defined earlier, we can invoke the method by writing

```
double result = compute(temperature[3])
```

An entire array can also be a single argument to a method. For example, the following method

```
public static void incrementArrayBy2(double[] array)
{
   for (int index = 0; index < array.length; index++)
      array[index] = array[index] + 2;
} // end incrementArrayBy2
```

will accept any array of `double` values as its single argument. We specify the parameter `array` in the method's signature just as we would declare an array: by specifying the type of the array elements followed by square brackets. We do not specify the length of the array.

The following statement is an example of how we would invoke this method:

```
incrementArrayBy2(temperature);
```

You use no square brackets when you pass an entire array as an argument to a method. Notice that the method can take any length array as an argument. The method `incrementArrayBy2` adds 2 to each element in the argument array `temperature`. That is, the method actually changes the values in the argument array.

Note: A method can change the values in an argument array.

A.76   **Arrays as return values.** In Java, a method can return an array. For example, rather than modifying its array argument, the previous method `incrementArrayBy2` could return an array whose values are 2 more than the corresponding values in the array argument. You specify the method's return type in the same way that you specify a type for an array parameter. The method would then look like this:

```
public static double[] incrementArrayBy2(double[] array)
{
   double[] result = new double[array.length];
   for (int index = 0; index < array.length; index++)
      result[index] = array[index] + 2;
   return result;
} // end incrementArrayBy2
```

The following statements invoke this method:

```
double[] originalArray = new double[10];
< Statements that place values into originalArray >
 . . .
double[] revisedArray = incrementArrayBy2(originalArray);
< At this point, originalArray is unchanged. >
```

Programming Tip: Notice that you do not write

```
double[] revisedArray = new double[10]; // WRONG!
revisedArray = incrementArrayBy2(originalArray);
```

to invoke the method in the previous example. The first statement allocates ten locations for a new array, but these locations are discarded when the second statement executes.

Initializing Arrays

A.77   You can provide initial values for the elements in an array when you declare it. To do this, you enclose the values for the individual elements in braces and place them after the assignment operator, as in the following example:

```
double[] reading = {3.3, 15.8, 9.7};
```

The array's length is the minimum number of locations that will hold the given values. This initializing declaration is equivalent to the following statements:

```
double[] reading = new double[3];
reading[0] = 3.3;
```

```
reading[1] = 15.8;
reading[2] = 9.7;
```

If you do not initialize the elements of an array, they are given initial default values according to their type. For example, if you do not initialize an array of integers, each element of the array will be initialized to zero. In an array of objects, each element is initialized to null. However, it is usually clearer to do your own explicit initialization, either when you declare the array or later by using a loop and assignment statements.

Array Index Out of Bounds

A.78   When programming with arrays, making a mistake with an index is easy. This is especially true if that index is an expression. If the array temperature has seven elements, but an index is some integer other than 0 through 6, the index is said to be **out of bounds** or **illegal.** An out-of-bounds index expression will compile without any error message, but will cause an error when you run your program. In particular, you will get an IndexOutOfBoundsException. (See Appendix B for a discussion of exceptions.)

Use of = and == with Arrays

A.79   **The operator =.** All array locations are together in one section of memory so that one memory address can specify the location of the entire array. Recall that a variable for an object really contains the memory address of the object. The assignment operator copies this memory address. For example, if a and b are arrays of the same size, the assignment b = a gives the array variable b the same memory address as the array variable a. In other words, a and b are two different names for the same array. These variables are **aliases.** Thus, when you change the value of a[2], you are also changing the value of b[2]. Chapter 1 talks more about aliases and references.

Because of the complications discussed in the previous paragraph, it is best not to use the assignment operator = with entire arrays. If you want the array b to have the same values as the array a, then instead of the assignment statement you must use something like the following:

```
for (int index = 0; index < a.length; index++)
    b[index] = a[index];
```

A.80   **The operator ==.** The equality operator == tests two arrays to see if they are stored in the same place in the computer's memory. It does not test whether the arrays contain the same values. To do so, you must compare the two arrays element by element. For example, if the arrays a and b contain primitive values and have the same length, the following code could be used:

```
boolean match = true;
int index = 0;
while (match && (index < a.length))
{
  if (a[index] != b[index])
    match = false;
  else
    index++;
} // end while

if (match)
  System.out.println("Arrays have the same contents");
```

```
    else
        System.out.println("Arrays have different contents");
```

If the arrays contained objects instead of primitive values, we would use the boolean expression `!a[index].equals(b[index])` instead of `a[index] != b[index]`.

Note: Are arrays really objects?
Arrays behave very much like objects. On the other hand, it is hard to come up with any commonly used name for the classes to which the arrays belong. There are also other features of objects that do not apply to arrays, such as inheritance (which we discuss in Chapter 2). So whether or not arrays should be considered objects is not absolutely clear. However, that is primarily an academic debate. Whenever Java documentation says that something applies to all objects, it also applies to arrays.

Note: Array methods
The only methods for an array object are a small number of predefined methods. Because arrays were used by programmers for many years before classes and objects (as we have used them) were invented, arrays use a special notation of their own to invoke those few predefined methods, and most people do not even call them methods.

Note: Array types are reference types
A variable of an array type holds only the address where the array is stored in memory. This memory address is often called a **reference** to the array object in memory. For this reason, an array type is often called a **reference type.** A reference type is any type whose variables hold references—that is, memory addresses—as opposed to the actual item named by the variable. Array types and class types are both reference types. Primitive types are not reference types.

Multidimensional Arrays

A.81   You can have an array with more than one index. For example, suppose we wanted to store the dollar amounts shown in Figure A-7 in some sort of array. The bold items are just labeling. There are 60 entries. If we use an array with one index, the array will have a length of 60 and it would be almost impossible to keep track of which entry goes with which index. On the other hand, if we allow ourselves two indices, we can use one index for the row and one index for the column. This arrangement is illustrated in Figure A-8.

Note that, as was true for the simple arrays you have already seen, you begin numbering indices with 0 rather than 1. If the array is named `table` and it has two indices, the Java notation `table[3][2]` specifies the entry in row number 3 and column number 2. Arrays that have exactly two indices can be displayed on paper as a two-dimensional table and are called **two-dimensional arrays.** By convention, we think of the first index as denoting the row and the second as denoting the column. More generally, an array is said to be an *n*-**dimensional array** if it has *n* indices. Thus, the ordinary one-index arrays that we have used up to now are **one-dimensional arrays.**

A.82   Arrays with multiple indices are handled much like arrays with one index. To declare and create the array `table` with 10 rows and 6 columns, we write

```
    int[][] table = new int[10][6];
```

You can have arrays with any number of indices. To get more indices, you just use more square brackets in the declaration.

Figure A-7   A table of values

The effect of various interest rates on $1000 when compounded annually (rounded to whole dollars)						
Year	5.00%	5.50%	6.00%	6.50%	7.00%	7.50%
1	$1050	$1055	$1060	$1065	$1070	$1075
2	$1103	$1113	$1124	$1134	$1145	$1156
3	$1158	$1174	$1191	$1208	$1225	$1242
4	$1216	$1239	$1262	$1286	$1311	$1335
5	$1276	$1307	$1338	$1370	$1403	$1436
6	$1340	$1379	$1419	$1459	$1501	$1543
7	$1407	$1455	$1504	$1554	$1606	$1659
8	$1477	$1535	$1594	$1655	$1718	$1783
9	$1551	$1619	$1689	$1763	$1838	$1917
10	$1629	$1708	$1791	$1877	$1967	$2061

Figure A-8   Row and column indices for an array named `table`

Row index 3   `table[3][2]`   Column index 2

Indices	0	1	2	3	4	5
0	1050	1055	1060	1065	1070	1075
1	1103	1113	1124	1134	1145	1156
2	1158	1174	1191	1208	1225	1242
3	1216	1239	1262	1286	1311	1335
4	1276	1307	1338	1370	1403	1436
5	1340	1379	1419	1459	1501	1543
6	1407	1455	1504	1554	1606	1659
7	1477	1535	1594	1655	1718	1783
8	1551	1619	1689	1763	1838	1917
9	1629	1708	1791	1877	1967	2061

Indexed variables for multidimensional arrays are just like indexed variables for one-dimensional arrays, except that they have multiple indices, each enclosed in a pair of square brackets. For example, the following statements set all the elements in `table` to zero:

```
for (int row = 0; row < 10; row++)
    for (int column = 0; column < 6; column++)
        table[row][column] = 0;
```

Note that we used two `for` loops, one nested within the other. This is a common way of stepping through all the indexed variables in a two-dimensional array. If we had three indices, we would use three nested `for` loops, and so forth for higher numbers of indices.

As was true of the indexed variables for one-dimensional arrays, indexed variables for multidimensional arrays are variables of the array's base type and can be used anywhere that a variable of the base type is allowed. For example, for the two-dimensional array `table`, an indexed variable such as `table[3][2]` is a variable of type `int` and can be used anyplace that an ordinary `int` variable can be used.

A multidimensional array can be a parameter of a method. For example, the following method signature has a two-dimensional array as a parameter:

```java
public static void clearArray(double[][] array)
```

A.83 Java implements multidimensional arrays as one-dimensional arrays. For example, consider the array

```java
int[][] table = new int[10][6];
```

The array `table` is in fact a one-dimensional array of length 10, and its base type is `int[]`. Thus, each entry in the array `table` is a one-dimensional array of length 6. In other words, multidimensional arrays are arrays of arrays.

Normally, you do not need to be concerned with this fact, since this detail is handled automatically by the compiler. However, sometimes you can profit from this knowledge. For example, consider the previous nested `for` loops that filled the two-dimensional array `table` with zeros. We used the constants 6 and 10 to control the `for` loops, but it would be better style to use the data field `length` instead. To do so, we need to think in terms of arrays of arrays. For example, the following is a rewrite of the nested `for` loops:

```java
for (int row = 0; row < table.length; row++)
    for (int column = 0; column < table[row].length; column++)
        table[row][column] = 0;
```

Here, `table.length` is the number of rows in `table`, and `table[row].length` is the number of columns.

Wrapper Classes

A.84 Java makes a distinction between the primitive types, such as `int`, `double`, and `char`, and the class types, such as `String` and the classes that you write. Java sometimes treats primitive types and class types differently. For example, an argument to a method and the assignment operator = behave differently for primitive types and class types. To make things uniform, Java provides a **wrapper class** for each of the primitive types that enables us to convert a value of a primitive type to an object of a corresponding class type.

For example, the wrapper class for the primitive type `int` is the predefined class `Integer`. If we want to convert an `int` value, such as 42, to an object of type `Integer`, we write

```java
Integer intObject = new Integer(42);
```

This statement creates an object `intObject` of the class `Integer` that has the `int` value 42 stored in its data field. Notice that we cannot now write

```java
intObject = 198; // ILLEGAL
```

but we could write

```java
intObject = new Integer(198);
```

We can extract the `int` value of `intObject` by writing

```
intObject.intValue()
```

The method `intValue` returns the equivalent `int` value from an object of type `Integer`.

The wrapper classes for the primitive types `long`, `float`, `double`, and `char` are `Long`, `Float`, `Double`, and `Character`, respectively. And, of course, rather than the method `intValue`, these classes use the methods `longValue`, `floatValue`, `doubleValue`, and `charValue`, respectively.

Many of the classes that we study in this book represent collections of objects. If your data has a primitive type, an appropriate wrapper class enables you to represent the data as objects so that you can use these classes.

A.85   Wrapper classes also contain some useful static constants. For example, you can find the largest and smallest values of any of the primitive number types by using the associated wrapper class. The largest and smallest values of type `int` are

```
Integer.MAX_VALUE and Integer.MIN_VALUE
```

The largest and smallest values of type `double` are

```
Double.MAX_VALUE and Double.MIN_VALUE
```

A.86   Wrapper classes have static methods that can be used to convert a string to the corresponding number of type `int`, `double`, `long`, or `float`. For example, suppose your program needs to convert the string `"199.98"` to a `double` value (which will turn out to be 199.98, of course). The static method `parseDouble` of the wrapper class `Double` will convert a string to a value of type `double`. So if `theString` is a variable of type `String` whose value is `"199.98"`,

```
Double.parseDouble(theString)
```

returns the `double` value 199.98. The other wrapper classes `Integer`, `Long`, and `Float` have analogous methods `parseInt`, `parseLong`, and `parseFloat`.

If there is any possibility that the string named by `theString` has extra leading or trailing blanks, you should instead use

```
Double.parseDouble(theString.trim())
```

The method `trim`, included in the class `String`, trims off leading or trailing whitespace, such as blanks. If the string is not a correctly formed number, the invocation of `Double.parseDouble` will crash your program. The use of `trim` helps some in avoiding this problem.

A.87   Each of the numeric wrapper classes also has a static method called `toString` that will convert in the other direction—that is, it will convert from a primitive numeric value to a string representation of the numeric value. For example,

```
Integer.toString(42)
```

returns the string value `"42"`, and

```
Double.toString(199.98)
```

returns the string value `"199.98"`. Additionally, each wrapper class, like all other classes, has a non-static version of `toString`. For example, if we define `n` as follows:

```
Integer n = new Integer(198);
```

then `n.toString()` returns the string `"198"`.

> ## Note: Wrapper classes
> Every primitive type has a wrapper class. Wrapper classes allow you to represent values of a primitive type as a class type. Wrapper classes also contain a number of useful predefined constants and methods.

A.88   `Character` is the wrapper class for the primitive type `char`. The following piece of code illustrates some of the basic methods for this class:

```
Character c1 = new Character('a');
Character c2 = new Character('A');
if (c1.equals(c2))
  System.out.println(c1.charValue() + " is the same as "
                       + c2.charValue());
else
  System.out.println(c1.charValue() + " is not the same as "
                       + c2.charValue());
```

This displays

```
a is not the same as A
```

The `equals` method checks for equality of characters, so uppercase and lowercase letters are considered different.

Some of the static methods in the class `Character` follow:

```
/** Task: Returns the lowercase equivalent of ch, if ch is a letter;
 *  otherwise returns ch. */
public static char toLowerCase(char ch);
```

Examples:

```
Character.toLowerCase('a') returns 'a'
Character.toLowerCase('A') returns 'a'
Character.toLowerCase('5') returns '5'
```

```
/** Task: Returns the uppercase equivalent of ch, if ch is a letter;
 *  otherwise returns ch. */
public static char toUpperCase(char ch);
```

Examples:

```
Character.toUpperCase('a') returns 'A'
Character.toUpperCase('A') returns 'A'
Character.toUpperCase('5') returns '5'
```

```
/** Task: Returns true if ch is a lowercase letter. */
public static boolean isLowerCase(char ch);
```

Examples:

```
Character.isLowerCase('a') returns true
Character.isLowerCase('A') returns false
Character.isLowerCase('5') returns false
```

```
/** Task: Returns true if ch is an uppercase letter. */
public static boolean isUpperCase(char ch);
```

Examples:

```
Character.isUpperCase('a') returns false
Character.isUpperCase('A') returns true
Character.isUpperCase('5') returns false
```

```
/** Task: Returns true if ch is a letter. */
public static boolean isLetter(char ch);
```

Examples:

```
Character.isLetter('a') returns true
Character.isLetter('A') returns true
Character.isLetter('5') returns false
```

```
/** Task: Returns true if ch is a digit. */
public static boolean isDigit(char ch);
```

Examples:

```
Character.isDigit('a') returns false
Character.isDigit('A') returns false
Character.isDigit('5') returns true
```

```
/** Task: Returns true if ch is either a letter or a digit. */
public static boolean isLetterOrDigit(char ch);
```

Examples:

```
Character.isLetterOrDigit('a') returns true
Character.isLetterOrDigit('A') returns true
Character.isLetterOrDigit('5') returns true
Character.isLetterOrDigit('%') returns false
```

```
/** Task: Returns true if ch is a whitespace character. */
public static boolean isWhitespace(char ch);
```

Examples:

```
Character.isWhitespace('a') returns false
Character.isWhitespace(' ') returns true
```

A.89   Java also has a wrapper class `Boolean`. This class has the two constants `Boolean.TRUE` and `Boolean.FALSE`. However, the Java reserved words `true` and `false` are much easier to use for these constants. So the constants in the class `Boolean` will not be of much help to us. The methods of the class `Boolean` are also not used very often. Although the class `Boolean` is not useless, it will be of little use to us in this text and we will discuss it no further.

PROGRAMMING TIPS

- Some programmers always use compound statements within other statements such as `if-else`, even when the compound statement contains only a single statement between braces. Doing so makes it easier to add another statement to the compound statement, but more importantly, it avoids the error that would occur if you did not remember to add the braces.

- Indentation within an **if-else** statement does not affect the action of the statement. For clarity, you should use indentation that matches the logic of the statement.

- If you test a program that contains a **switch** statement and it executes two cases when you expect it to execute only one case, you probably have forgotten to include a **break** statement where one is needed.

- The body of a **while** loop can execute zero times. When a **while** loop executes, its first action is to check the value of the boolean expression. If the boolean expression is false, the loop body is not executed even one time. Perhaps the loop adds up the sum of all your expenses for the day. If you did not go shopping on a given day, you do not want the loop body to execute at all.

- Although declaring a variable within a **for** statement is convenient, realize that the variable's scope is then the **for** loop. The variable is not available after the loop completes its execution.

- If you have used other programming languages that have a general-purpose comma operator, be warned that the comma operator in Java can appear only in **for** statements.

- Be sure to include a semicolon at the end of a **do-while** statement.

- A **while** loop can do anything that another loop can do.

- When applied to two strings (or any two objects), the operator **==** tests whether they are stored in the same memory location. Sometimes that is sufficient, but if you want to know whether two strings in different memory locations contain the same sequence of characters, use the method **equals**.

- When a method returns an array that you want to assign to an array variable, you should declare the variable but not allocate memory for an array. For example, you should write

```
double[] revisedArray = myMethod(originalArray);
```

instead of

```
double[] revisedArray = new double[10]; // WRONG!
revisedArray = myMethod(originalArray);
```

The 10 locations that are allocated for a new array are discarded when the last statement executes.

B

Exception Handling

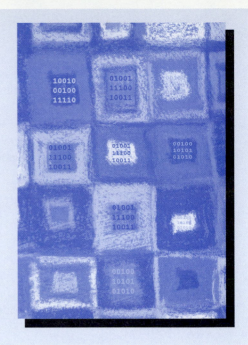

CONTENTS

Basic Exception Handling
Predefined Exception Classes
Defining Your Own Exception Classes
Multiple **catch** Blocks
Declaring Exceptions
Exceptions That Do Not Need to Be Caught

PREREQUISITES

Appendix A   Java Essentials
Chapter   1   Java Classes
Chapter   2   Creating Classes from Other Classes

Java provides a way to handle certain kinds of special conditions in your program. This facility enables you to divide a program or method definition into separate sections for the normal case and for the exceptional case. This appendix will show you how to handle an exceptional case within a method or to tell another method that an exceptional case has occurred.

Basic Exception Handling

B.1   An **exception** is an object that is created as a signal that an unusual event has occurred during the execution of a program. The process of creating an exception is called **throwing an exception.** You place the code that deals with the exceptional case at another place in your program—perhaps in a separate class or method. The code that detects and deals with the exception is said to **handle the exception.**

Using exceptions is most important when a method has a special case that some programs will treat in one way and that others will treat in another way. As you will see, such a method can throw an exception if the special case occurs. In this way, the special case can be handled outside of the method in a way that is appropriate to the situation.

B.2

E

Example. Let's begin with a simple example that does not use exceptions. Here, an if-else statement avoids a division by zero—which is an error—if there is no milk:

```java
System.out.println("Enter number of donuts:");
int donutCount = SavitchIn.readLineInt();

System.out.println("Enter number of glasses of milk:");
int milkCount = SavitchIn.readLineInt();

if (milkCount < 1)
{
  System.out.println("No Milk!");
  System.out.println("Go buy some milk.");
}
else
{
  double donutsPerGlass = donutCount/(double)milkCount;
  System.out.println(donutCount + " donuts.");
  System.out.println(milkCount + " glasses of milk.");
  System.out.println("You have " + donutsPerGlass +
                        " donuts for each glass of milk.");
} // end if
```

Now let's see how we can rewrite this code so that it uses Java's exception-handling facilities:

```java
try
{
  System.out.println("Enter number of donuts:");
  int donutCount = SavitchIn.readLineInt();

  System.out.println("Enter number of glasses of milk:");
  int milkCount = SavitchIn.readLineInt();

  if (milkCount < 1)
    throw new Exception("Exception: No Milk!");

  double donutsPerGlass = donutCount/(double)milkCount;
  System.out.println(donutCount + " donuts.");
  System.out.println(milkCount + " glasses of milk.");
  System.out.println("You have " + donutsPerGlass +
                        " donuts for each glass of milk.");
}
catch(Exception e)
{
  System.out.println(e.getMessage());
  System.out.println("Go buy some milk.");
}
```

This code is basically the same as the previous version, except that instead of the big if-else statement, we have the following smaller if statement:

```
if (milkCount < 1)
    throw new Exception("Exception: No Milk!");
```

This `if` statement says that if there is no milk, do something exceptional. That something exceptional is described after the word `catch`. In other words, the normal situation is dealt with by the code following the word `try`, and the code following the word `catch` is used only in exceptional circumstances. So we have separated the normal case from the exceptional case. In this simple example, that separation does not really buy us much, but in other situations, it will prove to be very helpful. Let's look at the details.

B.3 The basic way of handling exceptions in Java consists of a `try-throw-catch` threesome, as you saw in the previous segment. A **try block** contains the code for the basic algorithm. It is called a `try` block because we are not completely sure that all will go smoothly, but we want to give it a try. If something does go wrong, either we throw an exception or an invoked method throws one. The try block has the syntax

```
try
{
    Code_to_try
    Possibly_throw_an_exception
    More_code
}
```

The `throw` statement
```
throw new Exception("Exception: No Milk!");
```

in the previous segment creates a new object of the class `Exception` and throws it. `Exception` is a predefined class that is supplied with Java. You can use it, other predefined classes for exceptions, or your own class. The string `"Exception: No Milk!"` is an argument for the constructor of the class `Exception`. The `Exception` object contains that string in a data field. This object—and this string—is available to the `catch` block.

B.4 When an exception is thrown, execution of the code in the `try` block ends and another portion of code, known as a **catch block,** begins execution. Executing the `catch` block is called **catching the exception.** When an exception is thrown, it should ultimately be caught by some `catch` block. The `catch` block or blocks immediately follow the `try` block.

A `catch` block looks a little like a method definition that has a parameter. *It is not a method definition*, but in some ways, a `catch` block is like a method that the `throw` statement calls. The identifier e in

```
catch(Exception e)
```

is the **catch block parameter.** It represents the object thrown by the `throw` statement. Its type—`Exception` in this example—is the name of a class of exceptions. This class indicates the kind of exception the `catch` block can handle. Since all exception classes are derived from `Exception`, this `catch` block will handle any exception. You can have several `catch` blocks, one for each kind of exception you want to handle. For now, we'll consider only one `catch` block.

Every exception has a method called `getMessage` that retrieves the string given to the exception object by its constructor when the exception was thrown. So in the `catch` block

```
catch(Exception e)
{
    System.out.println(e.getMessage());
    System.out.println("Go buy some milk.");
}
```

e.getMessage() returns the string *Exception: No Milk!*. Thus, when the catch block executes, the following is displayed on the screen:

Exception: No Milk!
Go buy some milk.

B.5   To summarize, a try block contains some code that includes either a throw statement or a call to a method that contains a throw statement. The throw statement is normally executed only in exceptional circumstances, but when it is executed, it throws an exception of some exception class. (So far, Exception is the only exception class we know of, but there are others as well.) When an exception is thrown, an exception object is created. All the rest of the code in the try block is ignored and control passes to a suitable catch block. The exception object is represented by the catch block parameter, and the statements in the catch block are executed.

A catch block applies only to the nearest preceding try block. For now, we will assume that every try block is followed by an appropriate catch block. Later, we will discuss what happens when there is no appropriate catch block.

If no exception is thrown in the try block—that is, if a throw statement does not execute—the try block completes its execution. Program execution then continues with the code after the catch block. In other words, any catch blocks that follow the try block are ignored if no exception is thrown. Most of the time, the throw statement will not execute, and so in most cases, the code in the try block will run to completion and the code in the catch block(s) will be ignored completely.

Predefined Exception Classes

B.6   When you learn about the methods of predefined classes, you will sometimes be told that they might throw certain types of exceptions. Usually, these are predefined exception classes. If you use one of these methods, you can put the method invocation in a try block and follow it with a catch block to catch the exception. The names of predefined exceptions are designed to be self-explanatory. Some samples are

```
ArithmeticException
ClassCastException
ClassNotFoundException
FileNotFoundException
IndexOutOfBoundsException
IOException
NullPointerException
```

When you catch an exception of one of these predefined exception classes, the string returned by the getMessage method will usually provide you with enough information to identify the source of the exception. Thus, if you have a class called SampleClass and it has a method called doStuff that throws exceptions of the class IOException, you might use the following code:

```
SampleClass object = new SampleClass();
try
{
    < Possibly some code >
    object.doStuff(); // can throw IOException
    < Possibly some more code >
}
```

```
catch(IOException e)
{
  < Code to handle the exception, probably including the following: >
  System.out.println(e.getMessage());
}
```

If the cause of the exception makes it unwise to continue program execution, you can end execution by calling System.exit(0) within the catch block.

Every exception class is a descendant of the class Exception. You can use the class Exception itself, as we did earlier in this appendix, but catching specific exceptions enables you to provide more accurate messages.

Defining Your Own Exception Classes

B.7   You can define your own exception classes, but they must be derived classes of some already defined exception class. You can derive an exception class from any predefined exception class or from any exception class that you have already successfully defined. Our examples will be derived classes of the class Exception, but you can use any existing exception class.

When you define an exception class, the constructors are the most important and often the only methods, other than those inherited from the base class. For example, consider the following exception class called DivideByZeroException:

```
public class DivideByZeroException extends Exception
{
  public DivideByZeroException()
  {
    super("Dividing by Zero!");
  } // end default constructor

  public DivideByZeroException(String message)
  {
    super(message);
  } // end constructor
} // end DivideByZeroException
```

The only methods are a default constructor and a constructor with one String parameter. For our purposes, that is all we need to define. However, the class does inherit all the methods of the class Exception.[1] In particular, the class DivideByZeroException inherits the method getMessage, which returns a string message. In the default constructor, for example, this string message is set by the statement super("Dividing by Zero!"). This is a call to a constructor of the base class Exception. As we have already noted, passing a string to the constructor for the class Exception sets the value of a String data field that later can be recovered by a call to getMessage. The class DivideByZeroException inherits this String data field as well as the method getMessage.

For example, if we throw an exception by executing

```
throw new DivideByZeroException();
```

---

1. Some programmers would prefer to derive the class DivideByZeroException from the class ArithmeticException, but that would make it a kind of exception that we are not required to catch in our code, and so we would lose the help of the compiler in keeping track of uncaught exceptions. For more details, see the section "Exceptions That Do Not Need to Be Caught," later in this appendix.

and the corresponding `catch` block contains the statement

```
System.out.println(e.getMessage());
```

the following line will appear on the screen:

Dividing by Zero!

The definition of the class `DivideByZeroException` has a second constructor with one parameter of type `String`. This constructor allows us to choose any message we wish when we throw an exception. If the `throw` statement is

throw new `DivideByZeroException("Oops. Didn't mean to use zero.");`

and the corresponding `catch` block contains

```
System.out.println(e.getMessage());
```

the following line will appear on the screen:

Oops. Didn't mean to use zero.

Note: **Guidelines for programmer-defined exception classes:**
- Each exception class must be derived from an already existing exception class.
- If you have no compelling reason to use a particular class as the base class, use the class `Exception`.
- You should define a default constructor and at least one other constructor that has a `String` argument.
- Each constructor definition should begin with a call to the constructor of the base class by using `super`. The default constructor should call `super` with a `String` argument that indicates the kind of exception. The second constructor should call `super` with the string that was passed to the constructor as its argument. This string can then be recovered using the `getMessage` method.
- Your exception class inherits the method `getMessage`. Normally, you do not need to add any other methods, but it is legal to do so.

Programming Tip: As a general rule, if you insert a `throw` statement in your code, it is probably best to define your own exception class. In that way, when your code catches an exception, your `catch` blocks can tell the difference between your exceptions and exceptions thrown by methods in predefined classes.

Multiple catch Blocks

B.8   A `try` block potentially can throw any number of exceptions, and the exceptions can have different types. Each `catch` block can catch exceptions of only one type. You can, however, place more than one `catch` block after a `try` block, to catch exceptions of different types.

The order in which you place the `catch` blocks can be important. When an exception is thrown in a `try` block, the `catch` blocks are considered in order. The first `catch` block that matches the type of the exception thrown is the one that is executed. Thus, the following sequence of `catch` blocks would not be good:

```
catch(Exception e)
{
    . . .
}
catch(DivideByZeroException e)
{
    . . .
}
```

With this ordering, the `catch` block for `DivideByZeroException` will never be used, because all exceptions will be caught by the first `catch` block. Recall that all exceptions are derived from `Exception`. Fortunately, the compiler will probably warn you about this. The correct ordering is to reverse the `catch` blocks so that the more specific exception comes before its parent exception class, as follows:

```
catch(DivideByZeroException e)
{
    . . .
}
catch(Exception e)
{
    . . .
}
```

Programming Tip: Catch the most specific exception first.

Declaring Exceptions

B.9   Sometimes it makes sense to delay handling an exception. For example, you might have a method with code that throws an exception if there is an attempt to divide by zero, but you might not want to catch the exception in that method. Perhaps some programs that use that method should simply end if the exception is thrown, while others should do something else, so you would want to leave the handling of the exception to the invoking program. In these cases, it makes sense not to catch the exception in the method definition. Instead, any program (or other code) that uses the method would place the method invocation in a `try` block and catch the exception in a subsequent `catch` block.

When a method does not catch an exception, it must warn programmers that any invocation of the method might possibly throw an exception. This warning is called a **throws clause.** For example, a method that might possibly throw a `DivideByZeroException` but does not catch the exception would have a signature similar to the following:

```
public void sampleMethod() throws DivideByZeroException
```

The part `throws DivideByZeroException` is a `throws` clause. It says that an invocation of the method `sampleMethod` might throw a `DivideByZeroException`.

The `throws` clause absolves `sampleMethod` of the responsibility to catch any exceptions of type `DivideByZeroException` that might occur during its execution. If, however, some `methodB` calls sampleMethod, then methodB must deal with the exception. It can do so either by handling the exception with try and catch blocks or by passing the exception on to whoever calls it by including the same throws clause in its definition. In a well-written program, every exception that is thrown should eventually be caught somewhere by a catch block.

A throws clause can contain more than one exception type. In such cases, you separate the exception types with commas, as in the following example:

public int myMethod() **throws** IOException, DivideByZeroException

Note: Most exceptions that can occur during the execution of a method should be accounted for in one of two ways:

1. Catch the possible exception in a catch block that is within the method definition.
2. Declare the possible exception in a throws clause in the method's signature. Then whoever uses the method must either handle the exception or declare it in another throws clause.

In any one method, you can catch some exceptions and declare other exceptions in a throws clause.

Note: If an exception is thrown but never caught, either the program ends or its behavior may be unreliable from then on.

Exceptions That Do Not Need to Be Caught

B.10   Exceptions in Java are said to be either checked or unchecked. A **checked exception** must either be caught in a catch block or declared in a throws clause. Such exceptions indicate serious problems that likely should lead to program termination.

An **unchecked** or **runtime exception** need not be caught in a catch block or declared in a throws clause. These exceptions usually indicate that something is wrong with your code and that you should fix it. Normally, they are thrown by predefined classes that you use. That is, you would not have written a throw statement for these exceptions. For example, an ArrayIndexOutOf-BoundsException occurs if your program attempts to use an array index that is out of bounds. A NoSuchMethodException occurs when you use a method but you have not provided a definition for that method name. For such exceptions, you should repair your code, not add a catch block. Note that an uncaught runtime exception terminates program execution.

Note: Unchecked exceptions are descendants of the class RuntimeException or any of its descendants. They do not need to be caught. All other exceptions are checked. Checked exceptions are descendants of the class Exception.

How do you know if an exception is checked or unchecked? You could consult the documentation for a predefined exception, but usually an exception that you explicitly throw in your code is checked. However, you need not worry too much about the nature of an exception. If you fail to account for a checked exception, the compiler will tell you. You then can either catch it or add it to a `throws` clause.

Note: **A throws clause in a derived class**

If you redefine a method in a derived class, you cannot add exceptions to its `throws` clause. This, of course, means that you cannot throw any exceptions that are not either caught in a `catch` block or already listed in the `throws` clause of the method in the base class. You can, however, declare fewer exceptions in the `throws` clause of the redefined method.

B.11   **The class Error.** The class `Error` and its descendant classes are not considered to be exception classes, as they are not descendants of the class `Exception`. However, objects of the class `Error` are similar to unchecked exceptions in that you need not catch or declare them, even though you could. Errors are more or less beyond your control. For example, an `OutOfMemoryError` occurs if your program has run out of memory. This means that you must either revise your program to make it more efficient in its use of memory, change a setting to let Java access more memory, or buy more memory for your computer. Adding a `catch` block will not help in this case.

PROGRAMMING TIPS

- As a general rule, if you insert a **throw** statement in your code, it is probably best to define your own exception class. In that way, when your code catches an exception, your **catch** blocks can tell the difference between your exceptions and exceptions thrown by methods in predefined classes.

- Catch the most specific exception first.

APPENDIX

C

File Input and Output

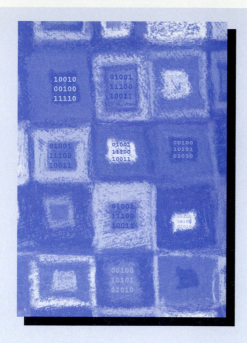

CONTENTS

Overview
    Streams
    The Advantage of Files
    Kinds of Files
    File Names
    The Package `java.io`
Writing to a Text File Using `PrintWriter`
    Flushing an Output File
    Appending to a Text File
Reading a Text File Using `BufferedReader`
    Testing for the End of a Text File
    Reading a File Name from the Keyboard
    Defining a Method to Open a Stream
I/O with Binary Files
    Writing to a Binary File Using `DataOutputStream`
    Reading from a Binary File Using `DataInputStream`
The Class `File`
Object Serialization

PREREQUISITES

Chapter   3   Designing Classes
Appendix A   Java Essentials
Appendix B   Exception Handling

Program input and output is also known as **I/O.** Input can be taken from the keyboard or from a file. Similarly, output can be sent to the screen or to a file. In this appendix, we explain how you can read input from a file and send output to another file. One advantage of files is that they give you a copy of your data that exists after your program completes its execution.

Overview

A **file** is a collection of data that is in a particular storage medium such as a disk. You already use files to store your Java classes and programs. You also can use files to store input for a program or to hold output from a program. Before you see how to write and read files, you need to know more about them, including some terminology.

Streams

C.1 In Java, all I/O is handled by **streams.** A stream is an object that either delivers data to its destination, such as a file or the screen, or takes data from a source, such as a file or the keyboard, and delivers it to your program. Thus, a stream is a flow of data. The data might be characters, numbers, or bytes consisting of binary digits. If the data flows into your program, the stream is called an **input stream.** If the data flows out of your program, the stream is called an **output stream.**

For example, if an input stream is connected to the keyboard, the data flows from the keyboard into your program, as Figure C-1 illustrates. If an input stream is connected to a file, data flows from the file into your program. In Java, streams are objects of special stream classes. The object `System.out` is an example of an output stream. The class `SavitchIn` behaves like an input stream (and, in fact, has an input stream embedded in its definition). `SavitchIn` is described in Appendix A and is on this book's companion website at www.prenhall.com/carrano.

Note: Input and output are done from the perspective of the program. Thus, "input" means that data moves *into your program*, not into a file. The word "output" means that data moves *out of your program*, not out of a file.

Figure C-1   Input and output streams

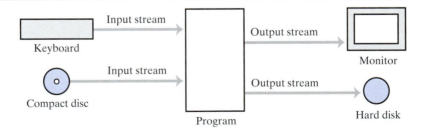

The Advantage of Files

C.2 When a program ends, the data typed at the keyboard and the data left on the screen go away. In other words, the data is temporary. In contrast, data in a file exists after the program has finished running. The contents of a file remain until a person or program changes the file.

An input file can be read over and over again by different programs without the need to type in the data separately for each program. Files also provide us with a convenient way to deal with large quantities of data.

Kinds of Files

C.3   All data in any file is stored as binary digits, or bits, that is, as a sequence of zeros and ones. However, we think of the contents of some files as sequences of characters. Such files are called **text files** and can be created and read with an editor. Files whose contents must be handled as sequences of bits are called **binary files.**

Although it is not technically precise and correct, you can safely think of a text file as containing a sequence of characters, and you can think of a binary file as containing a sequence of binary digits. When you write a Java program, it is stored in a text file. Another way to phrase the distinction between binary files and text files is to note that text files can be read by human beings, and binary files are read only by programs. Binary files represent data in a way that is not convenient to read with a text editor, but that can be written to and read from a program in a very efficient way. Thus, a binary file is a good place to store data that a program reads or writes.

One advantage of text files is that they are usually the same on all computers. You can move your text files from one computer to another with few or no problems. The implementation of binary files in languages other than Java usually differs from one platform to another. So your binary data files ordinarily must be read only on the same type of computer, and with the same programming language, as the program that created that file. But in Java, you can move your binary files from one computer to another and your Java programs will still be able to read the binary files.

The advantage of binary files is that they are more efficient to process. But the one big advantage of text files is that a text editor can read and write them. With binary files, all the reading and writing must normally be done by a program. (Some editors may be able to read some of the information in some binary files.)

File Names

C.4   You name files according to the rules of your operating system; Java does not have its own file-naming rules. Most common operating systems allow you to use letters, digits, and the dot symbol when spelling file names. Typically, file names have a suffix, such as .txt or .dat. This suffix has no special meaning to a Java program. Using a suffix is simply a convention, not a rule. In this book, we use the suffix .txt to indicate a text file and the suffix .dat to mean that a binary file can be used as data for a Java program.

The Package `java.io`

C.5   Every program or class that does file I/O using any of the techniques given in this appendix must begin with the following statement:

```
import java.io.*;
```

This statement tells the Java compiler and linker that our program uses the `java.io` package (library) that contains the definitions of classes necessary to do file I/O.

Writing to a Text File Using `PrintWriter`

C.6   When you write a program to send output to a text file, you use a method named `println` that behaves like `System.out.println`, but that is a method in the class `PrintWriter`. The class `PrintWriter` is the preferred stream class for writing to a text file. The following simple example reads three lines from the keyboard and writes them to a text file. The relevant statements appear in color.

```java
PrintWriter outStream = null;
try
{
  outStream = new PrintWriter(new FileOutputStream("data.txt"));
}
catch(FileNotFoundException e)
{
  System.out.println("Error opening the file data.txt.");
  System.exit(0);
}
System.out.println("Enter three lines of text:");

for (int count = 1; count <= 3; count++)
{
  String line = SavitchIn.readLine();
  outStream.println(count + " " + line);
} // end for

outStream.close();
System.out.println("Three lines were written to data.txt.");
```

These statements create a text file named `data.txt` that an editor or another Java program can read.
The first step is to **open the file** by writing

```java
outStream = new PrintWriter(new FileOutputStream("data.txt"));
```

This statement connects the stream `outStream` to the file named `data.txt`. When you connect a file to a stream in this way, your program always starts with an empty file. If the file `data.txt` already exists, its old contents will be lost. If the file `data.txt` does not exist, a new empty file named `data.txt` will be created.

The class `PrintWriter` has no constructor that takes a file name as its argument, so you use the class `FileOutputStream` with the class `PrintWriter` in the way shown previously. However, you can simply view this as one slightly cumbersome operation and still write and understand Java programs. Note that instead of writing a string constant for the file name, you could store the file name into a `String` variable and give that variable to the constructor. Segment C.16 will show you how.

C.7   Opening a text file by using the `FileOutputStream` constructor can possibly throw a `FileNotFoundException`, and any such exception should be caught in a `catch` block. Notice that the `try` block encloses only the opening of the file, as this is the only place an exception might be thrown.

The `FileNotFoundException` is poorly named, since in this case it does not mean that the file was not found. Remember that if you are creating a new file, it doesn't exist. An exception is thrown if the file could not be created because, for example, the file name is already used for a directory (folder) name.

A `FileNotFoundException` is a kind of `IOException`, so a `catch` block for an `IOException` would also work and would seem more sensible. However, it is usually best to catch the most specific exception that you can, since doing so can give more information.

C.8   The variable `outStream` names the stream associated with the actual file. The file has a name like `data.txt` that the operating system uses. But after you connect the file to the stream, your program always refers to the file by using the **stream name.** Notice that the variable `outStream` is declared outside of the `try` block so that `outStream` is available outside of the `try` block. Remember, anything declared in a block—even a `try` block—is local to the block.

The method `println` of the class `PrintWriter` works the same for writing to a text file as the method `System.out.println` works for writing to the screen. The class `PrintWriter` also has the method `print`, and it behaves just like `System.out.print`, except that the output goes to a text file.

C.9   When your program is finished writing to a file, it should **close** the stream connected to that file. In our previous example, the statement

```
outStream.close();
```

closes the stream connected to the file `data.txt`. When you close a stream, the system releases any resources used to connect the stream to the file and does some other housekeeping. If your program does not close a file before the program ends, Java will close it for you when the program ends. However, it is safest to close the file with an explicit call to `close`. All classes for file I/O include a method named `close`.

You should call `close` for at least two reasons. First, if your program ends abnormally, Java might not be able to close the file for you. The file might then be left open with no program connected to it, and this can damage the file. The sooner you close a file, the less likely it is that this will happen. Second, if your program writes to a file and later reads from the same file, it must close the file after it is through writing to the file and then reopen the file for reading. (Java does have a class that allows a file to be open for both reading and writing, but we will not cover that class in this book.)

Flushing an Output File

C.10   Like most programming languages, Java does not always send output immediately to its destination, such as a file; sometimes it waits to send a larger packet of data to the output destination. Thus, the output from a `println`, for example, might not be sent to the output file immediately. Instead, it might be saved and placed into memory called a **buffer** along with the output from the next invocation of `println`. Then the output from both method invocations might be sent to the file at the same time. This technique is called **buffering** and is done for efficiency reasons.

You can force any pending output to be written to its destination file by calling `PrintWriter`'s method `flush`, as follows:

```
outStream.flush();
```

The method `close` automatically calls the method `flush`, so for most simple applications, you do not need to call `flush` explicitly. However, if you continue to program, you will eventually encounter situations where you want to use `flush`.

Programming Tip: **Close a file when you are finished with it**
When you write data to a file, the data may not immediately reach its destination. Closing a file forces any pending output to be written to the file before it is closed. If you do not close a file and your program terminates abnormally, data can be lost.

Appending to a Text File

C.11   In our previous example, if the file data.txt had already existed, its old contents would be lost and replaced with new output. Sometimes that is not what you want. Sometimes you want to add a program's output to the end of the file. This is called **appending to a file.** If you want to append program output to the file data.txt, you would connect the file to the stream outStream, as follows:

```
outStream = new PrintWriter(new FileOutputStream("data.txt", true));
```

The effect is similar to our previous example. If the file data.txt already exists, the old file contents will remain, and the program's output will be placed after the old contents of the file. If the file data.txt does not already exist, Java will create an empty file of that name and write the output to this empty file.

Reading a Text File Using BufferedReader

C.12   **Example.** Suppose that the text file data.txt was created by either a text editor or a Java program—like the code in Segment C.6—that uses the class PrintWriter. The following simple example reads the lines from such a text file and displays them on the screen:

```
try
{
   BufferedReader inStream =
            new BufferedReader(new FileReader("data.txt"));

   String line = inStream.readLine();
   System.out.println("The first line in data.txt is:");
   System.out.println(line);

   line = inStream.readLine();
   System.out.println("The second line in data.txt is:");
   System.out.println(line);
   inStream.close();
}
catch(FileNotFoundException e)
{
   System.out.println("File data.txt was not found");
   System.out.println("or could not be opened.");
}
catch(IOException e)
{
   System.out.println("Error reading from file data.txt.");
}
```

Figure C-2 shows the file data.txt and the output when these statements read the file.

C.13   We open the file data.txt by writing

```
BufferedReader inStream = new BufferedReader(new FileReader("data.txt"));
```

The class BufferedReader is the preferred stream class for reading from a text file. As was true of the class PrintWriter, the class BufferedReader has no constructor that takes a file name as its argument, so we need to use another class—FileReader in this case—to help with opening the file. FileReader's constructor will accept a file name as its argument and produce a stream that is a

Reader. The constructor for BufferedReader will accept a Reader as an argument. Reader is an abstract class that is the base class of all streams with "Reader" in their name.

Figure C-2   (a) The text file data.txt and (b) the output of the code in Segment C.12 after reading the first two lines of the file

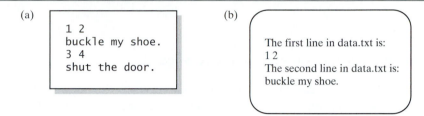

(a)

```
1 2
buckle my shoe.
3 4
shut the door.
```

(b)

The first line in data.txt is:
1 2
The second line in data.txt is:
buckle my shoe.

The method readLine of the class BufferedReader reads the next line of input from the input stream and returns that line. If the read goes beyond the end of the file, null is returned. Notice that readLine reads from a text file just as the method readLine of the class SavitchIn reads a line of text from the keyboard. After we are finished reading from the text file, we close it by invoking the method close, just as we did when we were finished writing a file.

Notice that we catch two kinds of exceptions, FileNotFoundException and IOException. Opening the file might throw a FileNotFoundException, and any invocation of inStream.readLine() might throw an IOException. Because a FileNotFoundException is a kind of IOException, we could choose to catch only IOException. However, if we do this, we would not know the reason for an exception. Was it caused by opening the file or by reading from the file after it was opened?

C.14   The class BufferedReader does not have any methods, such as readLineInt in SavitchIn, that can read a number. The only way that you can read a number from a text file using the class BufferedReader is to read it as a string and then convert the string to a number. Some techniques for converting strings to numbers are discussed in Segment A.86 of Appendix A.

The class BufferedReader does, however, have a method read that reads a single character. This method returns a positive integer of type int that corresponds to the character read; it does not return the character itself. Thus, to get the character, you must use a type cast, as in

```
char nextChar = (char)(inStream.read());
```

This statement sets nextChar to the first character that has not yet been read from the file. If the read goes beyond the end of the file, read returns –1.

Testing for the End of a Text File

C.15   When using the class BufferedReader, what happens if your program tries to read beyond the end of a text file? The method readLine returns null, and the method read returns –1. Your program can test for the end of a file by checking the return values of these methods. Notice that an EOFException is not thrown.

The following statements indicate how you could read all the lines of a text file without knowing how many lines are present:

```
String line = inStream.readLine();
while (line != null)
{
  < Process line here >
  . . .
  line = inStream.readLine();
} // end while
```

Reading a File Name from the Keyboard

C.16   Thus far, we have used literals—that is, string constants—to name the files in our examples when we connected the file to a stream. For example, we used the following to connect the file data.txt to the stream inStream:

```
BufferedReader inStream = new BufferedReader(new FileReader("data.txt"));
```

However, you can also ask the user to type the file name at the keyboard when the program is run. Simply have the program read the file name the user types into a variable of type String, and use that String variable in place of the file name. Thus, you can write the following:

```
System.out.println("Enter file name:");
String fileName = SavitchIn.readLineWord();
BufferedReader inStream = new BufferedReader(new FileReader(fileName));
```

You can use a String variable when you open text files and binary files, regardless of whether you open them for input or output.

Defining a Method to Open a Stream

C.17   Imagine that we want to write a method that opens a file. We will use a text file here and open it for output, but the idea is applicable to any kind of file. Our method has a String parameter that represents the file name. The client of this method could either read the file name from the user, as shown in the previous segment, or use a literal for the file name. The method creates an output stream, connects it to the given file, and returns the stream to the client. The following is such a method:

```
public static PrintWriter openOutputFile(String fileName)
                                    throws FileNotFoundException
{
  PrintWriter tempOutStream =
          new PrintWriter(new FileOutputStream(fileName));
  return tempOutStream;
} // end openOutputFile
```

We could invoke this method as follows:

```
PrintWriter outStream = openOutputFile("data.txt");
```

and go on to use outStream to write to the file.

What if we had written the method as follows instead?

```
// This method does not do what we want it to do.
public static void openFile(String fileName, PrintWriter streamName)
                                throws FileNotFoundException
{
   streamName = new PrintWriter(new FileOutputStream(fileName));
} // end openFile
```

This looks like a fairly reasonable method to include in some class, but it has a problem. For example, consider the following statements that invoke the method:

```
PrintWriter outStream = null;
openOutputFile("data.txt", outStream);
```

After this code is executed, the value of `outStream` is still `null`. The file that was opened in the method `openOutputFile` went away when the method ended. The problem has to do with how Java handles arguments of a class type. These arguments are passed to the method by reference—that is, as a memory address that cannot be changed. The object at the memory address normally can be changed, but the memory address itself cannot be changed. Thus, you cannot change `outStream`.

Once a stream is connected to a file, however, you can pass the stream name as an argument to a method, and the method can change the file. Also note that this applies only to arguments of methods. If the stream name is either a local variable or a data field, you can open a file and connect it to a stream and this problem will not occur.

I/O with Binary Files

C.18   Binary files store data in the same format in which data is stored in the computer's main memory, that is, as a sequence of bytes. This fact is the reason why a program can process binary files so efficiently. You can use a Java program to create a binary file on one computer and have it read by a Java program on another computer. Normally, you cannot use a text editor to read binary files.

The most commonly used stream classes for processing binary files are `DataInputStream` and `DataOutputStream`. Each class has methods to read or write data one byte at a time. These streams can also convert numbers and characters to bytes that can be stored in a binary file. They allow your program to write data to or read data from a binary file as if the data were not just bytes but strings or items of any of Java's primitive data types. If you do not need to access your files with an editor, the easiest and most efficient way to read and write data to files is to use `DataOutputStream` and `DataInputStream` with a binary file.

Writing to a Binary File Using `DataOutputStream`

C.19   If you want to create a binary file to store either `String` values or values of any of the primitive data types, you can use the stream class `DataOutputStream`. The following example uses the method `writeInt` of this class to write an `int` value to the file `numbers.dat`:

```
try
{
   DataOutputStream outStream =
       new DataOutputStream(new FileOutputStream("numbers.dat"));

   System.out.println("Enter nonnegative integers, one per line.");
   System.out.println("Place a negative number at the end.");
```

```
      int number;
      do
      {
        number = SavitchIn.readLineInt();
        outStream.writeInt(number);
      } while (number >= 0);

      outStream.close();
      System.out.println("Numbers and sentinel value");
      System.out.println("written to the file numbers.dat.");
    }
    catch(FileNotFoundException e)
    {
      System.out.println("Error opening the file numbers.dat.");
      System.exit(0);
    }
    catch(IOException e)
    {
      System.out.println("Problem with output to file numbers.dat.");
    }
```

Note that most of these statements appear within a try block, since any of the I/O statements that we are using here can throw an exception. A problem with opening a file causes a FileNotFoundException, regardless of whether the file is a text file or a binary file. The other I/O statements in our example can cause an IOException if something has gone wrong with our program I/O. We catch each of these exceptions in its own catch block, so that if an exception occurs, we get an appropriate error message.

C.20   The output stream for writing to the file numbers.dat is created and named when we open the file:

```
DataOutputStream outStream =
    new DataOutputStream(new FileOutputStream("numbers.dat"));
```

If the file numbers.dat does not exist, this statement will create an empty file named numbers.dat. If the file numbers.dat exists already, this statement will erase its contents so that the file starts out empty.

The class DataOutputStream has no constructor that takes a file name as its argument. Thus, when you connect a file to a stream of the class DataOutputStream, you must take a two-step process. First, you connect the file to another type of output stream—FileOutputStream—that does work with a file name, and then you connect this other output stream to a stream in the class DataOutputStream.

The stream named outStream is an object of the class DataOutputStream. It has some similarity to the stream System.out in that it has methods for handling program output. However, System.out and objects of the class DataOutputStream have output methods that have different names and that behave somewhat differently. Objects of the class DataOutputStream do not have a method named println. Instead, they have a method named writeInt that can write a single int value to a file. They also have other output methods that we will discuss shortly.

C.21   Once a stream in the class DataOutputStream is connected to a file, you can write integers to the file by using the method writeInt, as in

```
outStream.writeInt(number);
```

This statement writes the value of the int variable number to the file numbers.dat. The numbers in a binary file are not written in a human-readable form. There are no lines or other separators between the numbers. Instead, the numbers are written in the file one immediately after the other, and they are encoded as a sequence of bytes in the same way that the numbers would be encoded in the computer's main memory. These coded `int` values cannot be read with a text editor. Realistically, they can be read only by another Java program.

Notice that our example sends output to two different places by using two different output streams. The stream named `outStream` is connected to the binary file `numbers.dat` and sends its output to that file. The other output stream is `System.out`. You may be so used to using it that you don't think of `System.out` in this way, but it is an output stream that is connected to the screen. So output statements that use `System.out.println` send their output to the screen.

C.22   You can use a stream from the class `DataOutputStream` to write values of any primitive type and also to write data of the type `String`. `DataOutputStream` has the methods `writeLong`, `writeDouble`, and `writeFloat` that are similar to `writeInt`. All of these methods can throw an `IOException`. The method `writeChar` writes a single character, but `writeChar` expects its argument to be of type `int`. If you start with a value of type `char`, the `char` value must be type-cast to an `int` before it is passed it to the method `writeChar`. Java will automatically convert a `char` value to an `int` value for you, so you do not need to write the type cast explicitly. Thus, you could write, for example,

```
outStream.writeChar('A');
```

and have it mean

```
outStream.writeChar((int)'A');
```

The method `writeBoolean` writes a single boolean value:

```
outStream.writeBoolean(false);
```

To write a string to a binary file, you use the method `writeUTF`. For example, if `outStream` is a stream of type `DataOutputStream`, the following will write the string *Hi Mom* to the file connected to that stream:

```
outStream.writeUTF("Hi Mom");
```

Of course, with `writeUTF` or any of the write methods, you can use a variable of the appropriate type (in this case, the type `String`) as an argument to the method.

Note: Recall that Java uses the Unicode character set, a set of characters that includes many letters used in Asian languages and other languages whose character sets are very different from English. Most editors and operating systems use the ASCII character set, which is the character set normally used for English and for typical Java programs. The ASCII character set is a subset of the Unicode character set, so the Unicode character set has a lot of characters we do not need. There is a standard Unicode way of coding all the Unicode characters, but for English-speaking countries, it is not a very efficient coding scheme. The **Unicode Text Format,** or **UTF,** coding scheme is an alternative coding scheme that uses one byte for each ASCII character but two bytes for other Unicode characters.

You can write output of different types to the same file. For example, you can write a combination of `int`, `double`, and `String` values. However, mixing types in a file does require special care so that you can read them from the file later. To read a file of mixed types, you need to know the order in which the various types appear in the file because, as you will see, a program that reads from the file uses a different method to read data of each different type.

Like `PrintWriter`, `DataOutputStream` has a method `flush` that you can use to empty the output buffer at any time. It also has a method `close` that you should call when you are finished writing to the file.

C.23   **Appending to a binary file.** To add a program's output to the end of the data already in a binary file—that is, to append data to the file—you would open the file as follows:

```
DataOutputStream outStream =
        new DataOutputStream(new FileOutputStream("numbers.dat", true));
```

If `numbers.dat` does not exist already, Java will create an empty file of that name and write the output to this empty file.

Reading from a Binary File Using `DataInputStream`

C.24   If you use `DataOutputStream` to write data to a binary file, you can read that file by using the stream class `DataInputStream`. Each output method in `DataOutputStream` corresponds to an input method in `DataInputStream`. For example, if you use the method `writeInt` to write an integer to a binary file, you can read that integer back by using the method `readInt`. If you write a number to a file using the method `writeDouble`, you can read that number back by using the method `readDouble`, and so forth.

The following statements demonstrate how to read from a binary file of integers:

```java
try
{
    DataInputStream inStream =
            new DataInputStream(new FileInputStream("numbers.dat"));
    System.out.print("Reading all the integers ");
    System.out.println("in the file numbers.dat.");
    try
    {
        while (true)
        {
            int n = inStream.readInt();
            System.out.println(n);
        } // end while
    }
    catch(EOFException e)
    {
        System.out.println("End of reading from file.");
    }
    inStream.close();
}
catch(FileNotFoundException e)
{
    System.out.println("Cannot find file numbers.dat.");
}
catch(IOException e)
{
    System.out.println("Problem with input from file numbers.dat.");
}
```

You open a binary file for input by using `DataInputStream` in a manner similar to what you have already seen for `DataOutputStream`. You use the class `DataInputStream` instead of `DataOutputStream`, and you use the class `FileInputStream` instead of `FileOutputStream`.

C.25   The code in Segment C.24 assumes that the file contains integers. We read the entire file and display its contents on the screen. When a method such as readInt reaches the end of a binary file, an EOFException occurs. Thus, our example uses a while statement whose boolean expression is the constant true. The loop ends when the exception occurs, and processing continues with the first catch block. At that point, we call the method close to close the file. Program execution continues with the statement that is after the last of the three catch blocks.

You can use a stream from the class DataInputStream to read values of any primitive type and also to read data of the type String. In addition to readInt, DataInputStream has the methods readLong, readDouble, and readFloat that are similar to readInt.

The method readChar reads a single character that was written using writeChar. Likewise, readBoolean reads a single boolean value that was written using writeBoolean. To read a string from a binary file that was written using writeUTF, you use the method readUTF. All of these methods can throw either an IOException or an EOFException.

A binary file can contain data of differing types, and you can use DataInputStream to read such a file. You must be careful, however, to match read methods with data of the appropriate type. If a data item in the file is not of the type expected by the reading method, the result is likely to be a mess. For example, if your program writes an integer using writeInt, any program that reads that integer should read it using readInt. If you instead use readDouble, for example, your program will misbehave.

C.26   When the method writeInt writes an integer to a binary file, it stores the same number of bytes for each value of type int. All the write methods except for writeUTF write out the same number of bytes every time they write a value of their respective type. (But the methods each use a different number of bytes.) The method writeUTF uses differing numbers of bytes to store different strings in a file. Longer strings require more bytes than shorter strings. This can present a problem, because there are no separators between data items in a binary file. Thus, Java writes some extra information at the start of each string. This extra information tells how many bytes the string occupies in the file, so readUTF knows how many bytes to read.

Programming Tip: Binary files and text files encode their data in different ways. A stream that expects to read a binary file, such as a stream in the class DataInputStream, will have problems reading a text file. If you attempt to read a text file with a stream in the class DataInput-Stream, your program either will read "garbage values" or will encounter some other error condition.

Programming Tip: **Check for the end of a file**
If your program makes no provisions for detecting the end of a file, nothing good will happen when you reach the end of a file. If your program tries to read beyond the end of a file, it may enter an infinite loop or it might end abnormally. Always be sure your program checks for the end of a file and does something appropriate when it reaches the end of the file. Even if you think your program will not read past the end of the file, you should provide for this eventuality just in case things do not go exactly as you planned.

Programming Tip: **Ways to check for the end of a file**
When reading from a file, you must be careful to test for the end of the file in the correct way. If you do not, your program most likely will go into an unintended infinite loop or will terminate abnormally. Here are some possible ways to test for the end of a file:

- End the file with a special value to serve as a **sentinel value.** Then your program can stop reading when it reads the sentinel value. For example, a file of nonnegative integers could use a negative integer at the end as a sentinel value. Using a sentinel value, however, restricts the values that you can place in the file.
- Catch an `EOFException`, if the read method that you use throws one when it reaches the end of the file. This technique is applicable when you use a method in `DataInputStream` to read from a binary file.
- When reading from a text file, the methods in `BufferedReader` return a special value, such as `null`, when they try to read beyond the end of a file. You can test for this value.

The Class `File`

C.27   Java provides a class named `File` that you can use to check certain properties of files. For example, you can check whether a file with a specified name exists and whether a file is readable. The class `File` is like a wrapper class for file names. A string like `"data.txt"` might be a file name, but it has only string properties. It has no file-name properties. A `File` object, on the other hand, knows that it is supposed to name a file.

You can create a `File` object named `fileObject` by writing the following statement:

```java
File fileObject = new File("data.txt");
```

You usually—but not always—can pass an object of type `File` to a stream constructor as an argument whenever you can use a string as the argument. In particular, the classes `FileInputStream`, `FileOutputStream`, and `FileReader` each accept a `File` object as an argument.

You can use the method `exists` of the class `File` to test whether any file with the name `data.txt` exists, as in this example:

```java
if (!fileObject.exists())
  System.out.println("No file by that name.");
```

Most operating systems let you designate some files as not readable or as readable only by certain people. So if you know that a file exists and has a certain name, you can see whether the operating system will let you read from the file. You can make this test by using the method `canRead`, as follows:

```java
if (!fileObject.canRead())
  System.out.println("Not allowed to read from that file.");
```

The class `File` has the following additional methods:

```java
/** Task: Tests whether the program can write to the file. */
public boolean canWrite();

/** Task: Deletes the file and signals whether deletion was possible. */
public boolean delete();

/** Task: Returns the length of the file in bytes. */
public long length();

/** Task: Returns the name of the file. */
public String getName();

/** Task: Returns the path name of the file. */
public String getPath();
```

Note: **Path names**

When passing a file name as an argument to a constructor of classes like `File` and `FileReader`, you can use a simple file name. Java assumes that the file is in the same directory (folder) as the one that contains the program. You also can use a full or relative path name. A **path name** gives not only the name of the file, but also tells what directory (folder) the file is in. A **full path name,** as the name suggests, give a complete path name. A **relative path name** gives the path to the file starting in the directory that contains your program. Path names depend on your operating system rather than the Java language.

Object Serialization

C.28   You have seen how to write primitive values and strings to a file, and how to read them again. How would you write and read objects other than strings? You could, of course, write an object's data fields to a file and invent some way to reconstruct the object when you read the file. When you consider that a data field could be another object that itself could have an object as a data field, completing this task sounds formidable.

Fortunately, Java provides a simple way—called **object serialization**—to represent an object as a sequence of bytes that can be written to a file. This process will occur automatically for any object that belongs to a class that implements the interface `Serializable`. This interface, which is in the package `java.io`, is empty, so you have no additional methods to implement. Adding only the words `implements Serializable` to the class's definition is enough.

For example, we would begin a class `Student` as follows:

```
public class Student implements Serializable
{
    . . .
```

The `Serializable` interface tells the compiler that `Student` objects can be serialized. To serialize an object and write it to a file, you use the method `writeObject` from the class `ObjectOutput-Stream`. To read a serialized object from a file, you use the method `readObject` from the class `ObjectInputStream`.

C.29   **Example.** To serialize a `Student` object `aStudent` and write it to a binary file, we would write the following statements:

```
FileOutputStream outFile = new FileOutputStream("objects.dat");
ObjectOutputStream outStream = new ObjectOutputStream(outFile);
    . . .
outStream.writeObject(aStudent);
```

Any objects that are data fields of aStudent must also belong to a class that implements `Serializable`. Such objects are serialized when aStudent is serialized. Many classes in the Java Class Library—including `String`—implement `Serializable`.

To read the `Student` object from the file, we would write

```
FileInputStream inFile = new FileInputStream("objects.dat");
ObjectInputStream inStream = new ObjectInputStream(inFile);
    . . .
Student joe = (Student)inStream.readObject();
```

C.30 We will call a class **serializable** if

- It implements the interface `Serializable`
- Any of its object data fields are instances of a serializable class
- Its direct super class, if any, is either serializable or defines a default constructor

Note that any subclass of a serializable class is serializable.

C.31 **Arrays.** Since Java treats arrays as objects, you can use `writeObject` to write an array to a binary file, and you can use `readObject` to read it from the file. For example, suppose that `group` is an array of `Student` objects like the object `joe` that was defined in Segment C.29. If `outStream` is an instance of `ObjectOutputStream` that is associated with a binary file, we can write the array to that file by executing the statement

```
outStream.writeObject(group);
```

After creating the file, we can read the array by using the statement

```
Student[] myArray = (Student[])inStream.readObject();
```

where `inStream` is an instance of `ObjectInputStream` that is associated with the file that we just created.

PROGRAMMING TIPS

- When you write data to a file, the data may not immediately reach its destination. Closing a file forces any pending output to be written to the file before it is closed. If you do not close a file and your program terminates abnormally, data can be lost.

- Binary files and text files encode their data in different ways. A stream that expects to read a binary file, such as a stream in the class `DataInputStream`, will have problems reading a text file. If you attempt to read a text file with a stream in the class `DataInputStream`, your program either will read "garbage values" or will encounter some other error condition.

- When reading from a file, your program should check for the end of the file and do something appropriate when it reaches it. Even if you think your program will not read past the end of the file, you should provide for this eventuality just in case things do not go exactly as you planned.

- You must be careful to test for the end of a file in the correct way. If you do not, your program most likely will go into an unintended infinite loop or will terminate abnormally. Here are some possible ways to test for the end of a file:
    - End the file with a special value to serve as a **sentinel value.** Then your program can stop reading when it reads the sentinel value. For example, a file of nonnegative integers could use a negative integer at the end as a sentinel value. Using a sentinel value, however, restricts the values that you can place in the file.
    - Catch an `EOFException`, if the read method that you use throws one when it reaches the end of the file. This technique is applicable when you use a method in `DataInputStream` to read from a binary file.
    - When reading from a text file, the methods in `BufferedReader` return a special value, such as `null`, when they try to read beyond the end of a file. You can test for this value.

D

Documentation and Programming Style

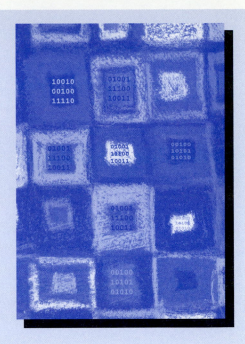

CONTENTS

Naming Variables and Classes
Indenting
Comments
    Single-Line Comments
    Comment Blocks
    When to Write Comments
    Java Documentation Comments
    Running `javadoc`

PREREQUISITES

Appendix   A   Java Essentials
Chapter   1   Java Classes

Most programs are used many times and are changed either to fix bugs or to accommodate new demands by the user. If the program is not easy to read and to understand, it will not be easy to change. It might even be impossible to change without heroic efforts. Even if you use your program only once, you should pay some attention to its readability. After all, you will have to read the program to debug it.

In this appendix, we discuss three techniques that can help make your program more readable: meaningful names, indenting, and comments.

Naming Variables and Classes

D.1   Names like x and y are almost never good variable names. The name you give to a variable should suggest what the variable is used for. If the variable holds a count of something, you might name it count. If the variable holds a tax rate, you might name it taxRate.

In addition to choosing names that are meaningful and legal in Java, you should also follow the normal practice of other programmers. That way it will be easier for them to read your code and to combine your code with their code, should you work on a project with more than one person. By convention, variable and class names are made up entirely of letters and digits. Begin each variable name with a lowercase letter and each class name with an uppercase letter. If the name consists of more than one word, use capital letters at the word boundaries, as in `numberOfTries` and `SavitchIn`.

Use all uppercase letters for named constants to distinguish them from other variables. Use the underscore character to separate words, if necessary, as in `INCHES_PER_FOOT`.

Indenting

D.2 A program has a structure: Smaller parts are within larger parts. You use indentation to indicate this structure and thereby make your program easier to read. Although Java ignores any indentation you use, indenting consistently is essential to good programming style.

Each class begins at the left margin and uses braces to enclose its definition. For example, you might write

```java
public class CircleCalculation
{
    . . .
} // end CircleCalculation
```

The data fields and methods appear indented within these braces. In a simple program, you might have the following:

```java
public class CircleCalculation
{
    public static final double PI = 3.14159;

    public static void main(String[] args)
    {
        double radius; // in inches
        double area;   // in square inches
        . . .
    } // end main
} // end CircleCalculation
```

Within each method, you indent the statements that form the method's body. These statements in turn might contain compound statements that are indented further. The program then has statements nested within statements.

Each level of nesting should be indented to show the nesting more clearly. The outermost structure is not indented at all. The next level of nested structure is indented. The nested structure within that is double indented, and so on. Typically, you should indent two or three spaces at each level of indentation. You want to see indentation clearly, but you want to use most of the line for the Java statement.

If a statement does not fit on one line, you can write it on two or more lines. However, when you write a single statement on more than one line, indent the successive lines more than the first line, as in the following example:

```java
System.out.println("The volume of a sphere whose radius is " + radius +
                   " inches is " + volume + " cubic inches.");
```

Ultimately, you need to follow the rules for indenting—and for programming style in general—given by your instructor or project manager. In any event, you should indent consistently within any one program.

Comments

D.3   The documentation for a program describes what the program does and how it does it. The best programs are **self-documenting.** That is, their clean style and well-chosen names make the program's purpose and logic clear to any programmer who reads the program. You should strive for such self-documenting programs, but your programs will also need a bit of explanation to make them completely clear. This explanation can be given in the form of **comments.**

Comments are notations in your program that help a person understand the program, but that are ignored by the compiler. Many text editors automatically highlight comments in some way, such as showing them in color. In Java, there are several ways of forming comments.

Single-Line Comments

D.4   To write a comment on a single line, begin the comment with the two symbols //. Everything after the symbols // through to the end of the line is treated as a comment and is ignored by the compiler. These sorts of comments are handy for short comments, such as

```
String sentence; // Spanish version
```

If you want a comment of this form to span several lines, each line must contain the symbols //.

Comment Blocks

D.5   Anything written between the matching pairs of symbols /* and */ is a comment and is ignored by the compiler. This form usually is not used to document a program. Instead, the pair /* and */ is handy during debugging to temporarily disable a group of Java statements. However, Java programmers do use the pair /** and */ to delimit comments written in a certain form, as you will see in Segment D.7.

When to Write Comments

D.6   It is difficult to explain just when you should write a comment. Too many comments can be as bad as too few comments. Too many comments can hide the really important ones. Too few comments can leave a reader baffled by things that were obvious to you. Just remember that you also will read your program. If you read it next week, will you remember what you did?

Every program file should have an explanatory comment at the beginning of the file. This comment should give all the important information about the file: what the program does, the name of the author, how to contact the author, the date that the file was last changed, and in a course, what the assignment is. Every method should have a comment that explains the method.

Within methods, you need a comment to explain any nonobvious details. Notice the poor comments on the following declarations of the variables radius and area:

```
double radius; // the radius
double area;   // the area
```

Because we chose descriptive variable names, these comments are obvious. But rather than simply omitting these comments, can we write something that is not obvious? What units are used for the radius? Inches? Feet? Meters? Centimeters? We will add a comment that gives this information, as follows:

```java
double radius; // in inches
double area;   // in square inches
```

Java Documentation Comments

D.7 The Java language comes with a utility program named **javadoc** that will generate HTML documents that describe your classes. These documents tell people who use your program or class how to use it, but omit all the implementation details.

The program javadoc extracts the signature for your class, the signatures for all public methods, and comments that are written in a certain form. No method bodies and no private items are extracted.

For javadoc to extract a comment, the comment must satisfy three conditions:

1. The comment must occur immediately before a public class definition or the signature of a public method.
2. The comment must begin with /** and end with */.
3. Each line of the comment must begin with *.

Segment D.12 contains an example of a comment in this style.

Placing extra asterisks is both allowed and common. You can insert HTML commands in your comments so that you gain more control over javadoc, but that is not necessary and we will not do so in this book.

D.8 **Tags.** Comments written for javadoc usually contain special **tags** that identify such things as the programmer and a method's parameters and return value. Tags begin with the symbol @. We will describe only four of the tags in this appendix.

The tag @author identifies the programmer's name and is required of all classes and interfaces. (To save space, we will ignore this requirement in this book.) The other tags of interest to us are for methods. They must appear within a comment in the following order:

```
@param
@return
@throws
```

D.9 **The @param tag.** You must write a @param tag for every parameter in a method. You should list these tags in the order in which the parameters appear in the method's signature. After the @param tag, you give the name and description of the parameter. Typically, you use a phrase instead of a sentence to describe the parameter, and you mention the parameter's data type first. Do not use punctuation between the parameter name and its description, as javadoc inserts one dash when creating its documentation.

For example,

```
* @param code      the character code of the ticket category
* @param customer  the string that names the customer
```

D.10 **The @return tag.** You must write a @return tag for every method that returns a value, even when you have already described the value in the method's description. Try to say something more specific about this value here. This tag must come after any @param tags in the comment. Do not use this tag for void methods and constructors.

D.11   **The @throws tag.** If a method throws a checked exception, you name it next by using a @throws tag. Recall that any checked exceptions that a method throws will also appear in a throws clause in the method's signature. You also should list any unchecked exception—other than NullPointerException—that a client might catch.

Include a @throws tag for each exception, and list them alphabetically by name.

D.12   **Example.** Here is a sample javadoc comment for a method. We usually begin such comments with a brief description of the method's purpose. Often, we will precede that description with the word "Task." This is our convention, as javadoc has no tag for this purpose.

```
/** Task: Adds a new entry to a list.
 *   @param newEntry     the object to be added to the list
 *   @param newPosition  the position of the new entry within the
 *                       list
 *   @return true if the addition is successful
 *   @throws ListException if newPosition < 1 or newPosition >
 *                         1 + the length of the list */
public boolean add(Object newEntry, int newPosition) throws ListException
```

To save space in this book, we sometimes omit portions of a comment that we would include in our actual programs. For example, some methods might have only a description of their purpose, and some might have only a @return tag.

The documentation that javadoc prepares from the previous comment appears as follows:

add

```
public abstract boolean add(java.lang.Object newEntry,
                            int newPosition) throws ListException
```

Task: Adds a new entry to a list.

Parameters:
     newEntry - the object to be added to the list
     newPosition - the position of the new entry within the list
Returns:
     true if the addition is successful

Running javadoc

D.13   You run javadoc on an entire package. However, if you want to run it on a single class, you can make the class into a package simply by inserting the following at the start of the file for the class:

package *package_name* ;

Remember that the package name should describe a relative path name for the directory or folder containing the files of classes.

To run javadoc, you must be in the directory that contains the package directory, but not in the package directory itself. To phrase it another way, you must be one directory above the directory that contains the class (or classes) in the package for which you want to generate documentation. Then all you need to do is give the following command:

javadoc -d *document_directory package_name*

Replace *document_directory* with the name of the directory in which you want `javadoc` to place the HTML documents it produces. For example, *document_directory* can simply be the name of the subdirectory you are in when you run the preceding command. The directory must already exist; `javadoc` will not create it for you.

For example, suppose you want to use `javadoc` to generate documentation for the class `SavitchIn`. First, go to a directory on your CLASSPATH. Create a subdirectory to hold a package; for example, you might call the subdirectory `ExtraSavitchStuff`. Place the file `SavitchIn.java` in the directory `ExtraSavitchStuff`, and place the following at the start of the file `SavitchIn.java`:

package `ExtraSavitchStuff;`

The package `ExtraSavitchStuff` now contains the class `SavitchIn`.

Next, create a directory to receive the HTML documents. For example, you might call this directory `SavitchDocs`. Make the directory a subdirectory of the directory containing `ExtraSavitchStuff`. (Do not make it a subdirectory of `ExtraSavitchStuff`.)

Finally, be sure you are in the directory that has both `ExtraSavitchStuff` and `SavitchDocs` as subdirectories, and give the following command:

```
javadoc -d SavitchDocs ExtraSavitchStuff
```

If you then look in the subdirectory `SavitchDocs`, you will see a number of HTML documents whose names end in `.html`. You can view these files by using your browser. The HTML documents will describe the package `ExtraSavitchStuff`, including the class `SavitchIn`.

If you wish, you can use the directory `ExtraSavitchStuff` in place of `SavitchDocs` so that both the source file `SavitchIn.java` and the HTML documents end up in the same directory.

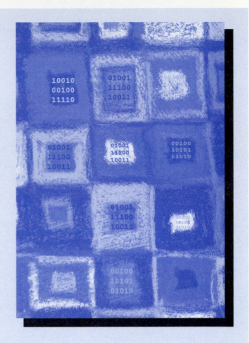

Chapter 1

1. ```
   Name myName = new Name();
   myName.setFirst("Joseph");
   myName.setLast("Brown");
   ```

2. `System.out.println(myName.getLast() + ", " + myName.getFirst());`

3. Valued: `getFuelLevel`, `getSpeed`, `getMileage`.

   Void: `goForward`, `goBackward`, `accelerate`, `decelerate`.

4. Mutator.

5. Valued.

6. Void.

7. A client could set the data field to an illegal value.

8. `number` is 5 and `aName` references `jamie`.

9. Yes, by using `Name`'s set methods.

10. No.

11. A default constructor is a constructor that has no parameters.

12. You invoke a constructor by using the `new` operator.

13. If you do not define a constructor, the compiler defines a default constructor.

14. The compiler does not define additional constructors. Thus, the class will not have a default constructor.

15. An object that is not referenced is marked for garbage collection. Eventually, the Java run-time environment deallocates the object by returning its memory locations to the operating system so that they can be used again.

16. Each instance (object) of a class will have a copy of a constant data field that is not static.
   ```

Chapter 2

1. Some possibilities are `roomNumber` and `dorm`, or `street`, `city`, `state`, `zip`.
2. `private Address residence;`
   Add the methods `setAddress` and `getAddress`.
3. The constructors, `setStudent`, `toString`.
4. The `Vehicle` class has two subclasses, `WheeledVehicle` and `WheellessVehicle`. The subclasses of `WheeledVehicle` are `Automobile` and `Wagon`. `Boat` is the subclass of `WheellessVehicle`. The remaining subclasses are the same as given in the figure.
5. Overloading.
6. Overriding. The revised version of `setStudent` in `CollegeStudent` has the same signature as the version in the base class `Student`.
7. Yes. You can assign an object of a class to a variable of any ancestor type. An object of type `HighSchoolStudent` can do anything that an object of type `Student` can do.
8. No. The `Student` object does not have all the operations expected of a `HighSchoolStudent` object.
9. `String`.
10. `if (sue.equals(susan))`
11. Overload. The two methods have different signatures: One has a parameter, one does not.
12. Overriding. The methods have the same signatures.
13. At one time, overloading was an example of polymorphism. Today, polymorphism describes a situation in which an object determines at execution time which action of a method it will use for a method name that is overridden either directly or indirectly.
14. No. Each call to `displayAt` will invoke the correct version of `display`.

Chapter 3

1. A client interface describes how to use the class. It contains the signatures for the class's public methods, the comments that tell you how to use these methods, and any publicly defined constants of the class. The implementation consists of all data fields and the definitions of all methods, including those that are public, private, and protected.
2. A television. The remote control and the controls on the TV form the client interface. The implementation is inside the TV itself.
3. Precondition: `radius > 0`; the constant `PI` is defined.
   Postcondition: The area of the circle is returned.
4. `// Assertion: max is the largest of array[0],..., array[index]`
5. ```
   public interface StudentInterface
   {
     public void setStudent(Name studentName, String studentId);
     public void setName(Name studentName);
     public Name getName();
     public void setId(String studentId);
     public String getId();
     public String toString();
   } // end StudentInterface
   ```
6. `public class Student implements StudentInterface`
7. ```
   public class Name implements Comparable
   {
     . . .
   ```

```
    public int compareTo(Object other)
    {
        Name otherName = (Name)other;

        int result = last.compareTo(otherName.last);

        // if last names are equal, check first names
        if (result == 0)
            result = first.compareTo(otherName.first);

        return result;
    } // end compareTo
    . . .
```

8. No.

9.

Student
Responsibilities
Set name and ID
Set name
Set ID
Get name
Get ID
Get a string that represents a student
Collaborations
String
Name

10.

Name
first
last
setName(firstName, lastName)
getName()
setFirst(firstName)
getFirst()
setLast(lastName)
getLast()
giveLastNameTo(aName)
toString()

11. Add a unidirectional association (arrow) from AllCourses to Course with a cardinality of 1 on its tail and * on its head.

Chapter 4

1. `myList.add(c)`
   `myList.add(1, a)`

```
myList.add(2, b)
myList.add(4, d)
```
2.
```
seven = myList.remove(7)
three = myList.remove(3)
myList.add(3, seven)
myList.add(7, three)
```
3.
```
bob = alphaList.remove(3);
ellen = alphaList.remove(2);
alphaList.add(2, bob);
alphaList.add(3, ellen);
drew = alphaList.remove(4);
ellen = alphaList.remove(3);
alphaList.add(3, drew);
alphaList.add(4, ellen);
```
4. **a.** When you use `println` to display an object, the method `toString` is called implicitly. It returns a string.

   b. No.

Chapter 5

1. When the name comes after the name of the student in the last desk; the new student then sits at the desk after the last one that is currently occupied.
2. The students remain in consecutively numbered positions.
3. Time is saved by not moving the students.
4. (1) Set elements of `entry` to `null`; (2) repeatedly remove the last entry by repeatedly calling `remove(length)`; (3) reallocate the array `entry`.
5. Advantage: It is easier to implement this add method. Your code will more likely be correct if the other add method is correct.

   Disadvantage: Invoking another method takes more time. Additionally, the second add method invokes `makeRoom` needlessly.
6. **a.** a b c d w e

   b. a b c d e w

   c. Part *a*
7. `myList.add(newEntry)`. The other add method validates the position 6 and then needlessly invokes `makeRoom`.
8. `null`. Since `(givenPosition >= 1) && (givenPosition <= 0)` is always false, the initial value of `result` is returned.
9. Advantage: You can access any array location directly if you know its index.

   Disadvantage: You likely will need to move entries within the array. The array has a fixed size, so you will either waste space or run out of room.
10.
```
public boolean add(int newPosition, Object newEntry)
{
    boolean isSuccessful = true;

    if ((newPosition >= 1) && (newPosition <= length+1))
    {
        if (isArrayFull())
            doubleArray();
```

```
      makeRoom(newPosition);
      entry[newPosition-1] = newEntry;
      length++;
   }
   else
      isSuccessful = false;

   return isSuccessful;
} // end add
```

Chapter 6

1. **a.** First.
   b. The student who arrived last (most recently).
2. At the beginning.
3. **a.** First.
   b. The student who arrived first.
4. At the end.
5. Advantage: You use only as much memory as you need; moving data is unnecessary.
   Disadvantage: You must traverse the chain to access items that are not first.
6. The student whose name is alphabetically first is in the first desk. You know the address of that desk. The student whose name is alphabetically last is in the last desk. You must traverse the chain to locate it.
7. deskBefore = address of first desk
   deskBefore = address on deskBefore
   deskToRemove = address on deskBefore
   Copy address on deskToRemove to deskBefore
   Return deskToRemove to the hallway
8. By asking the instructor, locate the first desk
   Give the address that is written on the first desk to the instructor
   Return the first desk to the hallway
9. When the chain is empty, `firstNode` is `null`. Setting `newNode.next` to `firstNode` sets it to `null`. Since `newNode.next` already is `null` as necessary, no harm is done by the additional assignment.
10. The method `replace` given in this chapter requires more effort than an array-based `replace` because it must traverse the chain to locate the entry to replace. An array-based `replace` can locate the desired entry directly, given its array index.
11. ```
    public void display()
    {
       Node currentNode = firstNode;
       while (currentNode != null)
       {
          System.out.println(current.data);
          currentNode = currentNode.next;
       } // end while
    } // end display
    ```
12. ```
    public boolean isEmpty()
    {
       return firstNode == null;
    } // end isEmpty
    ```

13. Add `Serializable` to the `implements` clause in the first line of the definition of `LList`. Add `implements Serializable` to the definition of `Node`.

14. The constructor and the methods `add`, `remove`, and `clear`. It probably would be a good idea to revise `clear` so that it sets `lastNode` to `null`. But as long as `isEmpty` checks `length` to determine whether a list is empty, you could leave `clear` as is.

Chapter 7

1. **a.** `nameList.reset();`
   `nameList.advance();`
   `nameList.advance();`
   `System.out.println(nameList.getCurrent());`

   b. `nameList.reset();`
   while `(nameList.advance())`
   `{`
   `   System.out.println(nameList.getCurrent());`
   `   nameList.advance();`
   `} // end while`

2. The output is
   Rachel
   Joey Rachel Jamie

3. Ben.

4. False, since the second call to `hasCurrent` within `advance` returns false.

5. Before: The first node would contain `null` in its next field.
   After: `firstNode`, `priorNode`, and `currentNode` would each be `null`.

6. Before: `currentNode` would reference the last node.
   After: `currentNode` would be `null`.

7. The last entry.

8. False, because `currentNode` is `null`.

9. Before: The node that `currentNode` references would contain `null` in its next field.
   After: The new node would contain `null` in its next field.

Chapter 8

1. `nameIterator.next();`
   `nameIterator.next();`
   `System.out.println(nameIterator.next());`

2. `nameIterator.next(); // list has > 1 entry`
   while `(nameIterator.hasNext())`
   `{`
   `   System.out.println(nameIterator.next());`
   `   if (nameIterator.hasNext())`
   `     nameIterator.next();`
   `} // end while`

3. **while** `(nameIterator.hasNext())`
   `{`
   `   nameIterator.next();`

```
    nameIterator.remove();
} // end while
```

4. **a.** Deb.
   b. Deb.

5. ```
   ListIterator listTraverser = aList.getListIterator();
   while (listTraverser.hasNext())
     listTraverser.next();

   while (listTraverser.hasPrevious())
     System.out.println(listTraverser.previous());
   ```

6. ```
   traverse.next(); // return doug
   traverse.next(); // return jill
   traverse.set("Jennifer"); // replace jill
   ```

7. ```
   traverse.next(); // return doug
   traverse.add("Miguel"); // adds after doug
   ```

Chapter 9

1. If you follow the hint given in the question, you will get the sum of n occurrences of $n + 1$, or $(n + 1) + (n + 1) + \ldots + (n + 1)$. This sum is simply the product $n * (n + 1)$. To get the sum, we added $1 + 2 + \ldots + n$ to itself. Thus, $n * (n + 1)$ is $2 * (1 + 2 + \ldots + n)$. The desired conclusion follows immediately from this fact.

2. Algorithm A: The loop iterates n times, so there are n additions and a total of $n + 1$ assignments. Algorithm B: For each value of i, the inner loop iterates i times, and so performs i additions and i assignments. The outer loop iterates n times. Together, the loops perform $1 + 2 + \ldots + n$ additions and the same number of assignments. By the identity given in Question 1, the number of additions is $n (n + 1) / 2$. The additional assignment to set sum to zero makes the total number of assignments equal to $1 + n (n + 1) / 2$.

3. $3n^2 + 2^n < 2^n + 2^n = 2 * 2^n$ when $n \geq 8$. So $3n^2 + 2^n = O(2^n)$, using $c = 2$ and $N = 8$.

4. The inner loop requires a constant amount of time, and so is $O(1)$. The outer loop is $O(n)$, so the entire computation is $O(n)$.

5. Twice as fast.

6. Four times as fast.

7. Let's tabulate the maximum number of times the inner loop executes for various values of index:

index	Inner Loop Iterations
0	$n - 1$
1	$n - 2$
2	$n - 3$
. . .	. . .
$n - 2$	1

   Thus, the maximum number of times the inner loop executes is $1 + 2 + \ldots + n - 1$, which is $n(n - 1) / 2$. Thus, the algorithm is $O(n^2)$ in the worst case.

8. $O(n)$.

9. $O(1)$.

10. $O(1)$.
   ```

11. O(n).
12. O(n).
13. O(n).
14. O(n).
15. O(n).
16. O(n).

Chapter 10

1.
```
public static void skipLines(int givenNumber)
{
   if (givenNumber >= 1)
   {
      System.out.println();
      skipLines(givenNumber - 1);
   } // end if
} // end skipLines
```

2. *Algorithm* **drawConcentricCircles(givenNumber, givenDiameter, givenPoint)**
```
if (givenNumber >= 1)
{
```
   Draw a circle whose diameter is givenDiameter *and whose center is at* givenPoint
```
   givenDiameter = 4 * givenDiameter / 3
   drawConcentricCircles(givenNumber - 1, givenDiameter, givenPoint)
}
```

3.
```
public static void countUp(int n)
{
   if (n >= 1)
   {
      countUp(n - 1);
      System.out.println(n);
   } // end if
} // end countUp
```

4.
```
public static int productOf(int n)
{
   int result = 1;
   if (n > 1)
      result = n * productOf(n - 1);
   return result;
} // end productOf
```

5.
```
public static void displayArray(int[] array, int first, int last)
{
   if (first == last)
      System.out.print(array[first] + " ");
   else if (first < last)
   {
      int mid = (first + last)/2;
      displayArray(array, first, mid-1);
      System.out.print(array[mid] + " ");
      displayArray(array, mid+1, last);
   }
} // end displayArray
```

6. The order of events is as follows:

```
displayBackward()
displayChainBackward(firstNode)
displayChainBackward(a reference to the second node)
displayChainBackward(a reference to the third node)
displayChainBackward(null)
Print the data in the third node
Print the data in the second node
Print the data in the first node
Advance to the next line
```

A trace of the stack of activation records appears as follows (dCB is an abbreviation for displayChainBackward; the stack is shown top to bottom):

```
dCB(firstNode)
dCB(reference to second node)  dCB(firstNode)
dCB(reference to third node)  dCB(reference to second node)  dCB(firstNode)
dCB(null)  dCB(reference to third node)  dCB(reference to second node)  dCB(firstNode)
dCB(reference to third node)  dCB(reference to second node)  dCB(firstNode)
Print the data in the third node
dCB(reference to second node)  dCB(firstNode)
Print the data in the second node
dCB(firstNode)
Print the data in the first node
```

7. $O(n)$. You can use the same recurrence relation that was shown in Segments 10.22 and 10.23 for the method countDown.

8. a. $t(n) = 1 + t(n - 1)$ for $n > 1$, $t(1) = 1$.
   b. $O(n)$.

9. Move a disk from pole 1 to pole 2
Move a disk from pole 1 to pole 3
Move a disk from pole 2 to pole 3
Move a disk from pole 1 to pole 2
Move a disk from pole 3 to pole 1
Move a disk from pole 3 to pole 2
Move a disk from pole 1 to pole 2
Move a disk from pole 1 to pole 3
Move a disk from pole 2 to pole 3
Move a disk from pole 2 to pole 1
Move a disk from pole 3 to pole 1
Move a disk from pole 2 to pole 3
Move a disk from pole 1 to pole 2
Move a disk from pole 1 to pole 3
Move a disk from pole 2 to pole 3

10. 2 and 6, respectively.

11. Directly. A recursive solution requires time that grows exponentially with n. An iterative solution is $O(n)$. If you use multiplication to compute a^n and b^n, the direct approach is also $O(n)$. If you use Java's pow method, or if your programming language has an exponentiation operator, multiplication would not be used to raise a number to a power. In those cases the direct approach is $O(1)$.

Chapter 11

1. 9 6 2 4 8
   2 6 9 4 8
   2 4 9 6 8
   2 4 6 9 8
   2 4 6 8 9

2. 9 6 2 4 8
   6 9 2 4 8
   2 6 9 4 8
   2 4 6 9 8
   2 4 6 8 9

3. No; `insertInOrder` changes the link portion of the first node in the unsorted part to `null`. If the line in question occurred next, it would set `unsortedPart` to `null`.

4. First, you consider the subarray of equally spaced integers at the indices 0, 4, and 8 (they appear in bold):

   9 8 2 7 **5** 4 6 3 **1**

   Now sort them to get

   1 8 2 7 **5** 4 6 3 **9**

   The indices 0, 4, and 8 have a separation of 4. Next, consider the integers at indices 1 and 5:

   1 **8** 2 7 5 **4** 6 3 9

   Sort them to get

   1 **4** 2 7 5 **8** 6 3 9

   Then sort the integers at indices 2 and 6; they already are in order:

   1 4 **2** 7 5 8 **6** 3 9

   Next, consider the integers at indices 3 and 7. Sort them to get

   1 4 2 **3** 5 8 6 **7** 9

   Now decrease the separation between indices to 2. You consider the integers at the indices 0, 2, 4, 6, and 8:

   1 4 **2** 3 **5** 8 **6** 7 **9**

   You find that they are sorted. Then consider the integers at indices 1, 3, 5, and 7:

   1 **4** 2 **3** 5 **8** 6 **7** 9

   Sort them to get

   1 **3** 2 **4** 5 **7** 6 **8** 9

   Decreasing the separation to 1 results in an ordinary insertion sort of an array that is almost sorted.

5. **9** 6 2 4 **8** 7 5 3
   8 6 2 4 **9** 7 5 3
   8 **6** 2 4 9 **7** 5 3
   8 6 **2** 4 9 7 **5** 3
   8 6 2 **4** 9 7 5 **3**
   8 6 2 **3** 9 7 5 **4**

8 6 **2** 3 **9** 7 **5** 4

2 6 **5** 3 **8** 7 **9** 4

2 **6** 5 **3** 8 **7** 9 4

2 **3** 5 **4** 8 **6** 9 **7**

Now apply regular insertion sort.

Chapter 12

1.   9 6 2 4 8 7 5 3

  9 6 2 4   8 7 5 3

  9 6   2 4   8 7   5 3

  9 6   2 4   8 7   5 3

  6 9   2 4   7 8   3 5

   2 4 6 9   3 5 7 8

      2 3 4 5 6 7 8 9

2. *Algorithm* `mergeSort(a, first, last)`

```
if (first < last)
{
  mid = (first + last)/2
  mergeSort(a, first, mid)
  mergeSort(a, mid+1, last)
  if (array[mid].compareTo(array[mid+1]) > 0)
    Merge the sorted halves a[first..mid] and a[mid+1..last]
}
```

3. `quickSort(array, 0, 7)`

`partition(array, 0, 7)`

 9 6 2 4 8 7 5 3

 3 6 2 4 8 7 5 9

 3 6 2 5 8 7 4 9

 3 2 6 5 8 7 4 9

 3 2 4 5 8 7 6 9

`quickSort(array, 0, 1)`

`insertionSort(array, 0, 1)`

 2 3 4 5 8 7 6 9

`quickSort(array, 3, 7)`

 2 3 4 5 8 6 7 9

 2 3 4 5 6 8 7 9

 2 3 4 5 6 7 8 9

`quickSort(array, 3, 4)`

`insertionSort(array, 3, 4)`

 2 3 4 5 6 7 8 9

`quickSort(array, 6, 7)`

`insertionSort(array, 6, 7)`

 2 3 4 5 6 7 8 9

4. 6340 1234 0291 0003 6325 0068 5227 1638
    6340 0291 0003 1234 6325 5227 0068 1638
    0003 6325 5227 1234 1638 6340 0068 0291
    0003 0068 5227 1234 0291 6325 6340 1638
    0003 0068 0291 1234 1638 5227 6325 6340
    0003 0068 0291 1234 1638 5227 6325 6340

5. *Algorithm* `radixSort(a, first, last, maxDigits)`
    // *Sorts the array of lowercase words* `a[first..last]` *into ascending order;*
    // *treats each word as if it was padded on the right with blanks to make all words have*
    // *the same length,* `wordLength`.
    for (i = 1 *to* wordlength)
    {
          Clear `bucket['a']`, `bucket['b']`, . . . , `bucket['z']`, `bucket[' ']`
          for (index = first *to* last)
          {
             letter = *i*th *letter from the right of* `a[index]`
             Place `a[index]` *at end of* `bucket[letter]`
          }
          Place contents of `bucket['a']`, `bucket['b']`, . . . , `bucket['z']`, `bucket[' ']`
             into the array a
    }

Chapter 13

1.  ```
    SortedListInterface sortedWordList = new SortedLinkedList();
    int numberOfWords = wordList.getLength();
    for (int position = 1; position <= numberOfWords; position++)
      sortedWordList.add((Comparable)wordList.getEntry(position));
    ```

2. **a.** ```
    int length = sortedList.getLength();
    String lastEntry = sortedList.getEntry(length);
    System.out.println(lastEntry);
    ```

    b. `sortedList.add((Comparable)sortedList.getEntry(1));`

3. Before the first occurrence of the entry.

4. Before the first occurrence of the entry.

5. The class `SortedLinkedList`, the private inner class `Node`, and the class of objects in the sorted list must all implement the interface `java.io.Serializable`. Thus, `SortedLinkedList` begins as
    ```
    public class SortedLinkedList implements SortedListInterface,
                                             java.io.Serializable
    ```
    and the class `Node` begins as
    ```
    private class Node implements java.io.Serializable
    ```

6. Before the first occurrence of the entry. Note that `getPosition` returns the position of the first occurrence of the entry within the list.

7. The first occurrence of the object. Note that `getPosition` returns the position of the first occurrence of the entry within the list.

8. **a.** 2; **b.** −1; **c.** −5; **d.** 4; **e.** −3.

9. ```
   public boolean contains(Object anEntry)
   {
     return getPosition((Comparable)anEntry) > 0;
   } // end contains
   ```
10. The implementation that invokes `getPosition` will be more efficient, because calling the list's method `contains` will search the entire list when the entry is not present.
11. Advantage: The implementation is easy to write.

    Disadvantage: The implementation is not efficient, especially when the implementation of the underlying list is linked.

Chapter 14

1. No, since the client will be unaware of what happened and will not know where in the sorted list the addition was made.
2. Advantage: The implementation is easy to write.

    Disadvantage: The implementation is not efficient, especially when the implementation of the underlying list is linked. Using inheritance in this way is as inefficient as using composition.
3. ```
   public void addToBeginning(Object newEntry)
   {
     Node firstNode = getFirstNode();
     Node newNode = new Node(newEntry, firstNode);
     setFirstNode(newNode);
   } // end addToBeginning
   ```

Chapter 15

1. ```
   // Create an object of the class Name
   Name derek = new Name("Derek", "Greene");
   // Convert the object to an immutable object; don't change its data fields
   ImmutableName derekI = derek.getImmutable();
   // Add the object to the sorted list nameList
   SortedListInterface nameList = new SortedLinkedList();
   nameList.add(derekI);
   ```
2. ```
   // Create an object of the class ImmutableName
   ImmutableName lila = new ImmutableName("Lila", "Bleu");
   // Convert the object to a mutable object; don't change its data fields
   Name changer = lila.getMutable();
   // Change the last name of the new object
   changer.setLast("Greene");
   // Convert the revised mutable object to an immutable object
   ImmutableName unchanger = changer.getImmutable();
   ```
3. a. A new Name object is created. Its first name and last name are the same as the corresponding fields of the original object.

    b. No.

4. **a.** No. The clone y has a name object that is distinct from x's name object, because a deep copy was made. (See Figure 15-8.)

   b. Yes. Both objects share one name object. (See Figure 15-9.)

5.
```
Node newRef = theCopy.firstNode;
for (Node oldRef = firstNode.getNextNode(); oldRef != null;
          oldRef = oldRef.getNextNode())
{
  newRef.setNextNode((Node)oldRef.clone());
  newRef = newRef.getNextNode();
} // end for
```

Chapter 16

1.
```
public int contains(Object anEntry)
{
  boolean found = false;
  int result = -1;
  for (int index = 0; !found && (index < length); index++)
  {
    if (anEntry.equals(entry[index]))
    {
      found = true;
      result = index;
    } // end if
  } // end for

  return result;
} // end contains
```

2.
```
public static boolean contains(AList theList, Object anEntry)
{
  boolean found = false;
  int length = theList.getLength();
  for (int position = 1; !found && (position <= length); position++)
  {
    if (anEntry.equals(theList.getEntry(position)))
      found = true;
  } // end for

  return found;
} // end contains
```

3. The object o6 is compared with o1, then o2, o3, o4, and o5.

4.
```
public static boolean contains(AList theList, Object anEntry)
{
  return search(theList, 1, theList.getLength(), anEntry);
} // end contains

private static boolean search(AList theList, int first, int last,
                              Object desiredItem)
{
  boolean found;
  if (first > last)
    found = false;
```

```
        else if (desiredItem.equals(theList.getEntry(first)))
          found = true;
        else
          found = search(theList, first+1, last, desiredItem);

        return found;
    } // end search
```

5. Searching for 8:

    Sequential search: 5 comparisons

    Binary search: 4 comparisons

  Searching for 16:

    Sequential search: 9 comparisons

    Binary search: 4 comparisons

  Thus, the recursive binary search requires fewer comparisons in each case.

6. **a.** 12 and 4.

  b. 12, 4, and 8.

  c. 12, 20, and 14.

7.
```
public int contains(Object desiredItem)
{
    return binarySearch(0, length-1, (Comparable)desiredItem);
} // end contains

private int binarySearch(int first, int last, Comparable desiredItem)
{
    int result = -1;
    int mid = (first + last)/2;
    if (first > last)
      result = -1;
    else if (desiredItem.equals(entry[mid]))
      result = mid;
    else if (desiredItem.compareTo(entry[mid]) < 0)
      result = binarySearch(first, mid-1, desiredItem);
    else
      result = binarySearch(mid+1, last, desiredItem);

    return result;
} // end binarySearch
```

8. In the second else if, change < to >.

9. 20 (log 1,000,000 rounded up).

Chapter 17

1. `DictionaryInterface myDictionary = new Dictionary();`

2. `myDictionary.add("Joe", "555-1234");`

3.
```
if (myDictionary.contains("Brittany"))
    System.out.println("Brittany's phone number is "
                     + myDictionary.getValue("Brittany"));
else
    System.out.println("Brittany is not in the dictionary.Brittany);
```

or

```
String phoneNumber = (String)myDictionary.getValue("Brittany");
if (phoneNumber == null)
  System.out.println("Brittany is not in the dictionary.Brittany);
else
  System.out.println("Brittany's phone number is " + phoneNumber);
```

4. ```
public Object remove(Name personName)
{
  return phoneBook.remove(personName);
} // end remove
```

5. ```
public Object changePhoneNumber(Name personName, String phoneNumber)
{
  return phoneBook.add(personName, phoneNumber);
} // end replace
```

Chapter 18

1. The memory requirements for the search keys and the values are the same for each representation, so let's ignore them. The memory requirement for the representation shown in Figure 18-1a uses three references for each entry in the dictionary: one in the array and two in the Entry object. Each of the other two representations requires only two references for each dictionary entry. Thus, the representation in Part *a* uses 50 percent more memory than either of the other two representations.

2. In the method add, pass (Comparable)key to locateIndex instead of passing key.
   In the method locateIndex, you can remove the cast of key to Comparable and use key instead of cKey.

Chapter 19

1. Since the implementation defines both the hash table and the dictionary entry, you have a choice as to where to add a field to indicate the state of a location in a hash table. You could add a field to each table location that has three states, but you really need only a boolean field, since a null location is empty. If the field is true, the location is occupied; if it is false, it is available.

   Adding a similar data field to the dictionary entry instead of to the hash table leads to a cleaner implementation. As before, if the table location is null, it is empty. If the entry's field is true, the location is occupied; if it is false, it is available. Note that the implementation that begins in Segment 19.31 uses this scheme.

2. The add algorithm is the same as the one given in Segment 19.22, but it would use a different search of a chain. Regardless of whether the chain is sorted, you would stop the search as soon as you found the desired search key. However, if the key is not in the chain, you have to search an entire unsorted chain to learn this. If the chain is sorted, you can stop the search when you reach the point where the key should have occurred if it were present.

3. No. If *a*, *b*, *c*, and *d* are search keys in sorted order that are in the table, *b* and *d* might appear in one chain while the other keys appear in another. Traversing the chains in order will not visit the keys in sorted order.

4. In each method, replace the statements

```
index = locate(index, key);
if (index != -1)
```

with

```
index = probe(index, key);
if ((hashTable[index] != null) && (hashTable[index].isIn()))
```

5. No. The table size has increased, so rehashing is not necessary.

Chapter 20

1. *Jill* is at the top, and *Jim* is at the bottom.
2. **a.**
```
StackInterface myStack = new LinkedStack();
while (!myStack.isEmpty())
    yourStack.push(myStack.pop());
```

   b. myStack is empty, and yourStack contains the strings that were in myStack but in reverse order.
3. The following stacks are shown bottom to top.

a.	**b.**	**c.**
[	{	[
[{	{ [	[{
[{ (	{ [(	[{ [
[{	{ [	[{ [(
{ { (	{	[{ [
[{		[{
[		[
empty		

4. **a.** *a b c * +*
   b. *a b * c d − /*
   c. *a b / c d − +*
   d. *a b / c + d −*
5. Always. Segment 20.15 showed that you push ∧ onto the stack if another ∧ is already at the top of the stack. But if a different operator is at the top, ∧ has a higher precedence, so you push it onto the stack.
6. **a.** *a b + c d − /*
   b. *a b c * − d e * f * g + /*
7. **a.** −4.
   b. −58.

8. **a.** 5.
   b. –4.
   c. 22.

Chapter 21

1. No. Although a tail reference would enable you to efficiently access the top of the stack or push a new entry onto the stack, it is not enough to pop the stack. You need a reference to the next-to-last node to remove the chain's last node. To get that reference, you could either traverse the chain or maintain a reference to the next-to-last node in addition to the tail reference. Thus, placing the top of the stack at the end of the chain is not as efficient as placing it at the beginning.
2. Change `Object` to the primitive type and do not assign `null` to `stack[topIndex]`.
3. Each push or pop would need to move all of the entries currently in the stack.
4. The bottom. You can then push entries onto the stack without moving the other elements already in the array.
5.
```
public void clear()
{
   for (; topIndex > -1; topIndex--)
      stack[topIndex] = null;
} // end clear
```
6.
```
while (!isEmpty())
   pop();
```
7. No. Since `Vector` uses an array and dynamic expansion, each push would need to move all of the entries in the stack to vacate the first entry in the vector.

Chapter 22

1. *Jill* is at the front, *Jess* is at the back.
2. *Jill* is at the front, *Jane* is at the back.

Chapter 23

1. The back of the queue is at the end of the chain. Since you add to the back of a queue, you need to add a node to the end of the chain. A tail reference allows you to do this without first traversing the chain to locate its last node. Thus, a tail reference enables an efficient enqueue operation.
2. Entries in a list have a particular position within the list and, thus, the array. Queue entries have positions that are relative to one another, but not to the queue and not to the array.
3. Each enqueue operation needs to move all of the entries in the queue to vacate `queue[0]` before it adds a new entry.
4.
```
public void clear()
{
   int frontIndexLimit = (backIndex + 1) % queue.length;
```

```
    for (int frontIndex = 0; frontIndex != frontIndexLimit;
            frontIndex = (frontIndex + 1) % queue.length)
    {
        queue[frontIndex] = null;
    } // end for

    frontIndex = 0;
    backIndex = queue.length -1;
} // end clear
```

5. ```
public void clear()
{
    while (!isEmpty())
        dequeue();
} // end clear
```
This version of clear is easier to write than the version given in Question 4.

6. Repeatedly call dequeue until the queue is empty, as in the answer to the previous question, or set the data fields of each node in the queue to null.

7. ```
public Object getBack()
{
    Object back = null;

    if (!isEmpty())
        back = lastNode.getData();

    return back;
} // end getBack
```

Chapter 24

1. **a.** N, O, P, G, H, Q, R, S, T, L, M.

   b. I, J.

   c. F, G.

   d. F, G, N, O, P.

   e. F, B, A.

2. A tree that represents the organization of this book is a general tree, such as the following:

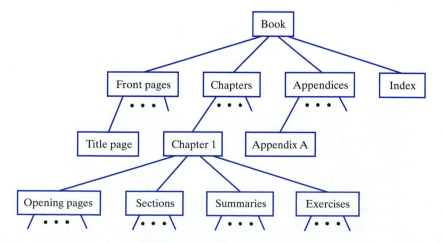

3. 4, 3, and 3, respectively.

4. **a.** For the tree in Figure 24-6a, n is 7 and h is 3. Since the tree is full and $7 = 2^3 - 1$, the relationship $n = 2^h - 1$ is true.

　b. For the tree in Figure 24-6b, n is 10 and h is 4. Since the tree is complete and $\log_2 (10 + 1)$ rounded up is 4, the relationship $h = \log_2 (n + 1)$ rounded up is true.

5. 63.

6. 4.

7. Preorder: Jared, John, James, Mary, Jennifer, Robert, Carole.
Postorder: James, Mary, John, Robert, Carole, Jennifer, Jared.
Inorder: James, John, Mary, Jared, Robert, Jennifer, Carole.
Level order: Jared, John, Jennifer, James, Mary, Robert, Carole

8.

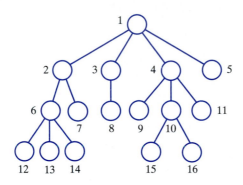

9.

(a) $a + b * c$

(b) $(a + b) * c$

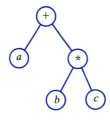   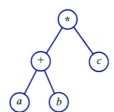

10. Figure 24-14a
Preorder: $/\ a\ b$
Inorder: $a\ /\ b$
Postorder: $a\ b\ /$

Figure 24-14c
Preorder: $*\ a + b\ c$
Inorder: $a * b + c$
Postorder: $a\ b\ c + *$

Figure 24-14d
Preorder: $/ * a + b * c\ d\ e$
Inorder: $a * b + c * d / e$
Postorder: $a\ b\ c\ d * + * e /$

11. The tree in Figure 24-14a is full; the tree in Figure 24-14b is complete.

12. 17.

13. The method `learn` augments the tree under conditions that the class `GuessingGame` must control. It would be inappropriate for a client to invoke this method.

14. 5.

15. The shortest tree has height 2; the tallest tree has height 3.

16. The root of a maxheap contains the object with the largest value. If this object is unique in the set of objects, the root is unique. If another object has the same value, the value of the object in the root is unique. In Figure 24-20a, only 9 can be the root.

17. No. The order of siblings is not specified in a heap, so several different heaps can contain the same data. For example, in Figure 24-20a, you could exchange 2 and 5, or you could exchange the root's two subtrees, and still have a maxheap.

18.

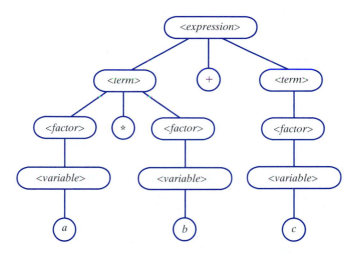

Chapter 25

1. No. Setting `rightTree` to `null` affects only the local copy of the reference argument `rightTree`.

2. The data in the objects d, b, e, a, f, g, and c is displayed on separate lines.

3.
```java
public void preorderTraverse()
{
  preorderTraverse(root);
} // end preorderTraverse

private void preorderTraverse(BinaryNode node)
{
  if (node != null)
  {
```

```
        System.out.println(node.getData());
        preorderTraverse((BinaryNode)node.getLeftChild());
        preorderTraverse((BinaryNode)node.getRightChild());
    } // end if
} // end preorderTraverse
```

4. 27.

5.

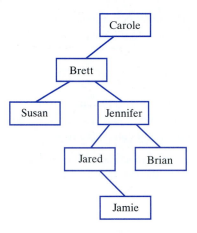

Chapter 26

1. As a left child of the node that contains *Whitney*.

2. No; `BinarySearchTree` inherits these methods from `BinaryTree`.

3. *Chris* is a right child of *Chad*. *Jason* is a left child of *Jim*. *Kelley* is a right child of *Jim*.

4. *Miguel* is a left child of *Whitney*, and *Nancy* is a right child of *Miguel*.

When you add *Nancy* first, *Nancy* is a left child of *Whitney*, and *Miguel* is a left child of *Nancy*. The order of the additions affects the tree that results.

5.

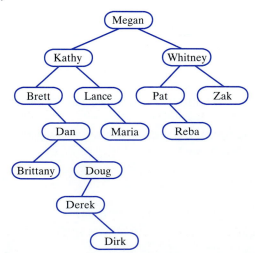

6.

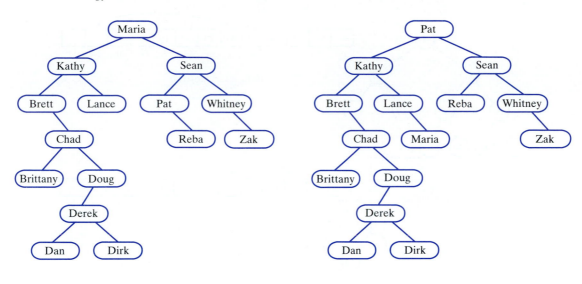

7. O(log *n*).

8. O(1).

9.
```
public int getSize()
{
    return bst.getNumberOfNodes();
} // end getSize

public boolean isEmpty()
{
    return bst.isEmpty();
} // end isEmpty

public boolean contains(Object key)
{
    Entry findEntry = new Entry(key, null);

    return bst.contains(findEntry);
} // end contains

public void clear()
{
    bst.clear();
} // end clear
```

10. In the method `contains` given previously, replace the `return` statement with
```
return getValue(key) != null;
```

Chapter 27

1. Place 100 as a right child of 80. Then swap 100 with 80, swap 100 with 85, and finally swap 100 with 90.

2.

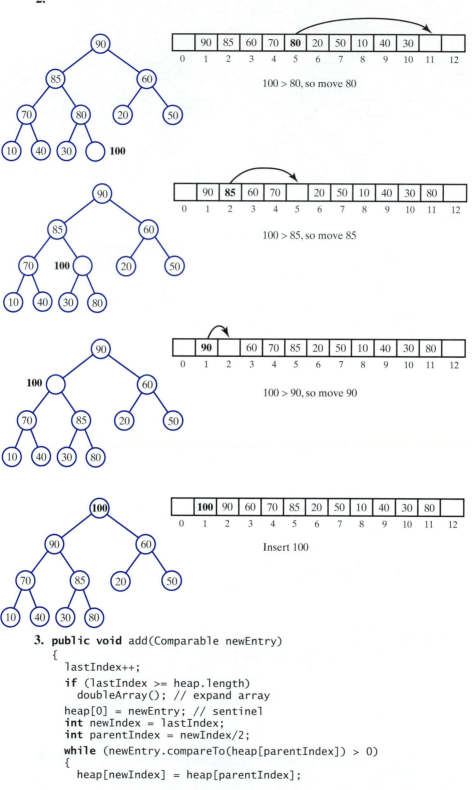

	90	85	60	70	**80**	20	50	10	40	30		
0	1	2	3	4	5	6	7	8	9	10	11	12

100 > 80, so move 80

	90	**85**	60	70		20	50	10	40	30	80	
0	1	2	3	4	5	6	7	8	9	10	11	12

100 > 85, so move 85

	90		60	70	85	20	50	10	40	30	80	
0	1	2	3	4	5	6	7	8	9	10	11	12

100 > 90, so move 90

	100	90	60	70	85	20	50	10	40	30	80	
0	1	2	3	4	5	6	7	8	9	10	11	12

Insert 100

3.
```java
public void add(Comparable newEntry)
{
    lastIndex++;
    if (lastIndex >= heap.length)
        doubleArray(); // expand array
    heap[0] = newEntry; // sentinel
    int newIndex = lastIndex;
    int parentIndex = newIndex/2;
    while (newEntry.compareTo(heap[parentIndex]) > 0)
    {
        heap[newIndex] = heap[parentIndex];
```

```
        newIndex = parentIndex;
        parentIndex = newIndex/2;
    } // end while
    heap[newIndex] = newEntry;
} // end add
```

4.

(a)

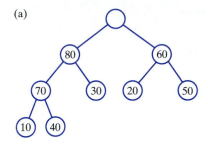

(b)

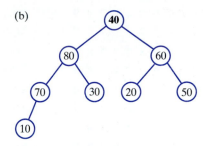

(c)

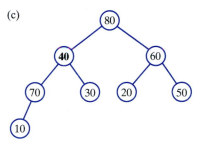

(d)

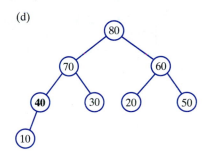

5.

(a)

85 is larger child of 30; 30 < 85, so move 85

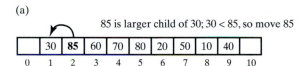

(b)   80 is larger child of vacated node; 30 < 80, so move 80

	85		60	70	**80**	20	50	10	40	
0	1	2	3	4	5	6	7	8	9	10

(c)

Reached leaf

	85	80	60	70		20	50	10	40	
0	1	2	3	4	5	6	7	8	9	10

(d)

Insert 30

	85	80	60	70	**30**	20	50	10	40	
0	1	2	3	4	5	6	7	8	9	10

6. 9 6 2 4 8 7 5 3   Original array
  9 8 7 4 6 2 5 3   After reheap
  3 8 7 4 6 2 5 **9**   After swap

  8 6 7 4 3 2 5 **9**   After reheap
  5 6 7 4 3 2 **8 9**   After swap

  7 6 5 4 3 2 **8 9**   After reheap
  2 6 5 4 3 **7 8 9**   After swap

  6 4 5 2 3 **7 8 9**   After reheap
  3 4 5 2 **6 7 8 9**   After swap

  5 4 3 2 **6 7 8 9**   After reheap
  2 4 3 **5 6 7 8 9**   After swap

  4 2 3 **5 6 7 8 9**   After reheap
  3 2 **4 5 6 7 8 9**   After swap

  3 2 **4 5 6 7 8 9**   After reheap
  2 **3 4 5 6 7 8 9**   After swap
  2 3 4 5 6 7 8 9   Done

Chapter 28

1.

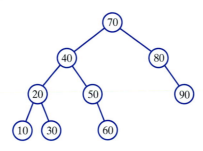

2. The following binary search tree is taller than the previous AVL tree, and it is not balanced:

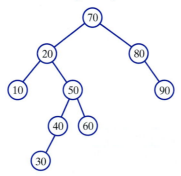

3. a. 60, 20, 10.
   b. 60, 20, 50, 55.
   c. 60, 20, 50, 35, 40.
   d. 60, 20, 50, 35.

4.

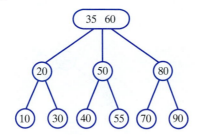

5.

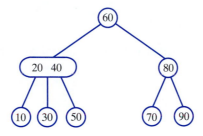

6. It is shorter and balanced.

7. a. 20, 10.
   b. 20, 50, 80, 55, 60.
   c. 20, 50, 35, 40.
   d. 20, 50, 35.

8.

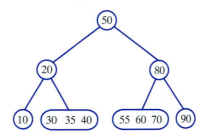

9.

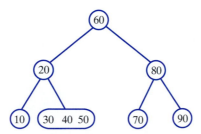

10. Both trees are completely balanced, and they have the same height. The 2-4 tree has fewer nodes.

11. a. 2-4: 20, 50, 80, 55, 60; Red-black: 50, 80, 60.
   b. 2-4: 20, 50, 80, 55; Red-black: 50, 80, 60, 55.

12. The first three properties follow immediately by observing the tree. Every path from the root to a leaf contains two black nodes.

13.

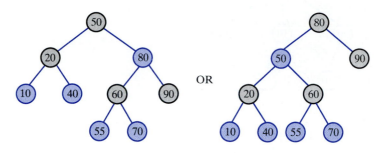

OR

14. The first three properties follow immediately by observing the tree. Every path from the root to a leaf contains two black nodes.

Chapter 29

1. **a.** 3.
   b. 36.
   c. Truro-Orleans-Barnstable-Sandwich.
   d. Truro-Orleans-Barnstable-Sandwich, with a weight of 48.
2. Electric (or telephone or TV) wires, plumbing, hallways or other connections between rooms.
3. The graph is connected but not complete.
4. No; cs8 and cs10 each have 2 parents.
5. **a.** No; **b.** Yes; **c.** No; **d.** No.
6. E F H C I B.
7. E F C B H I.
8. cs1 cs2 cs4 cs7 cs9 cs5 cs10 cs6 cs8 cs3.
9. $A \rightarrow E \rightarrow F \rightarrow C$.
10. $A \rightarrow B \rightarrow E \rightarrow F \rightarrow C$ with weight 10.
11. In the two calls to addEdge, you would add the edge weight as a third argument.
12. The method getShortestPath finds the path that contains the fewest number of edges; getCheapestPath finds the path with the smallest weight sum.

Chapter 30

1.

	0	1	2	3
0		T	T	T
1	T		T	T
2	T	T		T
3	T	T	T	

2. Vertex 0 references the list 1, 2, 3.
   Vertex 1 references the list 0, 2, 3.
   Vertex 2 references the list 0, 1, 3.
   Vertex 3 references the list 0, 1, 2.

3.
```java
Vertex vertexA = new Vertex("A");
Vertex vertexB = new Vertex("B");
Vertex vertexC = new Vertex("C");
vertexA.addEdge(vertexB, 2);
vertexB.addEdge(vertexC, 3);
vertexC.addEdge(vertexA, 4);
vertexA.addEdge(vertexC, 5);
```

4.
```java
DirectedGraph myGraph = new DirectedGraph();
myGraph.addVertex("A");
myGraph.addVertex("B");
myGraph.addVertex("C");
myGraph.addEdge("A", "B", 2);
myGraph.addEdge("B", "C", 3);
myGraph.addEdge("C", "A", 4);
myGraph.addEdge("A", "C", 5);
```

5.
```java
QueueInterface bfs = myGraph.getBreadthFirstTraversal("A");
while (!bfs.isEmpty())
  System.out.print(bfs.dequeue() + " ");
System.out.println();
```

6.
```java
StackInterface path = myGraph.getShortestPath("A", "C");
while (!path.isEmpty())
  System.out.print(path.pop() + " ");
System.out.println();
```

Index

A

Abstract base class, 46
Abstract classes, 45–46
  interfaces vs., 69–70
Abstract data type (ADT), 2, 3, 79, 81, 93
Abstract methods, 12, 45–46
Abstraction, 59, 75
Access methods, 11
Access modifiers, 11, 12, 22
Activation record, 229–31, 470
Actor, 70
Acyclic graphs, 675
Adapter class, 32–33
add algorithm, hashing, 413, 439–41
add method. *See* Adding an entry
addAfterCurrent method
  internal iterators, 161
  IteratorInterface class, 161
addElement method, Vector class, 110,
    112
addFirst method, LinkedList class, 147
Adding an entry
  AVL tree, 644–650, 650–653
  binary search tree, 598–606
  deque, 503, 532–33
  dictionary, 377, 396, 397–400, 401–2,
    405–6, 413, 439–41
  graph, 692, 708
  heap, 561, 630–33
  list, 81, 143–44, 144–45, 304–11, 326–28
  ListIterator interface, 186–87, 191, 195
  priority queue, 505, 562
  queue, 491, 492–93, 503, 513, 520, 524,
    530
  red-black tree, 664–69
  sorted list, 301, 302, 304–11, 312–17,
    326–28
  stack, 451, 474, 479, 480, 482, 503
  2-4 tree, 659–61
  2-3 tree, 655–57
addLast method, LinkedList class, 147
addNode private method, search trees, 652–53
Address, 118
addToBack method, deque, 532–33
addToFront method, deque, 533
Adjacency list, 701–2, 712
Adjacency matrix, 700–701, 712
Adjacent vertices, 676–77

ADT. *See* Abstract data type (ADT)
advance method
  IteratorInterface class, 159
  iterators, 154–59
  internal, 159
Airline routes, 677
Algorithm efficiency, 199–221
  analysis of algorithms, 202
  array-based implementation, 214–15
    adding to end of list, 214
    adding to list at given position, 214–15
  best-case time, 203
  Big Oh notation, 205–7
    formal definition of, 208
  Big Omega notation, 210
  Big Theta notation, 210
  comparing implementations, 216–17
  formalities, 208–10
  linked implementation, 215–16
    adding to end of list, 215–16
    adding to list at given position, 216
    retrieving an entry, 216
  measuring, 202–7
  motivation, 200–202
  time complexity, 202
  time efficiency, 202, 210–13
    of implementations of the ADT list, 210–13
  worst-case time, 203
Aliases, 9–10
AList class, 347
  ListInterface interface, 100–101, 108
Allocation of memory, 140
Analysis of algorithms, 202
Ancestor class, 34, 51
API (Application Programming Interface), 22
Applets, 715
Applications, Java, 715
Arguments
  methods, 8, 10, 718, 728
  objects, 10
  passing, 14–16
Arithmetic expressions, 724–25
Arithmetic operators, 724–25
  precedence of, 726
Array-based implementation(s), 99
  dictionaries, 394–400
    entries, 394–95
    sorted array-based dictionary, 397–400
    unsorted array-based dictionary, 395–96

Iterator interface, 179–82
  beginning the inner class, 179–80
  hasNext method, 180
  next method, 180
  remove method, 180–82
lists
  add methods, 102–4
  contains method, 105–6
  efficiency of adding to, 214–15
  getEntry method, 105
  Java implementation, 100–106
  remove method, 104–5
  replace method, 105
ListIterator interface, 188–95
  add method, 191, 195
  data fields, 188–89
  hasNext method, 189, 195
  hasPrevious method, 190, 195
  IteratorForArrayList inner class,
    188–94
  next method, 189–90, 195
  nextIndex method, 190–91, 195
  previous method, 190, 195
  previousIndex method, 190–91, 195
  remove method, 191–94, 195
queues, 515–23
  circular array, 516–17
  circular array with one unused location,
    518–24
stacks, 480–84
  adding to the top, 482
  data field and constructors, 481–82
  removing the top, 482–83
  retrieving the top, 482
ArrayList class, 113, 194–95
ArrayListWithIterator class, 179
ArrayQueue class, 520
Arrays, 755–64. *See also* Searching
  = operator, 758
  == operator, 758–59
  array table, 761
  array types, as reference types, 759
  cloning, 347–48
  compared to objects, 759
  initializing, 757–58
  methods, 759
  multidimensional, 759–61
  n-dimensional, 759
  object serialization, 792

one-dimensional, 759, 761
out-of-bounds index, 758
parameters, 756–57
recursion, 234–36
  displaying a list, 236
  dividing an array in half, 235
  starting at one end, 234
as return values, 757
sorted, merging, 278
two-dimensional, 759–61
wrapper classes, 761–64
Arrays class, 283
ArrayStack class, 481–82
ASCII character set, 748
Assertions, 62
Assignment compatibilities, 723
Assignment operator, 722
Assignment statements, 722
Associations, 74
Attributes (data fields), class diagram, 73
Automatic garbage collection, 19
Automobile class, 33–34
Average-case time, 203
AVL trees, 644–53
  binary search trees vs., 650
  defined, 644
  implementation, 650–53
    rebalancing, 651–53
    rotations, 650–51
  rotations
    double, 646–50
    single, 645–46

B

B-trees, 669–70
  of order m, 669
Bags, 2
BalanceChecker class, 458–59
Balanced expression, 455
Balanced search trees, 619–20, 643–72
  AVL trees, 644–53
    defined, 644
    double rotations, 646–50
    implementation, 650–53
    single rotations, 645–46
  B-trees, 669–70
  red-black trees, 662–69
    adding entries to, 664–69
    defined, 662
    properties, 663–64
  2-3 trees, 653–58
    adding entries to, 655–57
    searching, 654–55
    splitting nodes during addition, 657–58
    3-node, 653
    2-node, 653

2-4 trees, 658–62
  adding entries to, 659–60
  compared to AVL and 2-3 trees, 661–62
  defined, 658
  4-node, 658
Base case, 226–27
Base class, 33, 51, 328
  calling the constructor of, 36–37
  designing, 322–26
  private fields/methods of, 37–38
  private methods of, 38
  and type compatibility, 42–46
BasicGraphInterface interface, 692–93
BasicIteratorInterface interface, 153,
    155–57, 174
Best-case time, 203
Bidirectional arrow, 74
Big Oh notation, 205–7
  complexities of program constructs, 209–10
  formal definition of, 208
  identities, 209
Big Omega notation, 210
Big Theta notation, 210
Binary files, 779
  I/O, 785–90
    DataInputStream class, 788–90
    DataOutputStream class, 785–88
Binary operator, 724
Binary search
  sorted arrays, 361–67
    efficiency of, 365–67
  sorted chain, 369–70
Binary search trees, 3, 557–60, 565, 591–626
  adding an entry, 598–606
    iterative implementation, 599–601
    recursive implementation, 601–6
  balanced, 619–20
  beginning the class definition, 596–97
    disallowing setTree, 596–97
  completely balanced, 619–20
  defined, 557–58, 592
  duplicate entries, 595–96
  efficiency of operations, 618–21
    balance, 619–20
  efficiency of searching, 559–60
  height balanced, 619–20
  implementation, 591–626
  interface for, 593–95
    operations, 593
    specifications, 593–95
  nodes, order of addition, 620–21
  removing an entry, 606–15
    findLargest private method, 617
    iterative implementation, 611–15
    node has one child, 607
    node has two children, 607–10

node is a leaf, 606
    recursive implementation, 615–18
    remove private method, 616
    remove public method, 615
    removeEntry private method, 616–17
    removeLargest private method, 617–18
    in the root, 610–11
  search process, 558–59
  searching and retrieving, 597–98
    contains method, 598
    getEntry method, 597–98
    search algorithm, 597
  traversing, 598
Binary trees, 543, 544–45. See also Binary
    search trees and Heaps
  ancestors, 542
  children, 542
  clear method, 577, 587
  complete, 545, 564
    height, 545–46
  decision trees, 554–57
    expert systems, 554
    guessing game example, 555–57
  defined, 543, 695
  descendants, 542
  empty, 543
  expression trees, 552–54
    evaluating an algebraic expression,
        553–54
    implementation, 583–84
  full, 544–45
    height, 545–46
  getHeight method, 577–78, 587
  getNumberOfNodes method, 577–78,
    587
  getRootData method, 577, 587
  height of, 543
    alternate definition, 544
  hierarchical organizations, 540–42
  implementation
    accessor and mutator methods, 577
    BinaryNode methods, 578
    BinaryTree methods, 577–78
    computing height and counting nodes,
        577–78
    creating a basic binary tree, 573–74
    privateSetTree method, 574–76
    traversals, 578–83
  interface for, 550–52
  isEmpty method, 577, 587
  left child node, 544
  left subtree, 544
  level of nodes, 543, 544
  nodes in, 542–43, 570–72
    BinaryNode implementation, 571–72
    interface for a node, 570–71

interior (nonleaf) node, 542
  leaf node, 542
parent, 542
path, 543
right child node, 544
right subtree, 544
siblings, 542
subtree, 543
terminology, 542–46
traversals, 546–49
  breadth-first, 548
  depth-first, 549
  inorder, 547, 565
  InorderIterator class, 581–82
  iterative version of inorderTraverse,
      580–81
  level-order, 548, 565
  postorder, 548, 565, 582–83
  preorder, 547, 565, 582–83
  recursive, 578–79
  using an iterator, 580
BinaryNode class
  implementation, 571–72
  methods, 578
BinaryNodeInterface interface, 570–71,
    584
binarySearch method, 363–65, 473–74
BinarySearchTree interface, 596
BinaryTree class, 573–74
  methods, 577–78
BinaryTreeInterface interface, 551, 573
Blocks, 670
Body
  loops, 742
  methods, 12
Boolean expressions, 734–36
boolean type, 9
Breadth-first traversals, 548
  graphs, 680, 695
bstSearch algorithm, 559, 597
Bubble sort, 273–74
Bucket, 427
Bucket sort, 294–95
Buffer, 781
BufferedReader class, 782–84
Buffering, 781
byte type, 9

C

Call-by-value parameter mechanism, 14
Calling objects, 8, 716
Capital gain computations
  StockLedger class, 500–502
    design, 500–501
    implementation, 501–502

StockPurchase class, 500–502
  design, 500–501
  implementation, 501–502
Cardinality, associations, 74
Ceiling, 207
Chain. See Linked chain
char type, 9
charAt method, String class, 751
checkBalance algorithm, 457–58
Checked exceptions, 774–75
Children, trees, 542
Circle class, 69
CircleBase class, 69–70
Circular array
  array-based queue implementation, 516–24
    complications, 517
Circular array with one unused location
  array-based queue implementation, 518–24
    adding to the back, 520
    clear method, 523
    data fields and constructors, 519–20
    doubleArray method, 522
    isEmpty method, 522
    isFull method, 522
    removing the front, 521
    retrieving the front, 520
Circular interface, 68–69
Circular linked chains, 525
  doubly linked, 537
  two-part, 525–31
Circular linked implementations, 525–31
  circular linked chains, 525
    doubly linked, 537
    two-part, 525–31
  linear linked chains, 525
  queues, 525–31
    circular linked chains, 525
    linear linked chains, 525
    two-part circular linked chain, 525–31
  two-part circular linked chain, 525–31
Class definition, 6
Class diagram, 73, 75
Class file, 790–91
Class methods, 21
Class-responsibility-collaboration (CRC)
    cards, 71–75
Class types, 9, 720
  computing hash code for, 415–16
Classes, 5–27, 716
  choosing, 70–75
  class-responsibility-collaboration (CRC)
      cards, 71–75
  clients, 8
  collaborations among, 72
  constructors, 8
  defined, 6

defining, 10–22
designing, 57–78
identifying, 71–72
implementation, writing a test program prior
    to, 87
inheritance, 33–36
instance, 6
and interfaces, 63
methods, 7–10
naming, 13, 793–94
packages, 22
read-only, 334
responsibilities, 72
reusing, 74–75
testing, 87
using methods in, 7–10
views of, 7
clear method, 81
  queues, 491
    linked implementation, 515
  stack, 451, 480, 484, 485
  Vector class, 111
Client interface, 59–60
Clients, 8
clone method, Object class, 45
Cloneable interface, 64, 339–40
Cloneable objects, 339–44
  clone method, 45, 339–41, 343, 348, 352
  Cloneable interface, 64, 339–40
  CloneNotSupportedException, 340
  deep clone, 341
  shallow clone, 341
Clones, 332
  cloning a chain, 349–52
    methods, 351–52
    nodes, 350–51
  cloning an array, 347–48
  deep, 341
  defined, 339
  shallow, 341
  sorted lists of, 344–46
Clustering, in hashing, 424
  primary, 424
  secondary, 425
Coefficients, 318
Collaborations, among classes, 72
Collection, 2
CollegeStudent class, 35–43
Collision resolution, 419–29
  comparing schemes for, 434–35
  open addressing with double hashing,
      425–26
  open addressing with linear probing,
      419–24
    additions that collide, 420–21
    clustering, 424

removals, 421–22
  reusing locations in the hash table during an
      addition, 422–24
  open addressing with quadratic probing,
      424–25
  separate chaining, 427–29
Collisions, 414
Color flip, 665–66
Comments, 60–62, 795–97. *See also* `javadoc`
  comment blocks, 795
  Java documentation comments, 796–97
  and Java interfaces, 64
  single-line comments, 795
  when to write, 795–96
Companion classes, 335–36
  `ImmutableName` class, 336–37
  `Name` class, 337–39
  using inheritance to form, 336–39
`Comparable` interface, 64–66, 345
`compareTo` method, 63, 75, 506
  `Object` class, 66–67
  `String` class, 752
Complete binary trees, 544–45, 564
  height, 545–46
Complete graphs, 676, 695
Completely balanced search trees, 619–20. *See
    also* Balanced search trees
Complexity, of algorithms, 202. *See also*
    Algorithm Efficiency
Composition, 30–33, 51, 328
  adapter class, 32–33
Compound statement, 733
`concat` method, `String` class, 750–51
Concatenation, 749–50
  operator, 749
Concordance of words, 387–89
  `display` method, 388–89
  `readFile` method, 387–88
Conditional operator, 739
Conditional operator expression, 739
Connected graphs, 676, 695
Constants, 721
  named, 728
Constructors, 8, 18–20, 23
  default, 18
  defining, 18
  invoking from within constructors, 36–37
  using `this` to invoke, 37
Container, 2
`contains` method, 82, 357–59, 365, 367–68
  binary search trees, 598
  dictionaries, 378
  lists, 105–6
  `Vector` class, 112
`convertToPostFix` algorithm, 462–64
Costs, graphs, 675–76

`countDown` method, 224–39, 247–48
  time efficiency of, 238–40
`CourseSchedule` class, 73–74
CRC cards. *See* Class-responsibility-
    collaboration (CRC) cards
Cycle, 675, 695

D

Data abstraction, 59, 93. *See also* Abstract data
    type (ADT)
Data fields, 10–11, 23, 73
  inherited, accessing, 37–38
Data members, 10–11
Data portion, node, 129
Data structure, 2, 81
Data types, 9
`DataInputStream` class, 788–90
`DataOutputStream` class, 785–88
Deallocation of memory, 19, 140
Decision trees, 554–57, 565
  expert systems, 554
  guessing game example, 555–57
`DecisionTreeInterface` interface, 555
Declaration of a method, 12
Decrement operator (`--`), 726–27
`decrementLength` method, `LList` class, 325
Deep clones, 341
  of a single field, creating, 342–44
Deep copy, 341
Default constructor, 18
Degree of a polynomial, 318
Delimiters, 384
Depth-first traversals, 549
  graphs, 680–82, 695
Deques
  computing capital gain using, 504–5
  doubly linked implementation, 531–34
    adding an entry, 532–33
    data fields and constructors, 532
    removing an entry, 533–34
    retrieving an entry, 534
    reuse of, 534
  specifications of, 502–4
`dequeue` method, queue, 491, 521–22, 530
Derived classes, 33, 36, 51
  constructor, 36
  object types of, 42–43
  and `private` methods of the base class, 38
  `throws` clause in, 775
Descendant class, 34, 51
Descendants, trees, 542
Dictionaries, 3, 375–91
  `add(key, value)` method, 377
  adding an entry, 377, 396, 397–400, 401–2,
      405–6, 413, 439–41
  array-based implementations, 394–400

  entries, 394–95
    sorted array-based dictionary, 397–400
    unsorted array-based dictionary, 395–96
  `clear` method, 378
  comments, 623–24
  concordance of words, 387–89
    `display` method, 388–89
    `readFile` method, 387–88
  `contains` method, 378
  data, 377
  defined, 376
  `Dictionary` class, 622–23
  distinct search keys, 379
  duplicate search keys, 379
  entries, 377–78, 621–22
  frequency of words, 385–87
    creating the dictionary, 385–86
    displaying the dictionary, 386–87
    `FrequencyCounter` class, 385–87
  `getKeyIterator` method, 378
  `getSize` method, 378
  `getValueIterator` method, 378
  `getValue(key)` method, 378
  implementations, 393–409, 621–24
  `isEmpty` method, 378
  `isFull` method, 378
  iterators, 380–81, 623
  Java interface, 379–80
  linked implementations, 402–7
    entries, 402–3
    sorted linked dictionary, 404–7
    unsorted linked dictionary, 403–4
  `Map` interface, 389
  operations, 377–78
  `remove(key)` method, 377
  specifications for, 376–89
    refining, 379
  `TelephoneDirectory` class, 382–85
    class design, 382–83
    `getPhoneNumber` method, 384–85
    implementation, 383–84
  using, 381–89
  vector-based implementations, 400–402
    `add` method, 401–2
    `locateIndex` method, 402
`DictionaryInterface` interface, 379–80
Digraph, 675
Directed edges, 675
Directed graphs, 675
Directed path, 675
Directly proportional value of a function, 203
Directories, 540
Disconnected graphs, 676
`display` method, 82, 386–89
`displayArray` method, 236
`displayBackward` method, 237

`displayChain` method, 236
Divide and conquer algorithm, 278
`DivideByZeroException` class, 771–72
Division operator (/), 725
`do-while` statement (loop), 745–46
  defined, 745
  general form, 745
Documentation/programming style, 793–98
  classes, naming, 793–94
  comments, 795–97
  indenting, 794–95
  variables, naming, 793–94
Dot, 718
Double-ended queues. *See* Deques
Double hashing, open addressing with, 425–26
Double rotations, AVL trees, 646–50
  left-right, 648–49
  right-left, 646–48
`double` type, 9
`doubleArray` method, 108–9, 522
Doubly linked chain, 531, 537
Doubly linked implementation, deque
  adding an entry, 532–33
  data fields and constructors, 532
  removing an entry, 533–34
  retrieving an entry, 534
  reuse of, 534
Dummy head node, 149
Dummy node, 537
Dynamic array expansion, 108–9
Dynamic binding, 47–51
  type checking and, 50–51
Dynamic type, 48

E

`Edge` class, 704–5, 712
Edges
  graphs, 674
    directed edges, 675
  trees, 542
Efficiency of algorithms. *See* Algorithm
    efficiency
`elementAt` method, `Vector` class, 112
Empty trees, 543
Encapsulation, 58–60, 75
  abstraction, 59
  client interface, 59–60
  data abstraction, 59
  defined, 58–59
  implementation, 59–60
  information hiding, 58
  Java interface, 60
`enqueue` method, queue, 491, 520, 530
`Entry` class, 394–95
`equals` method, `Object` class, 44–45
`Error` class, 775

Escape characters, 748–49
`evaluate(expressionTree)` algorithm, 554
`evaluateInFix` algorithm, 468–69
`evaluatePostFix` algorithm, 467
Exception classes
  defining your own, 771–72
  predefined, 770–71
  programmer-defined, guidelines for, 772
Exception handling, 767–75
  basics, 767–70
  `catch` block parameter, 769
  `catch` blocks, 769–70
    multiple, 772–73
  catching the exception, 769
  throwing an exception, defined, 767
  `try` block, 769
Exceptions
  checked, 774–75
  declaring, 773–74
  defined, 767
  runtime, 774–75
  unchecked, 774–75
Exclusive or operation, 417
Expression trees, 552–54, 565
  evaluating an algebraic expression, 553–54
  implementation, 583–84
`ExpressionTree` class, 584
`ExpressionTreeInterface` interface, 583
Extending an interface, 67–68
  deriving from several interfaces, 68
External iterators, 162–66, 168
`ExternalIterator` class, 164–66

F

Fibonacci algorithm, time efficiency of,
    246–47
Fibonacci, Leonardo, 245
Fibonacci numbers (sequence), 245–47, 250
Files, 777–92
  advantage of, 778–79
  binary, 779
  closing, 781
  defined, 778
  flushing an output file, 781–82
  input/output, 777–92
  kinds of, 779
  names, 779
    reading from the keyboard, 784
  text, 779
    appending to, 782–83
    testing for the end of, 783–84
    writing to using `PrintWriter` class,
        780–82
Final class, 41
Final method, 41
`final` modifier, 41

`FirstProgram` class, 717
`float` type, 9
Floating-point number, 721
Floor, 207
Folders, 540
Folding, 417
`for` statement (loop), 743–45
  comma in, 744–45
  general form, 743–44
Formal parameters, 12–14, 23
Frame. *See* Activation record
Frequency of words, 385–87
  creating the dictionary, 385–86
  displaying the dictionary, 386–87
  `FrequencyCounter` class, 385–87
Full path name, 791
Full trees, 544–45
  height, 545–46

G

Game trees, 563–64
Garbage collection, 19
General trees, 543, 583–85
  game trees, 563–64
  node for, 583
  parse trees, 562–63
  traversals, 549
  using a binary tree to represent, 583–85
    traversals, 584–85
Generalizations, 73
`GeneralNodeInterface` interface, 585
Get methods (getters), 11
`getBreadthFirstTraversal` algorithm,
    graph, 680
`getCheapestPath` algorithm, graph, 691–92
`getCurrent` method
  internal iterators, 158
  `IteratorInterface` class, 158
  iterators, 154–58
`getDepthFirstTraversal` algorithm, graph,
    681–82
`getEntry` method, 82, 113, 140, 597–98
`getFirst` method, `LinkedList` class, 147
`getFirstNode` method, `LList` class, 324
`getFront` method, queue, 491, 520–21, 530
`getHashIndex` method, 414
`getHeight` method, binary tree, 578
`getHeightDifference` method, search trees,
    652
`getImmutable` method, `ImmutableName`
    class, 335–38
`getInorderIterator` method, 580
`getKeyIterator` method, 380–81
`getLast` method, `LinkedList` class, 148
`getLength` method, list, 82
`getListIterator` class, 166–67, 175, 177

getNodeAt method, LList class, 132–33, 136–37, 325

getNodeBefore private method, sorted list, 306–7

getNumberOfNodes method, binary tree, 578

getPhoneNumber method, TelephoneDirectory class, 384–85

getPosition(anEntry) method
  efficiency of, 313–15
  implementation, 313–15
  sorted list, 301–2

getRadius method, Circle class, 69

getRootData method, binary tree, 577

getShortestPath algorithm, graph, 687–88

getTopologicalSort method, graph, 684

getValueIterator method, dictionary, 380–81

getValue(key) algorithm, dictionary, 413, 429, 437

GradStudent class, 49, 73

Grammar
  for algebraic expressions, 562
  Java language, 719

GraphAlgorithmsInterface interface, 694

Graphs, 1, 3, 673–98
  acyclic, 675
  adjacency list, 701–2, 712
  adjacency matrix, 700–701, 712
  adjacent vertices, 676–77
  airline routes, 677
  algorithms, 710–12
    breadth-first traversal, 710–11
    depth-first traversal, 680
    shortest path, 687–88, 691–92, 711–12
    topological sort, 684
  basic operations, 707–10
  beginning the class, 707–8
  complete, 676, 695
  connected, 676
  costs, 675–76
  course prerequisites, 678
  defined, 674, 695
  directed (digraph), 675, 695–96
  directed edges, 675
  disconnected, 676
  Edge class, 704–5
  edges, 674, 702–6
    adding, 708
  implementations, 699–713
    adjacency list, 701–2
    adjacency matrix, 700–701
  Java interfaces for, 692–95
  mazes, 677–78
  miscellaneous methods, 709
  paths, 675, 684–92
    finding, 686

shortest path in an unweighted graph, 686–88, 711–12
shortest path in a weighted graph, 688–92
roadmaps, 674–77
subgraphs, 674, 677, 696
testing for an edge, 708–9
topological order, 678, 683–85
traversals, 679–82
  breadth-first traversal, 679, 680, 695
  depth-first traversal, 679, 680–82, 695
trees, 678–79
undirected, 675–76
Vertex class, 702–4
  addEdge methods, 706
  adjacency list, 702, 706
  beginning the class, 705
  identifying vertices, 702
  implementation, 705–6
  Java interface, 703–4
  path operations, 702–3
  visiting vertices, 702
vertices, 674, 702–6
  adding, 708
  resetting, 709–10
  visiting, 702
weighted, 675–76

Growth-rate function, 203

GuessingGame class, 556–57

H

Handling an exception. *See* Exception handling
Has a relationship, 30–31
hasCurrent method
  internal iterators, 158
  IteratorInterface class, 158
  iterators, 154–58
Hash code, 414
  compressing, 414
  compressing into an index for the hash table, 418–19
  computing, 415–19
    for a class type, 415–16
    for a primitive type, 417–18
    for a string, 416–17
Hash table, 412
  sparse, 414
hashCode method, guidelines for, 416
HashedMapOpenAddressing class, 437
Hashing, 411–48
  collision resolution, 414, 419–29
    comparing schemes for, 434–35
  defined, 412
  dictionary implementation using, 435–44
    add method, 439–41
    data fields and constructors, 436–37
    entries in the hash table, 435–36

getValue method, 437–38
locate method, 438–39
probe method, 441–42
rehash method, 442–43
remove method, 438
double, 425–26
efficiency, 430–33
  load factor, 430
  open addressing, cost of, 431–32
  separate chaining, cost of, 432–33
hash code
  compressing into an index for the hash table, 418–19
  computing, 415–19
hash functions, 412, 415–19
  general characteristics, 415
  perfect, 414
hash index, 413
hash table, 412
  sparse, 414
HashMap class, 444–45
ideal, 413–14
iterators, 443–44
open addressing, potential problem with, 426–27
perfect, 414
rehashing, 434
typical, 414–15
hasNext method
  Iterator interface, 178, 180
  IteratorForArrayList class, 180
  LinkedListWithIterator class, 178
  ListIterator interface, 189, 195
hasPrevious method, ListIterator interface, 190, 195
Head reference, 130
Heading of a method, 12
Heaps, 535, 560–62, 565, 628
  adding an entry, 630–33
    add method, 633
    avoiding swaps, 631–32
    basic algorithm, 630–31
    refined algorithm, 632–33
  creating, 637–39
    add method, 637
    reheap method, 637–38
  defined, 560
  heapsort, 639–41
    implementation, 641
    time efficiency of, 641
    trace of, 640
  implementation, 627–42
  maxheap, 560
  minheap, 560
  operations, 561
  priority queues, 561–62

removing an entry, 634–37
  basic algorithm, 634
  `reheap` method, 636–37
  `removeMax` method, 636
  transforming a semiheap into a heap,
      634–36
  using an array to represent, 628–30
    `MaxHeap` class, beginning, 629–30
    sentinel, 629
Heapsort, 639–41
  implementation, 641
  time efficiency of, 641
  trace of, 640
Height balanced search trees, 619–20
Hierarchical organizations, 540–42
Hierarchy of classes, 33–35
Higher-precedence operators, 726
Horner's method, 416

I

Identifiers, 719
`if-else` statement, 733–39
  boolean expressions, 734–36
  conditional operator, 739
  multiway, 738–39
  nested statements, 736–38
`IllegalStateException`, 176–77, 180
Immutable objects, 91
  companion classes, 335–36
    `ImmutableName` class, 334–39
    `Name` class, 337–39
    using inheritance to form, 336–39
  defined, 334
  sharing, 334
`ImmutableName` class, 334–39
  `getImmutable` method, 335–38
`implements` clause, 65, 75
Increment operator (++), 726–27
`incrementalInsertionSort`, 271, 273
`incrementLength` method, `LList` class, 325
`indexOf` method, `String` class, 751
Indirect recursion, 249–50
Infinite loops, 743
Infinite recursion, 227
Infix expression, 454
  checking for balanced delimiters in, 454–59
  evaluating, 467–69
    algorithm, 468–69
    example, 467–68
  Java implementation, 458–59
  transforming to a postfix expression, 459–66
Information hiding, 58
Inheritance, 30, 33–36, 51
  ancestors, 34
  base class, 33, 51
    calling the constructor of, 36–37

designing, 322–26
private fields/methods of, 37–38
private methods of, 38
and type compatibility, 42–46
constructors, invoking from within
    constructors, 36–37
defined, 33–34
derived classes, 33, 36, 51
  constructor, 36
  object types of, 42–43
  and `private` methods of the base class, 38
descendants, 34
hierarchy of classes, 33–35
and *is a* relationships, 34
and lists, 319–20
multiple, 42
`Object` class, 44–45
overriding/overloading methods, 38–41
protected access, 41–42
purpose of, 34
sorted list, efficient implementation of,
    326–28
subclasses, 33
superclasses, 33
using to implement a sorted list, 320–26
Inner class, 129, 162–64, 166–68, 169
Inner class iterator, 162–64, 166–68, 169
  defined, 168
Inorder predecessor, 607–10
Inorder successor, 607–10
Inorder traversals, 547, 565
`inorderIterator` method, 581–82
`inorderTraverse` method, 579, 580–81
Input/output (I/O), 729, 777–92
  with binary files, 785–90
    `DataInputStream` class, 788–90
    `DataOutputStream` class, 785–88
  class file, 790–91
  files, 778–9
    advantage of, 778–79
    kinds of, 779
    names, 779
  `java.io` package, 779
  object serialization, 114, 791–92
    arrays, 792
  path names, 791
  streams, 778
    defining a method to open, 784–85
  with text files, 780–85
    `BufferedReader` class, 782–84
    `PrintWriter` class, 780–82
Input stream, 778
`insertElementAt` method, `Vector` class,
    110–12
`insertInOrder`
  algorithm

final draft, 265–66
first draft, 264–65
method, 262, 264–69
Insertion sort, 261–69, 273
  of an array, 261–66
    efficiency of, 266
    iterative, 262–64
    recursive, 264–66
  of a chain of linked nodes, 266–69
    efficiency of, 269
    `insertionSort` algorithm, 262, 264,
        268–69
Instance, 6
Instance variables, 10–11
Instantiation, 6–7, 140
`int` type, 9, 721
Integer, 721
Interfaces, 75. *See also* Java interfaces
Interior (nonleaf) node, 542
Internal iterators, 153, 168
  `addAfterCurrent` method, 161
  `advance` method, 159
  `getCurrent` method, 158
  `hasCurrent` method, 158
  implementing, 157–62
  `removeCurrent` method, 159–61
  `replaceCurrent` method, 159
  `reset` method, 162
Interpolation search, 372–73
Invocation, 716
  methods, 6, 10, 23
    arguments in, 10
  recursive, 226
I/O. *See* Input/output (I/O)
Is a relationship, 30–31, 51
`isArrayFull` private method, list, 108
`isEmpty` method
  list, 82, 101
  queue, 491, 515
  stack, 451, 480, 483, 484, 485
  `Vector` class, 112
`isFull` method, list, 82, 108–9, 141
`isHashTableTooFull` method, 440
Iteration, 99
  defined, 152
  loops, 742
Iterative binary search, program stack, 472–73
Iterative insertion sort, 262–64
Iterative merge sort, 282–83
Iterative search, choosing between recursive
    search and, 371
Iterative selection sort, 258–60
Iterative sequential search
  unsorted arrays, 357–58
  unsorted chain, 367
`Iterator` interface, 174–82, 195

array-based implementation, 179–82
  beginning the inner class, 179–80
  `hasNext` method, 180
  `next` method, 180
  `remove` method, 180–82
implementing, 177–82
linked implementation, 177–79
  `hasNext` method, 178
  `next` method, 178
  `remove` method, 178–79
Iterator interfaces, 173–97
  `ArrayList` class, 194–95
  `Iterator` interface, 174–82, 195
    implementing, 177–82
  `IteratorInterface` interface, 155–57
  `LinkedList` class, 194–95
  `ListIterator` interface, 174, 182–94
    array-based implementation, 188–94
    current entry, 184
    indices of current/previous entries,
                184–85
    previous entry, 184
    using, 185–87
`IteratorForArrayList` class, 179–80
  `hasNext` method, 180
  `ListIterator` interface, 188–94
  `next` method, 180
  `remove` method, 180–82
`IteratorInterface` interface, 155–57
Iterators, 151–72
  basic, 153–55
  defined, 151, 152, 168
  external, 162–66, 168
  inner class, 162–64, 166–68, 169
  internal, 153, 168
    implementing, 157–62
  methods, 153–55
    effect on a list, 154, 156
    and modification of ADT, 155–57

J

Java, 3
  applets, 715
  applications, 715
    first program, 717–19
  arithmetic operators/expressions, 724–25
  arrays, 755–64
  assignment compatibilities, 723
  assignment statements, 722
  case sensitivity of, 719
  class types, 720
  classes. See Classes
  constants, 721
    named, 728
  data types, 9
  decrement operator, 726–27

essentials, 715–65
  grammar, 719
  identifiers, 719
  increment operator, 726–27
  input/output (I/O), 729, 777–92
  interfaces. See Java interfaces
  iterator interfaces, 173–97
  keyboard input, using `SavitchIn` class,
        731–33
  keywords, 719–20
  loops. See Loops
  method definitions, 11–14, 23, 716
  objects, 715–16
  parentheses, 725–26
  precedence rules, 726
  primitive types, 720–21
  reference types, 720
  reserved words, 719–20
  scope of a variable, 741–42
  screen output, 729–31
  special assignment operators, 727
  syntax, 719
  type casting, 723–24
  Unicode character set, 719
  variables, 720
Java Application Programming Interface
        (API), 22
Java Class Library, 22
  `ArrayList` class, 113, 194–95
  `Arrays` class, 283, 290
  `binarySearch` method, 365
  `HashMap` class, 444–45
  `LinkedList` class, 147–48, 194–95
  `List` interface, 91–92
  `Map` interface, 389
  merge sort, 283
  quick sort, 290
  `Serializable` interface, 114
  `sort` method, 283, 290
  `Stack` class, 473–74
  `TreeMap` class, 669
  `Vector` class, 112
Java documentation comments, 796–97. See
        also Comments and `javadoc`
Java interfaces, 60, 63–70
  abstract classes vs., 69–70
  and comments, 64
  as data types, 66
  defined, 63
  example, 64
  extending, 67–68
  implementation, 65–66
    type casts within, 66–67
  named constants within, 68–69
  naming, 64
  writing, 63–64

Java stack. See Program stack
`javadoc`, 60–61, 796–98
  `@param` tag, 61, 796
  `@return` tag, 61, 796–97
  running, 797–98
  tags, 796
  `@throws` tag, 61, 797
`java.io`, 779
`java.lang`, 22
`java.util`, 109–10, 113, 174, 384, 389, 390
Jump search, 372

K

Key, 3. See also Search keys
Keyboard input, using `SavitchIn` class,
        731–33
`KeyIterator` class, 443–44
Keywords, 719–20

L

Last-in, first out (LIFO) behavior, 450
Late binding. See Dynamic binding
Leaf node, 542, 564
Left child node, 544
Left-right double rotations, AVL trees, 648–49
Left rotation, AVL trees, 644
Left subtree, 544
`length` method, `String` class, 750
Length of a path, 675
Level-order traversals, 548, 565
Linear linked chains, 525
Linear probing
  defined, 419
  open addressing with, 419–24
    additions that collide, 420–21
    clustering, 424
    removals, 421–22
    reusing locations in the hash table during an
                addition, 422–24
Link portion, node, 129
Linked chain. See also Searching
  adding to a particular place in, 123–26
  circular, 525
    doubly linked, 531, 537
  cloning, 349–52
  defined, 118
  forming, 119–28
  linear, 525
  recursion, 236–37
    displaying a chain backwards, 237
  removing an item from, 126–28
Linked data, 118–28
`LinkedDeque` class, 532
`LinkedList` class, 147–48, 194–95
  `addFirst` method, 147

addLast method, 147
getFirst method, 147
getLast method, 148
removeFirst method, 147
removeLast method, 147
LinkedListWithInternalIterator class,
        157–62
    addAfterCurrent method, 161–62
    advance method, 159
    getCurrent method, 158
    hasCurrent method, 158
    removeCurrent method, 159–60
    replaceCurrent method, 159
    reset method, 162
LinkedListWithIterator class, 167–68,
        177–79
    hasNext method, 178
    next method, 178
    remove method, 178–79
LinkedQueue class, 492–93, 512
LinkedStack class, 478
List interface, 91–92, 147
Listable interface, 347
ListInterface interface, 86–89, 100,
        109–10, 130, 153
    AList class, 100–101, 108
    ListClient class, 88–89
ListIterator interface, 174–77, 182–94, 195
    add method, 183, 186–87, 191, 195
    array-based implementation, 188–95
        add method, 191, 195
        data fields, 188–89
        hasNext method, 189, 195
        hasPrevious method, 190, 195
        IteratorForArrayList inner class,
                188–94
        next method, 189–90, 195
        nextIndex method, 190–91, 195
        previous method, 190, 195
        previousIndex method, 190–91, 195
        remove method, 191–94, 195
    current entry, 184
    indices of current/previous entries, 184–85
    previous entry, 184
    remove method, 187, 191–94, 195
    set method, 187
    traversals, 185–86
    using, 185–87
Lists, 2–3, 79–96
    data, 81
    efficiency of, 327–28
    empty list, effect of operations on, 83
    implementation, dynamic array expansion,
        106–9
    implementation, fixed-size array, 98–106
        add method, 102–4

contains method, 105–6
    getEntry method, 105
    Java implementation, 100–106
    remove method, 104–5
    replace method, 105
implementation, linked, 130–42
    adding at a given point within list, 134–36
    adding to the end of list, 131–33
    add method, 136
    contains method, 141
    getEntry method, 140–41
    getNodeAt method, 136–37
    isFull method, 141
    OutOfMemory error, 136
    remove method, 137–140
    replace method, 140
implementation, vector-based, 109–12
List interface, 91–92
operations, 81–82
pros/cons of using array to implement, 113
specifications, 80–87
    first draft, 85
    refining, 83–87
using, 88–91
ListWithInternalIterator class, using,
        153–55
ListWithIteratorInterface interface,
        166, 177
Literals, 721
LList class, 130–32, 142–43, 322–25, 349
    decrementLength method, 325
    getFirstNode method, 324
    getNodeAt method, 132–33, 325
    incrementLength method, 325
    setFirstNode method, 324
    setLength method, 324
Load factor, 430, 433
Local variables, 13, 23
locate(index, key) algorithm, hashing, 439
locateIndex private method, dictionary,
        399–400, 402
long type, 9
Loops, 742, 746–47
    body, 742
    break statement in, 747
    choosing a loop statement, 746
    continue statement in, 747
    do-while statement, 745–46
    exit method, 747
    iteration, 742
    for statement, 743–45
    while statement, 742–43

M

Magic square, 27
main method, 21, 23, 24, 382–83

Map, 414. *See also* Dictionary
Map interface, 389, 390
Math class, 22, 728–29
Maxheap, 560
MaxHeap class, 629–30, 638–39
MaxHeapInterface interface, 561
Mazes, 677–78
Median, 297
Members, objects, 13
Memory leaks, 19
Merge sort, 278–83, 293
    algorithm, 279–82
    defined, 278
    efficiency of, 281–82
    iterative, 282–83
    in the Java Class Library, 283
    merging arrays, 278
    recursive, 279–81
        tracing the steps in the algorithm, 280–81
    time efficiency of, 282
Methods, 6, 7–10, 22, 51, 716
    alternate names for, 451, 491
    arguments, 8, 10, 718, 728
    body, 12
    calling objects, 8
    declaration, 12
    defined, 6
    definitions, 11–14, 23
        overloading, 40
    heading, 12
    invoking, 6, 10, 23
        arguments, 10
    iterators, 153–55
        effect on a list, 154, 156
        and modification of ADT, 155–57
    naming, 13
    overloading, 38–39, 52
    overriding, 38–39, 52
    postconditions, 61–62
    preconditions, 61–62
    as self-contained units, 13
    signature, 12
    specifying, 60–62
    tags, 61
    valued, 8–9
    void, 8–9, 12
Minheap, 560
Modulo (mod) operator, 725
Motivation for efficiency, 200–202
Multidimensional arrays, 759–61
Multiple inheritance, 42
Multiplicity, associations, 74
Multiway branches, 738
Multiway if-else statements, 738–39
Multiway search tree of order *m* (*m*-way search
        tree), 669

Mutable objects, 91, 332–39
  defined, 332
  sharing, 335
Mutator methods, 11
Mutual recursion, 249–50
  defined, 249
  example, 250

N

n-dimensional arrays, 759
Name class, 64
  constructors, 18–20
  default constructor, 18
  definition of, 16–18
  method definitions, 11–14
  passing arguments, 14–16
  shallow clone, 341–42
  static fields, 20–21
  static methods, 20
  toString method, 20
Name object, cloning, 340
Named constants, 728
NameInterface interface, 64
Navigability, 74
Neighbors, 676–77
Nested statements, 736–38
new operator, 8, 18–19
next method
  Iterator interface
    array-based implementation, 180
    linked implementation, 178
  IteratorForArrayList class, 180
  LinkedListWithIterator class, 178
  ListIterator interface, 189–90, 195
nextIndex method, ListIterator interface,
    190–91, 195
Node class, 129–30, 142–43, 350–52, 515
  getData method, 325
  getNextNode method, 325
  with set and get methods, 142
  setData method, 325
  setNextNode method, 325
Nodes, 542–43
  defined, 129
  interior (nonleaf) node, 542
  leaf node, 542
Nonlinear organizations, 540

O

Object class, 44–45, 52
  clone method, 45
  compareTo method, 66–67
  equals method, 44–45
  toString method, 44
Object-oriented programming (OOP), 6

  advantage of, 29–30
  design concepts, 58
Object serialization, 114, 791–92
  arrays, 792
ObjectInputStream class, 114
ObjectOutputStream class, 114
Objects, 6–7, 22, 715–16
  aliases, 9–10
  arguments, 10
  constructors, 18–20
  defined, 6
  invocation, 6
  members, 13
  reference types, 9–10
  type, 6
One-dimensional arrays, 759, 761
Open addressing
  cost of, 431–32
    double hashing, 432
    linear probing, 431
    quadratic probing, 432
  defined, 419
  with double hashing, 425–26
  with linear probing
    additions that collide, 420–21
    clustering, 424
    removals, 421–22
    reusing locations in the hash table during an
        addition, 422–24
  potential problem with, 426–27
  with quadratic probing, 424–25
Operands, 724
Operations (methods), class diagram, 73
Origin vertex, 679
Out-of-bounds index, 758
Outer class, 129
OutOfMemoryError, 141
Output stream, 778
Overflow, stack, 230
Overloading methods, 39–41, 52
Overriding methods, 38–39, 52

P

Packages, 22, 23
  package access, 22
Palindrome, 476
Parallel array, 402–7
@param tag, 61, 796
Parameters, 12
Parent, trees, 542
Parentheses, 725–26
Parse trees, 562–63
Partitioning, and iterative insertion sort, 262
Passing arguments, 14–16
Path names, 791
Paths, 675, 684–92, 695

  finding, 686
  shortest path in an unweighted graph, 686–88
  shortest path in a weighted graph, 688–92
peek method, stack, 451, 474, 480
Perfect hash function, 414
Pivot, 283, 285–86
Pivot selection, 286
play method, GuessingGame class, 557
Poisson distribution, 500
Polymorphic variables, 47
Polymorphism, 30, 46–51, 52
  defined, 46–47
  dynamic binding, 47–51
    type checking and, 50–51
  example, 47
  polymorphic variables, 47
Polynomial, 318
pop method, stack, 451, 474
Positions in a string, 751
Postconditions, 61–62
  as assertions, 62
PostFix class, 464–66
Postfix expression, 454
  evaluating, 466–67
  transforming an infix expression to, 459–66
    basics of a conversion algorithm, 460
    infix-to-postfix algorithm, 462–64
    Java implementation, 464–66
    pencil and paper scheme, 460
    successive operators with the same
        precedence, 460–62
Postorder traversals, 548, 565
Precedence, 454
Precedence rules, 725–26
Preconditions, 61–62
  as assertions, 62
  and responsibility, 61–62
Prefix expression, 454
Preorder traversals, 547, 565
previous method, ListIterator interface,
    190, 195
previousIndex method, ListIterator
    interface, 190–91, 195
Primary clustering, 424
Primitive types, 720–21
  computing hash code for, 417–18
PrintWriter class, 780–82, 784–85
Priority queues
  computing capital gain using, 506–7
  possible implementations of, 534–35
  PriorityQueue class, 561–62
  PriorityQueueInterface interface, 505
  specifications of, 505
private, 10–12, 22, 23
  making data fields private using, 11
privateSetTree method, 574–76

Probe sequence, 419, 423
`probe` private method, hashing, 440–42
Program stack, 229–31, 470–71
  activation record (frame), 470
  defined, 470
  iterative binary search, 472–73
  overflow, 230
  program counter, 470
  recursive methods, 470–72
Proof by induction, 239
Protected access, 41–42
Protected methods, 51
Pseudorandom numbers, 500
`public`, 11–12, 22, 23
`push` method, stack, 451, 474, 480

Q

Quadratic probing, open addressing with,
    424–25
Query methods, 11
`QueueInterface` interface, 492
Queues, 3, 489–502. *See also* Deques, Priority
    queues, *and* Waiting-line simulation
  array-based implementations, 515–23
    circular array, 516–17
    circular array with one unused location,
        518–23
  back of the queue, 490
  capital gain computations, 500–502
  circular linked implementations, 525–31
    circular linked chains, 525
    linear linked chains, 525
    two-part circular linked chain, 525–31
  `clear` method, 491
  data, 491
  defined, 490
  `dequeue` method, 491, 521–22, 530
  double-ended (deque), 490
  `enqueue` method, 491, 520, 530
  front of the queue, 490
  function of, 490
  `getFront` method, 491
  implementations, 511–37
    array-based, 515–23
    linked, 512–15
    vector-based, 523–24
  `isEmpty` method, 491, 515
  linked implementations, 512–15
    adding to the back, 513
    `clear` method, 515
    data fields and constructors, 512
    `isEmpty` method, 515
    removing the front, 514–15
    retrieving the front, 514
  methods, demonstrating, 492–93
  priority queue, 490

  specifications, 490–93
  vector-based implementations, 523–24
    adding to the back, 524
    data fields and constructors, 523
    efficiency, 524
    removing the front, 524
    retrieving the front, 524
  waiting-line simulation, 494–500
Quick sort, 283–90, 293
  algorithm, 283–84
  creating the partition, 284–87
  defined, 283
  efficiency of, 284
  in the Java Class Library, 290
  Java code for, 287–90
    partitioning, 288–89
    pivot selection, 287–88
    `quickSort` method, 289–90
  median-of-three pivot selection, 286
  method, `quickSort`, 289–90
  partition algorithm, adjusting, 286–87
  partition of the array, 283–84
  pivot, 283, 285–86
  pivot selection, 286
  time efficiency of, 284
`quickSort` algorithm, 283–84
`quickSort` method, 289–90

R

Radix sort, 290–92, 294
  buckets, 290
  defined, 290
  efficiency of, 292
  origin of, 291–92
  pseudocode for, 292
`radixSort` algorithm, 292
Read-only class, 334
`readFile` method, 387–88
`rebalance` algorithm, search trees, 651–52
`Record` class, program stack, 472–73
Recurrence relation
  defined, 238, 250
  solving, 238–39
Recursion, 223–54
  arrays, 234–36
    displaying a list, 236
    dividing an array in half, 235
    starting at one end, 234
  computing x^n, time efficiency of, 239–40
  countdown example, 224–26
  `countDown` method, 224–39
    time efficiency of, 238–40
  defined, 223–24
  designing a solution
    guidelines, 227
    questions for, 226

  Fibonacci numbers (sequence), 245–47
    indirect, 249–50
    infinite, 227
    linked chain, 236–37
      displaying a chain backwards, 237
    mutual, 249–50
    recurrence relation
      defined, 238, 250
      solving, 238–39
    recursive call, 226
    recursive invocation, 226
    recursive method, 226
      debugging, 233
      time efficiency of, 237–40
      tracing, 228–31, 232
      valued methods, 231–33
    tail, 247–49
    Towers of Hanoi problem, 240–45, 250
Recursive insertion sort, 264–66
  `insertInOrder` algorithm
    final draft, 265–66
    first draft, 264–65
Recursive invocation, 226
Recursive methods, program stack, 470–72
Recursive selection sort, 260
Recursive sequential search
  unsorted arrays, 358–59
  unsorted chain, 368
Red-black trees, 662–69
  adding entries to, 664–69
    adding a leaf, 664–65
    splitting a 4-node with black parent, 665–66
    splitting a 4-node with red parent, 667–69
  defined, 662
  properties, 663–64
  `TreeMap` class, 669
Reference types, 9, 720, 759
Reference variables, 9
References, 9, 118
`rehash` method, 440, 442–43
Rehashing, 434
Reheap
  algorithm, 636
  private method, 636
Relative path name, 791
`remove` method. *See also* Removing an entry
  `Iterator` interface
    array-based implementation, 180–82
    linked implementation, 178–79
  `IteratorForArrayList` class, 180–82
  iterators, 156–57
  `LinkedListWithIterator` class, 178–79
  `ListIterator` interface, 186–87, 191–94,
      195
`removeAllElements` method, `Vector` class,
    112

removeBack method, deque, 533–34
removeCurrent method
  internal iterators, 159–61
  IteratorInterface class, 159–60
removeElementAt method, Vector class,
  111–12
removeFirst method, LinkedList class,
  147
removeFront method, deque, 533
removeGap private method, list, 104
removeLast method, LinkedList class,
  147
Removing an entry
  binary search tree, 606–15
  deque, 503, 533–34
  dictionary, 377, 379, 396
  heap, 561, 634–37
  list, 81, 84, 86, 104–5, 111, 137–40,
    145–47
  priority queue, 505
  queue, 491, 492–93, 503, 514–15, 517–18,
    521–22, 524, 530
  sorted list, 301, 302, 313
  stack, 451, 474, 479–80, 482–83, 485, 503
replace method, 82
  iterators, 156–57
  list, 105, 156–57
replaceCurrent method
  internal iterators, 159
  IteratorInterface class, 159
Reserved words, 719–20
reset method
  internal iterators, 162
  IteratorInterface class, 162
Retrieving an entry
  binary search tree, 593, 597–98, 618
  deque, 503, 534
  dictionary, 378, 380, 413, 429, 437–38
  heap, 561, 628, 629–30
  list, 82, 84, 87
  priority queue, 505
  queue, 491, 492, 503, 514, 520, 524, 530
  sorted list, 301, 302, 315
  stack, 451, 452, 479, 482, 485, 503
  2-3 tree 654–55
@return tag, 61, 796–97
Right child node, 544
Right-left double rotations, AVL trees, 646–48
Right rotation, AVL trees, 644
Right subtree, 544
Roadmaps, 674–77
  adjacent vertices, 676–77
  connected graphs, 676
  paths, 675
  weights, 675–76
Root, 542, 564

rotateLeft algorithm, search trees, 646
rotateLeftRight algorithm, search trees,
  649
rotateRightLeft algorithm, search trees,
  648
rotateRight algorithm, search trees, 646
Runtime (unchecked) exceptions, 774–75

S

SavitchIn class, keyboard input using,
  731–33
Scope of a variable, 741–42
Screen output, 729–31
Search keys, 376, 394
  distinct, 379
  duplicate, 379
  iterator for, in sorted linked dictionary,
    406–7
  shifting, 417
Search trees, 557
search23Tree algorithm, 654–55
Searching, 355–74
  interpolation search, 372–73
  jump search, 372
  search method, choosing, 370–71
  search trees, 557
  sorted arrays, 360–69
    binary search, 361–67
    binarySearch method, 365
    efficiency of a binary search, 365–67
    sequential search, 360–61
  sorted chain, 369–70
    binary search, 369–70
    sequential search, 369
  target, 356
  2-3 tree, 654–55
  unsorted arrays, 357–59
    efficiency of a sequential search, 360
    iterative sequential search, 357–58
    recursive sequential search, 358–59
  unsorted chain, 367–69
    efficiency of a sequential search, 368–69
    iterative sequential search, 367
    recursive sequential search, 368
SearchTreeInterface interface, 593, 598
Secondary clustering, 425
Selection sort, 256–61, 273
  efficiency of, 260–61
  iterative, 258–60
  method, 260
  recursive, 260
  time efficiency of, 261
Semiheap, 634–636
Sentinel value, 790
Separate chaining, 427–29
  cost of, 432–33

Sequential search, 106
  choosing between binary search and, 370
  sorted arrays, 360–61
  sorted chain, 369
Serializable interface, 114, 395, 791–92
set method, ListIterator interface,
  186–87
Set methods (setters), 11
setElementAt method, Vector class, 112
setFirstNode method, LList class, 324
setLength method, LList class, 324
setRadius method, Circle class, 69
setStudent method, 32, 40
Sets, 116
setTree method, 596–97
Shallow clones, 341
Shallow copy, 341
Shell, Donald, 269–72
Shell sort, 269–72, 273
  defined, 269
  efficiency of, 272
  Java code, 271–72
  time efficiency of, 272
Shifting, in hashing, 417
short type, 9
Shortest path in an unweighted graph,
  686–88
  algorithm
    developing, 686–88
    pseudocode for, 687–88
    tracing, 688
  example, 686
Shortest path in a weighted graph, 689–92
  algorithm, 689–92
  example, 689
Siblings, trees, 542
Signature of a method, 12
Simple cycle, 675, 695
Simple path, 675
Single-line comments, 795
Single rotations, AVL trees, 645–46
Singly linked chain, 531
size method, Vector class, 112
SortArray class, 258–61
  indexOfSmallest method, 259
  swap method, 260
Sorted array-based dictionary, 397–400
  adding an entry, 398–99
  beginning the implementation, 398
  locateIndex method, 399–400
Sorted arrays, 360–69
  binary search, 361–67
    efficiency of, 365–67
  binarySearch method, 365
  searching, 360–69
    binary search, 361–67

`binarySearch` method, 365
  efficiency of a binary search, 365–67
  sequential search, 360–61
Sorted chains
  binary search, 369–70
  searching, 369–70
    binary search, 369–70
    sequential search, 369
  sequential search, 369
Sorted linked dictionary, 404–7
  adding an entry, 405–6
  iterator for search keys, 406–7
Sorted lists, 3, 299–318
  `add(newEntry)` method, 301, 304–11, 313, 316, 320, 326–28
    algorithm, 305
    efficiency of, 312–17
    `getNodeBefore` private method, 306–7
    implementation, iterative, 306
    implementation, recursive, 307, 308
    implementation, using a list, 312–17, 320–322, 326–328
    locating the insertion point, 304–5
    thinking recursively, 307
    tracing an addition, 308–11
  of clones, 344–46
  data, 301
  efficiency issues, 315–17
  `getPosition(anEntry)` method, 301–2
    efficiency of, 313–15
    implementation, 313–15
  implementation, 312–17
    and containment, 317
    efficient, 326–28
    inheritance, using, 320–322, 326–328
    linked, 304–12
  linked implementation, 304–12
    class outline, 304
    efficiency of, 311–12
  operations, 301
  recursive calls, 309–11
  `remove(anEntry)` method, 301
    implementation, 313
  specifications for, 300–304
  tracing returns from the recursive method, 311
  using, 303–4
`SortedArrayDictionary` class, 398–400
`SortedDictionary` class, 405–7
`SortedLinkedList` class, 304–11
`SortedList` class, 313–15, 320–22, 326–28
`SortedListInterface` interface, 302–3, 321–22
`SortedVectorDictionary` class, 400–402
Sorting, 255–76

algorithms, comparison of, 272–73, 293
  bubble sort, 273–74
  bucket sort, 294–95
  defined, 256
  faster sorting methods, 277–97
  insertion sort, 261–69, 273
    of a chain of linked nodes, 266–69
    efficiency of, 266
    iterative, 262–64
    recursive, 264–66
  merge sort, 278–83, 293
    defined, 278
    efficiency of, 281–82
    iterative, 282–83
    in the Java Class Library, 283
    merging arrays, 278
    recursive, 279–81
    time efficiency of, 282
  quick sort, 283–90, 293
    creating the partition, 284–87
    defined, 283
    efficiency of, 284
    in the Java Class Library, 290
    Java code for, 287–90
    median-of-three pivot selection, 286
    partition algorithm, adjusting, 286–87
    partition of the array, 283–84
    pivot, 283, 285–86
    pivot selection, 286
    time efficiency of, 284
  radix sort, 290–92, 294
    buckets, 290
    defined, 290
    efficiency of, 292
    origin of, 291–92
    pseudocode for, 292
  selection sort, 256–61, 273
    efficiency of, 260–61
    iterative, 258–60
    recursive, 260
  Shell sort, 269–72, 273
    defined, 269
    efficiency of, 272
    Java code, 271–72
  stable sorting algorithm, 295
Space complexity, algorithms, 202
Sparse hash table, 414
Special assignment operators, 727
Stable sorting algorithm, 295
Stack of activation records. *See* Program stack
`StackInterface` interface, 452
Stacks, 3, 229–31, 449–76
  and access to entries, 450
  array-based implementation, 480–84
    adding to the top, 482
    data field and constructors, 481–82

  removing the top, 482–83
  retrieving the top, 482
  balanced expression, 455
  `clear` method, 451, 480, 484, 485
  data, 451
  implementations, 477–87
  infix expression, 454
    checking for balanced delimiters in, 454–59
    evaluating, 467–69
    Java implementation, 458–59
    transforming to a postfix expression, 459–66
  interface, 452
  `isEmpty` method, 451, 480, 484, 485
  last-in, first out (LIFO) behavior, 450
  linked implementation, 477–80
    adding to the top, 479
    data field and constructor, 478–79
    removing the top, 479–80
    retrieving the top, 479
  methods, demonstration of, 452–53
  `peek` method, 451, 474, 480
  `pop` method, 451, 474
  `push` method, 451, 474, 480
  postfix expression, 454
    evaluating, 466–67
    transforming an infix expression to, 459–66
  prefix expression, 454
  processing algebraic expressions using, 453–69
  program stack, 229–31, 470–71, 472–73
  specifications of, 448–53
  top, 450
  `Stack` class, 473–74
  unbalanced expression, 456–57
  using instead of recursion, 471–73
  vector-based implementation, 484–86
    data fields and constructors, 484–85
    removing the top, 485
    retrieving the top, 485
Stand alone program, 716
Static field, 20–21, 23
Static method, 12, 21, 23, 728
Static type, 48
`StockLedger` class, 500–502
  design, 500–501
  implementation, 501–502
`StockPurchase` class, 500–502
  design, 500–501
  implementation, 501–502
Stopping cases, 226–27
Streams, 778
  defining a method to open, 784–85
  input, 778
  output, 778

String class, 30, 747–52
  characters within strings, 748–49
  charAt method, 751
  compareTo method, 752
  concat method, 750–51
  concatenation of strings, 749–50
  indexOf method, 751
  indices, 751
  length method, 750
  methods, 750–52
  toLowerCase method, 751
  trim method, 751
String, computing hash code for, 416–17
StringBuffer class, 752–53
StringTokenizer class, 384, 390, 753–54
Student class, 31–32, 35–43, 45–46, 73–74, 342–43
  displayAt method, 46–47
Subclass, 33
Subgraphs, 674, 677, 696
Subtree, 543
super, 52
  multiple use of, 40–41
Superclass, 33
switch statement, 739–41
  break statement, omission of, 741
  controlling expression, 739–41
  list of cases, 740
Syntax, definition of, 719
System.out.println, 31

T

Table. *See* Dictionary
TableEntry class, hashing, 436
Tail recursion, 247–49, 250
  defined, 248
  last action, 249
Tail references, 142–47
  problem, 142–43
  revised implementation of list, 143–48
    adding to end of list, 143–44
    adding to list at a given position, 144–45
    constructor, 143
    removing entry from list, 145–47
  solution, 143
TelephoneDirectory class, 382–85
  class design, 382–83
  getPhoneNumber method, 384–85
  implementation, 383–84
Ternary operator, 739
Test program for a class, 87
Text files, 779
  appending to, 782–83
  testing for the end of, 783–84

writing to using PrintWriter class, 780–82
Throwing an exception, defined, 767
@throws tag, 61, 796
Time complexity, algorithms. *See* Algorithm efficiency
Time-driven simulation, 494
Time efficiency, algorithms. *See* Algorithm efficiency
Tokens, 384
toLowerCase method, String class, 751
Topological order, graphs, 678, 683–85
Topological sort, graphs, 684
toString method, 20
  CollegeStudent class, 38–39
  Name class, 20, 32
  Object class, 44
Towers of Hanoi problem, 240–45, 250
Traversals, 99, 578–83
  of graphs, 679–82
    breadth-first, 679, 680, 695
    depth-first, 679, 680–82, 695
    InorderIterator class, 581–82
    iterative version of inorderTraverse, 580–81
    postorder, 582–83
    preorder, 582–83
  of trees, 546–49
    breadth-first, 548
    depth-first, 549
    inorder, 547, 565
    level-order, 548, 565
    postorder, 548, 565
    preorder, 547, 565
    recursive, 578–79
  using an iterator, 580
TreeInterface interface, 550, 593
TreeIteratorInterface interface, 550
TreeMap class, 669
TreeRotations class, 651
Trees, 1, 3, 539–67. *See also* AVL trees, B-trees, Binary search trees, Binary trees, General trees, Red-black trees, 2-4 trees, *and* 2-3 trees
trim method, String class, 751
Truncation, 207
Two-dimensional arrays, 759–61
2-4 trees, 658–62
  adding entries to, 659–61
  compared to AVL and 2-3 trees, 661–62
  defined, 658
  4-node, 658
Two-part circular linked chain, 525–31
  adding to the back, 528–30
  data fields and constructors, 528
  linked implementation, choosing, 531

  removing the front, 530
  retrieving the front, 530
2-3 trees, 653–58
  adding entries to, 655–57
  searching, 654–55
  splitting nodes during addition, 657–58
    splitting a leaf, 657–58
    splitting the root, 658
  3-node, 653
  2-node, 653
TwoPartCircularLinkedQueue class, 526
Type-cast returned objects, 91
Type casting, 723–24
Type checking, dynamic binding and, 50–51
Type compatibility, and base classes, 42–46
Type, variables, 720

U

Unary operator, 724
Unbalanced expression, 456–57
Unchecked (runtime) exceptions, 774–75
UndergradStudent class, 40, 43, 47–51, 73
Undirected graphs, 675–76
Unicode character set, 719, 748
Unicode Text Format (UTF), 787
Unidirectional arrow, 74
Unified Modeling Language (UML), 72–74, 75
Uninitialized variables, 722
Unsorted array-based dictionary, 395–96
Unsorted arrays, searching, 357–59
  efficiency of a sequential search, 360
  iterative sequential search, 357–58
  recursive sequential search, 358–59
Unsorted chain, searching, 367–69
  efficiency of a sequential search, 368–69
  iterative sequential search, 367
  recursive sequential search, 368
Unsorted linked dictionary, 403–4
  and add method, 407
Use case diagrams, 70–71, 75–76
Use modifier, 12

V

Valued methods, 8–9, 23, 716
  and return statement, 12
Variables, 720
  declaration, 720
  instance, 10–11
  local, 13, 23
  naming, 793–94
  polymorphic, 47
  reference, 9
  scope of, 741–42

uninitialized, 722
value of, 720
wider-type, 722
Vector-based implementations
  dictionary, 400–402
    locateIndex method, 402
  list, 109–111
    adding an entry, 110–111
    data fields and constructors, 110
    removing an entry, 111
    retrieving an entry, 111
  queue, 523–24
    adding to the back, 524
    data fields and constructors, 523
    efficiency of operations, 524
    removing the front, 524
    retrieving the front, 524
  stack, 484–86
    data fields and constructors, 484–85
    removing the top, 485
    retrieving the top, 485
Vector class, 109–14
  addElement method, 110, 112
  clear method, 111

contains method, 112
default constructor, 110
elementAt method, 112
insertElementAt method, 110–12
isEmpty method, 112
removeAllElements method, 112
removeElementAt method, 111–12
setElementAt method, 112
size method, 112
VectorList class, 111
Vehicle class, 33–34
Vertex class, 702–4, 712
  addEdge methods, 706
  adjacency list, 702, 706
  beginning the class, 705
  identifying vertices, 702
  implementation, 705–6
  Java interface, 703–4
  path operations, 702–3
  visiting vertices, 702
VertexInterface interface, 703–4
Visibility modifiers, 11
"Visiting a node," use of term, 545–46, 679
Void methods, 8–9, 12, 716

W

Waiting-line simulation, 494–500
  class design, 494–95
  Customer class, 494–95
  sample output, 499
  simulate method, 495–99
    implementation details for, 497–99
  WaitLine class, 494–95, 497–99
Weighted graphs, 675–76
while statement (loop), 742–43
  infinite loops, 743
  and zero iterations, 743
Whitespace characters, 731
Wider-type variables, 722
Worst-case time, 203
Wrapper classes, 86, 761–64
  Character class, 763–64
  static methods, 762
writeObject method, 114

Z

Zero iterations, and while statement, 743

Unicode Character Codes

The printable characters shown are a subset of the Unicode character set known as the ASCII character set. The numbering is the same whether the characters are considered to be members of the Unicode character set or members of the ASCII character set. (Character number 32 is the blank.)

32		56	8	80	P	104	h
33	!	57	9	81	Q	105	i
34	"	58	:	82	R	106	j
35	#	59	;	83	S	107	k
36	$	60	<	84	T	108	l
37	%	61	=	85	U	109	m
38	&	62	>	86	V	110	n
39	'	63	?	87	W	111	o
40	(	64	@	88	X	112	p
41	)	65	A	89	Y	113	q
42	*	66	B	90	Z	114	r
43	+	67	C	91	[	115	s
44	,	68	D	92	\	116	t
45	-	69	E	93	]	117	u
46	.	70	F	94	^	118	v
47	/	71	G	95	_	119	w
48	0	72	H	96	`	120	x
49	1	73	I	97	a	121	y
50	2	74	J	98	b	122	z
51	3	75	K	99	c	123	{
52	4	76	L	100	d	124	|
53	5	77	M	101	e	125	}
54	6	78	N	102	f	126	~
55	7	79	O	103	g		